GLOBAL POLITICAL ECONOMY

Praised for its authoritative coverage, *Global Political Economy* places the study of international political economy (IPE) in its broadest theoretical context—now updated to cover the continuing global economic crisis and regional relationships and impacts. This text not only helps students understand the fundamentals of how the global economy works but also encourages them to use theory to more fully grasp the connections between key issue areas like trade and development. Written by a leading IPE scholar, this text equally emphasizes theory and practice to provide a framework for analyzing current events and long-term developments in the global economy.

New to the Seventh Edition:

- Focuses on the ongoing global economic crisis and the continuing European sovereign debt crisis, along with other regional economic issues, including their implications for relationships in the global economy.
- Offers a fuller and updated discussion of critical perspectives like feminism and environmentalism, and includes new material differentiating between the terms neomercantilism, realism, mercantilism, and economic nationalism.
- Updated, author-written Test Bank is provided to professors as an eResource.

Theodore H. Cohn is Professor Emeritus of Political Science at Simon Fraser University.

 An eResource t
www.routledge.com/9781138958746

I have been using this wonderful text for the last few years for my upper division undergraduate course on Politics of the World Economy. This new edition brings all of the burning issues right up to date: the weight of China in the IPE, the immigration crisis in Africa and the Middle East, and the shift from multilateral to regional trade schemes. *Global Political Economy* gracefully weaves together theory and practice, and it strikes a perfect balance between institutions, interests and actors. I look forward to assigning this next edition.

Carol Wise, *University of Southern California*

With this new edition, Ted Cohn reaffirms his book's place among the very best texts available in the field of international political economy – well organized, articulate, and certainly up to date. Students will find it both enlightening and refreshing.

Benjamin J. Cohen, *University of California, Santa Barbara*

Cohn continues to produce an excellent textbook; I wouldn't think of using another. Among textbook authors, only Cohn consistently returns to the theories in each empirical chapter, driving home how the lenses we use shape our understanding of the global political economy.

Kathleen J. Hancock, *Colorado School of Mines*

The seventh edition of *Global Political Economy: Theory and Practice* is a fully updated, comprehensive textbook that builds on the strengths of the earlier editions but has been updated with a discussion of the ongoing global economic crisis. It contains both an excellent discussion of theoretical debates as well as the main issue areas. Issues are explained in plain language for an easy understanding for university students. This book is an excellent text for courses on international political economy and the like.

Amy Verdun, *University of Victoria*

Global Political Economy

Theory and Practice

Seventh Edition

THEODORE H. COHN

Routledge
Taylor & Francis Group

NEW YORK AND LONDON

To Shirley

Seventh edition published 2016
by Routledge
711 Third Avenue, New York, NY 10017

and by Routledge
2 Park Square, Milton Park, Abingdon, Oxon, OX14 4RN

Routledge is an imprint of the Taylor & Francis Group, an informa business

© 2016 Taylor & Francis

First edition published by Pearson Education, Inc. 2000
Second edition published by Pearson Education, Inc. 2002
Third edition published by Pearson Education, Inc. 2004
Fourth edition published by Pearson Education, Inc. 2008
Fifth edition published by Pearson Education, Inc. 2010
Sixth edition published by Pearson Education, Inc. 2012

Library of Congress Cataloging-in-Publication Data
Names: Cohn, Theodore H., 1940- author.
Title: Global political economy : theory and practice / Theodore H. Cohn.
Description: Seventh edition. | New York, NY : Routledge, 2016.
Identifiers: LCCN 2015044173| ISBN 9781138945654 (hardback) | ISBN 9781138958746 (pbk.) | ISBN 9781315659695 (ebook)
Subjects: LCSH: International economic relations. | International trade. | International finance.
Classification: LCC HF1359 .C654 2016 | DDC 337--dc23
LC record available at http://lccn.loc.gov/2015044173

ISBN: 9781138945654 (hbk)
ISBN: 9781138958746 (pbk)
ISBN: 9781315659695 (ebk)

Typeset in Sabon by
Printed at CPI on sustainably sourced paper
Servis Filmsetting Ltd, Stockport, Cheshire

BRIEF CONTENTS

Preface   xiii

Acknowledgments   xvii

Acronyms and Abbreviations   xix

PART I   Introduction and Overview   1

CHAPTER 1   Introduction   2
CHAPTER 2   Managing the Global Economy Since World War II:
                 The Institutional Framework   17

PART II   Theoretical Perspectives   51

CHAPTER 3   Neomercantilism   55
CHAPTER 4   Liberalism   77
CHAPTER 5   Critical Perspectives   103

PART III   The Issue Areas   129

CHAPTER 6   International Monetary Relations   131
CHAPTER 7   Financial Crises   172
CHAPTER 8   Global Trade Relations   215
CHAPTER 9   Regionalism and the Global Trade Regime   255
CHAPTER 10   Multinational Corporations and Global Production   293
CHAPTER 11   International Development   337

PART IV   Concluding Comments   383

CHAPTER 12   Current Trends in the Global Political Economy   384

Glossary   410

Index   420

DETAILED CONTENTS

Preface   xiii

Acknowledgments   xvii

Acronyms and Abbreviations   xix

PART I   Introduction and Overview   1

CHAPTER 1   Introduction   2

What is International Political Economy?   3

The IPE Theoretical Perspectives   4

Purposes and Themes of This Book   6
  Globalization 6 • North–North Relations 8 • North–South Relations 10

Focus of this Book   12
  Questions 13 • Key Terms 14 • Further Reading 14 • Notes 14

CHAPTER 2   Managing the Global Economy Since World
                 War II: The Institutional Framework   17

Global Economic Relations Before World War II   18
  *The Mercantilist Period 18 • The Industrial Revolution and British Hegemony 19 •
  The Decline of British Hegemony and World War I 20 • The Interwar Period 20 •
  The Institutional Framework Before World War II 21*

The Functions of the IMF, World Bank, and GATT   21

The KIEOs and the United Nations   22

The Postwar Economic Institutions and Changing North–South Relations   23
  *The IMF, World Bank, and WTO 26 • The OECD 28 • The G5, G7, G8,
  and G20 29*

The Postwar Economic Institutions and International Development   31

The KIEOs and the Centrally Planned Economies   39

Nonstate Actors   42

The 2008 Global Financial Crisis: A Turning Point?   43
  Questions 44 • Key Terms 45 • Further Reading 45 • Notes 46

PART II   Theoretical Perspectives   51

CHAPTER 3   Neomercantilism   55

Basic Tenets of Neomercantilism   55
  The Role of the Individual, the State, and Societal Groups 55 • The Nature and Purpose of International Economic Relations 56 • The Relationship Between Politics and Economics 56 • The Causes and Effects of Globalization 57

The Mercantilists   57

Neomercantilism and the Industrial Revolution   58

Neomercantilism in the Interwar Period   59

Neomercantilism After World War II   60

The Revival of Neomercantilist IPE   60

Hegemonic Stability Theory and U.S. Hegemony   61
  What Is Hegemony? 62 • What Are the Strategies and Motives of Hegemonic States? 62 • Is Hegemony Necessary and/or Sufficient to Produce an Open, Stable Economic System? 64 • What Is the Status of U.S. Hegemony? 65

Neomercantilism and North–South Relations   67

Present-Day Neomercantilism   68

Critique of the Neomercantilist Perspective   70
  Questions 71 • Key Terms 71 • Further Reading 71 • Notes 72

CHAPTER 4   Liberalism   77

Basic Tenets of the Liberal Perspective   77
  The Role of the Individual, the State, and Societal Groups 78 • The Nature and Purpose of International Economic Relations 78 • The Relationship Between Politics and Economics 79 • The Causes and Effects of Globalization 79

The Development of Liberal IPE: Adam Smith and David Ricardo   80

The Influence of John Maynard Keynes   81

Liberalism in the Postwar Period   83

A Return to Orthodox Liberalism   83

Liberalism and Institutions   85
  Interdependence Theory 85 • The Liberal Approach to Cooperation 86 • Regime Theory 88

Liberalism, Global Governance, and Regimes   89

Liberalism and Domestic–International Interactions   90

Liberalism and North–South Relations   92
   Orthodox Liberals and North–South Relations 93 • Interventionist Liberals and North–South Relations 93

Present-Day Liberalism   94

Critique of the Liberal Perspective   95
   Questions 97 • Key Terms 97 • Further Reading 97 • Notes 98

CHAPTER 5   Critical Perspectives   103

Basic Tenets of Historical Materialism   103
   The Role of the Individual, the State, and Societal Groups 103 • The Nature and Purpose of International Economic Relations 104 • The Relationship Between Politics and Economics 104 • The Causes and Effects of Globalization 105

Early Forms of Historical Materialism   106
   Karl Marx 106 • Vladimir Lenin: The Study of Imperialism 107 • Dependency Theory 108

Whither the Historical Materialist Perspective?   110
   World-Systems Theory 111 • Neo-Gramscian Analysis 112

Constructivism   114

Feminism   116

Environmentalism   118

Critique of the Critical Perspectives   121
   Questions 122 • Key Terms 123 • Further Reading 123 • Notes 124

PART III   The Issue Areas   129

CHAPTER 6   International Monetary Relations   131

The Balance of Payments   132

Government Response to a Balance-of-Payments Deficit   135
   Adjustment Measures 136 • Financing 136 • Adjustment, Financing, and the Theoretical Perspectives 139

The Functions and Valuation of Money   139

International Monetary Relations Before Bretton Woods   140
   The Classical Gold Standard (1870s to 1914) 140 • The Interwar Period (1918–1944) 141

The Formation of the Bretton Woods Monetary Regime   142

The International Monetary Fund   142

The Functioning of the Bretton Woods Monetary Regime   145
The Central Role of the U.S. Dollar 146 • A Shift Toward Multilateralism 148 •
The Demise of the Bretton Woods Monetary Regime 151

The Regime of Floating (or Flexible) Exchange Rates   151
The Plaza–Louvre Accords 153

Alternatives to the Current Monetary Regime   153

European Monetary Relations   154

What Is the Future of the U.S. Dollar as the Key Currency?   157
The Dollar Versus the Yen 158 • The Dollar Versus the Euro 159 • The Dollar
Versus the Renminbi 161 • The Future of the Dollar: Other Possible Scenarios 162

Considering IPE Theory and Practice   164
Questions 165 • Key Terms 166 • Further Reading 166 • Notes 167

CHAPTER 7   Financial Crises   **172**

Some Definitions and Terminology   173

The Origins of the 1980s Foreign Debt Crisis   174
Unexpected Changes in the Global Economy 174 • Irresponsible Behavior of
Lenders 175 • Irresponsible Behavior of Borrowers 175 • The South's Dependence
on the North 177

The Foreign Debt Regime   178
The IMF, World Bank, and Transition Economies 181 • The Paris and London
Clubs 184

Strategies to Deal with the 1980s Debt Crisis   185
Emergency Measures and Involuntary Lending: 1982–1985 186
• The Baker Plan: 1986–1988 187 • The Brady Plan: 1989–1997 188
• Initiatives for the Poorest LDCs 189 • Assessing the Effectiveness of the Debt
Strategies 189

Transition Economies and Foreign Debt   190

The IMF, the World Bank, and the Debt Crisis   192

The 1990s Asian Financial Crisis   194
Causes of the Asian Financial Crisis and Strategies to Deal with It 195
• The International Financial Architecture 196

The 2008 Global Financial Crisis   198

The European Debt Crisis   202
The European Debt Crisis and the Changing Relationship Between the EU and
IMF 204

Considering IPE Theory and Practice   205
Questions 207 • Key Terms 207 • Further Reading 208 • Notes 209

CHAPTER 8   Global Trade Relations   **215**

Trade Theory   216

Global Trade Relations Before World War II   220

GATT and the Postwar Global Trade Regime   221

Principles of the Global Trade Regime   222
  *Trade Liberalization 223 • Nondiscrimination 225 • Reciprocity 225
  • Safeguards 228 • Development 229*

Formation of the WTO   229

The WTO and the Global Trade Regime   232

The Transition Economies and Global Trade Relations   234

The South and Global Trade Issues   236
  *1940s to Early 1960s: Limited LDC Involvement 237 • 1960s to Early 1970s:
  Growing Pressures for Special Treatment 237 • 1970s to 1980: Increased
  North–South Confrontation 238 • 1980s to 1995: More LDC Participation in
  GATT 238 • 1995 to the Present: LDC Disillusionment with the Uruguay Round
  and Demands in the Doha Round 239 • The Emerging Economies: China, India, and
  Brazil 240*

Civil Society and Global Trade Relations   242

Trade and the Environment   244

Considering IPE Theory and Practice   246
  Questions 247 • Key Terms 248 • Further Reading 248 • Notes 249

CHAPTER 9   Regionalism and the Global Trade Regime   **255**

Regionalism and the IPE Theoretical Perspectives   257

Regionalism and Globalization   258

A Historical Overview of RTAs   258
  The First Wave of Regionalism 259 • The Second Wave of Regionalism 259

Explanations for the Rise of Regional Integration   261
  *Neomercantilist Explanations 261 • Liberal Explanations 262 • Historical
  Materialist Explanations 263*

The GATT/WTO and RTAs   263
  *Trade Diversion 264 • Trade Creation 264 • GATT Article 24 and RTAs 265 • The
  Effectiveness of GATT Article 24 265 • Special Treatment for LDCs 266*

The European Union   268
  *The Deepening of European Integration 269 • The Widening of European
  Integration 270 • Theoretical Perspectives and the EU 272*

The North American Free Trade Agreement   275
  The Formation of NAFTA 275 • NAFTA as a Free Trade Agreement 276

Mercosur   280

The Trans-Pacific Partnership   281

Considering IPE Theory and Practice   283
    Questions 285 • Key Terms 285 • Further Reading 286 • Notes 287

CHAPTER 10   Multinational Corporations and Global
                Production   293

Definitions and Terminology   294

Why Do Firms Become MNCs?   295

The Historical Development of FDI   297
    *The Pre-World War II Period 297 • The Mid-1940s to Mid-1980s 298
    • 1990 to the Present 301*

MNC–Host Country Relations: Determinants and Effects of FDI   304

Host Country Policies Toward MNCs   307
    The South 307 • The North 309

MNC–Home Country Relations   312
    *Home Country Policies Toward MNCs 312 • The Effects of MNCs on Labor Groups
    in Home Countries 315 • Competitiveness and Home Country–MNC Relations 316*

A Regime for FDI: What Is to Be Regulated?   318

Bilateral Investment Treaties   319

The United Nations   320

Regional Approaches: The EU and NAFTA   321

The GATT/WTO to the OECD and Back to the WTO   323

Private Actors   325

Considering IPE Theory and Practice   326
    Questions 328 • Key Terms 329 • Further Reading 329 • Notes 330

CHAPTER 11   International Development   337

IPE Perspectives and North–South Relations   339

Official Development Assistance   340

The World Bank Group   344

LDC Development Strategies   350

Import Substitution Industrialization   350

Socialist Development Strategies   353

Export-Led Growth   354
IPE Perspectives and the East Asian Experience 355 • The Asian Financial Crisis 357

The Revival of Orthodox Liberalism   359
Structural Adjustment and the Theoretical Perspectives 360 • Structural Adjustment and Questions About Orthodox Liberalism 361 • Structural Adjustment and Sub-Saharan Africa 361 • Structural Adjustment and LDC Women 362

Another Shift in Development Strategy?   363
The Late 1980s to 1994 364 • The Wolfensohn Period: 1995 to 2005 366 • 2005 to the Present 368 • China's Development Strategy 369 • A Diversity of Views on the UN's Development Goals 370

Considering IPE Theory and Practice   371
Questions 373 • Key Terms 373 • Further Reading 374 • Notes 374

PART IV　　Concluding Comments   **383**

CHAPTER 12　　Current Trends in the Global Political Economy   384

Globalization   384
Globalization and Triadization 385 • Globalization and the State 386 • Globalization, Inequality, and Poverty 387 • Globalization and Democracy 389 • Globalization and Civil Society 390 • Globalization and Neglected IPE Issues: Energy, the Environment, and Migration 391

North–North Relations   395
The Current State of U.S. Hegemony 395 • Is There a Candidate to Replace the United States as Global Hegemon? 397 • The Role of International Institutions 399

North–South Relations   401
Changing Concepts of Development 402 • Is There a "Best" Development Strategy? 403

A Final Word on IPE Theory and Practice   405
Notes 406

Glossary   410

Index   420

PREFACE

The seventh edition of this book emphasizes the challenge China is posing to the West in most areas of the global political economy, despite the country's economic slowdown and the need to reorient its economy. The book also examines how the focal point of the 2008 global financial crisis has shifted from the United States to the European Union (EU). Currently the EU is being buffeted by a sovereign debt crisis in Greece, a migration crisis from the Middle East and Africa, and anti-EU sentiments in Britain and some other member states. Scholars and policy-makers recognize the need for policies to limit the detrimental effects of financial crises and to prevent future crises. However, there are striking differences among analysts as to *what* policies should be adopted to prevent financial crises and hasten recovery from them. For example, some analysts refer to credit booms in which there is a rapid expansion of lending as a major cause of financial crises. However, a 2012 study of the International Monetary Fund (IMF) found that only about one-third of credit booms resulted in crises. A number of the booms produced long-term economic benefits. Whereas some policy-makers view more regulation of banking activities as essential to prevent financial crises, others argue that over-regulation can limit financial innovation. As for dealing with financial crises, some policy-makers emphasize austerity while others call for government stimulus. Noted economic scholars have also disagreed about policy priorities in response to financial crises. Whereas Niall Ferguson and Kenneth Rogoff believed that the United States had to control its deficits and foreign debt during the 2008 crisis, Paul Krugman argued that government stimulus was a more important priority.

The lack of consensus on how to deal with financial crises also applies to many other problems in the global political economy. Where we stand on issues often depends on where we sit, and our theoretical views can have a major effect on our policy prescriptions. Thus, this book puts considerable emphasis on the role of theory and the relationship between theory and practice. Theory helps us identify a degree of order in the complex world of international political economy (IPE), and enables us to go beyond description and engage in causal explanations and modest predictions. Our theoretical perspective also affects how we perceive and interpret issues. By applying theory to all the major issue areas in IPE, this book will help instructors draw connections between theory and practice for students. The book also focuses on three major themes: globalization, North–North relations (among developed countries), and North–South relations (among developed and developing countries). Despite the importance of globalization, it is *not* leading to a world society or world government. Indeed, considerable space is devoted to regional blocs and organizations such as the EU and the North American Free Trade Agreement (NAFTA), and Chapter 9 focuses specifically on regional trade agreements. Furthermore, the book discusses the interconnections between economic and security issues, and domestic and international issues.

NEW TO THIS EDITION

Some of the significant revisions in this edition include the following:

- I now use the term "neomercantilism" rather than "realism" to describe one of the three main IPE theoretical perspectives; and Chapter 3 discusses the similarities and differences between neomercantilism, realism, and economic nationalism. Chapters 3 and 4 include new sections on present-day neomercantilism and liberalism. Chapter 5 on the critical perspectives has extensive revisions.
- The data and discussion for the balance of payments are completely updated in Chapter 6 on monetary relations. Chapter 6 also updates the discussion of European monetary problems, and examines changes in the role of the U.S. dollar vis-à-vis the euro and the Chinese renminbi.
- To reflect the importance of financial crises, I have moved the subject from Chapter 11 in the sixth edition to Chapter 7 in this edition. The chapter devotes more space to the 2008 global financial crisis and the European sovereign debt crisis, and to the effect of these crises on relations between the developed countries (DCs) and the emerging economies.
- Chapter 8 examines the reasons why the Doha Round of multilateral trade negotiations has still not been concluded, and discusses the implications of this stalemate for the global trade regime.
- The discussion of trade regionalism in Chapter 9 is updated to include current challenges confronting the EU and the NAFTA, and the negotiations for a Trans-Pacific Partnership (TPP) agreement. The discussion of regional integration theory is also expanded and updated.
- Chapter 10 on multinational corporations (MNCs) devotes much more attention to the increasing role of emerging economies such as China, India, and Brazil as both host and home countries for MNCs.
- Chapter 11 on international development substantially updates the discussion of development strategies, and examines how China's policies toward less-developed countries differ from those of the United States, the IMF, and the World Bank.
- Chapter 12 and several other chapters discuss issues that require more attention in the study of IPE, including energy, the environment, and migration.

This edition provides a fully updated Test Bank for instructors. All of the data in the text, and the Questions, Key Terms, and Further Reading sections at the end of the chapters are also updated. In sum, the seventh edition of this text is fully updated and contains many revisions that reflect the changes occurring in the global political economy and in the academic study of IPE.

FEATURES

This book has a number of distinguishing features that have been consistently maintained through the seven editions:

- Emphasis on the interaction between theory and practice. Students understand theory better when they see its practical applications, and theory gives meaning to the substantive IPE issues. Chapters 3–5 discuss the IPE theoretical perspectives, and Chapters 6–11 on substantive issues (monetary relations, financial crises, global and regional trade, multinational corporations, and international development) conclude with a boxed item on "Considering IPE Theory and Practice."
- Attention to the role of formal and informal institutions. With globalization, there is a greater need for global governance in IPE. However, it is becoming more difficult to manage the global economy, and the IMF, World Bank, and World Trade Organization (WTO) are subject to numerous criticisms. Chapter 2 introduces the institutional framework for managing the global economy. Emphasis is also given to the role of private actors such as multinational corporations, nongovernmental organizations, and civil society groups in global economic governance.
- Attention to the historical evolution of issues. Some historical background is essential for understanding contemporary IPE issues. For example, knowing the history of the informal General Agreement on Tariffs and Trade (GATT) helps explain why the major trading economies replaced it with the formal WTO in 1995; and knowing the history of the 1980s foreign debt crisis helps explain why some developing countries are still plagued with foreign debt problems.
- Examination of North–South issues between developed and developing countries. Chapter 11 deals with international development, and the discussion of North–North and North–South issues is integrated throughout the book. This reflects the fact that most developing countries are increasingly integrated in the capitalist global economy, and that some Southern states such as China, India, and Brazil are becoming major economic actors.
- Focus on regional as well as global relations in IPE. Chapter 9 examines the proliferation of regional trade agreements, which is a highly controversial issue in IPE today; and regionalism is also discussed in other chapters.
- Examination of domestic–international interactions in IPE. One effect of globalization is the blurring of boundaries between international and domestic relations.
- Discussion of the broad range of IPE economic concepts, making them as clear as possible for students new to the subject, without oversimplifying them. To make the concepts more "user-friendly," examples are often provided.

■ Inclusion of a number of study and research aids to make the complexities of IPE understandable to students. At the end of the chapters are sections focusing on Questions, Key Terms, and Further Reading. All of the key terms are defined in a Glossary at the end of the book.

ACKNOWLEDGMENTS

I am grateful for the comments, advice, and support of a number of individuals in writing and revising this book. First, I want to thank the late Professor Mark Zacher for the discussions, advice, and friendship we shared over the years. Michael Webb of the University of Victoria also gave me extensive feedback and advice for most of the editions of the book; and Benjamin Cohen of the University of California–Santa Barbara provided some helpful advice and comments. The emphasis of this IPE text on international institutions and governance owes a great deal to the interest I developed in the subject years ago when the late Professor Harold K. Jacobson of the University of Michigan was my Ph.D. supervisor. Furthermore, I want to thank John Craig, the Dean of Arts and Social Sciences at Simon Fraser University, for a research grant which was helpful in completing this edition. I also want to thank Peter McLaren for his assistance in preparing the tables and figures for this edition; and Joel Fox, Paul Tubb, Malcolm Toms, and Pierre Dansereau for their assistance.

The competent editorial staff at Routledge have given me considerable support and encouragement in revising this book for the seventh edition. I especially want to thank Jennifer Knerr, Ze'ev Sudry, and Carrie Bell for their time and assistance. I also appreciate the support of the editorial staff at Pearson Longman for earlier editions of this book.

I am also indebted to the following external reviewers, whose helpful comments contributed to the various editions of this book: Katherine Barbieri, University of South Carolina; Sherry L. Bennett, Rice University; Vicki Birchfield, Georgia Institute of Technology; Kurt Burch, University of Delaware; Jeffrey Cason, Middlebury College; Robert A. Daley, Albertson College; Vincent Ferraro, Mount Holyoke College; David N. Gibbs, University of Arizona; Vicki L. Golich, California State University–San Marcos; Robert Griffiths, University of North Carolina at Greensboro; Beverly G. Hawk, University of Alabama at Birmingham; Michael J. Hiscox, University of California–San Diego; Tobias Hoffman, College of William and Mary; Matthias Kaelberer, University of Northern Iowa; Quan Li, Florida State University; Waltraud Q. Morales, University of Central Florida; Thomas Oatley, University of North Carolina at Chapel Hill; James Quirk, Catholic University of America; Howard Richards, Earlham College; David E. Spiro, University of Arizona; Kenneth P. Thomas, University of Missouri–St. Louis; John Tuman, University of Nevada, Las Vegas; Robert S. Walters, University of Pittsburgh; Ming Wan, George Mason University; and Jin Zeng, Florida International University. In addition, I want to thank four anonymous reviewers of the sixth edition of my book. Thanks are also due to several colleagues at Simon Fraser University, including James Busumtwi-Sam, Anil Hira, Stephen McBride, David Laycock, Sandra MacLean, Tsuyoshi Kawasaki, and Michael Howlett.

My acknowledgments would not be complete without mentioning the important role of my students over the years in asking insightful questions, raising important issues, and providing feedback on the aspects of IPE they found clear or confusing. My sons Daniel and Frank have given me assistance and advice, especially on issues related to the work they both do in international development. Finally, I am dedicating this book to my wife Shirley, for her caring advice, support, and encouragement. She makes it all seem so much more meaningful and worthwhile.

THEODORE H. COHN

ACRONYMS AND ABBREVIATIONS

ACP: African, Caribbean, and Pacific
ADB: Asian Development Bank
ADDs: antidumping duties
AFL: American Federation of Labor
AFTA: ASEAN Free Trade Area
AIDS: acquired immunodeficiency syndrome
AIIB: Asian Infrastructure Investment Bank
ASEAN: Association of Southeast Asian Nations
BIS: Bank for International Settlements
BITs: bilateral investment treaties
BRIC: Brazil, Russia, India, and China
BRICS: Brazil, Russia, India, China, and South Africa
CDF: Comprehensive Development Framework
CDOs: collateralized debt obligations
CEECs: Central and Eastern European countries
CET: common external tariff
CFCs: chlorofluorocarbons
CFIUS: Committee on Foreign Investment in the United States
CIA: Central Intelligence Agency
CIO: Congress of Industrial Organizations
CMEA: Council for Mutual Economic Assistance
CPEs: centrally planned economies
CRTA: Committee on Regional Trade Agreements
CSO: civil society organization
CSR: corporate social responsibility
CTE: Committee on Trade and Environment
CU: customs union
CUSFTA: Canada–U.S. Free Trade Agreement
CVDs: countervailing duties
DAC: Development Assistance Committee
DC: developed country
DDA: Doha Development Agenda

DISC: Domestic International Sales Corporation
EBRD: European Bank for Reconstruction and Development
EC: European Community
ECB: European Central Bank
ECSC: European Coal and Steel Community
EFTA: European Free Trade Association
EMS: European Monetary System
EMU: Economic and Monetary Union
ERM: exchange-rate mechanism
EU: European Union
Euratom: European Atomic Energy Community
FDI: foreign direct investment
FDIC: Federal Deposit Insurance Corporation
FIRA: Foreign Investment Review Agency
FSU: former Soviet Union
FTA: free trade area
G5: Group of Five
G7: Group of Seven
G8: Group of Eight
G10: Group of 10
G20: Group of 20
G24: Group of 24
G77: Group of 77
GAB: General Arrangements to Borrow
GATS: General Agreement on Trade in Services
GATT: General Agreement on Tariffs and Trade
GDP: gross domestic product
GHG: greenhouse gas
GNI: gross national income
GNP: gross national product
GPE: global political economy
GSP: generalized system of preferences
HDI: human development index
HIPC: heavily indebted poor countries
HIV: human immunodeficiency virus

IBRD: International Bank for Reconstruction and Development (World Bank)

ICSID: International Center for Settlement of Investment Disputes

IDA: International Development Association

IDB: Inter-American Development Bank

IFC: International Finance Corporation

IHDI: inequality-adjusted human development index

IMF: International Monetary Fund

IO: international organization

IPE: international political economy

IR: international relations

ISDS: investor-state dispute settlement

ISI: import substitution industrialization

ITO: International Trade Organization

ITT: International Telephone and Telegraph Corporation

KIEOs: keystone international economic organizations

LAFTA: Latin American Free Trade Association

LDC: less-developed country

LIC: low-income country

LLDC: least developed country

M&As: mergers and acquisitions

MAI: Multilateral Agreement on Investment

MBS: mortgage-backed securities

MDG: Millennium Development Goals

MDRI: Multilateral Debt Relief Initiative

Mercosur: Southern Common Market Treaty

MFA: Multi-Fiber Arrangement

MFN: most favored nation

MIC: middle-income country

MIGA: Multilateral Investment Guarantee Agency

MNC: multinational corporation

MTNs: multilateral trade negotiations

NAFTA: North American Free Trade Agreement

NATO: North Atlantic Treaty Organization

NEM: New Economic Mechanism

NEP: National Energy Program

NGO: nongovernmental organization

NIE: newly industrializing economy

NIEO: New International Economic Order

NTB: nontariff barrier

OBM: obsolescing bargain model

ODA: official development assistance

ODF: official development finance

OECD: Organization for Economic Cooperation and Development

OEEC: Organization for European Economic Cooperation

OPEC: Organization of Petroleum Exporting Countries

PPP: purchasing power parity

PRB: Population Reference Bureau

PRC: People's Republic of China

PRSPs: Poverty Reduction Strategy Papers

PTA: preferential trade agreement

R&D: research and development

RCEP: Regional Comprehensive Economic Partnership

RMB: renminbi

RTA: regional trade agreement

RTAA: Reciprocal Trade Agreements Act

SAL: structural adjustment loan

SAP: structural adjustment program

SDRs: special drawing rights

SDT: special and differential treatment

SEA: Single European Act

SEC: Securities and Exchange Commission

SWF: sovereign wealth fund

TAN: transnational advocacy network

TOA: Treaty of Asunción

TPP: Trans-Pacific Partnership

TRIMs: Trade-Related Investment Measures

TRIPs: Trade-Related Intellectual Property Rights

TTIP: Transatlantic Trade and Investment Partnership

UN: United Nations

UNCTAD: United Nations Conference on Trade and Development

UNCTC: United Nations Center on Transnational Corporations

UNDP: United Nations Development Program
UNICEF: United Nations Children's Fund

USTR: U.S. Trade Representative
VERs: voluntary export restraints
WEF: World Economic Forum
WTO: World Trade Organization

Introduction and Overview

The global political economy has a major effect on people, societies, and states today. A country's economic growth depends on its productivity, and production has become increasingly global. For example, an automobile manufactured by a major U.S. auto company may be assembled in Britain with inputs from all over Europe, designs produced in the United States, and stages of processing in various locations. Some Japanese auto companies depend on lower-wage Asian countries for much of their auto parts production. With the globalization of production, we have become more dependent on multinational corporations (MNCs) for our employment. Many Americans work for MNCs, and U.S. MNCs locate some of their production in other countries to take advantage of lower wages and taxes. The global political economy also affects us as consumers. The United States exports fruit and vegetables to Canada, and a drought in California affects prices for Canadians as well as Americans. Furthermore, much of the clothing we buy is produced in lower-wage countries in Asia. In sum, the increase of global interdependence is affecting our most important economic activities, including production, employment, and consumption. Politics and economics are intertwined because of the importance of these economic activities to individuals, governments, and states. Thus, international political economy (IPE) is an important area of study. Chapter 1 introduces the subject of IPE, the IPE theoretical perspectives, and the main themes of this book. Chapter 2 provides an overview of global economic relations before World War II and the postwar institutional framework developed to manage the global economy. For ease of reference, all terms defined in the glossary are in **bold print** when they are first described in detail.

Introduction

The developed countries (DCs) of the North, particularly the West—the United States and the European Union (EU)—have been the predominant economic powers in the global political economy. However, cracks have appeared in this Western predominance and some economic power has been shifting toward Asia, especially China. The 2008 global financial crisis which began in the United States and the current EU sovereign debt crisis are dramatic signposts of this shift in economic power. We begin this introductory chapter with a brief discussion of these crises, because they are affecting all the substantive issue areas we examine in this book. This book also examines the challenge China is posing to the West in most areas of the global political economy, despite the country's economic slowdown and the need to reorient its economy.

Financial crises go back to at least the thirteenth century, but in the mid-1980s central banks seemed to become better at limiting deep recessions, and many economists believed that the U.S. Federal Reserve had learned how to "tame" the business cycle. Thus, the 25-year period from the mid-1980s to about 2006 was called the *Great Moderation*.[1] Since business cycle downturns seemed less of a threat, financial innovations and deregulation encouraged investors to overextend themselves, and U.S. mortgage lenders provided *subprime mortgages* to people with low incomes or poor credit ratings who did not qualify for regular mortgages at market interest rates. The increased demand for houses led to a building boom, which resulted in reduced U.S. housing prices by mid-2006. Mortgages were also coming up for renewal at higher interest rates, and many subprime borrowers had to default on their loans because they owed more than the value of their houses. A number of large U.S. banks and financial institutions had repackaged and sold the subprime mortgages as mortgage-backed securities to investors around the world. One of these institutions was Lehman Brothers, the fourth largest U.S. investment bank. When Lehman Brothers went bankrupt in September 2008, this caused a chain reaction that resulted in the worst financial crisis since the Great Depression of the 1930s. Chapter 7 discusses how the current EU sovereign debt crisis resulted from homegrown factors as well as the 2008 global financial crisis, and Chapter 6 discusses how the EU debt crisis is posing a threat to the viability of the euro currency. Ongoing difficulties in dealing with the crisis, especially in Greece, have increased the EU's vulnerability to Russia's assertive policies in Ukraine, the migration crisis from the Middle East and North Africa, and anti-EU sentiments in Britain and some other member states.

The study of IPE requires factual knowledge in areas such as trade, monetary and financial relations, foreign investment, and development. However, people interpret the "facts" differently depending on whether they view them "from a bank office in Zurich, a *maquiladora* [border factory] in Mexico, a shantytown in Peru, a rice paddy in Sri Lanka ... [or] a trade office in Washington, DC."[2] Our interpretation of the facts also depends on our theoretical views, and the only choice is whether these views are implicit or whether we explicitly examine the theories we use to interpret issues and events. For example, different accounts of the causes of financial crises (in Chapter 7) demonstrate how our theoretical views affect our interpretation of international events. Our theoretical views also determine what facts we consider important. For example, neomercantilists focus on the power relations among developed countries in the North, while many critical theorists argue that the North's exploitation of less-developed countries (LDCs) in the South is a more pressing issue. This book focuses on competing theoretical perspectives, because the study of IPE is "far too important and multifaceted to leave to one analytic or methodological perspective alone."[3] This book also emphasizes the interaction between theory and practice: Theory shapes our practice of IPE, and practical experience leads us to reassess our theories. Before introducing the main theoretical perspectives and themes of this book, we address the question "what is IPE?"

WHAT IS INTERNATIONAL POLITICAL ECONOMY?

IPE scholars believe that we must cross the boundary between economics and political science if we are to understand behavior, relationships, and change at the global level. The political side of IPE deals with the pursuit of power and influence by a wide range of public and private actors. The most important public actor is the **state**, a sovereign, territorial political unit. The economic side of IPE deals with the pursuit of wealth and prosperity in the **market**, a coordinating mechanism where buyers and sellers exchange goods and services at prices determined by supply and demand. The market, according to liberal economists, results in the efficient allocation of scarce resources, so that consumer preferences determine what is produced. Economists and political scientists also focus on the *distribution* of wealth and power. Economics is concerned with the production and distribution of goods and services. In a free market economy, scarce resources are allocated through a pricing mechanism where supply and demand determine the production levels and prices of various goods. However, wealth is not equally distributed, so the marketplace benefits some more than others. Prices are in fact determined by the balance between supply and *effective* demand, or demand backed by purchasing power. A consumer without purchasing power cannot compete for scarce resources. When a few large business firms dominate the market for a product they can also limit competition and raise prices to increase their profits. Politics is concerned with the distribution of power in society. Those with more power and influence can affect the distribution of resources through policies, rules, and institutions that determine tax levels, employment prospects, and the provision of public services such as health care and welfare payments.

It is difficult to separate economics from politics, because governments may intervene in the market in efforts to improve economic performance, ensure that wealth is distributed more equitably, or correct for **market failure**. "Market failure" refers to the failure of a market to produce an optimal allocation of resources; for example, the market may produce private benefits that have huge social costs. Governments may also intervene in the market for corrupt reasons, such as enriching government officials. As interdependence has increased, governments have been drawn into the competitive forces of the world economy. Thus, *competition states* seek to increase their competitiveness by restructuring industry, deregulating financial markets, and supporting research and development (R&D) in high-technology sectors.[4] As we discuss, the rapid growth of the East Asian economies from the 1960s to 1980s was related to their symbiotic relationship with the competitive marketplace.

The title of this book is *Global Political Economy (GPE)* to reflect changes in the world as a result of *globalization*—which is one of the main themes of this book. Although the state continues to be the most important actor, it must share the stage with a wide range of nongovernmental and governmental actors at the subnational and transnational levels. Whether we refer to our field as IPE or GPE, it is interdisciplinary and draws on contributions from political scientists, economists, sociologists, anthropologists, historians, and geographers. Thus, IPE theorists criticize some economists for **economism** (i.e., an overemphasis on the importance of economics) and some political scientists for **politicism** (i.e., an overemphasis on the importance of politics).[5] IPE scholars also devote considerable attention to domestic–international linkages. Whereas domestic groups often leave international security decisions to the government "experts," they demand a greater role in international economic decisions because trade and foreign investment are "bread and butter issues" that affect their economic welfare. The distribution of scarce economic resources can have major consequences for individuals and societies, and Chapters 3 to 5 show that the IPE theoretical perspectives have different views on the distributional issues.

THE IPE THEORETICAL PERSPECTIVES

Many students tend to avoid "theory," but without it we cannot assess the broader implications of our statistical and factual studies. Some critics point to our failure to develop an all-embracing IPE theory to explain events. However, the existence of different theoretical perspectives is necessary, because even more objective IPE theorizing is partly based on our values. Thus, Robert Cox asserts that social science theory "is always *for* someone and *for* some purpose."[6] Alan Blinder writes that "economists come in all political stripes— just like other people," and that he has "long been distressed by the high correlation between economists' political views and their allegedly objective research findings."[7] This book focuses on three IPE theoretical perspectives that will never be entirely compatible because they are based on different sets of values: neomercantilism, liberalism, and critical perspectives. Critics of this typology argue that some IPE concepts and theories cannot be neatly categorized under one of these three perspectives. However, we believe that students should first become familiar with the main IPE theoretical perspectives; with this background, they will be in a better position to develop alternative theoretical formulations. We take a flexible approach to IPE theory in several respects. First, we do *not* view the IPE perspectives as separate ideologies, and we examine how they overlap and influence each other over time. Second, we discuss various concepts and theories that do not neatly fit within one perspective; examples include hegemonic, regime, feminist, and environmental theory. This flexible approach encourages students to explore alternative theoretical routes once they have mastered the basics.

Chapters 3 and 4 focus on the two mainstream IPE perspectives: neomercantilism and liberalism. Whereas realism, a major perspective in international relations (IR), focuses more on the military-security aspects of power, neomercantilism as an IPE perspective focuses more on the economic aspects of power. Neomercantilists examine how states develop economic policies to increase their wealth and position in the international system. Since IPE is a "self-help" system without a centralized authority, states must build up their power or form alliances to prevent being dominated by others. Thus, neomercantilists view IPE as a *zero-sum game*, in which one state's gain is another state's loss, and they focus on *relative gains* or a state's gains in relation to the gains of other states. In IPE each state tries to manipulate the market to capture relative gains. The roots of neomercantilism in the mercantilist period (see Chapter 3) make it the oldest IPE theoretical perspective; but liberalism is the most important IPE perspective. We should note that the term *liberal* is used differently in IPE and in U.S. domestic politics. In the United States, "liberals" support greater government involvement in the market to prevent inequalities and stimulate growth, whereas "conservatives" support free markets and minimal government intervention. Orthodox liberals in IPE are more akin to U.S. conservatives, because they favor free markets, private property rights, and only a limited government role in economic activities. However, Keynesian liberals are more accepting of government intervention (see Chapter 4). Liberals are more optimistic than neomercantilists about the prospects for cooperation among states, and they believe that international institutions can promote cooperation. Thus, liberals view economic relationships as a *positive-sum game*, in which all states benefit, even if they do not benefit equally.

Chapter 5 discusses four *critical perspectives* that view the mainstream perspectives as favoring some groups or issues and marginalizing others. *Historical materialism* encompasses the largest group of critical theories. Stemming partly from Marxism, historical materialism is "historical" because it examines structural change over time, with an emphasis on class and North–South struggles. The perspective is "materialist" because it examines the role of material (especially economic) factors in shaping society.[8] Capitalism is the dominant system today, with the capitalist class (the bourgeoisie) exploiting the workers (the proletariat). Chapter 5 also discusses three other critical perspectives: *constructivism*, *feminism*, and *environmentalism*. They do not fully "fit" in the critical category, and all three of them have liberal variants. However, we include them in Chapter 5 because they all examine issues that the mainstream perspectives have traditionally overlooked.

Although the neomercantilist, liberal, and critical perspectives provide alternative lenses for viewing IPE issues, they have evolved and influenced each other over time. Hybrid theories such as hegemonic stability and regime theory are also linked with more than one perspective. Furthermore, the relationship between domestic institutions and IPE does not fit easily into a single perspective. In addition to the main theoretical perspectives, this book discusses hybrid theories and domestic–international interactions.

PURPOSES AND THEMES OF THIS BOOK

This book provides a comprehensive approach to the study of IPE. Part II discusses the theoretical perspectives, and Part III examines substantive issues—monetary relations, financial crises, global and regional trade, multinational corporations, and international development. To help draw connections between theory and the substantive issues, this book focuses on three major themes: globalization, North–North relations, and North–South relations. We also discuss South–South relations, but it is not one of the major themes of the book.

Globalization

The first theme of this book, **globalization**, involves the broadening and deepening of interdependence among peoples and states. Broadening refers to the extension of geographic linkages to all major societies and states, so that policies and events in one part of the world can have global repercussions. Deepening refers to the greater frequency and intensity of state and societal interactions. Although states continue to be the most important actors in IR, modern telecommunications and transportation have increased connections among people across territorial boundaries. Thus, states are confronting a more complex environment in which international organizations (IOs), MNCs, and nongovernmental organizations (NGOs) have important roles. Theorists have different definitions of globalization, and different views regarding its causes and effects. Whereas some theorists argue that globalization stems from technological advances, others emphasize the role of the state, the role of MNCs, the capitalist mode of production, and cultural and social-psychological factors.[9] We discuss several definitions of globalization here, and focus on its causes and effects in Chapters 3–5.

At one end of the spectrum are *extreme* or **hyperglobalists**, who view globalization as creating a "borderless world" in which MNCs lose their national identities, and regional and global markets replace national economies. For example, Kenichi Ohmae asserts that "traditional nation states have become unnatural, even impossible, business units in a global economy."[10] When there is no longer state interference, MNC decisions and consumer choices will result in the rational allocation of global resources. We devote less attention to the views of hyperglobalists, because there is little evidence that the state is withering away.[11] **Internationalists** recognize that interdependence is increasing and that nonstate actors have a role in IPE, but they believe that the world is no more "global" than it was in the nineteenth century. The international economy "is still fundamentally characterized by exchange between relatively distinct and national economies."[12] Events such as the persistence of violent international conflict and the current disunity within the European Union convince internationalists that violence, geopolitics, and the national interest continue to be central concerns.[13]

Moderate globalists take a mid-range position between hyperglobalists and internationalists. Although they reject the hyperglobalist view that the state is no longer viable, they differentiate *international* relations among states from *global* relations taking place without regard to territorial boundaries. Global linkages in finance, trade, and communications have existed in the past, but they now occur more frequently, intensely, and on a wider scale. For example, the Internet provides instantaneous linkages; MNCs control economic resources greater than those of many states; and global problems such as climate change and market volatility are increasing. Although states continue to be important, they must share the stage with private actors such as MNCs and NGOs, and with systems of global and regional governance. Moderate globalists view the world as *globalizing*, rather than fully *globalized*, because territorial and supraterritorial relations coexist.[14]

This book provides evidence that the internationalist and moderate globalist positions both have some validity. Relying on these two approaches, we briefly discuss some important points about globalization:

- Globalization is not uniform throughout the world. Its effects are more evident in urban centers than in rural areas, remote islands, and the poorest countries.
- Globalization is *not* causing the state to wither away. Although the autonomy of states is eroding in some respects, they are adopting new and more complex functions to deal with an interdependent world and they continue to have policy-making choices.
- Globalization can result in fragmentation and conflict as well as unity and cooperation. For example, it is often associated with an increase in

global competitiveness and the formation of regional economic blocs in Europe, North America, and East Asia. Although competitiveness is a "contested concept" with various meanings, this book shows that it causes states to be concerned with their relative positions in the global economy.

■ Interdependence and globalization are not unique to the present-day world, and it is possible that international events could cause some reversal. For example, there was a high degree of interdependence in trade and foreign investment before World War I which declined during the interwar period and began to increase again after World War II.[15]

Currently there are many indications that we may again be entering a period of some reversal of globalization. First, countries have been less interested in trade multilateralism through the World Trade Organization (WTO), and more interested in bilateral and regional trade agreements. Second, the European sovereign debt crisis has given populists who oppose many aspects of European integration more influence. Third, emerging economies such as China, India, and Brazil are increasingly dissatisfied with their limited influence in the International Monetary Fund (IMF) and World Bank. Fourth, Russian President Vladimir Putin's annexation of Crimea and intervention in eastern Ukraine have resulted in Western economic sanctions and a decline in Russia's linkages with the West. Fifth, there is increased fragmentation and conflict in the Middle East, with a growing number of "failed states" such as Syria, Iraq, and Libya.[16]

Despite the historical fluctuations, globalization is more encompassing today than at any time in the past. With advances in technology, communications, and transportation, state activities are being internationalized to a degree not previously experienced. Global interdependence today is also qualitatively different than previously. Although a number of corporations globalized their activities during the nineteenth century, the MNC's role in generating foreign investment, trade, and technology is a modern-day phenomenon.[17] The geographic reach of the capitalist economic system is also encompassing the entire globe, with LDCs and transition economies of Eastern Europe and the former Soviet Union (FSU) becoming more involved in the global economy. For the first time, membership in the IMF, World Bank, and WTO is becoming truly global. This book examines the implications of these changes and the differing views as to whether globalization is a positive or negative process.

North–North Relations

The second theme of this book concerns North–North relations. International management has been primarily a North–North issue, because the DCs in Western Europe, North America, and Japan are the only states that have had the wealth and power to look after international management of the global economy. However, emerging economies in the South such as China, India, and Brazil are posing a growing challenge to Northern management. This book discusses two factors that contribute to global economic management: hegemony and international institutions.

The United States was the undisputed leader or *hegemon* after World War II because of its economic and military power. An important measure of economic power is the **gross domestic product (GDP)**, the total value of goods and services produced within a country's borders in a given year. The GDP records income in terms of where it is earned rather than who owns the factors of production. Thus, the GDP includes the interest and profits domestic and foreign companies and individuals earn in a country; it does not include income the country's residents earn abroad. The **gross national product (GNP)** by contrast records income according to who owns the factors of production rather than where the income is earned; it includes the total value of goods and services produced by domestically owned factors of production in a given year. The GNP is derived by adding the income a country's residents earn from foreign activity to the GDP and subtracting the income foreigners earn from activity in the country. For example, the income a U.S. resident earns in France is part of the U.S. GNP but not the U.S. GDP; this income by contrast is included in the French GDP but not in the French GNP. A number of states and IOs now use a third indicator, the **gross national income (GNI)**, instead of the GNP. In practical terms, the GNI equals the GNP—it simply measures the income produced by the GNP rather than the value of the product itself.[18] This book usually uses the GDP, because most countries use it as their measure of national economic activity. However, a country's GDP and GNI (or GNP) normally do not differ greatly, and we use all these measures, depending on the source of the data. Whether we use the GDP or GNI, the United States was clearly the economic hegemon after World War II. During the war the U.S. GDP had increased by about 50 percent, whereas Western European states had lost one-quarter of their GDPs on average and the Soviet Union and Japanese economies were severely damaged. In 1950, the U.S. GDP was about three times larger than the Soviet Union's, five times larger than Britain's, and 20 times larger than Japan's. Western Europe and Japan also depended on U.S. aid and foreign investment for their postwar reconstruction.[19]

During the 1960s, the United States' *relative* economic position began to decline as Western Europe and Japan recovered from the war. The extent of the U.S. economic decline and the possibilities for U.S. hegemonic renewal are matters of intense debate, partly because IR and IPE theorists focus on different aspects of hegemony. IR theorists, focusing on *security*, often argue that U.S. hegemony has increased since the breakup of the Soviet bloc and Soviet Union. However, IPE theorists often assert that the United States' relative *economic* power has declined since the end of World War II. In 1971, the United States shifted from having annual balance-of-trade surpluses to having trade deficits (i.e., imports greater than exports). Since then, the United States has become a major recipient as well as source of foreign direct investment, and there has been less confidence in the U.S. dollar as the top international currency. The United States remains a major force in the global economy, and it accounts for about 22.5 percent of world GDP in nominal terms.[20] However, the relative

U.S. economic decline has resulted in a gradual shift from unilateral U.S. to collective management of the global economy. Today, an emerging economy—China—poses a growing challenge to U.S. hegemony. China is already the world's largest merchandise exporter and the second largest importer. China also holds the world's largest foreign exchange reserves, amounting to about $4 trillion. However, China is still a relatively poor country in terms of GDP *per capita* (income per person).

Another factor in global economic management is the role of international institutions. Under U.S. and British leadership, three international economic organizations were established in the 1940s to help manage the global economy: the IMF, the International Bank for Reconstruction and Development (IBRD or World Bank), and the General Agreement on Tariffs and Trade (GATT). The DCs were the dominant economic powers in these organizations, and they also created some institutions largely limited to DC membership, including the Organization for Economic Cooperation and Development (OECD) and the Group of Seven (G7). In 1995 the WTO replaced the GATT as the main global trade organization. This book examines the role of these institutions in managing the global economy.

Despite the joint efforts of DCs to manage the global economy, they also have some significant differences. Three major economic blocs emerged in Europe, North America, and East Asia with the decline of U.S. economic hegemony and the end of the Cold War. The competitiveness among these blocs has major consequences for the future of the global economy, and differences over security issues such as the 2003 U.S.-led war against Iraq have further exacerbated the divisions among DCs. Thus, the second theme of this text concerns the linkages and divisions among DCs of the North.

North–South Relations

The third theme of this book concerns North–South relations. The South includes almost all the countries of Latin America and the Caribbean, Asia, and Africa and the Middle East. These countries are mainly LDCs with colonial histories and lower levels of economic and social development. In 1950 the South accounted for almost 65 percent of the total world population, and today this figure has climbed to 85 percent of the world total. After passing the 7 billion mark in 2011, the world population grew to 7.06 billion in mid-2012, and countries in the South accounted for about 97 percent of this growth because of their high birth rates and young populations. A number of former Communist states in Eastern Europe and the FSU are now receiving foreign debt and development financing from the DCs and are, in effect, also a part of the South. When we speak of the world, we therefore must give a great deal of attention to the South.[21]

LDCs generally have lower per capita incomes, inadequate **infrastructure** (e.g., transportation and communications), and limited access to modern technology. Many LDCs also have inadequate educational facilities, health and sanitary facilities, and low literacy rates. Assessing political development in a country is a difficult and contentious issue; but LDCs are more likely than DCs to have unstable and authoritarian governments.[22] LDCs also have less influence in international economic organizations such as the IMF, World Bank, and WTO. It is important to note that many IOs and development theorists prefer the term *developing countries* to *LDCs* because they believe the term *LDC* suggests that these countries are inferior or are expected to follow the same path to development as the DCs. However, LDC is used as an abbreviation in this book simply to indicate that these countries are *economically* less developed. LDCs may have histories and cultures as rich or richer than those of DCs, and they may follow different paths to development.

LDCs in fact have become a highly diverse group of countries with major differences in income and economic development. Some analysts therefore question whether it is still meaningful to speak of the South as a single group. On the one hand, some countries in the South have dramatically increased their economic standing. For example, the East Asian newly industrializing economies (NIEs)—South Korea, Taiwan, Singapore, and Hong Kong—have relatively high per capita incomes and literacy rates and are competitive with DCs in some areas; some larger LDCs and transition economies such as the BRIC economies—Brazil, Russia, India, and China—have increased their political and economic influence; and some members of the Organization of Petroleum Exporting Countries (OPEC) such as Qatar, Kuwait, and Saudi Arabia have higher GDPs than many DCs. On the other hand, the UN list of 48 least developed countries (LLDCs)—mainly in Sub-Saharan Africa and Central Asia—have extremely low per capita incomes, literacy rates, and shares of manufacturing. One analyst estimates that 4 billion of the 5 billion people in LDCs are in fact benefiting from development; but the "bottom billion"— most of whom are in LLDCs—are caught in a "development trap" and falling further behind.[23]

Despite the economic disparities within the South, a major characteristic of the global economy is the inequality in wealth and power between DCs and most LDCs. Although China surpassed Japan in 2010 as the world's second largest national economy (in terms of GDP) after the United States, Japan, the United States, and Germany are still well above China in terms of GDP *per capita*; China ranked 121st among countries in GDP per capita in 2013.[24] Although some OPEC members such as Qatar and Kuwait have very high per capita incomes, their income is mainly based on oil wealth and in many respects they remain LDCs. Although China, India, Brazil, and Russia have growing economic and political influence, they have major problems to overcome. In 2005 the United Nations Development Program reported that "convergence is a relative concept. Absolute income inequalities between rich and poor countries are increasing even when developing countries have higher growth rates— precisely because the initial income gaps are so large."[25] This book explores the strategies LDCs have employed to promote economic development and increase their influence.

Although we focus mainly on inequalities between DCs and LDCs, there are also great differences of wealth and power within states. Brazil has one of the largest income gaps among LDCs, with the per capita income of the richest 10 percent of people 32 times higher than that of the poorest 40 percent.[26] As Chapter 11 discusses, women and children in LDCs are especially disadvantaged. (Disparities in wealth are of course also present within DCs.) This book examines the effects of changes in the global economy on inequalities both among and within states. Chapters 3–5 show that IPE theorists have different interpretations of the main themes in this book. In regard to globalization, neomercantilists emphasize the centrality of the state; liberals believe that globalization is an important and beneficial process; and historical materialists also view globalization as significant but as having negative consequences for poorer people, LDCs, and those marginalized because of gender, race, and ethnicity. In regard to North–North relations, liberals are more inclined than other theorists to see international institutions as having a positive role in promoting economic cooperation. In regard to North–South and gender-based relations, critical theorists place more emphasis than liberals or neomercantilists on inequalities and exploitation.

FOCUS OF THIS BOOK

This book introduces undergraduate and graduate students to the study of IPE, and we have already discussed some of its distinguishing features. First, it provides an in-depth background to IPE theory, current IPE issues in historical perspective, and the interplay between theory and practice. Without the organizing framework of theory, discussions about trade, foreign investment, and development simply become a series of disparate facts. Although we devote considerable attention to the mainstream perspectives of liberalism and neomercantilism, we do *not* accept the view that the breakup of the Soviet bloc marked an "end of history" leading to "the universalization of Western liberal democracy as the final form of human government."[27] Thus, we also examine major critical perspectives.

Second, we focus on three themes relating to globalization, North–North relations, and North–South relations. Third, we emphasize the role of global and regional organizations. Early scholarship on international organizations had a strong idealistic and legal focus on the bodies and rules of the League of Nations and UN, and post-World War II realists pointed out that these studies did not deal with the real world of power politics. In recent years, scholars have recognized the need to study IOs as part of international politics, and we examine the limitations as well as the strengths of international economic organizations.[28] IOs are to a large degree creatures of their member states, and they are having difficulty managing the international economy in an age of globalization; for example, the daily flows of foreign exchange on global markets are much greater than the total resources of the World Bank, IMF, and UN. Despite their limitations, IOs are important forums for negotiation that assist in upholding the principles, norms, and rules of the global economy.

Fourth, this book emphasizes regional as well as global relations in IPE. At one end of the spectrum, countries ranging from the United States to Japan, Singapore, and Mexico are negotiating a number of bilateral free-trade agreements. At the other end of the spectrum are much larger regional trade agreements (RTAs) such as the EU and the North American Free Trade Agreement (NAFTA). Although liberal economists fear that the many smaller bilateral RTAs could impede global trade liberalization, they believe that the larger EU and NAFTA may be "stepping stones" to global free trade. Reinforcing the idea that RTAs may be "stepping stones" is the trend to negotiate larger cross-continental regional agreements. Prime examples are the negotiations for Trans-Pacific Partnership (TPP) and Trans-Atlantic Trade and Investment Partnership (TTIP) agreements (see Chapter 9).

Fifth, this book focuses on North–South issues and integrates the North–North and North–South discussions as much as possible for several reasons. The IPE theoretical perspectives should be assessed in terms of their approach to all countries, and Chapters 3–5 discuss each perspective's approach to North–South as well as North–North relations. Part III also integrates the discussion of North–North and North–South relations because globalization in trade, foreign investment, and monetary relations is affecting the entire world.

Sixth, this book discusses Eastern Europe, the FSU, and China, which are in transition from centrally planned to market economies. They have established closer economic ties with the DCs and have become active members of international economic organizations. However, there have been growing tensions between the DCs and Russia under President Vladimir Putin.

Seventh, this book examines the challenges civil society groups and NGOs are posing to globalization and the policies of the IMF, World Bank, and WTO. Finally, this book devotes considerable attention to contemporary changes in IPE, such as the global financial crisis and the sovereign debt crisis in Europe; the growing influence of China, India, and Brazil as emerging economies; and the effects of environmental changes on the prospects for growth in the global political economy.

Chapter 2 provides an overview of the history and institutions of the postwar international economic order; Chapters 3–5 discuss the basic assumptions and historical evolution of the IPE theoretical perspectives; and Chapters 6–11 cover monetary relations, financial crises, global trade, trade regionalism, MNCs, and international development. To assist students in understanding the issues and concepts, Chapters 1–11 have Questions and Key Terms sections, together with suggestions for further reading.

QUESTIONS

1. What is IPE, and why do IPE scholars criticize some economists and political scientists? What is the relationship between "the state" and "the market"?
2. What was the 2008 global financial crisis, and what were some of its causes?
3. What is the importance of theory, and what are the main theoretical perspectives in IPE?
4. What are the hyperglobalist, moderate globalist, and internationalist views of globalization? Which group's views do you find most convincing, and why?

5. Why has the North been so important in managing the global economy? Do you think that the South is gaining in influence?
6. What are the East Asian NIEs, the BRIC economies, and the LLDCs? What do these groups tell us about economic disparities within the South?

KEY TERMS

economism
globalization
gross domestic product
gross national income
gross national product

hyperglobalists
infrastructure
internationalists
market
market failure

moderate globalists
politicism
state

FURTHER READING

The *Review of International Political Economy* has special issues on IPE as a field of study (vol. 20, no. 5, 2013) and on the American school of IPE (vol. 16, no. 1, 2009). Useful handbooks on IPE as a discipline include Ralph Pettman, ed., *Handbook on International Political Economy* (Hackensack, NJ: World Scientific, 2012), and Mark Blyth, ed., *Routledge Handbook of International Political Economy* (New York: Routledge, 2009). Other recommended books include Benjamin J. Cohen, *International Political Economy: An Intellectual History* (Princeton, NJ: Princeton University Press, 2008), and Robert Gilpin with Jean M. Gilpin's seminal study, *The Political Economy of International Relations* (Princeton, NJ: Princeton University Press, 1987).

Studies on globalization from different perspectives include Robert C. Feenstra and Alan M. Taylor, eds., *Globalization in an Age of Crisis* (Chicago: University of Chicago Press, 2014); Philip McMichael, "Globalization: A Project in Crisis," in Ronen Palan, ed., *Global Political Economy: Contemporary Theories*, 2nd ed. (New York: Routledge, 2013), pp. 75–88; David Held and Anthony McGrew, *Globalization/Anti-Globalization: Beyond the Great Divide*, 2nd ed. (Malden, MA: Polity Press, 2007); Ngaire Woods, *The Globalizers: The IMF, the World Bank and Their Borrowers* (Ithaca, NY: Cornell University Press, 2006); Jan Aart Scholte, *Globalization: A Critical Introduction*, 2nd ed. (New York: Palgrave Macmillan, 2005); Jagdish Bhagwati, *In Defense of Globalization* (New York: Oxford University Press, 2004); and Linda Weiss, *The Myth of the Powerless State* (Ithaca, NY: Cornell University Press, 1998).

NOTES

1. James H. Stock and Mark W. Watson coined the term "Great Moderation" in "Has the Business Cycle Changed and Why?" *NBER Macroeconomics Annual 2002*, Vol. 17, January 2003, p. 162; Carmen M. Reinhart and Kenneth S. Rogoff, *This Time Is Different: Eight Centuries of Financial Folly* (Princeton, NJ: Princeton University Press, 2009).
2. James A. Caporaso, "Global Political Economy," in Ada Finifter, ed., *Political Science: The State of the Discipline II* (Washington, DC: American Political Science Association, 1993), p. 451.
3. Kathleen R. McNamara, "Of Intellectual Monocultures and the Study of IPE," *Review of International Political Economy* 16, no. 1 (February 2009), p. 73.

4. Philip G. Cerny, "Paradoxes of the Competition State: The Dynamics of Political Globalization," *Government and Opposition* 32, no. 2 (April 1997), pp. 251–274.

5. Colin Hay and David Marsh, "Introduction: Towards a New (International) Political Economy?" *New Political Economy* 4, no. 1 (1999), pp. 9–10.

6. Robert W. Cox, "Social Forces, States and World Orders: Beyond International Theory," *Millennium* 10, no. 2 (1981), p. 128.

7. Alan S. Blinder, "What's the Matter with Economics?" *New York Review of Books*, December 18, 2014, pp. 56–57.

8. Mark Rupert and Hazel Smith, eds., *Historical Materialism and Globalization* (New York: Routledge, 2002).

9. Jan Aart Scholte, *Globalization: A Critical Introduction*, 2nd ed. (New York: Palgrave Macmillan, 2005); Aseem Prakash and Jeffrey A. Hart, "Globalization and Governance: An Introduction," in Aseem Prakash and Jeffrey A. Hart, eds., *Globalization and Governance* (London: Routledge, 1999), pp. 4–17.

10. Kenichi Ohmae, *The End of the Nation State: The Rise of Regional Economies* (New York: Free Press, 1995), p. 5.

11. Linda Weiss, ed., *States in the Global Economy: Bringing Domestic Institutions Back In* (Cambridge: Cambridge University Press, 2003), p. 3, ch. 1.

12. Paul Hirst and Grahame Thompson, *Globalization in Question: The International Economy and the Possibilities of Governance*, 2nd ed. (Cambridge, MA: Polity Press, 1999), p. 7.

13. David Held and Anthony McGrew, *Globalization/Anti-Globalization: Beyond the Great Divide*, 2nd ed. (Malden, MA: Polity Press, 2007), pp. 6–8.

14. Scholte, *Globalization: A Critical Introduction*, pp. 59–75.

15. Philip G. Cerny, "Globalization and Other Stories: The Search for a New Paradigm for International Relations," *International Journal* 51, no. 4 (Autumn 1996), pp. 617–637; David P. Rapkin and Jonathan R. Strand, "Competitiveness: Useful Concept, Political Slogan, or Dangerous Obsession?" in David P. Rapkin and William P. Avery, eds., *National Competitiveness in a Global Economy* (Boulder, CO: Rienner, 1995), pp. 1–20.

16. Philip Stephens, "'Fragmentation' and 'Identity' are Reshaping the World," *Financial Times*, December 18, 2014.

17. John H. Dunning, *Multinational Enterprises and the Global Economy* (Wokingham, MA: Addison-Wesley, 1993), pp. 14–15.

18. On the GNP and GNI, see Organization for Economic Cooperation and Development, *System of National Accounts, 1993—Glossary* (Paris: OECD, 2000), p. 23; World Bank, *World Development Report—2003* (Washington, DC: World Bank, 2003), pp. 233, 245.

19. Joseph S. Nye, Jr., *Bound to Lead: The Changing Nature of American Power* (New York: Basic Books, 1990), p. 70.

20. Paul R. Krugman and Maurice Obstfeld, *International Economics: Theory and Policy*, 7th ed. (New York: Pearson Addison-Wesley, 2006), pp. 11–14 and 280–283.

21. Mike Mason, *Development and Disorder: A History of the Third World Since 1945* (Toronto: Between the Lines, 1997), p. 1; William A. McEachern, *Macroeconomics: A Contemporary Introduction* (Independence, KY: South-Western, 2009), p. 124; Carl Haub, "Fact Sheet: World Population Trends 2012," *Population Reference Bureau,* Washington, DC, 2012.

22. Howard Handelman, *The Challenge of Third World Development* (Upper Saddle River, NJ: Prentice-Hall, 1996), pp. 3–10.

23. Paul Collier, *The Bottom Billion: Why the Poorest Countries Are Failing and What Can Be Done About It* (New York: Oxford University Press, 2007).

24. Central Intelligence Agency, *World Fact Book*.

25. United Nations Development Program (UNDP), *Human Development Report 2005*, p. 36, http://hdr.undp.org/reports/global/2005, p. 37.

26. UN Department of Economic and Social Affairs, *The Inequality Predicament: Report on the World Social Situation 2005* (New York: United Nations, 2005), p. 49.

27. Francis Fukuyama, "The End of History?" *The National Interest* 16 (Summer 1989), p. 4.

28. On the inadequate attention given to IOs see J. Martin Rochester, "The Rise and Fall of International Organization as a Field of Study," *International Organization* 40, no. 4 (Autumn 1986), pp. 777–813.

Managing the Global Economy Since World War II: The Institutional Framework

In July 1944, delegates from 44 countries convened the **Bretton Woods Conference** in New Hampshire, and within 22 days they endorsed a framework for international economic cooperation after World War II. The Bretton Woods negotiations were "the first successful attempt ... by a large group of nations to shape and control their economic relations."[1] Two international economic organizations resulted from the conference—the **International Monetary Fund (IMF)** and **International Bank for Reconstruction and Development (IBRD)** or **World Bank**—and in 1948 the **General Agreement on Tariffs and Trade (GATT)** became the main global trade organization. These organizations were part of a complex institutional framework to manage the postwar global economy. The conventional view is that only a small number of states had a critical role in the negotiating process. The three years of prenegotiations before Bretton Woods and the conference itself were described as "very much an Anglo-American affair, with Canada playing a useful mediating role."[2] However, Eric Helleiner argues in a recent book that "Southern countries played a more active and significant role in shaping and supporting the Bretton Woods outcomes than conventional wisdom suggests."[3] Discussions between U.S. and Latin American officials had an effect on both the U.S.-British prenegotiations and the Bretton Woods negotiations. While recognizing that Southern countries had some influence, we should not overstate their influence. The chief conference planners were Harry Dexter White of the U.S. Treasury and John Maynard Keynes of Britain, and American and British dominance resulted from their more favored position at the time. Although French delegates were at the conference, France was still occupied by Germany; and Germany, Italy, and Japan as enemy states were not represented. Despite some

17

basic differences of outlook, the Western DCs generally agreed on the postwar institutional order. Above all, they wanted to avoid a repetition of the interwar period experience, when exchange controls and trade protectionism contributed to the 1930s Great Depression and World War II.

After providing some background on economic relations before World War II, this chapter introduces the postwar institutional framework the North developed to manage the global economy. The chapter also focuses on two other groups of states that had only a limited role in establishing the postwar economic order and at times sought to form an alternative order: the South and the former East bloc led by the Soviet Union. Although many developing countries were colonies at the time of the Bretton Woods Conference, those attending included 19 Latin American states, 4 African states, and 5 delegations from Asia. Three Eastern European countries and the Soviet Union were represented at Bretton Woods; but the Soviet Union refused to sign the final agreements. Instead of joining the IMF, World Bank, and GATT, the Soviets established their own economic institutions. Finally, this chapter discusses the role of nongovernmental actors (business groups and NGOs) in the liberal economic order.

GLOBAL ECONOMIC RELATIONS BEFORE WORLD WAR II

This section introduces some general historical benchmarks before World War II, and Chapters 6 to 11 provide historical background on each issue area, such as trade and monetary relations.

The Mercantilist Period

The origins of IPE are closely associated with the development of modern European states and their global markets.[4] The modern European state gained official recognition at the 1648 Treaty of Westphalia, which marked the defeat of the Catholic Hapsburg countries by mostly Protestant countries in Northern Europe. The Peace of Westphalia upheld state sovereignty and territorial integrity by preventing external religious and secular authorities (e.g., the Pope and the Holy Roman Emperor) from interfering in a state's internal affairs. A major factor enabling the state to establish its authority vis-à-vis internal and external forces was the development of *mercantilism*. Adam Smith, an eighteenth-century liberal economist who was highly critical of the mercantilists, used the term in reference to economic thought and practice in Europe from about 1500 to 1750.[5] (Since mercantilism usually refers to this early historical period, we use the term *neomercantilism* for one of our three theoretical perspectives. Neomercantilism refers to thought and practice any time after about 1750.) Mercantilists were acutely aware of the linkage between politics and economics, viewing both power and wealth as essential goals of national policy. Mercantilist states could use their wealth to build up their armed forces, hire mercenaries, and influence their enemies and allies. In efforts to enlarge their gold and silver stocks, mercantilist states sought to increase their exports and decrease their imports of manufactured goods. They also restricted raw material and technology exports to prevent others from developing manufacturing capabilities. The colonies provided mercantilist states with raw materials and served as markets for their manufactures; thus, manufacturing in the colonies was usually prohibited. Although Smith criticized mercantilists for following beggar-thy-neighbor policies that would lead to conflict, their emphasis on national power helped establish state authority and territorial unification.[6] The establishment of the European state system under mercantilism provided the foundation for the eventual development of the global political economy.[7]

Although sovereignty in principle gives states supreme authority within their own territory, there is a pecking order in which some states are more powerful than others. Chapter 3 discusses hegemonic stability theory, which deals with the role of hegemonic powers in leading the international system. Some scholars have examined the role of "world powers" such as Portugal, Spain, the Netherlands, and Britain during the mercantilist period, but it is debatable whether these states were dominant enough to be hegemonic.[8] Most hegemonic stability theorists refer to only two global hegemonic periods, both of them after the mercantilist period: under Britain in the nineteenth century and the United States in the twentieth century.

The Industrial Revolution and British Hegemony

The mercantilist period lasted only until about 1750. When the Industrial Revolution began in about 1780, it initially progressed from region to region rather than involving entire countries. Britain became the first state to industrialize, and this enabled it to become the hegemonic power. By 1860 Britain accounted for about 37 percent of European industrial production, 20 percent of world industrial production, and 80 percent of newer technology industries.[9] In view of its competitive edge, Britain shifted from mercantilist policies toward free trade: It removed most of its industrial trade restrictions by the 1830s, and in 1846 it repealed its *Corn Laws* which had restricted agricultural imports. Britain's decision to liberalize agricultural trade stemmed from both domestic and external factors. Domestically, industrial groups gained seats in the British Parliament through legislative and demographic changes, and the agricultural elite could no longer prevent the repeal of the Corn Laws. Externally, Britain opened its markets to agricultural and raw material imports so that other countries would accept its manufactured goods. The division of labor served Britain's hegemonic interests in promoting its industrial exports. Other states complied with Britain's preferences because it was the largest market for their exports. Thus, Britain's policies contributed to an extended period of free trade during the nineteenth century, and the 1860 *Cobden–Chevalier Treaty* between Britain and France resulted in a network of treaties lowering tariffs.[10]

The Decline of British Hegemony and World War I

Although free trade flourished during part of the nineteenth century, it was based on bilateral trade agreements because no IO such as GATT existed. Thus, trade faltered in the late nineteenth century because of depressed economic conditions, a decline of British hegemony, and industrial protectionism on the European continent. A decrease in Britain's productivity relative to the United States and Germany made it less competitive and less able to serve as a market for other countries' exports. Banks and the state helped increase U.S. and German productivity through investment in industrial production and infrastructure such as railroads and canals, and the two countries built up their infant industries through protectionist trade policies. Whereas Britain's share of world trade fell from 24 percent in 1870 to 14.1 percent in 1913, Germany's share rose from 9.7 to 12.2 percent and the U.S. share rose from 8.8 to 11.1 percent. On the eve of World War I, the United States had become the largest industrial power; but Britain continued to dominate in international finance.[11] London was the main international financial center, the British pound sterling was the key international currency, and in 1913 Britain accounted for 43 percent of the world's foreign investment. During World War I, Britain's foreign liabilities substantially increased and the United States emerged as a net creditor. Thus, financial preeminence finally shifted from London to New York after the war.[12]

The Interwar Period

World War I completely disrupted international monetary relations. Under British hegemony, the monetary regime was based on a classical gold standard, in which currencies were convertible; thus, gold was almost like a common currency among states. This stability decreased transaction costs among states and facilitated international trade. However, World War I disrupted the classical gold standard, and this hindered international economic transactions during the interwar period. Some theorists believe that the monetary instability resulted from Britain's inability as a declining hegemon to stabilize policies, but others argue that countries were no longer willing to sacrifice domestic goals such as full employment for the sake of currency stability.

World War I also disrupted trade relations. The United States emerged from the war as the world's largest industrial power and the only major net creditor. Although it lent about $10 billion to cash-short countries during the 1920s, the United States initially insisted that Britain and France repay all their war debts, and it imposed import barriers that made it difficult for Europeans to gain export revenue. The 1922 Fordney–McCumber Act raised U.S. tariffs, and when the U.S. economy moved into depression, the 1930 Smoot–Hawley Act increased U.S. tariffs to their highest level in the twentieth century. European states retaliated with their own import restrictions, and world trade declined from $35 billion in 1929 to $12 billion in 1933.[13] Hegemonic stability theorists attribute the economic instability in the interwar period to the lack of a global hegemon. Britain was no longer able, and the United States was not yet willing, to assume the hegemon's role. Other theorists argue that domestic U.S. politics was responsible for the economic disarray. The U.S. Constitution gives Congress the authority to regulate foreign commerce, but as a large unwieldy body, Congress catered to protectionist demands of special interests. Thus, U.S. tariffs increased because of domestic politics despite the growth of U.S. economic power.[14]

To reverse the damage caused by the Smoot–Hawley tariff, the U.S. Congress passed the *Reciprocal Trade Agreements Act (RTAA)* in 1934. The RTAA delegated tariff-setting authority to the president, who could resist special interests and negotiate tariff reductions more effectively than Congress. The RTAA agreements resulted in a substantial reduction of some tariffs, but tariff rates were so high in the early 1930s that the agreements were not sufficient to stem the forces of protectionism.

The Institutional Framework Before World War II

The first financial IO, the **Bank for International Settlements (BIS)**, was established in Basle, Switzerland in 1930 to oversee the settlement of German reparations after World War I, but its main purpose was to promote cooperation among central banks (see Chapter 6).[15] Other than the BIS, economic IOs in the interwar period were mainly concerned with developing international standards for facilities, equipment, and installations required for the global economy. These organizations could not deal with international economic problems such as the Great Depression. As economic differences among states increased in the 1920s–30s, several international conferences were convened to confront the trade and financial problems; but these conferences failed to resolve the problems of war reparations and debt, disorderly currency exchange conditions, and a decline in world trade. This experience emphasized the need for international bodies to promote open and stable economic relations after World War II and as a result the IMF, World Bank, and GATT were formed.[16]

THE FUNCTIONS OF THE IMF, WORLD BANK, AND GATT

The United States emerged as a more mature power after World War II, and under U.S. leadership the North established institutions to prevent a recurrence of the interwar problems. The United States had the most influence over the formation of the institutions, but the British economist John Maynard Keynes also had an important role. We refer to the IMF, World Bank, and GATT as *keystone international economic organizations (KIEOs)* because of their central role in monetary relations, development, and trade.[17] The IMF was created to monitor a system of *pegged* or *fixed exchange rates*, in which each currency had an official exchange rate in relation to gold and the U.S. dollar. This system was designed to avoid the competitive devaluation of currencies that led to trade wars during the interwar period. *Devaluation* refers to a reduction in the official rate at which one currency is exchanged for another. States with balance-of-payments deficits (with more money leaving than entering the country) may devalue their currencies to make their goods cheaper so they can increase their exports and decrease their imports. Thus, the IMF provided short-term loans to help states deal with temporary balance-of-payments deficits and maintain the fixed exchange rates of their currencies. In contrast to the IMF's short-term loans, the IBRD or World Bank provided long-term loans for postwar European reconstruction and LDC economic development. GATT lowered tariffs in multilateral trade negotiations, established international trade rules, and developed trade dispute settlement procedures. These functions were designed to avoid the protectionist trade barriers of the interwar period.

The KIEOs' functions evolved after World War II. For example, European reconstruction was a larger task than anticipated, and the United States established the European Recovery Program (or Marshall Plan) in 1948 to give bilateral aid to Western Europe. The World Bank therefore shifted its loans almost completely to LDCs for economic development. The IMF lost one of its main functions when fixed exchange rates for currencies collapsed in the 1970s and were replaced by floating exchange rates. However, the IMF's role increased again in the 1980s–90s when it became the lead international agency for the foreign debt and financial crises. GATT was formed under special circumstances. After the Bretton Woods Conference, negotiations were held to create an international trade organization (ITO) comparable to the IMF and World Bank. However, the U.S. Congress refused to ratify the ITO treaty, and the "temporary" GATT which had initiated postwar trade negotiations became the global trade organization by default. Since GATT was designed to be only a treaty, states joining it were called "contracting parties" rather than members (this book uses the term *GATT members* for the sake of brevity). Despite its humble origins, GATT was quite effective in liberalizing trade; but its dispute settlement system was weak, its regulations were often circumvented, and it could not deal with new areas of trade. Thus, the formal **World Trade Organization** (**WTO**) superseded GATT as the global trade organization in 1995. Unlike GATT, the WTO deals not only with trade in goods but also with trade in services, intellectual property rights, and trade-related investment measures (see Chapter 8).

THE KIEOS AND THE UNITED NATIONS

Figure 2.1 shows that the IMF and World Bank are *specialized agencies* and that the World Bank is in fact a World Bank group of five institutions (see Chapter 11). As specialized agencies, the IMF and World Bank are autonomous organizations affiliated with the UN. Although they report on their activities to the *Economic and Social Council* (*ECOSOC*) once a year, the UN has little authority over them. Indeed, the UN signed an agreement with the World Bank (and one with the IMF), acknowledging that "it would be sound policy to refrain from making recommendations to the Bank with respect to particular loans or with respect to terms or conditions of financing."[18] The UN General Assembly has at times tried to influence World Bank lending decisions, but it has been largely unsuccessful.[19] The WTO was established in 1995 as a "related organization" rather than a specialized agency (see Figure 2.1); so it is not even required to issue a yearly report to the ECOSOC.[20]

A major reason for the UN's lack of leverage is that the IMF, World Bank, and WTO do not depend on UN funding. The DCs have directed most of their funds for multilateral economic management to the IMF and World Bank because they prefer their weighted voting systems to the UN's one-nation, one-vote system (see Chapters 6 and 11). Despite the UN's limited leverage, it has sometimes induced the KIEOs to revise their policies and adopt new programs. Examples include the UN role in the World Bank's creation of the International Development Association as a soft-loan agency (see Chapter 11), the IMF's establishment of a compensatory financing facility (see Chapter 6), and the IMF and World Bank's decision to introduce human and social dimensions in their lending programs. The World Bank also cooperates with UN bodies such as the United Nations Development Program (UNDP) in providing development assistance.[21]

THE POSTWAR ECONOMIC INSTITUTIONS AND CHANGING NORTH–SOUTH RELATIONS

The North has had the dominant role in most international economic institutions. However, some emerging economies have posed a challenge to this Northern dominance, especially since the 2008 global financial crisis. The North's role in the global economy has had several characteristics:

- The United States has been the most powerful single state, but its economic hegemony is giving way to a triad composed of North America, Western Europe, and East Asia.
- The triad has been responsible for the largest share of global economic transactions, including foreign investment, trade in manufactures and services, and capital flows.
- Countries within the triad have conducted most of their international economic transactions with each other.[22]

Although the DCs have occupied the dominant position in the global economy, some LDCs and transition economies are challenging this dominance. Four groups (that are somewhat overlapping) have posed the biggest challenge:

- The **Organization of Petroleum Exporting Countries (OPEC)** is a group of LDC oil exporters that has acted as a resource cartel to manipulate oil supplies and prices. Formed in 1960, OPEC posed a challenge to DCs in 1973–74 when it limited supplies and drastically increased prices. OPEC's influence has varied widely depending on supply and demand,

The United Nations System

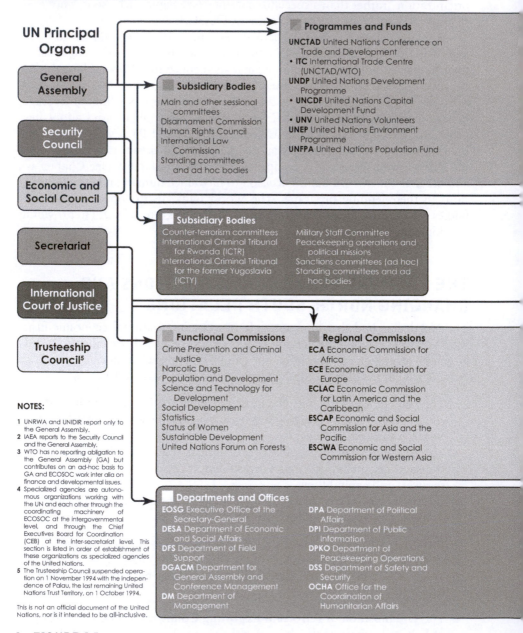

UN Principal Organs

- General Assembly
- Security Council
- Economic and Social Council
- Secretariat
- International Court of Justice
- Trusteeship Council[5]

Programmes and Funds

UNCTAD United Nations Conference on Trade and Development
- **ITC** International Trade Centre (UNCTAD/WTO)

UNDP United Nations Development Programme
- **UNCDF** United Nations Capital Development Fund
- **UNV** United Nations Volunteers

UNEP United Nations Environment Programme

UNFPA United Nations Population Fund

Subsidiary Bodies

Main and other sessional committees
Disarmament Commission
Human Rights Council
International Law Commission
Standing committees and ad hoc bodies

Subsidiary Bodies

Counter-terrorism committees
International Criminal Tribunal for Rwanda (ICTR)
International Criminal Tribunal for the former Yugoslavia (ICTY)

Military Staff Committee
Peacekeeping operations and political missions
Sanctions committees (ad hoc)
Standing committees and ad hoc bodies

Functional Commissions

Crime Prevention and Criminal Justice
Narcotic Drugs
Population and Development
Science and Technology for Development
Social Development
Statistics
Status of Women
Sustainable Development
United Nations Forum on Forests

Regional Commissions

ECA Economic Commission for Africa
ECE Economic Commission for Europe
ECLAC Economic Commission for Latin America and the Caribbean
ESCAP Economic and Social Commission for Asia and the Pacific
ESCWA Economic and Social Commission for Western Asia

Departments and Offices

EOSG Executive Office of the Secretary-General
DESA Department of Economic and Social Affairs
DFS Department of Field Support
DGACM Department for General Assembly and Conference Management
DM Department of Management

DPA Department of Political Affairs
DPI Department of Public Information
DPKO Department of Peacekeeping Operations
DSS Department of Safety and Security
OCHA Office for the Coordination of Humanitarian Affairs

NOTES:

1 UNRWA and UNIDIR report only to the General Assembly.
2 IAEA reports to the Security Council and the General Assembly.
3 WTO has no reporting obligation to the General Assembly (GA) but contributes on an ad-hoc basis to GA and ECOSOC work inter alia on finance and developmental issues.
4 Specialized agencies are autonomous organizations working with the UN and each other through the coordinating machinery of ECOSOC at the intergovernmental level, and through the Chief Executives Board for Coordination (CEB) at the inter-secretariat level. This section is listed in order of establishment of these organizations as specialized agencies of the United Nations.
5 The Trusteeship Council suspended operation on 1 November 1994 with the independence of Palau, the last remaining United Nations Trust Territory, on 1 October 1994.

This is not an official document of the United Nations, nor is it intended to be all-inclusive.

FIGURE 2.1

The United Nations System

UN-HABITAT United Nations Human Settlements Programme
UNHCR Office of the United Nations High Commissioner for Refugees
UNICEF United Nations Children's Fund
UNODC United Nations Office on Drugs and Crime
UNRWA[1] United Nations Relief and Works Agency for Palestine Refugees in the Near East
UN-Women United Nations Entity for Gender Equality and the Empowerment of Women
WFP World Food Programme

Research and Training Institutes

UNICRI United Nations Interregional Crime and Justice Research Institute
UNIDIR[1] United Nations Institute for Disarmament Research

UNITAR United Nations Institute for Training and Research
UNRISD United Nations Research Institute for Social Development
UNSSC United Nations System Staff College
UNU United Nations University

Other Entities

UNAIDS Joint United Nations Programme on HIV/AIDS
UNISDR United Nations International Strategy for Disaster Reduction
UNOPS United Nations Office for Project Services

Related Organizations

CTBTO PrepCom Preparatory Commission for the Comprehensive Nuclear-Test-Ban Treaty Organization
IAEA[2] International Atomic Energy Agency
OPCW Organisation for the Prohibition of Chemical Weapons
WTO[3] World Trade Organization

Advisory Subsidiary Body

UN Peacebuilding Commission

Other Bodies

Committee for Development Policy
Committee of Experts on Public Administration
Committee on Non-Governmental Organizations
Permanent Forum on Indigenous Issues
United Nations Group of Experts on Geographical Names
Other sessional and standing committees and expert, ad hoc and related bodies

Specialized Agencies[4]

ILO International Labour Organization
FAO Food and Agriculture Organization of the United Nations
UNESCO United Nations Educational, Scientific and Cultural Organization
WHO World Health Organization
World Bank Group
• **IBRD** International Bank for Reconstruction and Development
• **IDA** International Development Association
• **IFC** International Finance Corporation
• **MIGA** Multilateral Investment Guarantee Agency
• **ICSID** International Centre for Settlement of Investment Disputes

IMF International Monetary Fund
ICAO International Civil Aviation Organization
IMO International Maritime Organization
ITU International Telecommunication Union
UPU Universal Postal Union
WMO World Meteorological Organization
WIPO World Intellectual Property Organization
IFAD International Fund for Agricultural Development
UNIDO United Nations Industrial Development Organization
UNWTO World Tourism Organization

OHCHR Office of the United Nations High Commissioner for Human Rights
OIOS Office of Internal Oversight Services
OLA Office of Legal Affairs
OSAA Office of the Special Adviser on Africa
OSRSG/CAAC Office of the Special Representative of the Secretary-General for Children and Armed Conflict
UNODA United Nations Office for Disarmament Affairs

UNOG United Nations Office at Geneva
UN-OHRLLS Office of the High Representative for the Least Developed Countries, Landlocked Developing Countries and Small Island Developing States
UNON United Nations Office at Nairobi
UNOV United Nations Office at Vienna

and the political relations of OPEC members. For example, OPEC's influence declined in the 1980s–1990s, increased in the early 2000s, and then declined again in 2014. OPEC members include Algeria, Angola, Ecuador, Iran, Iraq, Kuwait, Libya, Nigeria, Qatar, Saudi Arabia, the United Arab Emirates, and Venezuela.

- The **newly industrializing economies** (NIEs) in East Asia and Latin America presented a competitive challenge to the North in the early 1980s. They include Hong Kong, Singapore, South Korea, Taiwan, Argentina, Brazil, and Mexico.
- Brazil, Russia, India, and China—the **BRIC economies** as coined by a Goldman Sachs researcher in 2001—pose a major challenge to the North. The term **BRICS economies** includes South Africa. The BRICS have been holding summit meetings, but there are in fact major differences between them. For example, China's economic power clearly exceeds that of the other BRICS.
- The **emerging market economies** are developing and transition economies that have adopted many elements of a free-market system and have achieved rapid economic growth. They include many BRIC, NIE, OPEC, and other economies.[23]

The following discussion shows that although the North continues to have the most influence in the KIEOs, pressure from the emerging economies for change is increasing.

The IMF, World Bank, and WTO

Most of the funding for IMF and World Bank loans has come from the **Group of Five (G5)**: the United States, Japan, Germany, Britain, and France. Until recently these five countries have also had the most votes in these institutions. In 2010, China leapfrogged over Germany, Britain, and France, and now has the third largest number of votes in the IBRD after the United States and Japan. However, the G5 countries still have the most votes in the IMF (see Chapters 6 and 11). Although the WTO has a one-nation, one-vote system, the agenda for multilateral trade negotiations has been set mainly by the North. Moreover, the North has had a dominant position in the bureaucracies of these institutions. By tacit agreement, the World Bank president has always been American, and the IMF managing director has always been European. The GATT/WTO directors general have all been from DCs except Supachai Panitchpakdi of Thailand (2002–2005), and Roberto Azevêdo of Brazil (2013–the present). The South is also underrepresented on the KIEO professional staffs.[24] The KIEOs have made some moves to give the South more voice, especially since the 2008 global financial crisis. For example, the IBRD won an increase in its capital in April 2010 in return for transferring some voting power from smaller European countries to China, India, and Brazil. However, as of August 2015 the U.S. Congress has refused to approve similar changes in the IMF. This has angered the emerging economies, and threatens the IMF's legitimacy as an international institution. Recent moves by China to establish an *Asian Infrastructure Investment Bank (AIIB)* stem from its dissatisfaction with the North's dominance in the IMF and World Bank, and with Japan's dominant position in the *Asian Development Bank* (see Chapter 11).

The KIEOs are often credited with contributing "to almost unprecedented global economic growth and change over the past five decades."[25] However, the type of growth these institutions foster has followed the prescriptions of the North. The KIEOs support a liberal economic approach, which holds that the free flow of goods and capital promotes prosperity. (Critical theorists argue that the liberal economic approach benefits some states and individuals at the expense of others.) In the 1950s–1960s, the liberal economic order contributed to economic growth and stability for several reasons. First, the Cold War increased U.S. economic cooperation with Western Europe and Japan; economic recovery was viewed as a prerequisite for a strong anti-Soviet alliance. Second, the United States as the global hegemon helped establish principles and rules for conducting postwar trade, financial, and monetary relations, and the major DCs generally accepted U.S. leadership. Third, the KIEOs enabled governments to abide by international rules and obligations without jeopardizing domestic policy objectives such as full employment.[26]

In the 1970s, however, several changes began to pose problems for the KIEOs. First, the United States became less supportive of economic liberalism as its economic dominance declined; for example, U.S. protectionism increased after it began to have balance-of-trade deficits in 1971. Second, Europe and Japan began to question U.S. leadership, and frictions among DCs increased with the decline of the Cold War. Third, oil prices increased when the Arab OPEC countries limited supplies after the October 1973 Middle East War; this disrupted the global economy and challenged the KIEOs' management capabilities. Fourth, the KIEOs had difficulty managing the forces of globalization, because their economic resources "pale in comparison to daily market-driven foreign exchange cash flows," and no IO regulates the MNCs and international banks that contribute to these capital flows.[27] Finally, the growing membership of the KIEOs made them more broadly representative, but their large, diverse memberships posed an obstacle to consultation, coordination, and decision-making.

The large memberships of the IMF, World Bank, and WTO caused some analysts to argue that "they must be led by a much smaller core group whose weight confers on them the responsibility of leadership."[28] The decline of U.S. economic hegemony also contributed to the need for collective leadership, and DCs have often conferred among themselves before seeking the KIEOs' endorsement of their policies.[29] As Table 2.1 and Figure 2.2 show, the smaller DC-led groups include the **Organization for Economic Cooperation and Development** (**OECD**), the G5, and the **Group of Seven** (G7). Whereas liberal economists believe that these groups have promoted economic leadership and stability, critical theorists argue that they have excluded LDCs from decision-making. As the economic importance of emerging countries increased, the DCs had to

TABLE 2.1

Members of the OECD (Year of Admission)

Australia	1971	Hungary	1996	Poland	1996
Austria*	1961	Iceland*	1961	Portugal*	1961
Belgium*	1961	Ireland*	1961	Slovak Republic	2000
Canada*	1961	Israel	2010	Slovenia	2010
Chile	2010	Italy*	1962	South Korea	1996
Czech Republic	1995	Japan	1964	Spain*	1961
Denmark*	1961	Luxembourg*	1961	Sweden*	1961
Estonia	2010	Mexico	1994	Switzerland*	1961
Finland	1969	Netherlands*	1961	Turkey*	1961
France*	1961	New Zealand	1973	United Kingdom*	1961
Germany*	1961	Norway*	1961	United States*	1961
Greece*	1961				

*Founding members

expand the circle of decision-making in these smaller groups. Table 2.1 shows that the OECD has gradually increased its membership, and Figure 2.2 shows that the G7 has expanded to the **Group of Twenty** (**G20**) which includes a number of emerging economies.

The OECD

The OECD, which is in Paris, has 34 mainly DC members (see Table 2.1). Created in 1961 as a successor to the all-European *Organization for European Economic Cooperation (OEEC)*, the OECD also included two non-European members: the United States and Canada. The United States wanted Western Europe to begin sharing the burden of promoting economic growth, and it viewed the OECD as a forum where it "could sit down together on equal terms" with "the Europeans and other 'industrial democracies'."[30] The OECD is committed to liberalizing trade and capital flows, and it also serves as a forum for the member states to discuss and coordinate their economic policies. In an age of globalization, a state's domestic policies often have international consequences, and OECD members try to reach a consensus on domestic policies that will minimize conflict. The OECD usually operates through a system of mutual persuasion, in which members exert peer pressure on each other to meet their commitments.[31] The North has also used the OECD to develop a more unified position on issues in the IMF, World Bank, and WTO. For example, the OECD's work on services trade helped the North legitimize the idea that the WTO should include rules for trade in services as well as goods.[32] Although the OECD normally maintains a low profile, its efforts to negotiate a Multilateral Agreement on Investment (MAI) in the 1990s were highly controversial. The MAI negotiations were suspended in 1998 because of divisions among OECD members and strong opposition by LDCs and civil society groups (see Chapter 10).

In earlier years, the DC economies in the OECD accounted for the predominant share of world production, trade, and advances in science and technology. Thus, the new OECD members accepted in the 1960s–1970s were all DCs, including Japan, Finland, Australia, and New Zealand (see Table 2.1). No new members were accepted in the 1980s, but two major changes caused the OECD to reassess its policies in the early 1990s: Eastern European countries were interested in joining after the breakup of the Soviet Union, and the OECD members' share of global production and trade was declining. As Table 2.1 shows, ten countries outside the industrial core group became OECD members after 1992: Mexico in 1994; the Czech Republic in 1995; Hungary, Poland, and South Korea in 1996; the Slovak Republic in 2000; and Chile, Slovenia, Israel, and Estonia in 2010. The OECD has also had accession talks with Russia, and has offered "enhanced engagement" to Brazil, China, India, Indonesia, and South Africa. Critics argue that further enlargement will jeopardize the OECD's strength as an organization of like-minded members, and that China and Russia do not meet the democratic requirements of OECD members. However, others question whether the OECD can retain its importance if it does not include the emerging economies. In 2010 the 34 OECD members accounted for only 50 percent of global GDP and 60 percent of global exports. The question also arises whether large emerging economies such as China, India, and Brazil will *want* to join the OECD, because it continues to support ideas endorsed by Western DCs, and DC nationals hold most of the positions in the OECD bureaucracy. The OECD has developed valuable techniques to reach consensus on major issues in the global economy. However, to maintain its relevance the OECD must expand its membership and "break decades of Western dependence and put into practice deep and difficult internal reform to emerge as a much more inclusive, diverse and open organization."[33]

The G5, G7, G8, and G20

This section focuses on smaller informal groups that deal with the global economy as a whole, and other issue-oriented groups are discussed in subsequent chapters. For a number of years the most influential groups (the G5, G7, and G8) were largely comprised of DCs; but more recently the G20 (composed of DCs and emerging economies) has become much more important (see Figure 2.2). In the 1970s the main focus of policy coordination shifted from the OECD to the G5 and G7 for several reasons: They were smaller groups without formal constitutions, they included the most powerful DCs in the global economy, and top political leaders with authority to implement agreements often attended their meetings.[34]

The G5 included the finance ministers and **central bank** governors of the five largest DC economies with the most votes in the IMF and World Bank: the United States, Japan, Germany, France, and Britain (see Figure 2.2). In 1967 the G5 finance ministers and central bank governors began holding informal discussions to coordinate their economic policies, and in 1975 the heads of state or government of the G5 countries held an annual summit in which Italy

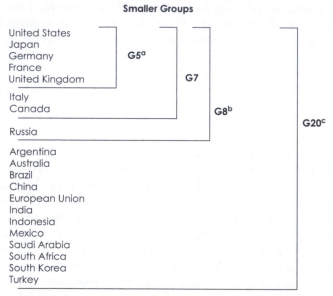

Smaller Groups

^a The G5 was superseded by the G7.
^b Russia was admitted to full G8 membership in 1998 but was suspended in 2014 following the Ukraine crisis. The G8 now functions as the G7.
^c The G20 has 19 member countries plus the EU.

FIGURE 2.2
Groups of Developed Countries and Emerging Economies

was also invited to attend. Italy and Canada were invited to the 1976 summit, and the G7 was created. The G7 summits signaled a move toward collective leadership with the decline of U.S. economic hegemony, the 1973–74 OPEC oil crisis, and the world economic recession. G7 members have used the summits to reach a consensus on key issues at the highest political level. From 1976 to 1986, the G5 finance ministers and central bank governors continued to meet, while the G7 met at the level of heads of state or government. However, the G7 superseded the G5 in 1986–87 and now meets at two levels: The G7 heads of state or government meet in annual summits, and the G7 finance ministers also meet. In 1991 the G7 members started inviting Russia to their summits to help it come to terms with its loss of superpower status and to encourage it to continue with economic and political reforms; and the **Group of Eight (G8)** was established in the 1998 Birmingham Summit when Russia joined as a full participant. However, Russia was more involved in the political discussions at the heads of state and government level, and the G7 countries' finance ministers and central bank governors continued to meet separately.[35] On March 24, 2014 the G7 countries suspended Russia from the G8 for its annexation of Crimea, which had been part of Ukraine. The G7 statement did not mention expulsion or any time-frame for the suspension, but the G7 currently functions without Russia's participation. Thus, the following discussion refers to the functioning of the G7 rather than the G8.

The G7 has no constitution or legal status, no headquarters or formal meeting place, no formal rules of membership, and no means to enforce its decisions. Its main objectives are "to raise consciousness, set an agenda, create networks, prod other institutions to do things that they should be doing, and, in some cases to help create institutions."[36] Although the G7 has been quite successful in some areas such as managing the end of the Cold War and addressing the issue of debt relief for LDCs, its influence has declined because of DC divisions with the demise of the Cold War and the difficulties in coping with globalization; for example, massive international capital flows interfere with the ability of G7 monetary authorities to influence currency markets. Most importantly, the G7 could not deal with the problems such as the 2008 global financial crisis alone, and it was necessary to include "systematically important" emerging as well as developing economies.[37] Figure 2.2 shows that the G20 includes 19 countries and the EU. As with the G7, the G20 is not a decision-making body, has no charter or permanent staff, and does not take votes or make legally binding decisions. Instead, the G20 finance ministers and central bank governors try to reach a consensus on economic and financial issues, shape the international agenda, and lead by example.

The G7 members accounted for about 65 percent of global economic output from 1965 to 2002, but by 2008 their share had fallen to 52 percent. The G20 countries represent about two-thirds of the world's population and 85 percent of the global GNP. With the onset of the 2008 global financial crisis, the G20 rather than the G7 was seen as the most effective forum to lead the global response. In September 2009 the G20 Pittsburgh Summit leaders therefore agreed to permanently shift the main discussions of global economic issues from the G7 to the G20. This was a recognition that China and other emerging economies had a central role in dealing with the global financial crisis. G20 meetings often occur in parallel with, and sometimes before, IMF meetings. Although G20 agreements have no legal status in the IMF, they have considerable influence on IMF decision-making. The larger, more diverse G20 is more vulnerable to divisions than the G7, but the G20 has clearly eclipsed the G7 as the main informal group dealing with global economic issues.[38]

THE POSTWAR ECONOMIC INSTITUTIONS AND INTERNATIONAL DEVELOPMENT

As Figure 2.2 shows, the G20 includes a number of "systematically important" emerging economies (Argentina, Brazil, China, India, Indonesia, Mexico, Saudi Arabia, South Africa, South Korea, and Turkey), but has no seats for the poorest LDCs. Poverty, disease, and hunger are still prevalent in much of the world, and a major gulf remains between the North and much of the South. This section focuses on the South's position vis-à-vis the North, and on divisions within the South. We also look at growing inequalities *within* countries, in both the North and the South. The most common measure economists use to compare the economic development of states is *per capita* GNI or GDP (a country's GNI or GDP divided by its population). We use **exchange rates,** or the rates at which currencies are exchanged for one another, to convert per capita GNI figures in other currencies into the U.S. dollar. However, a country's per capita GNI does not tell us fully about its standard of living because the exchange rate does not accurately reflect the *purchasing power* of the local currency in a country. Countries often have different price levels for comparable goods, and prices are generally lower in LDCs than in DCs. In comparing per capita GNIs, we therefore often convert the figures into **purchasing power parity** (**PPP**) based exchange rates. PPP rates are "the number of units of a country's currency required to buy the same amount of goods and services in the domestic market as a United States dollar would buy in the United States."[39] For example, *The Economist* has used a "Big Mac index" to compare PPP rates for hamburgers. If a Big Mac costs 2.75 euros in countries using the euro and $2.65 in the United States, the PPP exchange rate for Big Macs would be 2.75/2.65, or 1.0377.[40] The PPP rates for different goods and services are weighted according to their importance in the economy. PPP exchange rates have limitations because they are based on price comparisons of "comparable items," but the quality of these items may differ across countries. Nevertheless, they are more accurate in comparing living standards, and this book sometimes provides PPP-adjusted per capita GNI figures.

Even PPP-weighted figures are an imperfect indicator of well-being because they do not take account of income inequalities. A country where a relatively small number of people are extremely rich and most are extremely poor has less well-being than a country with the same per capita GNI that has less extreme wealth and poverty.[41] The most common measure of income inequality in a country is the **Gini coefficient,** which measures the deviation of income distribution among individuals or households in a country from an equal distribution. The coefficient may range from 100 (absolute inequality) to 0 (absolute equality). Furthermore, PPP-adjusted per capita GNI figures only measure a country's *economic* development. Since 1990 the United Nations Development Program (UNDP) has published a *Human Development Report* with a **human development index** (**HDI**) that measures social as well as economic development. The HDI includes three dimensions: a long life measured by life expectancy at birth; knowledge measured by adult literacy rates and school enrollments; and a decent standard of living measured by PPP-adjusted per capita GNIs. A major problem with the HDI is collecting accurate data; for example, national and international data may differ because of the use of different methodologies, and international agencies may not have access to the most recent national data. Thus, the 2014 *Human Development Report* does not provide an HDI for eight UN members because of a lack of reliable data, and the statistics are incomplete for a number of countries.[42]

Table 2.2 compares HDI rank and values and per capita GNIs for a selected list of countries. As the table shows, countries with higher HDI values also tend to have higher per capita GNIs. For example, the seven countries on the list with the highest HDI values (Norway, the United States, Canada, Japan,

TABLE 2.2

Human Development Index (HDI), Rank, and Gross National Income (GNI) Per Capita—Selected Countries—2013

HDI Rank	Country	HDI Value	GNI per Capita *(2011 PPP$)
1	Norway	0.904	63,909
5	United States	0.914	52,308
8	Canada	0.902	41,887
17	Japan	0.890	36,747
20	France	0.884	36,629
31	Qatar	0.851	119,029
40	United Arab Emirates	0.827	58,068
50	Uruguay	0.790	18,108
57	Russian Federation	0.778	22,617
68	Costa Rica	0.763	13,012
71	Mexico	0.756	15,854
78	Brazil	0.744	14,275
91	China	0.719	11,477
108	Indonesia	0.684	8,970
109	Botswana	0.683	14,792
110	Egypt	0.682	10,430
118	South Africa	0.658	11,788
135	India	0.586	5,150
142	Bangladesh	0.558	2,713
147	Kenya	0.535	2,158
152	Nigeria	0.504	5,353
159	Tanzania	0.488	1,702
173	Ethiopia	0.435	1,303
183	Sierra Leone	0.374	1,815
186	Congo, D.R.	0.338	444

* Purchasing Power Parity using the US$ as of 2011

Source: Adapted from United Nations Development Program, *Human Development Report, 2014.* http://hdr.undp.org/en/data-hdr14_statisticaltables.xls, table 1

France, Qatar, and the United Arab Emirates or UAE) also have the highest per capita GNIs. The four countries with the lowest HDI values (Tanzania, Ethiopia, Sierra Leone, and the Democratic Republic of the Congo) also have the lowest per capita GNIs. This is not surprising, because the poorest LDCs cannot provide adequate education and health care facilities. However, there are also some significant variations. For example, Qatar has the highest per capita GNI on the list ($119,029), but its HDI ranking (31) is below that of Norway, the United States, Canada, Japan, and France; and the UAE has a lower HDI ranking but a higher per capita GNI than four DCs. A second example is the case of Costa Rica, which has a higher HDI ranking, but a lower per capita GNI than Brazil. A third example is the case of Nigeria, which has a lower HDI ranking, but a higher per capita GNI than India, Bangladesh, and Kenya. What accounts for these differences in per capita GNI and HDI rankings? In the first example, Qatar and the UAE are oil-rich states, but a number of people have not benefited from advances in health care and education. The UAE's high per capita GNI is skewed—not only toward UAE nationals over foreign laborers, but also toward Abu Dhabi and Dubai over the other principalities. The society also discourages women from meeting their economic potential.[43] In the second example, Costa Rica has a higher HDI than Brazil because of its advances in meeting education and health care needs. In 1949 Costa Rica adopted a constitutional amendment calling for comprehensive measures on education, public health, and social security. Although Brazil has some affirmative action programs, it continues to have high levels of inequality. It also has significant racial disparities for its Afro-Brazilian and mixed race populations.[44] In the third example, Nigeria, like Qatar and the UAE, is a member of OPEC and has been subject to the so-called *resource curse*—the thesis that LDCs which are overly dependent on resources may have high levels of inequality, corruption, authoritarianism, and poor governance.

Critics of the resource curse thesis correctly point out that some natural-resource-rich countries have developed better than others. For example, Norway is an oil-rich DC in which health care, education, and social benefits are widespread throughout the population. Another example is the case of Botswana and Sierra Leone, which are both rich in diamonds. Although Botswana has been seriously affected by HIV/AIDS, Table 2.2 shows that its HDI ranking and GNI per capita are much higher than those of Sierra Leone, which has been adversely affected by years of civil strife. However, the resource curse thesis does have some validity for several reasons. First, natural resources can often be extracted without participation of most domestic workers. Second, natural resources are nonrenewable and may produce considerable wealth for the few. Third, LDCs rich in natural resources have often had a colonial history with long-term negative effects on development.[45]

Table 2.3 shows that there are also some notable differences among the regions. Many countries in East Asia and the Pacific, and in Europe and Central Asia, rank higher in human development than in per capita GNI. Many countries in the Arab states and Sub-Saharan Africa by contrast rank lower in human development than in per capita GNI. Note that the rankings for the regions for 2013 are given in parentheses in Table 2.3. Whereas the Arab states rank first on per capita GNI among the regions, they rank fourth in HDI, mean years of schooling, and life expectancy at birth. East Asia and the Pacific, by contrast, ranks fourth in per capita GNI, but third in HDI and mean years of schooling, and second in life expectancy at birth. A number of factors account for the disparity in per capita GNI and HDI rankings for LDC regions. First, LDCs with less inequality in access to health care and education tend to have higher HDI rankings.[46] A second factor involves the inclusiveness of the society in terms of gender and ethnicity. A third factor, which we already discussed, relates to the resource curse. A fourth factor relates to the extent to which a

TABLE 2.3

Human Development Index, Less Developed Country Regions 2010 and 2013 Rankings

Human Development Group or Region (Less Developed Countries)	Human Development Index Value		Life expectancy at Birth (years)			Mean Years of Schooling (years)			Expected Years of Schooling (years)			Gross national income per capita (2011 PPP$)*		
	2010	2013	Rank 2013	2010	2013	2010	2013	Rank 2013	2010	2013	Rank 2013	2010	2013	Rank 2013
Latin America and the Caribbean	0.734	0.740	(1)	74.2	74.9	7.9	7.9	(2)	13.8	13.7	(1)	12,926	13,767	(2)
Europe and Central Asia	0.726	0.738	(2)	70.7	71.3	9.6	9.7	(1)	13.3	13.6	(2)	11,280	12,415	(3)
East Asia and the Pacific	0.688	0.738	(3)	73.5	74.0	7.4	7.4	(3)	12.3	12.5	(3)	8,628	10,499	(4)
Arab states	0.675	0.682	(4)	69.7	70.2	6.2	6.3	(4)	11.7	11.8	(4)	15,281	15,817	(1)
South Asia	0.573	0.588	(5)	66.4	67.2	4.7	4.7	(6)	10.6	11.2	(5)	4,732	5,195	(5)
Sub-Saharan Africa	0.468	0.502	(6)	55.2	56.8	4.8	4.8	(5)	9.4	9.7	(6)	2,935	3,152	(6)

*PPP: Purchasing Power Parity

Source: Adapted from United Nations Development Program, Human Development Report 2014, Chapter 2, Table 2.1, p. 34
http://hdr.undp.org/sites/default/files/hdr14-report-en-.pdf

country or region is subject to violence, which of course prevents people from gaining access to adequate health care and education.

Despite the differences, LDCs in general have been achieving higher levels of human development as measured by the HDI. The HDI gap has also narrowed between the DCs and some emerging economies such as China, India, Brazil, Indonesia, South Africa, and Turkey. The South as a whole is also becoming more important in the global economy. For example, the South's share of world merchandise trade increased from 25 percent in 1980 to 47 percent in 2010, and its share of world output rose from 33 percent to 45 percent. Furthermore, South–South trade increased from less than 8 percent of world merchandise trade in 1980 to 26 percent in 2011.[47] However, not all LDCs have shared in this growth, and the North–South gap continues to persist. In 2013 the 14 countries with the highest HDIs were all DCs.[48]

Although the North–South gap is the most important division, there are also major differences within the South. Table 2.3 shows that Latin America, East Asia, Europe and Central Asia, and the Arab states score higher in terms of most socioeconomic indicators than South Asia and Sub-Saharan Africa. For example, in 2013 the HDI index ranged from 0.740 in Latin America and the Caribbean to 0.502 in Sub-Saharan Africa; life expectancy at birth ranged from 74.9 years in Latin America and the Caribbean to 56.8 years in Sub-Saharan Africa; mean years of schooling ranged from 9.7 years in Europe and Central Asia to 4.7 years in South Asia; and the PPP-adjusted GNI per capita ranged from $15,817 in the Arab States to $3,152 in Sub-Saharan Africa.

In 1971 the UN compiled a list of 24 **least developed countries (LLDCs)**, which grew to 48 countries by 2014. The LLDCs have low per capita GNIs, weak human assets (i.e., health and education), and high economic vulnerability. Thirty-four of the 48 LLDCs are in Africa, 13 are in Asia, and one is in Latin America and the Caribbean. The LLDCs had fairly strong economic growth from 2002 to 2007, with their real GDP increasing at an average annual rate of 7 percent. However, LLDC economic growth slowed considerably from 2008 to 2012 due to the global financial crisis. LLDCs have lost export revenue because of a decline in global demand, commodity prices, and foreign direct investment. LLDCs were able to decrease their average level of indebtedness to 28 percent of their GNIs in 2012, partly because of debt relief provided by bilateral and multilateral donors (see Chapters 7 and 11). However, some LLDCs continue to have high debt burdens. In 2012, for example, debt as a percentage of GNI was 59 percent for Gambia, 82 percent for Mauritania, 87 percent for Bhutan, and 73 percent for Laos.[49] From 2001 to 2012, 50.8 percent of people in LDCs subsisted on less than $1.25 (U.S.) a day. Many LLDCs continue to have limited production and export bases, high transport costs, lack of infrastructure, and greater vulnerability to shocks such as economic crises, natural disasters, and the spread of disease. Thus, the African countries most severely affected by the recent Ebola virus—Guinea, Liberia, and Sierra Leone—are all LLDCs.[50]

It is also important to consider inequities *within* states. The per capita income of a country is an average figure that does not tell us about the *distribution* of income. As discussed, the Gini coefficient measures income inequality, and countries on average now have more income inequality than in the 1980s.[51] The HDI, like the per capita GNI, provides only an *average* figure for a country. Thus, the 2010 *Human Development Report* introduced an **inequality-adjusted HDI (IHDI)**; if there was no inequality within a country, the HDI would equal the IHDI. In all countries, the IHDI is in fact lower than the HDI, and the difference between the two figures measures the loss in human development because of inequality.[52] Before looking at the IHDI data it is important to note that the 2014 *Human Development Report* does *not* provide IHDI values for 36 of the 187 countries it surveys.[53] DCs generally have less inequality in human development than LDCs, and people in the poorest LDCs tend to have the most multidimensional inequality. However, there is also great variation in inequality among both DCs and LDCs. Table 2.4 shows the loss of HDI value (in percent) due to inequality in a small number of selected countries. In 2013 losses of HDI value due to inequality for very high HDI countries ranged from 19.6 percent for Chile to 5.5 percent for Finland; for high HDI countries, from 33.6 percent for Iran to 7.2 percent for Montenegro; for medium HDI countries, from 43.6 percent for Namibia to 11.5 percent for Mongolia; and for low HDI countries, from 44.3 percent for Sierra Leone to 27.1 percent for Tanzania. Although there has been some progress in reducing disparities in health and education within countries, income disparities within countries have been increasing. Globalization, deregulation of labor markets, and countries' macroeconomic policies are some of the factors contributing to the growing income disparities within states.

A book entitled *Capital in the Twenty-First Century* by Thomas Piketty introduces statistical methods to trace inequalities in income and wealth from the early twentieth century to the present. Piketty points out that income disparities are increasing in many DCs as well as LDCs, and he focuses considerable attention on the United States and Britain. In 1910 the top 1 percent received about 20 percent of total income in the United States and Britain, but that share had decreased by more than half by 1950. Since 1980, however, the top 1 percent's share has been rapidly increasing, and in the United States it is back to about 20 percent of total income. Notably, the United States today has a much more unequal distribution of income than other DCs, which redistribute more wealth through transfers and taxes. For example, of the three DCs listed in Table 2.4, the United States' loss of HDI value due to inequality in 2013 was 17.4 percent compared with 7.6 percent for Canada and 5.5 percent for Finland. Piketty attributes the growing income disparity to capital income, inherited wealth, and super-salaries for senior executives, and he argues that this level of inequality can "lead to a capture of the political process by a tiny high-income and high-wealth elite."[54]

Although this book discusses within-country inequities and inequities among LDCs, it gives more emphasis to North–South inequities. Since most LDCs are in a weak position individually, only collective action provides some opportunity to extract concessions from the North. This chapter briefly discusses the **United Nations Conference on Trade and Development**

TABLE 2.4

Loss of HDI Value (in percent)
Due to Inequality—Selected Countries 2013

HDI Rank*	Country	Inequality Adjusted HDI (IHDI) Loss %
Very high human development		
5	United States	17.4
8	Canada	7.6
24	Finland	5.5
41	Chile	19.6
High human development		
51	Montenegro	7.2
71	Mexico	22.9
75	Iran	33.6
79	Brazil	27.0
Medium human development		
103	Mongolia	11.5
127	Namibia	43.6
135	India	28.6
141	Zambia	35.0
Low human development		
145	Nepal	28.8
152	Nigeria	40.3
159	Tanzania	27.1
183	Sierra Leone	44.3

Source: United Nations Development Program,
Human Development Report, 2014, Table 3, pp. 168–171.
* HDI: Human Development Index

(**UNCTAD**), which gives priority to the interests of LDCs. In the 1960s many LDCs gained political independence, and the number of African and Asian states in the UN increased from 10 in 1955 to 55 in 1966. In 1964, the 77 LDCs in the UN from Africa, Asia, and Latin America ("the Third World") met to express their dissatisfaction with the KIEOs, and this LDC caucus, which now has 134 members, is still referred to as the **Group of 77 (G77)**.[55] The G77 was highly critical of GATT, which it viewed as a rich countries' club, and it was instrumental in organizing the first UN Conference on Trade and Development, or UNCTAD I, in March 1964. UNCTAD subsequently became a permanent forum or conference under the UN General Assembly, with facilities to do research and policy analysis (see Figure 2.1). Unlike the KIEOs, UNCTAD depends on UN funds for its operating budget and its technical cooperation activities. Although all UN members are in UNCTAD, its secretariat openly supports LDC interests, and the UNCTAD secretary general has always been from the South. UNCTAD established some international commodity agreements and has induced the GATT/WTO to give more priority to LDC trade interests (see Chapter 8). However, the DCs refused to accept UNCTAD as a major forum for trade negotiations, and the WTO continues to be the unrivaled global trade organization. UNCTAD acts as a pressure group for Southern interests and as a source of technical expertise. UNCTAD has toned down its critical approach in recent years, but its 2009 *Least Developed Countries Report* warns that "the current financial crisis is the result of weaknesses in the neoliberal model that has been shaping global economic policies in the last three decades."[56]

THE KIEOS AND THE CENTRALLY PLANNED ECONOMIES

The centrally planned economies (CPEs) of Eastern Europe, the Soviet Union, and China were either nonmembers of the KIEOs or had a very limited role for many years. The U.S. negotiator Harry Dexter White thought that universalism would create a more secure environment, and his 1942 draft Bretton Woods plan asserted that to exclude "Russia would be an egregious error. Russia, despite her socialist economy could both contribute and profit by participation."[57] The West also expected Eastern European states to become KIEO members. Although the Soviet Union feared capitalist encirclement, it participated in the Bretton Woods Conference and wanted financial aid to reconstruct its war-damaged economy. As the only Communist state at Bretton Woods (Poland and Czechoslovakia were not yet Communist), the Soviet Union criticized proposals for IMF and World Bank voting procedures, rules on state-trading, and requirements that members provide detailed economic information. Although the West made limited concessions to the Soviet Union and it signed the Bretton Woods agreements, the Soviets continued to oppose the IMF and World Bank voting systems, the transfer of gold to U.S. territory, and IMF conditions on its loans. Cold War issues also intruded (e.g., disputes over Berlin and the Soviet occupation of Eastern Europe), and the Soviet Union decided not to become a member of the KIEOs.[58]

In 1947, the United States created the European Recovery Program or Marshall Plan to help Western Europe build up its foreign exchange reserves. Although U.S. Secretary of State George C. Marshall invited the Soviet Union and Eastern Europe to participate, the Soviets refused and prevented participation by Eastern Europe. The Soviets objected to provisions that would give the United States advisory authority over the internal budgets of Marshall Plan recipients, require European states to cooperate with each other in using Marshall Plan aid, and tie most of the aid to the purchase of U.S. exports. Only Western Europe participated in the Marshall Plan, and the Soviets established the *Council for Mutual Economic Assistance* (*CMEA*) in 1949 as a counterweight. Composed of the Soviet Union and Eastern European states other than Yugoslavia, CMEA solidified the East–West divide.[59] In contrast to the market-oriented Bretton Woods system, CMEA emphasized central economic planning, nationalization of the factors of production, the collectivization of agriculture, and insulation of the domestic economy from external influences. However, CMEA performed poorly because it contributed to bilateralism, inward-looking policies, and a currency (the ruble) with unrealistic conversion rates that limited trade.[60] U.S. policies were also responsible for the growing East–West economic rift. For example, the United States restricted trade with Communist countries and pressured its allies to participate in embargoes of strategic goods to the Soviet bloc. The liberal economic orientation of the KIEOs also contributed to the East–West split. Although the IBRD Articles of Agreement state that "only economic considerations shall be relevant" to the Bank's decisions, the KIEOs in fact base their decisions on political and ideological as well as economic factors.[61]

In view of the East–West divisions, most linkages between Communist states and the KIEOs were severed. Czechoslovakia, Poland, Yugoslavia, China, and Cuba were founding members of the IMF and World Bank, but their status changed after they became Communist (the sole exception was Yugoslavia). As Table 2.5 shows, Poland withdrew from the IMF and World Bank in 1950, charging that they were controlled by the U.S. government, and the World Bank and IMF expelled Czechoslovakia in 1954 ostensibly for failing to pay its capital subscription.[62] Yugoslavia, which maintained its independence from the Soviet Union, was the only Eastern European state that remained in these institutions in the 1950s. Taiwan occupied the China seat in the IMF and World Bank after the People's Republic of China took over the mainland in 1949, and Fidel Castro's Cuba withdrew from the Bank in 1960 and the IMF in 1964. Table 2.5 shows that China and Czechoslovakia were founding members of GATT in 1948, but the Chiang Kai-shek government (which had fled to Taiwan) withdrew from GATT in 1950, purportedly on behalf of China. Czechoslovakia remained in GATT, but its membership was inactive for many years. This was possible because of GATT's status as an informal organization.

As nonmembers of the KIEOs, the Soviet bloc countries joined the South in supporting alternative organizations such as UNCTAD. However, some Eastern Europeans turned to the KIEOs in the late 1960s because of their economic problems, their growing dependence on exporting to Western markets, and their efforts to gain more independence from the Soviet Union. Thus, Table 2.5 shows that Poland, Romania, and Hungary joined the KIEOs beginning in the late 1960s, and China replaced Taiwan in the IMF and World Bank in 1980. The most dramatic change occurred in the early 1990s after the breakup of the Soviet Union, when Russia and other FSU republics joined the IMF and World Bank, and a number of former East bloc countries joined GATT. China, Taiwan, and Ukraine became WTO members in 2001, 2002, and 2008; and Russia joined the WTO in 2012.

TABLE 2.5

Membership of Transition Economies in the Keystone International Economic Organizations

	IMF/World Bank	GATT/WTO[b]
[a]1945	China, Czechoslovakia, Yugoslavia	
[a]1946	Poland, Cuba	
1948		China, Czechoslovakia, Cuba—founding members
1950	Poland withdraws from IMF/World Bank	Republic of China—Taiwan withdraws from GATT
1954	Czechoslovakia ousted from IMF/World Bank	
1960	Cuba withdraws from World Bank	
1964	Cuba withdraws from IMF	
1966		Yugoslavia
1967		Poland
1971		Romania
1972	Romania	
1973		Hungary
1980	People's Republic of China (replaces Taiwan) IMF/WB	
1982	Hungary	
1986	Poland readmitted	
1990	Czechoslovakia readmitted, Bulgaria	East Germany—due to German reunification
1991	Albania, Mongolia	
1992	Federal Republic of Yugoslavia ceased membership	
1992–97	Russian Federation, Azerbaijan, Belarus, Bosnia and Herzegovina, Croatia, Czech Republic, Estonia, Georgia, Kazakhstan, Kyrgyz Republic, Latvia, Lithuania, Macedonia, Moldova, Slovak Republic, Slovenia, Serbia, Tajikistan, Turkmenistan, Ukraine, Uzbekistan	Bulgaria, Czech Republic, Slovak Republic, Slovenia, Mongolia
1998–2001	Serbia/Montenegro (IMF/World Bank)	Kyrgyz Republic, Estonia, Croatia, Albania, Georgia, Latvia, Lithuania, Moldova, China
2002		Chinese Taipei (Taiwan)

TABLE 2.5 (continued)		
2003		Armenia, Macedonia
2004		Cambodia
2006	Montenegro (IMF/World Bank) (Serbia continues membership of former Serbia/Montenegro)	
2008		Ukraine
2009	Kosovo	
2012		Montenegro, Russian Federation
2013		Tajikistan

[a]Original Members 1945–46; [b]In 1995 WTO replaced GATT

Sources:
www.imf.org/external/np/sec/memdir/memdate.htm
www.worldbank.org/en/about/leadership/members
www.wto.org/english/thewto_e/whatis_e/tif_e/org6_e.htm

NONSTATE ACTORS

Business firms, which often support the neoliberal globalization process, are the most influential nonstate actors in the global economy. They have established their own business institutions, influenced KIEO policies, and interacted with governments and IOs in the **World Economic Forum (WEF)**. The WEF's origins stem from the *European Management Forum*, a group of European business leaders that began meeting in Davos, Switzerland in 1971 to help Europe reclaim some leadership of the international business community from the United States. The group gradually shifted to a global focus; changed its name to the WEF in 1987; and became a venue in which business executives, political leaders, and multilateral institutions discuss global problems. The WEF's core members are the top 1,200 global firms and banks in terms of global sales or capital. In addition to its annual meeting in Davos, the WEF holds regional summits and issues influential publications such as the *Global Competitiveness Report* and the *Global Information Technology Report.* Although the WEF is a private institution with no publicly sanctioned authority, it has considerable influence in the public sphere. For example, the Mexican president initiated discussions at the WEF in 1990 that led to negotiation of the NAFTA.[63] Many liberals believe that business entrepreneurs in the WEF are acting in the public interest, and they note that the WEF's founder (Klaus Schwab) adheres to a multistakeholder model that takes account of the interests of a wide range of private and public actors. Critical theorists by contrast argue that NGOs account for less than 2 percent of those at the Davos meetings, and that the WEF governing boards are "overwhelmingly male, predominantly white and substantially from the wealthiest nations of Europe, North America and Japan."[64]

In contrast to global business firms, NGOs and social movements focusing on labor, women, the environment, development, and human rights have been largely excluded from positions of power. These diverse groups are often categorized together as **civil society**, which can be defined as a wide range of nongovernmental, noncommercial groups that seek to either reinforce or alter existing norms, rules, and social structures. Scholars discuss three types of civil society organizations (CSOs): conformist, reformist, and transformist or rejectionist.[65] Although much of the literature focuses on civil society protests aimed at the IMF, World Bank, and WTO, most civil society groups are *conformist CSOs* "that seek to uphold and reinforce existing norms."[66] They include professional associations, business lobbies, philanthropic foundations, research groups such as the Institute for International Economics and Brookings Institution, and the WEF. *Reformist CSOs* want the KIEOs to become more democratic, transparent, and open to participation by underrepresented groups, but they do not seek to replace the underlying structure of capitalism. Although reformists often engage in peaceful protest such as passive marches, they also interact with the KIEOs through lobbying, discussions, briefing sessions, and negotiations. *Transformist or rejectionist CSOs* seek "a comprehensive change of the social order (whether in a progressive or a reactionary fashion)."[67] Leftist rejectionists are anticapitalist and see the KIEOs as unreformable. Although rejectionists employ a diversity of tactics, they are generally committed to confrontational and disruptive actions; extreme rejectionists such as anarchists may engage in property destruction, clashes with the police, and violence. Some scholars refer to rejectionists as "anti-globalizers" because they oppose international trade and financial integration, but others argue that rejectionists do not oppose globalization *per se*; they oppose the current neoliberal form of globalization.[68]

A major obstacle to scholarly analysis of civil society groups is that "civil society" is a vague concept used in "many different theoretical, practical, and historical contexts."[69] Some scholars view **transnational advocacy networks** (**TANs**) as a more useful concept for analyzing the relations between NGOs and other actors. A TAN "includes those relevant actors working internationally on an issue, who are bound together by shared values, a common discourse, and dense exchanges of information and services."[70] TANs support value-laden causes and are important in areas such as the environment, women, infant health, and indigenous peoples; but they are also involved with economic matters such as trade, development, and foreign debt. TANs incorporate NGOs, social movements, the media, trade unions, consumer organizations, religious institutions, intellectuals, and various parts of IOs and governments.[71]

THE 2008 GLOBAL FINANCIAL CRISIS: A TURNING POINT?

This chapter has examined the institutional framework for managing the postwar global economy. Subsequent chapters discuss the role of these institutions in greater detail. The DCs at Bretton Woods believed that international institutions could promote economic stability and growth, and the three KIEOs have contributed to postwar prosperity. However, there is a hierarchy of states in the IMF, World Bank, and WTO, with the North having the most votes in the IMF and World Bank and the most influence over multilateral trade negotiations in the WTO. The South has tried to alter the KIEOs and establish alternative organizations such as UNCTAD. However, the South's gains have been limited, and financial crises in the 1980s and 1990s induced many LDCs to become more closely integrated with the KIEOs. For many years the centrally planned economies did not participate in the KIEOs, and the Soviet Union established the CMEA as an alternative organization. However, these countries began to join the KIEOs because of growing economic problems and dependence on the West. The breakup of the Soviet bloc and Soviet Union sped up this integration process.

The KIEOs are therefore universal membership organizations, but it is increasingly difficult for them to reach a consensus and manage global economic relations. Emerging economies such as the BRICS have been growing more rapidly than the DCs, and are less willing to accept the North's dominance in international institutions. The 2008 global financial crisis marked a turning point because the crisis began in the United States, and emerging economies such as China, Brazil, and India played a major role in the recovery process. In September 2009 the G7 ceded responsibility for steering the global economy to the G20, and this was the first sign of a significant change in the global institutional framework. The G20 has discussed the issue of reforming the IMF and World Bank, and some votes have been redistributed in the World Bank from smaller European countries to emerging economies such as China, India, and Brazil. However, the U.S. Congress has not yet ratified similar changes in the IMF, and this jeopardizes the legitimacy of the IMF as an institution. Furthermore, the LDCs in the G20 are emerging economies and there is no representation for the 48 LLDCs.[72] In sum, the 2008 global financial crisis has been somewhat of a turning point in giving emerging countries such as the BRIC economies more influence, but the influence of the poorest LDCs continues to be extremely limited. The next three chapters examine the IPE theoretical perspectives.

QUESTIONS

1. Why were the IMF, World Bank, and GATT created, and how did they evolve over time?
2. What is the role of smaller organizations and groups such as the OECD, G7/G8, and G20? Why was the G20 formed, and why is it now more important than the G7?
3. What are the advantages of using PPP-adjusted per capita GDP figures, and what are its shortcomings? What is the Gini coefficient?
4. What is the HDI, and what are its strengths and weaknesses? What is the IHDI?
5. What is the resource curse, and does it apply to all countries that are rich in natural resources?

6. Why were the G77 and UNCTAD formed, and how successful have they been? Is the growing influence of the G20 likely to benefit all LDCs?
7. What are the most significant divisions within the South? What are OPEC, the NIEs, the BRICS, and the emerging economies? Do these groups have anything in common with the LLDCs?
8. How has the relationship changed between the former centrally planned economies and the KIEOs?
9. What is the WEF, and in what way does it contribute to a blurring of lines between "public" and "private" in the global political economy?
10. What are civil society groups, and how do they differ in terms of tactics and goals? What are TANs?

KEY TERMS

Bank for International
Settlements
Bretton Woods Conference
BRIC economies
BRICS economies
central bank
civil society
emerging market
economies
exchange rates
General Agreement on
Tariffs and Trade
Gini coefficient
Group of Five

Group of Seven
Group of Eight
Group of 20
Group of 77
human development
index
inequality-adjusted
HDI
International Monetary
Fund
least developed
countries
newly industrializing
economies

Organization for
Economic Cooperation
and Development
Organization of Petroleum
Exporting Countries
purchasing power parity
transnational advocacy
networks
United Nations
Conference on Trade
and Development
World Bank
World Economic Forum
World Trade Organization

FURTHER READING

Studies with alternative perspectives on the KIEOs include Eric Helleiner, *Forgotten Foundations of Bretton Woods* (New York: Cornell University Press, 2014); Liam Clegg, *Controlling the World Bank and the IMF* (New York: Palgrave Macmillan, 2013); Gustav Ranis, James Raymond Vreeland, and Stephen Kosack, *Globalization and the Nation State: The Impact of the IMF and the World Bank* (New York: Routledge, 2006); Ngaire Woods, *The Globalizers: The IMF, the World Bank, and Their Borrowers* (Ithaca, NY: Cornell University Press, 2006); and Richard Peet, *Unholy Trinity: The IMF, World Bank and WTO* (New York: Zed Books, 2003). Studies on the OECD include Judith Clifton and Daniel Diaz-Fuentes, "The OECD and Phases in the International Political Economy, 1961–2011," *Review of International Political Economy* 18, no. 5 (December 2011), pp. 552–569; Kerstin Martens and Anja P. Jakobi, eds., *Mechanisms of OECD Governance* (New York: Oxford University Press, 2010); Richard Woodward, *The Organisation for Economic Co-operation and Development (OECD)* (New York: Routledge, 2009); and Rianne Mahon and Stephen McBride, eds., *The OECD and Transnational Governance* (Vancouver: University of British Columbia Press, 2008). On the G20 see Peter I. Hajnal, *The G20: Evolution, Interrelationships, Documentation* (Burlington, VT: Ashgate, 2014); and Andrew F. Cooper and Ramesh Thakur, *The Group of Twenty*

(New York: Routledge, 2013). On the G7/G8 see Hugo Dobson, *The Group of 7/8* (New York: Routledge, 2007); and Robert D. Putnam and Nicholas Bayne's classic study *Hanging Together: Cooperation and Conflict in the Seven-Power Summit*, rev. ed. (London: Sage, 1987). John J. Kirton has been series editor for a number of books dealing with the G7/G8, G20, and global governance.

On UNCTAD see Ian Taylor and Karen Smith, *United Nations Conference on Trade and Development* (New York: Routledge, 2007); and Shigehisa Kasahara and Charles Gore, eds., *Beyond Conventional Wisdom in Development Policy: An Intellectual History of UNCTAD 1964–2004* (New York: United Nations, 2004). For differing views on the World Economic Forum, see Geoffrey Allen Pigman, *The World Economic Forum: A Multi-Stakeholder Approach to Global Governance* (New York: Routledge, 2007); and Jean-Christophe Graz, "How Powerful Are Transnational Elite Clubs? The Social Myth of the World Economic Forum," *New Political Economy* 8, no. 3 (November 2003), pp. 321–340. A good study of TANs is Sanjeev Khagram, James V. Riker, and Kathryn Sikkink, eds., *Restructuring World Politics: Transnational Social Movements, Networks, and Norms* (Minneapolis, MN: University of Minnesota Press, 2002).

On the resource curse see Brenda Shaffer and Taleh Ziyadov, *Beyond the Resource Curse* (Philadelphia: University of Pennsylvania Press, 2012); and Macartan Humphreys, Jeffrey D. Sachs, and Joseph E. Stiglitz, *Escaping the Resource Curse* (New York: Columbia University Press, 2007).

NOTES

1. Armand Van Dormael, *Bretton Woods: Birth of a Monetary System* (London: Macmillan, 1978), p. ix.
2. Richard N. Gardner, "The Political Setting," in A. L. Keith Acheson, John F. Chant, and Martin F. J. Prochowny, eds., *Bretton Woods Revisited* (Toronto: University of Toronto Press, 1972), p. 20; Richard N. Gardner, "The Bretton Woods System After Fifty Years: A Balance Sheet of Success and Failure," in Orin Kirshner, ed., *The Bretton-Woods-GATT System* (Armonk, NY: M.E. Sharpe, 1996), pp. 201–207.
3. Eric Helleiner, *Forgotten Foundations of Bretton Woods* (Ithaca, NY: Cornell University Press, 2014), p. 2.
4. Herman M. Schwartz, *States Versus Markets: The Emergence of a Global Economy*, 2nd ed. (New York: St. Martin's Press, 2000), p. 11.
5. Adam Smith used the term *mercantile system,* and only later did the term *mercantilism* become standard. Jacob Viner, "Mercantilist Thought," in David L. Sills, ed., *International Encyclopedia of the Social Sciences,* vol. 4 (New York: Free Press, 1968), p. 436; David A. Baldwin, *Economic Statecraft* (Princeton, NJ: Princeton University Press, 1985), p. 72.
6. Adam Smith, *The Wealth of Nations*, vol. 1 (London: Dent, Everyman's Library no. 412, 1910), bk. 4, p. 436.
7. On mercantilism, see Eli F. Heckscher, *Mercantilism*, vols. 1 and 2, 2nd ed., trans. Mendel Shapiro (London: George Allen & Unwin, 1955); Jacob Viner, *Studies in the Theory of International Trade* (New York: Augustus M. Kelley, 1965), chs. 1 and 2.
8. George Modelski, "The Long Cycle of Global Politics and the Nation-State," *Comparative Studies in Society and History* 20, no. 2 (April 1978), pp. 214–235; Joshua S. Goldstein, *Long Cycles: Prosperity and War in the Modern Age* (New Haven, CT: Yale University Press, 1988), pp. 99–147.

9. Paul Kennedy, *The Rise and Fall of the Great Powers: Economic Change and Military Conflict from 1500 to 2000* (New York: Random House, 1987), p. 151; Paul Bairoch, "International Industrialization Levels from 1750 to 1980," *Journal of European Economic History* 11, no. 2 (Fall 1982), pp. 291–292.

10. Edward John Ray, "Changing Patterns of Protectionism: The Fall in Tariffs and the Rise in Non-Tariff Barriers," *Northwestern Journal of International Law & Business* 8 (1987), pp. 294–295; Stephen D. Krasner, "State Power and the Structure of International Trade," *World Politics* 28, no. 3 (April 1976), pp. 330–335.

11. David A. Lake, *Power, Protection, and Free Trade: International Sources of U.S. Commercial Strategy, 1887–1939* (Ithaca, NY: Cornell University Press, 1988), pp 30–32; Bairoch, "International Industrialization Levels from 1750 to 1980," pp. 292–293, 297.

12. Kennedy, *The Rise and Fall of the Great Powers*, p. 230; Albert Fishlow, "Lessons from the Past: Capital Markets During the 19th Century and the Interwar Period," *International Organization* 39, no. 3 (Summer 1985), p. 390; David A. Lake, "British and American Hegemony Compared: Lessons for the Current Era of Decline," in Michael Fry, ed., *History, The White House and The Kremlin: Statesmen as Historians* (London: Pinter, 1991), p. 108.

13. Sally Marks, *The Illusion of Peace: International Relations in Europe 1918–1933* (New York: St. Martin's Press, 1976), p. 47; Charles P. Kindleberger, *The World in Depression 1929–1939*, rev. ed. (Berkeley: University of California Press, 1986), pp. 23–26.

14. Elmer E. Schattschneider, *Politics, Pressures and the Tariff: A Study of Free Private Enterprise in Pressure Politics, as Shown in the 1929–1930 Revision of the Tariff* (Hamden, CT: Archon Books, 1963).

15. Age F. P. Bakker, *International Financial Institutions* (New York: Longman, 1996), ch. 6; Hazel J. Johnson, *Global Financial Institutions and Markets* (Oxford: Blackwell, 2000), pp. 410–411.

16. Margaret G. de Vries, "The Bretton Woods Conferences and the Birth of the International Monetary Fund," in Orin Kirshner, ed., *The Bretton Woods-GATT System: Retrospect and Prospect After Fifty Years* (Armonk, NY: M.E. Sharpe, 1996), pp. 3–4.

17. Harold Jacobson and Michel Oksenberg use the term *KIEOs* in *China's Participation in the IMF, the World Bank, and GATT: Toward a Global Economic Order* (Ann Arbor, MI: University of Michigan Press, 1990).

18. Quoted in Sidney Dell, "Relations Between the United Nations and the Bretton Woods Institutions," *Development* 4 (1989), p. 28.

19. See Samuel A. Bleicher, "UN v. IBRD: A Dilemma of Functionalism," *International Organization* 24, no. 1 (Winter 1970), pp. 31–47.

20. Communication from a Counsellor, WTO External Relations Division, November 8, 2001.

21. Dell, "Relations Between the United Nations and the Bretton Woods Institutions," pp. 27–38; Edward S. Mason and Robert E. Asher, *The World Bank Since Bretton Woods* (Washington, DC: Brookings Institution, 1973), pp. 566–576.

22. UNCTAD, *World Investment Report 1996* (New York: United Nations, 1996), pp. 239–247; World Trade Organization, *WTO Annual Report 1996*, vol. 2 (Geneva: WTO, 1996), pp. 24, 67.

23. Robert E. Hoskisson, Lorraine Eden, Chung Ming Lau, and Mike Wright, "Strategy in Emerging Economies," *Academy of Management Journal* 43, no. 3 (June 2000), pp. 249–267.

24. Miles Kahler, *Leadership Selection in the Major Multilaterals* (Washington, DC: Institute for International Economics, 2001); Theodore Cohn, "Developing Countries in the International Civil Service: The Case of the World Bank Group," *International Review of Administrative Sciences* 41, no. 1 (1975), pp. 47–56.
25. Bretton Woods Commission, *Bretton Woods: Looking to the Future* (Washington, DC: Bretton Woods Committee, 1994), p. B–3.
26. John G. Ruggie, "International Regimes, Transactions, and Change: Embedded Liberalism in the Postwar Economic Order," in Stephen D. Krasner, ed., *International Regimes* (Ithaca, NY: Cornell University Press), pp. 195–231.
27. "United Nations-Bretton Woods Collaboration: How Much Is Enough?" *Report of the Twenty-Sixth United Nations Issues Conference* (Muscatine, IA: Stanley Foundation, February 24–26, 1995), p. 2.
28. C. Fred Bergsten and C. Randall Henning, *Global Economic Leadership and the Group of Seven* (Washington, DC: Institute for International Economics, 1996), p. 15.
29. On the smaller DC-led groups see Theodore H. Cohn, *Governing Global Trade: International Institutions in Conflict and Convergence* (Burlington, VT: Ashgate, 2002).
30. Nicholas Bayne, "Making Sense of Western Economic Policies: The Role of the OECD," *The World Today* 43, no. 2 (February 1987), p. 27.
31. David Henderson, "The Role of the OECD in Liberalising International Trade and Capital Flows," in Sven Arndt and Chris Miller, eds., special issue of *The World Economy* on "Global Trade Policy" (1996), pp. 11–28; David Howarth and Tal Sadeh, "In the Vanguard of Globalization: The OECD and International Capital Liberalization," *Review of International Political Economy* 18, no. 5 (December 2011), pp. 622–645.
32. William J. Drake and Kalypso Nicolaïdis, "Ideas, Interests, and Institutionalization: 'Trade in Services' and The Uruguay Round," *International Organization* 46, no. 1 (Winter 1992), pp. 37–100.
33. Robert Wolfe, "From Reconstructing Europe to Constructing Globalization: The OECD in Historical Perspective," in Rianne Mahon and Stephen McBride, eds., *The OECD and Transnational Governance* (Vancouver: University of British Columbia Press, 2008), pp. 32–33; Judith Clifton and Daniel Diaz-Fuentes, "The OECD and Phases in the International Political Economy, 1961–2011," *Review of International Political Economy* 18, no. 5 (December 2011), pp. 559–567.
34. Michael C. Webb, *The Political Economy of Policy Coordination: International Adjustment Since 1945* (Ithaca, NY: Cornell University Press, 1995), pp. 176–177.
35. Robert D. Putnam and Nicholas Bayne, *Hanging Together: Cooperation and Conflict in the Seven-Power Summits*, rev. ed. (London: Sage, 1987), pp. 150–154; Nicholas Bayne, *Hanging in There: The G-7 and G-8 Summit in Maturity and Renewal* (Burlington, VT: Ashgate, 2000), pp. 116–118.
36. Michael R. Hodges, "The G8 and the New Political Economy," in Michael R. Hodges, John J. Kirton, and Joseph P. Daniels, eds., *The G8's Role in the New Millennium* (Brookfield, VT: Ashgate, 1999), p. 69.
37. Peter I. Hajnal, *The G20: Evolution, Interrelationships, Documentation* (Burlington, VT: Ashgate, 2014), p. 13.
38. "The Group of Twenty: A History," www.g20.utoronto.ca/docs/g20history.pdf; Annys Shin and Michael D. Shear, "Reflecting New Global Economic Order, More Expansive G-20 to Replace G-8," *Washington Post*, September 25, 2009.

39. World Bank, *World Development Indicators—2001* (Washington, DC: World Bank, 2001), p. 293; Ian Castles and David Henderson, "International Comparisons of GDP," *World Economics* 6, no. 1 (January–March 2005), pp. 75–80.
40. For example, see "Big MacCurrencies," *The Economist*, April 11, 1998, p. 58.
41. OECD, *Going for Growth—2006* (Paris: OECD, 2006), pp. 135–136.
42. United Nations Development Program, *Human Development Report 2014* (New York: UNDP, 2014), p. 155. The eight excluded countries are listed on p. 163.
43. Timothy N. Walters, Alma Kadragic, and Lynne M. Walters, "Miracle or Mirage: Is Development Sustainable in the United Arab Emirates?" *Middle East Review of International Affairs* 10, no. 3 (September 2006), pp. 77–91.
44. UNDP, *Human Development Report 2014*, pp. 39, 87, and 103–104.
45. Philippe Le Billon, "The Resource Curse," *The Adelphi Papers* 45, no. 373 (2005), pp. 11–27; Macartan Humphreys, Jeffrey D. Sachs, and Joseph E. Stiglitz, eds., *Escaping the Resource Curse* (New York: Columbia University Press, 2007), pp. 2–4; Frederick van der Ploeg, "Natural Resources: Curse or Blessing?" *Journal of Economic Literature* 49, no. 2 (June 2011), pp. 366–420.
46. UNDP, *Human Development Report 2010* (New York: UN, 2010), p. 58.
47. UNDP, *Human Development Report 2013* (New York: UN, 2013), pp. 1–2.
48. UNDP, *Human Development Report 2014*, p. 160.
49. UNCTAD, *State of the Least Developed Countries 2014* (New York: UN, 2014), pp. 74–75.
50. UNCTAD, *The Least Developed Countries Report 2009* (New York: UN, 2009), pp. 1–7; UNCTAD, *The Least Developed Countries Report 2014* (New York: UN, 2014), p. 2; UN Office of the High Representative for the Least Developed Countries, Landlocked Developing Countries and Small Island Developing States, *State of the Least Developed Countries 2014*, pp. 3–5.
51. UNDP, *Human Development Report 2010*, p. 72.
52. UNDP, *Human Development Report 2010*, pp. 87–89.
53. See UNDP, *Human Development Report 2014*, Table 3, pp. 168–171.
54. "Q & A: Thomas Piketty on the Wealth Divide," The New York Times Blogs, March 11, 2014; Thomas Piketty, *Capital in the Twenty-First Century* (Cambridge, MA: Belknap Press, 2014), p. 249 and chs. 9–11; UNDP, *Human Development Report 2014*, p. 39; Paul Krugman, "Why We're in a New Gilded Age," *New York Review of Books*, May 8, 2014.
55. David A. Kay, *The New Nations in the United Nations, 1960–1967* (New York: Columbia University Press, 1970), pp. 2–3.
56. UNCTAD, *The Least Developed Countries Report 2009*, p. i.
57. Quoted in Joseph Gold, *Membership and Nonmembership in the International Monetary Fund: A Study in International Law and Organization* (Washington, DC: IMF, 1974), p. 129.
58. Valerie J. Assetto, *The Soviet Bloc in the IMF and the IBRD* (Boulder, CO: Westview Press, 1988), pp. 56–66, 185; Jozef M. van Brabant, *The Planned Economies and International Economic Organizations* (Cambridge, UK: Cambridge University Press, 1991), pp. 45–48.
59. Michael Kaser, *Comecon: Integration Problems of the Planned Economies* (London: Oxford University Press, 1965), pp. 9–12.
60. Klaus Schröder, "The IMF and the Countries of the Council for Mutual Economic Assistance," *Intereconomics* 2 (March/April 1982), p. 87; Brabant, *The Planned Economies and International Economic Organizations*, p. 70.

61. *IBRD—Articles of Agreement*, as amended effective February 16, 1989 (Washington, DC: IBRD, August 1991), Article 4, Section 10; David A. Baldwin, "The International Bank in Political Perspective," *World Politics* 18, no. 1 (October 1965), pp. 68–81; Theodore H. Cohn, "Politics in the World Bank Group: The Question of Loans to the Asian Giants," *International Organization* 28, no. 3 (Summer 1974), pp. 561–571.

62. Gold, *Membership and Nonmembership in the International Monetary Fund*, pp. 342–379; Assetto, *The Soviet Bloc in the IMF and the IBRD*, pp. 69–93.

63. Geoffrey A. Pigman, *The World Economic Forum: A Multi-Stakeholder Approach to Global Governance* (New York: Routledge, 2007), p. 15.

64. Quoted in Mark Rupert and M. Scott Solomon, *Globalization and International Political Economy: The Politics of Alternative Futures* (Lanham, MD: Rowman & Littlefield, 2006), pp. 59–61.

65. Jan A. Scholte, "Civil Society and Democracy in Global Governance," *Global Governance* 8 (2002), pp. 281–304; Jeffrey M. Ayres, "Global Governance and Civil Society Collective Action: The Challenge of Complex Transnationalism," *International Journal of Political Economy* 33, no. 4 (Winter 2003–2004), pp. 84–100.

66. Scholte, "Civil Society and Democracy in Global Governance," p. 284.

67. Scholte, "Civil Society and Democracy in Global Governance," p. 284; Pigman, *The World Economic Forum*, p. 58.

68. Ayres, "Global Governance and Civil Society Collective Action," pp. 92–94; Leslie E. Armijo, "The Terms of the Debate: What's Democracy Got to Do with It?" in Leslie E. Armijo, ed., *Debating the Global Financial Architecture* (Albany, NY: State University of New York Press, 2002), pp. 51–53.

69. Mark N. Jensen, "Concepts and Conceptions of Civil Society," *Journal of Civil Society* 2, no. 1 (May 2006), p. 39.

70. Margaret E. Keck and Kathryn Sikkink, *Activists Beyond Borders: Advocacy Networks in International Politics* (Ithaca, NY: Cornell University Press, 1998), p. 2.

71. Sanjeev Khagram, James V. Riker, and Kathryn Sikkink, eds., *Restructuring World Politics: Transnational Social Movements, Networks, and Norms* (Minneapolis, MN: University of Minnesota Press, 2002).

72. "The Group of Twenty: A History," pp. 36–39.

Theoretical Perspectives

The discussion of the theoretical perspectives has some major revisions in this edition of the text. We now use the term "neomercantilism" rather than "realism" to describe one of the three main IPE perspectives, and Chapter 3 discusses the similarities and differences between the terms neomercantilism, realism, and economic nationalism. Chapters 3 and 4 also include new sections on present-day neomercantilism and liberalism, and the discussion of the critical perspectives in Chapter 5 is updated. Before turning to the theoretical perspectives, we briefly outline the role of theory and methodology. Theory helps us identify meaningful patterns and a degree of order in the complex world of IPE. Theory also enables us to go beyond description and provide causal explanations and modest predictions. For example, one scholar might hypothesize that average real incomes increase with free trade, while another might hypothesize that free trade results in greater economic inequality. Some theorists use mathematical and statistical techniques to test their hypotheses, while others rely on qualitative studies. A third group of theorists questions whether value-free theorizing is even possible, because scholars are affected by the historical and cultural setting in which they operate (constructivism is discussed in Chapter 5). Most theorists agree that theory helps us deal with the wide array of IPE issues and events by focusing on some and disregarding others; but theorists from different perspectives do *not* agree on which issues and events are the most important![1]

This book examines theories within the *neomercantilist, liberal,* and *critical* perspectives. In a seminal study of IPE, Robert Gilpin grouped the theories into three competing "ideologies": liberalism, nationalism, and Marxism.[2] This book alters Gilpin's approach to theory in several respects.

First, the theoretical perspectives are based on different sets of assumptions, but they influence each other over time. Many IPE theories such as hegemonic stability theory and regime theory are hybrids that draw on more than one perspective. Second, Marxism, one of Gilpin's perspectives, has declined in importance with the breakup of the Soviet bloc and Soviet Union. We focus on a wider range of *critical perspectives*: *historical materialism*, which stems partly from Marxism; *constructivism*; *feminism*; and *environmentalism*. (As we discuss, feminism and environmentalism draw on more than one theoretical perspective.) Third, we point to the wide diversity of writings *within* each theoretical perspective. For example, Chapter 4 discusses the diversity of liberal views regarding the relationship between government and the market.

Despite the diversity of views within liberalism, neomercantilism, and the critical perspectives, authors within each perspective generally agree on a core set of assumptions. Chapters 3–5 begin with a discussion of each theoretical perspective's approach to four questions: (1) What is the role of domestic actors? (2) What are the nature and purpose of international economic relations? (3) What is the relationship between politics and economics? (4) What are the causes and effects of globalization? The chapters then examine the historical development of the perspectives, with particular emphasis on the diversity within each perspective. Most importantly, the book emphasizes the fact that no single theoretical perspective explains all phenomena in IPE. Different theoretical perspectives help us understand various issues and events, and "our empirical task is to sort out under what condition each logic operates—including the recognition that they operate together in some circumstances."[3]

Although this book focuses mainly on substantive theories, we also devote some attention to two methodologies or methods of theory construction used by IPE theorists: *rational choice* and *constructivism*. It is important to note that many IPE scholars do not explicitly identify their work with either rational choice or constructivism, and that a number of scholars implicitly draw on both methodologies. We discuss rational choice here because it is closely associated with the mainstream liberal and neomercantilist assumptions that individuals and states are rational actors with specified interests. Constructivists by contrast see reality as being socially constructed. Although there are both critical and liberal versions of constructivism, we discuss constructivism with the critical perspectives in

Chapter 5 because even liberal constructivists are critical of the rationalist assumptions of mainstream theorists.

Rational choice analysis is a highly influential method of theory construction, and one scholar describes it as "the most powerful paradigm in the political science discipline, especially in the United States."[4] (Whereas political scientists prefer the term *rational choice*, economists prefer *public choice*.) Rational choice theorists apply an economic model of human behavior to the social, political, and economic spheres, and develop propositions that simplify the real world and can be tested through quantitative methods. (Although mathematical models are often central, they are not a *necessary* feature of rational choice.)[5] Rational choice theorists assume that individuals have goals and some freedom of choice, and that they take actions they believe will help achieve their goals. Individuals are "utility maximizers," who seek to further their self-interest by weighing the expected costs and benefits of their actions. For example, political leaders weigh the costs and benefits of adopting certain policies in terms of their re-election (i.e., political survival); and individuals weigh the benefits of voting (having an effect on the election results) against the costs (the effort involved in going to vote). Although the pure rational choice model posits that rational individuals have an *optimal* amount of information before making decisions, "rationality applies only to endeavor not to outcome; failure to achieve an objective because of ignorance or some other factor does not invalidate the premise that individuals act on the basis of a cost/benefit or means/ends calculation."[6] Thus, most studies assume that individuals achieve *satisfactory* rather than optimal outcomes because of limits to their knowledge and abilities.[7] The actions of individuals also have limits because they make choices under conditions of scarcity; for example, an individual may rent a house because she is unable to purchase one. Although rational choice analysis is grounded in liberalism with its emphasis on the individual, some neomercantilists use it to explain the international behavior of states, and some critical theorists use it as well.[8]

In many cases the rational choice model seems to accurately describe human behavior; for example, politicians may support policies favored by their constituents to increase their chances for re-election. However, rational choice analysis has been criticized on a number of grounds. Politicians may take actions that rational choice analysts do not consider "rational"; for example, they may adopt policies that accord with their ethical principles even if this decreases their chances for re-election. Some politicians may also support unpopular policies to honor prior commitments, and this could also decrease their re-election chances. Furthermore, rational choice analysis assumes that the actor is a rational, self-interested person who makes decisions without regard to historical and cultural context. It takes individual preferences as a "given" without seeking to explain why an individual or state has some preferences rather than others. Some other IPE approaches such as constructivist theory take more account of historical and sociological factors (see Chapter 5). Constructivists seek to explain why actors have particular norms, values, beliefs, perceptions, and preferences, and how these affect actions and outcomes. This book examines several areas where rational choice is explicitly applied to the study of IPE. For example, Chapter 3 discusses public goods theory, and Chapter 4 discusses a type of game theory—prisoners' dilemma. In game theory, two or more people interact, with each person acting according to the rational choice model.[9]

NOTES

1. James N. Rosenau and Mary Durfee, *Thinking Theory Thoroughly: Coherent Approaches to an Incoherent World*, 2nd ed. (Boulder, CO: Westview Press, 2000), ch. 1.
2. Robert Gilpin with Jean M. Gilpin, *The Political Economy of International Relations* (Princeton, NJ: Princeton University Press, 1987), ch. 2.
3. Duncan Snidal, "Rational Choice and International Relations," in Walter Carlsnaes, Thomas Risse, and Beth A. Simmons, eds., *Handbook of International Relations* (Thousand Oaks, CA: Sage, 2002), p. 80.
4. John S. Dryzek, *Deliberative Democracy and Beyond: Liberals, Critics, Contestations* (New York: Oxford University Press, 2000), p. 31.
5. Snidal, "Rational Choice and International Relations," p. 77.
6. Robert Gilpin, *War and Change in World Politics* (New York: Cambridge University Press, 1981), p. x.
7. Herbert A. Simon, "A Behavioral Model of Rational Choice," in Herbert A. Simon, ed., *Models of Man: Social and Rational* (New York: John Wiley & Sons, 1957), pp. 20–21.
8. Stephen Parsons, *Rational Choice and Politics: A Critical Introduction* (New York: Continuum, 2005), pp. 1–23; George T. Crane and Abla Amawi, eds., *The Theoretical Evolution of International Political Economy* (New York: Oxford University Press, 1997), pp. 21–22.
9. Lisa J. Carlson, "Game Theory: International Trade, Conflict and Cooperation," in Ronen Palan, ed., *Global Political Economy: Contemporary Theories* (New York: Routledge, 2000), pp. 117–129.

Neomercantilism

Liberalism is the dominant theoretical perspective in IPE. However, we begin with neomercantilism because it is the oldest school of thought in IPE. We use the term *neomercantilist* perspective, because *mercantilism* usually refers only to economic thought and practice in Europe from about 1500 to 1750. Neomercantilism is the IPE counterpart of **realism,** which is the oldest school of thought in international relations (IR). Realists and neomercantilists both view power as central in the global arena. However, realists focus more on the military aspects of power while neomercantilists emphasize the economic aspects. Unlike realism, neomercantilism "is overt with regard to, and emphatic about, the economic instruments and strategies of competition."[1] Neomercantilists are interested in the struggle among states for economic resources and the economic strategies the great powers use to further their national interests.

BASIC TENETS OF NEOMERCANTILISM

The Role of the Individual, the State, and Societal Groups

Neomercantilists view the international system as "anarchic," because there is no central authority above the state. Conflict and war are an ever-present danger, and each state must look after its own national interests. Neomercantilists see the state as the principal actor in IR, and they emphasize the need to preserve national sovereignty. Both realists and neomercantilists see the state as having primacy over both domestic actors such as interest groups and transnational actors such as multinational corporations. However, neomercantilists address individual choices in the domestic arena more than realists because of their focus on economic issues. For example, neomercantilists examine relations between states and firms, the emphasis of an economy on manufacturing versus

55

agriculture, and strategies to promote exports and decrease imports. Thus, the neomercantilist scholar Stephen Krasner writes in his book *Defending the National Interest: Raw Materials Investments and U.S. Foreign Policy* that "a state must deal with private actors in its own society as well as with other actors in the international arena." Although Krasner views "the state as an autonomous actor" that "has purposes of its own," he also argues that it is "constrained by domestic as well as international structures."[2]

The Nature and Purpose of International Economic Relations

In the absence of a central authority above the state, a *security dilemma* results because the actions a state takes to bolster its security may increase the fear and insecurity of others; thus, states must always consider the possibility of conflict and war. In view of the security dilemma, neomercantilists see each state as being most concerned with **relative gains**, or its position vis-à-vis other states. Even if two states are "gaining absolutely in wealth, in political terms it is the effect of these gains on relative power positions which is of primary importance."[3] The neomercantilist emphasis on relative gains stems from their view that IR is a **zero-sum game**, in which one group's gain equals another group's loss. Liberals by contrast focus on **absolute gains**, with each state seeking to maximize its own gains and less concerned about the gains of others; thus, liberals see IR as a **variable-sum game**, in which groups may gain or lose together. Liberal and neomercantilist views of international institutions exemplify this difference in outlook. Whereas liberals see the IMF, World Bank, and WTO as benefiting all states adhering to their liberal economic guidelines, neomercantilists see these IOs as "arenas for acting out power relationships" in which the most powerful states shape the rules to fit their national interests.[4]

Despite their concern with relative gains, neomercantilists focus on the redistribution of power *within* the capitalist system, whereas historical materialists believe that power and wealth cannot be more equitably distributed with unfettered capitalism. Historical materialists see only two "modes of development in contemporary history: capitalist and redistributive," and neomercantilism fits with liberalism in the capitalist mold.[5]

The Relationship Between Politics and Economics

Although neomercantilists focus explicitly on economic issues, like realists they give priority to politics over economics and view "the economy as a creature of the state."[6] Neomercantilists like liberals recognize the importance of the market, but they believe that the state must ensure that the market serves its interests and its relative standing vis-à-vis other states. To further its relative gains, the state should "play an active part in promoting trade, shaping investment policy, and supporting national firms."[7] Neomercantilists also believe that the distribution of political power has a major effect on international economic relations. Thus, this chapter discusses "hegemonic stability theory," which examines the effect of a predominant state (Britain in the nineteenth century and the United States in the twentieth century) on the global political economy.

The Causes and Effects of Globalization

Neomercantilists have a range of views on globalization. They tend to see globalization mainly as an economic process that does not affect the international political structure in which states predominate. Globalization increases only when states permit it to increase, and the largest states can open or close world markets to improve their power positions vis-à-vis weaker states. Thus, neomercantilists see "no evidence that globalization has systematically undermined state control ... Transnational activities have challenged state control in some areas, but these challenges are not manifestly more problematic than in the past."[8] In the areas where globalization has challenged state control, states may take actions to protect their interests. For example, a state may take defensive actions if globalization reduces its ability to tax its citizens, or weakens the identity citizens feel with the state. Whereas liberals see globalization as imposing pressure on states to adopt a single model of capitalism, neomercantilists argue that different national capitalisms can coexist in a world of separate states. For example, the state has a greater socioeconomic role in France, Scandinavia, Japan, and South Korea than it has in the United States, Britain, and Canada.[9] Some neomercantilists argue that globalization has enabling as well as constraining effects on the state. Thus, many states have "increased direct tax yields, maintained or expanded social spending, and devised more complex systems of trade and industrial governance in order to cope with deepening integration."[10]

THE MERCANTILISTS

Mercantilism refers to economic thought and practice that prevailed in Europe from about 1500 to 1750.[11] As discussed in Chapter 2, mercantilism's emphasis on national power played an important role in state building after the demise of feudalism. Mercantilists called on the state to solidify its power by establishing primacy over other domestic actors and protecting its sovereignty vis-à-vis outside forces. Mercantilists also believed that a state could use its gold and silver to build up its armed forces, hire mercenaries, and influence its enemies and allies. States therefore took all necessary measures to accumulate precious metals by increasing their exports and decreasing their imports. Because it is impossible for all states to have a balance-of-trade surplus, mercantilists viewed IR as a zero-sum game in which relative gains were most important.[12] In the late eighteenth century, critics argued that mercantilist states encroached on individual freedom and engaged in the continuous cycle of European wars. For example, Adam Smith, the eighteenth-century liberal economist, asserted that mercantilism encouraged states to "beggar ... all their neighbours" and cause trade and commerce to become a "fertile source of discord and animosity."[13]

These criticisms were highly effective, and liberal views of free trade became dominant in England for much of the nineteenth century.

NEOMERCANTILISM AND THE INDUSTRIAL REVOLUTION

Mercantilism was a preindustrial doctrine, and the Industrial Revolution gave new impetus to neomercantilists who viewed industrialization as essential for a state's military power, security, and economic self-sufficiency. Foremost among the neomercantilist thinkers at this time were Alexander Hamilton (1755–1804), the first U.S. secretary of the treasury, and Friedrich List (1789–1846), a German civil servant, professor, and politician who was imprisoned and exiled for his dissident political views. Hamilton and List wanted the United States and Germany to maintain a positive balance of trade, and to increase industrial exports which had long-term advantages over raw material exports. Hamilton's 1791 *Report on the Subject of Manufactures* "contains the intellectual origins of modern economic nationalism and the classic defense of economic protectionism."[14] The report argued that the United States could preserve its independence and security only by promoting economic development through industrialization, government intervention, and protectionism. Industrialization was especially important because the "independence and security of a Country, appear to be materially connected with the prosperity of manufactures."[15] Hamilton viewed U.S. government intervention as necessary to promote industrialization, because Britain as the only industrialized power discouraged manufacturing in its colonies. To counter Britain's advantages, the U.S. government had to promote the use of foreign technology, capital, and skilled labor and adopt protectionist policies such as tariffs and quotas to bolster its fledgling industries.

List also emphasized the importance of manufacturing for a state's economic development. In *The National System of Political Economy* (1841), he wrote that "a nation which exchanges agricultural products for foreign manufactured goods is an individual with *one* arm, which is supported by a foreign arm."[16] Thus, Germany and the United States could catch up with the British only by providing protection for their **infant industries**. (Infant industries are not yet able to compete with established industries in more developed countries.) Britain had attained manufacturing supremacy by adopting protectionist policies, and it did not turn to free trade until the nineteenth century to retain its lead in manufacturing; thus, it traded industrial products for U.S. wool and cotton. List also emphasized the importance of national unity so a state could impose external trade barriers, launch national projects such as railroads, and develop "human capital" (e.g., human skills, training, and enterprise); this was especially important for Germany, which was a group of principalities that did not become a country until 1871.[17]

Although List was highly critical of Adam Smith's brand of liberalism, List and Hamilton were influenced by Smith's arguments for free trade. Despite List's support for protectionism to promote industrialization, he criticized the mercantilists for supporting *agricultural* protectionism. List believed that protection should be targeted, not excessive, and temporary. Thus, List viewed free trade as valuable in the long term for states that had achieved industrial supremacy. The United States and Germany had to adopt protectionist policies to increase their productive potential, but after they were "raised by artificial measure," List wrote, "freedom of trade" could then "operate naturally."[18]

It is important to note that IPE scholars have different interpretations of List's writings. Many scholars describe List as an economic nationalist and also as a neomercantilist. For example, Robert Gilpin writes that "all nationalists are realists in their emphasis on the crucial role of the state, security interests, and power in international affairs."[19] However, some IPE scholars argue that List was an economic nationalist, but *not* a neomercantilist. A **state** is a sovereign, territorial political unit, and a *nation* is a group of people who feel tied by a common ethnicity, culture, language, history, or religion. Although state and nation may largely coincide in a nation-state, there are many examples where this is not the case; for example, the Kurds in Iran, Iraq, Turkey, and Syria. Thus, Rawi Abdelal argues that "nationalism is not equivalent to statism; economic nationalism is not equivalent to mercantilism";[20] and Eric Helleiner writes that List's economic nationalism "can be associated with a wide range of policy projects, including the endorsement of liberal economic policies."[21]

It is true that economic nationalism is not synonymous with neomercantilism. However, economic nationalism and neomercantilism can overlap (in a nation-state), and List as an economic nationalist adhered to neomercantilism in some important respects. For example, List wrote that liberal arguments for free trade do "not take into account the influence of war on the necessity for a protective system."[22] He also showed how the state had facilitated economic development in Britain, France, and the United States, and he criticized Adam Smith for seeking "almost entirely to exclude politics and the power of the State."[23] Only when a state had achieved industrial supremacy did List believe that it could benefit from free trade. Thus, one IPE scholar writes that "the achievements of nineteenth-century neomercantilists" such as Hamilton and List resulted from "integrating the advances in economic thought produced by the liberal school with realist … assumptions about politics."[24]

NEOMERCANTILISM IN THE INTERWAR PERIOD

Britain ushered in a period of free trade with the repeal of its Corn Laws in 1846, but changes in the late nineteenth century caused trade liberalization to falter. World War I and economic crises during the interwar years caused states to protect their national interests with trade barriers, competitive currency devaluations, and foreign exchange controls. The dire economic conditions also encouraged extreme ideologies such as fascism, which "took advantage of the economic dislocation to attack the entire liberal-capitalist system and to call for assertive 'national' policies, backed if necessary by the sword."[25] For example, Germany sought to create a self-sufficient sphere of influence in southern and eastern Europe that would block Britain's access to the area. Germany exported manufactured products to these countries in return for agricultural goods, and prevented the establishment of industries in these countries. By increasing self-sufficiency and stockpiling strategic materials and food imports, Hitler prepared the economy and the army for war.[26] The extreme nationalism and protectionism contributed to the Great Depression and World War II and gave the leaders at Bretton Woods the impetus to establish a liberal economic system.

NEOMERCANTILISM AFTER WORLD WAR II

Although neomercantilists such as Hamilton and List had been highly attuned to economic issues, U.S. realist scholars after World War II focused almost exclusively on security issues. Security was a major concern with the emergence of the Cold War, and economic issues seemed to have less political importance. A consensus formed under U.S. leadership at Bretton Woods ushered in a period of economic stability and prosperity, and LDCs that did not share in this prosperity had little influence. The KIEOs had an important role in strengthening the capitalist economies vis-à-vis the Soviet bloc, but the Cold War had little effect on these organizations because most Soviet bloc countries were not members; the KIEOs functioned well without the Soviet bloc because it accounted for only a small share of global economic transactions. Thus, U.S. realist scholars considered economic issues to be "low politics" and not worthy of much attention.[27] Postwar realists were also influenced by liberal views on the separability of economics and politics. However, unlike liberals such as Adam Smith who favored a laissez-faire economy free of political constraints, realist scholars emphasized politics and largely ignored economics. The U.S. view that the state *should be* separated from the economy also influenced postwar realists. Although U.S. government involvement in military defense matters was accepted, government involvement in the economy was considered less legitimate. Finally, America's superpower status led U.S. realists to focus so firmly on the struggle with the Soviet Union that they "overlooked the economic relations beneath the flux of political relations."[28] Thus, liberalism and Marxism clearly overshadowed neomercantilism as IPE perspectives during the 1950s–1960s.

THE REVIVAL OF NEOMERCANTILIST IPE

In the 1970s–1980s, theorists such as Robert Gilpin and Stephen Krasner returned "to a realist conception of the relationship of economics and politics that had disappeared from postwar American writings."[29] Two factors contributed to the revival of neomercantilism as an IPE perspective. First, the decline of the Cold War and increasing disarray in the global economy induced many realists to devote more attention to economic issues. Although Western economic relations had prospered under U.S. leadership during the 1950s–1960s, major changes in the 1970s–1980s—the OPEC price increases, the relative decline of U.S. hegemony, and the 1980s foreign debt crisis—destabilized the global economy. These issues forced U.S. realists to revise their view that economic issues were low politics. Second, a number of developments demonstrated the need for neomercantilist studies focusing on the economic role of the state. For example, the "Keynesian Revolution" caused DC governments to become heavily involved in macroeconomic management; the decline of colonialism led to the creation of newly independent states that differed from the Western liberal democratic model; and growing international competition induced states to promote industry and technology through targeted investments and strategic trade policy. Thus, neomercantilists had to "bring the state back in" to the study of IPE.[30]

Whereas liberals believed that postwar international economic relations had flourished because of the growth of interdependence, neomercantilists argued that *the distribution of power among states* was a more important factor. A major issue was whether a global hegemonic state with predominant power was willing and able to provide leadership. Thus, neomercantilists strongly supported hegemonic stability theory. Hegemonic stability theory is a hybrid theory that also draws on liberalism and historical materialism, but we discuss it here because it has been central to the neomercantilist approach to IPE.

HEGEMONIC STABILITY THEORY AND U.S. HEGEMONY

Hegemonic stability theory asserts that the international economic system is more likely to be open and stable when a dominant or hegemonic state is *willing* and *able* to provide leadership, and when most other major states view the hegemon's policies as beneficial. When a global hegemon is lacking or declining in power, economic openness and stability are difficult—but not impossible—to maintain. Scholars generally agree that Britain was a global hegemon during the nineteenth century and the United States was a hegemon after World War II. Some studies assert that Portugal, Spain, the United Provinces (or present-day Netherlands), and the British were world powers before the nineteenth century.[31] However, most scholars view these states as less influential than the British and American hegemons of the nineteenth and twentieth centuries. Hegemonic stability theory "remained atop the agenda of IPE in the United States" for two decades.[32] Scholars critiqued all aspects of the theory, and many criticisms were based on empirical grounds. For example, critics questioned whether theorists could draw meaningful conclusions about hegemonic behavior from only two global hegemons during limited historical periods. Theorists also lacked consistent definitions and measures of hegemony, with different authors focusing on the military, political, economic, or cultural aspects. Thus, there was no consensus on when British hegemony declined, and on whether U.S. hegemony was declining. Some critics questioned the premise that a global hegemon contributes to economic openness and stability. These criticisms gradually caused scholars to become less interested in hegemonic stability theory. However, the theory "has sensitized the current generation of scholars to the international political underpinnings of the international economy. This insight should be preserved and built upon, not abandoned."[33] Economic openness and stability are dependent on decisions and policies of the most powerful state or states. Furthermore, scholars have continued to examine the effects of the U.S. foreign debt, the 2008 global financial crisis, and the growing influence of emerging powers on U.S. hegemony. This section focuses on some key questions related to hegemonic stability theory:

- What is hegemony?
- What are the strategies and motives of hegemonic states?
- Is hegemony necessary and/or sufficient to produce an open, stable economic system?
- What is the status of U.S. hegemony?

What Is Hegemony?

Neomercantilists define **hegemony** as an extremely unequal distribution of power, in which "a single powerful state controls or dominates the lesser states in the system."[34] However, this definition does not tell us how much control a state must have to be a hegemon. Most theorists have stringent conditions and believe that only two or three states have been global hegemons. For example, Susan Strange defines hegemony as a state's *structural power* or ability to design the rules and customs in global economic relations in four areas: security, production, finance, and knowledge.[35] The critical theorist Immanuel Wallerstein limits hegemony to a relationship in which one state "can largely impose its rules and wishes (at the very least by effective veto power) in the economic, political, military, diplomatic and even cultural arenas."[36] Whereas neomercantilists define hegemony in state-centric terms, *Gramscian* theorists use the term in a cultural sense to connote the *ideas* social groups use to exert their authority; for example, Gramscians refer to the hegemony of ideas such as capitalism and to the global predominance of American culture (see Chapter 5). Neo-Gramscians assert that globalization in trade, foreign investment, and finance is enabling a "transnational capitalist class" to establish its hegemony and remove all impediments to the free flow of capital.[37] Although the Gramscian views alert us to other aspects of hegemony, mainstream scholars usually define hegemony in state-centric terms.

To be a hegemon a state must not only have superior *material capabilities* in the economic, security and other areas. A state must also be *willing* to lead; we must therefore look at the motivations of states. Furthermore, other major states must be *willing to accept the hegemon's leadership*. Other states may accept the hegemon's leadership because of persuasion, coercion, common views, or the desire for protection.

What Are the Strategies and Motives of Hegemonic States?

One model portrays the hegemon as benevolent—promoting general benefits rather than its self-interest, and using rewards rather than threats to ensure compliance by other states. A second, mixed model portrays the hegemon as seeking both general and personal benefits, and as relying on both threats and rewards to achieve its goals. A third model portrays the hegemon as exploitative—pursuing only its self-interest and using coercion to enforce compliance. Benevolent hegemons focus on absolute gains, coercive hegemons seek relative gains, and hegemons with mixed strategies and motives seek both absolute and relative gains.[38]

Liberals view the hegemon in benevolent terms as willing to "take on an undue share of the burdens of the system" by providing public goods.[39] **Public goods** (or *collective goods*) are *nonexcludable* and *nonrival.* Nonexcludability means that others can benefit from the good, even if they do not contribute to it. For example, a sidewalk is nonexcludable because individuals who do not help pay for it through taxes can use it. Nonrivalness means that a state or individual's use of the good does not decrease the amount available to others. A sidewalk is nonrival because many people can use it. In the liberal view, a benevolent hegemon provides public goods to sustain economic openness and stability. After World War II the United States provided security as a public good through the U.S. nuclear umbrella so that Western Europe and Japan could focus on economic recovery. The United States also permitted its currency to be used as the main reserve asset, supplied U.S. dollars for the Marshall Plan, provided finance for LDC economic growth, and maintained an open market for other countries' exports. **Rational choice** theorists point out that public goods are underproduced even though states benefit from them, because states receive public goods even if they are free riders. *Free riders* benefit from the use of a public good without contributing to it. To convince states that they will benefit from contributing to public goods, it is necessary to overcome *collective action problems*. A **collective action problem** occurs when the uncoordinated actions of states do not produce the best possible outcome for them. Liberals assume that the hegemon will use rewards rather than coercion to induce others to contribute to public goods.[40]

Neomercantilists are more inclined than liberals to portray the hegemon as furthering its national interest rather than the general good. They expect a rising hegemonic state to prefer an open international system because this contributes to its economic growth and political power.[41] They also often portray the hegemon as coercive, threatening to cut off trade, investment, and aid to force other states to contribute to public goods. However, many neomercantilists believe that hegemonic states have mixed motives and that the effects of hegemony may be beneficial. Thus, Gilpin asserts that

> the creation of a system of multilateral trade relations was in the interests of the United States … It does not follow from this fact, however, that American efforts to achieve such a system were solely self-serving … Nor does it follow that what is good for the United States is contrary to the general welfare of other nations.[42]

Historical materialists are most likely to view a hegemon as coercive. Some see the hegemon as coordinating the actions of DCs in the core of the global economy to ensure that they dominate LDCs in the periphery. Only when the hegemon declines is there disarray among the leading capitalist states, which undermines their ability to extract surplus from the periphery. Gramscian theorists encourage disadvantaged groups to develop a "counterhegemony" to extricate themselves from subservience to hegemonic forces in the core.[43]

Is Hegemony Necessary and/or Sufficient to Produce an Open, Stable Economic System?

Hegemonic stability theorists believe that a hegemon promotes openness and stability by helping to create liberal **international regimes,** or "sets of implicit or explicit principles, norms, rules, and decision-making procedures around which actors' expectations converge in a given area of international relations."[44] The regime concept refers to the fact that some governance exists above the state in the absence of a centralized world government. For example, WTO members abide by trade regime principles, norms, and rules. The United States as the postwar hegemon helped create and maintain open and stable monetary, trade, and aid regimes by providing public goods and using coercion when necessary. When there is no hegemonic leader, hegemonic stability theorists foresee more instability and less openness because national leaders will feel increased pressure to "defect" (i.e., not cooperate) for short-term gains. If too many states defect and become free riders this can lead to economic uncertainty, political tensions, and even war.[45] Thus, hegemonic stability theorists make several assertions about British and U.S. hegemony: British hegemony was a major force behind trade liberalization in the nineteenth century; Britain's hegemonic decline after 1875 led to increased trade protectionism; protectionism increased between World Wars I and II because there was no hegemon willing and able to lead; and the United States as global hegemon after World War II helped create open and stable international regimes.

Despite these claims, a number of empirical studies question whether hegemony is in fact necessary or sufficient to produce economic openness. For example, some critics argue that World War I, *not* Britain's hegemonic decline, "sounded the death knell for liberalized international trade."[46] Some liberal critics also argue that a hegemon that helped create open international regimes may not be necessary for *maintaining* them. Other states that benefit from open regimes may collectively maintain them. Thus, we should ask not only whether there is a hegemon to *supply* open regimes, but also whether there is sufficient *demand* to maintain the regimes after a hegemon declines.[47] Some liberals go even further and argue that hegemony is not necessary for the creation of regimes. *Negotiated regimes* may arise among states, and *spontaneous regimes* may arise when countries' expectations converge even without negotiating an explicit agreement.[48] Others note that hegemonic states do not always support open regimes because domestic groups may oppose the free flow of goods, services, or capital. For example, in response to domestic interests the United States insisted that GATT treat agriculture as an exception and supported a Multi-Fiber Agreement limiting textile imports (see Chapter 8).[49]

Some writers assert that factors other than hegemony can account for economic openness and stability. World prosperity can result in open economic regimes, whereas economic downturns may cause states to adopt protectionist policies. Furthermore, industries tend to support trade openness during periods of shortages, and trade protectionism when surpluses accumulate.[50] In sum, while there may be some connection between hegemony and economic openness, critics question whether hegemony is necessary or sufficient to create and maintain open, stable regimes.

What Is the Status of U.S. Hegemony?

Some theorists are "declinists," who see hegemony as inherently unstable. They predict that the hegemon will overextend or overreach itself, that free riders will gain more than the hegemon from economic openness, and that dynamic economies will challenge the hegemon's predominance.[51] For example, a historian writes that "the only answer to … whether the United States can preserve its existing position is 'no'—for it simply has not been given to any one society to remain *permanently* ahead of all the others"; and a political scientist claims that "one of the most important features of American hegemony was its brevity."[52] "Renewalists" by contrast question whether the United States is in fact declining. Most renewalists concede that U.S. economic power has declined in a *relative* sense since 1945. However, they argue that U.S. predominance at the end of the war was so great that its hegemony is largely intact. For example, Stephen Gill asserts that U.S. economic power continues to be "quite enormous when compared to that of any other country, and has an international aspect which gives the U.S. government a unique prerogative *vis-à-vis* the rest of the world."[53] Joseph Nye argues that the United States not only has **hard power** based on coercion and payments, but also has *structural* or **soft power** based on attraction and co-option; that is, the United States can persuade "other countries to *want* what it wants."[54]

Declinists were prominent in the 1970s–1980s when the United States had chronic trade deficits and economic **stagflation**. (Stagflation occurs when an economy has inflation, stagnant economic growth, and relatively high unemployment.) Japan by contrast had impressive economic growth, and one scholar wrote that "if any country surpasses the United States as the leading economic power, it will be Japan."[55] However, events in the late 1980s–1990s resulted in an upsurge of renewalist writing. In the security sphere, the end of the Cold War led some scholars to argue that we were entering a "unipolar" period with the United States as the only superpower.[56] The 1990s East Asian financial crisis and Japan's inability to revive its lackluster economy led renewalists to argue that the United States was also regaining its economic predominance.

Declinists and renewalists can be found on all ends of the political spectrum. Prominent among the renewalists are U.S. *neoconservatives*, who called for greater U.S. activism when the Soviet bloc and Soviet Union imploded in the late 1980s–1990s. For example, William Kristol and Robert Kagan argued that the United States achieved its recent position of strength not by prac-ticing a foreign policy of live and let live, nor by passively waiting for threats to arise, but by actively promoting American principles of gov-ernance abroad—democracy, free markets, respect for liberty.[57]

The tragic terrorist events in the United States on September 11, 2001 increased the resolve of neoconservatives to follow an activist foreign policy combining moral purpose with the national interest. For example, after 9/11 Charles Krauthammer wrote that "the new unilateralism argues explicitly and unashamedly for maintaining unipolarity, for sustaining America's unrivaled dominance for the foreseeable future."[58] However, the results of the Iraq War show that neoconservatives overestimated the U.S. ability to replace coercive regimes in complex developing societies with Western-style governments. More importantly, the neoconservatives overestimated U.S. power because they defined unipolarity mainly in security terms. Growing U.S. economic problems resulted in a reassessment; thus Francis Fukuyama, who had previ-ously identified with neoconservatism, shifted his views and wrote that "the neoconservative moment appears to have passed."[59] This book discusses both the sources of U.S. strength and the challenges the EU, Japan, and now most importantly emerging economies such as China, India, and Brazil have posed to U.S. hegemony.

Currently the main question is whether China will displace the United States as the global hegemon. A cursory look at U.S.–China relations shows that both declinists and renewalists offer important arguments. After China began to reform its economy in 1978, its annual GDP growth rate averaged 9.4 percent, and its foreign trade increased from $20.6 billion in 1978 to $851 billion in 2005. China has become the world's largest economy if measured by PPP-adjusted GDP, but the U.S. economy is still the largest if GDP is measured in pure market exchange terms; the IMF predicts that China will overtake the United States on this measure also by the early 2020s. China is already the world's largest exporter of goods and the second largest importer. China also holds the world's largest foreign exchange reserves, amounting to about $4 trillion. China's massive trade surplus, and American dependence on China's purchase of its government bonds to deal with U.S. foreign debt, gives China considerable influence.

Declinists point not only to the relative decline in U.S. material capabili-ties, but also to its ability and willingness to use them. For example, one analyst argues that "an economic hegemon is supposed to solve global economic crises, not cause them."[60] However, the U.S. subprime mortgage crisis plunged the world into the worst financial crisis since the Great Depression of the 1930s. As discussed, a hegemon must not only be able and willing to lead, but other major states must be willing to accept its leadership. In view of President George W. Bush's penchant to follow unilateral policies, Joseph Nye advised U.S. leaders to use "hard power in a manner that does not undercut … [their] soft power."[61] China on the other hand has been quite successful of late in building up its own soft power. The financial crisis raised questions about the

U.S. brand of free-market capitalism and raised the appeal of China's government-directed model to others. China's willingness and ability to extend investment and assistance to other states without interfering with their internal political arrangements is another source of its growing soft power.[62]

The arguments declinists present are compelling, but renewalists also present strong arguments. A country's GDP is not the only factor to consider. Per capita GDP gives us an indication of how much surplus capital an economy can accumulate above the amount individuals require for basic goods and services. In 2013 the United States ranked tenth with a PPP-adjusted per capita GDP of $53,001, whereas China ranked ninety-seventh with a PPP-adjusted per capita GDP of $9,800. China ranked below such countries as Peru, Cuba, Thailand, and Tunisia.[63] Some renewalists also argue that to promote global cooperation and exchange, a hegemon must lead others in respecting private property and patent rights. These rights are less clearly defined in China; for example, piracy of intellectual property in film, computer software, and music is much more common in China. Another issue is the role of the hegemon as the key currency country. The two global hegemons to this point (Britain and the United States) have been willing and able to provide the key currency to the global economy. As we discuss in Chapter 6, China is neither able nor willing to do this at present. Most countries believe that the United States is likely to have more political stability than China, and there is usually a rush to accumulate U.S. dollars during unstable periods such as financial crises.[64] We draw further comparisons between the United States and China in Chapters 6 to 11.

In sum, declinists and renewalists present sharply divergent points of view, and this book addresses the changing role of the United States as global hegemon in monetary relations, trade, foreign investment, and international development.

NEOMERCANTILISM AND NORTH–SOUTH RELATIONS

The preoccupation of neomercantilists with power and relative gains leads them to emphasize distributional issues among the most powerful states. The neomercantilist tendency to ignore the poorest countries in the South was especially evident in earlier years. For example, Friedrich List advised the United States and Germany to adopt protectionist policies to develop their manufacturing industries, but he ruled out industrialization for the South: Northern states were "specially fitted by nature for manufacturing," whereas Southern states should provide the North with "colonial produce in exchange for their manufactured goods."[65] Neomercantilist scholars have directed more attention to the South in recent years, but they are mainly interested in LDCs that pose a challenge to the North's predominance. In the 1970s neomercantilists became interested in OPEC when it wrested control over oil prices from the international oil companies and launched "the most effective exercise of power by the South against the North since the conclusion of the Second World War."[66] When OPEC supported the G77's demands in the UN for a **New**

International Economic Order (NIEO), neomercantilists examined the NIEO's possible impact. In the 1980s–1990s neomercantilists devoted attention to the East Asian NIEs, which posed a new economic challenge to the North. More recently, neomercantilists have focused on the challenge posed by the BRIC economies, and on "resource nationalism" of the OPEC countries, Russia, and other oil exporters.[67] Neomercantilists, by contrast, do not have a sustained interest in the poorest LDCs and the poorest groups within LDCs.

Whereas liberals see LDCs as seeking wealth and prosperity, neomercantilists assert that LDCs also seek increased power. LDC problems result not only from poverty but also from their weak position in the international system. Thus, even when LDCs have absolute economic gains they feel vulnerable because of their relatively weak position vis-à-vis the North.[68] LDCs can employ various strategies to decrease their vulnerability. In line with Hamilton and List's view that late industrializers require state involvement, LDC governments can facilitate development; for example, they can provide government assistance to their infant industries.[69] As we discuss in Chapter 11, LDCs have adopted policies such as import substitution and export-led growth in which the government supplements the market. In Chapters 7 and 11 we discuss the neomercantilist concept of the *developmental state*, which helped promote economic development in the East Asian NIEs.[70] LDCs can also engage in collective action because they lack power individually. For example, the G77 has been a vehicle for Southern pressure on the North. Finally, LDCs can try to alter international economic regimes and organizations. After World War II the United States as hegemon helped establish liberal economic regimes, but LDCs often prefer more authoritative, less market-oriented regimes in which IOs redirect some power and wealth from the North to the South.[71]

Although neomercantilists examine the redistribution of power and wealth from the North to the South, they assume that such a redistribution is possible within the capitalist system. As discussed in Chapter 5, historical materialists by contrast believe that such a redistribution can only occur under socialism.

PRESENT-DAY NEOMERCANTILISM

States currently employ a wide range of neomercantilist policies, which we discuss in Chapters 6 to 11. Oil and natural gas are highly strategic raw materials, and in this section we examine present-day energy neomercantilism in Russia, China, and the United States.

President Vladimir Putin has been employing neomercantilist policies to advance Russia's power as a supplier of these commodities. After the breakup of the Soviet Union, the energy sector was largely privatized under President Boris Yeltsin. When Putin became president, he viewed oil and gas as critical to reviving Russia's great-power status, and he reasserted state influence and control over these commodities. Russia's energy neomercantilism under Putin is especially evident in its policies toward the EU. More than half of the EU's energy consumption comes from imports, and a number of EU countries depend on Russia's state-owned company *Gazprom* for a large share of these imports. Gazprom has taken actions to prevent central Europe from diversifying its gas imports, and to assert control over the region's major pipelines, wholesale infrastructure, and storage facilities that deliver gas to distributors. The EU is seeking to diversify its sources of natural gas to decrease its dependence on Russia, especially because Russia's manipulation of gas supplies to Ukraine has at times interfered with supplies for EU countries. One source of EU influence is that Russia also depends on the EU for a large share of its energy export revenue, so the EU–Russian energy relationship is highly interdependent. However, this has not prevented Russia from following energy neomercantilist policies in efforts to re-establish some of the control it lost with the breakup of the Soviet Union.[72]

China has also followed neomercantilist policies, but as an energy consumer. Energy supplies are critical if China is to maintain its rapid economic growth rate, and it has relied on three national oil companies to increase its energy security through securing access and diversifying supplies. The national oil companies have been acquiring energy assets throughout the world and forming partnerships with foreign firms. For example, Chinese energy corporations initiated 71 investment projects in 16 African countries from 2003 to 2010.[73] Although China's oil policies are often government-directed, "the extent of state dominance should not be overstated and is markedly less pronounced than in Russia."[74] The Chinese government is mainly concerned that foreign investments contribute to energy security, whereas Chinese energy corporations are concerned with profitability. The government recognizes that the corporations require a degree of independence to pursue their objectives, but China's main motivation continues to be long-term assurance of adequate supplies.

Russian and Chinese energy neomercantilism has also been motivated by an effort to counter U.S. hegemony. The welfare of every industrial economy, including the United States, depends on assured supplies of energy at reasonable prices. In addition to ensuring its own supplies, U.S. dominance in oil-rich areas gives it structural power in being able to assure that other major powers receive adequate supplies. U.S. support for private international oil companies accords with its liberal economic policies that involve a minimal role for the state. However, the United States also draws linkages between its control over oil markets and its hegemonic position in the global economy; in this sense, it also follows neomercantilist policies in the energy sector. These policies involve using force when necessary to ensure that oil flows smoothly, and the United States has stationed military forces in strategic regions of the South. For example, a major reason for the invasion and occupation of Iraq was to ensure that oil supplies would continue to flow from this strategic region of the Middle East. Thus, some analysts assert that "U.S. global hegemony has been—and remains—underpinned by unchallenged control over vast quantities of oil."[75]

In recent years U.S. oil production has increased dramatically because of *hydraulic fracturing*, or *fracking*, which fractures rocks by injecting fluid into cracks and forcing them to open further. As a result, more oil and gas can flow out of the fissures and be extracted. U.S. oil output from fracking increased from about 1 million barrels per day in 2010 to more than 3 million barrels per day in late 2013. Access to this huge reservoir of energy supplies puts the United States in a stronger position in some respects. However, the U.S. ability to perform its hegemonic role of ensuring global oil supplies over the longer term is in question for several reasons. First, fracking oil and gas from deep shales is expensive and, to be productive, requires higher oil prices. There are also uncertainties about the ability of the United States to continue producing large quantities of oil over the longer term, and the detrimental effects of fracking on the environment. Second, instability in the Middle East could threaten major oil-rich states such as Saudi Arabia, the United Arab Emirates, and Kuwait, which have maintained good relations with the United States. Third, Russia under President Putin has not hesitated to use oil and natural gas as a weapon in his dispute with Ukraine, and many EU countries continue to rely heavily on Russian energy supplies. Thus, the United States as global hegemon is not able to assure the EU that it will receive adequate oil and gas. Fourth, China has established linkages with countries throughout the South to gain assured access to oil, gas, and other resources outside of the global energy market. Thus, continued U.S. hegemony based partly on its ability to ensure global energy security is by no means certain. In sum, the struggle among the major powers for control over oil and natural gas is one example of present-day neomercantilism.

CRITIQUE OF THE NEOMERCANTILIST PERSPECTIVE

Because neomercantilists focus on economic issues, they address individual choices in the domestic arena more than realists. Nevertheless, neomercantilists like realists see the state as the principal actor in IR. As interdependence and globalization have increased, liberals and critical theorists have been more attuned than neomercantilists to the importance of nonstate actors such as multinational corporations, international banks, and international and transnational organizations. Liberal and critical theorists are also more attuned to the importance of domestic variables such as the history, social structure, and cultural values of a state in determining its role in IPE. Neomercantilists often correctly criticize liberals and historical materialists for "economism," but neomercantilists by contrast tend to overemphasize the centrality of politics. Neomercantilists often downgrade the importance of economic issues that are not related to concerns with power, security, and relative gains; for example, they do not have a sustained interest in the effects of IPE on the poorest LDCs. Neomercantilists also emphasize relative gains because of their concern with state survival and security in an anarchic self-help system. Relative gains are of primary concern in some interstate relationships, such as U.S.–Soviet relations during the Cold War; but absolute gains are often of greater concern in interdependent relationships among states that do not threaten each other with force. Even when neomercantilists study international economic organizations, they are more attuned to relative gains. For example, one neomercantilist study of the EU concludes that the weaker members "will seek to ensure that the rules" give them the opportunity "to voice their concerns and interests and thereby prevent their domination by stronger partners."[76] The preoccupation of neomercantilists with relative gains causes them to be highly skeptical about the influence of international institutions. However, the IMF, World Bank, WTO, EU, and NAFTA all have a significant effect in IPE. This book now turns to liberalism, the most important IPE theoretical perspective.

QUESTIONS

1. What is rational choice, and what are its strengths and shortcomings as an approach to the study of IPE?
2. What were the similarities and differences between the mercantilists and Friedrich List in their approach to IPE? Did liberalism have any effect on List's views?
3. What are the similarities and differences between realism, neomercantilism, and economic nationalism?
4. What is hegemony, and what are theorists' views regarding the strategies and motives of hegemonic states? Is a hegemon necessary to create and maintain open, stable economic regimes?
5. What are "public goods"? Why are they necessary, and why does their provision present "collective action" problems? What is the relationship between hegemony and public goods?
6. How do theorists differ in their views regarding the current status of U.S. hegemony? Is any other actor likely to replace the United States as the global hegemon?
7. What aspects of North–South relations are of most, and least, interest to neomercantilists?
8. What are the strengths and weaknesses of the neomercantilist perspective?

KEY TERMS

absolute gains
collective action
   problem
hard power
hegemonic stability
   theory
hegemony

infant industries
international
   regimes
mercantilism
New International
   Economic Order
public goods

rational choice
realism
relative gains
soft power
stagflation
variable-sum game
zero-sum game

FURTHER READING

General studies on the history of economic thought include Jurgen Georg Backhaus, ed., *Handbook of the History of Economic Thought* (New York: Springer, 2012); and Agnar Sandmo, *Economics Evolving: A History of Economic Thought* (Princeton, NJ: Princeton University Press, 2011).

On the neomercantilist approach to IPE see Charles E. Ziegler and Rajan Menon, "Neomercantilism and Great-Power Energy Competition in Central Asia and the Caspian," *Strategic Studies Quarterly* (Summer 2014), pp. 17–41; and Jonathan Kirshner, "Realist Political Economy: Traditional Themes and Contemporary Challenges," in Mark Blyth, ed., *Routledge Handbook of International Political Economy* (New York: Routledge, 2009), pp. 36–47. On economic nationalism see

Eric Helleiner and Andreas Pickel, eds., *Economic Nationalism in a Globalizing World* (Ithaca, NY: Cornell University Press, 2005).

On neomercantilist views of the state's role in IPE, see Linda Weiss, *America Inc.? Innovation and Enterprise in the National Security State* (New York: Cornell University Press, 2014); Jonathan Perraton and Ben Clift, eds., *Where Are National Capitalisms Now?* (New York: Palgrave Macmillan, 2004); and Stephen D. Krasner's classic study *Defending the National Interest: Raw Materials Investments and U.S. Foreign Policy* (Princeton, NJ: Princeton University Press, 1978).

On hegemony, see Kristen P. Williams, Steven E. Lobell, and Neal G. Jesse, eds., *Beyond Great Powers and Hegemons* (Stanford, CA: Stanford University Press, 2012); Andrew C. Sobel, *Birth of Hegemony* (Chicago: University of Chicago Press, 2012); and Doug Stokes and Sam Raphael, *Global Energy Security and American Hegemony* (Baltimore, MD: Johns Hopkins University Press, 2010). On neoconservativism and U.S. renewal, see Robert Kagan and William Kristol, eds., *Present Dangers: Crisis and Opportunity in American Foreign and Defense Policy* (San Francisco, CA: Encounter Books, 2000). On soft power, see Joseph S. Nye, Jr., *The Paradox of American Power: Why the World's Only Superpower Can't Go It Alone* (New York: Oxford University Press, 2002).

On neomercantilist views of North–South relations, see David A. Lake, "Power and the Third World: Toward a Realist Political Economy of North-South Relations," *International Studies Quarterly* 31, no. 2 (June 1987), pp. 217–234; and Stephen D. Krasner, *Structural Conflict: The Third World Against Global Liberalism* (Berkeley, CA: University of California Press, 1985).

NOTES

1. Charles E. Ziegler, "Neomercantilism and Energy Interdependence: Russian Strategies in East Asia," *Asian Security* 6, no. 1 (2010), p. 76.
2. Stephen D. Krasner, *Defending the National Interest: Raw Materials Investments and U.S. Foreign Policy* (Princeton, NJ: Princeton University Press, 1978), pp. 13 and 330.
3. Robert Gilpin, *U.S. Power and the Multinational Corporation: The Political Economy of Foreign Direct Investment* (New York: Basic Books, 1975), p. 34; Kenneth N. Waltz, *Theory of International Politics* (Reading, MA: Addison Wesley, 1979), p. 126.
4. Tony Evans and Peter Wilson, "Regime Theory and the English School of International Relations: A Comparison," *Millennium* 21, no. 3 (Winter 1992), p. 330.
5. Robert W. Cox, *Production, Power, and World Order: Social Forces in the Making of History* (New York: Columbia University Press, 1987), p. 6.
6. Hannes Lacher, "Putting the State in Its Place: The Critique of State-Centrism and Its Limits," *Review of International Studies* 29 (2003), p. 526.
7. Ziegler, "Neomercantilism and Energy Interdependence," p. 78.
8. Stephen D. Krasner, *Sovereignty: Organized Hypocrisy* (Princeton, NJ: Princeton University Press, 1999), p. 223.
9. Jonathan Perraton and Ben Clift, *Where Are National Capitalisms Now?* (New York: Palgrave Macmillan, 2004).
10. Linda Weiss, "The State-Augmenting Effects of Globalisation," *New Political Economy* 10, no. 3 (September 2005), p. 352.
11. Adam Smith used the term *mercantile system*, and *mercantilism* became a standard

English term later. Jacob Viner, "Mercantilist Thought," in David L. Sills, ed., *International Encyclopedia of the Social Sciences*, vol. 4 (New York: Free Press, 1968), p. 436; David A. Baldwin, *Economic Statecraft* (Princeton, NJ: Princeton University Press, 1985), p. 72.

12. Eli F. Heckscher, *Mercantilism*, vol. 2 (London: Allen and Unwin, 1934).
13. Adam Smith, *The Wealth of Nations*, vol. 1 (London: Dent & Sons, Everyman's Library, 1910), bk. 4, p. 436.
14. Robert Gilpin with Jean M. Gilpin, *The Political Economy of International Relations* (Princeton, NJ: Princeton University Press, 1987), p. 180.
15. Alexander Hamilton, "The Report on the Subject of Manufactures," in Harold C. Syrett, ed., *The Papers of Alexander Hamilton, December 5, 1791*, vol. 10 (New York: Columbia University Press, 1966), p. 291.
16. Friedrich List, *The National System of Political Economy*, trans. Sampson S. Lloyd (London: Longmans, Green 1916), p. 130.
17. David Levi-Faur, "Friedrich List and the Political Economy of the Nation-State," *Review of International Political Economy* 4, no. 1 (Spring 1997), pp. 154–178.
18. List, *The National System of Political Economy*, p. 107; Mehdi Shafaeddin, "What Did Freiderich List Actually Say?—Some Clarifications on the Infant Industry Argument," UNCTAD Discussion Paper no. 149, July 2000.
19. Robert Gilpin, *Global Political Economy* (Princeton, NJ: Princeton University Press, 2001), p. 14.
20. Rawi Abdelal, "Nationalism and International Political Economy in Eurasia," in Eric Helleiner and Andreas Pickel, eds., *Economic Nationalism in a Globalizing World* (Ithaca, NY: Cornell University Press, 2005), p. 22.
21. Eric Helleiner, "Economic Nationalism as a Challenge to Economic Liberalism? Lessons from the 19th Century," *International Studies Quarterly* 46 (2002), p. 308.
22. List, *The National System of Political Economy*, p. 253.
23. Christopher Winch, "Listian Political Economy: Social Capitalism Conceptualised?" *New Political Economy* 3, no. 2 (1998), p. 303; List, *The National System of Political Economy*, p. 277.
24. Jonathan Kirshner, "Realist Political Economy: Traditional Themes and Contemporary Challenges," in Mark Blyth, ed., *Routledge Handbook of International Political Economy* (New York: Routledge, 2009), p. 38.
25. Paul Kennedy, *The Rise and Fall of the Great Powers: Economic Change and Military Conflict from 1500 to 2000* (New York: Random House, 1987), p. 283; David Levi-Faur, "Economic Nationalism: From Friedrich List to Robert Reich," *Review of International Studies* 23, no. 3 (July 1997), p. 359.
26. Steven E. Lobell, *The Challenge of Hegemony* (Ann Arbor, MI: University of Michigan Press, 2003), pp. 92–94; Albert O. Hirschman, *National Power and the Structure of Foreign Trade*, expanded ed. (Berkeley, CA: University of California Press, 1980), pp. 36–39.
27. On the difference between U.S. government officials and U.S. realist scholars see Michael Mastanduno, "Economics and Security in Statecraft and Scholarship," *International Organization* 52, no. 4 (Autumn 1998), p. 835.
28. Robert G. Gilpin, "The Richness of the Tradition of Political Realism," *International Organization* 38, no. 2 (Spring 1984), p. 294.
29. Gilpin, *The Political Economy of International Relations*, p. xii.
30. Theda Skocpol, "Bringing the State Back In: Strategies of Analysis in Current Research," in Peter B. Evans, Dietrich Rueschemeyer, and Theda Skocpol, eds., *Bringing the State Back In* (New York: Cambridge University Press, 1985), pp. 6–7.

31. George Modelski, *Long Cycles in World Politics* (Seattle, WA: University of Washington Press, 1987), ch. 2; Joshua S. Goldstein, *Long Cycles: Prosperity and War in the Modern Age* (New Haven, CT: Yale University Press, 1988), pp. 126–133.
32. Benjamin J. Cohen, *International Political Economy: An Intellectual History* (Princeton, NJ: Princeton University Press, 2008), p. 67.
33. David A. Lake, "Leadership, Hegemony, and the International Economy: Naked Emperor or Tattered Monarch with Potential," *International Studies Quarterly* 37, no. 4 (December 1993), p. 485.
34. Robert Gilpin, *War and Change in World Politics* (New York: Cambridge University Press, 1981), p. 29.
35. Susan Strange, *States and Markets*, 2nd ed. (New York: Pinter Publishers, 1994), pp. 24–32.
36. Immanuel Wallerstein, "The Three Instances of Hegemony in the History of the Capitalist World-Economy," in Immanuel Wallerstein, ed., *The Politics of the World-Economy: The States, the Movements and the Civilizations* (London: Cambridge University Press, 1984), p. 38.
37. Stephen Gill, ed., *Gramsci, Historical Materialism and International Relations* (New York: Cambridge University Press, 1993).
38. Duncan Snidal, "The Limits of Hegemonic Stability Theory," *International Organization* 39, no. 4 (Autumn 1985), pp. 585–586.
39. Charles P. Kindleberger, *The World in Depression 1929–1939* (Berkeley, CA: University of California Press, 1973), p. 28.
40. Snidal, "The Limits of Hegemonic Stability Theory," pp. 590–592; Robert O. Keohane, *After Hegemony: Cooperation and Discord in the World Political Economy* (Princeton, NJ: Princeton University Press, 1984), p. 65; Mancur Olson, *The Logic of Collective Action: Public Goods and the Theory of Groups* (Cambridge, MA: Harvard University Press, 1965), pp. 14–15.
41. Stephen D. Krasner, "State Power and the Structure of International Trade," *World Politics* 28 (April 1976), p. 322.
42. Robert Gilpin, "The Politics of Transnational Economic Relations," in Robert O. Keohane and Joseph S. Nye, Jr., eds., *Transnational Relations and World Politics* (Cambridge, MA: Harvard University Press, 1972), p. 58.
43. Wallerstein, "The Three Instances of Hegemony in the History of the Capitalist World-Economy," pp. 44–46; Robert W. Cox, "Gramsci, Hegemony and International Relations: An Essay in Method," in Stephen Gill, ed., *Gramsci, Historical Materialism and International Relations* (New York: Cambridge University Press, 1993), pp. 64–65.
44. Stephen D. Krasner, "Structural Causes and Regime Consequences: Regimes as Intervening Variables," in Stephen D. Krasner, ed., *International Regimes* (Ithaca, NY: Cornell University Press, 1983), p. 2.
45. Andrew C. Sobel, *Birth of Hegemony* (Chicago: University of Chicago Press, 2012), p. 5.
46. Arthur A. Stein, "The Hegemon's Dilemma: Great Britain, the United States and the International Economic Order," *International Organization* 38, no. 2 (Spring 1984), p. 373.
47. Keohane, *After Hegemony*; Robert O. Keohane, "The Demand for International Regimes," in Stephen D. Krasner, ed., *International Regimes* (Ithaca, NY: Cornell University Press, 1983), pp. 141–171.
48. Oran R. Young, "Regime Dynamics: The Rise and Fall of International Regimes,"

in Stephen D. Krasner, ed., *International Regimes* (Ithaca, NY: Cornell University Press, 1983), pp. 98–101.

49. Eric Helleiner, *States and the Reemergence of Global Finance: From Bretton Woods to the 1990s* (Ithaca, NY: Cornell University Press, 1994), p. 4; Theodore H. Cohn, "The Changing Role of the United States in the Global Agricultural Trade Regime," in William P. Avery, ed., *World Agriculture and the GATT, International Political Economy Yearbook*, vol. 7 (Boulder, CO: Rienner, 1993), pp. 20–24; Vinod K. Aggarwal, *Liberal Protectionism: The International Politics of Organized Textile Trade* (Berkeley, CA: University of California Press, 1985), pp. 77–81.

50. Timothy J. McKeown, "Hegemonic Stability Theory and Nineteenth Century Tariff Levels in Europe," *International Organization* 37, no. 1 (Winter 1983), p. 89; Peter F. Cowhey and Edward Long, "Testing Theories of Regime Change: Hegemonic Decline or Surplus Capacity?" *International Organization* 37, no. 2 (Spring 1983), pp. 157–188.

51. Samuel P. Huntington, "The Lonely Superpower," *Foreign Affairs* 78, no. 2 (March/April 1999), pp. 35–49.

52. Kennedy, *The Rise and Fall of the Great Powers*, p. 533; Keohane, *After Hegemony*, p. 139.

53. Stephen Gill, "American Hegemony: Its Limits and Prospects in the Reagan Era," *Millennium* 15, no. 3 (Winter 1986), p. 331.

54. Joseph S. Nye, Jr., "Soft Power," *Foreign Policy* 80 (Fall 1990), p. 166.

55. Ronald A. Morse, "Japan's Drive to Pre-Eminence," *Foreign Policy* 69 (Winter 1987–1988), pp. 3–21. See also Tsumeo Akaha and Frank Langdon, eds., *Japan in the Posthegemonic World* (Boulder, CO: Lynne Rienner, 1993).

56. Charles Krauthammer, "The Unipolar Moment," *Foreign Affairs* 70, no. 1 (1990/1991), pp. 23–33.

57. William Kristol and Robert Kagan, "Toward a Neo-Reaganite Foreign Policy," *Foreign Affairs* 75, no. 4 (July/August 1996), pp. 21–22.

58. Charles Krauthammer, "The Unipolar Moment Revisited," *The National Interest* 70 (Winter 2002/2003), p. 17.

59. Francis Fukuyama, "After Neoconservatism," *The New York Times Magazine*, February 19, 2006, p. 67.

60. Christopher Layne, "Conclusion," in Kristen P. Williams, Steven E. Lobell, and Neal G. Jesse, eds., *Beyond Great Powers and Hegemons* (Stanford, CA: Stanford University Press, 2012), p. 228.

61. Joseph S. Nye, Jr., *The Paradox of American Power: Why the World's Only Superpower Can't Go It Alone* (New York: Oxford University Press, 2002), pp. 140–141; Neal G. Jesse, Steven E. Lobell, Galia Press-Barnathan, and Kristen P. Williams, "The Leader Can't Lead When the Followers Won't Follow," in Kristen P. Williams, Steven E. Lobell, and Neal G. Jesse, eds., *Beyond Great Powers and Hegemons* (Stanford, CA: Stanford University Press, 2012), pp. 1–30.

62. Layne, "Conclusion," in Williams, Lobell, and Jesse, eds., *Beyond Great Powers and Hegemons*, pp. 230–232.

63. IMF, World Economic Outlook Database, October 2014.

64. Sobel, *Birth of Hegemony*, pp. 202–222.

65. List, *The National System of Political Economy*, p. 154.

66. Stephen D. Krasner, *Structural Conflict: The Third World Against Global Liberalism* (Berkeley, CA: University of California Press, 1985), pp. 108–109.

67. Vlado Vivoda, "Resource Nationalism, Bargaining and International Oil Companies:

Challenges and Change in the New Millennium," *New Political Economy* 14, no. 4 (December 2009), pp. 517–534.

68. Krasner, *Structural Conflict*, p. 3; Robert L. Rothstein, *The Weak in the World of the Strong: The Developing Countries in the International System* (New York: Columbia University Press, 1977), p. 8.

69. On the government and late industrializers see Alexander Gerschenkron, *Economic Backwardness in Historical Perspective: A Book of Essays* (Cambridge, MA: Harvard University Press, 1962).

70. Chalmers Johnson, "Introduction—The Taiwan Model," in James C. Hsiung, ed., *Contemporary Republic of China: The Taiwan Experience 1950–1980* (New York: Praeger, 1981), pp. 9–18.

71. Krasner, *Structural Conflict*, p. 7.

72. Ziegler, "Neomercantilism and Energy Interdependence," pp. 74–81; Anita Orban, *Power, Energy, and the New Russian Imperialism* (Westport, CT: Praeger Security International, 2008).

73. Hui-Chi Yeh and Chi-Wei Yu, "China's Energy Diplomacy: SOE Relations in the Context of Global Distribution and Investment Pattern," *Advances in Applied Sociology* 2, no. 4 (2012), p. 332.

74. Charles E. Ziegler and Rajan Menon, "Neomercantilism and Great-Power Energy Competition in Central Asia and the Caspian," *Strategic Studies Quarterly* (Summer 2014), p. 28.

75. Doug Stokes and Sam Raphael, *Global Energy Security and American Hegemony* (Baltimore, MD: Johns Hopkins University Press, 2010), p. 16.

76. Joseph M. Grieco, "The Maastricht Treaty, Economic and Monetary Union and the Neo-realist Research Programme," *Review of International Studies* 21 (January 1995), p. 34.

Liberalism

Liberalism is the most influential perspective in IPE. Most international economic organizations and the economic policies of most states today are strongly influenced by liberal principles. It is important to note that the term *liberal* is used differently in IPE and in U.S. politics. Whereas U.S. conservatives support free markets and minimal government intervention, U.S. liberals support government involvement in the market to prevent inequalities and stimulate growth. Liberal economists, by contrast, have similarities with U.S. conservatives; they emphasize the importance of the free market and private property and seek to limit the government's role in economic affairs. However, this chapter shows that there are also variations among economic liberals. Although some liberal economists favor minimal government involvement, others believe that some government intervention is necessary for the effective functioning of markets.

BASIC TENETS OF THE LIBERAL PERSPECTIVE

Neomercantilists and Marxists place more emphasis than liberals on developing parsimonious theories that rely on a small number of concepts and variables.[1] Whereas neomercantilists focus on the centrality of the state and Marxists view the world in terms of class relations, liberals deal with a wider range of actors and levels of analysis. Although this broader outlook enables liberals to capture complexities that neomercantilists and Marxists overlook, it also hinders the development of a coherent liberal international theory. This chapter focuses on three types of liberalism relevant to IPE: **Orthodox liberals** promote "negative freedom," or freedom of the market to function with minimal interference from the state. **Interventionist liberals** believe that negative freedom is not sufficient, and they support some government involvement to promote more equality and justice in a free **market economy** (an economy in which the market coordinates individual choices to determine the types of goods and services produced). **Institutional liberals** also view some outside involvement as necessary to supplement the market, and they favor strong international institutions such as the WTO, IMF, and World Bank. In addition to these three variants, liberals also employ different methods of studying IPE; they may rely on *rationalism*, *constructivism*, or some combination of the two. We discussed rational choice in the introduction to Part II; we discuss constructivism in Chapter 5 because liberal as well as critical constructivists view the rationalist assumptions of most mainstream theorists as too limiting.

The Role of the Individual, the State, and Societal Groups

Liberals see politics in "bottom-up" terms, in which individuals and groups seek to achieve their goals through political means. In IPE, liberals therefore give primacy to the individual consumer, firm, or entrepreneur.[2] They place considerable emphasis on domestic–international interactions, and view individuals as having inalienable rights that must be protected from collectivities such as labor unions, churches, and the state. Thus, the orthodox liberal Adam Smith (1723–1790) argued that the welfare of society depends on the individual's ability to pursue his or her interests:

> Every individual is continually exerting himself to find out the most advantageous employment for whatever capital he can command. It is his own advantage, indeed, and not that of the society, which he has in view. But the study of his own advantage naturally, or rather necessarily, leads him to prefer that employment which is most advantageous to the society.[3]

Because this "invisible hand" of the market performs efficiently, society can regulate itself with minimal interference from the state. Even among orthodox liberals there is a variance of views, and Adam Smith did argue that there was some role for the government. Interventionist liberals such as John Maynard Keynes favor more government activism than orthodox liberals, because of the market's limitations in dealing with economic problems such as unemployment.

The Nature and Purpose of International Economic Relations

The IMF, World Bank, and WTO uphold liberal economic principles, and liberals therefore have a positive view of international economic relations as currently structured. They believe that the KIEO liberal principles are politically neutral and that states benefit from economic growth and efficiency when their policies conform to those principles. If governments do not pursue liberal economic principles, resources will be allocated inefficiently and economic growth will falter. Liberals also assume that international economic interactions can be mutually beneficial, or a positive-sum game, if they operate freely. All states can gain from open economic relationships, even if they do not gain equally.

Thus, liberals are often less concerned with *distributional* issues and less likely to differentiate between rich and poor states. Liberalism in fact encompasses a range of views on distributional issues, with interventionist liberals emphasizing a more equitable distribution of benefits and social democracy as well as liberty and efficiency. However, all liberals believe that the international economic system functions best if it ultimately depends on the price mechanism and the market.

Many liberals assume that the South faces the same challenges as the North did during the nineteenth century. Unlike the nineteenth century, however, the South benefits from the North's diffusion of advanced technology and modern forms of organization. Integration with the DC centers of activity therefore spurs LDC economic growth, whereas isolation from these centers results in LDC backwardness. The purpose of international economic activity is to achieve optimum use of the world's scarce resources and to maximize economic efficiency and growth. Thus, liberals consider aggregate measures of economic performance such as the growth of GNI, trade, foreign investment, and per capita income as more important than relative gains among states.

The Relationship Between Politics and Economics

Liberals tend to view economics and politics as separate and autonomous spheres of activity. Orthodox liberals argue that the role of governments should be limited to creating an open environment in which individuals and private firms can freely express their economic preferences. Thus, the state should prevent restraints on competition and provide infrastructure (roads and railways) and national defense to facilitate production and transportation. If governments permit the market to operate freely, a natural division of labor develops in which each state produces goods for which it has a comparative advantage and everyone benefits from the efficient use of scarce resources. As this chapter discusses, interventionist liberals accept a greater degree of government involvement.

The Causes and Effects of Globalization

Liberals attribute globalization to technological change, market forces, and international institutions. For example, one liberal argues that "our new international financial regime ... was not built by politicians, economists, central bankers or by finance ministers ... It was built by technology."[4] Some liberals argue that governments can do nothing to stop globalization, because technological advances in transportation and communications are rapidly shrinking time and space. Other liberals believe that governments have choices but that technological progress makes it more costly for them to close their economies. In addition to technology, liberals attribute globalization to the competitive marketplace and to legal and institutional arrangements. Thus, they examine the role of the KIEOs in facilitating globalization.[5] Kenichi Ohmae argues that globalization is leading to the demise of the state, but this is an extreme view (see Chapter 2). Most liberals believe that the state cannot deal with many global issues such as climate change, capital mobility, and financial crises. Thus, globalization is constraining the state and forcing it to vie with other significant actors such as MNCs, IOs, and NGOs. Liberals generally view these changes as positive developments, but this chapter discusses the fact that there is a range of liberal views.

THE DEVELOPMENT OF LIBERAL IPE: ADAM SMITH AND DAVID RICARDO

The liberal tradition dates back at least to John Locke (1632–1704), who believed that all men were free and equal in the "state of nature," and that this gave them inalienable rights beyond the laws of any government. Although governments should be able to levy taxes and require military service, Locke wrote that the state's primary role was to ensure the "*Preservation* of ... [people's] Lives, Liberties and Estates, which I call by the general Name, *Property*."[6] Locke did some writing about economic issues, but François Quesnay (1694–1774) was the most significant forerunner of Adam Smith. One of Quesnay's economic principles was that the government should support an economy based on free competition and free trade, or as some of his followers phrased it, "laissez faire, laisser passer." Quesnay's followers, who became known as the *physiocrats*, were also the first group to call for a liberal economic order which would develop spontaneously through the actions of self-interested individuals. This idea pre-dated Adam Smith's concept of self-interested individuals and the invisible hand.[7] Smith was the first to outline a detailed liberal approach to political economy. His first book, *The Theory of Moral Sentiments* (1759), describes people as basically moral and altruistic;[8] and his second more widely known book, *The Wealth of Nations* (1776), focuses on self-interest as the motive force behind human action. Some analysts believe there is a contradiction between these two books. However, Smith explains how the concern for justice is expressed through rules for acceptable behavior. Within this framework of rules, people can be motivated by self-interest in various areas.[9] He is associated with the orthodox liberal approach, because he opposed mercantilism and favored only limited government involvement in the economy. Whereas the mercantilists assumed that a state could gain power and wealth only at the expense of other states, Smith cautioned that

> By such maxims as these ... nations have been taught that their interest consisted in beggaring all their neighbours. Each nation has been made to look with an invidious eye upon the prosperity of all the nations with which it trades, and to consider their gain as its own loss. Commerce, which ought naturally to be ... a bond of union and friendship, has become the most fertile source of discord and animosity.[10]

Despite Smith's criticism of the mercantilists, he recognized that some government involvement was necessary, but only in three areas: to protect society from violence and invasion; to promote the administration of justice; and to erect public works and institutions that individuals would not establish on their own. Although Smith strongly supported free trade, he did not view it as an unconditional policy. For example, a state should be able to retaliate against unfair trade restrictions, and it might implement free trade gradually to give domestic industry and labor time to adjust to international competition. Despite Smith's support for some government involvement, he believed "that the system of natural liberty was in general the best practical guide to policy, especially because government was often incompetent and more often subject to special interest pressures."[11] Smith argued that free trade encourages a division of labor and greater productivity; enables people to buy a broader range of goods at the cheapest source; and enables each state to specialize in goods it produces most efficiently.

David Ricardo (1772–1823) went well beyond Smith in his arguments for free trade. Smith argued that the gains from trade are due to *absolute advantage*, in which all states benefit by specializing in the goods they produce most efficiently and trading them with other states. For example, if France produces wine more cheaply than England, and England produces cloth more cheaply than France, both states can benefit from specialization and trade. Ricardo's theory of *comparative advantage* is less intuitive and more powerful, because it posits that two countries can benefit from trade in two commodities even if one of the countries produces *both* products more cheaply. Although Portugal was more productive than England in producing both wine and cloth, Portugal had a greater cost advantage in producing wine. Thus, both countries could benefit from trade if Portugal specialized in wine production and England specialized in cloth production.[12] The theory of comparative advantage is explained more fully in Chapter 8.

Ricardo, like Smith, diverged from orthodox liberalism in some respects. For example, Ricardo had social concerns about the poor. Some draw parallels between Ricardo's views on the conflict between landowners and other classes, and Marx's later writings on class conflict between the bourgeoisie and proletariat (see Chapter 5). However, Ricardo was clearly an orthodox liberal economist in his defense of free trade and limited government control over the market.

THE INFLUENCE OF JOHN MAYNARD KEYNES

A number of scholars view John Maynard Keynes (1883–1946) as "the most influential economist of his generation."[13] In a 1926 essay entitled "The End of Laissez-Faire," Keynes clearly indicated the dangers of depending on the "invisible hand" to promote the public good:

> The world is *not* so governed from above that private and social interest always coincide … It is *not* a correct deduction from the Principles of Economics that enlightened self-interest always operates in the public interest. Nor is it true that self-interest generally *is* enlightened … Experience does *not* show that individuals, when they

make up a social unit, are always less clear-sighted than when they act separately.[14]

In contrast to the orthodox liberal view, Keynes argued that a market-generated equilibrium might occur at a point where labor and capital are underutilized. Economic adjustment often results in unemployment rather than wage cuts because labor unions resist the downward movement of wages; this unemployment in turn leads to reductions in demand, production, and investment. To lower the unemployment rate and revive the economy, it is necessary to turn to the government. In his major book *The General Theory of Employment, Interest, and Money* (1936), Keynes therefore called on governments to implement fiscal (and to a lesser extent monetary) policies to increase demand, and he supported government investment when necessary in public projects.[15]

Keynes's support for government involvement resulted in a greater "willingness to accept public sector deficits in order to finance public works or other spending programs designed to lower unemployment."[16] His emphasis on full employment also caused him to place less priority than orthodox liberals on specialization and international trade. When unemployment reached record highs in the 1930s, Keynes wrote that goods should "be homespun whenever it is reasonably and conveniently possible."[17] Limits on imports are sometimes justifiable to bolster domestic employment, even if the goods can be produced more cheaply abroad. As Britain's chief negotiator at Bretton Woods, Keynes was mainly concerned with establishing an international monetary system with enough flexibility to deal with postwar economic problems. He also supported internationalist solutions because of his preference for planning on a global scale. Keynes was the world's leading monetary economist at the time, but the United States was in the dominant position because Britain would be bankrupt without American support. Thus, the Bretton Woods agreement was closer to the proposals of the U.S. chief negotiator Harry Dexter White. Keynes also pressured the Labour government to pursue open liberal policies, and in return the United States provided the British with $3.75 billion in loans.[18]

When Keynes's *General Theory* was first published there was concern that it called for socialism, and there were even attempts to prevent U.S. university students from learning Keynesian economics.[19] However, Keynes refused to join the British Labour Party, which he referred to as "a class party," and he remained a member of the Liberal Party. He was highly critical of socialists for nationalizing industry in efforts to produce goods more efficiently than the private sector:

> The most important *Agenda* of the State relate not to those activities which private individuals are already fulfilling, but to those functions which fall outside the sphere of the individual, to those decisions which are made by *no one* if the State does not make them. The important thing for Government is not to do things which individuals are doing already ... but to do those things which at present are not done at all.[20]

In sum, Keynes believed in the importance of individual initiative and the efficiency of the market, but he called for greater management to facilitate the efficient functioning of market forces. Thus, he favored government intervention, not to replace capitalism but to rescue and revitalize it; this perspective gave rise to interventionist liberalism.[21]

LIBERALISM IN THE POSTWAR PERIOD

The ideas of Karl Polanyi (1886–1964) as well as Keynes were important for avoiding economic problems like those of the interwar years. Polanyi argued that markets and other economic relations are embedded in complex social relations. In modern capitalist society market relations *seem* to be autonomous, but the failure to recognize the linkages with society is putting civilization in crisis. In *The Great Transformation*, Polanyi warned that the orthodox liberal commitment to the "self-regulating market" had produced disasters such as the Great Depression, and that society would move to protect itself from unregulated market activities.[22] The planners who designed the postwar international economic order were strongly influenced by the ideas of Keynes and Polanyi. John Gerard Ruggie's term *embedded liberal compromise* referred to the fact that postwar efforts to maintain an open liberal international economy were embedded in societal efforts to provide domestic security and stability for individuals.[23] Thus, policies to promote economic liberalization included government measures to cushion domestic economies, and government policies to provide domestic stability in turn were designed to minimize interference with liberalization efforts. In trade policy, for example, Western leaders called for multilateral tariff reductions, but they permitted states to use safeguards to protect their balance of payments and promote full employment. Underlying the embedded liberal compromise was a domestic class compromise. Business induced labor unions to temper their demands for socialism by agreeing to collective bargaining and the welfare state. As a result, business won broad acceptance of trade liberalization, private ownership, and the market.[24] In sum, postwar liberals favored government intervention to counter socially unacceptable aspects of the market, but they opted for government measures that would reinforce rather than replace the market.

A RETURN TO ORTHODOX LIBERALISM

Although postwar policy-makers supported interventionist liberalism, orthodox liberals continued to have influence in some circles. In his 1944 study *The Road to Serfdom*, Friedrich Hayek (1898–1992) criticized Keynes's preference for economic planning. Instead of trying to direct the operation of markets, Hayek argued, governments should simply facilitate the orderly operation of markets so that private property and private contracts are protected. Free markets would regulate themselves, allocate resources efficiently, and promote economic freedom.[25] In 1947, Hayek organized what became known as the Mont Pelerin Society, a private transnational forum of scholars and political figures committed to orthodox liberalism. Prominent members such as Hayek, Ludwig von Mises, and Milton Friedman (1912–2006) favored competitive markets and a strict separation between politics and economics.[26] Thus, Milton Friedman and Rose Friedman wrote:

> Wherever we find any large element of individual freedom, some measure of progress in the material comforts at the disposal of ordinary citizens, and widespread hope of further progress in the future, there we also find that economic activity is organized mainly through the free market. Wherever the state undertakes to control in detail the economic activities of its citizens ... ordinary citizens are in political fetters, have a low standard of living, and have little power to control their own destiny.[27]

Most Western leaders followed interventionist liberal policies during the expansive years of the 1950s–1960s; but the 1973 OPEC price increases and the global recession that followed made welfare and full-employment policies more costly. As economic growth declined, policies that redistributed some of the wealth posed a threat to capital accumulation by business groups. Thus, Hayek and Friedman's writings had more influence on government policy-makers in the late 1970s–1980s. Foremost among political leaders pushing for a revival of orthodox liberalism were British Prime Minister Margaret Thatcher and U.S. President Ronald Reagan. Critics argued that the Thatcher–Reagan policies revitalized business confidence by rejecting the attempt to ease the effects of liberalism on vulnerable groups. Thus, governments felt pressure to adopt orthodox liberal policies such as privatization, deregulation, and free trade; these policies resulted in open conflict with government employees, trade unions, and welfare recipients.[28] In contrast to Adam Smith's liberalism, the return to orthodox liberalism was global in extent for several reasons:

- Advances in technology, communications, and transportation enabled MNCs and international banks to shift their activities and funds around the world.
- The conditions on IMF and World Bank loans have included privatization, deregulation, and liberalization of indebted LDC economies.
- With the breakup of the Soviet bloc, orthodox liberal pressures also spread to transition economies.

Scholars use the term *neoliberalism* to differentiate this new liberal orthodoxy from the liberalism of Smith and Ricardo. In his book *Great Transformations*, Mark Blyth discusses the role of *ideas*, first in building embedded liberalism and then in disembedding it.[29] (We discuss constructivism in Chapter 5.) In the 1980s–1990s there was a strong negative reaction to neoliberalism and globalization, which was intensified with the 2008 global financial crisis; and today some call for a revival of interventionist liberalism. After focusing on institutional liberalism, we assess the ongoing tensions between orthodox and interventionist liberalism.

LIBERALISM AND INSTITUTIONS

Robert Keohane defines **institutions** as "persistent and connected sets of rules (formal and informal) that prescribe behavioral roles, constrain activity and shape expectations."[30] International institutions can take three forms: international organizations (IOs), international regimes, and international conventions. A liberal scholar first used the term *regime* in an IPE context, and a neomercantilist scholar edited a definitive volume on regimes.[31] However, we discuss institutions in this chapter because liberals attach the most importance to them. International regimes promote cooperation in areas such as trade and monetary relations, where there is a high degree of interdependence. Before turning to regimes, we therefore discuss interdependence and cooperation in IPE.

Interdependence Theory

Interdependence can be defined as "mutual dependence," in which "there are reciprocal (although not necessarily symmetrical) costly effects of transactions."[32] Richard Cooper's *The Economics of Interdependence* (1968) was the first systematic study of economic interdependence among states.[33] Cooper argues that growing interdependence due to advances in transportation, communications, and technology "negates the sharp distinction between internal and external policies," and limits the ability of states "to achieve their desired aims, regardless of their formal retention of sovereignty."[34] States should respond to interdependence by coordinating their policies in "taxation, the regulation of business ... [and] the framing of monetary policy."[35] However, Cooper devotes only limited attention to the *political* aspects of interdependence.

Liberals generally have a positive view of the political effects of interdependence. For example, Immanuel Kant (1724–1804) wrote in *Perpetual Peace* that "the *spirit of commerce sooner* or later takes hold of every people, and it cannot exist side by side with war";[36] and Bruce Russett and John Oneal find empirical evidence that "countries that are interdependent bilaterally or economically open to the global economy whether democratic or not, have an important basis for pacific relations and conflict resolution."[37] However, the benefits from interdependence between two countries are rarely symmetrical, because the smaller country is likely to be the more dependent partner. In *Power and Interdependence*, Robert Keohane and Joseph Nye analyze how asymmetrical interdependence transforms international politics:

> Asymmetrical interdependence [i.e., mutual dependence that is not evenly balanced] can be a source of power ... A less dependent actor in a relationship often has a significant political resource, because changes in the relationship ... will be less costly to that actor than to its partners.[38]

Nevertheless, Keohane and Nye have a rather benign view of the effects of asymmetrical interdependence on smaller states. For example, they conclude that Canada is often successful in conflicts with the United States because of the "complex interdependence" between the two countries. In complex interdependence, multiple channels (nongovernmental and governmental) connect societies, there is no hierarchy among issues (military security does not dominate the agenda), and one government does not use military force against another.[39] However, critics of the Keohane–Nye study argue that the United States as the larger power does not let market transactions dictate its interdependence with Canada and instead demands a wide array of "side payments." For example, side payments in NAFTA include Canadian concessions to U.S. demands regarding openness to foreign investment and the sharing of energy resources.[40]

Interdependence theorists question the neomercantilist assumptions that states are the central actors in IR, and that they can use military force to promote their national interest. Military force is of little use in dealing with interdependence issues such as environmental pollution, monetary and trade relations, and sustainable development.

The Liberal Approach to Cooperation

The possibilities for *both* cooperation and conflict increase between interdependent states, simply because they interact more and have a greater impact on each other:

> Significant interdependence, especially when accompanied by disrupting events, forces government and corporate elites to deal with problems arising from such worldwide interconnections. The greater the interdependence, the greater the compulsion for elites to take action. Such action can be defensive or conflictual, as well as collaborative or cooperative.[41]

This section examines how one type of game theory—prisoners' dilemma—is used to study cooperation among interdependent actors in an anarchic international system. *Game theory* investigates the interaction of two or more individuals, states, or private groups, in which the decisions of each player affect outcomes. Each player must assess what the other player(s) is likely to do before taking action.[42] **Prisoners' dilemma** is a "mixed-motive game," in which two players can benefit from mutual cooperation but have an incentive to "defect" or cheat on each other and become free riders. The term *prisoners' dilemma* derives from the description of the game: The police arrest two individuals, A and B, for committing a minor crime, and suspect that they have also committed a serious crime (robbery) but cannot prove it. To get A and B to confess and testify against each other, the police put them in different cells so they cannot communicate, and question them separately. In Figure 4.1, prisoners A and B "cooperate" with each other if they do not confess to robbery, and they "defect" (or cheat on each other) if they confess and testify against each other. The sentences the prisoners receive depend on their decisions. The numbers in **bold** at the top right-hand corners of the squares are A's years in

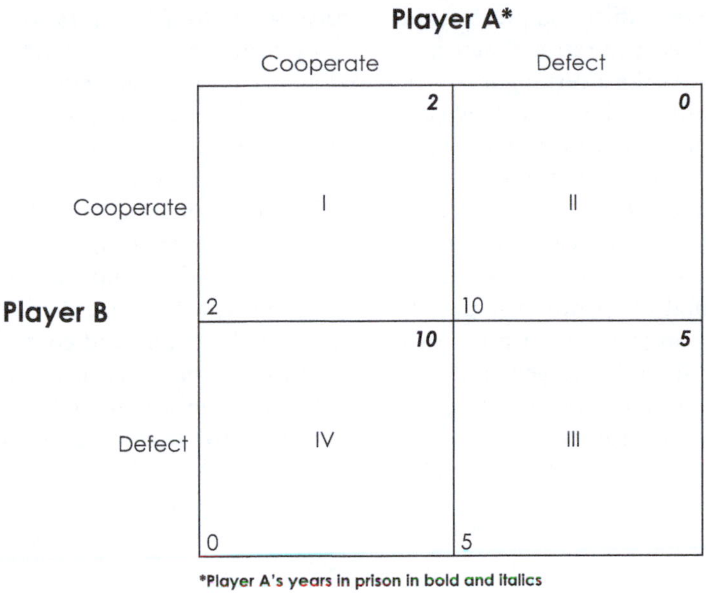

Player A*

<table>
<tr><td></td><td colspan="2">Cooperate</td><td colspan="2">Defect</td></tr>
<tr><td rowspan="2">Cooperate</td><td colspan="2">2</td><td colspan="2">0</td></tr>
<tr><td colspan="2">I</td><td colspan="2">II</td></tr>
<tr><td></td><td>2</td><td></td><td>10</td><td></td></tr>
</table>

Player B

*Player A's years in prison in bold and italics

FIGURE 4.1
Prisoners' Dilemma

prison, and the numbers at the bottom left-hand corners are B's years in prison. The police make a tempting offer to induce A to confess and testify against B (i.e., defect). They inform A that conviction for the minor crime is certain and will result in a two-year sentence for both prisoners if they do not confess (square I in Figure 4.1). However, if A confesses to robbery and testifies against B (defects) and B does not confess (cooperates), A will go free and B will get 10 years (square II). If both A and B defect and confess to robbery, they will get a reduced sentence of five years (square III). Finally, if A does not confess (cooperates) but B confesses (defects), A will get 10 years and B will go free (square IV). The police provide the same offer to B.

What will the prisoners do? If B defects (confesses), A is better off defecting (5 years in prison) than cooperating (10 years). If B cooperates (does not confess), A is also better off defecting (goes free) than cooperating (2 years). Thus, *individual* rationality pushes A to defect regardless of what B does, and the same reasoning applies to B. Furthermore, A and B mistrust each other, and they both fear receiving the worst penalty by cooperating (10 years) if the other prisoner defects. As a result, A and B are both likely to defect (confess) and spend five years in prison (square III), even though both would get only two years (square I) if they cooperated with each other. Square I is the best *collective* outcome or the **Pareto-optimal outcome** for A and B, because no actor can become better off without making someone else worse off (if A defects and goes free, B will get 10 years). Square III is an inferior collective outcome or **Pareto-deficient outcome**, because *both* A and B would prefer another outcome (square I).

Prisoners' dilemma presents a *collective action problem* in rational choice analysis, because rational actors may be "unable to reach a Pareto-optimal solution, despite a certain degree of convergence of interests between them."[43] The dilemma in both the provision of public goods (see Chapter 3) and prisoners' dilemma is that *individual* and *collective* rationality differ: The decisions of rational, self-interested states may interfere with the provision of public goods, and may lead to a Pareto-deficient outcome.[44] In IPE, we ask how states can move from a Pareto-deficient to a Pareto-optimal outcome. Defecting or cheating by states can inhibit cooperation, and liberals believe that mutual cooperation is possible if cheating can be controlled. A global hegemon can prevent cheating by providing public goods and coercing other states to abide by agreed rules and principles. International institutions can also prevent cheating by bringing states together on a regular basis; a state that interacts regularly with others is less likely to cheat because the others have many opportunities to retaliate. Institutions also enforce principles and rules to ensure that cheaters are punished; collect information on members' policies which increases confidence that cheaters will be discovered; and contribute to a learning process in which states realize that mutual gains can result from cooperation.[45]

Neomercantilists are more skeptical that international institutions can move states to a Pareto-optimal outcome. Since international institutions serve the interests of the most powerful states, they cannot enforce meaningful rules and instill confidence that there will be transparency and that cheaters will be punished. Each state is therefore likely to defect, and to assume that other states will do the same. Neomercantilists also see state concerns with *relative gains* as posing an obstacle to cooperation. Even if two states have common interests, they may not cooperate because of each state's concern that it will receive lesser gains. Institutions can promote cooperation only if they can ensure that all members' gains are balanced and equitable; this is difficult to achieve because gains are rarely equal.[46]

Regime Theory

Regime theory first developed from efforts to explain why international interactions are more orderly in some issue areas than in others. *Regimes* are "sets of implicit or explicit principles, norms, rules, and decision-making procedures around which actors' expectations converge in a given area of international relations."[47] Regime *principles* and *norms* refer to general beliefs and standards of behavior that guide relations; for example, principles of the global trade regime include liberalization, reciprocity, and nondiscrimination. Rules and decision-making procedures stem from the broader principles and norms; for example, to promote the "trade liberalization" principle, WTO rules and decision-making procedures limit protectionism and increase transparency. International regimes are normally associated with **international organizations** (**IOs**), which are institutions with formal functions and procedures, and at least three members. IOs are concrete, formal institutions that are often embedded in regimes; for example, the WTO is embedded in the global trade regime and the IMF is embedded in the monetary regime.

Theorists focus on the formation, maintenance, and results of regimes. Researchers disagree as to whether a hegemon is necessary for the *formation* of regimes (see Chapter 3), and they examine the strategies and processes that lead to regime formation. Some writers such as Robert Keohane argue that it is easier to *maintain* regimes than to create them and that states benefiting from a regime may collectively maintain it after a hegemon declines (see Chapter 3).[48] Theorists have examined regime *results* in areas such as global debt, the environment, transportation, and communications.[49] To assess regime results, they examine whether states abide by regime principles, norms, and rules; whether regimes effectively manage international problems; and whether regimes cause states to broaden their perceptions of self-interest.[50]

Whereas liberal theorists have devoted considerable attention to international regimes, the traditional realist view is that the most powerful states establish regimes that further their national interests, and do not adhere to the regime principles, norms, and rules when they conflict with their interests. For example, one realist asserts that "all those international arrangements dignified by the label regime are only too easily upset when either the balance of bargaining power or the perception of national interest ... change among those states who negotiate them."[51] Some neomercantilists such as Stephen Krasner by contrast acknowledge that regimes may be important in certain areas such as international trade and monetary relations.[52] However, Krasner continues to emphasize the centrality of the state and national power, and sees regimes as existing only under rather restrictive conditions. Many liberals by contrast view regimes as a pervasive and significant phenomenon. Despite the interest of liberals in regimes, some critics note that most regime studies have either explicitly or implicitly accepted "the realist view of states as the central actors of international politics."[53]

This book assumes that regimes have a significant impact in certain areas of IPE. Regime principles, norms, and rules can increase understanding and cooperation, and help establish standards that states and nonstate actors use to assess each other's behavior. Regimes can also induce states to follow consistent policies, limit actions that adversely affect others, and become less responsive to special interests. We do not assume that the effect of regimes is always positive. As neomercantilists and historical materialists point out, a regime may further the interests of the most powerful actors, often at the expense of the least powerful. Despite the value of regime theory, it has some shortcomings, and many liberal theorists now focus instead on *global governance*.

LIBERALISM, GLOBAL GOVERNANCE, AND REGIMES

Governance refers to formal and informal processes and institutions that organize collective action, and **global governance** describes formal and informal arrangements that produce some order and collective action above the state in the absence of a global government.[54] As globalization has increased, states have had more difficulty managing their economic affairs individually; thus, global governance has become a central issue in IPE. Some liberal theorists believe that the global governance concept avoids the limitations of regime analysis in several respects. First, most regime studies are state-centric, whereas global governance studies are attuned to the relocation of some authority from states to subnational, transnational, and supranational actors.[55] Second, regime theorists often overlook the broader aspects of global management because they focus on specific issue areas; for example, most regime studies do not examine the crucial linkages between the trade and environmental regimes. Global governance by contrast examines the linkages among issue areas and the significance of these linkages. Third, regime theorists are criticized for assuming that "everyone wants ... more and better regimes" and that "order and managed interdependence should be the collective goal."[56] Global governance studies are less obsessed with order and cooperation, and more open to NGO demands for greater equity and justice.[57]

Despite the advantages of global governance studies, they also have shortcomings. Most importantly, the global governance literature does *not* offer a consistent theoretical framework for testing the coherence or utility of its ideas; it uses a number of different theoretical approaches.[58] Furthermore, regime theorists have responded to the critics by altering their studies. For example, some regime analysts examine private and transnational regimes, and devote more attention to the linkage among issue areas. Thus, the international regimes and global governance concepts are not incompatible.[59] Part III of this book relies on regime theory because it permits us to analyze specific issue areas. However, we are attuned to the criticisms of regime analysis and also refer to some broader issues of global governance.

LIBERALISM AND DOMESTIC–INTERNATIONAL INTERACTIONS

Literature on domestic–international interactions cannot be categorized under a single IPE perspective, but we discuss this issue here because liberals often focus on domestic societal pressures on the state. Neomercantilists devote less attention to domestic issues with their emphasis on the state as the central actor. (Some Marxists view the state as an "instrument" of the dominant capitalist class; see Chapter 5.) This section examines theoretical advances in the study of domestic–international interactions, and the chapters in Part III give examples in specific IPE issue areas.[60]

In a 1977 study, Peter Katzenstein and others identified domestic political structure as a factor explaining different national responses to international economic events. For example, more centralized states such as Japan and France responded more decisively than decentralized states such as the United States to the 1973 OPEC price increase. The U.S. government was less able to respond promptly because of the separation of powers between the president and Congress, and the division of powers between the federal government and the states.[61] Later studies found that states are not *uniformly* strong or weak across different issue areas or time periods.[62] For example, the U.S. executive has more leeway in making monetary than trade policy because societal groups view their economic fortunes as being more affected by trade. More centralized states such as Japan also do not act decisively on every economic issue. During the East Asian financial crisis in the late 1990s, Japan had great difficulty in adopting bold policy measures to deal with the crisis.

IPE scholars have done a considerable amount of research on domestic–international interactions in international trade. If import tariffs are phased out, consumers may benefit from lower prices and a greater variety of goods, but local producers may suffer because of increased competition from imports. Although consumers greatly outnumber producers, the gains of free trade to consumers are more *diffuse,* whereas the losses to producers are more *concentrated.* Rational choice theorists argue that the concentrated protectionist interests of industries have more influence over policy-makers than the diffuse free-trade interests of consumers, because politicians adopt policies that improve their chances for re-election.[63] However, concentrated interest groups do not necessarily have common interests. Concentrated "anti-protection interests" such as exporters, import-using industries, retailers, and multinational corporations often counteract the influence of concentrated protectionist interests. Second, concentrated producer interests do not *always* exert more influence, because the general public sometimes reacts strongly to policies affecting employment, taxation, and inflation, and threatens to express its views in the ballot box.[64]

The influence of producer groups on trade policy also depends on a country's domestic governmental institutions. For example, the U.S. president, who is elected by the entire voting public, is less susceptible to pressure from concentrated protectionist interests than members of the U.S. Congress, who are elected by smaller constituencies. As Chapter 8 discusses, U.S. trade policy became less protectionist after the Congress began delegating trade negotiating authority to the president in 1934. Parliamentary systems with strong party discipline are better equipped to limit protectionist forces; but legislators in parliamentary systems with weaker party discipline are more responsive to protectionist demands. Peter Gourevich and others point out that domestic structure is a *consequence* as well as a *cause* of foreign economic policy-making. For example, interdependence and globalization have altered domestic structure, causing governmental actors to share more power with private actors such as MNCs.[65]

Two-level game theory, a term coined by Robert Putnam, describes international negotiations as a two-level game involving a state's *international interests and obligations* on the one hand, and *domestic interactions within the state* on the other.[66] At the international level (level 1 in Figure 4.2), state representatives negotiate with each other to reach an agreement; at the domestic level (level 2), the representatives negotiate with domestic actors whose concurrence is needed for the agreement to have legitimacy. Game theorists try to identify *win-sets*, or all possible level 1 agreements that would win ratification at level 2 within each state involved in the negotiations. The negotiations between two countries will

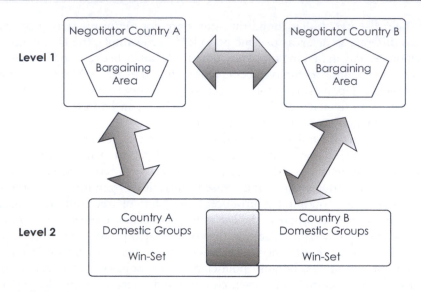

FIGURE 4.2

Putnam's Two-level Game

Source: Derived from the description in Robert D. Putnam, "Diplomacy and Domestic Politics: The Logic of Two-Level Games," *International Organization* 42, no. 3 (Summer 1983), pp. 427–460.

only be successful if the negotiators reach an agreement that falls within an area where the two countries' domestic win-sets overlap (the shaded area in Figure 4.2). If the two countries' domestic win-sets do not overlap, the negotiations will fail. Putnam notes that "larger win-sets make Level I agreement more likely, *ceteris paribus*."[67] Two-level game theory is also used to assess the leverage and strategies of states in negotiations. For example, Putnam notes the irony that "the stronger a state is in terms of autonomy from domestic pressures, the weaker its relative bargaining position internationally."[68] A state with smaller win-sets can make fewer concessions, and the other state must make more concessions if the negotiations are to succeed. As Figure 4.2 shows, country A has a larger win-set than country B; thus, B has less room to make concessions, and this may give it a bargaining advantage over A. Chapter 8 shows that the U.S. Congress's constitutional powers on trade often limit the executive's options and give the president more leverage in international trade negotiations. A minority government in a parliamentary system may also have more leverage if it can convince others that its domestic position limits its win-set.[69]

LIBERALISM AND NORTH–SOUTH RELATIONS

Liberals usually consider the key factors in development to be the efficient use of scarce resources and economic growth, which they often define as an increase in a state's per capita income. Beyond these broad areas of agreement, orthodox and interventionist liberals often diverge in their views of development.

Orthodox Liberals and North–South Relations

Orthodox liberals assume that development problems stem largely from inefficient LDC policies. *Modernization theory* asserts that the DCs achieved economic development by abandoning traditional practices and that LDCs must also replace their traditional practices with Western norms and institutions if they are to achieve development.[70] Although some modernization theorists suggested that LDCs might follow different routes to development, most were deterministic.[71] Walt Rostow's book *The Stages of Economic Growth* was highly deterministic, claiming that societies move through five stages on the path to modernity: traditional society, the preconditions for takeoff, the takeoff, the drive to maturity, and the age of high mass consumption.[72] Despite the initial appeal of this model, Rostow's prediction that an LDC's growth would become self-sustaining when it reached the takeoff stage raised false hopes that LDC development was readily achievable and irreversible. Critics of modernization theory point out that the challenges facing LDCs today are very different from those confronting early developers because of globalization, MNCs, and the difficulty in competing with the North.[73] Critics also question whether the Western experience is the best path to development, and they question the assumption that there is a single Western development model. For example Sweden's social democratic development differed in important respects from U.S. development. Despite these criticisms, many orthodox liberals continue to view the Western model as the only legitimate path to development. In the late 1980s, for example, one liberal wrote that "third-world countries are much like those of the first world and will, with a modicum of external aid and internal stability, follow in the path of their predecessors," and another predicted that we may be witnessing "not just the end of the Cold War" but "the universalization of Western liberal democracy as the final form of human government."[74]

Internationally, orthodox liberals view North–South relations as a positive-sum game that benefits the South, and they often argue that "the late-comers to modern economic growth tend to catch up with the early-comers."[75] The South needs foreign investment, the diffusion of advanced technologies, and export markets. Thus, LDCs that achieve development are integrated in the global economy through freer trade and capital flows, whereas the least developed LDCs have few economic linkages with the North.

Interventionist Liberals and North–South Relations

Interventionist liberals, like orthodox liberals, believe that LDCs with efficient, market-oriented policies are most likely to achieve economic growth. However, interventionists point to North–South inequalities, and some argue that "economic forces left entirely to themselves tend to produce growing inequality."[76] Interventionists therefore call on the North to consider the South's special needs, and they recommend some intervention by governments and international organizations in the market. For example, they propose that DCs remove trade barriers to LDCs, permit some protectionism for LDC industries, and provide IMF and World Bank financing to indebted LDCs. Interventionists see the North's assistance to the South as a matter of enlightened self-interest because "the countries of the North, given their increasing interdependence with the South, themselves need international economic reform to ensure their own future prosperity."[77] Interventionists believe that the necessary changes can occur within the liberal order and that a radical redistribution of wealth and power between North and South is not necessary. They also believe in private enterprise and agree with orthodox liberals that many LDC development problems stem from domestic inefficiencies.[78]

PRESENT-DAY LIBERALISM

As discussed, there was a revival of orthodox liberalism (or neoliberalism) in the 1970s. However, there was a strong reaction against neoliberalism among some individuals, groups, and states beginning in the 1980s, and this negative reaction was intensified with the 2008 global financial crisis. After discussing the negative reaction in the 1980s to early 2000s, we briefly assess the effects of the 2008 financial crisis on present-day liberalism.

As discussed in Chapters 7 and 11, with globalization most countries were integrated with global financial markets, and this helped create the conditions for financial crises in the 1980s–1990s. The 1980s foreign debt crisis not only threatened Latin American and African LDCs, but also the international banking system. The IMF and World Bank provided structural adjustment loans to the indebted LDCs, but imposed neoliberal conditions on the loans calling for privatization, deregulation, and greater openness to trade and foreign investment. Many LDCs questioned whether these conditions were conducive to promoting their economic growth, and similar questions were raised about the IMF and World Bank's response to the 1990s East Asian financial crisis.

Dissatisfaction was also developing with neoliberalism and globalization in the North. Many MNCs were relocating their operations from the North to the South because they could pay lower wages and taxes, and were subject to less strict environmental, health, and safety regulations. Although industrial mechanization and technological change also contributed to DC workers' problems, competitive imports from emerging economies were certainly a factor. Labor unions, environmentalists, students and others protested against the perceived threats to DC economic, social, and environmental conditions in the West throughout the 1990s. For example, about 50,000 protesters joined in the "Battle of Seattle" to oppose globalization pressures at the WTO's Third Ministerial Conference in Seattle, Washington in November 1999. LDCs had their own globalization concerns. Globalization was occurring under principles and rules established by the KIEOs, which were dominated by the North. The protests involved groups from both the North and the South. For example, about 15,000 people protested against market globalization and militarism at the October 2002 IMF and World Bank annual meetings in Washington, DC; and thousands of Mexican farmers marched during the WTO's fifth ministerial conference in Cancun, Mexico in September 2003.[79]

The opposition to neoliberalism and globalization increased sharply as a result of the 2008 global financial crisis. As discussed in Chapter 7, U.S. investment banks packaged risky subprime mortgages in large mortgage-backed securities, and firms, banks, and other groups from around the world invested in them. The investors assumed that these mortgage-backed securities were a safe and profitable investment, but this proved not to be the case. Regulations imposed on the U.S. banking system instituted after the 1930s Great Depression had gradually been relaxed since the mid-1970s and this enabled the banks to engage in more risky behavior. The globalization process also contributed to the rapid spread of the financial crisis, and this created a standoff between orthodox and interventionist liberalism:

> On the one hand, there was the set of free-market beliefs which Alan Greenspan admitted were no longer working as an economic argument, but which still animated many people's beliefs about the legitimacy of the state. On the other hand, there was the ideology that underlay the post-Second World War settlement, including the recovery of Europe from the political turmoil of the 1920s and 1930s, and is best labeled social democracy.[80]

The 2008 financial crisis also led to a revival of interest in many of Keynes's ideas regarding the need for government stimulus in times of instability and high levels of unemployment.[81] As discussed in Chapter 7, the EU is undergoing a sovereign debt crisis, and there is a bitter split between those calling for more government austerity and those calling for more stimulus to promote economic growth. In sum, the standoff between orthodox and interventionist liberalism shows that some of the biggest divisions in IPE today are *within* the liberal perspective.

CRITIQUE OF THE LIBERAL PERSPECTIVE

As this chapter notes, orthodox liberals believe that all states benefit from free trade and foreign investment in a competitive market. They are not concerned about the fact that all states do not benefit equally, because the economic linkages produce mutual benefits. Interventionist liberals note that unemployment can occur under market conditions and that LDCs may require special treatment, but they believe that these problems can be remedied by supplementing rather than replacing the liberal economic system. Both neomercantilists and critical theorists (historical materialists and dependency theorists) criticize liberals for devoting too little attention to power and distributional issues. Neomercantilists argue that relative gains are more important than absolute gains, because the most powerful states capture the largest share of the benefits. Economic exchanges are rarely free and equitable, and bargaining power based on monopoly and coercion can have important political effects. Thus, weaker states should be wary of highly interdependent relationships. Powerful states can harm weaker states simply by reducing trade, aid, and investment.[82] Historical materialists accuse liberals of legitimizing inequality and exploitation. Domestically, liberals mislead the working class into believing that it will benefit from economic growth along with the capitalist class. Internationally, liberals disguise exploitation and dependency relations under the cloak of "interdependence."

Critics also question the liberal view that advances in technology, transportation, and communication can solve the world's economic and environmental problems. Even with technological advances, the liberal international order that seemed so positive-sum in the immediate postwar years is becoming more competitive as global resources such as energy, water, and food become less abundant. Furthermore, technological advances may in fact contribute to greater North–South inequalities. **Endogenous growth theory** posits that technological change is not the result of fortunate breakthroughs in knowledge exogenous to the factors of production. Instead, technological knowledge is an *endogenous* factor of production along with labor and capital. In other words, technological progress depends on investment in science and education, and on research and development (R&D). Because DCs and their firms have more resources than LDCs to subsidize education and R&D, they continue to increase their productivity and "grow indefinitely at a faster pace" than small and poor economies.[83] Although some claims of endogenous growth theorists are controversial, they raise important questions about the orthodox liberal assumption that "the late-comers to modern economic growth tend to catch up with the early-comers."[84]

Orthodox liberals also assume that open economic policies and interdependence will improve LDC conditions, without considering North–South political power relationships. Aside from cases such as OPEC, the East Asian NIEs, and the BRIC economies, North–South relations are highly asymmetrical. Thus, Tanzania's president Julius Nyerere remarked to a G77 meeting,

> What we have in common is that we are all, in relation to the developed world, dependent—not interdependent—nations. Each of our economies has developed as a by-product and a subsidiary of development in the industrialized North, and is externally oriented.[85]

This dependent relationship provides the North with a potent source of power over the South. Economic liberals tend to discount the effects of this power asymmetry by arguing that North–South relations are a positive-sum game in which everyone benefits. One liberal assessment of NAFTA, for example, indicates that the United States, Canada, and Mexico agreed to "a partial surrender of autonomy in order to achieve the benefits that are available from mutual relaxation of protectionism."[86] However, orthodox liberals avoid asking whether LDCs (i.e., Mexico in NAFTA) must surrender more autonomy than DCs (the United States and Canada). Liberals are also criticized for putting too much faith in the market and for disregarding the role of the state. Interventionist liberals view states as performing corrective functions, but even interventionists are criticized for undertheorizing the role of the state. Thus, neomercantilists argue that we should "bring the state back in" to our research because of its central role in policy-making.[87]

Whereas liberals and neomercantilists accept the capitalist system as a given, historical materialists view capitalism as an exploitative system that should—and will—eventually be replaced by socialism. We discuss historical materialists and other critical theorists in the next chapter.

QUESTIONS

1. What are the similarities and differences among orthodox, interventionist, and institutional liberals?
2. Why did John Gerard Ruggie's "embedded liberalism" become so important after World War II, and how did it draw upon the ideas of John Maynard Keynes and Karl Polanyi?
3. When did neoliberalism emerge, and why? How did it draw on the ideas of Milton Friedman? How did it differ from the liberalism of Adam Smith?
4. In what way do both the provision of public goods and prisoners' dilemma demonstrate "collective action problems"? How and why do liberals and neomercantilists differ in their views regarding the possibilities for cooperation under prisoners' dilemma?
5. What are international regimes, and what are the views of regime theorists regarding the formation, maintenance, and results of regimes?
6. In what way does regime theory draw on both the liberal and neomercantilist perspectives? What are the major criticisms of regime theory? Is "global governance" a more useful concept than "regimes"?
7. In what ways have studies of foreign economic policy-making, concentrated and diffuse domestic interests, and two-level game theory increased our understanding of domestic–international interactions in IPE?
8. How do orthodox and interventionist liberals approach the issue of North–South relations? What are some of the criticisms of their approach?

KEY TERMS

endogenous growth
  theory
global governance
governance
institutional liberals
institutions

interdependence
international
  organizations
interventionist liberals
market economy
orthodox liberals

Pareto-deficient outcome
Pareto-optimal outcome
prisoners' dilemma
two-level game theory

FURTHER READING

Studies on economic liberalism include Mark R. Reigg, *Exploitation and Economic Justice in the Liberal Capitalist State* (New York: Oxford University Press, 2013); Mark Blyth, *Great Transformations* (New York: Cambridge University Press, 2002); John G. Ruggie, "International Regimes, Transactions, and Change: Embedded Liberalism in the Postwar Economic Order," in Stephen D. Krasner, ed., *International Regimes* (Ithaca, NY: Cornell University Press, 1983), pp. 195–231; and Karl Polanyi's classic study *The Great Transformation* (Boston, MA: Beacon Press, 1965).

On Adam Smith, see David Hardwick and Leslie Marsh, eds., *Propriety and Prosperity: New Studies in the Philosophy of Adam Smith* (New York: Palgrave Macmillan, 2014). On Keynesianism see Peter Temin, *Keynes: Useful Economics for the World Economy* (Cambridge, MA: MIT Press, 2014); Roger E. Backhouse and Bradley W. Bateman, *Capitalist Revolutionary: John Maynard Keynes* (Cambridge, MA: Harvard University Press, 2011); and Robert Skidelsky, *Keynes: A Very Short Introduction* (New York: Oxford University Press, 2010).

The literature on global governance includes Roman Goldbach, *Global Governance and Regulatory Failure: The Political Economy of Banking* (New York: Palgrave Macmillan, 2015); Thomas G. Weiss, *Global Governance* (Malden, MA: Polity, 2013); and David Held and Charles Roger, eds., *Global Governance at Risk* (Malden, MA: Polity, 2013). Studies on regime theory include Robert M. A. Crawford, *Regime Theory in the Post-Cold War World* (Brookfield, VT: Dartmouth, 1996); Volker Rittberger with Peter Mayer, eds., *Regime Theory and International Relations* (New York: Oxford University Press, 1993); and Stephen D. Krasner, ed., *International Regimes* (Ithaca, NY: Cornell University Press, 1983). On private regimes, see A. Claire Cutler, "Private International Regimes and Interfirm Cooperation," in Rodney B. Hall and Thomas A. Biersteker, eds., *The Emergence of Private Authority in Global Governance* (New York: Cambridge University Press, 2002), pp. 23–40.

On domestic–international interactions, see Robert O. Keohane and Helen Milner, eds., *Internationalization and Domestic Politics* (New York: Cambridge University Press, 1996); G. John Ikenberry, David A. Lake, and Michael Mastanduno, eds., "The State and American Foreign Economic Policy," special issue of *International Organization* 42, no. 1 (Winter 1988); and Peter J. Katzenstein, ed., "International Relations and Domestic Structures: Foreign Policies of the Advanced Industrial States," special issue of *International Organization* 31, no. 4 (Autumn 1977). On two-level game theory, see Peter B. Evans, Harold K. Jacobson, and Robert D. Putnam, eds., *Double-Edged Diplomacy* (Berkeley, CA: University of California Press, 1993); and Robert D. Putnam, "Diplomacy and Domestic Politics: The Logic of Two-Level Games," *International Organization* 42, no. 3 (Summer 1988), pp. 427–460.

NOTES

1. Robert. D. McKinlay and Richard Little, *Global Problems and World Order* (London: Pinter, 1986), p. 41.
2. Andrew Moravcsik, "Taking Preferences Seriously: A Liberal Theory of International Politics," *International Organization* 51, no. 4 (Autumn 1997), p. 517.
3. Adam Smith, *The Wealth of Nations*, vol. 1 (London: Dent, Everyman's Library no. 412, 1910), bk. 4, p. 398.
4. Walter Wriston, "Technology and Sovereignty," *Foreign Affairs* 67, no. 2 (Winter 1988–1989), p. 71.
5. Geoffrey Garrett, "The Causes of Globalization," *Comparative Political Studies* 33, no. 6/7 (August/September 2000), pp. 941–991.
6. John Locke, *Two Treatises of Government* (Cambridge, UK: Cambridge University Press, 1964), ch. 9 of the Second Treatise, p. 368.
7. Agnar Sandmo, *Economics Evolving: A History of Economic Thought* (Princeton, NJ: Princeton University Press, 2011), pp. 24–25; Luis Argemi d'Abadal, "The Physiocrats," in Jurgen Georg Backhaus, ed., *Handbook of the History of Economic Thought* (New York: Springer, 2012), pp. 137–159.

8. Adam Smith, *The Theory of Moral Sentiments*, ed. Knud Haakonssen (New York: Cambridge University Press, 2002).

9. Sandmo, *Economics Evolving*, pp. 32–34.

10. Smith, *The Wealth of Nations*, p. 436.

11. Andrew Wyatt-Walter, "Adam Smith and the Liberal Tradition in International Relations," *Review of International Studies* 22, no. 1 (1996), pp. 7–11; Smith, *The Wealth of Nations*, vol. 2, bk. 4, pp. 180–181.

12. See David Ricardo, *Principles of Political Economy and Taxation* (Amherst, NY: Prometheus Books, 1996).

13. Peter A. Hall, "Introduction," in Peter A. Hall, ed., *The Political Power of Economic Ideas: Keynesianism Across Nations* (Princeton, NJ: Princeton University Press, 1989), p. 4.

14. "The End of Laissez-Faire (1926)," in John Maynard Keynes, *Essays in Persuasion* (New York: W.W. Norton, 1963), p. 312.

15. John M. Keynes, *The General Theory of Employment, Interest, and Money* (New York: Harcourt, Brace & World, 1936), pp. 378–379; Jeffry A. Frieden, *Global Capitalism* (New York: W.W. Norton, 2006), p. 152.

16. Hall, "Introduction," p. 7.

17. John M. Keynes, "National Self-Sufficiency," *The Yale Review* 22 (1933), p. 758. On Keynes's changing view of trade protection, see Barry Eichengreen, "Keynes and Protection," *Journal of Economic History* 44, no. 2 (June 1984), pp. 363–373.

18. Roger E. Backhouse and Bradley W. Bateman, *Capitalist Revolutionary: John Maynard Keynes* (Cambridge, MA: Harvard University Press, 2011), pp. 104–108; Fred L. Block, *The Origins of International Economic Disorder: A Study of United States International Monetary Policy from World War II to the Present* (Berkeley, CA: University of California Press, 1977), pp. 62–69.

19. David Colander and Harry Landreth, *The Coming of Keynesianism to America* (Brookfield, VT: Edward Elgar, 1996), pp. 11–13.

20. "The End of Laissez-Faire (1926)," p. 317.

21. Anthony Arblaster, *The Rise and Decline of Western Liberalism* (New York: Basil Blackwell, 1984), p. 292; Donald Winch, "Keynes, Keynesianism, and State Intervention," in Peter A. Hall, ed., *The Political Power of Economic Ideas: Keynesianism Across Nations* (Princeton, NJ: Princeton University Press, 1989), pp. 109–110.

22. Karl Polanyi, *The Great Transformation* (Boston, MA: Beacon Press, 1965).

23. John G. Ruggie, "International Regimes, Transactions, and Change: Embedded Liberalism in the Postwar Economic Order," in Stephen D. Krasner, ed., *International Regimes* (Ithaca, NY: Cornell University Press, 1983), pp. 204–214.

24. Peter Gourevitch, *Politics in Hard Times: Comparative Responses to International Economic Crises* (Ithaca, NY: Cornell University Press, 1986), pp. 166–169; Adam Przeworski, *Capitalism and Social Democracy* (New York: Cambridge University Press, 1985), pp. 205–211.

25. Friedrich A. Hayek, *The Road to Serfdom* (Chicago: University of Chicago Press, 1944).

26. Hayek gave priority to social as well as economic relationships. See Walter Block, "Hayek's Road to Serfdom," *Journal of Libertarian Studies* 12, no. 2 (Fall 1996), p. 365; Charles R. McCann, "F. A. Hayek: The Liberal as Communitarian," *Review of Austrian Economics* 15, no. 1 (2002), pp. 5–34.

27. Milton Friedman and Rose Friedman, *Free to Choose: A Personal Statement* (New York: Harcourt Brace Jovanovich, 1980), pp. 54–55.

28. Robert Cox, *Production, Power, and World Order: Social Forces in the Making of History* (New York: Columbia University Press, 1987), pp. 286–288; Alain Lipietz, *Towards a New Economic Order: Postfordism, Ecology and Democracy*, trans. Malcolm Slater (New York: Oxford University Press, 1992), pp. 30–31.

29. Mark Blyth, *Great Transformations: Economic Ideas and Institutional Change in the Twentieth Century* (New York: Cambridge University Press, 2002).

30. Robert O. Keohane, "Neoliberal Institutionalism: A Perspective on World Politics," in Robert O. Keohane, ed., *International Institutions and State Power: Essays in International Relations Theory* (Boulder, CO: Westview Press, 1989), pp. 3–4.

31. John G. Ruggie first used the term *regime* in IPE in "International Responses to Technology: Concepts and Trends," *International Organization* 29, no. 3 (Summer 1975), pp. 570–573; Krasner, *International Regimes*.

32. Robert O. Keohane and Joseph S. Nye, *Power and Interdependence,* 2nd ed. (Glenview, IL: Scott, Foresman, 1989), pp. 8–9.

33. Richard N. Cooper, *The Economics of Interdependence: Economic Policy in the Atlantic Community* (New York: McGraw-Hill, 1968).

34. Richard N. Cooper, "Economic Interdependence and Foreign Policy in the Seventies," *World Politics* 24 (January 1972), p. 179.

35. Cooper, "Economic Interdependence and Foreign Policy in the Seventies," pp. 170–171.

36. Immanuel Kant, *Perpetual Peace: A Philosophical Sketch*. Reprinted in Hans Reiss, ed., *Kant's Political Writings* (New York: Cambridge University Press, 1970), p. 114.

37. Bruce Russett and John R. Oneal, *Triangulating Peace: Democracy, Interdependence, and International Organizations* (New York: W.W. Norton, 2001), p. 155.

38. Keohane and Nye, *Power and Interdependence*, p. 11.

39. See Keohane and Nye, *Power and Interdependence*, pp. 24–29, and ch. 7.

40. Ricardo Grinspun and Maxwell A. Cameron, eds., *The Political Economy of North American Free Trade* (Montreal: McGill-Queen's University Press, 1993).

41. Raymond F. Hopkins and Donald Puchala, "The Failure of Regime Transformation: A Reply," *International Organization* 34, no. 2 (Spring 1980), pp. 304–305; Theodore H. Cohn, *The International Politics of Agricultural Trade* (Vancouver: University of British Columbia Press, 1990), pp. 16–32.

42. James D. Morrow, *Game Theory for Political Scientists* (Princeton, NJ: Princeton University Press, 1994), pp. 1–8.

43. Robert O. Keohane, *After Hegemony: Cooperation and Discord in the World Political Economy* (Princeton, NJ: Princeton University Press, 1984), p. 68.

44. Robert Axelrod, *The Evolution of Cooperation* (New York: Basic Books, 1984), p. 9. *Pareto-optimal* and *Pareto-deficient* are named after an Italian sociologist, Vilfredo Pareto (1848–1923).

45. Keohane, "Neoliberal Institutionalism," pp. 1–20; Robert Axelrod and Robert O. Keohane, "Achieving Cooperation Under Anarchy: Strategies and Institutions," in Kenneth A. Oye, ed., *Cooperation Under Anarchy* (Princeton, NJ: Princeton University Press, 1986), pp. 226–254.

46. Arthur A. Stein, "Neoliberal Institutionalism," in Christian Reus-Smit and Duncan Snidal, eds., *The Oxford Handbook of International Relations* (New York: Oxford University Press, 2008), p. 206.

47. Stephen D. Krasner, "Structural Causes and Regime Consequences," in Stephen D. Krasner, ed., *International Regimes* (Ithaca, NY: Cornell University Press, 1983), p. 2; Mark W. Zacher with Brent A. Sutton, *Governing Global Networks:*

International Regimes for Transportation and Communications (New York: Cambridge University Press, 1996), p. 1.

48. Keohane, *After Hegemony*, pp. 49, 244–245.
49. Oran R. Young, *International Cooperation: Building Regimes for Natural Resources and the Environment* (Ithaca, NY: Cornell University Press, 1989), p. 206.
50. Olav S. Stokke, "Regimes as Governance Systems," in Oran R. Young, ed., *Global Governance: Drawing Insights from the Environmental Experience* (Cambridge, MA: MIT Press, 1997), pp. 27–63.
51. Susan Strange, "Cave! Hic Dragones: A Critique of Regime Analysis," in Stephen D. Krasner, ed., *International Regimes* (Ithaca, NY: Cornell University Press, 1983), p. 345.
52. Krasner, *International Regimes*.
53. Stein, "Neoliberal Institutionalism," p. 203.
54. Oran R. Young, *Governance in World Affairs* (Ithaca, NY: Cornell University Press, 1999), p. 2.
55. John Vogler, "Taking Institutions Seriously: How Regime Analysis Can Be Relevant to Multilevel Environmental Governance," *Global Environmental Politics* 3, no. 2 (May 2003), pp. 32–35; James N. Rosenau, "Governance in the Twenty-First Century," *Global Governance* 1, no. 1 (Winter 1995), pp. 18–20.
56. Strange, "Cave! Hic Dragones," p. 345.
57. Anil Hira and Theodore H. Cohn, "Toward a Theory of Global Regime Governance," *International Journal of Political Economy* 33, no. 4 (Winter 2003–2004), pp. 9–11.
58. For other criticisms of the global governance literature see Hira and Cohn, "Toward a Theory of Global Regime Governance," pp. 12–16.
59. Stokke, "Regimes as Governance Systems," p. 31.
60. Jeffry Frieden and Lisa L. Martin, "International Political Economy: Global and Domestic Interactions," in Ira Katznelson and Helen V. Milner, eds., *Political Science: The State of the Discipline* (New York: W.W. Norton, 2002), pp. 118–120.
61. Peter J. Katzenstein, ed., "International Relations and Domestic Structures: Foreign Policies of the Advanced Industrial States," special issue of *International Organization* 31, no. 4 (Autumn 1977), pp. 587–920; Benjamin J. Cohen, *International Political Economy: An Intellectual History* (Princeton, NJ: Princeton University Press, 2008), pp. 124–129.
62. G. John Ikenberry, David A. Lake, and Michael Mastanduno, eds., "The State and American Foreign Economic Policy," special issue of *International Organization* 42, no. 1 (Winter 1988), pp. 1–243.
63. Bruno S. Frey, "The Public Choice View of International Political Economy," *International Organization* 38, no. 1 (Winter 1984), pp. 207–214; Guido Pincione and Fernando R. Tesón, *Rational Choice and Democratic Deliberation* (New York: Cambridge University Press, 2006), pp. 5–7.
64. I. M. Destler and John S. Odell, *Anti-Protection: Changing Forces in United States Trade Policy* (Washington, DC: Institute for International Economics, 1967), pp. 125–128.
65. Peter Gourevitch, "The Second Image Reversed: The International Sources of Domestic Politics," *International Organization* 32, no. 4 (Autumn 1978), pp. 881–912; Frieden and Martin, "International Political Economy," pp. 132–136.
66. Robert D. Putnam, "Diplomacy and Domestic Politics: The Logic of Two-Level Games," *International Organization* 42, no. 3 (Summer 1988), pp. 427–460.
67. Putnam, "Diplomacy and Domestic Politics," p. 437.

68. Putnam, "Diplomacy and Domestic Politics," p. 449.
69. See Andrew Moravcsik, "Introduction," in Peter B. Evans, Harold K. Jacobson, and Robert D. Putnam, eds., *Double-Edged Diplomacy* (Berkeley, CA: University of California Press, 1993), pp. 3–42.
70. Cyril E. Black, *The Dynamics of Modernization: A Study in Comparative History* (New York: Harper & Row, 1966), p. 27; Daniel Lerner, "Modernization: Social Aspects," in David Sills, ed., *International Encyclopedia of the Social Sciences*, vol. 10 (New York: Macmillan, 1968), pp. 386–388.
71. Less deterministic studies include Gabriel A. Almond and James S. Coleman, eds., *The Politics of the Developing Areas* (Princeton, NJ: Princeton University Press, 1960); Samuel P. Huntington, *Political Order in Changing Societies* (New Haven, CT: Yale University Press, 1968).
72. W. W. Rostow, *The Stages of Economic Growth: A Non-Communist Manifesto* (Cambridge, UK: Cambridge University Press, 1960), pp. 4–92.
73. Alejandro Portes, "On the Sociology of National Development: Theories and Issues," *American Journal of Sociology* 82, no. 1 (July 1976), p. 60.
74. Lloyd G. Reynolds, *Economic Growth in the Third World, 1850–1980* (New Haven, CT: Yale University Press, 1985), p. 6; Francis Fukuyama, "The End of History?" *The National Interest* 16 (Summer 1989), p. 4.
75. W. W. Rostow, *Why the Poor Get Richer and the Rich Slow Down* (Austin, TX: University of Texas Press, 1980), p. 259.
76. Independent Commission on International Development Issues (henceforth, Brandt Commission I), *North–South: A Program for Survival* (Cambridge, MA: MIT Press, 1980), pp. 103–104.
77. Brandt Commission I, *North–South*, p. 33.
78. Stephen D. Krasner, *Structural Conflict: The Third World Against Global Liberalism* (Berkeley, CA: University of California Press, 1985), pp. 22–25.
79. Frieden, *Global Capitalism*, pp. 457–472; Manfred B. Steger, *Globalisms*, 3rd ed. (Lanham, MD: Rowman & Littlefield, 2009), pp. 97–130.
80. Backhouse and Bateman, *Capitalist Revolutionary*, pp. 146–147.
81. See, for example, Robert Skidelsky, *Keynes: The Return of the Master* (New York: Allen Lane, 2009).
82. Charles E. Lindblom, *Politics and Markets: The World's Political–Economic Systems* (New York: Basic Books, 1977), p. 48.
83. Michael Burda and Charles Wyplosz, *Macroeconomics*, 4th ed. (New York: Oxford University Press, 2005), pp. 65–66.
84. Rostow, *Why the Poor Get Richer and the Rich Slow Down*, p. 259.
85. "Address by His Excellency Mwalima Julius K. Nyerere, President of the United Republic of Tanzania, to the Fourth Ministerial Meeting of the Group of 77," *Arusha*, February 12–16, 1979, in Karl P. Sauvant, *The Group of 77: Evolution, Structure, Organization* (New York: Oceana Publications, 1981), p. 133.
86. Steven Globerman and Michael Walker, "Overview," in Steven Globerman and Michael Walker, eds., *Assessing NAFTA: A Trinational Analysis* (Vancouver, BC: The Fraser Institute, 1993), p. ix.
87. Theda Skocpol, "Bringing the State Back In: Strategies of Analysis in Current Research," in Peter B. Evans, Dietrich Rueschemeyer, and Theda Skocpol, eds., *Bringing the State Back In* (New York: Cambridge University Press, 1985), p. 6.

Critical Perspectives

This chapter discusses four *critical perspectives* that do *not* agree on a core set of assumptions: historical materialism, constructivism, feminism, and environmentalism. Three of these perspectives—constructivism, feminism, and environmentalism—have liberal as well as critical variants; but we include them in this chapter for two reasons. First, constructivism, feminism, and environmentalism were not traditionally of interest to mainstream IPE theorists, and many mainstream theorists continue to devote little attention to them. Second, it is useful to compare the liberal and critical variants of these three perspectives in the same chapter. This chapter devotes more attention to historical materialism than to the other perspectives because it encompasses the largest group of critical theories, including Marxism, dependency theory, world-systems theory, and Gramscian analysis. Although these approaches all have some roots in Marxism, they often diverge substantially from classical Marxist thought. **Historical materialism** is "historical" because it examines structural change in terms of class and sometimes North–South struggles over time, and it is "materialist" because it examines the role of material (especially economic) factors in shaping society.[1]

BASIC TENETS OF HISTORICAL MATERIALISM

The Role of the Individual, the State, and Societal Groups

Marxists see "class" as the main factor affecting the economic and political order. Each mode of production (e.g., feudalism and capitalism) is associated with an exploiting nonproducing class and an exploited class of producers. Classes are absent only in the simplest primitive-communal mode of production and in the future Communist mode. Thus, Karl Marx and Friedrich Engels wrote in *The Communist Manifesto* that "the history of all hitherto existing society is the history of class struggles." Modern bourgeois society "has not done away with class antagonisms. It has but established new classes, new conditions of oppression, new forms of struggle in place of the old ones."[2] Marx and Engels view the state as an agent of the dominant class, the bourgeoisie, which uses it as an instrument to exploit wage labor. Although the state may have some autonomy from a dominant class during transition periods when the power of classes is more equally balanced, the state cannot escape from its dependence on the capitalist class in the longer term.[3] Only when the proletarian revolution eliminates class distinctions based on private ownership will the state no longer be an instrument of class oppression. Some historical materialists criticize Marx and Engels' position that state actions simply reflect the views of the dominant class (see discussion below).

The Nature and Purpose of International Economic Relations

Historical materialists see economic relations historically as conflictual, with one part of society exploiting another.[4] The views of historical materialists evolved along with changes in the international system. Thus, Marx and Engels predicted that contradictions within capitalism would contribute to poverty of the working class, surplus production, economic downturns, and the collapse of capitalism. Vladimir Lenin later attributed the survival of capitalism to *imperialism*, asserting that colonies provided the "metropole" states with a cheap source of raw materials and a market for their surplus production.[5] When capitalism persisted after decolonization, historical materialists attributed this to *neocolonialism*: Although the imperial powers had ceded *political* control, they retained *economic* control over their former colonies.[6] As we discuss, dependency, world-systems, and Gramscian theorists offer other explanations for capitalism's persistence. Historical materialists favor a redistribution of power and wealth, and they do not believe that this can occur with unfettered capitalism. Although historical materialists advocate for the poor and less powerful, they take different approaches to dealing with capitalism's inequities. Some accept certain elements of market capitalism whereas others totally reject it, and some believe in evolutionary reform whereas others advocate revolution.

The Relationship Between Politics and Economics

Marx describes history as a dialectical process, marked by a contradiction between the economic mode of production (e.g., feudalism and capitalism) and the political system. This contradiction is resolved when changes in the mode and relations of production eventually cause the political "superstructure" to change. Thus, Marx provided the foundation for **instrumental Marxism**, which—like liberal pluralism—sees government as responding in a rather passive manner to economic pressures.[7] Liberals see any societal group as having political influence, whereas instrumental Marxists believe that a state's policies reflect the interests of the capitalist class. To support their position, instrumental Marxists point to personal ties between capitalists and public officials and to the movement of individuals between business and government.[8] After World War II, many scholars criticized instrumental Marxism because DCs adopted welfare and unemployment insurance policies *despite* the opposition of business groups. As a result, **structural Marxism** emerged, which sees the state as relatively autonomous from direct political pressure of the capitalist class. Although some capitalists oppose state policies benefiting workers, they do not realize that these policies serve their long-term interests. By providing welfare and other benefits, the state placates the workers and gains their support for capitalism.[9] Structural Marxists differ from neomercantilists even though they both see the state as somewhat autonomous. In the structural Marxist view, the bourgeoisie does not *directly* control the state, but the two share a commitment to the survival of capitalism. Neomercantilists, by contrast, see the state as furthering the "national interest" independently of the economic interests of any societal group.

The Causes and Effects of Globalization

Marxists view the bourgeoisie as promoting globalization because it increases their profits and helps them control the proletariat. Marxists and liberals agree that technological advances can facilitate globalization. However, liberals see these technological advances as resulting from natural human drives for economic progress, whereas Marxists see them as resulting from "historically specific impulses of capitalist development."[10] Unlike liberals, Marxists view globalization as a negative process that prevents states from safeguarding domestic welfare and employment. Adjustment to global competitiveness is the new imperative, and states must adapt to the needs of the global economy; for example, indebted LDCs must impose adjustment measures on vulnerable groups such as women and children to become more globally competitive.

Globalization is also increasing the structural power of capital over labor. **Capital** is a factor of production, along with land and labor; it consists of physical assets such as equipment, tools, buildings, and other manufactured goods that can generate income and financial assets. Historical materialists focus on capital's exploitation of labor in the capitalist system. For example, states are dependent on foreign investment and must respond to business demands by disciplining trade unions and pressuring for lower wages. Furthermore, a new transnational managerial class has divided the labor force by shifting production from the mass production factory to many small component-producing and servicing units. Historical materialists also see globalization as a cause of environmental degradation, the illegal drug trade, intra-ethnic conflict, and civil society protests. Whereas some historical materialists oppose globalization in general, most focus their criticisms on capitalist globalization.[11]

EARLY FORMS OF HISTORICAL MATERIALISM

Karl Marx

Karl Marx (1818–1883) was one of the world's most influential economic theorists, but most mainstream economic textbooks devote little attention to him. Although *The Communist Manifesto* was Marx and Engels' (1820–1895) most politically influential publication, Marx's major work was *Das Kapital*, or *Capital* in English translation.[12] Marx focused on the growing gap between the wealthy *bourgeoisie* and the working class or *proletariat*, and on the exploitation of workers by the capitalists. Marx's *labor theory of value* describes a product's value as being determined, not by capital, but by the amount of labor put into its production. However, workers are paid less than the value of what they produce, because the capitalists expropriate the *surplus value* created by labor. Workers are paid only the minimum wage required for subsistence living so they will continue producing goods, and the growing ranks of the unemployed enable the capitalists to continue exploiting the workers. The division of labor under capitalism also causes *alienation* of the workers, with their work losing "all individual character, and consequently, all charm."[13] Marx describes each historical period as marked by a dominant mode of production with a particular set of property rights and institutions. The mode of production provides the basis for a particular ideological *superstructure* which includes the government, the legal system, and other elements of society. As productive forces develop through innovation and advances in technology, there is growing tension between the productive forces and the mode of production. This tension eventually results in a revolution leading to a new mode of production and ideological superstructure. This dialectical process explains the displacement of feudalism by capitalism, and the proletariat would soon rise against the bourgeoisie and replace capitalism with socialism and Communism. If Marx and Engels viewed the Communist revolution as inevitable, why did they regularly urge the workers to take action? This apparent contradiction made Marxism appealing both to the intellectual who simply wanted to sit back and watch the inevitable process occur, and to the activist who wanted to urge others to join the revolution. Marx also never clearly described what the characteristics of the new society would be under Communism. He seemed to portray a utopian society in which there would be an end to class oppression, and no further tension between productive forces and the mode of production.[14]

Although Marx did not write systematically about IR, his theory of capitalism and class struggle provided the framework for historical materialism in IPE. Marx wrote many articles about the effect of Western capitalism on non-European areas, but he had little direct experience with these areas.[15] He believed that capitalism emerged in Europe when feudal landholdings were converted into bourgeois property. India and China, by contrast, had an "Asiatic" mode of production outside the mainstream of Western development. The state's presence was much greater in the Asiatic mode, with the central governments in China and India developing large public work projects to provide water over extensive land areas. At the local level, small, self-sufficient village communities had communal rather than individual ownership. Thus, Marx saw no basis for a transformation to private capitalist holdings in the Asiatic mode. Marx argued that external pressure from Western colonialism was necessary for China and India to progress to capitalism and then to socialism.[16]

Marx harshly criticized England for preventing India from exporting cotton to Europe and for inundating it with British textiles; but he also criticized India for lacking capitalism's capacity for development.[17] In contrast to stagnating Asiatic societies, Marx viewed capitalism as a dynamic, expansive system with a historic mission to spread development throughout the world. Thus, Marx believed that England performed a dual function in India: destroying the old society and providing the foundation for Western society, which would provide the conditions for a Communist revolution in Asia:

> Can mankind fulfill its destiny without a fundamental revolution in the social state of Asia? If not, whatever may have been the crimes of England, she was the unconscious tool of history in bringing about that revolution.[18]

Marx's analysis of Asia had major defects due to his lack of direct experience and his Eurocentric prejudices, and later in life he repudiated some of his own ideas regarding the Asiatic mode of production.[19]

Vladimir Lenin: The Study of Imperialism

Although Marx wrote about the international effects of capitalism on non-European societies, systematic studies of imperialism depended on later writers. Theories of imperialism portray the world as hierarchical, with some societies engaging in conquest and control over others. John Hobson (1858–1940), a non-Marxist English economist, developed an economic theory of imperialism that identified three major problems of capitalist societies: low wages and underconsumption by workers, oversaving by capitalists, and overproduction. The workers had limited purchasing power because they were paid such low wages, and overproduction became a problem. The capitalists had to look to countries abroad as an outlet for their surplus goods and profits, and this gave rise to imperialism.[20] Despite Hobson's influence, Vladimir Lenin's (1870–1924) *Imperialism: The Highest Stage of Capitalism* became the most widely cited work in this area.[21] Lenin focused on imperialism of the late nineteenth century when "the dominance of monopolies and finance capital established itself" and "the division of all territories of the globe among the great capitalist powers [was] ... completed."[22] Although Hobson and Lenin agreed that imperialism resulted from low wages and underconsumption by workers, Hobson as a liberal assumed that imperialism would no longer be needed as an outlet for surpluses if workers' wages increased *within* the capitalist system. Lenin by contrast viewed exploitation of the workers and imperialism as *inevitable* outcomes of capitalism. Whereas Hobson believed in evolution within the capitalist system, Lenin saw revolution as the only alternative.

Lenin also invoked imperialism to explain why the revolution had not occurred in the most advanced European capitalist states as Marx had predicted. The export of capital and goods to colonial areas provided "super-profits," which the capitalists used to bribe the working class in their home countries with higher wages and social benefits. This created a "labor aristocracy" committed to the European metropole states that slowed the movement to Marxism. However, imperialism did not resolve capitalism's contradictions, and the revolution was still inevitable. Capitalist states were dividing the globe into colonial areas, and when there were no longer new areas to conquer, attempts to redistribute the spoils of colonialism would lead to inter-imperialist wars and the downfall of capitalism. Thus, Lenin viewed World War I as more related to control of the colonies than to control of Europe. Although Lenin viewed revolution as inevitable, like Marx he was somewhat contradictory on this issue. Thus, Lenin wrote that "the history of all countries shows that the working class, exclusively by its own effort, is able to develop only trade union consciousness."[23] Only a well-organized revolutionary party acting as a *vanguard of the proletariat* could cultivate a radical class consciousness among the workers. In other words, political forces were necessary to help bring about the (inevitable) revolution. Lenin's position on the effects of colonialism was also somewhat ambivalent. Although capitalist states opposed industrialization in the colonies and used them as a source of raw materials, Lenin viewed colonialism as a progressive force essential for Southern development. Western exports of capital and technology to the colonies would help create foreign competitors with lower wages, and the increased competition between rising and declining capitalist powers would lead to imperial rivalries and conflict. However, colonialism did not bring industrialization and development to the colonies as Marx and Lenin had predicted. Even after Latin American colonies gained their independence in the nineteenth century, they continued to depend on external capital and technology, and on primary product exports. The failure to bring about capitalist development led to major rifts among Marxists, with some arguing that imperialism was economically regressive.[24] As the following discussion shows, dependency theorists turned Marxism on its head and focused on capitalism's role in hindering rather than facilitating LDC development.

Dependency Theory

Dependency theory, the dominant approach to development among Latin American intellectuals in the 1960s, rejects the optimism of liberal modernization theory (see Chapter 4) and argues that advanced capitalist states either underdevelop LDCs or prevent them from achieving genuine autonomous development. Dependency theory stems from two theoretical traditions: *Marxism* and *Latin American structuralism*. Like Marxists, dependency theorists focus on capitalist development; use terms such as *class, mode of production*, and *imperialism*; and support replacing capitalism with socialism. However, dependency theorists reject orthodox Marxist views that DCs benefit LDCs in the long term by contributing to the spread of capitalism. Dependency theory stems from the ideas of the Argentinian economist Raúl Prebisch and other Latin American "structuralists," who focused on structural obstacles to LDC development. Prebisch rejected liberal assumptions that free trade was beneficial and argued that LDCs in the periphery suffer from declining **terms of trade** with DCs in the core. As people's incomes increase, they demand more industrial goods, *not* more primary products; if LDCs try to raise the prices for their raw materials, DCs can develop substitute or synthetic products. Thus, Prebisch advised LDCs to adopt *import substitution industrialization (ISI)* policies that impose import barriers on industrial goods, and produce the goods domestically; and in the 1960s–1970s many LDCs took his advice.[25] We discuss ISI in detail in Chapters 7 and 11; for our purposes here we simply note that ISI contributed to various problems such as growing balance-of-payments deficits. Thus, scholars challenged Prebisch's views from both the right and the left, and many leftists turned to dependency theory. Unlike Prebisch, dependency theorists argue that DCs will never permit LDCs to achieve genuine, autonomous development.[26]

There are two groups of dependency theorists: A group inspired by André Gunder Frank's *Capitalism and Underdevelopment in Latin America* takes a more doctrinaire position; and a group inspired by Fernando Henrique Cardoso and Enzo Faletto's *Dependency and Development in Latin America* takes a less doctrinaire approach.[27] They differ in several respects. First, dependency theorists argue that the North benefits from global capitalist linkages and dynamic development based on internal needs, whereas the South's development is severely constrained because of its interaction with the North. Whereas Frank focused on external factors inhibiting the South's development, Cardoso and Faletto rejected the idea that "external factors … were enough to explain the dynamic of societies," and they examined the relationship between "internal and external processes of political domination."[28] For example, they contend that elites in the South (*compradores*) act as a national bourgeoisie, forming alliances with capitalists in the North that reinforce LDC dependency. A second difference relates to their views regarding the possibilities for LDC development. Dependency theorists in the Frank strain argued that the development of capitalist economies in the core *required* the underdevelopment of the periphery. Although LDCs were *un*developed in the past, they became *under*developed as a result of their involvement with the core.[29] Theorists in the Cardoso–Faletto strain took a more nuanced approach, arguing that "associated dependent development" was sometimes possible in the periphery.[30] With dependent development, LDCs can begin to produce capital goods, but they are less sophisticated and depend on imports of machinery, technology, and foreign investment from the core. The Cardoso–Faletto strain gained support because industrialization *was* occurring in some LDCs, and even Frank began writing about dependent development in the East Asian NIEs.[31]

Dependency theorists became a major target of criticism in the 1970s–1980s for several reasons. First, they were criticized for lacking conceptual clarity: They see states as dependent or independent and do not measure different levels of dependence. Furthermore, "core" and "periphery" are overly broad categories; do we include Haiti with Brazil in the periphery, and Greece with the United States in the core? Second, dependency theorists only discuss capitalist exploitation. Critics argue that the most important factor in dependency is unequal power, and that capitalism and Soviet Communism were both marked by "asymmetric and unequal linkages between a dominant center and its weaker dependencies."[32] Third, dependency theorists often prescribe a breaking of linkages with the core and a socialist revolution. However, critics note that cutting linkages with the core does not ensure that a country will "emphasize distribution and participation rather than accumulation and exclusion."[33] Fourth, dependency theorists focus so much on the global economy that they do not adequately explain why LDCs may respond differently to similar external constraints. The Cardoso–Faletto strain examines the relationship between internal and external processes, but even it gives primacy to external factors.[34] Fifth, dependency theory's predictions regarding development are often incorrect. For example, theorists held up China as a model of agrarian self-reliance, but in 1976 it adopted more open policies that contributed to its rapid economic growth. Finally, orthodox Marxists assert that dependency theorists are overly nationalistic. They criticize dependency theorists for focusing more on "relations of exchange" (between core and peripheral states) than on "relations of production" (between classes).[35]

Although many of these criticisms have validity, it is unfortunate that they were often aimed at the more doctrinaire strain associated with Frank. Cardoso and Faletto's major book was not translated from Spanish into English until about eight years after it was published, so the early U.S. and Canadian "consumption" of dependency theory relied on the Frank approach.[36] Dependency theory served an important function in several respects. First, dependency theory often overemphasized external factors, but it counterbalanced the overemphasis of liberal modernization theory on internal factors. Second, the Cardoso–Faletto strain sensitized us to the relationship between internal and external factors affecting development. Third, dependency theorists sensitized us to the differences in wealth and power between some LDCs in the periphery and the DCs in the core. Although scholars today rarely identify themselves as dependency theorists, they continue to examine "many issues and areas of development where dependency plays a major role."[37]

WHITHER THE HISTORICAL MATERIALIST PERSPECTIVE?

With the breakup of the Soviet bloc and the end of the Cold War, some mainstream theorists see historical materialism as no longer relevant. For example, one liberal theorist argues that "the implosion of the Soviet Union, and domestic changes in Eastern Europe, have eliminated the significance of the socialist economic model," and another claims that we are witnessing the "victory of economic and political liberalism."[38] However, there are reasons to expect a renewed interest in historical materialism. First, the breakup of the Soviet bloc enables theorists to express Marxist ideas without having to defend the heavy-handed actions of the Soviet Union. Second, Marxist predictions that capitalism's contradictions would lead to serious crises have gained some support from financial crises since the 1980s (see Chapter 7). Third, growing inequalities between rich and poor in a number of states are reviving interest in alternatives to the liberal economic model. For example, the share of total income going to the top 1 percent of earners in the United States rose from 8.9 percent in 1976 to 23.5 percent in 2007.[39] Historical materialism continues to have appeal because of its focus on the poor, the weak, and distributive justice issues. The following sections discuss more recent theories with links to historical materialism.

World-Systems Theory

Whereas dependency theory focuses on core–periphery relations, **world-systems theory** focuses on the entire world-system, including relationships among core states and the rise and decline of hegemons.[40] The main unit of analysis in world-systems theory is the *world-system*, which has "a single division of labor and multiple cultural systems."[41] There are two types of world-systems: world-empires and world-economies. In a *world-empire*, a single political entity (such as ancient Rome) often uses coercive power to control the economic division of labor between the core and the periphery. The modern world-system is a *world-economy*, because no single state has conquered the entire core region. Instead, states engage in a "hegemonic sequence," in which various hegemonic states (the Netherlands, Britain, and the United States) rise and fall. Today the capitalist world-economy is the only world-system. Although states establish a power hierarchy through market mechanisms, the core states may use force when peripheral states challenge the market rules. Immanuel Wallerstein asserts that the capitalist world-economy emerged in Europe during the "long" sixteenth century (1450–1640), but some other theorists argue that it originated earlier in the Middle East or Asia.[42] The capitalist world-economy's main features are production for the market to gain the maximum profit, and unequal exchange relations between core and peripheral states.[43]

World-systems theorists do not consider states to be meaningful actors apart from their position in the world-economy; thus, long before the breakup of the Soviet Union, Wallerstein wrote that there are "no socialist systems in the world-economy any more than there are feudal systems because there is *one* [capitalist] world-system."[44] World-systems theorists also believe that a state's strength cannot be viewed separately from its position in the world-economy. Core states are strong because of their dominant position in the world-economy, whereas peripheral states are weak. In contrast to dependency theorists, world-systems theorists introduced the *semiperiphery* between the periphery and the core to account for the fact that some LDCs are industrializing. Some states have moved up or down in the hierarchy, but world-systems theorists are more pessimistic than liberals about the prospects for today's LDCs. Although some semiperipheral states *seem* to be models of economic success, they are simply "the more advanced exemplars of dependent development."[45] The semiperiphery divides the periphery so the core states do not face a unified opposition, and this stabilizes the capitalist world-economy. Despite this apparent stability, capitalism has contradictions, and world-systems theorists raise the prospect of its replacement by socialism. More recently, Wallerstein has focused on the decline of U.S. hegemony and on the growing crises facing capitalism. He argues that the capitalist world-economy cannot persist forever, and he examines the possibilities of developing a more equitable world-economy.[46]

Theorists have subjected world-systems theory to wide-ranging criticisms. Neomercantilists see world-systems analysts as undertheorizing the role of the state. Wallerstein only examines the incorporation of states into the world-economy, and he simply assumes that strong states are in the core and weak states are in the periphery.[47] In the sixteenth century, however, some strong states such as Spain and Sweden were in the periphery, while core states such as Holland and England had relatively weak state structures. Indeed, late industrializers often require strong states to promote their development.[48] Liberals argue that world-systems theorists generalize about capitalism, without noticing variations during different historical periods. For example, merchant capitalism under Dutch hegemony was quite different from competitive capitalism under U.S. hegemony. Marxists assert that world-systems theory puts more emphasis on "relations of exchange" among the core, semiperiphery, and periphery than on "relations of production" between capitalists and workers. Despite its shortcomings, world-systems theory offers a long-term historical view of economic and political change. Many liberals by contrast underestimate the historical differences between industrializing countries in the past and LDCs today, and the neomercantilist approach is often ahistorical. Although world-systems theorists overestimate the degree to which external exploitation causes LDC problems, orthodox liberals err in the opposite direction by downplaying the role of external exploitation in the capitalist world economy.

Neo-Gramscian Analysis

Neo-Gramscian analysis is "the most influential Marxist theory in ... contemporary international relations."[49] It draws on the writings of Antonio Gramsci (1891–1937), a theorist and social activist who was a former leader of the Italian Communist party. Despite his Marxist linkages, Gramsci saw Marxism as unable to explain the role of Catholicism and the rise of Mussolini in Italy because it was *economistic* (it exaggerated the importance of economics). In discussing capitalist domination and the reorganization of society under socialism, Gramsci examined the interaction of economics with politics, ideology, and culture. In the 1980s Robert Cox developed "neo-Gramscian IPE" by extending Gramsci's ideas about Italy to the international sphere.[50]

Whereas neomercantilists view hegemony in terms of a predominant state, Gramscians view hegemony in class terms. A dominant class that rules only by coercion is not hegemonic because its power does not extend throughout society and it can be overthrown simply by physical force. To attain hegemony, the dominant class must gain the active consent of subordinate classes based on shared values, ideas, and material interests. Thus, the dominant class portrays its policies as being beneficial for all classes, and provides incentives and rewards to subordinate groups to gain their support and divide the opposition. For example, the bourgeoisie gained the support of subordinate classes by offering them economic benefits and accepting labor unions. Gramscians use the term **historic bloc** to describe the congruence between state power, ideas, and institutions that guide the society and economy. It is difficult for subordinate groups to replace a historic bloc because it is supported by the power of ideas as well as physical power. Gramsci used his discussion of the bourgeois historic bloc to explain why revolution had not occurred in the most advanced European countries as Marx had predicted. However, Gramsci called for building a *counterhegemony*—an alternative ethical view of society—to challenge capitalism. The decline of government economic benefits in this age of global competitiveness could induce subordinate classes to develop a counterhegemony.[51]

Applying Gramsci's ideas to IPE, Cox writes that the KIEOs legitimized liberal norms and U.S. hegemony with a minimal amount of force. A *transnational historic bloc* composed of the largest MNCs, international banks, business groups, and IOs also extended class relations to the global level. Central to this historic bloc is the power and mobility of transnational capital, which is extending neoliberalism on a global scale. The ability of transnational capital and MNCs to shift location among states enables them to play off less mobile national labor groups against each other. Workers in MNCs also identify their interests with transnational capital, and this divides the working class and limits its ability to build a counterhegemony. Further solidifying this transnational historic bloc is a hegemonic ideology that sees capital mobility as beneficial.[52] However, civil society dissatisfaction with this transnational historic bloc could stimulate a counterhegemony. Although civil society protests at IMF, World Bank, and WTO meetings have not attained the status of a counterhegemonic alliance, they demonstrate concern about the effects of neoliberal globalization on people's lives.[53]

Neo-Gramscian theory has been criticized by groups on both the right and left. Liberal critics argue that concessions such as economic benefits are genuine changes that cannot be dismissed simply as attempts to co-opt subordinate classes. Some critical theorists charge that neo-Gramscians focus more on the durability of capitalism than on the process of developing a counterhegemony. Marxists criticize neo-Gramscians for focusing so much on ideology and culture that they underestimate the centrality of economics, and some even argue that "a recognizable Marxism has been largely purged from neo-Gramscian IR."[54] Feminist theorists criticize neo-Gramscians for treating gender as a side issue; this is curious for "a perspective that focuses on social relations" and emancipation.[55] Despite these criticisms, Gramscian analysis has many strengths. Because neomercantilists and liberals define hegemony in state-centric terms, their study of hegemony is limited to a small number of relatively brief historical periods. Neo-Gramscians, by contrast, use the term *hegemony* in a cultural sense that applies to a much wider range of relationships in the global economy. As discussed, neo-Gramscians focus on the interaction of ideas and material interests and thus avoid the economism of Marxists.

CONSTRUCTIVISM

The discipline of IPE developed with theoretical tools that were *rationalist* in assuming that states, firms, and classes make decisions by weighing the costs against the benefits. The tools were also *materialist* in assuming that international constraints on states and other actors stem from material factors such as armaments, money, and natural resources. For example, John Mearsheimer asserts that "the distribution of material capabilities among states is the key factor for understanding world politics"; and Marx's materialist view of history posited that "real living individuals," *not* their ideas, are central to understanding the laws of history.[56] **Constructivism** by contrast does not simply assume that an actor's preferences reflect rational choices; it examines the beliefs, traditions, roles, ideologies, and patterns of influence that shape preferences, behavior, and outcomes. Constructivists devote considerable attention to the role of collectively held or *intersubjective* ideas in IR. They are interested in understanding how our sense of identity and interests become established as *social facts*, or the meanings people attach to objects. Social facts result from collectively held beliefs, which exist only because people agree they exist. For example, shared understandings that a country's monetary reserves have value determine that they are not simply worthless pieces of paper. Social facts differ from *material facts*, or the physical properties of objects that exist regardless of shared beliefs. Constructivists do not reject material reality, but they note that the construction of material reality depends on ideas and interpretation. Constructivists also examine the relationship between structures and agents. Whereas *structures* are "the institutions and shared meanings that make up the context of international action" (e.g., the international system), *agents* are "any entity that operates as an actor in that context" (e.g., states are agents that operate in the international system).[57] Constructivists refer to the "co-constitution" of agents and structures, because the actions of states (agents) can alter the institutions and norms, and the institutions and norms (structures) can alter the way a state defines its situation. For example, states are concerned both with revising international trade rules and norms to condone their behavior, and with altering their behavior to adhere to the trade rules and norms.

Constructivism did not emerge as a social theory in IR until the 1980s, and Nicholas Onuf coined the term in 1989.[58] Whereas liberal constructivists are willing to engage in a dialogue with the mainstream perspectives, critical constructivists take a more extreme position; they seek to "deconstruct" what mainstream theorists assume as givens, and advocate a change in social structures and relationships.[59] As with other IPE theoretical approaches, the boundaries between constructivism and materialism are sometimes blurred. For example, an emerging branch of economic constructivism uses statistical methods to objectively compare the causal role of ideas with other variables. However, most constructivists have a strong preference for qualitative methods.[60] Despite some blurring of boundaries with materialists, all constructivists agree that to understand political processes and outcomes, we need to examine intersubjective or collectively held beliefs.

Liberal constructivists have increased their influence in the mainstream, and constructivism today has become "one of the main analytic orientations for mainstream IR research."[61] Even materialist theories now incorporate nonmaterial factors such as socially constructed ideas and interests, but they continue to attribute more importance to material factors. Whereas the most prominent debates in IR theory in the 1980s–1990s were between realism and liberalism, some argue that the most important IR mainstream debate today is between rationalism and constructivism.[62] However, many U.S. scholars are uncomfortable with constructivism because it devotes more attention to "social facts" than "material facts" and does not adhere to the systematic, objective testing of hypotheses. Even those who agree that ideas, cultures, and identities affect political actors often assume that *economic* actors rationally pursue *material* interests. Thus, security specialists have been more open to constructivism than IPE specialists. We discuss how constructivism has affected the study of IPE in the examples below and in the substantive chapters of this book.

Scholarly work in areas such as epistemic communities has enabled liberal regime theorists to benefit from the insights of constructivists.[63] An **epistemic community** is "a network of professionals with recognized expertise and competence in a particular domain and an authoritative claim to policy-relevant knowledge within that domain or issue-area."[64] The literature explores the role of knowledge-based experts in framing international issues and helping states define their interests. For example, an epistemic community composed mainly of American and British experts helped shape the Bretton Woods order. U.S. economic power was increasing, and State Department officials wanted an open trading system. Britain's economy by contrast was severely damaged by the war, and British cabinet officials favored a preferential trading system to bolster employment and economic stability. A set of policy ideas inspired by Keynes and supported by an epistemic community of U.S. and British specialists helped create a new system of interventionist liberalism acceptable to both countries (see Chapter 4).[65]

IPE concepts such as the gross domestic product (GDP) are also based on shared ideas and values. Although the GDP seems to be a "material fact" that measures the output of goods and services, it is also a "social fact," because shared values determine what is included. Whereas goods and services with market values are included in the GDP, economic activities within households are excluded. Feminist scholars argue that this decision reflects the downgrading of the role of women, who do most of the household work in the economy. Shared values also determine that environmental measures are not included in the GDP even though environmental degradation may have detrimental effects on economic productivity.[66]

Some constructivists believe that national identities influence how countries "interpret the material facts of their foreign economic relations."[67]

For example, some former Soviet republics viewed economic dependence on Russia as a threat to national security, while others saw it as a reason for closer ties with Russia. Thus, some adopted a Western orientation in finance and trade, while others joined Russia in the new Commonwealth of Independent States (CIS). Constructivists attribute these differences to each new state's sense of self, arguing that states with a stronger sense of national identity were more inclined to distance themselves from the CIS.[68] Constructivists have also analyzed the role of ideas in relation to the 2008 global financial crisis. Some examples relate to debates over the regulation of banks and the emphasis on government stimulus versus austerity. One highly relevant study is Mark Blyth's *Austerity: The History of a Dangerous Idea.*[69]

FEMINISM

This section provides a brief introduction to **feminist theory** and IPE, and it cannot cover the broad scope of feminist research. As a group that is often marginalized, feminist theorists are open to a diversity of thought and reject the idea of developing a single IR theory. Thus, one classification divides feminist thought into liberal, radical, socialist, psychoanalytic, existentialist, postmodern, multicultural, and ecofeminist variants.[70] We discuss feminist theorists in this chapter because they criticize the mainstream perspectives for their inattention to gender issues; thus, they often ask, "Where are the women?" in studies of IR and IPE.[71] Feminist theorists also generally agree that patriarchy exists in almost all societies. **Patriarchy** refers to a system of society or government in which men hold most of the power. However, it is important to differentiate the liberal and critical variants of feminism. *Liberal feminists* examine various aspects of women's subordination, such as income inequalities, the lack of women in positions of influence, and the plight of refugee and immigrant women. They accept the liberal institutions under capitalism, and propose that more inclusion of women in positions of influence is the best way to address gender inequality. Thus, liberal feminists are concerned with removing barriers so that women have the same opportunities as men. *Critical feminists* by contrast believe that inequality and exclusion are *inherent* characteristics of liberal institutions, because capitalism differentiates "production" from "reproduction." A major part of women's work is reproduction of the male work force, which does not count as a productive activity in an economic sense. Thus, critical feminists view the replacement of liberal institutions with more egalitarian models as the only way to move beyond patriarchy. Legal changes will not give women equality without changing social perceptions of what are "natural" occupations for men and women.[72] Whereas sex refers to biological differences between male and female, feminist scholars view *gender* as "a structural feature of social life" that "shapes how we identify, think, and communicate."[73] A *gendered division of labor* has divided people according to what is considered appropriate work for men and women. Whereas men are associated with the public sphere as wage earners, women are associated with the private sphere as housewives, mothers, and caregivers. When women work outside the home they often receive lower wages than men for similar work, because their pay is seen as supplemental to family income.[74] Thus, feminist scholars examine "the unequal gender hierarchies that exist in all societies and their effects on the subordination of women and other marginalized groups."[75]

Feminist studies came later to IR, partly because IR specialists after World War II focused on the "high politics" of diplomacy, war, and statecraft. Scholars simply assumed that political and military leaders, and soldiers were male. When IPE emerged as a discipline in the 1970s, its emphasis on international finance, trade, and production and its rationalist methodology also left little room for studying gender relations. Development theory was the one exception, but the literature on women and development was "marginalized from mainstream theories of political and economic development."[76] A major theme of the women and development literature is that pre-existing gender relations affect the outcome of development policies. For example, IMF and World Bank structural adjustment loans required indebted LDCs to reduce spending on social services such as health care, education, and food subsidies; this downloaded more responsibility to women as the main caregivers in households (see Chapter 11).

Feminist scholars argue that the main IPE perspectives largely ignore the role of women. Liberalism measures production and participation in the labor force only in terms of the market, or working for pay or profit. However, women often work in the subsistence sector of LDC economies or provide basic household needs. Because this work does not involve payment for goods and services, these women are considered "nonproducers" who should not share in the benefits of global economic production.[77] Deregulation, privatization, and other neoliberal strategies have been damaging to women because of their dependence on the state for public services that support families. Neomercantilism views the state as the main unit of analysis, but in many respects the state is a gendered construct. Men are normally responsible for advancing the state's security interests, and women are in an inferior position because of gender differences in inheritance rights and wages for comparable work, and the inattention to domestic and sexual violence.[78] Neomercantilism also gives priority to maximizing wealth and power, but it does not consider the effects on women who are near the bottom of the economic scale. Historical materialism focuses on class-based oppression of workers, but it does not consider patriarchy-based oppression of women. Thus, some feminist scholars assert that by ignoring gender, historical materialism "mirrors the tactics that have so commonly been wielded by the mainstream against the fringes."[79] Some claim that the main IPE perspectives are "gender neutral, meaning that … the interaction between states and markets … can be understood without reference to gender distinctions."[80] However, feminists argue that those who ignore gender distinctions simply reinforce the unequal economic relations between men and women. Many feminist theorists take a constructivist or postmodern approach to increase our understanding of "subjectivity, reflexivity, meaning, and value."[81]

ENVIRONMENTALISM

Environmentalism has become a more central concern for some IPE theorists because of the growing interaction between global economic and environmental issues. IPE specialists are concerned with two types of environmental problems: the problem of *additions*, through the spread of pollution and other contaminants over the land, air, and water; and the problem of *withdrawals*, or the *depletion* of nonrenewable resources such as oil and gas.[82] Economic development will not be "sustainable" if it seriously exacerbates the problems of environmental additions and withdrawals. **Sustainable development** refers to development that meets "the needs of the present without compromising the ability of future generations to meet their own needs."[83] Environmental theory is discussed in this chapter because the mainstream IPE perspectives for many years devoted little attention to environmental concerns. However, some environmentalists identify more closely with mainstream IPE theorists, whereas others identify with critical theorists.

Neomercantilists often describe environmental issues as peripheral to the main concerns of states with power and wealth. States are not going to fulfill environmental commitments that disadvantage them economically or pose a threat to their security. Thus, neomercantilists can point to the failure of most states to fulfill the objectives of global environmental conferences. In 1992, shortly after the end of the Cold War, the *UN Conference on Environment and Development* (the *Rio Earth Summit*) developed the Rio Declaration to promote sustainable development, and a 350-page voluntary action plan. However, in the 24 years since the Rio Earth Summit global environmental goals have rarely been met: "Of the ninety most important global environmental goals, only four showed progress in 2012."[84] Furthermore, the outcome of the 2012 *UN Conference on Sustainable Development (Rio+20)* was ambiguous, because major participants had more pressing concerns. The United States was preoccupied with the effects of the financial crisis and preparations for the 2010 presidential election; China and India had growth and stability concerns; and there was growing turmoil in the Middle East. The failure to establish a strong global environmental regime is not surprising, because the most powerful states only establish and adhere to regime principles, norms, and rules that further their national interests.

Although neomercantilists do not see much of a future for environmental conference diplomacy, they do view states as having some major environmental concerns related to natural resources. The issue of *energy security* has strong geopolitical as well as environmental linkages, and oil is central to energy security concerns because it is a finite resource that has a vital role in national economies. Conflicting views about the extent of global petroleum reserves and the economic and environmental consequences of exploiting them have made oil an important source of power and influence. Neomercantilists first began to view energy security as a major issue when Arab OPEC countries limited supplies, and oil prices quadrupled after the October 1973 Middle East war. Oil prices have declined recently, partly because of *hydraulic fracturing* or *fracking* in the United States and elsewhere. Fracking is a process of creating fractures in rocks by injecting liquid at high pressure to extract oil and gas. Neomercantilists concerned with energy security cannot easily avoid examining such controversial issues as the long-term effects of fracking on the environment.

Liberals are optimistic about people's ability to improve environmental conditions through progress in science and technology. However, orthodox, interventionist, and institutional liberals have different views regarding the role of the market, government, and institutions in effectuating environmental change. *Orthodox liberals* believe that economic growth is the main factor behind better environmental policies. Even if some business activities adversely affect air and water quality in the short term, they contribute to economic growth which will improve environmental conditions over time. Rapid economic growth may exacerbate income inequalities between the rich and poor, but orthodox liberals view this as a positive-sum game, in which everyone will benefit in the longer term. As the income of people increases, they have more ability and incentive to improve the environment. Thus, the best policy for the environment is to promote economic growth through open trade and foreign investment policies without government interference. In globally integrated markets, business firms recognize that their competitiveness will improve in the longer term if they are sensitive to environmental issues.

Interventionist liberals also prefer market-based solutions to environmental problems, but they favor some government involvement to address the market's inadequacies and ensure that business firms follow environmentally friendly policies. Governments should use market-based rather than mandatory policies whenever possible to protect the environment, such as environmental taxes, tradable pollution permits, and market incentives to encourage firms to produce environmental products. Governments should also encourage firms to adopt voluntary measures to improve environmental conditions.

Institutional liberals also prefer market-based solutions, but they call for strong global institutions to coordinate efforts to deal with environmental degradation, pollution, and resource scarcity. Despite the shortcomings of institutional efforts to this point, they believe that institution-building is essential to confront environmental challenges. For example, institutional liberals such as Oran Young have examined the effectiveness of international environmental regimes in dealing with oil pollution, the management of fisheries, and acid rain.[85] Institutional liberals also support World Bank, UN Environment Program, and Global Environment Facility efforts to provide technology, finance, and knowledge to help LDCs promote sustainable development. Achieving positive results has been difficult, but institutional liberals firmly believe in the continuing efforts to promote environmental awareness and increased cooperation through UN conference diplomacy. Whereas the IMF, World Bank, and WTO have measures in place to significantly affect state behavior (see Chapters 6, 8, and 11), international environmental organizations rarely have any enforcement measures.[86] Thus, institutional liberals have been a driving force behind efforts to promote more effective global environmental governance in four major UN conferences over a 40-year period: the

1972 UN Conference on the Human Environment in Stockholm; the 1992 UN Conference on Environment and Development in Rio de Janeiro; the 2002 World Summit on Sustainable Development in Johannesburg; and the 2012 UN Conference on Sustainable Development in Rio de Janeiro.

Critical environmental theorists, whom Jennifer Clapp, Peter Dauvergne, and others refer to as the *social greens* (or the *greens*), argue that DCs follow environmentally exploitative practices; that economic growth *causes* global environmental problems; and that environmental degradation affects some people and states more than others because of globalization and inequality. Some greens are historical materialists, arguing that capitalism is the main source of environmental degradation. Some greens also take a neo-Gramscian approach; they examine how DCs and large corporations as a hegemonic bloc frame environmental issues in a way that furthers their hegemonic interests. Furthermore, the greens criticize the World Bank, IMF, and WTO, and call for a radical restructuring of the global economy. Many greens reject economic globalization and favor a return to autonomy for local and indigenous communities.[87]

The greens believe that overconsumption of resources threatens the earth's ability to support life, and the concept of "common property goods" is central to this problem. Figure 5.1 lists four types of goods. In Chapter 4 we discussed *public goods*, which are nonexcludable and nonrival. *Private goods* are excludable and rival; for example, I must have money to buy food and clothing (they are excludable), and I must purchase items that are in short supply before someone else does (they are rival). *Club goods* are excludable but not rival; for example, cable television and private golf club memberships are usually not rival, but the fees charged make them excludable. The greens, and liberal institutional theorists, argue that major problems stem from **common property**

Excludability

		Yes	No
Rivalness	Yes	Private goods	Common property goods
	No	Club goods	Public goods

FIGURE 5.1
Types of Goods

goods, which are rival but nonexcludable. Resources such as the air, water, fish outside territorial waters, and outer space can be depleted (they are rival), but no one owns them (they are not excludable). Common property goods present a collective action problem because we see little benefit as individuals from conserving the resource; but we all lose when the resource is depleted. Garrett Hardin described this as the "tragedy of the commons."[88] Comparing the unregulated use of the atmosphere and the oceans to the preindustrial overuse of the English commons, Hardin predicted this would be detrimental to all. In terms of prisoners' dilemma (Chapter 4), individual rationality leads us to deplete our common property resources. To avoid this outcome, the greens call for limits on economic growth and population growth. Institutional liberals, by contrast, call for international institutions and agreements to ensure that common property goods do not become a source of environmental degradation.[89]

CRITIQUE OF THE CRITICAL PERSPECTIVES

It is difficult to provide a general critique of the critical perspectives, because they do not agree on a core set of assumptions. As discussed, constructivism, feminism, and environmentalism also have liberal and critical variants. However, in some respects all of these perspectives are critical of neomercantilism and liberalism, which traditionally devoted little attention to constructivism, feminism, and environmentalism. It is important to assess the validity of their arguments, and whether they supplement or provide viable alternatives to the mainstream IPE perspectives.

A major criticism of historical materialism stems from its repeated tendency to overestimate the degree to which capitalism is in decline. As discussed, Marx and Engels predicted that contradictions within capitalism would lead to its collapse, and when this did not occur, Lenin asserted that *imperialism* explained the survival of capitalism. After decolonization, historical materialists argued that capitalism persisted because Western countries maintained economic control in their former colonies through *neocolonialism*. The breakup of the Soviet bloc led Francis Fukuyama to declare that the capitalist liberal system had triumphed, but the world-systems theorist Wallerstein went to the opposite extreme and predicted that the end of the Cold War would lead to "the collapse of liberalism," because the breakup of the Soviet Union "undid the major justification for U.S. leadership."[90] Neo-Gramscian theorists call for a counterhegemony to topple capitalist hegemony, but they rarely venture to guess when or how this counterhegemony will materialize. More recently, historical materialists have reacted to the 2008 global financial crisis by again predicting the end of capitalism; for example, Wallerstein boldly states that "neo-liberal globalization ... is now dead."[91] In sum, one can ask whether historical materialist predictions regarding capitalism's demise (like Fukuyama's predictions regarding liberalism's triumph) are affected by wishful thinking.

Some mainstream theorists also argue that the critical perspectives have little influence on the theory and practice of IPE. Of the critical perspectives, only constructivism is involved in one of the major mainstream debates (rationalism versus constructivism). Many critical theorists would concede that they have little effect on the mainstream. For example, a feminist theorist asserts that "in spite of the consistently high quality and quantity of gender analysis, gender has not been able to achieve more than a marginal status in International Political Economy."[92] When critical perspectives do enter the mainstream arena, they often must do so on the mainstream's terms. For example, Steven Bernstein argues that "liberal environmentalism legitimates the primacy of the global marketplace ... rather than adapting the marketplace to operate in sympathy with requirements of ecological integrity and sustainability."[93] The most important IOs generally give priority to economic over environmental concerns.

Critics also question whether the critical perspectives can provide viable alternatives to the mainstream perspectives, because of the major divisions within the ranks of critical theorists. Although feminists, constructivists, and others view this multiplicity of views as consistent with their acceptance of marginalized voices, mainstream theorists question whether such a diversity of voices can offer coherent and meaningful alternatives. Indeed, the most vehement critics of critical theorists are often other critical theorists. For example, Marxists criticize dependency and world-systems theorists for giving priority to relations of exchange (between North and South) over relations of production (between classes); and feminists argue that Marxists are so focused on class that they devote little attention to gender issues.

Although the mainstream has devoted little attention to most of the critical perspectives, it is important to note that critical theorists play a vital role in the study of IPE. Constructivists increase our awareness of the effects of historical and social contexts on our preferences and decisions; historical materialists and feminists give a voice to poorer, marginalized people and states; and environmentalists alert us to the risks of ignoring the long-term effects of the environment on the economy and on the future of the planet. Furthermore, the 2008 global financial crisis, the European sovereign debt crisis, and current instability in financial, trade, and foreign investment relations indicate that alternatives to dependence on the unrestrained market are necessary. Although some critical theorists advocate the replacement of the capitalist global economy, others seek to make it more inclusive, equitable, and socially responsible.

QUESTIONS

1. What are the similarities and differences between Marxism, dependency theory, and world-systems theory?
2. What are the main features of Gramscian and neo-Gramscian analysis and how does it differ from classical Marxism?
3. How does the constructivist approach differ from the rationalist approach to IPE?
4. In what ways do the mainstream IPE perspectives not adequately address gender issues, and how do you think gender issues should be dealt with in IPE?
5. What are the differences between neomercantilist, liberal, and critical environmental theorists? What are the differences between liberal and critical constructivists? How significant are the differences among feminist theorists?

6. What are the differences between public goods, private goods, club goods, and common property goods? In what way do common property goods present a collective action problem?
7. Do you believe that historical materialism is *passé* as a result of the breakup of the Soviet bloc and the end of the Cold War?
8. What are some of the criticisms of the critical perspectives, and how valid do you think they are?

KEY TERMS

capital
common property goods
constructivism
dependency theory
epistemic community

feminist theory
historic bloc
historical materialism
instrumental Marxism
neo-Gramscian analysis

patriarchy
structural Marxism
sustainable development
terms of trade
world-systems theory

FURTHER READING

Studies of Marxism and historical materialism include William J. Davidshofer, *Marxism and the Leninist Revolutionary Model* (New York: Palgrave Macmillan, 2014); Alexander Anievas, ed., *Marxism and World Politics* (New York: Routledge, 2010); and Mark Rupert and Hazel Smith, eds., *Historical Materialism and Globalization* (New York: Routledge, 2002). On world-systems theory see Immanuel Wallerstein et al., *Does Capitalism Have a Future?* (New York: Oxford University Press, 2013); and Thomas R. Shannon, *An Introduction to the World-System Perspective*, 2nd ed. (Boulder, CO: Westview Press, 1996). On neo-Gramscian theory see Alison Ayers, ed., *Gramsci, Political Economy, and International Relations Theory*, rev. ed. (New York: Palgrave Macmillan, 2013); and Stephen Gill, ed., *Gramsci, Historical Materialism, and International Relations* (New York: Cambridge University Press, 1993).

Overviews of constructivism include Andre Broome, "Constructivism in International Political Economy," in Ronen Palan, ed., *Global Political Economy: Contemporary Theories*, 2nd ed. (New York: Routledge, 2013), pp. 193–204; Rawi Abdelal, "Constructivism as an Approach to International Political Economy," in Mark Blyth, ed., *Routledge Handbook of International Political Economy* (New York: Routledge, 2009), pp. 62–76; and Ian Hurd, "Constructivism," and Richard Price, "The Ethics of Constructivism," in Christian Reus-Smit and Duncan Snidal, eds., *The Oxford Handbook of International Relations* (New York: Oxford University Press, 2008), pp. 298–326.

Books focusing on gender and IPE include Penny Griffin, *Popular Culture, Political Economy and the Death of Feminism* (New York: Routledge, 2015); V. Spike Peterson, *A Critical Rewriting of Global Political Economy* (New York: Routledge, 2003); and J. Ann Tickner, *Gendering World Politics: Issues and Approaches in the Post-Cold War Era* (New York: Columbia University Press, 2001).

On environmentalism and IPE see Jennifer Clapp and Peter Dauvergne, *Paths to a Green World: The Political Economy of the Global Environment*, 2nd ed. (Cambridge, MA: MIT Press, 2011); and Simon Dalby, Ryan Katz-Rosene, and Mathew Paterson, "From Environmental to Ecological Political Economy," in Ronen Palan, ed., *Global Political Economy: Contemporary Theories*, 2nd ed. (New York: Routledge, 2013), pp. 219–231. On liberal environmentalism with a strong IPE emphasis see Steven Bernstein,

Compromise of Liberal Environmentalism (New York: Columbia University Press, 2001). Writings on energy security include Carlos Pascual and Jonathan Elkind, eds., *Energy Security: Economics, Politics, Strategies, and Implications* (Washington, DC: Brookings Institution Press, 2010); and Daniel Moran and James A. Russell, eds., *Energy Security and Global Politics* (New York: Routledge, 2009).

NOTES

1. Mark Rupert and Hazel Smith, eds., *Historical Materialism and Globalization* (New York: Routledge, 2002).
2. Karl Marx and Friedrich Engels, *The Communist Manifesto* (New York: International Publishers, 1948), p. 9.
3. Bob Jessop, *The Capitalist State: Marxist Theories and Methods* (Oxford, UK: Martin Robertson, 1982), pp. 1–31.
4. Marx and Engels, *The Communist Manifesto*, p. 29.
5. V. I. Lenin, *Imperialism: The Highest Stage of Capitalism*, rev. trans. (New York: International Publishers, 1939).
6. Jack Woddis, *An Introduction to Neo-Colonialism* (London: Lawrence & Wishart, 1967); Harry Magdoff, "Imperialism Without Colonies," in Roger Owen and Bob Sutcliffe, eds., *Studies in the Theory of Imperialism* (London: Longman, 1981), pp. 144–169.
7. Some authors argue that Marx was not a strict economic determinist. See David McLellan, *Marx*, 7th ed. (London: Fontana/Collins, 1980), p. 41.
8. On instrumental Marxism, see David A. Gold, Clarence Y. H. Lo, and Erik O. Wright, "Recent Developments in Marxist Theories of the Capitalist State," *Monthly Review* 27, no. 5 (October 1975), pp. 32–35.
9. On structural Marxism, see Gold et al., "Recent Developments in Marxist Theories of the Capitalist State," pp. 35–40; Pat McGowan and Stephen G. Walker, "Radical and Conventional Models of U.S. Foreign Economic Policy Making," *World Politics* 33, no. 3 (April 1981), pp. 357–360.
10. Jan A. Scholte, *Globalization: A Critical Introduction*, 2nd ed. (New York: Palgrave Macmillan, 2005), pp. 128–130.
11. Robert W. Cox, "Structural Issues of Global Governance: Implications for Europe," in Stephen Gill, ed., *Gramsci, Historical Materialism and International Relations* (New York: Cambridge University Press, 1993), pp. 259–262; Jackie Smith and Hank Johnston, eds., *Globalization and Resistance: Transnational Dimensions of Social Movements* (Lanham, MD: Rowman & Littlefield, 2002).
12. Karl Marx, *Capital: A Critical Analysis of Capitalist Production*, translated from the third German edition by Samuel Moore and Edward Aveling, and edited by Friedrich Engels, vols. 1–3 (Moscow: Foreign Languages Publishing House, 1957).
13. Marx and Engels, *The Communist Manifesto*, p. 16.
14. Agnar Sandmo, *Economics Evolving: A History of Economic Thought* (Princeton, NJ: Princeton University Press, 2011), pp. 120–126.
15. For Marx's writings on non-European areas, see Shlomo Avineri, ed., *Karl Marx on Colonialism and Modernization: His Dispatches and Other Writings on China, India, Mexico, the Middle East and North Africa* (Garden City, NJ: Doubleday, 1968).
16. Brendan O'Leary, *The Asiatic Mode of Production: Oriental Despotism, Historical Materialism and Indian History* (New York: Basil Blackwell, 1989), p. 263; Lawrence

Krader, *The Asiatic Mode of Production: Sources, Development and Critique in the Writings of Karl Marx* (The Netherlands: Van Gorcum & Comp., 1975).

17. Karl Marx, "The British Rule in India," in Shlomo Avineri, ed., *Karl Marx on Colonialism and Modernization: His Dispatches and Other Writings on China, India, Mexico, the Middle East and North Africa* (Garden City, NJ: Doubleday, 1968), pp. 86–88.

18. Marx, "The British Rule in India," p. 481.

19. B. N. Ghosh, *Dependency Theory Revisited* (Aldershot, UK: Ashgate, 2001), p. 19.

20. John. A. Hobson, *Imperialism: A Study* (Ann Arbor, MI: University of Michigan Press, 1965), p. 81.

21. For differing views of Lenin's contribution see Anthony Brewer, *Marxist Theories of Imperialism: A Critical Survey*, 2nd ed. (New York: Routledge, 1990), p. 116; Tom Kemp, "The Marxist Theory of Imperialism," in Roger Owen and Bob Sutcliffe, eds., *Studies in the Theory of Imperialism* (London: Longman, 1972), pp. 26–30.

22. Lenin, *Imperialism,* p. 89.

23. V. I. Lenin, *What Is to Be Done? Burning Questions of our Movement*, 3rd rev. ed. (Moscow: Progress Publishers, 1964), p. 30.

24. Thomas Biersteker, "Evolving Perspectives on International Political Economy: Twentieth-Century Discontinuities," *International Political Science Review* 14, no. 1 (January 1993), p. 12.

25. Raúl Prebisch, "The Economic Development of Latin America and Its Principal Problems," *Economic Bulletin for Latin America* 7, no. 1 (February 1962), pp. 1–22 (published in Spanish in 1950).

26. Joseph L. Love, "The Origins of Dependency Analysis," *Journal of Latin American Studies* 22 (February 1990), pp. 143–160.

27. André G. Frank, *Capitalism and Underdevelopment in Latin America: Historical Studies of Chile and Brazil* (New York: Monthly Press, 1967); Fernando H. Cardoso and Enzo Faletto, *Dependency and Development in Latin America*, trans. Marjory M. Urquidi (Berkeley, CA: University of California Press, 1979).

28. Cardoso and Faletto, *Dependency and Development in Latin America*, p. xviii.

29. André G. Frank, "The Development of Underdevelopment," *Monthly Review* 18, no. 4 (September 1966), pp. 17–31.

30. Cardoso and Faletto, *Dependency and Development in Latin America*, p. 174.

31. André G. Frank, "Asia's Exclusive Models," *Far Eastern Economic Review* 116, no. 26 (June 25, 1982), pp. 22–23; Peter Evans, *Dependent Development: The Alliance of Multinational, State, and Local Capital in Brazil* (Princeton, NJ: Princeton University Press, 1979); Thomas B. Gold, *State and Society in the Taiwan Miracle* (Armonk, NY: M.E. Sharpe, 1986).

32. Cal Clark and Donna Bahry, "Dependent Development: A Socialist Variant," *International Studies Quarterly* 27, no. 3 (September 1983), p. 286.

33. Evans, *Dependent Development*, p. 329.

34. Tony Smith, "The Underdevelopment of Development Literature: The Case of Dependency Theory," *World Politics* 31, no. 2 (January 1979), pp. 257–258.

35. Ernesto Laclau, "Feudalism and Capitalism in Latin America," *New Left Review* 67 (May–June 1971), p. 25.

36. Fernando Henrique Cardoso, "The Consumption of Dependency Theory in the United States," *Latin American Research Review* 12, no. 3 (1977), pp. 7–24.

37. Ghosh, *Dependency Theory Revisited*, p. 133; Peter Evans, "After Dependency: Recent Studies of Class, State, and Industrialization," *Latin American Research Review* 20, no. 2 (1985), p. 158.

38. John G. Ruggie, "Multilateralism: The Anatomy of an Institution," in John G. Ruggie, ed., *Multilateralism Matters: The Theory and Praxis of an Institutional Form* (New York: Columbia University Press, 1993), p. 33; Francis Fukuyama, "The End of History?" *The National Interest* 16 (Summer 1989), pp. 3, 11.

39. Robert H. Frank, "Income Inequality: Too Big to Ignore," *New York Times*, October 16, 2010.

40. On the differences between dependency and world-systems theory, see Peter Evans, "Beyond Center and Periphery: A Comment on the Contribution of the World System Approach to the Study of Development," *Sociological Inquiry* 49, no. 4 (1979), pp. 15–20.

41. Immanuel Wallerstein, "The Rise and Future Demise of the World Capitalist System: Concepts for Comparative Analysis," in Immanuel Wallerstein, *The Capitalist World-Economy* (New York: Cambridge University Press, 1979), p. 5.

42. Janet L. Abu-Lughod, *Before European Hegemony: The World System A.D. 1250–1350* (New York: Oxford University Press, 1989); André G. Frank and Barry Gills, eds., *The World System: Five Hundred Years or Five Thousand?* (London: Routledge, 1996).

43. Wallerstein, "The Rise and Future Demise of the World Capitalist System," pp. 18–19.

44. Wallerstein, "The Rise and Future Demise of the World Capitalist System," p. 35.

45. Evans, *Dependent Development*, p. 33.

46. Immanuel Wallerstein, *Alternatives: The United States Confronts the World* (Boulder, CO: Paradigm Publishers, 2004); Immanuel Wallerstein, *After Liberalism* (New York: The New Press, 1995).

47. Gold, *State and Society in the Taiwan Miracle*, pp. 13–14.

48. Theda Skocpol, "Wallerstein's World Capitalist System: A Theoretical and Historical Critique," *American Journal of Sociology* 82, no. 5 (March 1977), pp. 1084–1088; Alexander Gerschenkron, "Economic Backwardness in Historical Perspective," in Alexander Gerschenkron, ed., *Economic Backwardness in Historical Perspective: A Book of Essays* (Cambridge, MA: Belknap Press of Harvard University Press, 1962), pp. 16–21.

49. Benno Teschke, "Marxism," in Christian Reus-Smit and Duncan Snidal, eds., *The Oxford Handbook of International Relations* (New York: Oxford University Press, 2008), p. 173.

50. Antonio Gramsci, *Selections from the Prison Notebooks of Antonio Gramsci*, ed. and trans. Quintin Hoare and Geoffrey N. Smith (New York: International Publishers, 1971).

51. Robert W. Cox, "Gramsci, Hegemony and International Relations: An Essay in Method," *Millennium* 12, no. 2 (1983), pp. 162–175.

52. Robert W. Cox, "Social Forces, States and World Orders: Beyond International Relations Theory," in Robert O. Keohane, ed., *Neorealism and Its Critics* (New York: Columbia University Press, 1986), pp. 204–254; Stephen Gill and David Law, "Global Hegemony and the Structural Power of Capital," in Stephen Gill, ed., *Gramsci, Historical Materialism and International Relations* (New York: Cambridge University Press, 1993), pp. 93–124.

53. Robert W. Cox, "Civil Society at the Turn of the Millennium: Prospects for an Alternative World Order," *Review of International Studies* 25 (1999), p. 4.

54. Julian Saurin, "The Formation of Neo-Gramscians in International Relations and International Political Economy," in Alison Ayers, ed., *Gramsci, Political Economy, and International Relations Theory* (New York: Palgrave Macmillan, 2008), p. 26.

55. Jill Steans and Daniela Tepe, "Gender in the Theory and Practice of International Political Economy," in Alison Ayers, ed., *Gramsci, Political Economy, and International Relations Theory* (New York: Palgrave Macmillan, 2008), p. 135.

56. John J. Mearsheimer, "A Realist Reply," *International Security* 20, no. 1 (Summer 1995), p. 91; Erich Fromm, *Marx's Concept of Man* (New York: Frederick Ungar, 1961), p. 13; Rawi Abdelal, "Constructivism as an Approach to International Political Economy," in Mark Blyth, ed., *Routledge Handbook of International Political Economy* (New York: Routledge, 2009), pp. 62–63.

57. Ian Hurd, "Constructivism," in Christian Reus-Smit and Duncan Snidal, eds., *The Oxford Handbook of International Relations* (New York: Oxford University Press, 2008), p. 303.

58. See Nicholas G. Onuf, *World of Our Making: Rules and Rule in Social Theory and International Relations* (Columbia, SC: University of South Carolina Press, 1989).

59. On constructivism as critical theory, see Richard Price and Christian Reus-Smit, "Dangerous Liaisons? Critical International Theory and Constructivism," *European Journal of International Relations* 4, no. 3 (1998), pp. 259–294. On the different types of constructivism, see Emanuel Adler, "Seizing the Middle Ground: Constructivism in World Politics," *European Journal of International Relations* 3, no. 3 (1997), pp. 335–336.

60. Andre Broome, "Constructivism in International Political Economy," in Ronen Palan, ed., *Global Political Economy: Contemporary Theories*, 2nd ed. (New York: Routledge, 2013), pp. 197–200.

61. Benjamin J. Cohen, *International Political Economy: An Intellectual History* (Princeton, NJ: Princeton University Press, 2008), p. 132.

62. On the realist–liberal debates, see David A. Baldwin, ed., *Neorealism and Neoliberalism: The Contemporary Debate* (New York: Columbia University Press, 1993); Charles W. Kegley, Jr., ed., *Controversies in International Relations Theory: Realism and the Neoliberalism Challenge* (New York: St. Martin's Press, 1995).

63. Jeffrey T. Checkel, "The Constructivist Turn in International Relations Theory," *World Politics* 50, no. 2 (January 1998), p. 329.

64. Peter M. Haas, "Introduction: Epistemic Communities and International Policy Coordination," *International Organization* 46, no. 1 (Winter 1992), pp. 2–3.

65. G. John Ikenberry, "Creating Yesterday's New World Order: Keynesian 'New Thinking' and the Anglo-American Postwar Settlement," in Judith Goldstein and Robert O. Keohane, eds., *Ideas and Foreign Policy: Beliefs, Institutions, and Political Change* (Ithaca, NY: Cornell University Press, 1993), pp. 57–86.

66. Rawi Abdelal, Mark Blyth, and Craig Parsons, "Constructivist Political Economy," January 14, 2005: www.jhfc.duke.edu/ducis/GlobalEquity/pdfs/ABP.pdf.

67. Rawi Abdelal, *National Purpose in the World Economy: Post-Soviet States in Comparative Perspective* (Ithaca, NY: Cornell University Press, 2001), p. 151.

68. Abdelal, *National Purpose in the World Economy*, p. 151; Andrei P. Tsygankov, *Pathways After Empire: National Identity and Foreign Economic Policy in the Post-Soviet World* (Lanham, MD: Rowman & Littlefield, 2001).

69. Mark Blyth, *Austerity: The History of a Dangerous Idea* (New York: Oxford University Press, 2013).

70. Rosemarie P. Tong, *Feminist Thought: A More Comprehensive Introduction*, 2nd ed. (Boulder, CO: Westview Press, 1998).

71. Cynthia Enloe, *Bananas, Beaches and Bases: Making Feminist Sense of International Politics*, updated ed. (Berkeley, CA: University of California Press, 2000), p. 11.

72. Sandra Whitworth, *Feminism and International Relations* (New York: St. Martin's Press, 1994), p. 69.
73. V. Spike Peterson, *A Critical Rewriting of Global Political Economy: Integrating Reproductive, Productive and Virtual Economies* (New York: Routledge, 2003), p. 31.
74. See Elisabeth Prügl, *The Global Construction of Gender: Home-Based Work in the Political Economy of the 20th Century* (New York: Columbia University Press, 1999).
75. J. Ann Tickner, "On the Frontlines or Sidelines of Knowledge and Power? Feminist Practices of Responsible Scholarship," *International Studies Review* 8, no. 3 (September 2006), p. 386.
76. J. Ann Tickner, *Gender in International Relations: Feminist Perspectives on Achieving Global Security* (New York: Columbia University Press, 1992), p. 70.
77. Marilyn Waring, *Counting for Nothing: What Men Value and What Women Are Worth*, 2nd ed. (Toronto: University of Toronto Press, 1999), p. 1.
78. Jill Steans, *Gender and International Relations: An Introduction* (Cambridge, UK: Polity Press, 1998), p. 149.
79. Penny Griffin, "Refashioning IPE: What and How Gender Analysis Teaches International (Global) Political Economy," *Review of International Political Economy* 14, no. 4 (October 2007), p. 735.
80. Tickner, *Gender in International Relations*, pp. 69–70.
81. Peterson, *A Critical Rewriting of Global Political Economy*, pp. 22–25. On feminism and constructivism, see Prügl, *The Global Construction of Gender*.
82. Simon Dalby, Ryan Katz-Rosene, and Matthew Paterson, "From Environmental to Ecological Political Economy," in Ronen Palan, ed., *Global Political Economy: Contemporary Theories*, 2nd ed. (New York: Routledge, 2013), p. 219.
83. World Commission on Environment and Development, *Our Common Future* (New York: Oxford University Press, 1987), p. 8.
84. Maria Ivanova, "The Contested Legacy of Rio + 20," *Global Environmental Politics* 13, no. 4 (November 2013), pp. 2–3.
85. Oran R. Young, ed., *The Effectiveness of International Environmental Regimes: Causal Connections and Behavioral Mechanisms* (Cambridge, MA: MIT Press, 1999).
86. Jennifer Clapp and Peter Dauvergne, *Paths to a Green World: The Political Economy of the Global Environment*, 2nd ed. (Cambridge, MA: MIT Press, 2011), pp. 3–9.
87. Clapp and Dauvergne, *Paths to a Green World*, pp. 12–14.
88. Garrett Hardin, "The Tragedy of the Commons," *Science* 162, no. 3859 (December 1968), pp. 1243–1248.
89. Clapp and Dauvergne, *Paths to a Green World*, pp. 9–14.
90. Fukuyama, "The End of History?" p. 4; Wallerstein, *After Liberalism*, p. 1; Wallerstein, *Alternatives*, p. 104.
91. Wallerstein, *Alternatives*, p. 151.
92. Griffin, "Refashioning IPE," p. 719.
93. Steven Bernstein, "Environment, Economy, and Global Environmental Governance," in Richard Stubbs and Geoffrey D. Underhill, eds., *Political Economy and the Changing Global Order*, 3rd ed. (New York: Oxford University Press, 2006), p. 246; Steven Bernstein, *The Compromise of Liberal Environmentalism* (New York: Columbia University Press, 2001).

The Issue Areas

Part III focuses on the substantive issue areas in IPE and has significant revisions to reflect changes in the field. Chapter 6 on international monetary relations updates the discussion of the balance of payments, and compares the U.S. payments balance with that of China and Germany. Comparisons are also drawn between the role of the U.S. dollar, the euro, and the Chinese renminbi. To reflect its importance, we have moved the discussion of financial crises from Chapter 11 in the sixth edition to Chapter 7 in this edition of the text. Financial crises are also closely related to international monetary relations, and can occur in both DCs and LDCs. We devote considerable attention to the 2008 global financial crisis and the European sovereign debt crisis. Chapter 8 on global trade relations provides necessary background on the General Agreement on Tariffs and Trade and the emergence of the World Trade Organization. It also examines the reasons why the Doha Round of multilateral trade negotiations has still not been concluded, and discusses the implications of this stalemate for the global trade regime. Chapter 9 on regional trade relations expands and updates the discussion of regional integration theory. The chapter also examines the current challenges confronting the EU and the North American Free Trade Agreement (NAFTA), and the negotiations for a Trans-Pacific Partnership (TPP) Agreement. Chapter 10 on multinational corporations (MNCs) provides essential background on MNCs as private actors, and devotes more attention to the increasing role of emerging economies such as China, India, and Brazil as both host and home countries for MNCs. Chapter 11 on international development updates the discussion of development strategies, and compares China's policies toward less-developed countries with those of the United States, the International Monetary Fund (IMF), and the World Bank. The final section of each chapter in Part III has a boxed item that draws linkages between the issue areas and the IPE theoretical perspectives.

International
Monetary Relations

The first issue area we discuss in this book is international monetary relations, because "the international monetary system is the glue that binds national economies together ... it is impossible to understand the operation of the international economy without also understanding its monetary system."[1] Although monetary issues are difficult for students to master, some background in this area provides a sound basis for understanding other IPE issues such as trade and investment. The 2008 financial crisis is a prime example of how international monetary and financial transactions can reshape the global economy. Indeed, the amount of money foreign exchange markets handle *daily* increased from negligible amounts in the late 1950s, to $590 billion in 1989, $1.5 trillion in 1998, and $1.9 trillion in 2008.[2] Neomercantilists argue that financial transactions have increased with the permission and sometimes encouragement of the most powerful states, and that these states continue to dictate the terms for such transactions. Liberals by contrast assert that the increased transactions result from advances in communications, transportation, and technology, and that it is difficult for states to regulate global financial activities.

Neomercantilists also point to the fact that international monetary transactions rely mainly on separate national currencies, even though 19 EU members now use the *euro*. However, a liberal monetary specialist argues that the concept of one state, one currency is a myth today, because "international relations ... are being dramatically reshaped by the increasing interpenetration of national monetary spaces."[3] About 29 percent of the world's circulating currency is located outside the country issuing it, and during the mid-1990s at least $300 billion of the three top currencies at the time (the U.S. dollar, German deutsche mark, and Japanese yen) were circulating outside the country of origin. The U.S. dollar continues to be the top international currency, but cross-border currency competition is a reality today.[4] Although monetary flows and cross-border currency competition are eroding some governmental powers, monetary relations continue to function in a world of states. It is therefore necessary to discuss the balance of payments, which tells us about a state's overall financial position.

THE BALANCE OF PAYMENTS

The **balance of payments** records the *debit* and *credit* transactions that residents, firms, and governments of one state have with the rest of the world over a one-year period. All payments to foreigners are recorded as debits, and all payments received from foreigners are recorded as credits. The two most important components of the balance of payments are the **current account**, which mainly consists of a country's exports and imports of goods and services; and the **financial account**, which includes all movements of financial capital into and out of a state. A third component of the balance of payments, the *capital account*, is usually smaller than the first two accounts; it consists of specialized payments such as debt forgiveness, and the transfer of goods and financial assets by migrants entering or leaving a state. As Table 6.1 shows, the current account comprises four types of transactions:

1. *Merchandise trade*, or trade in tangible goods. The difference between the value of merchandise exports and imports is the *merchandise trade balance*.
2. *Services trade*, or trade in intangible items such as insurance, information, transportation, banking, and consulting. A state's merchandise and services exports minus imports (items 1 and 2 in the table) are equal to its overall *balance of trade*.
3. *Primary income* measures interest and dividend payments on investments by citizens of a country to foreigners and by foreigners to citizens of the country. It is important to note that this item does *not* record the foreign investment itself, which is in the financial account. This item is in the current account, because the investment income is compensation for providing foreign investment at an earlier date.
4. *Secondary income* includes current transfers between residents of a country and nonresidents such as workers' remittances (income that migrant workers or foreign companies send out of a country), donations, official assistance, and pensions.

Table 6.1 shows that in 2013 China had a current account *surplus* of $182.81 billion (U.S.), Germany had a current account *surplus* of $251.80 billion, and the United States had a current account *deficit* of $400.25 billion. The critical item for all countries was the merchandise trade balance: China had a merchandise trade *surplus* of $351.77 billion, Germany had a merchandise trade *surplus* of $275.87 billion, and the United States had a merchandise trade *deficit* of $701.67 billion. As Chapter 7 discusses, the United States has had merchandise trade deficits since 1971. For a number of years the largest U.S. trade deficits were with Japan, but in recent years they have often been

TABLE 6.1

Balance of Payments Data US Dollars, Billions

Balance of Payments	United States 2013	China 2013	Germany 2013
Current Account			
1. Merchandise Trade			
Exports	1,592.79	2,147.53	1,439.20
Imports	-2,294.45	-1,795.76	-1,163.32
Merchandise trade balance	-701.67	351.77	275.87
2. Services Trade			
Exports	687.41	215.11	261.01
Imports	-462.14	-331.49	-324.53
Services trade balance	225.28	-116.39	-63.52
Balance of Trade (1 + 2)	-476.39	235.38	212.35
3. Primary Income			
Credit	780.12	185.51	276.80
Debit	-580.47	-229.34	-179.74
Primary income balance	199.65	-43.84	97.06
4. Secondary Income			
Credit	118.43	53.16	68.64
Debit	-241.94	-61.90	-126.25
Secondary income balance	-123.52	-8.73	-57.62
Income Balance (3 + 4)	76.14	-52.57	39.44
Current Account (1+2+3+4)	-400.25	182.81	251.80
Financial Account			
Direct Investment Assets (outward)	-408.25	-162.88	-80.94
Direct Investment Liabilities (Inward)	294.97	347.85	51.27
Portfolio Investment Assets	-489.88	-5.35	-186.66
Portfolio Investment Liabilities	490.95	65.90	-32.10
Other Investment Assets*	248.01	-136.53	219.98
Other Investment Liabilities	231.75	214.16	-297.30
Financial Account Balance	367.56	323.15	-325.75
Capital Account	-0.41	3.05	2.65
Net Errors and Omissions	30.03	-77.63	72.47
Reserves and Related Items	3.08	-431.38	-1.16
proof of balance	400.26	-182.81	-251.79

* Includes financial derivatives and employee stock options

Source: IMF data library: BOP data reported to the IMF on a BPM6 basis. http://elibrary-data. imf.org/DataReport.aspx?c=20303469. (Differences in proof of balance relate solely to rounding errors.)

with China. Table 6.1 shows that in contrast to merchandise trade, the United States had a services trade *surplus* of $225.28 billion in 2013. China and Germany by contrast had services trade deficits in 2013 of $116.39 billion and $63.52 billion, respectively. The strong U.S. export position in services results from its skilled consultants and its highly developed markets in insurance and banking. Thus, the United States applied pressure to include services trade in the GATT/WTO and the NAFTA. The U.S. income balance (primary plus secondary income) was also positive in 2013 ($76.14 billion) because of interest and dividend payments received on past investments. However, the positive balances on services trade and income were not sufficient to overcome the large U.S. merchandise trade deficit. Thus, the United States had a current account deficit of $400.25 billion in 2013.

The second major item in the balance of payments is the *financial account*, which measures the inflow and outflow of investment assets. A country's capital exports are *debit* items because they involve the purchase of financial assets from foreigners, and its capital imports are *credit* items because they involve the sale of financial assets to foreigners. (This is the opposite of merchandise trade, in which exports are credits and imports are debits.) As Table 6.1 shows, the financial account includes foreign direct investment (FDI) and portfolio investment assets and liabilities. FDI is capital investment in physical or tangible assets such as a branch plant or subsidiary of an MNC in which the investor has some operating control. Portfolio investment, by contrast, refers to the purchase of paper assets such as stocks and bonds that do not give the purchaser operating control.

A country often seeks to offset a current account deficit with an inflow of foreign investment into its financial account; a current account surplus by contrast permits a country to have a financial account deficit through investment abroad or the purchase of foreign assets. As Table 6.1 shows, Germany (with a current account *surplus*) had a financial account *deficit* of $325.75 billion in 2013, and the United States (with a current account *deficit*) had a financial account *surplus* of $367.56 billion. The case of China which still has some characteristics of a developing country is somewhat different. Although China had a current account *surplus* in 2013, Table 6.1 shows that it also had a financial account *surplus* of $323.15 billion. China has often had a surplus on both its current and financial accounts in recent years, and this has enabled it to build up huge monetary reserves. The balance of payments also includes the *capital account*. As the small figures for the capital accounts of the three countries show in Table 6.1, the capital account is less important than the current and financial accounts.

The balance of payments includes two remaining items (see Table 6.1). The net errors and omissions item results partly from errors in data collection but mainly from a government's failure to include all the goods, services, and capital that cross its borders. The final item is the *change in official reserves*. Each country has a central bank such as the U.S. Federal Reserve or Bank of Canada that manages the money supply and holds official international reserves as a buffer against economic problems. When a country has an overall deficit in its current, investment, *and* capital accounts, it loses reserves; and when a country has an overall surplus in these three accounts, it adds to its reserves. A country's current, financial, and capital accounts, statistical discrepancy, and change in reserves always equals zero, hence the term *balance of payments*. Note in Table 6.1 that, by standard accounting procedures, a *minus* figure equals an *increase* in reserves and a *plus* figure equals a *decrease* in reserves. This is merely a bookkeeping exercise so the balance of payments will equal zero. Thus, in 2013, U.S. reserves *declined* by $3.08 billion, Germany's reserves *increased* by $1.16 billion, and China's reserves increased by the substantial sum of $431.38 billion.

Why does the balance of payments always balance (i.e., equals zero)? Because a country's current account is always counterbalanced by the sum of its financial and capital accounts, its net errors and omissions, and its changes in reserves. For example, note in Table 6.1 that the U.S. current account in 2013 was *minus* $400.25 billion. The total of the U.S. financial and capital accounts, net errors and omissions, and change in reserves in 2013 was *plus* $400.26 billion. (See the *proof of balance* item at the bottom of the table. The slight difference in the two figures is due to rounding.) Although the balance-of-payments account always balances (i.e., equals zero) in a bookkeeping sense, countries can have payments difficulties. When a country has a *balance-of-payments surplus* or a *balance-of-payments deficit*, these terms refer only to the current, financial, and capital accounts and exclude any changes in official reserves. A government with a balance-of-payments surplus reduces its liabilities and/or adds to its official reserves, whereas a government with a balance-of-payments deficit increases its liabilities and/or reduces its official reserves. The main body of the balance of payments therefore informs us about a state's overall financial position.

GOVERNMENT RESPONSE TO A BALANCE-OF-PAYMENTS DEFICIT

A country with large balance-of-payments surpluses may feel some pressure to correct its imbalances in the longer term. Large payments surpluses can force up the value of its currency making its exports more expensive for foreigners, and excessive official reserves can lead to inflationary pressures and rising domestic prices. However, countries with payments deficits feel more pressure to correct the imbalances than countries with surpluses, because their liabilities increase and their official monetary reserves can be depleted. Thus, surplus countries normally view their payments disequilibrium as an economic asset, and we focus here on a country's response to a payments deficit. A government with a payments deficit has two policy options: to *finance* the deficit or *adjust* to it. Adjustment measures have political risks because some societal groups must bear the adjustment costs in the present; thus, governments often prefer financing measures that defer the adjustment costs to the future.[5]

Adjustment Measures

Governments opting for adjustment rely on monetary, fiscal, and commercial policy instruments. **Monetary policy** influences the economy through changes in the money supply. A central bank uses monetary policy to deal with a balance-of-payments deficit by limiting public access to funds for spending purposes and making such funds more expensive. For example, a central bank raises interest rates to make borrowing more costly, decreases the amount of money available for loans by requiring commercial banks to hold larger reserves, and sells government bonds to withdraw money from the economy. These policies can lower the payments deficit through a contraction of the economy and decreased spending on goods and services. A government uses **fiscal policy** to deal with a payments deficit by lowering government expenditures and raising taxes to withdraw purchasing power from the public. (Countries with payments surpluses by contrast often seek to expand the money supply, increase the budget deficit, and inflate the economy.) *Commercial policy* lowers a country's payments deficit through trade by increasing the country's exports and decreasing its imports.

A government's use of monetary, fiscal, and commercial policies depends on whether it opts for external or internal adjustment measures. *External adjustment measures* such as tariffs, import quotas, export subsidies, and currency devaluation are used to decrease imports and foreign investment outflows and increase exports and foreign investment inflows. External adjustment measures impose most of the adjustment costs on foreigners; foreigners often retaliate and everyone loses in the long run. For example, external adjustment measures can result in the competitive devaluation of currencies, with every country trying to lower the relative price of its exports. Although a government may adopt external measures to avoid politically unpopular decisions, even external measures impose some costs on domestic groups. For example, a reduction of imports adversely affects importing businesses and the products available to consumers. *Internal adjustment measures* include deflationary monetary and fiscal policies to slow business activity and decrease the deficit; for example, higher taxes and interest rates reduce spending by individuals, business firms, and the government. Internal adjustment measures cause individuals and groups at home to pay more of the adjustment costs through unemployment, lower living standards, business bankruptcies, and fewer publicly financed programs. However, internal adjustment can also affect foreigners by deflating the economy and lowering the demand for imports.

Financing

A country may also seek *financing* for its balance-of-payments deficit by borrowing from external sources or decreasing its foreign exchange reserves. Financing is often the preferred option when access to credit is available because it is easier to postpone difficult adjustment measures. However, financing may not be available over the long term; a country's reserves may be depleted, and foreigners are reluctant to invest in a country with chronic foreign debt problems. The United States has depended mainly on financing through its financial account (plus $367.56 billion in 2013, in Table 6.1) to counter its current account deficit (minus $400.25 billion in 2013). The United States has had persistently high current account deficits in recent years, and its dependence on financing has resulted in a growing foreign debt. As Table 6.2 shows, the U.S. current account *deficit* decreased from $677.1 billion in 2008 during the financial crisis, to $400.3 billion in 2013; and the U.S. merchandise trade *deficit* declined from $827.1 billion in 2008 to $701.7 billion in 2013. However, high U.S. merchandise trade and current account deficits have persisted for many years, and as a result the United States has the world's highest **external debt**, or the total of public and private debt owed to nonresidents by residents of an economy. In marked contrast to the United States, Table 6.2 shows that Germany had current account *surpluses* of $226.3 billion in 2008 and $251.8 billion in 2013, and merchandise trade *surpluses* of $267.2 billion in 2008 and $275.9 billion in 2013. However, many other countries in the euro zone (those EU countries that use the euro currency) were in a less favorable position. Thus, Table 6.2 shows that France had merchandise trade *deficits* of $87.3 billion in 2008 and $56.5 billion in 2013. China and Germany are the world's largest merchandise exporters. Thus, Table 6.2 shows that China had current account *surpluses* of $420.6 billion in 2008 and $182.8 billion in 2013; and China had merchandise trade *surpluses* of $360.7 billion in 2008 and $351.8 billion in 2013. However, Japan which was an export leader in the 1980s has lagged behind China. Table 6.2 shows that Japan had a merchandise trade *surplus* of $38.1 billion in 2008, but it had a merchandise trade *deficit* of $89.7 billion in 2013. Table 6.2 also shows that there is considerable variation among the BRIC economies. In marked contrast to China's large trade surpluses, India had merchandise trade *deficits* of $93.1 billion in 2008 and $114.7 billion in 2013.

TABLE 6.2

Current Account Balance and Merchandise Trade Balance

Billions of Dollars (U.S.) 2008 and 2013

Country	2008		2013	
	CAB[1]	MTB[2]	CAB	MTB
Canada	6.4	43.8	−54.7	−7.0
China	420.6	360.7	182.8	351.8
France	−49.9	−87.3	−40.2	−56.5
Germany	226.3	267.2	251.8	275.9
India	−31.0	−93.1	−49.2	−114.7
Japan	159.4	38.1	34.1	−89.7
United States	−677.1	−827.1	−400.3	−701.7

[1] CAB: current account balance; [2] MTB: merchandise trade balance

Source: IMF data library: BOP data reported to the IMF on a BPM6 basis. http://elibrary-data.imf.org

The United States has had the highest current account and merchandise trade deficits, and this has been a major factor in its high external debt.

Some analysts have argued that the U.S. deficits and external debt are not a major concern for several reasons. First, although the United States has the highest external debt, a number of countries with smaller economies than the United States have higher external debts as a percentage of their GDPs. For example, in 2012 the U.S. foreign debt was considerably higher than the combined foreign debt of Poland, Hungary, Romania, and all the other Central and Eastern European countries. However, to assess the ability of a country to service its foreign debt, it is important to look at debt as a percent of GDP. The foreign debt of the Central and Eastern European countries amounted to about 67 percent of their combined GDP in 2012, while the U.S. net foreign debt amounted to only about 25 percent of its GDP.[6] Second, the negative U.S. trade balance is not a valid measure of U.S. competitiveness, because highly competitive U.S. firms often sell goods abroad through their foreign subsidiaries rather than exporting them from the United States. In 1998, for example, U.S. global exports of $933 billion were far less than U.S. foreign affiliate sales of $2.4 trillion. Third, the United States often has higher trade and current account deficits when U.S. productivity is increasing at a faster rate. The 1990s was a decade when the United States had sustained economic expansion, EU economic growth was largely stalled, and the Japanese economy was often in recession. During the late 1990s the United States had growing current account deficits while Japan and the euro area had current account surpluses. Thus, U.S. trade and current account deficits may indicate that a vibrant U.S. economy is serving as the largest market for other countries' exports. Fourth, some argue that the United States attracts so much foreign capital because others want to invest in the country. In view of this positive balance on its financial account, the United States balances its payments by incurring a deficit on its current account. Central banks in Europe and Asia will continue to buy U.S. dollars indefinitely, so there is no effective constraint on U.S. borrowing.[7]

A balance-of-trade surplus is certainly not the only measure of economic health, as Japan's economic problems demonstrate (see Chapters 7 and 11). However, arguments that the U.S. trade deficit is of little concern are not convincing. Regarding the first argument, serious questions are being raised about the sustainability of the U.S. external debt, especially since the 2008 global financial crisis (see Chapter 7). Regarding the second argument, a state's competitiveness is not synonymous with the competitiveness of its MNCs (see Chapter 10). In assessing U.S. trade competitiveness and employment prospects for U.S. workers, it is *not* sufficient to focus only on the sales of U.S. foreign affiliates. Regarding the third and fourth arguments, the United States does sometimes have higher deficits during periods of rapid economic growth, and it has been able to finance its deficits because its large economy and political stability attract foreign investors. However, a number of problems have resulted from the long-term U.S. deficits including a protectionist backlash against U.S. liberal trade policy, a loss of U.S. manufacturing jobs and disposable income, increased leverage of foreign governments with substantial U.S.

dollar holdings, and disruptive market volatility against the U.S. dollar. There are also geopolitical implications, because two of the largest holders of dollar reserves—China and Russia—are U.S. rivals rather than allies. The degree to which China and Russia diversify their holdings into other reserves can have a major effect on the future of the U.S. dollar as the top international currency.[8] This chapter discusses whether other currencies are likely to pose a challenge to the top position of the U.S. dollar.

Adjustment, Financing, and the Theoretical Perspectives

In reality, states usually employ a combination of external and internal adjustment and financing measures to deal with payments deficits. Liberals, neomercantilists, and historical materialists have different preferences regarding these policies. Orthodox liberals believe that governments should adopt internal adjustment measures as a necessary form of discipline because they see payments deficits as resulting from domestic inefficiencies. They oppose external adjustment measures that raise trade barriers and distort economic interactions, and they oppose external financing because it permits states to delay instituting internal reforms. Neomercantilists by contrast see internal adjustment methods as posing a threat to a state's policy-making autonomy, and historical materialists believe that LDCs should not have to bear internal adjustment costs in an international system that serves DC interests. External adjustment is much more acceptable to neomercantilists and historical materialists. Neomercantilists view external measures as "fair game" in a state's efforts to improve its competitive position. For example, some analysts argue that the United States should adopt external adjustment measures because Japan and China's manipulation of "their currencies to gain an unfair competitive advantage" has "a substantial impact on exchange rates and the U.S. trade deficit."[9] Historical materialists argue that LDCs should impose import controls because of their unfavorable terms of trade with DCs, and that DCs should provide LDCs with liberal financing to help alleviate their balance-of-payments problems.

THE FUNCTIONS AND VALUATION OF MONEY

Before tracing the development of monetary relations, it is important to be familiar with the concepts of *money* and *currency*, which is simply money used as a medium of exchange. Money serves three main functions:

- As *a medium of exchange*, money must be acceptable to others in payment for goods, services, or assets.
- As *a unit of account*, it places a value or price on goods, services, or assets.
- As *a store of value*, it helps preserve purchasing power or wealth in the private sector for investment purposes, or by governments in official foreign exchange reserves.

These functions depend on ideational as well as material factors, because "the key to all three of money's roles is *trust,* the reciprocal faith of a critical mass of like-minded transactors."[10] Without this trust, currencies would simply be worthless pieces of paper. A currency can serve effectively as a medium of exchange and a store of value only if individuals are confident that it can be used in financial transactions without significantly losing its value. Currencies can be priced by setting fixed exchange rates, by free markets, or by some combination of the two. **Devaluation** occurs when a state lowers its currency's official price, and **revaluation** occurs when it raises the official price. **Depreciation** refers to a *market-driven* reduction in a currency's price, and **appreciation** refers to a market-driven increase in its price.

INTERNATIONAL MONETARY RELATIONS BEFORE BRETTON WOODS

Four regimes have provided a degree of governance in international monetary relations: the classical gold standard from the 1870s to World War I, a gold exchange standard during the first part of the interwar period, the Bretton Woods system from 1944 to 1973, and a mixed system of floating and fixed exchange rates from 1973 to the present.[11] This chapter focuses mainly on the third and fourth regimes, but it is necessary to provide some background on the first two regimes.

The Classical Gold Standard (1870s–1914)

The classical **gold standard** was a regime based on **fixed exchange rates**, in which national currencies had specific exchange rates in relation to gold, and countries held their official international reserves in the form of gold. Governments were committed to converting domestic currency into gold at the fixed rate, and individuals could export and import gold. By stabilizing national currency values, the gold standard facilitated trade and other transactions. For example, if the U.S. dollar and British pound were pegged at $35 and £14.5 per ounce of gold, the exchange rate between the dollar and the pound would remain constant at $2.41 per £1 (35 divided by 14.5). Although some states adhered to the gold standard more closely than others, it functioned reasonably well because it was backed by British hegemony and cooperation among the major powers. Britain helped stabilize the gold standard by providing other states with public goods such as investment capital, loans, and an open market for their exports. The three states at the center of the regime—Britain, France, and Germany—also defended their central banks' gold reserves, maintained the convertibility of their currencies, and instituted domestic adjustments when necessary to preserve the gold standard. Thus, Western Europe and the United States maintained their official gold parities for about 35 years.[12]

The gold standard was based on the orthodox liberal objective of promoting monetary openness and stability by maintaining stable exchange rates. This was a period before Keynes introduced interventionist liberal ideas to combat unemployment, and states were expected to sacrifice domestic social objectives for the sake of monetary stability. Orthodox liberals sometimes refer to the gold standard in idealized terms, and in 1981 President Ronald Reagan created a special commission to determine whether the United States should return to the gold standard (its recommendation was negative).[13] However, critics argue that the gold standard imposed the largest burden of adjustment in welfare and employment on the poorest people and states.

The Interwar Period (1918–1944)

World War I completely disrupted international monetary relations. After the war, exchange rates floated freely and central banks did not intervene in the foreign exchange market. However, the floating exchange rates contributed to volatility in the value of currencies, and there were efforts to restore the gold standard. By 1927 the major states established a **gold exchange standard** regime, in which central banks held their reserves in major currencies as well as gold, and each central bank fixed the exchange rate of its currency to a key currency (the British pound) with a fixed price in gold. Although central banks had held reserve currencies in earlier years, the gold exchange standard institutionalized this practice. A gold exchange standard permits more flexibility in increasing international reserves than a gold standard because the reserves are not limited to the supply of gold. However, the gold exchange standard did not operate as planned because some states had persistent balance-of-payments deficits and others had persistent surpluses. The Great Depression of 1929 put further stress on the gold exchange standard, and in 1931, Britain suspended the convertibility of the pound sterling into gold. States gradually returned to floating their currencies, but unlike the early 1920s this was a *managed* float in which central banks intervened to deal with excessive fluctuations in exchange rates.

Some theorists argue that the failure to re-establish monetary stability in the interwar period resulted from Britain's inability as a declining hegemon to stabilize policies; but others argue that the main factor was the growing reluctance of states to sacrifice *domestic* goals such as full employment for the sake of currency stability. Before World War I, voting in most states was limited, labor unions were weak, farmers were not organized, and leftist parties were restricted. Thus, governments could stabilize their currencies through policies that caused domestic hardship such as raising interest rates and taxes and decreasing government expenditures. By the end of World War I, the extension of suffrage, legalization of labor unions, organization of farmers, and development of mass political parties gave domestic groups more influence. Thus, interventionist liberal views that some government involvement is necessary to deal with domestic economic problems took hold at this time, and governments could no longer sacrifice the welfare of their citizens to maintain monetary stability.[14]

THE FORMATION OF THE BRETTON WOODS MONETARY REGIME

World War II was marked by a breakdown of monetary cooperation and a period of exchange controls, and planning for a postwar monetary regime culminated in the 1944 Bretton Woods conference. To avoid the volatility of currency values experienced during the free float of the 1920s, the Bretton Woods planners established a gold exchange standard in which the value of each country's currency was pegged to gold or the U.S. dollar as the key currency. A *key currency* is the currency that nonresident private and public actors most often hold, use globally for cross-border transactions, and purchase in the form of financial instruments such as bonds. Other states are also most likely to peg their currencies to the key currency.[15] Unlike earlier monetary regimes, the Bretton Woods system was based on the embedded liberal compromise (see Chapter 4). The postwar planners assumed that the pegged (or fixed) exchange rates would provide the monetary stability needed for international trade, but they also provided for some flexibility and assistance so countries could adopt domestic policies to combat inflation and unemployment. This marked a contrast with the classical gold standard, in which exchange-rate stability took precedence over domestic requirements.[16] The embedded liberal compromise had three major elements. First, the gold exchange standard was an adjustable-peg rather than a fixed-exchange rate system. Although countries were to maintain the par value of their currencies in the short term, all countries other than the United States (as discussed later) could devalue their currencies under IMF guidance to correct chronic balance-of-payments problems. The IMF framework for changing currency values was designed to provide more flexibility than the classical gold standard and avoid competitive devaluations such as those of the interwar period. Second, the IMF would provide short-term loans to countries with balance-of-payments problems so they could maintain exchange-rate stability. Third, countries could impose national controls over capital flows. Speculative capital flows had led to instability during the interwar period, and the negotiators feared that such speculation could undermine postwar efforts to maintain pegged exchange rates and promote freer trade.[17]

THE INTERNATIONAL MONETARY FUND

The **International Monetary Fund (IMF)**, located in Washington, DC, was created to stabilize exchange rates and provide member states with short-term loans for temporary balance-of-payments problems. Under the IMF Articles of Agreement, members had to peg their currencies to gold or the U.S. dollar, which was valued at $35 per ounce of gold. Members also contributed to a pool of national currencies available for IMF loans to deficit countries. Each IMF member is given a *quota* based on several factors such as the member's GDP and economic openness. The country's quota determines the size of its *subscription* or contribution to IMF resources, its voting power in IMF decision-making bodies, and the amount it can borrow from the IMF. Under the

IMF's weighted voting system, the most economically powerful states have the largest subscriptions and the most votes. At regular intervals (usually every five years), the IMF adjusts members' quotas to accord with changes in their economic positions. However, some emerging economies are dissatisfied because they should have higher quotas based on their economic importance. IMF **conditionality** ensures that borrowers must agree to adopt specific economic policies in return for IMF loans, and the conditions become more stringent as a member borrows more from the IMF in relation to its quota. LDCs feel strong pressure to abide by IMF conditionality because they depend on IMF loans, and DCs and private banks often require the acceptance of IMF conditions before providing their own loans and development assistance. IMF officials usually require borrowers to adopt contractionary monetary and fiscal policies so they can correct their balance-of-payments problems and repay their IMF loans. However, many loan recipients feel that IMF conditionality infringes on their sovereignty and does not address the basic structural problems hindering their economic development (see Chapter 11).

The highest IMF decision-making body is the *Board of Governors*. Every IMF member appoints one governor to the board, but the voting power of each governor depends on the weighted voting system. The governors are usually finance ministers or central bank heads. For example, the U.S. governor is the Secretary of the Treasury and the alternate representative is the Federal Reserve Board chair; the Canadian governor is the Finance Minister and the alternate representative is the governor of the Bank of Canada. The Board of Governors meet once a year at the IMF–World Bank Annual Meetings and delegate most of their powers to the *Executive Board* (or Board of Executive Directors), which also has weighted voting and is composed of 24 directors appointed or elected by the IMF members. However, the Board of Governors retains the right to make several important decisions such as approving IMF quota increases and admitting new IMF members. The 24-member Executive Board is responsible for the IMF's daily business, including requests for financial assistance, economic consultations with members, and policy development. The IMF *managing director*, appointed by the Executive Board for a five-year renewable term, is the top executive officer who is head of the staff and is chair of the Executive Board. The IMF also has two ministerial committees that provide critical advice to the Board of Governors on the global economy, economic development, and changes in IMF policy and management: the *International Monetary and Financial Committee* and the *Development Committee* (a joint committee that advises both the IMF and World Bank Governors).[18]

The countries with the largest subscriptions and most votes in the IMF are the G5—the United States, Japan, Germany, France, and Britain. The DCs also have the most influence in the IMF operating staff. By tacit agreement, the IMF managing director has always been European, and the World Bank president has always been American. Furthermore, as of April 2014 Europeans, Americans, and Canadians occupied 55.9 percent of the IMF professional staff positions and 68.2 percent of the senior staff positions with managerial responsibilities. Underrepresented regions in the professional and managerial staff include Sub-Saharan Africa, East Asia, the Middle East and North Africa, and the European transition economies. Gender disparities are also evident. There has been some increase in representation of LDCs and women in staff positions, but they are still underrepresented. For example, women on the professional staff increased from 35.9 percent in 2007 to 38.4 percent in 2014, and women on the senior staff with managerial responsibilities rose from 15.6 percent in 2007 to 23.6 percent in 2014. In striking contrast, 84.7 percent of IMF support staff positions (secretaries and the administrative assistant) were occupied by women in 2014. However, the IMF is trying to increase diversity on its staff, and in June 2011 Christine Lagarde was the first woman to become Managing Director of the IMF.[19]

The emerging economies were increasingly dissatisfied with the dominance of the DCs and particularly the G5 in the IMF and World Bank. However, no significant changes were made until the 2008 global financial crisis, which has been marked by some shifting of power and influence from the United States and Europe toward emerging economies (see Chapter 7). Thus, the G20 leaders at their September 2009 Pittsburgh Summit agreed to increase the voice of the emerging economies in the IMF and the IBRD (or World Bank). The IBRD subsequently won a general increase in its capital in April 2010 in return for a transfer of some voting power from smaller European countries to emerging economies. As a result, China leapfrogged over Germany, Britain, and France, and now has the third largest number of votes in the IBRD after the United States and Japan (see Chapter 11). What about the IMF? The decision to reform the IBRD set a precedent for the IMF, and in October 2010 the G20 agreed to double the IMF's quota and to shift 6 percent of the total quota to developing countries. The EU was reluctant to accept a decrease in its voting power in the IMF (recall that the IMF is the more senior institution vis-à-vis the World Bank), but the United States persuaded Europe to accept this change in 2010.

However, much has changed since 2010. The U.S. political system has been quite dysfunctional of late, and it is the United States, not Europe, that has blocked the implementation of the changes in the IMF. Although the G20 agreed to the IMF changes in 2010, they had to be ratified by the separate governments. In January 2014, Republicans in the U.S. House of Representatives refused President Obama's request to ratify the IMF changes; the House's refusal to ratify was less related to dissatisfaction with the IMF than to domestic US politics.[20] As a result, the G5 developed countries continued to have the most votes in the IMF. The G5 had 37.37 percent of the votes in the IMF Executive Board in March 2015. As Table 6.3 shows, the United States had 16.75 percent, followed by Japan with 6.23 percent, Germany with 5.81 percent, and France and Britain with 4.29 percent each. The G5 countries have enough votes to always appoint their own executive directors, and three other countries—China, Saudi Arabia, and Russia (with 3.81, 2.80, and 2.39 percent of the votes, respectively)—have also appointed their own executive directors. Coalitions of member states elect the other 16 executive directors every two years.[21] How can the U.S. Congress prevent the IMF reforms approved by the G20 from going into effect? As discussed, the G20 tries to reach a consensus

TABLE 6.3

IMF Members with the Most Votes

Country	March 16, 2015 Number of Votes	Percent of Total
United States	421,961	16.75
Japan	157,022	6.23
Germany	146,392	5.81
France	108,122	4.29
United Kingdom	108,122	4.29

Source: IMF Executive Directors and Voting Power. www.imf.org/external/np/sec/memdir/eds.aspx

and shape views on issues, but it is not a decision-making body. The most important decisions in the IMF, including changing member quotas and voting power, require approval by an 85 percent majority. As Table 6.3 shows, the United States with 16.75 percent of the voting power is the only country that has a veto over these decisions. The failure to implement the IMF reforms leaves Europe overrepresented and is threatening to pose a serious threat to the IMF's legitimacy as an international institution. For example, China's anger over the U.S. Congress's refusal to ratify the 2010 agreement to increase the voting share of emerging economies in the IMF is a major factor in its decision to establish a new Beijing-based Asian Infrastructure Investment Bank (AIIB). The AIIB could compete with the World Bank and Asian Development Bank, which are dominated by the United States and Japan, respectively. (See Chapters 7 and 11.)[22]

THE FUNCTIONING OF THE BRETTON WOODS MONETARY REGIME

Bretton Woods was a gold exchange regime in which the main reserves were gold and the U.S. dollar. Economists ask three questions about the adequacy of reserve assets in upholding a monetary regime. First, are there sufficient reserves (e.g., gold and the U.S. dollar) for *liquidity*, or financing purposes? (**Liquidity** refers to the ease with which an asset can be used in making payments.) As interdependence increases, more liquidity is needed to cover the growing number of economic transactions. However, a surplus of liquidity can cause inflation and other problems. Second, is there *confidence* in the reserves? When countries lack confidence that an asset will retain its value, they are reluctant to hold it in their reserves. Confidence problems have led to periodic efforts to sell British pounds and U.S. dollars. Third, what *adjustment* options do countries have in dealing with balance-of-payments deficits? An effective regime should offer all deficit countries (including the top-currency country, the United States) adjustment options. The following discussion examines problems with liquidity, confidence, and adjustment in the Bretton Woods monetary regime.[23]

The Central Role of the U.S. Dollar

Central banks held their international reserves in gold and foreign exchange under the Bretton Woods monetary regime. However, the original attraction of gold—its scarcity—became a liability as increased trade and foreign investment led to a growing demand for reserves. Most countries also preferred U.S. dollars to gold, because dollars earned interest and did not have to be shipped and stored. U.S. dollars were therefore vital for global liquidity purposes, but large U.S. balance-of-trade surpluses in the late 1940s contributed to a shortage of dollars in other countries. To remedy this problem, the United States distributed dollars around the world from 1947 to 1958 through economic aid and military expenditures. Other countries could devalue their currencies under IMF guidance, but the dollar's value was to remain fixed at $35 per ounce of gold to ensure that it would be "as good as gold." The United States agreed to exchange all dollars held by foreigners for gold at the official rate, and this seemed feasible because it had larger gold reserves than any other country.

From the liberal perspective, the United States provided *public goods* by opening its market to imports from other counties, disbursing aid through the European Recovery Program or Marshall Plan, and supplying the U.S. dollar as the main source of international liquidity. However, the U.S. policies could also be explained as furthering the national interest in a neomercantilist sense. Marshall Plan aid to help Western European economic recovery was designed partly to strengthen the West in the emerging Cold War with the Soviet Union. Furthermore, the United States benefited from having the key currency in several respects: The United States could avoid exchange-rate risks and transaction costs by trading and borrowing in its domestic currency; it was largely exempt from the discipline the international financial system imposed on other states; and the dollar's role bolstered New York City as the world's financial capital. The United States has also gained additional revenue through **seigniorage**, or the ability of a national government to increase public spending through money creation. The extensive international use of the dollar gives the United States greater opportunities for seigniorage.[24] U.S. policy was therefore based on both altruism and self-interest, and others accepted U.S. leadership because of the benefits they received.

However, several changes in the late 1950s led to concerns about U.S. leadership. Although the United States had large current account surpluses because of its positive trade balance, it had even larger financial account deficits because of the economic and military finance it was providing. Thus, the United States began to have balance-of-payments deficits as early as 1950. U.S. payments deficits averaged $1.5 billion per year for most of the decade, but they increased rapidly in the late 1950s, and observers began to speak of a dollar glut rather than a dollar shortage. In 1960, foreign dollar holdings exceeded U.S. gold reserves for the first time, and European governments were reluctant to accumulate excessive dollar reserves. To some economists, the dollar's declining fortunes demonstrated the problems with a gold exchange standard regime that relied on a single key currency. The need for sufficient *liquidity* caused the United States to supply dollars by running balance-of-payments deficits; but these deficits lowered *confidence* in the U.S. dollar because the United States would not be able to continue exchanging dollars for gold at $35 per ounce. Any U.S. actions to restore *confidence* in the dollar by reducing its balance-of-payments deficit would contribute to global *liquidity* shortages. The **Triffin dilemma** (named after economist Robert Triffin) refers to the problem with a monetary regime that depends on a single key currency: The *liquidity* and *confidence* functions of the currency eventually come into conflict.[25]

A second change that raised questions about U.S. leadership was the growth of the **eurocurrency market**. A eurocurrency is a currency traded and deposited in banks outside the home country. (A *euromarket* is a broader term, referring not only to bank deposits, but also to eurobonds, equities, and derivatives outside the home country.) As early as 1917, the Russian Communist government deposited U.S. dollars in European banks to prevent the United States from seizing them, and the eurocurrency market developed after World War II when the Soviet Union continued to hold its U.S. dollars in Europe because of the Cold War. In the 1960s, the eurocurrency market developed further when President Lyndon B. Johnson responded to U.S. balance-of-payments deficits by limiting foreign lending by U.S. banks. U.S. companies responded by financing their foreign operations from offshore banks, which were not subject to U.S. banking regulations. The eurocurrency market also grew because European firms involved with international trade found it easier to use a single currency (the U.S. dollar). The 1973 OPEC oil crisis contributed to further growth, because Middle Eastern OPEC countries deposited large sums of *petrodollars*—the proceeds from their oil sales—in European banks. By using the eurocurrency market, the OPEC countries' funds were subject to fewer regulations and avoided the risk of seizure by the U.S. government. Thus, the eurocurrency market grew from a gross value of about $20 billion in 1964 to $110 billion in 1970 and $2.15 trillion in 1982.[26] As Chapter 7 discusses, the large volume of petrodollar loans to LDCs through the eurocurrency market was one factor contributing to the 1980s foreign debt crisis. Although eurocurrency activity first developed in Europe, in recent years it has expanded elsewhere. By the early 1990s, banks in Europe, North America, Asia, and the Caribbean had eurocurrency deposits; over half of these were *eurodollar* deposits held in banks outside the United States.

Eurodollars are not subject to the regulations governments impose on domestic banking activities. For example, the U.S. Federal Reserve requires banks to hold a certain percentage of their deposits as reserves and impose a ceiling on interest rates they pay on deposits; but the United States does not have this control over eurodollars. Thus, the growth of the eurocurrency market posed new obstacles to control over monetary relations by the United States and other countries. If a government tries to restrict credit to fight inflation, large firms can continue to borrow in the eurocurrency market; and the size and speed of eurocurrency flows can destabilize foreign exchange rates and domestic interest rates. Effective regulation of the eurocurrency market must be multilateral, but strong competition for eurobanking has made regulation more difficult.[27]

Liberal interdependence theorists point to the role international bankers played in the expansion of the eurocurrency market as a result of the increase in capital mobility and global lending and borrowing. Neomercantilists by contrast argue that the eurocurrency market grew with the approval and encouragement of the leading states. For example, Britain allowed the eurocurrency market to operate without regulation to promote London as a leading financial center, and the U.S. government permitted its bankers to retain their dominance in international finance by avoiding U.S. capital controls. In view of the declining confidence in the dollar, the U.S. government also believed that the eurocurrency market would enhance the appeal of its currency.[28] However, British and U.S. support for the eurocurrency market "may prove to have been the most important single development of the century undermining national monetary sovereignty."[29] In sum, the growth of the eurocurrency market and the persistent U.S. balance-of-payments deficits raised concerns about the U.S. ability to manage global monetary relations, and these concerns contributed to a shift toward multilateralism.

A Shift Toward Multilateralism

A *top currency* is favored for international monetary transactions because others have confidence in the economic position of the issuing state. A *negotiated currency* does not benefit from this high degree of confidence, so the issuing state must induce others to accept its leadership. As U.S. balance-of-payments deficits increased, the dollar slipped from top-currency to negotiated-currency status, and there was a shift toward multilateral management.[30] In 1962, 10 DCs, called the **Group of 10** (the **G10**), established the *General Arrangements to Borrow (GAB)*, an agreement to lend up to $6 billion in their own currencies as supplementary resources to the IMF if the Fund's resources could not meet member countries' needs. The G10 countries establishing the GAB were Belgium, Britain, Canada, France, Germany, Italy, Japan, Netherlands, Sweden, and the United States. Switzerland, which was not an IMF member at the time, joined the G10 in 1962 as the eleventh member (it is still called the G10). The creation of the GAB represented a shift from unilateral U.S. management toward collective management, because the G10 had to approve each request for supplementary support for the IMF.[31] Another indication of the shift to multilateral management was the increased role of the Swiss-based **Bank for International Settlements (BIS)**. Formed in 1930, the BIS is an important venue for promoting cooperation among central banks. However, the BIS was controversial in earlier years because of allegations that it had pro-Nazi sentiments and accepted looted gold from occupied countries. It resumed operations after returning the looted gold, but this stigma limited its role as an international financial institution. In the 1960s the BIS regained some stature by organizing mutual lines of credit among the central banks to stabilize exchange rates and alleviate the downward pressure on the U.S. dollar. The BIS has become the main forum for cooperation among DC central bankers, and it uses its deposits from the central banks to provide credit and deal with exchange-rate problems.[32]

Despite these moves toward collective management, LDCs were not represented in either the G10 or the BIS. In 1971, the South therefore formed its own **Group of 24 (G24)**, which includes finance ministers or central bank governors from the three main LDC regions—Africa, Asia, and Latin America and the Caribbean. China has been a "special invitee" in the G24 since 1981. The G24 tries to coordinate LDC monetary policies and responds to G10 reports on monetary reform, but its influence is limited because its members are IMF borrowers.[33] Although the G10 countries have considerable economic power, even their resources could not defend the dollar if it came under attack as U.S. payments deficits increased. The G10 therefore took actions to bolster the dollar, and the United States tried to improve its balance of payments by reducing capital outflows. However, U.S. gold stocks continued to fall, dollar claims against the U.S. gold supply rose, and by 1968 the dollar in effect had become inconvertible into gold.

Some observers attributed the U.S. balance-of-payments deficit to the public goods it provided such as the Marshall Plan, the U.S. dollar as the key currency, and an open market for other countries' exports; but critics argued that the United States was unwilling to balance its revenues and expenditures. For example, the U.S. Congress refused to raise taxes to pay for the Vietnam War, President Johnson refused to cut domestic social programs, and the United States had a low personal savings rate. The personal savings rate as a share of disposable income in 1980 was 19.2 percent for Japan, 12.3 percent for Britain, 11 percent for France, 10.9 percent for West Germany, and only 6 percent for the United States. Thus, high-saving Japan provided large-scale capital flows to the low-saving United States.[34] The U.S. payments deficit also resulted from its declining competitiveness as Western Europe and Japan recovered from the war. The Bretton Woods regime did not provide the United States with *adjustment* options, because it was the only country that could not devalue its currency. As the key currency, the U.S. dollar had to remain at $35 per ounce of gold.

The U.S. payments deficit was not the only problem confronting the Bretton Woods regime. The national controls on capital flows were becoming less effective because investors lacked confidence in the pegged currency exchange rates. Speculative activity in the eurocurrency market was difficult to regulate, and MNCs evaded controls through transactions among their affiliates. MNCs moved capital from one country to another to take advantage of interest rate spreads and expected exchange-rate adjustments, and this put growing pressure on states to realign their currency exchange rates. To prevent a run on their currencies, leaders often committed themselves to the established parities, severely limiting their policy options. Powerful domestic interests also prevented governments from realigning their currencies. Thus, modest changes in exchange rates were difficult to institute, and the monetary regime became overly rigid despite the need for flexibility.[35]

To support the Bretton Woods fixed exchange rate regime, IMF members agreed, with the G10's approval, to create an artificial reserve asset in 1969: **special drawing rights (SDRs)**. SDRs were designed to provide a new source of liquidity, because gold and the U.S. dollar were not providing adequate support for the expansion of global trade and finance. SDRs are *not* a currency, and only states can hold them. The IMF may allocate SDRs to member countries in proportion to their IMF quotas, and countries holding SDRs can obtain freely usable currencies of IMF members in exchange for them. IMF members may voluntarily exchange SDRs for convertible currencies, or the IMF may designate members with strong external payments to purchase SDRs from members with weaker payments positions. Those members that purchase SDRs earn interest, while those that sell SDRs pay interest on them. Initially, 35 SDRs were equal to $35 (U.S.) or an ounce of gold, but since the move to floating exchange rates in the 1970s (discussed later), the SDR value has been determined by a basket or weighted average of currencies. Today, the basket consists of the U.S. dollar, the euro, the Japanese yen, and the British pound sterling. In addition to providing more liquidity, the SDR has served as a stable unit of account for the IMF and other IOs, because some currencies in the basket rise while others fall in value.

Decisions to allocate SDRs require approval by three-fifths of the IMF members with 85 percent of the voting power. The first allocation was for 9.3 billion SDRs in 1970–72, and the second allocation was for 12.1 billion SDRs in 1979–81. However, there were no further allocations until 2009 for several reasons. First, DCs had less need for SDRs because the major currencies shifted to floating exchange rates and there was an end to national capital controls (discussed later), so creditworthy governments could readily borrow on capital markets. Second, SDRs are allocated in proportion to a country's IMF quota, and the G5 countries receive the most SDRs. The South proposed that the creation of new SDRs be linked to the transfer of resources for development to LDCs, but the North argued that LDC needs for development assistance would lead to the creation of excess SDRs in liquidity terms. This led to a long-term stalemate in the creation of new SDRs. However, the G20 responded to the 2008 global financial crisis by calling for another allocation of SDRs to provide financial resources to countries lacking liquidity. In August 2009, the IMF provided a third general allocation of 161.2 billion SDRs, and it also provided a special allocation of 21.5 billion SDRs to countries that joined the IMF after the 1970s and did not benefit from the first two SDR allocations. These allocations had a critical role in providing liquidity and supplementing countries' reserves during the financial crisis. With the decline in value of the U.S. dollar in recent years, countries with large U.S. dollar reserves such as China and Russia have called for a greater role for the more stable SDR in the global monetary regime. However, despite the large increase in SDRs allocated in 2009, as of April 2013 there were about $300 billion of SDR stocks which accounted for only 3 percent of global reserve assets. SDRs are not likely to ever *replace* the U.S. dollar or euro as a reserve asset because "no money has ever risen to a position of international preeminence that was not initially backed by a leading economy."[36]

The Demise of the Bretton Woods Monetary Regime

By the late 1960s, the Bretton Woods monetary regime had become untenable. France's president Charles de Gaulle was deliberately converting dollars into gold to bring about an end to U.S. "exorbitant privilege" as the key-currency state, and the United States was making it more difficult for foreign central banks to change their dollars into gold.[37] Although U.S. foreign investment and loans had been the main source of its balance-of-payments deficits, in 1971 the United States had its first balance-of-*trade* deficit since 1893. On August 15, 1971, President Richard M. Nixon suspended the official convertibility of the dollar into gold and imposed a 10 percent tariff surcharge on all dutiable imports. In December 1971, the G10 countries therefore agreed to devalue the dollar by 10 to 20 percent vis-à-vis other major currencies in the first Smithsonian Agreement (negotiated at the Smithsonian Institution in Washington, DC). This did not correct the problem, and a second Smithsonian Agreement devalued the dollar further in February 1973.[38]

By the early 1970s, the requirements for adequate reserves—liquidity, confidence, and adjustment—all presented serious problems: The U.S. balance-of-payments deficits created a crisis of confidence in the dollar; countries were therefore reluctant to hold large supplies of U.S. dollars for liquidity purposes; and the dollar could not be adequately adjusted through devaluation because the dollar was to be "as good as gold" (the Smithsonian agreements were "too little, and too late"). With the increased global capital flows, the Bretton Woods system of pegged exchange rates was also becoming untenable. IMF members tried to reform the international monetary regime, but their discussions failed because of differences among the Americans, Europeans, and LDCs; destabilizing changes such as the 1973 increase in OPEC oil prices; and Germany and France's preoccupation with establishing a *European Monetary System* (*EMS*). Thus, the Bretton Woods regime of pegged exchange rates collapsed and was replaced by a regime that permitted floating exchange rates.

THE REGIME OF FLOATING (OR FLEXIBLE) EXCHANGE RATES

By 1973, the major trading nations were "living in sin," because they were ignoring the Bretton Woods ban on freely floating exchange rates.[39] The 1976 IMF meeting in Jamaica finally legalized this situation by permitting each country to either establish a par value for its currency or shift to **floating exchange rates**. In a *free-floating* regime, countries do not intervene in currency markets, and the market alone determines currency values. IMF members often rely instead on *managed floating*, in which central banks intervene to deal with disruptive conditions such as excessive fluctuations in exchange rates. Although the IMF accepts managed floating, it opposes *manipulative floating*, which involves "manipulating exchange rates ... in order to prevent effective balance of payments adjustment or to gain an unfair competitive advantage."[40]

The current monetary regime is mixed in nature: Major DCs such as the United States, Japan, and Canada (and a number of LDCs) float their currencies; the EU members seek increased regional coordination of their policies; and many LDCs peg the value of their currencies to a key currency or basket of currencies. The choice of a pegged versus a floating currency can have consequences for domestic groups in a state, and domestic as well as international factors therefore determine whether a state decides to peg or float its currency.[41] In view of the variation among countries, some analysts describe the current monetary system as a "nonsystem."[42]

The move to floating exchange rates had an intellectual appeal for orthodox liberals, who argued that exchange rate adjustment should occur through the market rather than government involvement. As early as 1953 Milton Friedman had called for "a system of exchange rates freely determined in open markets, primarily by private transactions, and the simultaneous abandonment of direct controls over exchange transactions."[43] Although some liberals feared that floating rates would lead to speculative capital flows as they had in the 1930s, Friedman argued that instability during the 1930s had resulted more from fundamental economic and financial problems.[44] Floating rates also appealed to some neomercantilists and interventionist liberals, because they permit governments to establish their own independent monetary policies in a domestic context. As capital controls were abandoned, countries were finding it increasingly difficult to set their own monetary policies under the pegged exchange rate regime because of the so-called *Unholy Trinity*.[45] The three elements of the Unholy Trinity are exchange-rate stability, private capital mobility, and monetary policy autonomy. Economists assert that states can attain only two of these three goals simultaneously. With pegged exchange rates and capital mobility, a state's attempt to follow independent monetary policies can lead to capital flight and a downward pressure on the currency exchange rate until the state alters its monetary policies. For example, if domestic interest rates differ from global interest rates, capital flows can quickly eliminate the difference. Because most states have accepted a high degree of capital mobility and cannot reverse this trend, the Unholy Trinity involves a trade-off between pegged exchange rates and policy autonomy. In shifting to floating exchange rates, states opted for more policy autonomy.

Although the shift to floating rates has permitted larger DCs to follow more independent monetary policies, most economists underestimated the degree to which increased capital mobility would disrupt exchange rates. As orthodox liberalism returned, the United States and Britain rejected any further attempts to control capital flows, and other DCs soon followed because countries were competing for foreign investment. The integration of financial markets, combined with technological advances, contributed to a massive growth in speculative capital flows. Thus, volatility and misalignment of currencies have been serious problems with the floating exchange rate regime. *Volatility* refers to the short-term instability of exchange rates. Under the floating system, unpredictable capital flows can produce highly volatile exchange rates that create uncertainty, inhibit productive investments, and interfere with international trade. *Misalignment* refers to the long-term departure of exchange rates from competitive levels. Misalignment is even more serious than volatility because it leads to prolonged changes in international competitiveness. Depending on whether a currency is under- or overvalued, misalignment gives a country substantial price advantages or disadvantages vis-à-vis its competitors.[46]

The shift to floating rates also created a crisis of purpose for the IMF, because its role in stabilizing pegged exchange rates largely disappeared. The G5 and G7 discussed the floating regime outside of IMF auspices, and the G7 summits engaged in a limited degree of policy coordination. For example, at the 1978 Bonn Summit the United States agreed to reduce its balance-of-payments deficits, and Germany and Japan agreed to adopt expansionary economic policies to increase their demand for U.S. goods.[47] However, this limited policy coordination ended with the Reagan administration, which lowered taxes and raised spending for military-defense purposes. These policies contributed to an annual U.S. government deficit that exceeded $200 billion by the mid-1980s. To service its debt, the United States raised interest rates to attract foreign capital—but the increase in capital imports strengthened the U.S. dollar, and U.S. trade and payments deficits began to spiral out of control.

The Plaza–Louvre Accords

As its dollar appreciated and its deficits increased, the United States could no longer afford to neglect exchange rates. To lower the value of the dollar, U.S. Secretary of the Treasury James Baker III assembled the G5 finance ministers and central bank heads in New York City's Plaza Hotel in September 1985. The G5 agreed to raise the value of the major nondollar currencies through coordinated market intervention (i.e., by buying and selling currencies), and the United States in return promised to reduce government spending. The dollar depreciated significantly after the Plaza Agreement, and the G7 therefore met at the Louvre in Paris in February 1987 to prevent its value from slipping even further. The Plaza and Louvre accords marked a shift to managed floating, in which governments intervened to correct currency volatility and misalignment. However, the major economies have not coordinated their interventions on a consistent basis since the Louvre accord. Although policy coordination is important for maintaining currency stability, international capital flows and governments' unwillingness to accept constraints on their fiscal and monetary policies preclude such coordination. Thus, the current monetary regime is much more unstable than liberal economists had predicted.[48]

ALTERNATIVES TO THE CURRENT MONETARY REGIME

Some economists point to the problems of volatility and misalignment under the floating regime and favor a return to a pegged exchange rate regime.[49] However, most analysts feel that efforts "to reestablish a system of pegged

TABLE 6.4

Membership of the European Union

Year of Membership	Members
1957	France*, West Germany, Italy*, Belgium*, Netherlands*, Luxembourg*
1973	United Kingdom, Denmark, Ireland*
1981	Greece*
1986	Spain*, Portugal*
1990	Germany unified*
1995	Austria*, Finland*, Sweden
2004	Cyprus*, Czech Republic, Estonia*, Hungary, Latvia*, Lithuania*, Malta*, Poland, Slovakia*, Slovenia*
2007	Bulgaria, Romania
2013	Croatia

*Eurozone Members

Sources: Europa—Member states of the EU, updated August 20, 2015. Europa—Which members use the euro. http://europa.eu/about-eu/countries/index_en.htm. http://europa.eu/about-eu/basic-information/money/euro/index_en.htm

but adjustable rates will ... prove futile."[50] States would find it difficult to defend pegged exchange rates because of the rise in international financial transactions; and any effort to enforce capital controls would require policy coordination, a highly unlikely possibility. Thus, the global monetary regime is likely to retain floating exchange rates. In looking to alternatives to the current regime, the noted monetary specialist Barry Eichengreen wrote in the 1990s that the only "serious experiment" in international monetary reform was taking place in Europe.[51] It is therefore important to discuss Europe's **euro zone**, in which the members have substituted a common currency—the euro—for their national currencies. This chapter discusses European monetary relations, and Chapter 9 examines the EU as a regional trade agreement. To reflect a name change in the EU, we use the term *European Community* *(EC)* when discussing the events from 1957 to 1992 and the term *European Union (EU)* when discussing events from 1993 to the present. Table 6.4 shows that the EC gradually enlarged from 6 members in 1957 to the 28-member EU in 2013. As Table 6.4 shows, only 19 of the 28 EU members have joined the euro zone and adopted the euro as a common currency. The euro zone members are identified with an asterisk.

EUROPEAN MONETARY RELATIONS

The Treaty of Rome creating the EC in 1957 focused on eliminating trade barriers, but a series of events starting in the 1960s also gave concrete form to the idea of a European monetary union. In January 1999, 11 EU members formed the euro zone and agreed to adopt the euro in place of their national currencies: Austria, Belgium, Finland, France, Germany, Ireland, Italy, Luxembourg, the Netherlands, Portugal, and Spain. Eight more EU members joined later, and the euro zone now has 19 members. The following discussion examines the challenges in creating and maintaining the euro zone, and the implications of the euro zone for European and global monetary relations.

From 1958 to the late 1960s, the Bretton Woods pegged exchange rate regime provided the EC with some stability. However, two changes in the 1960s caused the EC to consider regional monetary integration: Growing U.S. balance-of-payments deficits decreased confidence in the U.S. dollar; and Europe's rapid progress in developing a customs union and a common agricultural policy increased the need for exchange-rate stability among EC members. In 1970, the Werner Plan (developed by Pierre Werner, the Luxembourg prime minister) recommended that the EC countries adopt similar fiscal and monetary policies and reduce fluctuations in their currency exchange rates. One element of the plan was a "snake agreement" that limited exchange-rate fluctuations among EC currencies to a narrow band of +2.25 to –2.25 percent. However, France, Ireland, Italy, and Britain could not adhere to the band because they had weaker currencies, and they soon left the snake agreement. Other factors contributing to the failure of the snake agreement were the increase in capital mobility, the divergent macroeconomic policies of EC members, and global events such as the 1973–74 oil price rise and the 1975 global recession. As discussed, states can attain only two of the three "Unholy Trinity" goals (exchange-rate stability, capital mobility, and monetary policy autonomy). Capital mobility was increasing, and the EC members could stabilize their currency exchange rates only by sacrificing monetary policy autonomy. However, the EC members' divergent economic policies led to differential inflation rates, and speculative capital flows against the weaker currencies split the "snake" apart.

After the snake agreement failed, the EC launched a European Monetary System (EMS), and this time they were more successful. Kathleen McNamara argues from a constructivist perspective that a neoliberal policy consensus among EC leaders in the late 1970s induced them to give up autonomous monetary policies to achieve exchange-rate stability. To become more competitive internationally, the EMS members gave priority to exchange-rate stability and inflation control over social issues and were "willing to rule out the use of monetary policy as a weapon against broader societal problems, such as unemployment and slow growth."[52] Like the Werner Plan, the EMS had an *exchange-rate mechanism (ERM)* that limited exchange-rate fluctuations to a +2.25 to –2.25 percent band, and central banks intervened to keep the exchange rates within these levels. If this effort failed, a state could realign its currency after consultations with other EMS members. Although the EMS helped to stabilize exchange rates, some EC members could not keep their exchange rates within the narrow ERM band because of increased financial flows, and they were permitted to move to a broader band of +6 to –6 percent.[53]

The problems of the EMS stemmed from the fact that it was only a partial monetary union, and the need for monetary stability increased as EC integration progressed. Hence, there were pressures for a full monetary union that would create a single European currency and give Europe a greater voice in international economic negotiations. In 1992, the *Treaty on European Union* or *Maastricht Treaty* included a three-stage plan for monetary union, involving the coordination of monetary policies, the realignment of currency exchange rates, and the creation of a single currency under a European central bank.[54] However, the steps toward monetary union were difficult because the Maastricht agreement (at Germany's insistence) had rigid requirements for developing a single currency. To join the euro zone, a country's budget deficit had to be no greater than 3 percent of its GDP and its public debt no greater than 60 percent of its GDP. Some EU countries did not meet these criteria, and the required budgetary cuts caused considerable discontent. For example, French workers staged massive strikes in 1995 to protest planned cutbacks in social programs. Many Germans also did not want to sacrifice the deutsche mark, which reflected the country's economic strength, for what could be a weaker euro; but Germany's chancellor Helmut Kohl strongly supported the euro zone. Other countries had different concerns. For example, Britain wanted to preserve its monetary sovereignty, and Britain and France opposed the decision to locate the new European Central Bank in Frankfurt, Germany. Britain, Sweden, and Denmark decided not to join the euro zone, and Greece was too weak economically to be a founding member. Despite the obstacles, 11 EU members formed the euro zone in 1999 and agreed to replace their national currencies with the euro. Greece was admitted to the euro zone in 2001, Slovenia in 2007, Cyprus and Malta in 2008, Slovakia in 2009, Estonia in 2011, Latvia in 2014, and Lithuania in 2015.

The euro zone and the EU itself are facing major challenges today as a result of the European sovereign debt crisis (see Chapter 7). However, debate has continued over the costs and benefits of the euro zone. The benefits of a monetary union include reduced exchange-rate volatility, lower transaction costs, greater price transparency, and a better functioning internal market. The costs of a monetary union result from the loss of the exchange rate as a policy instrument; that is, euro zone members can no longer pursue independent monetary policies by altering their exchange rates. As we discuss in Chapter 7, a monetary union cannot respond well to financial crises if there is a lack of fiscal or political unity. The Nobel laureate Robert Mundell framed this debate on costs versus benefits many years earlier. Mundell argued that an **optimum currency area**, which maximizes the benefits of using a common currency, has certain characteristics: It is subject to common economic shocks, has a high degree of labor mobility, and has a tax system that transfers resources from strong to weak economic areas. Mundell's ideas have been highly influential (albeit controversial), and he has been called the "Father of the Euro."[55] When the euro zone was created, there were serious questions as to whether countries with such different characteristics should be forming a common currency. Whereas more competitive countries such as Austria, Finland, and Germany had currencies that persistently appreciated, less competitive countries such as Portugal, Spain, Italy, and Greece (which joined the euro zone later) had currencies that persistently depreciated. "Euro-optimists" hoped that the common currency would make the poorer countries more competitive. However, low interest rates within the euro zone lured governments and households in these countries to engage in unwise budgetary policies and excessive consumption.

Greece, Portugal, and Spain could also rely on large inflows of foreign capital, because membership of these countries in the euro zone *seemed* to make their bonds safe investments. However, the 2008 global financial crisis caused revenues to plunge, and capital inflows to countries where fiscal discipline was inadequate precipitously declined. Greece was the country hit hardest, and there are questions as to whether it will remain within the euro zone (see Chapter 7). If Greece were outside the euro zone, it could devalue its currency and become more competitive. However, Greece's creditworthiness and ability to avoid a sovereign default would be severely compromised. Fears that Greece's deficit and debt problems would spread to other countries such as Portugal, Ireland, Spain, and even Italy sparked efforts by the IMF and EU to provide Greece with an economic rescue package. However, political as well as economic factors will determine the outcome of this crisis in the euro zone. For example, there is political opposition in Germany (the strongest member) to bailing out euro zone countries because of their overspending habits, and there is opposition in the deficit countries to the stringent terms (e.g., cutbacks in wages and other economic benefits) the IMF, EU, and European Central Bank require for economic assistance. An examination of these economic–political linkages is critical to an understanding of the crisis facing the euro zone and the EU.[56]

To this point, we have looked mainly at the regional implications of the euro zone. However, many have raised questions about the future of the U.S. dollar and whether it may be displaced as the key international currency. The next section addresses this issue.

WHAT IS THE FUTURE OF THE U.S. DOLLAR AS THE KEY CURRENCY?

Analysts offering predictions about the future of the dollar take different approaches depending on their theoretical perspectives. This section draws on three approaches outlined in *The Future of the Dollar*, edited by Eric Helleiner and Jonathan Kirshner.[57] Liberal economists generally favor a *market-based approach*, which assumes that the assessments of market actors such as business firms and other financial institutions determine an international currency's importance. For example, the chronic U.S. government deficits and the growing U.S. foreign debt problem have an adverse effect on confidence in the dollar. However, other factors such as the size of the U.S. economy, U.S. political stability, and the depth and openness of U.S. financial markets help account for the continued role of the dollar as the key international currency. Whereas liberals favor a market-based approach, neomercantilists favor instrumental and geopolitical approaches because of their focus on the state. An *instrumental approach* focuses on the involvement of governments in determining the relative position of an international currency. Instrumentalists believe that the importance of a particular currency (currency A) stems from foreign governments holding currency A in their reserves, and from foreign governments pegging their own currencies—formally or informally—to currency A. For example, in the 1950s–1960s, Japan and Germany benefited from pegging their currency to the U.S. dollar. As these two countries recovered from the war, their currencies did not rise in value relative to the U.S. dollar to reflect their increased competitiveness. This gave them an advantage in selling their goods to the United States which was the world's largest domestic market, because the dollar could not be devalued in the Bretton Woods regime. In recent years, countries such as China, Taiwan, and South Korea have informally undervalued their currencies in relation to the dollar to increase their exports, and they have built up substantial reserves which are largely composed of U.S. dollars. In sum, maintaining the dollar as the key international currency has been of instrumental value to many foreign governments in exporting to the large U.S. market. A *geopolitical approach* is also favored by neomercantilists, who believe that geopolitics and power have a major role in determining a currency's international position. For example, Japan's continued support for the U.S. dollar as the key international currency is closely related to the country's reliance on U.S. military support. In reality, the market-based, instrumental, and geopolitical approaches *all* help in making predictions about the future of the dollar as the key international currency. In the following discussion we assess the prospects for the dollar vis-à-vis the three most likely competitors: the Japanese yen, the euro, and the Chinese renminbi.

The Dollar Versus the Yen

The yen's status as an international currency increased significantly in the 1970s–1980s when Japan experienced impressive economic growth. Japan became the world's second largest economy in 1968, and the yen became one of the most widely used currencies in the 1970s because Japan had large annual trade surpluses, a sizable financial market, and political stability. Whereas Japan became the world's largest creditor nation in the 1980s, the United States by contrast had chronic trade deficits, a weak dollar, and economic stagflation; so some analysts speculated that the yen might replace the dollar as the key international currency. However, the international appeal of the yen had its limits even during the 1970s–1980s, partly because of Japan's efforts to maintain tight control over its monetary policy. The Japanese financial system lacked openness, and its capital markets were highly regulated and protected until the 1990s. Other factors limiting Japan's willingness and ability to vie with the United States in developing the key international currency were bitter memories among other Asian countries of Japan's role in World War II, and Japan's dependence on the United States for military security. In the late 1980s, Japan began to experience serious economic problems that have resulted in two decades of economic stagnation and deflation, and as a result the international status of the yen has declined. Japan's problems include low economic growth, a rapidly aging population, and a very high public debt level. Thus, the yen's share in foreign exchange markets declined from 27 percent of global turnover in 1989 to about 20 percent in 2004. In recent years the Japanese government has done more to promote the yen as an international currency, but its efforts have been largely unsuccessful. Although the yen has a regional role in Asia, it poses no challenge to the dollar today as the key international currency. Even in Asia, there is the increasing prospect that the yen will be overshadowed by the Chinese yuan.[58]

The Dollar Versus the Euro

In the years before the 2008 global financial crisis, a number of analysts speculated as to whether the euro might supplement or even replace the U.S. dollar as the key international currency. Euro-optimists could point to a number of economic benefits of having a common currency. For example, it has stimulated trade and foreign investment within the euro zone, which has benefited consumers and enabled firms to merge and become more competitive. The euro zone also benefited from having political stability, a low inflation rate, a large combined GDP, and a European Central Bank (ECB). Although by all measures the U.S. dollar remained the key international currency, there were clear signs that the international use of the euro was increasing. In comparing currencies, it is important to look at their three main functions. In 2007, the dollar was used as a *medium of exchange* in 86 percent of all foreign exchange transactions, compared with 37 and 16.5 percent for the euro and Japanese yen, respectively. Almost two-thirds of all countries that peg their currencies peg them to the U.S. dollar as a *unit of account*, compared with one-third to the euro. The share of dollars as a *store of value* in central bank holdings declined from 70.9 percent in 1999 to 64 percent in 2007, while the share of euros rose from 17.9 to 26.5 percent. Although the dollar continued to be the key international currency, the euro had made impressive gains since its creation in 1999.[59]

However, euro-pessimists have pointed to structural flaws in the design of the euro zone and the economic policies of its members. Although European financial markets could pose a challenge to U.S. dominance, decentralization and fragmentation in the euro zone is a disadvantage relative to the more unified U.S. financial structure. The ECB has less supervisory capacity over EU financial markets than the U.S. Federal Reserve; and Britain, which has the most developed financial markets in Europe, has not adopted the euro. The transactional network of the euro is limited by the fact that only 19 of the 28 EU members have adopted it. Some political security factors also give the dollar an advantage over the euro. For example, U.S. military power and political stability contribute to confidence in the dollar. The EU by contrast lacks political unity, and EU members have difficulty asserting their power collectively on international political issues. The difficulties the euro zone has had in confronting the financial problems of its weaker members also show the problems of monetary union without political union. These problems were addressed in a 2001 debate between two Nobel Prize winners, Robert Mundell (a Canadian), who has been called "the father of the euro," and Milton Friedman, who was a euro-sceptic. In that debate Friedman predicted that the euro zone's "real Achilles heel will prove to be political; that a system under which the political and currency boundaries do not match is bound to prove unstable."[60]

Another problem stems from the fact that the value of the euro reflects the average economic strength of the euro zone members. Thus, the euro's exchange rate is much lower for Germany than the exchange rate of the deutsche mark would be, and this has contributed to the strength of Germany as an export giant (Germany's exports are less expensive for foreigners). As Table 6.2 shows, in 2013 Germany's merchandise trade surplus was $275.9 billion, second only to China's surplus of $351.8 billion. The euro exchange rate by contrast is too high for two-thirds of the euro zone countries, and it is crippling the economies of a third of them. The southern European countries have the biggest competitiveness problems, and they have no exchange-rate flexibility; that is, they cannot become more competitive by devaluing their currencies. Thus, Greece, Portugal, Spain, and Italy are finding it difficult to escape from their debt traps. Another problem is that the less competitive countries were able to borrow more easily when the euro zone was formed, because confidence in the euro reflected Germany's economic strength. Whereas Germany became more efficient, other members let the cheap borrowing rates via the euro lull them into complacency. Budget deficits increased, wages rose rapidly, and speculation in real estate escalated out of control.

These flaws in the design of the euro made the euro zone countries more vulnerable to the 2008 global financial crisis. As Chapter 7 discusses, the crisis has resulted in a marked decline in the euro's role as an international currency. In 1999 a strong political coalition of states had joined around a German–French core to establish the euro; but the sovereign debt crisis has caused that coalition to fragment. Northern euro zone countries with surpluses have been reluctant to provide the large fiscal transfers required to support the southern euro zone countries facing major adjustment costs. The German Chancellor Angela Merkel has viewed austerity programs as the best answer to the debtor countries' problems. As Chapter 7 discusses, some analysts argue that the austerity policies in Europe have exacerbated the debt crisis, and several euro zone countries have faced the danger of default. The crisis has threatened to spread throughout the euro zone and has caused financial markets to turn away from the euro. The European sovereign debt crisis strengthens the position of those who argue that a disparate group of countries, ranging from Germany and its powerful economy at one extreme to Greece at the other, should not have been joined in a single currency bloc without deeper economic, fiscal, and political integration. In a May 2013 article, Kenneth Rogoff supports this view, writing that "without further profound political and economic integration—which may not end up including all current euro zone members—the euro may not make it even to the end of the decade."[61] Rogoff's statement may be too extreme, but it is difficult to find an analyst today predicting that the euro will replace the dollar as the key international currency. The main problem, according to Eichengreen, is that the euro is "a currency without a state."[62]

The Dollar Versus the Renminbi

The *renminbi* (*RMB*) is the official name of China's currency introduced by the Communist People's Republic of China at the time it was founded in 1949; it means "the people's currency." The *yuan* is the unit of account for the renminbi currency. A similar example would be the British pound sterling. The pound is the unit of account of the sterling currency just as the yuan is the main unit of the renminbi currency. The terms renminbi and yuan are often used interchangeably. This section addresses the question as to whether the Chinese renminbi will replace the U.S. dollar as the key international currency. It is understandable that people would ask this question, because China's economy is huge, and growing. In 2014, China displaced the United States as the country with the largest GDP adjusted for purchasing power parity (PPP). Its PPP-adjusted GDP was about $17.6 trillion, compared with $17.4 trillion for the United States. The United States was still far ahead of China in terms of the more commonly used unadjusted GDP. In 2014, the U.S. unadjusted GDP was about $17.4 trillion, compared with $10.4 trillion for China. However, a number of analysts predict that China's unadjusted GDP will surpass that of the United States by the early 2020s. China is already the world's largest merchandise exporter and the second largest importer. China also holds the world's largest foreign exchange reserves, amounting to about $4 trillion.[63] China's large role in trade makes it valuable to hold RMB, largely as a means of paying for goods. China is also beginning to develop the foundations for a Chinese-centered financial system. It wants to create an RMB zone to balance the U.S. dollar zone which has been dominant since the end of World War II. This involves encouraging the use of the renminbi as a medium of exchange, a unit of account, and a store of value. China has made notable progress in a short period. Trading in the RMB tripled in a three-year period, and in September, 2013 the RMB became the ninth most actively traded currency internationally. The RMB is in the currency reserves of a growing number of countries, including Chile, Kenya, Malaysia, and Nigeria. Furthermore, China has signed currency swap agreements with 23 countries and regions, including Japan, South Korea, Australia, Brazil, and Turkey. In a currency swap, companies in two countries can acquire each other's currencies by exchanging them on a specified date. This exchange enables companies to minimize foreign borrowing costs and to hedge their exposure to exchange-rate risks. The strong competition among countries and cities to become a hub for RMB trading is another indication that the Chinese currency is becoming increasingly internationalized. London and Singapore have signed similar agreements to become trading hubs for the renminbi, and in March, 2015 Toronto became the site of the first trading hub for China's currency in the Americas. Since the 2008 global financial crisis, China has decided to accelerate the process of RMB internationalization, and this would enable states to diversify their reserve holdings.[64]

However, China's policies would have to change substantially before the RMB could pose a serious challenge to the dollar, because the requirements for foreign currency reserves are demanding. In his book entitled *The Dollar Trap*,

Eswar Prasad of Cornell University puts forth three conditions for a currency to become a widely used reserve currency: capital account convertibility, a floating exchange rate, and internationalization. Regarding *capital account convertibility*, China has eased its restrictions on capital flows to promote the use of the RMB as an international currency. However, it still imposes more restrictions than any of the reserve currency economies. The U.S. dollar, British pound sterling, Japanese yen, and Canadian and Australian dollars are fully convertible currencies. A fully convertible currency can be traded and converted into gold or another currency with minimal or no restrictions. The RMB by contrast is not fully convertible. Regarding *a floating exchange rate*, the exchange rate of the RMB is freer to float than it was in earlier years. From 1997 to 2005 the RMB exchange rate was pegged to the U.S. dollar. China let the RMB appreciate vis-à-vis the dollar in 2005, but it pegged the RMB to the dollar again during the 2008 financial crisis, and relaxed controls again only in 2010. Thus, China's willingness to accept a floating RMB is still limited and conditional. Regarding *internationalization*, there is a clear limitation on integration of Chinese financial institutions and markets with the rest of the world. A major obstacle to the internationalization of the RMB is that China does not yet have well-developed financial markets or widely trusted public institutions. China's domestic record on governance is marked by widespread official corruption, favoritism to state-owned companies over private companies, and a lack of transparency in financial dealings. The government views the financial system as an instrument of control because it is fearful of economic, political, and social instability. Thus, it is unlikely that the RMB will replace the U.S. dollar as the key international currency in the foreseeable future. U.S. dollars still accounted for about 62 percent of the world's currency reserves in early 2013, and a recent global survey shows that, of the $5 trillion a day foreign exchange market, the U.S. dollar was on one side of 87 percent of the transactions.[65]

The Future of the Dollar: Other Possible Scenarios

As discussed, no other major currency poses a challenge to the U.S. dollar as the key international currency at the current time. However, the high U.S. foreign debt is a potential source of instability for both the U.S. dollar and the global monetary regime. The growing U.S. debt has been financed largely by foreign countries, and the most prominent of these is China. From 2008 to 2012, China purchased about $750 billion of U.S. treasury bonds, almost a quarter of total foreign investors' purchases of $3.2 trillion.[66] Other countries such as Japan, South Korea, and some OPEC exporters also have large dollar holdings. Many of these countries have expressed resentment of the United States' "exorbitant privilege"; that is, its ability to have large current account deficits and high foreign debt levels because others will continue to seek U.S. dollars as the key international currency. As a result, they are shifting some of their reserves from U.S. dollars to euros and other reserve currencies. However, liberal economists point out that it is not in the economic interests of China, Japan, and South Korea to shift too much of their reserves and cause a rapid decline in the value of the U.S. dollar. They are highly dependent on the large U.S. market for their exports, and U.S. consumers with a cheaper dollar would purchase less. The value of these countries' dollar reserves would also fall with the declining value of the dollar. Thus, liberal economists note that the countries with large dollar reserves have a highly interdependent relationship with the United States. This interdependence should stabilize the value of the dollar as the key international currency despite the high U.S. foreign debt levels.

Neomercantilists, however, argue that China may decide to sell a certain percentage of its treasury bond holdings for geopolitical reasons, even if this resulted in an economic cost to China. Japan and South Korea are likely to continue to support the dollar for political as well as economic reasons, because of their dependence on U.S. military support. China by contrast has geopolitical tensions with the United States which could trump the interdependence between the two countries. For example, U.S. support for Taiwan in its efforts to avoid incorporation into China, or U.S. support for Japan and Taiwan in their island territorial disputes with China, could induce China to shift from U.S. treasury bonds despite the economic damage it could cause for both countries.

Concerns about the high U.S. foreign debt levels and resentment against the country's "exorbitant privilege" have resulted in a search for other alternatives to the current dollar-based regime. For example, the governor of the People's Bank of China has proposed that SDRs should be given a more important role as a major global monetary reserve. China would also want the RMB to be included with the U.S. dollar, euro, Japanese yen, and pound sterling in determining the value of this upgraded SDR. As discussed, however, SDRs cannot be used in private transactions, and they are not backed by a strong economy with fiscal authority. For the SDR to be a global currency, the IMF would have to act as a form of global central bank that could issue new SDRs as emergency liquidity during a financial crisis. Eichengreen refers to SDRs as "funny money," because it is highly unlikely that the major economies would give the IMF so much authority.[67] Thus, it is unlikely that the SDR will ever replace the dollar as the key international currency. Other possible alternatives to the U.S. dollar as the key international currency such as more dependence on gold or on electronic money such as Bitcoins are neither practical nor feasible in the present world. The most likely scenario is that currencies such as the renminbi, the euro, and the yen will gradually become more important along with the U.S. dollar in other countries' reserves, and that a different mix of currencies will be the dominant reserves in different regional areas. For example, the RMB and to a lesser extent the Japanese yen will gain an increasing foothold in Asia, and the euro (assuming it deals with the European sovereign debt crisis) could increase its hold in Europe and in various parts of Africa. Whether this diversification of currency reserves leads to cooperation, or to fragmentation and conflict, remains to be seen. As for the present, the dollar is maintaining its position as the key international currency, because of the size of the U.S. economy, its political stability, and the quality and depth of its financial markets.[68]

Considering IPE Theory and Practice

In the 1940s, the Bretton Woods negotiators opted for a monetary regime based on interventionist liberalism, in which states pegged their exchange rates to gold and the U.S. dollar, the IMF provided short-term loans for balance-of-payments problems, and states controlled capital flows to maintain exchange-rate stability. However, growing U.S. balance-of-payments deficits, combined with pressures for a return to orthodox liberalism, contributed to a shift from pegged to floating exchange rates in 1973 and to a gradual freeing of capital controls. Liberal theorists point out that, with the globalization of capital flows, countries had to choose between independent monetary policies and pegged exchange rates because of the "Unholy Trinity." To preserve their independence in monetary policy, the major countries shifted from pegged to floating exchange rates. In the orthodox liberal view, the shift to floating currencies and the freeing of capital flows are positive developments enabling markets to function more freely, with little state interference. Historical materialists by contrast see the increased capital mobility as a negative development because the fear of capital outflows forces governments to adopt policies that adversely affect the poorest and weakest in society. If governments do not adopt capital-friendly policies, MNCs and international banks can shift their funds to more welcoming locations. Thus, governments often lower their tax rates on corporate income, even if this means sacrificing social programs. Increased capital mobility also adversely affects the working class, because countries with weak labor unions draw investment away from countries with stronger unions. Neomercantilists argue that the globalization of monetary and financial relations is greatly exaggerated. To the extent that global financial flows have increased, this has occurred with the permission and sometimes encouragement of the most powerful states, and these states continue to dictate the terms for such transactions. Whereas neomercantilists are correct that powerful states supported financial globalization, liberals correctly point out that this globalization has had unintended consequences, because restoring national controls on capital flows would be like putting the genie back in the bottle.

To insulate themselves from global monetary instabilities, some countries are seeking regional alternatives, and the most important of these is the euro zone. Ideational as well as material factors have played a role in the euro zone, because a neoliberal policy consensus among EC leaders in the late 1970s induced them to give up autonomous monetary policies to achieve exchange-rate stability. As this chapter discusses, the euro has emerged as an alternative reserve currency to the U.S. dollar. A currency's effectiveness as a medium of exchange, a unit of account, and a store of value depends on ideational as well as material factors, because individuals must feel confident that the currency will not significantly lose its value. Growing U.S. current account deficits and foreign debt have decreased confidence in the U.S. dollar, but the euro zone's difficulty in forging political and economic unity among the member countries has also detracted from confidence in the euro. As discussed, the European sovereign debt crisis has raised major questions about the future of the euro, the euro zone, and the EU. China's currency, the RMB, must also be considered, because the country's monetary influence is increasing along with the growth of its economic power. With financial globalization the future of the dollar depends not only on the United States and its traditional European allies, but also on the actions of emerging economies with large U.S. dollar reserves such as China and a number of OPEC countries. These countries are dissatisfied with the fact that the United States' "exorbitant privilege" as the key currency country has enabled it to avoid dealing with its current account deficits and high foreign debt levels. Thus, China has argued for a greater role for SDRs as an alternative to the dollar, has taken some action to diversify its large reserves into other currencies, and has moved to increase the role of the renminbi as a reserve currency. Liberals argue that the interdependence between China and the United States will prevent China from withdrawing too much of its funds from U.S. treasuries. Such withdrawals could precipitate a major depreciation of the value of the dollar, which would adversely affect China because of its large holdings of dollar reserves. However, neomercantilists point out that China might act to undercut the dollar for geopolitical reasons such as U.S. support for Japan or Taiwan in their territorial disputes with China. For neomercantilists, China's geopolitical interests might trump its economic interests if conflict with the United States escalates. Despite China's growing influence, this chapter discusses the fact that the U.S. dollar is likely to retain its role as the key international currency for a number of years. However, different currencies such as the euro and the RMB are likely to have increased influence in various regional areas. Whereas liberals believe that global interdependence will result in cooperation among the various regions, neomercantilists see fragmentation and conflict as the most likely outcome of monetary regionalization.

QUESTIONS

1. What options does a country have in dealing with a balance-of-payments deficit, and what are the preferred options of the three main theoretical perspectives?
2. When did the United States first have a balance-of-payments deficit, and when did it first have a balance-of-trade deficit? Why was the Bretton Woods monetary regime unsustainable, and what role did the "Triffin dilemma" and the eurocurrency market play in the breakdown of the regime?
3. How much influence have DCs and LDCs had in IMF decision-making? Do you think this is likely to change in the future?
4. What have the IMF's functions been in the global monetary regime? How did the shift from pegged to floating exchange rates affect the role of the IMF vis-à-vis the G7? How has the role of the G20 changed in relation to the G7, and what is the reason for this change?
5. What are the characteristics of the current global monetary regime, and in what ways has it contributed to instability? What is the "Unholy Trinity," and does it limit the changes that IMF members can make in the current monetary regime?
6. Why was the euro zone formed, and what are its strong and weak points?

7. Are the Japanese yen, the euro, and the Chinese renminbi likely to pose a challenge to the U.S. dollar as the key international currency? What are SDRs, and could they pose a challenge to the U.S. dollar?
8. Do you think the U.S. deficit and debt problems pose an economic and geopolitical threat to the country? Is external financing a good solution for U.S. debt problems?

KEY TERMS

appreciation	external debt	International Monetary
balance of payments	financial account	Fund
Bank for International	fiscal policy	liquidity
Settlements	fixed exchange rates	monetary policy
conditionality	floating exchange rates	optimum currency area
current account	gold exchange standard	revaluation
depreciation	gold standard	seigniorage
devaluation	Group of 10	special drawing rights
eurocurrency market	Group of 24	Triffin dilemma
euro zone		

FURTHER READING

On the changing role of the U.S. dollar see Eswar S. Prasad, *The Dollar Trap* (Princeton, NJ: Princeton University Press, 2014); Barry Eichengreen, *Exorbitant Privilege: The Rise and Fall of the Dollar* (New York: Oxford University Press, 2011); Eric Helleiner and Jonathan Kirshner, eds., *The Future of the Dollar* (Ithaca, NY: Cornell University Press, 2009); and "At Home Abroad? The Dollar's Destiny as a World Currency," a special issue of *Review of International Political Economy* 15, no. 3 (August 2008). On China's growing monetary power see Eric Helleiner and Jonathan Kirshner, eds., *The Great Wall of Money: Power and Politics in China's International Monetary Relations* (Ithaca, NY: Cornell University Press, 2014). On the euro in crisis see Roger Bootle, *The Trouble with Europe* (Boston, MA: Nicholas Brealey, 2014); and Ivan T. Berend, *Europe in Crisis* (New York: Routledge, 2013). On the euro and integration theory see Amy Verdun, ed., *The Euro: European Integration Theory and Economic and Monetary Union* (Lanham, MD: Rowman & Littlefield, 2002).

On monetary governance and the competition among currencies, see Benjamin J. Cohen, *Currency Power: Understanding Monetary Rivalry* (Princeton, NJ: Princeton University Press, 2015); and Benjamin J. Cohen, *The Future of Money* (Princeton, NJ: Princeton University Press, 2004). Useful historical overviews of international monetary and financial relations include Barry Eichengreen, *Globalizing Capital: A History of the International Monetary System*, 2nd ed. (Princeton, NJ: Princeton University Press, 2008); Benjamin J. Cohen, *Global Monetary Governance* (New York: Routledge, 2008); and Harold James, *International Monetary Cooperation Since Bretton Woods* (New York: Oxford University Press, 1996). Studies on the governance of global finance include Tony Porter, *Globalization and Finance* (Malden, MA: Polity Press, 2005); and Michele Fratianni, Paolo Savona, and John J. Kirton, eds., *Governing Global Finance: New Challenges, G7 and IMF Contributions* (Burlington, VT: Ashgate, 2002).

On domestic politics and international finance see J. Lawrence Broz and Jeffry A. Frieden, "The Political Economy of International Monetary Relations," in *Annual*

Review of Political Science 4 (Norwood, NJ: Ablex, 2001), pp. 317–343. On the relation between capital mobility, policy coordination, and domestic autonomy, see Michael C. Webb, *The Political Economy of Policy Coordination: International Adjustment Since 1945* (Ithaca, NY: Cornell University Press, 1995).

NOTES

1. Barry Eichengreen, *Globalizing Capital: A History of the International Monetary System*, 2nd ed. (Princeton, NJ: Princeton University Press, 2008), p. 1; Susan Strange, "Protectionism and World Politics," *International Organization* 39, no. 2 (Spring 1985), p. 257.
2. Benjamin J. Cohen, *The Future of Money* (Princeton, NJ: Princeton University Press, 2004), pp. 11–12.
3. Benjamin J. Cohen, *The Geography of Money* (Ithaca, NY: Cornell University Press, 1998), p. 3.
4. Susan Strange, *Casino Capitalism* (Oxford, UK: Basil Blackwell, 1986), p. 29; Benjamin J. Cohen, "Life at the Top: International Currencies in the Twenty-First Century," *Essays in International Economics*, no. 221 (Princeton, NJ: Princeton University, International Economics Section, December 2000), pp. 2–4.
5. Mordechai E. Kreinin, *International Economics: A Policy Approach*, 6th ed. (San Diego, CA: Harcourt Brace Jovanovich, 1991), pp. 123–124; Richard N. Cooper, *The Economics of Interdependence: Economic Policy in the Atlantic Community* (New York: McGraw-Hill, 1968), pp. 13–23, chs. 7–9.
6. Paul R. Krugman, Maurice Obstfeld, and Marc J. Melitz, *International Economics: Theory and Policy*, 10th ed. (New York: Pearson, 2015), pp. 334–337.
7. Joseph Quinlan and Marc Chandler, "The U.S. Trade Deficit: A Dangerous Obsession," *Foreign Affairs*, May/June 2001, pp. 87–97; William R. Cline, "The Impact of U.S. External Adjustment on Japan," and Kathryn M. Dominguez, "Foreign Exchange Intervention: Did It Work in the 1990s?" in C. Fred Bergsten and John Williamson, eds., *Dollar Overvaluation and the World Economy* (Washington, DC: Institute for International Economics, 2003), pp. 179, 218.
8. Eric Helleiner, "Political Determinants of International Currencies: What Future for the U.S. Dollar?" *Review of International Political Economy* 15, no. 3 (August 2008), p. 370.
9. Ernest H. Preeg, "Exchange Rate Manipulation to Gain an Unfair Competitive Advantage," in C. Fred Bergsten and John Williamson, eds., *Dollar Overvaluation and the World Economy* (Washington, DC: Institute for International Economics, 2003), p. 270.
10. Cohen, *The Geography of Money*, p. 11; Kathleen R. McNamara, "A Rivalry in the Making? The Euro and International Monetary Power," *Review of International Political Economy* 15, no. 3 (August 2008), pp. 446–448; Eric Helleiner and Jonathan Kirshner, "The Future of the Dollar: Whither the Key Currency," in Eric Helleiner and Jonathan Kirshner, eds., *The Future of the Dollar* (Ithaca, NY: Cornell University Press, 2009), p. 3.
11. See Kenneth W. Dam, *The Rules of the Game: Reform and Evolution in the International Monetary System* (Chicago, IL: University of Chicago Press, 1982), p. 6; Benjamin J. Cohen, *Organizing the World's Money: The Political Economy of International Monetary Relations* (New York: Basic Books, 1977), ch. 3.

12. Barry Eichengreen, *Golden Fetters: The Gold Standard and the Great Depression, 1919–1939* (New York: Oxford University Press, 1992), ch. 2, pp. 204–207.
13. Paul R. Krugman and Maurice Obstfeld, *International Economics: Theory and Policy*, 3rd ed. (New York: HarperCollins, 1994), p. 507.
14. Peter A. Gourevitch, "Squaring the Circle: The Domestic Sources of International Cooperation," *International Organization* 50, no. 2 (Spring 1996), pp. 349–373; Beth A. Simmons, *Who Adjusts? Domestic Sources of Foreign Economic Policy During the Interwar Years* (Princeton, NJ: Princeton University Press, 1994).
15. McNamara, "A Rivalry in the Making?" p. 441.
16. John G. Ruggie, "International Regimes, Transactions, and Change: Embedded Liberalism in the Postwar Economic Order," in Stephen D. Krasner, ed., *International Regimes* (Ithaca, NY: Cornell University Press, 1983), pp. 209–214.
17. Eric Helleiner, "From Bretton Woods to Global Finance: A World Turned Upside Down," in Richard Stubbs and Geoffrey R. D. Underhill, eds., *Political Economy and the Changing Global Order* (Toronto: McClelland & Stewart, 1994), p. 164; J. Keith Horsefield, ed., *The International Monetary Fund 1945–1965: Twenty Years of International Monetary Cooperation, Vol. 3: Documents* (Washington, DC: IMF, 1969), p. 67.
18. International Monetary Fund, "IMF Quotas," *Factsheet*, October 3, 2014; and "How the IMF Makes Decisions," *Factsheet*, September 30, 2014, www.imf.org/external/np/exr/facts/.
19. IMF, *IMF Diversity & Inclusion Annual Report, FY 2014*, pp. 12 and 34, www.imf.org/external/np/div/2014/index.pdf; IMF, *IMF Annual Report—2008* (Washington, DC: IMF, 2008), CD-ROM.
20. Robert Harding, "US Fails to Approve IMF Reforms," *Financial Times*, January 14, 2014; Richard McGregor, "Congressional Impasse on IMF Shows the Tight Spot Obama Is in," *Financial Times*, January 27, 2014.
21. IMF website: www.imf.org/external/np/sec/memdir/eds.htm.
22. Paul Taylor and William James, "Fumbles, Mixed Signals Led to Tiff over China-Led Institution," *Globe and Mail*, March 23, 2015, pp. B1 and B7; "U.S. Allies, Lured by China's Bank," *International New York Times*, March 20, 2015.
23. A group of economists noted the liquidity, confidence, and adjustment problems: Fritz Machlup and Burton G. Malkiel, eds., *International Monetary Arrangements: The Problem of Choice: Report on the Deliberations of an International Study Group of 32 Economists* (Princeton, NJ: Princeton University International Finance Section, 1964), p. 24.
24. Cohen, *The Geography of Money*, pp. 39–42.
25. Robert Triffin, *Gold and the Dollar Crisis: The Future of Convertibility*, rev. ed. (New Haven, CT: Yale University Press, 1961).
26. Tony Porter, "Eurocurrency Market," in R. J. Barry Jones, ed., *Routledge Encyclopedia of International Political Economy*, vol. 1 (New York: Routledge, 2001), pp. 464–465.
27. Harold James, *International Monetary Cooperation Since Bretton Woods* (Washington, DC and New York: IMF and Oxford University Press, 1996), pp. 179–181.
28. Eric Helleiner, *States and the Reemergence of Global Finance: From Bretton Woods to the 1990s* (Ithaca, NY: Cornell University Press, 1994), pp. 81–100; Michael C. Webb, *The Political Economy of Policy Coordination: International Adjustment Since 1945* (Ithaca, NY: Cornell University Press, 1995), p. 16.

29. Susan Strange, *Sterling and British Policy: A Political Study of an International Currency in Decline* (London: Oxford University Press, 1971), p. 209.
30. Strange, *Sterling and British Policy*, pp. 5, 17.
31. C. Fred Bergsten and C. Randall Henning, *Global Economic Leadership and the Group of Seven* (Washington, DC: Institute for International Economics, 1996), pp. 22–23.
32. Hazel J. Johnson, *Global Financial Institutions and Markets* (Oxford, UK: Blackwell, 2000), p. 411; Age F. P. Bakker, *International Financial Institutions* (New York: Longman, 1996), ch. 6.
33. C. Randall Henning, "The Group of Twenty-Four: Two Decades of Monetary and Financial Cooperation Among Developing Countries," in UNCTAD, *International Monetary and Financial Issues for the 1990s*, vol. 1 (New York: UN, 1992), pp. 137–154.
34. Krugman and Obstfeld, *International Economics*, pp. 311–313; Marin Bronfenbrenner and Yasukichi Yasuba, "Economic Welfare," in Kozo Yamamura and Yasukichi Yasuba, eds., *The Political Economy of Japan: The Domestic Transformation*, vol. 1 (Stanford, CA: Stanford University Press, 1987), p. 100.
35. John Williamson and C. Randall Henning, "Managing the Monetary System," in Peter B. Kenen, ed., *Managing the World Economy: Fifty Years After Bretton Woods* (Washington, DC: Institute for International Economics, 1994), p. 89.
36. Cohen, "Life at the Top," pp. 5–6; IMF, "Special Drawing Rights (SDRs)," *Fact Sheet*, October 3, 2014, www.imf.org.external/np/exr/facts/sdr.htm; Eswar S. Prasad, *The Dollar Trap* (Princeton, NJ: Princeton University Press, 2014), p. 280.
37. The "exorbitant privilege" term was used by de Gaulle's Finance Minister, Valery Giscard d'Estaing. See Barry Eichengreen, *Exorbitant Privilege: The Rise and Fall of the Dollar* (New York: Oxford University Press, 2011), p. 4.
38. Robert Solomon, *The International Monetary System, 1945–1981*, 2nd ed. (New York: Harper & Row, 1982), pp. 176–234.
39. Cohen, *Organizing the World's Money*, p. 115. The IMF permitted Canada to float its currency from 1950 to 1962 because of its "special relationship" with the United States. See Arthur F. W. Plumptre, *Three Decades of Decision: Canada and the World Monetary System, 1944–75* (Toronto: McClelland and Stewart, 1977).
40. *Articles of Agreement of the International Monetary Fund*, adopted July 22, 1944, as amended in 1978 (Washington, DC: IMF, 1993), Article 4, section 1–iii.
41. See J. Lawrence Broz and Jeffry A. Frieden, "The Political Economy of International Monetary Relations," *Annual Review of Political Science* 4 (Norwood, NJ: Ablex, 2001), pp. 317–343.
42. Yusuke Kashiwagi, "Future of the International Monetary System and the Role of the IMF," in Bretton Woods Commission, *Bretton Woods: Looking to the Future, Background Papers* (Washington, DC: Bretton Woods Committee, 1994), p. C–1.
43. Milton Friedman, "The Case for Flexible Exchange Rates," in *Essays in Positive Economics* (Chicago, IL: University of Chicago Press, 1953), p. 203.
44. Helleiner, *States and the Reemergence of Global Finance*, pp. 116–117.
45. Benjamin Cohen coined the term *Unholy Trinity*, based on a model developed by Robert Mundell. See Robert Mundell, "Capital Mobility and Stabilization Policy Under Fixed and Flexible Exchange Rates," *Canadian Journal of Economics and Political Science* 29, no. 4 (November 1963), pp. 475–485; Benjamin J. Cohen, "The Triad and the Unholy Trinity: Lessons for the Pacific Region," in Richard Higgott, Richard Leaver, and John Ravenhill, eds., *Pacific Economic Relations in the 1990s: Cooperation or Conflict* (Boulder, CO: Rienner, 1993), pp. 133–158.

46. Helleiner, *States and the Reemergence of Global Finance*, pp. 115–116; John Williamson, *The Exchange Rate System*, rev. ed. (Washington, DC: Institute for International Economics, 1985), pp. 9–10, 39.
47. Michael Devereux and Thomas A. Wilson, "International Co-ordination of Macroeconomic Policies: A Review," *Canadian Public Policy* 15 (February 1989), pp. S23–S24.
48. Williamson and Henning, "Managing the Monetary System," p. 100. On the difficulties in bringing about policy coordination, see Webb, *The Political Economy of Policy Coordination*.
49. Robert Mundell has been a strong (and controversial) defender of fixed exchange rates and the gold standard.
50. Barry Eichengreen, *International Monetary Arrangements for the 21st Century* (Washington, DC: Brookings Institution, 1994), p. 5.
51. Barry Eichengreen, "Prerequisites for International Monetary Stability," in Bretton Woods Commission, *Bretton Woods: Looking to the Future, Background Papers* (Washington, DC: Bretton Woods Committee, 1994), p. C-50.
52. Kathleen R. McNamara, *The Currency of Ideas: Monetary Politics in the European Union* (Ithaca, NY: Cornell University Press, 1998), p. 10.
53. Malcolm Levitt and Christopher Lord, *The Political Economy of Monetary Union* (London: Macmillan, 2000), pp. 29–42.
54. McNamara, *The Currency of Ideas*, pp. 166–170; Sylvester C. W. Eijffinger and Jakob de Haan, *European Monetary and Fiscal Policy* (Oxford, UK: Oxford University Press, 2000), pp. 4–7.
55. Robert A. Mundell, "A Theory of Optimum Currency Areas," *American Economic Review* 51, no. 4 (September 1961), pp. 657–665.
56. "Briefing: The Euro Zone's Debt Crisis," *The Economist*, May 1, 2010, pp. 63–65; Paul Krugman, "The Euro Trap," *New York Times*, April 20, 2010.
57. Helleiner and Kirshner, "The Future of the Dollar," pp. 6–17.
58. Benjamin J. Cohen, "Toward a Leaderless Currency System," in Eric Helleiner and Jonathan Kirshner, eds., *The Future of the Dollar* (Ithaca, NY: Cornell University Press, 2009), pp. 152–154; Benjamin J. Cohen, "The China Question," in Eric Helleiner and Jonathan Kirshner, eds., *The Great Wall of Money* (Ithaca, NY: Cornell University Press, 2014), pp. 33–35.
59. Helleiner, "Political Determinants of International Currencies," p. 356; McNamara, "A Rivalry in the Making?" p. 444; Cohen, *The Geography of Money*, pp. 156–161; Helleiner and Kirshner, "The Future of the Dollar," p. 3; Cohen, "Toward a Leaderless Currency System," p. 148.
60. "One World, One Money?" *Policy Options*, May 2001, p. 10; Jonathan Kirshner, "Dollar Primacy and American Power: What's at Stake?" *Review of International Political Economy* 15, no. 3 (August 2008), pp. 419–420.
61. Kenneth Rogoff, "Keynes Never Met the Euro Zone," *Globe and Mail*, May 24, 2013, p. A11.
62. Eichengreen, *Exorbitant Privilege*, pp. 130–135.
63. International Monetary Fund, *World Economic Outlook*, www.imf.org/external/ns/cs.aspx?id+28; Josh Noble, "China's Foreign Exchange Reserves Near Record $4tn," *Financial Times*, April 15, 2014.
64. John Shmuel, "Renminbi Trading Hub Opens in Toronto," *National Post*, March 23, 2015; Gregory Chin, "China's Rising Monetary Power," in Eric Helleiner and Jonathan Kirshner, eds., *The Great Wall of Money* (Ithaca, NY: Cornell University Press, 2014), pp. 208–209.

65. Prasad, *The Dollar Trap*, pp. 229–245; Martin Wolf, "Even Beijing Balks at Price to Pay for Renminbi to Become a Reserve Currency," *Financial Times*, September 30, 2014; "Beijing's Challenge to the World of Bretton Woods," *Financial Times*, October 30, 2014.
66. Prasad, *The Dollar Trap*, p. 286.
67. Eichengreen, *Exorbitant Privilege*, pp. 137–143.
68. Prasad, *The Dollar Trap*, pp. 262–293; Cohen, "Toward a Leaderless Currency System," pp. 156–163; Paul Bowles and Baotai Wang, "The Rocky Road Ahead: China, the US and the Future of the Dollar," *Review of International Political Economy* 15, no. 3 (August 2008), pp. 335–353.

Financial Crises

Financial crises have existed since at least the thirteenth century, and they come in many forms. In their book *This Time Is Different* Carmen Reinhart and Kenneth Rogoff discuss inflation, currency, and banking crises, and external and domestic debt crises. Reinhart and Rogoff write that during prosperous times we begin to assume that "this time is different." We have learned from our past mistakes and can avoid serious financial crises in the future. However, the authors conclude that this is only wishful thinking. The 2008 global financial crisis and European sovereign debt crisis show that financial crises continue to pose an ever-present danger in today's world.[1] This chapter compares and contrasts four major financial crises. First, we discuss the 1980s foreign debt crisis, which was "one of the most traumatic international financial disturbances" of the twentieth century.[2] Although debt crises had occurred in earlier years, the world was unprepared for the 1980s crisis, which threatened many LDCs and the international banking system. Second, we examine the 1990s Asian financial crisis, in which "many of Asia's most rapidly advancing countries found themselves sliding down the rungs of the hierarchical world income ladder" instead of continuing their steady growth of earlier years.[3] Whereas the first two crises began in the South, the second two crises we examine began in the North. As Niall Ferguson writes in his book *The Ascent of Money*,

> just ten years ago, during the Asian Crisis of 1997–8, it was conventional wisdom that financial crises were more likely to happen on the periphery of the world economy—in the so-called emerging markets ... of East Asia or Latin America. Yet the biggest threats to the global financial system in this new century have come not from the periphery but from the core.[4]

The third crisis we discuss is the 2008 global financial crisis, which began with the U.S. subprime mortgage crisis and became the most severe financial crisis since the Great Depression of the 1930s. The fourth crisis, the European debt crisis, was partly an outgrowth of the 2008 global financial crisis, but also resulted from home-grown economic problems in Europe. The final outcome of this crisis will have major implications for the future of the euro zone and the EU. These four crises all demonstrate the degree to which globalization and interdependence have increased in the global political economy, and they also provide an indication of changing global power relations. Before discussing these crises, it is important to provide some basic definitions and terminology.

SOME DEFINITIONS AND TERMINOLOGY

A **financial crisis** can be defined as an escalation of financial disturbances such as a sharp decrease in the value of financial institutions or assets, the failure of large financial intermediaries, and disruption in foreign exchange markets. A financial crisis is often associated with a run on banks, where investors and depositors sell off assets and withdraw money because of fears about the future of financial institutions. A **debt crisis** is one type of financial crisis that occurs when some major debtor states lack foreign exchange to pay the interest and/ or principal on their debt obligations. As discussed in Chapter 6, a country that finances rather than adjusts to its current account deficits must borrow from external credit sources and/or decrease its foreign exchange reserves. If the country continues to borrow, its foreign debt will increase. The severity of a country's debt problem depends not only on the size of the debt but also on whether it has the ability and commitment to service its debt repayment obligations. Debt crises vary in severity and in the measures required to resolve them. If a state's debt problem is temporary, it has a *liquidity* problem: It may defer some payments or obtain a new loan to meet its repayment obligations and then repay later on terms acceptable to the creditors. If a state is unable to service its debts indefinitely, it has a *solvency* problem. In this case, the debtor can regain its creditworthiness only if its creditors reduce the interest or principal payments on its debt. Debt crises may begin as liquidity problems and become solvency problems. Indebted countries may require *debt restructuring agreements* that alter the terms between the creditor and debtor for servicing a debt. These agreements can take two different forms. First, **debt rescheduling agreements** defer debt service payments and apply longer maturities to the deferred amount. These agreements can give countries with a liquidity problem some extra time to repay their debts. However, debt rescheduling will not be sufficient for countries with a solvency problem. In cases of insolvency, **debt reduction agreements** (also called *debt relief* or *debt forgiveness*) are required to decrease the overall debt burden.[5]

As the following discussion of the 1980s foreign debt crisis and the European sovereign debt crisis shows, creditors are more willing to support debt rescheduling agreements, and they often only agree to debt reduction after debtor countries' insolvency problems become severe.

THE ORIGINS OF THE 1980s FOREIGN DEBT CRISIS

The foreign debt crisis began in August 1982, when Mexico announced that it could no longer service its public sector debt obligations. This produced shock waves because Mexico had an external debt of about $78 billion, $32 billion of which was owed to commercial banks. However, earlier warning signs of a possible debt crisis had been largely ignored. A number of LDCs, including Zaïre, Argentina, Peru, Sierra Leone, Sudan, and Togo, required debt rescheduling negotiations from 1976 to 1980, and the South's external debt increased sixfold to $500 billion between 1972 and 1981. Foreign debt was also a problem in Eastern Europe, and Poland's debt had reached serious proportions by 1981. After Mexico's 1982 announcement, the debt crisis spread rapidly as private creditor banks moved to decrease their loan exposure to other LDC borrowers. Thus, 25 LDCs requested a restructuring of their commercial bank debt by late 1982, and in 1983 the World Bank reported that "almost as many developing countries have had to reschedule loans in the last two years as in the previous twenty-five years."[6] Analysts with different theoretical perspectives do not agree on the causes of the 1980s debt crisis. Whereas some analysts focus on unexpected changes in the global economy, others emphasize the irresponsible behavior of lenders, the irresponsible behavior of borrowers, or the South's dependence on the North.

Unexpected Changes in the Global Economy

Some observers attribute the debt crisis to unexpected changes such as the sharp increase in international grain and oil prices. Major surpluses of wheat and grain during the 1960s led to production cutback programs in grain-exporting countries such as the United States and Canada. As a result, the world's grain supply was highly vulnerable to inclement weather and unexpected crop shortfalls in the Soviet Union in the early 1970s. In 1972–73 global food stocks fell to their lowest level in 20 years, food grain prices sharply increased, and food aid was drastically reduced.[7] Oil prices also increased sharply when the Arab OPEC countries limited supplies after the October 1973 Middle East war. Whereas LDC oil and food importers were doubly hit by the price increases, the OPEC states accumulated huge "petrodollar" reserves. They deposited a large share of these petrodollars in commercial banks, and the banks recycled them through loans to middle-income LDCs. From 1974 to 1979 non-OPEC LDCs received about 60 percent of their external finance from commercial bank credits.[8]

Another doubling of OPEC prices in 1979 (the "second oil shock") led to a new wave of bank loans to oil-importing LDCs. The second oil shock contributed to a severe economic contraction in the North and a sharp decline in its demand for the South's commodity exports, which made it difficult for LDCs to earn foreign exchange to service their debts. The South's problems were compounded when the U.S. Reagan administration raised interest rates to limit inflation resulting from the 1979 oil price increases and to facilitate

U.S. borrowing abroad to cover its huge federal deficits. The higher interest rates had a severe effect on LDC debt levels because the banks were providing short-term loans to LDCs at variable interest rates.[9] It may seem odd that the debt crisis began with Mexico—an oil exporter. However, oil-exporting LDCs had also borrowed private funds to launch ambitious development projects without anticipating that oil prices would fall sharply after 1979. Thus, unexpected changes in the global economy contributed to external debt problems for LDC oil exporters as well as importers.

Both commercial banks and debtor states often favor this external shocks explanation for the 1980s debt crisis because it awards "primary responsibility to economic policy shifts beyond their control."[10] However, external shocks do not explain why East Asian debtors fared so much better than Latin American debtors (see the following discussion). Thus, the policies of lenders and borrowers must also be considered as explanations for the crisis.

Irresponsible Behavior of Lenders

Historical materialists and some interventionist liberals consider irresponsible behavior of creditor banks to be a major cause of the debt crisis. Banks in New York, London, and elsewhere with a surfeit of OPEC petrodollars aggressively increased loans to LDCs without giving attention to their creditworthiness or the activities they were financing. Because of competition among the lenders, the banks charged low interest rates on these loans, which did not give LDCs adequate signals as to when to stop borrowing. After LDC debtors had become overly dependent on commercial bank loans, interest rates rose sharply in the early 1980s, and this heightened the severity of the debt crisis. Thus, "loan pushing" by commercial banks encouraged "debtor countries to increase their liabilities."[11]

Critics also argue that DC governments and the IMF shared responsibility for the bank overlending. After the first oil shock in 1973, DC policies encouraged the flow of private bank funds to the South; for example, central banks in the G10 states provided assurances that they would assist banks recycling petrodollars if they encountered financial problems. The IMF also introduced new lending programs for LDC oil importers such as the 1974 oil facility, which encouraged private banks to upgrade their lending activities. Furthermore, the gradual lifting of capital controls (discussed in Chapter 6) eased the process by which U.S. and European banks could recycle petrodollars to the South. From this perspective, creditor banks, DCs, and the IMF shared responsibility for overlending, which was a major cause of the debt crisis.[12]

Irresponsible Behavior of Borrowers

Many liberal theorists, especially orthodox liberals, attribute primary responsibility for the debt crisis to the behavior of the borrowing states. LDCs borrowed from private banks in the 1970s to avoid the conditionality requirements of IMF loans, because private banks did not impose policy conditions on their loans to sovereign governments. Basic IMF principles—that indebted governments should not have unlimited access to balance-of-payments financing and should undergo adjustment measures—were jeopardized because private funds were so accessible. Thus, the IMF warned that

> Access to private sources of balance of payments finance may ... permit countries to postpone the adoption of adequate domestic stabilization measures. This can exacerbate the problem of correcting payments imbalances, and can lead to adjustments that are politically and socially disruptive when the introduction of stabilization measures becomes unavoidable.[13]

Liberals point out that LDC governments sometimes secretly seek IMF conditionality to help them push through unpopular economic reforms. As Robert Putnam notes, international negotiations are a two-level game that may enable "government leaders to do what they privately wish to do, but are powerless to do domestically." For example, in Italy's negotiations with the IMF, "domestic conservative forces exploited IMF pressure to facilitate policy moves that were otherwise infeasible internally."[14] Uruguay also made use of an IMF agreement to impose painful, unpopular economic austerity measures. The agreement raised the cost to domestic interests of opposing economic reform "because a rejection was no longer a mere rejection of ... [Uruguay's] president, but also of the IMF."[15] In most cases, however, LDC governments were inclined to follow the path of least resistance and seek private bank loans without instituting necessary reforms.

In addition to imprudent borrowing, liberals also attribute the debt crisis to the domestic policies of borrowing states. Although some LDCs used commercial bank loans to finance productive investments and economic growth, a number used the funds to make poor investments, increase public expenditures, import luxury goods, and pay off corrupt officials. Some LDCs reacted to the debt crisis in a timely manner with readjustment policies, but many others were unwilling or unable to change. Liberal economists often contrasted the strong economic performance of Asian debtors that employed export-led growth policies with the weak performance of Latin American debtors that followed more protectionist import substitution policies (see Chapter 11). The East Asians' outward-oriented export-led growth policies put them in a stronger position because exports provided foreign exchange for servicing their debts.[16] Thus, Table 7.1 shows that the three largest debtors were Latin American when the debt crisis erupted in 1982; the debts of Brazil, Mexico, and Argentina exceeded $92, $86, and $43 billion, respectively. Table 7.1 shows that South Korea, Indonesia, and the Philippines also had substantial debts in 1982, exceeding $37, $24, and $24 billion, respectively; but the stronger export position of the Asians (except the Philippines) enabled them to service their debts better than the Latin Americans. To assess a country's ability to service its debt, economists use the **debt service ratio** which measures the ratio of a country's interest and principal payments on its debt to its export income. Countries with lower debt service ratios (and debt-to-export ratios) are more likely to meet their debt

TABLE 7.1

Total Debt, and Debt Indicators, 1982 (millions of dollars)

	Total Debt	Debt/Exports (%)	Debt Service Ratio* (%)
Latin America			
Argentina	43,634	447.3	50.0
Brazil	92,990	396.1	81.3
Chile	17,315	335.9	71.3
Colombia	10,306	204.3	29.5
Mexico	86,019	311.5	56.8
Peru	10,712	255.9	48.7
Venezuela	32,153	159.8	29.5
East and Southeast Asia			
Indonesia	24,734	116.3	18.1
Malaysia	13,354	93.4	10.7
Philippines	24,551	297.8	42.6
South Korea	37,330	131.6	22.4
Thailand	12,238	130.0	20.6

*Debt service ratio: the ratio of a country's interest and principal payments to its export income.

Source: World Bank, *World Debt Tables 1992–93, Vol. 2: Country Tables* (Washington, DC: IBRD, 1992).

obligations. Table 7.1 shows that in 1982 the debt service ratios of Malaysia and Indonesia were 10.7 and 18.1 percent, respectively, much lower than the debt service ratios of Brazil, Chile, and Mexico which were 81.3, 71.3, and 56.8 percent, respectively.

Those who question the orthodox liberal view that LDC behavior was the main factor explaining the debt crisis point out that LDC governments with good intentions often lacked the political capacity and support to institute economic reforms. They also argue that the debt crisis was *systemic* in nature; "the simultaneous onset of the crisis in more than forty developing countries" indicates that some contributing factors were external and largely beyond LDCs' control.[17] Furthermore, Asian LDCs such as Thailand, Malaysia, Indonesia, and South Korea, which liberals identified as following responsible policies during the 1980s debt crisis, experienced a severe financial crisis in the late 1990s (see later discussion).

The South's Dependence on the North

Historical materialists argue that the 1980s debt crisis stemmed from the structural nature of capitalism. Dependency and world-systems theorists view debt crises as extreme instances of a "debt trap" that exploits LDCs in the periphery and binds them to DCs in the core. Some writers draw linkages between debt crises and the legacy of colonialism. The colonial powers established a division of labor in which the colonies provided agricultural products and raw materials to the metropole and served as markets for the metropole's manufactures. This legacy still affects the exports and imports of many LDCs, preventing them from earning the foreign exchange necessary for development. Although some LDCs are industrializing, they cannot escape from their indebtedness because they continue to depend on DCs for technology and finance.[18] Historical materialists also point to foreign aid as a cause of debt crises because more than half of all official development assistance (ODA) is disbursed as loans (see Chapter 11). Development assistance is another mechanism for transferring surpluses from the periphery to the core, because a large share of foreign aid is required simply to cover LDC repayments of past aid disbursements. Thus, public as well as private external finance perpetuates LDC debt and dependency:

> If they seek official help on softer than commercial terms, they have to accept outside scrutiny ... and accept conditions which doom their efforts at industrial, diversified development. If they accept suppliers' credits on commercial terms in order to go through with their cherished projects, they are caught anyway when the payments come due before they are able to meet them.[19]

Like other interpretations of the debt crisis, critics question the views of historical materialists. Liberals argue that dependency theorists attribute LDC debt problems solely to external causes beyond their control and avoid looking at the *domestic* sources of LDC problems—traditional attitudes, domestic inefficiencies, corrupt political leaders, and a reluctance to follow liberal economic policies. It is safe to conclude that *all* the preceding views on the origins of the debt crisis have some validity. Unexpected food and oil price increases during the 1970s encouraged LDCs to increase their borrowing, and the world recession after the 1979 oil price increase added to the LDC debt load. Although these unexpected global changes were important, irresponsible behavior of commercial banks, DCs, and LDCs exacerbated the debt crisis. Furthermore, the South's structural dependence on the North increased LDC vulnerability to protracted debt problems. A Mexican finance minister identified the shared responsibility for the debt crisis and the widespread failure to foresee it, when he stated,

> The origin of the debt itself is clearly traceable to a decision by both developing and developed countries that resulted in the channeling of tens of billions of dollars to the debtor community of today ... The whole world congratulated itself on the success, smoothness, and efficiency with which the recycling process was achieved. *We all were responsible.*[20]

THE FOREIGN DEBT REGIME

Before discussing the world reaction to the 1980s debt crisis, we describe the foreign debt regime that monitored and managed the crisis. The mechanisms for dealing with a debt crisis before World War II included unilateral actions by the creditors or debtors and two-party solutions in which debtors and creditors negotiated agreements. Postwar debt settlements, by contrast, were three-party affairs involving IOs such as the IMF and World Bank and informal groups such as the Paris and London Clubs. The United States also acted as a third-party hegemon in the postwar period, pressuring for debt settlements and coordinating settlement efforts. Later in the postwar period the members of the G7/G8 summits supplemented U.S. hegemony by taking collective responsibility for dealing with foreign debt issues.[21]

Some regimes encompass only one sector or issue while others are broader in scope, and specific regimes are nested within more diffuse regimes; for example, the textile and agricultural trade regimes are nested within the global trade regime.[22] Although the global trade regime principles, norms, and rules provide a general framework, textile and agricultural trade have their own unique characteristics. This chapter views the 1980s *foreign debt regime* as a specific regime nested within a more diffuse *balance-of-payments financing regime* because foreign debt crises are a specific, more extreme type of balance-of-payments problem.[23] Although creditors and debtors have often negotiated agreements, pressures resulting from the 1980s foreign debt crisis produced more coordinated, longer-term efforts to establish rules and decision-making procedures that we associate with an international regime. The first principle of the balance-of-payments financing regime is that an adequate but not unlimited amount of financing should be available to states to deal with their balance-of-payments deficits. The second principle is that those providing the financing may attach conditions to ensure that recipient states correct their balance-of-payments problems. The balance-of-payments regime principle of conditional lending was threatened in the 1970s because private banks recycled petrodollars as loans to debtor countries with minimal conditions and very low interest rates. Although these bank loans were readily available to middle-income countries (MICs) and NIEs during the 1970s, low-income countries (LICs) lacked creditworthiness and remained dependent on loans from the IMF and donor governments. Thus, Table 7.2 shows that private bank loans in 1980 accounted for only 6 percent of LIC debt but for 38 percent of MIC debt and 65 percent of NIE debt. ODA, by contrast, accounted for 67 percent of LIC debt in 1980 but for only 25 percent of MIC debt and 4 percent of NIE debt. The willingness of private banks to provide finance to the more creditworthy LDCs limited the IMF's ability to set conditions for these borrowers.

However, private banks responded to the 1980s debt crisis by quickly limiting their loan exposure, and the MICs and NIEs therefore had to look to the IMF, World Bank, and government aid agencies for assistance with their growing debt problems. This dependence on official financing provided the IOs and the U.S. government with considerable leverage in establishing the foreign debt regime. As with the pre-1970s balance-of-payments regime, the basic principle of the debt regime revolved around conditionality—the provision of new loans and debt rescheduling were contingent on the debtor countries' commitment to market-oriented reforms. However, the 1980s debt regime differed from the pre-1970s balance-of-payments regime in several respects. First,

TABLE 7.2

Total Debt, and Share of Debt Based on ODA and Private Bank Loans for Non-Oil LDCS

Income Group	1971			1975			1980			1982		
	Total Debt[a]	Percentage ODA	Percentage Private Banks	Total Debt	Percentage ODA	Percentage Private Banks	Total Debt	Percentage ODA	Percentage Private Banks	Total Debt	Percentage ODA	Percentage Private Banks
LICs	$18	74	2	$40	73	7	$86	67	6	$110	69	6
MICs	$25	45	14	$40	33	29	$107	25	38	$144	24	39
NIEs	$32	16	38	$72	9	60	$192	4	65	$266	3	67

[a]Total debt figures in billions.

Abbreviations: ODA = official development assistance; LICs = low-income countries; MICs = middle-income countries; NIEs = newly industrializing economies.

Source: External Debt of Developing Countries—1982 Survey, p. 34. Copyright © OECD, 1982. By permission of the Organization for Economic Cooperation and Development.

the IMF (with U.S. backing) adopted a new role when it pressured private commercial banks in the 1980s to continue providing loans to debtor LDCs. Second, creditor groups such as the Paris and London Clubs (discussed below) met more often in the 1980s and 1990s than in earlier periods. Third, the IMF and World Bank provided **structural adjustment loans** (**SALs**) to indebted LDCs and transition economies (see Chapter 11). The SALs were conditioned on more demanding requirements—that loan recipients adopt orthodox liberal reforms such as deregulation, privatization, and greater openness to trade and foreign investment. The following sections discuss two other actors in the global debt regime—the transition economies of Eastern Europe and the former Soviet Union (FSU) that became debtors along with the LDCs, and the Paris and London Clubs that coordinated the actions of creditors. The changing roles of the IMF and World Bank in the foreign debt regime are examined later in the chapter.

The IMF, World Bank, and Transition Economies

Chapter 2 noted that the Soviet bloc countries were not IMF and World Bank members for most of the early postwar period. Before examining the role of these countries in the foreign debt regime, this chapter discusses how they joined these institutions; a country cannot join the World Bank ("the Bank") without first becoming a member of the IMF. As Table 7.3 shows, Yugoslavia was a founding member of the IMF and the Bank; it defected from the Soviet bloc in 1948 and developed a nonaligned foreign policy. Yugoslavia also adopted worker self-management and market socialist policies that were more compatible with the liberal economic orientation of the Bretton Woods institutions. In contrast to Yugoslavia, Poland and Czechoslovakia left the IMF and the Bank in 1950 and 1954 (Czechoslovakia was expelled for not paying its dues), because membership was incompatible with their status as satellite countries in the Soviet bloc. Table 7.3 shows that Romania joined these institutions in 1972. Although Romania was still a Soviet bloc member, it had distanced itself politically from the Soviet Union and viewed the Soviet-led Council for Mutual Economic Assistance (CMEA) as hindering its development. As an IMF and Bank member, Romania could receive loans, upgrade its economic relations with the West, and further its political objectives. Western states admitted Romania despite its slow moves toward economic reform and its sizable foreign debt, because its membership produced divisions within the Soviet bloc. Although Romania provided sensitive economic information to the IMF and the Bank, they did not disclose this information in their statistical reports.[24]

The IMF and the Bank treated the case of the People's Republic of China (PRC) as a representation rather than a new membership issue, and in 1980 they permitted the PRC to take the China seat from Taiwan. The PRC's decision to "return" to these institutions followed a radical change in its policies. Mao Zedong had adopted an inward self-reliance policy in the 1950s, and China's policies became even more autarkic from 1966 to 1969 during the Cultural

TABLE 7.3

Membership of Transition Economies in IMF and the World Bank

	IMF	World Bank (IBRD)
*1945	China, Czechoslovakia, Yugoslavia	China, Czechoslovakia, Yugoslavia
*1946	Poland, Cuba	Poland, Cuba
1950	Poland withdraws from IMF/World Bank	
1954	Czechoslovakia ousted from IMF/World Bank	
1960		Cuba withdraws from the World Bank
1964	Cuba withdraws from IMF	
1966		Yugoslavia
1972	Romania	Romania
1980	People's Republic of China (replaces Taiwan in IMF/World Bank)	
1982	Hungary	Hungary
1986	Poland readmitted	Poland
1990	Czech & Slovak Federative Republic, Bulgaria	Bulgaria
1991	Albania, Mongolia	Albania, Czech & Skovak Federative Republic
1992	Federal Republic of Yugoslavia ceased membership Armenia, Azerbaijan, Belarus, Bosnia and Herzegovina, Croatia, Estonia, Georgia, Kazakhstan, Kyrgyz Republic, Latvia, Lithuania, Macedonia, Moldova, Russian Federation, Slovenia, Serbia, Tajikistan, Turkmenistan, Ukraine, Uzbekistan	Armenia, Azerbaijan, Belarus, Estonia, Georgia, Kazakhstan, Kyrgyz Republic, Latvia, Lithuania, Moldova, Russian Federation, Turkmenistan, Ukraine, Uzbekistan
1993	Czech Republic, Slovak Republic, Tajikistan, Croatia, Slovenia, Macedonia	Bosnia and Herzegovina, Croatia, Czech Republic, Macedonia, Serbia, Slovak Republic, Slovenia, Tajikistan
1995	Bosnia and Herzegovina	
2007	Montenegro	Montenegro
2009	Kosovo	Kosovo

*Original members 1945–46

Sources: IMF and World Bank Members; www.imf.org/external/np/sec/memdir/memdate.htm; www.worldbank.org/en/about/leadership/members

Revolution. However, problems caused by the Cultural Revolution pushed China to adopt more open policies. China's commercial contacts with the North increased, and the UN General Assembly voted to seat the PRC delegation in 1971. After Mao's death in 1976 and the arrest of cultural revolutionaries, the

PRC launched the Four Modernizations program to increase economic productivity, and it viewed IMF and Bank membership as a means of gaining access to capital for its development. Several factors facilitated China's re-entry application, including U.S. support and a compromise agreement on the Taiwan issue.[25] After the PRC's takeover of the China seat in 1980, Hungary and Poland requested accession in 1981. Unlike Romania, Hungary was much closer to meeting the IMF's normal economic requirements. Hungary's New Economic Mechanism had increased its economic decentralization, outward economic orientation, and international competitiveness in the late 1960s; and in the 1970s and 1980s it introduced other economic reforms. Hungary sought IMF membership to safeguard these reforms and get assistance with its foreign debt, which resulted partly from its development plans. Poland's debt problems were more serious, because it had borrowed in international financial markets during the 1970s instead of introducing meaningful economic reform. Poland needed to reassure the financial community that it would service its debt in the early 1980s, and IMF membership would be helpful in this regard. Although Hungary was admitted to the IMF and the Bank in 1982, Poland's application was stalled by its imposition of martial law in 1981; it was not until 1986 that Poland was admitted to the Bretton Woods institutions (see Table 7.3).[26]

Poland was the last Eastern European country to become an IMF and Bank member before upheaval in the Soviet bloc transformed East–West relations. Mikhail Gorbachev's attempts to revive the Soviet economy through economic restructuring (*perestroika*) and political openness (*glasnost*) failed. However, his policies contributed to a series of revolutionary changes, including the disintegration of Communist regimes in Eastern Europe in 1989, the unification of Germany in 1990, and the dissolution of the Soviet Union in 1991. Czechoslovakia and Bulgaria joined the IMF and the Bank in 1990 and 1991, but the most significant change was the accession of Russia and other FSU republics in 1992 and 1993. Russia was facing an economic crisis, and the IMF and Western donors offered it a $24 billion assistance package in return for its commitment to decrease its budget deficit and inflation rate.[27]

The Bretton Woods institutions have helped the transition economies move toward market reform. The IMF has taken the lead in this process, estimating financing needs, providing policy advice, and setting conditions for reform. The Bank has offered technical assistance and funding for infrastructure, the development of market incentives, the privatization of state monopolies, and the creation of a legal framework for the emerging private sector. However, tensions have existed between the transition economies and the Bretton Woods institutions because of their different economic outlooks. The addition of so many new members has also put pressure on IMF and Bank resources, and LDCs sometimes charge that the transition economies receive better treatment. These charges seem to have some validity. For example, one study revealed that Romania, Poland, and Hungary received more IMF loans than expected on the basis of economic criteria; and Russia was able to borrow more funds in relation to its IMF quota than other countries when it joined the IMF in 1992.[28] This favored treatment demonstrates that security as well as economic factors affect IMF lending decisions. However, the charges of favored treatment do not seem to apply to all transition economies; for example, a 1990 study concluded that the IMF and the Bank did not give special treatment to China.[29]

The Paris and London Clubs

Creditors and debtors held three types of negotiations to deal with the 1980s foreign debt crisis. First, the IMF and the Bank provided SALs to debtor governments in exchange for the debtors' commitment to follow specific policies to reduce their balance-of-payments deficits. The other two types of negotiations involved meetings between the debtors and creditor groups: the Paris and London Clubs. The **Paris Club** is an informal group of creditor governments, which in most cases are OECD members. The **London Clubs** (also called *private creditor committees* or *bank advisory committees*) are composed of the largest commercial banks. The Paris and London Clubs have no charters or formal institutional structures, and their memberships vary with each rescheduling negotiation. The ad hoc nature of these clubs stems from the creditors' view that negotiations should be low-profile and debt reschedulings should be infrequent. Thus, the Paris Club has no legal status or written rules, no voting procedure (decisions are made by consensus), and no regular office (it usually meets in the French Ministry of Finance). The Paris Club's origins stem from a 1956 meeting of 12 European creditor states to reschedule Argentina's foreign debt. Argentina was in arrears to the governments, and the meeting provided a multilateral rescheduling forum instead of uncoordinated bilateral reschedulings. Initially the Paris Club seldom met, but their meetings became more frequent as debt problems increased. Thus, the Paris Club concluded more than twice as many agreements in the seven years from 1978 to 1984 as it did in the previous 22 years, and deferred $27 billion of debt service obligations. Paris Club meetings include the debtor government; the main creditor governments; and representatives of the IMF, the Bank, UNCTAD, and regional development banks. Three basic principles guide its deliberations:

■ The *imminent default principle* limits debt rescheduling to states with a serious, justifiable need. The Paris Club will not even consider a request unless the debtor has substantial external payments arrears and is likely to default on its payments.
■ The *conditionality principle* seeks to ensure that the debtor services its debts on schedule. Thus, the debtor must conclude an IMF arrangement with conditionality requirements before the Paris Club will negotiate.
■ The *burden sharing principle* requires all creditor states to provide relief in proportion to their loan exposure to the debtor state. This principle helps avoid the problem of free riding, and it applies to creditor banks as well as states.[30]

The private creditor groups are called London Clubs because their meetings were often held in London in the 1980s. Like the Paris Club, a single debtor and its creditors negotiate London Club agreements, and the debtor must commit to IMF adjustment policies. However, the coordination problems for London Club meetings are greater because there are so many private creditors. They coordinate their activities by establishing bank advisory committees which include the largest international banks (those holding the most loans outstanding). The international banks on each committee bargain with each other and with the debtor country to reschedule debts and then present the agreement to smaller creditor banks for ratification. Although the largest creditors would like to limit their loan exposure to a troubled debtor, they realize that the debtor state could default if all creditors withheld loans. The major international banks have a common interest in debt restructuring because of their high loan exposure and their long-term interest in the stability of international capital markets. Smaller creditor banks, by contrast, have fewer loans at risk and less interest in maintaining the international credit system; thus, they are reluctant to support restructuring agreements that require them to provide additional loans. Because smaller creditor banks often think on the basis of individual rationality (see prisoners' dilemma in Chapter 4), there is a danger that all banks could defect and that massive debtor default could disrupt the international banking system. To prevent a Pareto-deficient outcome, the large international banks pressure the smaller banks to avoid free riding and participate in the debt restructuring agreements.[31] As we will discuss, the London Clubs worked effectively in earlier years but were insufficient to deal with the 1980s debt crisis.

As historical materialists note, creditors can exert strong pressures on debtor states in the Paris and London Clubs, because a single debtor meets with its major creditors at the bargaining table. The case-by-case approach also prevents debtors from developing a united front, and it ignores the systemic nature of the 1980s debt crisis by assuming that each debtor's situation can be treated individually. Furthermore, historical materialists criticize the two clubs for their emphasis on IMF conditionality as a prerequisite for negotiations.[32] At the UNCTAD V conference in 1979 the G77 sought to replace the Paris and London Clubs with an international debt commission more attuned to LDC interests. Although the creditor governments agreed to invite an UNCTAD observer to future Paris Club negotiations, it refused to create such a commission. Thus, the creditors continue to set the rules and procedures for Paris and London Club negotiations.

STRATEGIES TO DEAL WITH THE 1980s DEBT CRISIS

The debt crisis was more prolonged than expected, and the creditor states and international institutions adopted more activist strategies when milder measures proved to be insufficient. Although the IMF had lost some importance with the collapse of the pegged exchange rate system and the increase in private bank lending in the 1970s, the 1980s debt crisis put it "back at the center of the international financial system, first as a coordinator in a crisis, and then ... as a source of information, advice, and warning on the mutual consistency of national policies."[33] The IMF's central role stemmed largely from the U.S. view that multilateral institutions could best implement DC policies on debt issues. The IMF also could put pressure on LDC debtors and private banks without causing major protests over U.S. government interference. When G7 summit meetings began to address international debt issues in the late 1980s, the major economic powers to a degree replaced U.S. hegemony with collective responsibility for LDC debt problems.[34]

The international debt strategies had three major goals: to prevent the collapse of the international banking system, to restore capital market access for debtor countries, and to restore economic growth in debtor states. The strategies to achieve these goals can be divided into four phases:

1. Emergency loans and private "involuntary" loans to debtor states (1982–1985).
2. The Baker Plan, which continued the private involuntary lending and put new emphasis on official lending (1986–1988).
3. The Brady Plan, which emphasized debt reduction agreements (1989–1994).
4. Initiatives for the poorer LDCs (1996 to the present).

Emergency Measures and Involuntary Lending: 1982–1985

The United States, the IMF, and other creditors first reacted to the debt crisis with a "firefighting" strategy, providing short-term emergency loans to Mexico, Brazil, and other LDCs to avert a 1930s-style financial collapse.[35] This emergency lending was followed by IMF pressure on private banks to engage in *involuntary lending* (politely termed *concerted lending*). Involuntary lending refers to "the increase in a bank's exposure to a borrowing nation that is in debt-servicing difficulty and that ... would be unable to attract new lending from banks not already exposed in the country."[36] Before the debt crisis, the largest international banks in the London Clubs induced smaller banks to engage in involuntary lending in debt restructuring agreements. However, the large international banks could not cope with the massive scope of the 1980s debt crisis, and many small banks in the U.S. Southwest with loans outstanding to Mexico were unwilling to increase their loan exposure. Thus, the IMF had to pressure the banks.[37]

The IMF also insisted that debtor states develop adjustment programs as the price for debt rescheduling and new lending. In the neomercantilist view, the 1980s crisis posed such a major threat to the international financial system that only creditor *states* operating through the IMF could mobilize sufficient resources to deal with it. Only official pressures could induce banks to continue lending to debtors and force debtors to meet conditionality requirements. Liberals, by contrast, emphasize the IMF's role as an international institution in managing the debt crisis, and they reject the neomercantilist view that the IMF was simply following creditor state instructions. The IMF and creditor states in these early years assumed that the debt crisis was a short-term problem stemming from the temporary inability of LDCs to service their debts. However, many LDCs could not resolve their debt problems even after adjusting their policies. When James A. Baker III became U.S. Secretary of the Treasury in 1985, he therefore adopted a more structured approach to the debt crisis.

The Baker Plan: 1986–1988

The **Baker Plan** provided a more structured, longer-term approach, but it underestimated the insolvency problem confronting many LDCs and did not offer any debt forgiveness. Instead, the Baker Plan emphasized the postponement of debt payments, the provision of new loans, and changes in debtor country policies.[38] The Baker Plan also focused on 17 middle-income heavily indebted LDCs as the target group for international debt measures. As Table 7.4 shows, 12 of the "Baker-17" states were Latin American and Caribbean, and the list did not include low-income LDCs that were heavily indebted to official (rather than private) creditors. The four countries with the highest debts in 1985 (Brazil, Mexico, Argentina, and Venezuela) were all Latin American. However, a country's debt servicing abilities also depend on its debt service

TABLE 7.4				

Gross External Debt and External Debt as a Percent of GNI for the Baker-17 Countries, 1985 and 1997 (US$ millions)

	1985		1997	
	Debt	EDT/GNI%[b]	Debt	EDT/GNI%[b]
[a]Brazil	106,148	50.3	198,023	23.8
[a]Mexico	96,867	55.2	148,702	38.3
[a]Argentina	50,946	84.2	128,411	44.8
[a]Venezuela	35,334	–	35,797	41.5
Philippines	26,622	89.1	45,683	53.4
Former Yugoslavia	22,251	48.2	10,968	–
[a]Chile	20,384	143.3	22,809	31.4
Nigeria	19,550	25.1	28,455	83.7
Morocco	16,529	136.6	20,195	62.6
[a]Peru	12,884	85.3	29,265	50.6
[a]Colombia	14,245	42.6	31,800	30.5
Cote d'Ivoire	9,745	154.2	15,609	158.1
[a]Ecuador	8,703	77.4	15,419	81.8
[a]Bolivia	4,805	176.6	5,237	68
[a]Costa Rica	4,401	120.8	3,476	27.6
[a]Jamaica	4,068	234.9	3,920	56.9
[a]Uruguay	3,919	89.7	6,710	31.8

[a]Latin American and Caribbean countries.
[b]EDT/GNI%: Total external debt as a percentage of gross national income

Source: World Bank, *World Debt Tables, 1992–93, Vol. 2: Country Tables* (Washington, DC: IBRD, 1992); World Bank, *Global Development Finance 2002, Vol. 2: Country Tables* (Washington, DC: IBRD, 2002).

ratio (see Table 7.1) and its debt as a share of GNI. Table 7.4 shows that the LDCs with the highest gross external debts ranked well below some poorer and smaller LDCs in terms of debt as a percent of GNI. Thus, external debt as a percent of GNI for Brazil, Mexico, and Argentina in 1985 was 50.3, 55.2, and 84.2 percent, respectively. The debtors on the list with the highest debt-to-GNI ratios were Jamaica (234.9 percent), Bolivia (176.6 percent), and Cote d'Ivoire (154.2 percent).

Despite the Baker Plan's more structured approach, it failed to stimulate LDC economic growth, and many LDC debtors refused to comply with IMF conditionality requirements (e.g., Brazil declared a moratorium on paying its debts in 1987). Furthermore, commercial banks sought to reduce their loan exposure, and the lending risks continued to shift to governments and multilateral agencies. From 1981 to 1988, real per capita income in most South American LDCs declined in absolute terms, and living standards in many LDCs fell to levels of the 1950s–1960s. Thus, some analysts refer to the 1980s as a "lost development decade." Although the Baker Plan's failure resulted partly from unforeseen events, critical theorists view the plan as an "attempt to maintain the fiction that the debt crisis was only temporary and could be surmounted if all parties cooperated."[39] Many debtors were caught in a vicious circle in which their debt burdens hindered their economic growth, and their slow growth prevented them from overcoming their debt problems.

The Brady Plan: 1989–1997

The Baker Plan's failure to promote economic recovery raised concerns about U.S. exports to Latin America, and about the effects of debt problems on the revival of democratic governments in the region. Riots in Caracas, Venezuela, in February 1989 in reaction to government austerity measures provided further evidence that the Baker Plan was insufficient. In March 1989, U.S. Secretary of the Treasury Nicholas Brady therefore introduced the **Brady Plan**, which sanctioned the idea of *debt reduction*, or forgiving some LDC debts to commercial banks. Recognizing that debt rescheduling without debt reduction was not sufficient for some highly indebted LDCs, the Brady Plan stipulated that U.S. private banks that reduced the principal or interest on LDC debt would receive guarantees of repayment on the remaining debt. The IMF and the Bank would help finance these guarantees, and Japan also committed funds for this purpose.[40] Although the Brady Plan was an improvement over the Baker Plan, it did not resolve all the debt problems of the Baker-17 countries. Table 7.4 shows that the external debt for all but three of the Baker-17 countries (Yugoslavia, Costa Rica, and Jamaica) increased from 1985 to 1997 (the last year that a Brady Plan agreement was concluded). However, a country's creditworthiness depends more on its debt-to-GNI ratio than on its foreign debt, and the Brady Plan helped restore the creditworthiness of most of the Baker-17 countries. As Table 7.4 shows, the external-debt-to-GNI ratio was lower in 1997 than in 1985 for most countries other than Nigeria, Cote d'Ivoire, and Ecuador. (IMF data were not available for Venezuela and the former Yugoslavia.)

The Brady Plan's greatest shortcoming was that it dealt only with commercial bank debt. It offered little to low-income LDCs because most of their debt was to governments and international financial institutions. Thus, 11 of the 17 Brady Plan agreements were concluded with the Baker-17 countries, and two of the agreements were with Eastern European countries. Only after the Brady Plan helped restore the creditworthiness of the Baker-17 did the G7 finally begin to "tackle the debt problems of the poorest countries."[41]

Initiatives for the Poorest LDCs

The total external debt of Sub-Saharan African countries increased from $56.2 billion (U.S.) in 1980 to $147 billion in 1990, and their external debt service payments on long-term loans rose from $4.5 billion to $11.1 billion. The 1996 G7 summit in Lyon, France finally began to address this problem by establishing the **Heavily Indebted Poor Countries (HIPC) Initiative**, a plan to alleviate the debts of the poorest LDCs to multilateral institutions. The IMF and the Bank had previously refused to permit debt rescheduling of their loans because this could damage their high credit ratings.[42] The HIPC countries have high debt-to-export ratios and debt-to-GNI ratios, and low enough incomes to be eligible for the World Bank group's soft loans (see Chapter 11). Forty-one countries initially met these criteria: 33 in Sub-Saharan Africa and 8 in the Americas and Asia. However, a country seeking an HIPC loan had to go through a slow and demanding two-stage process, and the debt situation of the poorest LDCs was not improving.[43] The IMF and the Bank therefore established an Enhanced HIPC Initiative in 1999, which provided debt relief more rapidly to more countries. This plan was also insufficient, and in 2005, the World Bank listed 27 of the low-income LDCs as "severely indebted," 17 as "moderately indebted," and only 14 as "less indebted."[44] In view of the continuing problems of the poorest LDCs, the IMF and World Bank established a **Multilateral Debt Relief Initiative (MDRI)** in 2006. Low-income LDCs that had their debts reduced under the enhanced HIPC initiative are eligible to have the rest of their debt to the IMF, World Bank, and African Development Bank canceled under the MDRI.[45] Despite the gradual expansion of debt relief programs for low-income LDCs, these countries continue to have serious indebtedness problems. It is therefore necessary to look at the overall effectiveness of the debt reduction strategies.

Assessing the Effectiveness of the Debt Strategies

The international debt strategies had three main objectives: to prevent the collapse of the international banking system, to restore capital market access for the debtors, and to restore economic growth in the debtor countries. The Baker and Brady plans were most successful in achieving the first two objectives. In regard to the first objective, by the late 1980s "the banks were no longer in the serious jeopardy that they faced at the outset of the debt crisis."[46] From 1982 to 1992, the loan exposure of U.S. banks to the Baker-17 countries fell from

130 to 27 percent of the banks' capital and reserves, and the loan exposure of French banks fell from 135 to 23 percent. In regard to the second objective, Latin American debtors were able to return to the international financial markets far more rapidly after the 1980s debt crisis than after the 1930s crisis. Most liberal economic theorists view these two criteria as the most important, and they believe that the Baker and Brady plans were quite successful.[47] Some orthodox liberals question whether the HIPC and MDRI initiatives are necessary, because the two main liberal objectives of the debt strategies have been achieved. They argue that debt reduction is "too easy to get," allowing countries "to persist with bad economic policies."[48] Historical materialists and some interventionist liberals by contrast see the third objective—restoring economic growth in LDC debtor countries—as the most important, and they were highly critical of the Baker and Brady plans. For example, one critic argued that the IMF and major creditor states were concerned with increasing "the immediate payment capacity of the debtor nations and not their development."[49] Historical materialists also believe that the debt strategies required more from LDCs than DCs and international bankers, and they argue that "the debt crisis is by no means over yet; a banking crisis may have been tidied up, but a development crisis is in full swing."[50]

The Baker and Brady plans did have serious shortcomings in regard to the third objective of restoring LDC economic growth. This was especially true for the low-income LDC debtors that were not on the Baker-17 list. As discussed, the Baker and Brady plans focused on debt to commercial banks, and did not provide relief for debt to the IMF and World Bank. The North should be credited for gradually developing more assertive debt strategies, shifting from debt rescheduling under the Baker Plan to debt reduction under the Brady Plan to debt relief for the poorest LDCs under the HIPC and MDRI initiatives. However, it always took a new crisis before the IMF, the Bank, and DCs upgraded their debt relief efforts, and it remains to be seen whether the new initiatives will deal with the debt problems of the poorest LDCs. Successful debt management "depends on a country's ability to achieve high growth and foreign-exchange generation—thereby containing debt-to-GDP, debt-to-exports and debt-to-revenues at reasonable ('sustainable') levels."[51]

TRANSITION ECONOMIES AND FOREIGN DEBT

To this point, we have discussed the effects of the 1980s debt crisis on LDCs. However, the LDCs and transition economies in Eastern Europe and the FSU contended with some common economic problems such as balance-of-payments deficits, declining terms of trade, and stagnating economic growth. The need for financing also caused the transition economies to look to the IMF and World Bank for support; for example, Hungary and Poland joined these institutions in the 1980s, partly because of their growing debt problems. Eastern Europeans had borrowed heavily on international financial markets in the 1970s to finance industrial investment. However, the oil price shocks, poor investment decisions, lack of export competitiveness, and high interest rates on their foreign debt created severe economic problems. For example, Poland had financed an ambitious industrial investment program with external funding, but its exports were insufficient to service its debt. In 1981, an acute foreign exchange shortage forced Poland to negotiate a rescheduling of its debt with official and private creditors.[52]

The Eastern European countries followed two different strategies to deal with their foreign debt: the so-called Polish and Czech-Hungarian models. The Polish model involved large debt buildup followed by repeated debt reschedulings and eventually official debt reduction, partly based on political considerations. Poland's debt to the DCs increased from $7.6 billion in 1975 to $22.1 billion in 1980, and in 1981 it had the highest debt and debt service ratio in the Soviet bloc. Poland responded by instituting severe economic austerity measures, but this resulted in the formation of the anti-Communist Solidarity Movement and the Polish government's imposition of martial law in December 1981. As a result, Western governments suspended debt repayment talks with Poland and did not resume them until Poland ended martial law in 1983. Private banks refinanced some Polish debt during the 1981 to 1983 period, and from 1981 to 1990 Poland had seven reschedulings of its commercial bank debt and five reschedulings of its official debt. When a democratically elected government replaced the Communists in 1990, the West gave Poland assistance under the Brady Plan. Western governments also offered Poland a 50 percent forgiveness of its official bilateral debt at Paris Club negotiations in 1991; the Paris Club had previously offered a maximum forgiveness of only 33 percent to LDCs. Under pressure from the G7, commercial banks also reduced Poland's private debt by 45 percent. Bulgaria followed the Polish model, and the private banks agreed in principle to a substantial reduction of Bulgaria's debt in late 1993 (most of Bulgaria's debt was private).

Czechoslovakia and Hungary were also affected by the debt crisis, but they tried to maintain their creditworthiness with more prudent economic policies. In 1981, Hungary had the highest per capita debt in the Soviet bloc and the second highest debt service ratio after Poland. However, Hungary joined the IMF and the Bank in 1982 and instituted ambitious economic reforms. As a result, Hungary and Czechoslovakia did not require the debt relief measures offered to Poland and Bulgaria.[53]

The different debt strategies stemmed partly from domestic economics and politics. For example, the Polish government was unable to take decisive action to deal with its debt problems. Wladyslaw Gomulka's removal as first secretary of the Polish Communist Party in 1970 resulted in decentralization of the party and divisions among the political leaders. Thus, workers were able to resist government austerity moves in response to high oil prices and declining exports. When the leaders tried to raise prices and hold down wages, massive labor strikes forced them to reverse these moves. An austerity program was introduced in 1981 when the military took control in Poland and dominated the Solidarity Movement, but it resulted in hardship and further protests.[54] Unlike Poland, domestic politics in Hungary contributed to more prudent economic policies. Although Hungary instituted some austerity measures, it also adopted reforms to increase economic efficiency and give profits and prices a larger role in resource allocation. The suppression of the 1956 Hungarian revolt had led to several developments that contributed to these economic reforms. For example, Hungary turned from one-person to collective leadership and introduced a limited market mechanism and a more balanced development strategy. Hungarian reformers also "sought not to weaken the [Communist] party but to use it to pursue their particular economic goals."[55] Hungary's earlier reforms enabled it to meet its debt service obligations much more effectively than Poland.

The debt problems of Eastern European countries also resulted from external events largely beyond their control. They suffered from increased dependence on imports from nonsocialist states, the collapse of the Soviet bloc's Council for Mutual Economic Assistance (CMEA) in 1991 (see Chapter 9), and deteriorating terms of trade as the Soviet Union ended subsidized oil exports. Bulgaria is a prime example of a state affected by external events: The breakup of CMEA had major consequences because of Bulgaria's export dependence on the Soviet Union, the Gulf War adversely affected Bulgaria's exports to Iraq, and the war in Yugoslavia disrupted Bulgarian export routes to Western Europe. The structural transition to market-oriented economies produced further instability in Eastern Europe, and domestic output fell by almost 25 percent in 1990 and 1991. Thus, a combination of internal and external factors contributed to Eastern Europe's foreign debt problems.

THE IMF, THE WORLD BANK, AND THE DEBT CRISIS

The 1980s debt crisis altered the relationship between the IMF and World Bank as they adopted new overlapping functions. The Bretton Woods negotiators wanted the IMF and the Bank to have separate functions; thus, they excluded specific references to the South in the IMF Articles of Agreement and assigned the development function to the Bank. Whereas the IMF was to provide short-term loans to *any* country with balance-of-payments problems, the Bank was to provide long-term loans for reconstruction and development. (The South was later mentioned in the second amendment to the IMF Articles of Agreement.) The only direct linkage between the two organizations was that IMF membership was a prerequisite for Bank membership. However, the Bank began to infringe on IMF territory in the 1960s. Diverging from its practice of providing loans for specific development projects, the Bank provided *program lending* to India for balance-of-payments support; and it linked its loans with conditions that India reform its policies. The Bank justified its actions by asserting that India's balance-of-payments deficit resulted from long-term development problems. However, the IMF argued that the Bank's balance-of-payments funding with conditionality infringed on its functions. The two organizations signed an agreement to avoid further overlap in 1966, but this did not resolve the problem.[56]

Several changes in the 1970s increased the overlap problem. First, the IMF lost its role of stabilizing exchange rates with the shift to floating rates. The

IMF's role of providing loans, in which there is potential overlap with the Bank, therefore became more prominent. Second, the IMF initially provided loans to all countries, but by the late 1970s it was lending almost exclusively to LDCs—the same countries receiving Bank loans. Third, the Bank's *Articles of Agreement* (Article 3, Section 4) state that it should provide loans for specific projects "except in special circumstances"; but some LDCs needed development funding for other purposes. In 1971, the Bank therefore decided that program loans like its loan to India in the 1960s were sometimes appropriate. The Bank's program loans are very similar to IMF loans for balance-of-payments problems.[57] However, the main reason for increased overlap was the 1980s foreign debt crisis. The IMF's short-term loans for balance-of-payments problems with 3–5-year repayment periods were inadequate for LDCs with longer–term debt problems, and it began to provide *medium-term* SALs with repayment periods of 5–10 years. The Bank's long-term loans for development projects with repayment periods of 15–20 years were also not adequate to deal with LDC debtors' more immediate balance-of-payments problems, and the Bank also began to provide medium-term SALs to debtor countries. Although the IMF still provided short-term balance-of-payments loans and the Bank provided long-term development loans, they *both* were now providing medium-term SALs to indebted countries.

The greater overlap of IMF and Bank functions has increased both conflict and collaboration. The overlap also raises questions as to whether two institutions are necessary, and the *Economist* predicted in 1991 that a merger between the two "makes sense, and in time it will happen."[58] However, the IMF and the Bank both perform important functions. First, the Bank group is composed of five institutions, and it is already too large for efficient management (see Chapter 11). Second, development issues are highly complex, and a range of institutions are needed to provide advice and loans. Although historical materialists argue that IMF and Bank policies are virtually identical, liberal economists point to IMF–Bank disputes as an indication of competing perspectives. Third, IMF and Bank responsibilities extend well beyond providing loans. The IMF advises states on monetary and financial issues, and this role has become more important since the 2008 global financial crisis. As discussed in Chapter 11, the Bank by contrast is a source of economic expertise on development issues.[59]

Although IMF–World Bank collaboration is partly designed to avert institutional conflict, the South is highly suspicious of these moves. Historical materialists and debtor states often see IMF conditionality as infringing on LDC sovereignty, and they argue that the liberal economic conditions on IMF and World Bank loans hinder LDC development. IMF–Bank collaboration could result in *cross-conditionality*, in which an IMF decision that a loan applicant is uncreditworthy also prevents the applicant from receiving Bank funding. Although the IMF and the Bank rule out cross-conditionality in a formal, legal sense, they sometimes practice it informally.[60] Critics also charge that IMF and Bank SALs put the onus of adjustment on LDC debtors and vulnerable groups within LDCs, even though the North shared responsibility for the debt crisis.

The SAL prescription for improving LDC balance of payments is to reduce spending for social services, lower wages, produce more for export than for local consumption, and end subsidies for local industries. However, poorer LDC women who manage the household are the most severely affected by a reduction in funding for public services (see Chapter 11).[61] IMF and Bank officials argue that structural adjustment aimed at market efficiency and decreased public sector involvement can be compatible with social welfare goals, but they have not convinced their critics.

THE 1990s ASIAN FINANCIAL CRISIS

This section on the 1990s East and Southeast Asian financial crisis (the "Asian financial crisis") examines the challenges the crisis posed to the IMF and international financial stability, and proposals to improve the "international financial architecture." Chapter 11 discusses this crisis in the context of international development. As discussed, international bank lending to LDCs sharply declined during the 1980s as a result of the foreign debt crisis. In the 1990s, private capital flows to middle-income LDCs increased again, but there was a change in the source of capital. Whereas commercial bank lending was the primary source of capital in the 1970s and 1980s, *portfolio investment*, or the purchase of stocks, bonds, and money market instruments by foreigners, was much more important in the 1990s. *Foreign direct investment*, or the foreign ownership or control of assets, also increased during the 1990s (see Chapter 10). Indeed, the net private capital flows to 29 emerging market economies increased from $35 billion in 1990 to $334 billion in 1996.[62] This revival of capital flows resulted from LDC economic reforms in response to the debt crisis, the success of the Brady Plan debt reductions, higher interest rates in the South, and a freeing of capital controls on investment in LDCs. However, some economists warned that these capital flows were volatile and "could be reversed easily."[63] Their concerns were soon realized when capital flows to Mexico halted rather suddenly in 1994. This section focuses mainly on the 1997–99 Asian financial crisis, which "was the sharpest financial crisis to hit the developing world since the 1982 debt crisis."[64]

The Asian financial crisis began in Thailand in July 1997, when there was a massive run on its currency, the *baht*. The roots of this crisis can be traced to the early 1990s, when capital inflows to Thailand rose sharply even though its current account deficit was increasing, its property prices were declining, and Thai banks were incurring a sizable foreign currency debt. Like other East Asian currencies, the baht was pegged to the U.S. dollar, and Thai exports became less competitive when the dollar's exchange rate rose against the Japanese yen. Thus, Thailand had to allow its baht to float because of downward pressure on the currency. Despite government efforts to bolster the baht, capital outflows caused the currency to lose 48.7 percent of its value over the next six months, and this resulted in a sharp decrease in the country's assets and growth. After the baht began to depreciate, the currencies of Indonesia, South Korea, Malaysia, the Philippines, and Singapore also came under severe downward pressure. The widening of the crisis from Thailand to other Asian countries is referred to as **financial contagion**, or the transmission of a financial shock from one market or country to other interdependent markets or countries.

A financial crisis often develops when the failure of a single company, bank, or country spreads, often through panic, to other companies, banks and countries. Several factors cause financial contagion. First, as regional and global interdependence has increased, so has financial contagion. In the late 1990s the interconnections among East Asian economies caused the Thai crisis to spread to Indonesia, the Philippines, Malaysia, Hong Kong, and South Korea within a few months. The financial contagion was manifested in several ways. All of these countries experienced rapid outflows of capital, depreciation of their currencies, and dramatic declines in their stock markets. Most of these countries also had recessions, banking crises, and lower economic growth rates. Thus, Thailand, Indonesia, and South Korea had to seek IMF and World Bank loans. The economic problems also led to political unrest, with major demonstrations resulting in the resignation of Indonesia's president Suharto, and transfers of power in Thailand, South Korea, and the Philippines. As we discuss below, financial contagion was also a factor explaining how the U.S. subprime mortgage crisis spilled over into other economies and led to the 2008 global financial crisis. Second, there are common shocks. In both the Asian financial crisis and the 2008 global financial crisis, a number of countries were vulnerable because of real estate bubbles, current account deficits, and dependence on large capital inflows. Third, there is guilt by association. When Thailand devalued its currency in July 1997, investors feared that Indonesia, South Korea, Malaysia, and the Philippines would do the same because they had similar economic circumstances. Investors rushed to sell these currencies, causing more devaluation. In this way, fears of a crisis spreading can become a "self-fulfilling prophecy."[65]

Causes of the Asian Financial Crisis and Strategies to Deal with It

As was the case for the 1980s foreign debt crisis, IPE theorists from different perspectives did not agree on the causes of the Asian financial crisis. Many liberals—especially orthodox liberals—argued that Asian countries benefited from greater economic interdependence and the freeing of capital flows. The main cause of the Asian crisis according to liberals was the pervasive role of governments and government–business linkages in the region. As we discuss in Chapter 11, many East Asians lived in authoritarian developmental states. Liberals argued that these states had close government–business linkages that contributed to widespread nepotism, and that the operation of banks and access to credit depended more on political connections than on market forces. Thus, lenders and foreign investors expanded credit without sufficient safeguards to risky borrowers, and huge sums were spent for questionable building and real estate projects without clear sources of financing. Neomercantilists by contrast argued that the East Asian states had contributed to rapid development in the region, and that "deeper financial integration" was the main factor contributing to the Asian financial crisis. Most East Asian economies had opened their capital accounts, and the region received a dramatic increase of international capital inflows during the early 1990s. The financial crisis resulted from the vulnerability of these economies to the massive reversal of these capital flows. Deeper financial integration also contributed to contagion, with creditors engaging in speculative attacks on currencies not because of economic fundamentals, but because of the actions of other creditors. Historical materialists argued that the East Asian economies had not achieved genuine, autonomous development. Although the strong developmental state contributed to rapid East Asian economic growth in the 1970s and 1980s, this growth was highly dependent on U.S. and Japanese policies. As a result, the East Asian economies were highly vulnerable to changes in U.S. and Japanese policies in the 1990s that contributed to an outflow of capital from East and Southeast Asia (see Chapter 11).

The strategies to deal with the Asian financial crisis, like the 1980s foreign debt crisis, were determined largely by the creditors led by the United States and the IMF. The U.S. Treasury Secretary Robert Rubin, and the Federal Reserve Chair Alan Greenspan pressured the Asian economies to liberalize their financial systems and make their political systems more transparent. Taking its cue from the United States, the IMF did not support moves by Asian economies to offset the problems in the private sector by increasing government spending. The IMF also assumed that the crisis occurred because the East Asian economies were not open enough to foreign capital. However, critics have argued that the U.S./IMF approach ignored the fact that the 1990s Asian crisis was quite different from the 1980s foreign debt crisis. The main problem in the 1980s debt crisis was the high indebtedness of many LDC governments. In the Asian financial crisis by contrast the debts of most governments to private and official creditors were relatively small. Domestic banks and private companies in Asia, by contrast, had borrowed heavily from foreign creditors, and when capital flows were reversed the Asian governments had to overhaul insolvent banking systems and restructure corporate debt. Thus, the Asian crisis was due more to private sector problems than to government debt problems. In the view of many critics "it looked like the IMF and the United States were taking advantage of the [Asian] crisis to push forward their program of global financial liberalization."[66]

The International Financial Architecture

Although the 1990s financial crisis proved to be only a temporary setback and the Asian economies generally resumed their rapid growth rates, there were concerns that financial crises could recur because of globalization and increased capital flows. Thus, the major DC governments proposed a number of reforms to strengthen global governance in finance, or the *international financial architecture*. The annual G7 summits played an important role in the architecture exercise, which began in 1995 in response to the Mexican financial crisis and evolved in response to the Asian crisis and a financial crisis in

Russia. The architecture exercise led to the creation of new IMF lending facilities, efforts to strengthen the financial infrastructure in LDCs and transition economies, and a debate regarding the IMF's role. The main objectives were *crisis prevention*, which entailed identifying vulnerable countries before crises occurred and fostering compliance with international standards to increase financial stability; and *crisis resolution*, which entailed reforming IMF policies and involving private creditors in efforts to resolve financial problems of LDCs and transition economies.[67]

Not surprisingly, prescriptions for the best measures to reform the financial architecture depend on one's theoretical perspective.[68] Orthodox liberals see the problems with international finance as stemming from defective domestic policies and institutions, *not* from the freeing of capital flows. Capital flows maximize efficiency because they are directed to countries with balanced budgets, stable markets, and low inflation rates. International regulation to limit risky behavior in capital markets would be harmful, and all capital controls should be abolished. Some economists believe that a lender of last resort is necessary for states with financial problems and that the IMF could perform this function if it had more financial resources. A **lender of last resort** is "an institution that is willing and able to supply unlimited amounts of short-term credit to financial institutions when they are threatened by a creditor panic."[69] However, orthodox liberals argue that the best way to prevent capital flight and speculative attacks on a state's currency is to eliminate the problem of moral hazard. **Moral hazard** refers to the idea that protection against risk encourages a person, firm, or state to engage in riskier behavior. If a lender of last resort exists, states and banks facing financial crises are more likely to take risks because they can count on the lender to rescue them. Some orthodox liberals criticize the IMF and the Bank for contributing to moral hazard by providing development assistance, debt bailouts, and balance-of-payments support. Other orthodox liberals see an important role for the IMF and World Bank conditional loans in ensuring that LDCs and transition economies follow transparent, liberal economic policies. They favor strong IMF requirements to ensure that states are subject to the discipline of the marketplace, and IMF policies that "legitimize financial liberalization" and block efforts to increase "state regulation of international financial flows."[70]

Interventionist liberals agree that the failure of countries to follow liberal economic policies interferes with efficiently functioning markets. However, they also believe that *unrestrained* markets are not beneficial and that measures must be taken to protect society (see Chapter 4). In finance, currency traders often buy and sell for profit without taking account of fundamental economic conditions, and this produces volatility in capital flows and foreign exchange markets. Thus, financial markets are likely to perform better when regulated. Interventionist liberals also emphasize the need for a well-funded international lender of last resort to prevent financial crises from damaging global economic efficiency and development in LDCs and transition economies.[71] Some interventionists responded to the Asian financial crisis by supporting the *Tobin tax*, which Nobel Laureate James Tobin first proposed in 1972. Tobin's proposal called for "an internationally uniform tax on all spot conversions of one currency into another, proportional to the size of the transaction."[72] Although Tobin recommended a tax of only 1 percent, he believed that it would discourage short-term speculative capital flows and generate revenue that could be used for combating world poverty. However, critics of the Tobin tax range from orthodox liberals who insist there is nothing wrong with the financial markets, to others who argue that such a tax would be ineffective. Whereas currency traders in times of crisis would disregard a small tax, a larger tax would seriously interfere with financial markets. Interventionist liberals also propose numerous reforms in IMF and World Bank transparency, accountability, and conditionality requirements; and many support the idea that the IMF should become the lender of last resort.[73]

Historical materialists view the Asian financial crisis as another example of the corrupting power of international capital. Unlike interventionist liberals, they see the IMF and the Bank as unreformable, and they favor the abolition of these institutions. For example, one study concludes that "the international financial institutions require Third World countries to adopt policies that harm the interests of working people."[74]

THE 2008 GLOBAL FINANCIAL CRISIS

As discussed, the 1980s foreign debt crisis and the 1990s Asian financial crisis began in the South. The 2008 **global financial crisis** by contrast began with the subprime mortgage crisis in the United States, the world's largest and richest economy. Also called the "great recession," business cycle analysts now date the global financial crisis as beginning in December 2007 and ending in June 2009.[75] We refer to it as the 2008 financial crisis in this book. To explain how this crisis came about, it is necessary to discuss some historical aspects of banking and financial regulation in the United States. In the 1920s three Republican presidents adopted policies of government deregulation in order to stabilize and invigorate business. The antiregulatory policies led to rampant financial speculation, fueled by investment banks and other firms that sold and traded securities. The U.S. Federal Reserve set low interest rates which encouraged individuals and firms to borrow funds, and loose stock market regulations resulted in a stock market boom that was largely fueled by borrowing. This speculation combined with large amounts of borrowed money led to the 1929 stock market crash. Millions of Americans began to withdraw their money from banks because of fears that they would fail, resulting in the Great Depression and the collapse of about 11,000 of the 25,000 U.S. banks in 1933.

Before looking at the U.S. reaction to the Great Depression, it is important to discuss why banks are often central to financial crises. The worst financial crises usually involve banks because they are often highly leveraged, and there is a mismatch between their borrowing and lending behavior. **Leverage** is the process by which an individual, firm, or bank can use borrowed money as a lever to make larger investments than they could with their own financial resources. A measure of a bank or firm's leverage is its equity-to-asset ratio. The *equity-asset ratio* is the share of lending financed by the owner's capital (equity) rather than borrowed money. If investments by a highly leveraged bank turn out well, the bank can greatly increase its profit. However, a highly leveraged bank is taking more risk. If the investment turns out badly, the bank's losses are greater. Commercial banks can take a large percent of the money people leave on deposit and profitably lend it out to borrowers. Since depositors are unlikely to withdraw all their money at once, only a fraction of their money must be kept in the bank's reserves. By lending out a large share of their deposits, commercial banks perform the important function of credit creation. However, there is a *mismatch* between the funds a bank borrows and loans. Whereas commercial banks usually borrow in the form of deposits that people can withdraw on relatively short notice, the loans the banks make have a much longer maturity and are difficult to convert into cash on short notice. If depositors for some reason lose confidence and try to withdraw their funds *en masse*, the bank will be in serious trouble.[76]

As an interventionist liberal, President Franklin D. Roosevelt led the way in responding to the Great Depression with moves to protect society from the economic and political power of the largest banks. The **Glass–Steagall Act** or *Banking Act of 1933* was designed to insulate U.S. commercial banks from the risky activities of investment banks. An *investment bank* acts as a financial intermediary or underwriter, buying securities (stocks and bonds) and assuming the risk of distributing the securities to investors. The *Federal Deposit Insurance Corporation (FDIC)*, created in 1933, guaranteed commercial bank deposits from panic-induced runs on banks. In return, the commercial banks had to follow a number of regulations limiting the interest rates they could pay, the states they could enter, and their business activities. Most importantly, commercial banks could not underwrite securities; only investment banks could do this. Investment banking was riskier than commercial banking, and it had only minimal regulation by the *Securities and Exchange Commission (SEC)*. The SEC did *not* provide investment banks with a government guarantee as the FDIC did for commercial banks.

The United States had about 50 years of financial stability under the Glass–Steagall Act. In the 1980s, however, central banks in DCs seemed to become better at limiting deep recessions, and many economists argued that "this time is different" because the U.S. Federal Reserve had learned how to "tame" the business cycle. Thus, the 25 years from the mid-1980s to about 2006 was called the *Great Moderation*.[77] Since business cycle downturns seemed less of a threat, consumers took on more debt and risky mortgages for their homes and other assets. An influx of cheap foreign capital resulting from the huge U.S. trade balance and current account deficits kept interest rates low, and contributed to steady increases in mortgage financing and in housing prices. Financial deregulation and innovations in the United States and Europe also encouraged banks, businesses, and investors to overextend themselves. Early in the twentieth century, U.S. banks had equity–asset ratios of about 25 percent, but by the early 1990s their equity–asset ratios were about 7 percent. The U.S. Federal Reserve under Alan Greenspan also began to expand loopholes that enabled commercial banks to perform some functions of investment banks; and in return, investment banks performed some commercial bank functions. In 1999 the Glass–Steagall Act was repealed, and the *Gramm–Leach–Bliley Act* removed the remaining barriers between commercial and investment banks by letting holding companies own subsidiaries engaged in both businesses. Since commercial and investment banking could no longer be separated, the government guarantee for commercial banks was effectively extended to investment banking. Deposits could be invested in risky assets with assurance that the FDIC would make up the losses. Another critical change occurred in 2004, when the SEC allowed investment banks to increase their leverage. As the rivalry between investment banks and commercial banks increased, the investment banks took on more risk.[78]

These changes were the enabling factors behind the subprime mortgage crisis. **Subprime mortgages** are mortgages for borrowers who do not qualify for market interest rates because of income level, credit history, size of the down-payment, and/or employment prospects. With deregulation, banks found it highly profitable to package large numbers of subprime mortgages and sell them to investors as *mortgage bonds* or *mortgage-backed securities (MBS)*. When payments were made on the mortgages, they were passed on to the bondholders. MBSs permitted investors from around the world to get exposure to the U.S. home mortgage market. The investors basically loaned money to homeowners and were repaid through the mortgage payments. MBSs pool hundreds of thousands of mortgages so the theory was that even when some mortgage holders defaulted, the majority that did not default would permit repayment of the debt. Unfortunately this theory did not work out in practice. In the early 1990s, banks went even further and combined MBSs into much larger *collateralized debt obligations (CDOs)*. CDOs are securities created by banks that pool together various types of debt, and then sell shares of that pool to investors. These pools may consist of auto loans, credit card debt, corporate debt, or mortgages. At first, CDOs were a welcome innovation that provided more liquidity in the economy, but the extra liquidity created bubbles in housing and other assets. A *bubble* is "a *large* and *long-lasting* deviation of the price of some asset ... from its fundamental value."[79] CDOs also allowed banks to avoid having to collect on loans when they were due, because the loans were now owned by other investors. This made them less careful in adhering to strict lending standards, so many loans were made to uncreditworthy borrowers.

U.S. housing prices rose by 85 percent between 1997 and 2006, and as long as they were rising borrowers could always refinance if their mortgages became unaffordable. Even if a borrower defaulted on his/her mortgage payments, seizure of the house would provide more collateral than necessary to repay the loan to the investor. However, when housing prices began to fall in 2006, the house was no longer worth enough to repay the loan. As soon as U.S. housing prices stopped rising and people started defaulting, hundreds of billions of dollars' worth of CDOs were virtually wiped out. The large U.S. investment banks that were highly leveraged and had invested heavily in these CDOs were at great risk of defaulting. Lehman Brothers, the fourth largest U.S.

investment bank, was leveraged at 30.7 to 1 (the amount of debt to equity), and in September 2008 it had to file for bankruptcy. This was the biggest bankruptcy in U.S. history, and for some this marked the beginning of the global financial crisis.

Although the subprime crisis began in the United States, there are parallels between the U.S. subprime borrowers and LDCs in the 1980s crisis, because subprime borrowers (like LDCs) are poorer and more vulnerable to financial distress. Critical theorists and some interventionist liberals pointed to "loan pushing" by international banks recycling OPEC petrodollars as a cause of the 1980s crisis, and mortgage pushing by highly assertive lenders was also a cause of the 2008 crisis. As with the international banks in the 1970s, the mortgage lenders did little to assess borrowers' ability to repay their loans, and they encouraged people who were credit risks to borrow in the subprime mortgage market. Orthodox liberals by contrast focused on the responsibility of mortgage buyers in the 2008 crisis, just as they had focused on the responsibility of LDC borrowers for the 1980s crisis. Many mortgage buyers were complacent about their personal debts, accustomed to living beyond their means, and had unrealistic expectations. From 1980 to 2006, the U.S. household personal savings rate had declined from 8 to 0 percent, and total private sector debt (households, and financial and nonfinancial businesses) had increased from 120 percent to 300 percent of GDP.[80]

The strategies to deal with the two crises were also similar. As with the 1980s crisis, the first priority in the 2008 crisis was to rescue the largest banks so that access to credit would be maintained. Thus, the United States responded to the Lehman bankruptcy by creating the $700 billion *Troubled Assets Relief Program (TARP)* to recapitalize financial institutions facing threats to their liquidity or solvency. The Treasury Secretary Henry Paulson had considerable discretion in deciding who would receive the funding, and nine major banks were given $125 billion; these banks were considered "too big to fail."[81] Although some credited the TARP with containing the spread of the financial crisis, others viewed it as an unjustified bailout of Wall Street. In contrast, the Treasury Department did little to bailout homeowners (Main Street). Critics have also argued that bailing out the large banks without requiring them to take responsibility for their actions has contributed to moral hazard. The penalties that banks paid were small compared with their profits and bonuses. Whereas the U.S. Treasury and the IMF pressured for more severe restructuring of the financial industry in response to the Asian financial crisis, when the crisis occurred in the United States the U.S. Treasury opted for a bailout.[82]

In addition to the rescue efforts, the Obama administration sought to provide more regulation of financial institutions, just as occurred after the Great Depression. The most tangible result was the passage of the *Dodd–Frank Wall Street Reform and Consumer Protection Act*, signed into law in July 2010. Its main provisions are designed to monitor systemic risk, limit bank proprietary trading (the *Volcker rule*), put new regulations on derivatives, and protect consumers. (*Proprietary trading* is a bank's active buying and selling of securities for its own accounts, as opposed to accounts of its clients.)

Perceptions of the Dodd–Frank Act vary widely depending on one's theoretical perspective. When the Act was passed, the U.S. Council on Foreign Relations described it as "one of the most significant regulatory reform measures since the Great Depression."[83] Some analysts by contrast describe Dodd–Frank as "a hodgepodge of several unrelated regulations."[84] Major banking interests that oppose more government regulation have warned that the reforms will limit future growth by constraining the financial system and penalizing risk-taking. Interventionist liberals by contrast argue that the law does not go far enough to deal with banks that are "too big to fail" and the resulting moral hazard. Not surprisingly, it has been difficult to implement and strengthen some parts of the Dodd–Frank Act because of political divisions in the U.S. government. For example, the Treasury Department "consistently sided with Wall Street against proposals in the Senate that would have imposed more restrictions on big banks' size and activities."[85] In sum, after the 2008 global financial crisis, there were calls in some circles for a return to Keynesianism and interventionist liberalism, where the government would have a more active role in guiding and regulating the economy. However, the largest banks and financial institutions, including those that had received substantial assistance from the government during the financial crisis, have continued to resist pressures for greater government regulation. Thus, the conflict over the extent to which U.S. banks and other financial institutions should be regulated continues.

THE EUROPEAN DEBT CRISIS

This chapter introduces some of the issues related to the European debt crisis. Chapter 9 discusses other aspects of the European debt crisis in the context of the European Union (EU) as a regional trade agreement. The 2008 global financial crisis which began in the United States was a major factor leading to the European crisis, but it also resulted from home-grown economic problems. For example, a year before the Lehman Brothers' collapse, thousands of people tried to withdraw their deposits from Britain's Northern Rock bank. The rush on Northern Rock only stopped when the Bank of England guaranteed full coverage for their deposits. In the years before the 2008 financial crisis, banks in Britain, Germany, and France poured money into the bonds backed by U.S. subprime mortgages and underestimated the risk involved. The banks also financed rampant property speculation that contributed to a housing bubble in a number of European countries such as Spain, Latvia, and Ireland. We discuss European integration in detail in Chapter 9, but to understand the European debt crisis it is necessary to differentiate the EU, which is mainly a regional trade agreement, from the euro zone, which includes members of the EU that share a common currency, the euro. As Table 7.5 shows, the EU has 28 member countries today, 19 of which are in the euro zone (the countries with asterisks).

The European debt crisis has differences and similarities with the 1980s foreign debt crisis. As for *differences*, the 1980s crisis mainly affected developing countries, whereas the European crisis has mainly affected developed countries. A second difference is that sovereign or government debt was the main

TABLE 7.5

Members of the European Union

Year of Membership	Members
1957	France*, West Germany, Italy*, Belgium*, Netherlands*, Luxembourg*
1973	United Kingdom, Denmark, Ireland *
1981	Greece*
1986	Spain*, Portugal*
1990	Germany unified*
1995	Austria*, Finland*, Sweden
2004	Cyprus*, Czech Republic, Estonia*, Hungary, Latvia*, Lithuania*, Malta*, Poland, Slovakia*, Slovenia*
2007	Bulgaria, Romania
2013	Croatia

Source: European Commission—European Neighbourhood Policy and Enlargement Negotiations. http://ec.europa.eu/enlargement/policy/from-6-to-28-members/index_en.htm

cause of the 1980s crisis, whereas it has been more a result of the European crisis. In Europe, sovereign debt was the primary problem only in Greece. In other countries, the governments went into debt by bailing out the banks and dealing with other forms of private debt. For example, Ireland's government debt amounted to only 25 percent of its GDP in 2007. However, the government debt rose to 112 percent of GDP in 2011 as a result of bailing out the banks that lost huge sums of money when the housing market collapsed.[86] A third difference relates to changes in power and influence. Whereas the 1980s foreign debt crisis markedly increased the influence of the IMF and DCs over the LDC debtors, the European debt crisis was marked by a shift in some power and influence from the EU to emerging economies. There are also similarities between the 1980s debt crisis and the European debt crisis. First, in both crises banks were seriously affected, and the drying up of credit was a major problem. Second, in both crises some governments have been unable to repay the interest or principal on their debt without external assistance; that is, they have threatened to default on their loans. Third, in both cases, creditors first viewed the crises as liquidity crises, but then had to recognize that some debtor countries were facing solvency crises. Fourth, the international community upgraded the role of the IMF to deal with both crises.

Regarding the third difference above, we have already discussed several instances of the shift in some power and influence from the EU to emerging economies. For example, in Chapter 2 we discussed the pressure to shift some votes in the IMF and IBRD (World Bank) from the EU countries to the emerging economies. As a result of these pressures, China leapfrogged over Germany, France, and the UK in the IBRD in 2010, and it now has the third largest number of votes in the IBRD after the United States and Japan. The U.S. Congress's refusal to ratify similar changes in voting for the IMF is threatening to decrease the legitimacy of that institution. In Chapter 6 we discussed how the European debt crisis has decreased the relative importance of the euro as an international currency. In previous years, some scholars were predicting that the euro might replace the U.S. dollar as the key international currency, but today scholarly discussion is focusing much more on the Chinese renminbi. The EU's preoccupation with its internal economic problems has also prevented it from devoting more attention and resources to pressing foreign policy issues such as the standoff with Russia over Ukraine and the migration crisis (discussed in Chapter 12). In the section that follows, we examine the effects of the European debt crisis on the changing relationship between the EU and the IMF.

The European Debt Crisis and the Changing Relationship Between the EU and IMF

The European debt crisis is transforming the relationship between the EU and the IMF. The IMF had not lent to EU members for decades, and EU states and banks were mainly creditors in the Paris and London Clubs. However, several EU members have recently requested IMF financial support. The first wave of IMF-supported programs was in 2008–2009 for three EU countries that were not in the euro zone at the time: Hungary, Latvia, and Romania (Latvia joined the euro zone in January 2014). The IMF gave loans to these countries in conjunction with the *European Commission*, the executive body of the EU. Although the IMF and European Commission each provided their own loans, they coordinated their actions through joint lending. Then three euro zone countries requested IMF support: Greece, Ireland, and Portugal. For these countries the *European Central Bank (ECB)* was also involved, because all euro zone countries are ECB members. The term "troika" is now used for the IMF, European Commission, and ECB when they cooperate in lending to euro zone members. Thus, the euro is an important factor in the European debt crisis, but it is *not* the only factor.

Reaching agreement on the joint lending terms has caused some friction between the IMF and the EU. The IMF has often been criticized for the strict terms of its conditionality requirements for loans to developing countries. It is therefore interesting that the EU has favored stricter terms with an emphasis on austerity for the joint EU–IMF loans to EU countries, whereas the IMF has preferred a more flexible approach. Why is this the case? First, the IMF is an international organization, whereas the EU is a *supranational organization* in which member states have given up some of their sovereignty; thus, the EU has rule-based mandates as defined by the European Treaties (see Chapter 9). The EU has specific requirements for joining the euro zone; for example, a state's budget deficit should not exceed 3 percent of its GDP and its public debt should not exceed 60 percent of its GDP. Second, the IMF has become somewhat more flexible as a result of experience with the rigid terms on its loans during the 1980s foreign debt crisis and the 1990s Asian financial crisis (see Chapter 11). Third, European policy-makers have a common interest in preventing sovereign defaults. Even if a smaller country defaulted on its debt, the crisis could spread quickly and result in expensive bailouts of financial institutions throughout the EU. Fourth, Germany is the only euro zone member with sufficient resources to provide substantial economic assistance to the weaker members, and it opted for austerity in the euro zone.[87]

Although the IMF preferred a more flexible approach, the EU Commission led by Germany wanted more rigid requirements and its position prevailed. Thus, the troika's bailout programs in the euro zone have been linked with adopting austerity policies that have resulted in serious costs in human terms. Despite some limited easing up of austerity policies because of widespread dissatisfaction in the debtor countries, these policies have produced ongoing tensions within the troika. A prime example was the dispute between the EU and the IMF over Greece. In 2010 Greece was clearly insolvent. However, euro zone policy-makers instead portrayed the Greek government's problem as a liquidity problem and refused to give it any debt forgiveness. They agreed to provide Greece with some debt forgiveness only in 2012, but by then the country's economic problems were much greater. In June 2013 an IMF internal report strongly criticized the 2010 program negotiated for Greece. The IMF indicated that it would have been better to offer a partial forgiveness of Greece's public debt—a scenario that was ruled out at the time by Germany and France. The EU's economic commissioner Olli Rehn strongly rejected the IMF report, saying "I don't think it's fair and just for the IMF to wash its hands and throw the dirty water on the Europeans."[88] The IMF was also criticized by some developing countries for imposing less strict conditions for euro zone countries than for LDCs. They attribute this difference to the IMF voting quotas which favor DCs, and to the fact that the IMF managing director is always European. These criticisms helped shift the IMF towards a more aggressive stance on the euro zone crisis. Tensions have also grown between creditor and debtor countries within the EU; this is especially evident in the standoff between Germany and Greece.

In sum this chapter has dealt with four financial crises, two that began in LDCs, and two that began in DCs. In each of these crises there was a variance of views on the causes, the best actions to take, and the longer-term remedies. In the Considering IPE Theory and Practice section that follows we examine competing theoretical views on the benefits of austerity versus stimulating economic growth.

Considering IPE Theory and Practice

A major debate regarding financial crises is whether the best policy response is to focus on austerity or on stimulating economic growth. *Austerity* can be defined as an attempt to restore economic competitiveness by reducing wages, prices, and public spending.[89] Whereas orthodox liberals emphasize austerity, interventionist liberals give more priority to government stimulus of economic growth. This section briefly examines the arguments for each approach.

Interventionist liberals view government stimulus as necessary during financial crises, but they do not argue that austerity is *never* justified. Thus, John Maynard Keynes wrote that "The boom, not the slump, is the right time for austerity";[90] and during the 2008 global financial crisis Paul Krugman cautioned that "now is no time to be tightfisted ... for the time being credit must be easy and interest rates low."[91] Interventionist liberals maintain that premature austerity during the European debt crisis has resulted in more debt and economic hardship. A top priority of many interventionist liberals is to decrease unemployment during a downturn. They may posit this as a moral issue, but they also argue that unemployment reduces economic growth, because jobless workers may quit the labor force and lose their skills.[92] Interventionist liberals and historical materialists also point to the human costs of austerity, which are clearly evident in the euro zone. In 2013 Greece was experiencing a public health crisis. Its national health budget had been cut by 40 percent since 2008, partly to meet the troika's deficit reduction targets. About 35,000 doctors, nurses, and other health care workers lost their jobs, and hospital admissions soared after many Greeks stopped getting treatment. A related argument against austerity is that poorer people lose more, because they are more dependent on the government for health provision, unemployment insurance, and other services. Austerity policies have often been applied more to "Main Street" than to "Wall Street."[93] Another interventionist liberal argument concerns the *paradox of thrift*, a concept similar to prisoners' dilemma that was popularized by Keynes. Although a single state may try to reduce its debts through austerity during a recession, if many other states try to do the same thing, this may inhibit recovery. For someone to save more, others must spend more; for example, for a state to export more, another state must import more. Non-Keynesians, however, question the paradox of thrift idea; they note that if people increase their bank savings, banks tend to lower their interest rates which stimulates lending and spending.[94]

Those favoring austerity argue that governments as well as businesses or households cannot indefinitely increase their debt without becoming insolvent. As mentioned, Keynes argued that the right time for austerity was only during the boom, not the slump. However, the public choice theorist James Buchanan criticized this approach for ignoring the political difficulties democracies have in reversing their deficit policies when the economy improves. Spending programs create constituencies that lobby to continue them long after the crisis has passed. Politicians want to be re-elected, and are therefore reluctant to raise taxes or decrease spending on popular programs.[95] For example, it seems impossible under current political conditions to reach agreement on medium- to long-term reforms to lower the U.S. foreign debt. On a related note, austerity supporters warn that too much government involvement can cause serious economic problems. For example, austerity advocates attribute many of France's problems to the government's involvement in the economy. It has been almost impossible for French leaders to alter the country's statist economic model with its cradle-to-grave social safety net.[96] Austerity advocates also note that in fall 2011 private lenders began to refuse to finance further borrowing by Greece,

Portugal, Spain, and Italy. Austerity may be the only feasible policy if these euro zone countries are to regain the confidence of the market.

In some respects the austerity versus government stimulus debate oversimplifies the issue of how to deal with financial crises. First, countries experience financial crises for a variety of reasons. Depending on the reasons, different combinations of austerity and government stimulus may be necessary. Second, the austerity versus stimulus debate often does not clearly address the need for structural reform. Third, the debate oversimplifies the EU's problems, which also stem from structural flaws in the design of the euro zone and the economic policies of its members. As discussed in Chapter 6, the euro's exchange rate gives major advantages in exporting to more competitive Germany and major disadvantages to less competitive Greece, and prevents Greece from devaluing its currency. Chapter 9 on regional trade agreements examines other structural flaws in the euro zone.

QUESTIONS

1. What are the competing theoretical views regarding the causes of the 1980s foreign debt crisis?
2. What are the competing theoretical views regarding the causes of the 1990s Asian financial crisis? What were the similarities and differences between the 1980s foreign debt crisis and the 1990s Asian financial crisis?
3. What are the similarities and differences between the European debt crisis and the 1980s foreign debt crisis?
4. What are the views of orthodox, institutional, and interventionist liberals and historical materialists regarding the best means for reforming the international financial architecture? Was a new financial architecture developed as a result of the 1990s Asian financial crisis?
5. What is the relationship among the London Clubs, the IMF, and the Paris Club in dealing with foreign debt? How has the relationship between the IMF and World Bank changed as a result of the foreign debt and financial crises? Why do you think some of the most important institutional groupings such as the Paris Club, the London Clubs, the G7, and the G20 are so informal?
6. What were the strengths and weaknesses of the Baker Plan, the Brady Plan, and the HIPC and MDRI initiatives? How do you explain the fact that the Baker and Brady plans did not address the problems of the poorest LDC debtors?
7. What were the causes of the 2008 global financial crisis? What are the competing arguments of those calling for austerity versus government stimulus in response to financial crises? Which side's arguments do you find most convincing and why?
8. Why are banks so often central to financial crises? What was the Glass–Steagall Act and what is its current status? What are collateralized debt obligations, subprime mortgages, and mortgage-backed securities? How were they involved with the 2008 global financial crisis?

KEY TERMS

Baker Plan	debt crisis	debt rescheduling
Brady Plan	debt reduction agreements	agreements

debt service ratio	Heavily Indebted Poor	Multilateral Debt Relief
financial contagion	Countries Initiative	Initiative
financial crisis	lender of last resort	Paris Club
Glass–Steagall Act	leverage	structural adjustment
global financial	London Clubs	loans
crisis	moral hazard	subprime mortgages

FURTHER READING

Books with a longer-range perspective on financial crises include Jonathan Kirshner, *American Power After the Financial Crisis* (Ithaca, NY: Cornell University Press, 2014); Changyong Rhee and Adam S. Posen, eds., *Responding to Financial Crises: Lessons from Asia Then, the United States and Europe Now* (Washington, DC: Asian Development Bank and Peterson Institute for International Economics, 2013); Carmen M. Reinhart and Kenneth S. Rogoff, *This Time Is Different: Eight Centuries of Financial Folly* (Princeton, NJ: Princeton University Press, 2009); and Paul Krugman, *The Return of Depression Economics and the Crisis of 2008* (New York: W.W. Norton, 2009).

Some of the important books on the 2008 global financial crisis include Eric Helleiner, *The Status Quo Crisis* (New York: Oxford University Press, 2014); Alan S. Blinder, *After the Music Stopped* (New York: Penguin, 2013); Raghuram G. Rajan, *Fault Lines* (Princeton, NJ: Princeton University Press, 2010); and Michael Lewis, *The Big Short* (New York: W.W. Norton & Co., 2011). On the European sovereign debt crisis see Philippe Legrain, *European Spring* (New York: CB Books, 2014); David Marsh, *Europe's Deadlock* (New Haven, CT: Yale University Press, 2013); Ivan T. Berend, *Europe in Crisis: Bolt from the Blue?* (New York: Routledge, 2013); and Jean Pisany-Ferry, *The Euro Crisis and Its Aftermath* (New York: Oxford University Press, 2011). For background on austerity policies, which have been so controversial in the EU, see Mark Blyth, *Austerity: The History of a Dangerous Idea* (New York: Oxford University Press, 2013).

On the role of banks in financial crises see Anat Admati and Martin Hellwig, *The Bankers' New Clothes* (Princeton, NJ: Princeton University Press, 2013); and Simon Johnson and James Kwak, *13 Bankers* (New York: Vintage Books, 2011). On the role of central banks see Neil Irwin, *The Alchemists: Three Central Bankers and a World on Fire* (New York: Penguin, 2013). On regulation and financial crises, see James R. Barth, Gerard Caprio, Jr., and Ross Levine, *Guardians of Finance: Making Regulations Work for Us* (Cambridge, MA: MIT Press, 2012).

On the 1990s Asian financial crisis see Richard Carney, ed., *Lessons from the Asian Financial Crisis* (New York: Routledge, 2009); and T. J. Pempel, ed., *The Politics of the Asian Economic Crisis* (Ithaca, NY: Cornell University Press, 1999). On the 1990s crisis and the need to develop a new international financial architecture, see Ben Thirkell-White, *The IMF and the Politics of Financial Globalization: From the Asian Crisis to a New International Financial Architecture?* (New York: Palgrave, 2005); Barry Eichengreen, *Financial Crises and What to Do about Them* (New York: Oxford University Press, 2002); and Leslie E. Armijo, ed., *Debating the Global Financial Architecture* (Albany, NY: State University of New York Press, 2002).

Useful books on foreign debt crises include Barry Herman, José Antonio Ocampo, and Shari Spiegel, eds., *Overcoming Developing Country Debt Crises* (New York: Oxford University Press, 2010); A. Geske Dijkstra, *The Impact of International Debt*

Relief (New York: Routledge, 2008); Chris Jochnick and Fraser A. Preston, eds., *Sovereign Debt at the Crossroads: Challenges and Proposals for Resolving the Third World Debt Crisis* (New York: Oxford University Press, 2006); and Lex Rieffel, *Restructuring Sovereign Debt: The Case for Ad Hoc Machinery* (Washington, DC: Brookings Institution Press, 2003).

NOTES

1. Carmen M. Reinhart and Kenneth S. Rogoff, *This Time Is Different: Eight Centuries of Financial Folly* (Princeton, NJ: Princeton University Press, 2009).
2. William R. Cline, *International Debt Reexamined* (Washington, DC: Institute for International Economics, 1995), p. 1.
3. T. J. Pempel, "Introduction," in T. J. Pempel, ed., *The Politics of the Asian Economic Crisis* (Ithaca, NY: Cornell University Press, 1999), p. 1.
4. Niall Ferguson, *The Ascent of Money* (New York: Penguin, 2008), p. 284.
5. Lex Rieffel, *Restructuring Sovereign Debt: The Case for Ad Hoc Machinery* (Washington, DC: Brookings Institution, 2003), pp. 9–16 and 22–23.
6. World Bank, *World Bank Annual Report—1983* (Washington, DC: World Bank, 1983), p. 34; John T. Cuddington, "The Extent and Causes of the Debt Crisis of the 1980s," in Ishrat Husain and Ishac Diwan, eds., *Dealing with the Debt Crisis: A World Bank Symposium* (Washington, DC: World Bank, 1989), p. 15; World Bank, *World Debt Tables 1992–1993*, vol. 1 (Washington, DC: World Bank, 1992), pp. 41–45.
7. Theodore H. Cohn, *Canadian Food Aid: Domestic and Foreign Policy Implications* (Denver, CO: University of Denver, Graduate School of International Studies, 1979), pp. 25–26.
8. Charles Lipson, "The International Organization of Third World Debt," *International Organization* 35, no. 4 (Autumn 1981), p. 611; Benjamin J. Cohen, "Balance-of-Payments Financing: Evolution of a Regime," in Stephen D. Krasner, ed., *International Regimes* (Ithaca, NY: Cornell University Press, 1983), p. 329.
9. Albert Fishlow, "Lessons from the Past: Capital Markets During the 19th Century and the Interwar Period," *International Organization* 39, no. 3 (Summer 1985), p. 433.
10. Miles Kahler, "Politics and International Debt: Explaining the Crisis," *International Organization* 39, no. 3 (Summer 1985), pp. 358–359.
11. Barbara Stallings, *Banker to the Third World: U.S. Portfolio Investment in Latin America, 1900–1986* (Berkeley, CA: University of California Press, 1987), pp. 184–186.
12. Ethan B. Kapstein, *Governing the Global Economy: International Finance and the State* (Cambridge, MA: Harvard University Press, 1994), pp. 60–69.
13. International Monetary Fund, *IMF Annual Report—1977* (Washington, DC: IMF, 1977), pp. 40–41.
14. Robert D. Putnam, "Diplomacy and Domestic Politics: The Logic of Two-level Games," *International Organization* 42, no. 3 (Summer 1988), p. 457.
15. James R. Vreeland, "Why Do Governments and the IMF Enter into Agreements? Statistically Selected Cases," *International Political Science Review* 24, no. 3 (2003), pp. 338–339.
16. Jeffrey Sachs, "External Debt and Macroeconomic Performance in Latin America and East Asia," in William C. Brainard and George L. Perry, eds., *Brookings Papers*

on Economic Activity, vol. 2 (Washington, DC: Brookings Institution, 1985), pp. 523–535.

17. Sachs, "External Debt and Macroeconomic Performance in Latin America and East Asia," p. 526.

18. Cheryl Payer, *The Debt Trap: The IMF and the Third World* (Harmondsworth, UK: Penguin, 1974), pp. 45–49; Peter Körner, Gero Maass, Thomas Siebold, and Ranier Tetzlaff, *The IMF and the Debt Crisis: A Guide to the Third World's Dilemma* (London: Zed Books, 1986), pp. 30–31.

19. Payer, *The Debt Trap*, p. 48.

20. Jesús Silva-Herzog, "The Costs for Latin America's Development," in Robert A. Pastor, ed., *Latin America's Debt Crisis: Adjusting to the Past or Planning for the Future?* (Boulder, CO: Lynne Rienner, 1987), p. 33.

21. Peter H. Lindert and Peter J. Morton, "How Sovereign Debt Has Worked," in Jeffrey D. Sachs, ed., *Developing Country Debt and Economic Performance, Vol. 1: The International Financial System* (Chicago, IL: University of Chicago Press, 1989), pp. 66–77; Nicholas Bayne, *Hanging in There: The G7 and G8 Summit in Maturity and Renewal* (Burlington, VT: Ashgate, 2000), p. 38.

22. Vinod K. Aggarwal, *Liberal Protectionism: The International Politics of Organized Textile Trade* (Berkeley, CA: University of California Press, 1985); Theodore H. Cohn, "The Changing Role of the United States in the Global Agricultural Trade Regime," in William P. Avery, ed., *World Agriculture and the GATT, International Political Economy Yearbook*, vol. 7 (Boulder, CO: Lynne Rienner, 1993), pp. 17–38.

23. On the balance-of-payments financing regime, see Cohen, "Balance-of-Payments Financing," pp. 315–336.

24. Valerie J. Assetto, *The Soviet Bloc in the IMF and the IBRD* (Boulder, CO: Westview Press, 1988), pp. 186–187; Jozef M. van Brabant, *The Planned Economies and International Economic Organizations* (New York: Cambridge University Press, 1991), p. 126.

25. Harold K. Jacobson and Michel Oksenberg, *China's Participation in the IMF, the World Bank, and GATT: Toward a Global Economic Order* (Ann Arbor, MI: University of Michigan Press, 1990), pp. 46–52.

26. Klaus Schröder, "The IMF and the Countries of the Council for Mutual Economic Assistance," *Intereconomics* 2 (March/April 1982), pp. 88–90; Marie Lavigne, "Eastern European Countries and the IMF," in Béla Csikós-Nagy and David G. Young, eds., *East–West Economic Relations in the Changing Global Environment* (London: Macmillan, 1986), pp. 300–304.

27. Leah A. Haus, *Globalizing the GATT: The Soviet Union's Successor States, Eastern Europe, and the International Trading System* (Washington, DC: Brookings Institution, 1992), p. 104.

28. Assetto, *The Soviet Bloc in the IMF and the IBRD*, p. 50.

29. Jacobson and Oksenberg, *China's Participation in the IMF, the World Bank, and GATT*, p. 128; William Feeney, "Chinese Policy in Multilateral Financial Institutions," in Samuel S. Kim, ed., *China and the World: Chinese Foreign Policy in the Post-Mao Era* (Boulder, CO: Westview Press, 1984), p. 274; Richard W. Stevenson, "In Borrowing from the I.M.F., Did Yeltsin Get a Sweetheart Deal?" *New York Times*, March 3, 1996, p. A5.

30. Alexis Rieffel, *The Role of the Paris Club in Managing Debt Problems* (Princeton, NJ: Princeton University, Essays in International Finance, no. 161, December 1985), pp. 4–14; Barry Herman, "The Players and the Game of Sovereign Debt,"

in Christian Barry, Barry Herman, and Lydia Tomitova, eds., *Dealing Fairly with Developing Country Debt* (Malden, MA: Blackwell, 2007), pp. 25–28.

31. Charles Lipson, "International Debt and International Institutions," in Miles Kahler, ed., *The Politics of International Debt* (Ithaca, NY: Cornell University Press, 1986), pp. 222–226; Charles Lipson, "Bankers' Dilemmas: Private Cooperation in Rescheduling Sovereign Debts," in Kenneth A. Oye, ed., *Cooperation Under Anarchy* (Princeton, NJ: Princeton University Press, 1986), pp. 200–225.

32. See Cheryl Payer, *Lent and Lost: Foreign Credit and Third World Development* (London: Zed Books, 1991), pp. 52–56.

33. Harold James, *International Monetary Cooperation Since Bretton Woods* (New York: Oxford University Press, 1996), p. 347.

34. Benjamin J. Cohen, "International Debt and Linkage Strategies: Some Foreign-Policy Implications for the United States," *International Organization* 39, no. 4 (Autumn 1985), p. 722.

35. Paul Krugman, "LDC Debt Policy," in Martin Feldstein, ed., *American Economic Policy in the 1980s* (Chicago, IL: University of Chicago Press, 1994), pp. 692–694.

36. William R. Cline, *International Debt and the Stability of the World Economy* (Washington, DC: Institute for International Economics, 1983), p. 74.

37. Lipson, "Bankers' Dilemmas," p. 223; Lipson, "International Debt and International Institutions," pp. 220–227.

38. William R. Cline, "The Baker Plan and Brady Reformulation: An Evaluation," in Ishrat Husain and Ishac Diwan, eds., *Dealing with the Debt Crisis: A World Bank Symposium* (Washington, DC: World Bank, 1989), p. 177.

39. Payer, *Lent and Lost*, p. 97.

40. Ross P. Buckley, "The Facilitation of the Brady Plan: Emerging Markets Debt Trading from 1989 to 1993," *Fordham International Law Journal* 21, no. 5 (1998), p. 1805; Jeffrey Sachs, "Making the Brady Plan Work," *Foreign Affairs* 68, no. 3 (Summer 1989), pp. 87–92.

41. Rieffel, *Restructuring Sovereign Debt*, p. 178; David Roodman, "Creditor Initiatives in the 1980s and 1990s," in Chris Jochnick and Fraser A. Preston, eds., *Sovereign Debt at the Crossroads: Challenges and Proposals for Resolving the Third World Debt Crisis* (New York: Oxford University Press, 2006), pp. 23–26.

42. Bichaka Fayissa, "Foreign Debt, Capital Inflows, and Growth: The Case of the Sub-Sahara African Countries (SSACs)," *Scandinavian Journal of Development Alternatives and Area Studies* 16, nos. 3 & 4 (September and December 1997), p. 253.

43. U.S. General Accounting Office, "Status of the Heavily Indebted Poor Countries Debt Relief Initiative," GAO/NSIAD-98-229, September 1998, pp. 5–8, 27; Gerardo Esquivel, Felipe Larraín, and Jeffrey D. Sachs, "Central America's Foreign Debt Burden and the HIPC Initiative," *Bulletin of Latin American Research* 20, no. 1 (January 2001), p. 2.

44. World Bank, *Global Development Finance, Vol. I—2005* (Washington, DC: World Bank, 2005), pp. 166–169.

45. Tony Addison, "Debt Relief: The Development and Poverty Impact," in Tony Addison and George Mavrotas, eds., *Development Finance in the Global Economy: The Road Ahead* (New York: Palgrave Macmillan, 2008), p. 220.

46. Cline, *International Debt Reexamined*, pp. 70–76.

47. "Summary of Discussion on LDC Debt Policy," in Martin Feldstein, ed., *American Economic Policy in the 1980s* (Chicago, IL: University of Chicago Press, 1994), p. 737.

48. Nancy Birdsall and Brian Deese, "Beyond HIPC: Secure, Sustainable Debt Relief for Poor Countries," in Fantu Cheru and Colin Bradford, Jr., eds., *The Millennium Development Goals: Raising the Resources to Tackle World Poverty* (New York: Zed Books, 2005), p. 139.

49. Ricardo Ffrench-Davis, "External Debt, Adjustment, and Development in Latin America," in Richard E. Feinberg and Ricardo Ffrench-Davis, eds., *Development and External Debt in Latin America: Bases for a New Consensus* (South Bend, IN: University of Notre Dame Press, 1988), p. 31.

50. Richard E. Feinberg, "Latin American Debt: Renegotiating the Adjustment Burden," in Richard E. Feinberg and Ricardo Ffrench-Davis, eds., *Development and External Debt in Latin America: Bases for a New Consensus* (South Bend, IN: University of Notre Dame Press, 1988), pp. 57–58; and Stuart Corbridge, *Debt and Development* (Oxford, UK: Blackwell, 1993), p. 85.

51. Addison, "Debt Relief," p. 217.

52. Assetto, *The Soviet Bloc in the IMF and the IBRD*, pp. 189–190.

53. Cline, *International Debt Reexamined*, pp. 360–367; Assetto, *The Soviet Bloc in the IMF and the IBRD*, pp. 163–179.

54. Matthew Evangelista, "Domestic Structure and International Change," in Michael W. Doyle and G. John Ikenberry, eds., *New Thinking in International Relations Theory* (Boulder, CO: Westview Press, 1997), pp. 212–214; Kazimierz Poznanski, "Economic Adjustment and Political Forces: Poland Since 1970," *International Organization* 40, no. 2 (Spring 1986), pp. 455–488.

55. Ellen Comisso and Paul Marer, "The Economics and Politics of Reform in Hungary," *International Organization* 40, no. 2 (Spring 1986), p. 422.

56. Joseph Gold, "The Relationship Between the International Monetary Fund and the World Bank," *Creighton Law Review* 15 (1982), pp. 509–510; Richard E. Feinberg, "The Changing Relationship Between the World Bank and the International Monetary Fund," *International Organization* 42, no. 3 (Summer 1988), p. 547.

57. Hiroyuki Hino, "IMF-World Bank Collaboration," *Finance & Development* 23, no. 3 (September 1986), p. 11.

58. "Survey: The IMF and the World Bank," *The Economist*, October 12, 1991, p. 48.

59. James, *International Monetary Cooperation*, p. 326; Jacques J. Polak, *The World Bank and the International Monetary Fund: A Changing Relationship*, Brookings Occasional Papers (Washington, DC: Brookings Institution, 1994), pp. 44–45.

60. Feinberg, "The Changing Relationship Between the World Bank and the International Monetary Fund," pp. 552–556; Polak, *The World Bank and the International Monetary Fund*, pp. 16–17.

61. Diane Elson, "From Survival Strategies to Transformation Strategies: Women's Needs and Structural Adjustment," in Lourdes Benería and Shelley Feldman, eds., *Unequal Burden: Economic Crises, Persistent Poverty, and Women's Work* (Boulder, CO: Westview Press, 1992), pp. 26–48.

62. Rieffel, *Restructuring Sovereign Debt*, pp. 190–192.

63. Stijn Claessens and Sudarshan Gooptu, "Can Developing Countries Keep Foreign Capital Flowing In?" *Finance and Development* 31, no. 3 (September 1994), p. 64; Susan Schadler, "Surges in Capital Inflows: Boon or Curse?" *Finance and Development* 31, no. 1 (March 1994), pp. 20–23.

64. Steven Radelet and Jeffrey Sachs, "The Onset of the East Asian Financial Crisis," in Paul Krugman, ed., *Currency Crises* (Chicago, IL: University of Chicago Press, 2000), p. 105.

65. Stijin Claessens and Kristin J. Forbes, eds., *International Financial Contagion* (Boston, MA: Kluwer, 2001); T. J. Pempel, ed., *The Politics of the Asian Economic Crisis* (Ithaca, NY: Cornell University Press, 1999), pp. 1–2; Stephan Haggard, *The Political Economy of the Asian Financial Crisis* (Washington, DC: Institute for International Economics, 2000), pp. 3–7.

66. Simon Johnson and James Kwak, "Policy Advice and Actions During the Asian and Global Financial Crises," in Changyong Rhee and Adam S. Posen, eds., *Responding to Financial Crises* (Washington, DC: Asian Development Bank and Peterson Institute for International Economics, October 2013), pp. 143–148; Dilip K. Das, *Asian Economy and Finance: A Post-Crisis Perspective* (New York: Springer, 2005), p. 243.

67. Peter B. Kenen, *The International Financial Architecture: What's New? What's Missing?* (Washington, DC: Institute for International Economics, 2001), pp. 87–123.

68. This section draws from Leslie E. Armijo, "The Political Geography of World Financial Reform: Who Wants What and Why?" *Global Governance* 7, no. 4 (October–December 2001), pp. 379–396; Leslie E. Armijo, ed., *Debating the Global Financial Architecture* (Albany, NY: State University of New York Press, 2002); and Ben Thirkell-White, *The IMF and the Politics of Financial Globalization: From the Asian Crisis to a New International Financial Architecture?* (New York: Palgrave, 2005).

69. Kenen, *The International Financial Architecture*, p. 57.

70. Susanne Soederberg, "The Emperor's New Suit: The New International Financial Architecture as a Reinvention of the Washington Consensus," *Global Governance* 7, no. 4 (October–December 2001), p. 460.

71. Armijo, "The Political Geography of World Financial Reform," pp. 385–390.

72. James Tobin, "A Proposal for Monetary Reform," *Eastern Economic Journal* 4 (1978), p. 155.

73. See for example Shelendra D. Sharma, "Constructing the New International Financial Architecture: What Role for the IMF?" *Journal of World Trade* 34, no. 3 (2000), pp. 47–70; Tony Porter, "The Democratic Deficit in the Institutional Arrangements for Regulating Global Finance," *Global Governance* 7, no. 4 (October–December 2001), pp. 427–439.

74. Vincent Lloyd and Robert Weissman, "How International Monetary Fund and World Bank Policies Undermine Labor Power and Rights," *International Journal of Health Services* 32, no. 3 (2002), pp. 433–442.

75. "US Business Cycle Expansions and Contractions," National Bureau of Economic Research, May 24, 2015. www.nber/org/cycles.html.

76. Simon Johnson and James Kwak, *13 Bankers* (New York: Vintage Books, 2011), pp. 31–35; Anat Admati and Martin Hellwig, *The Bankers' New Clothes* (Princeton, NJ: Princeton University Press, 2013), pp. 17–18.

77. Reinhart and Rogoff, *This Time Is Different*, p. 208. James Stock coined the term "the great moderation" in James H. Stock and Mark W. Watson, "Has the Business Cycle Changed and Why?" National Bureau of Economic Research (NBER) Working Paper 9127, September 2002.

78. Admati and Hellwig, *The Bankers' New Clothes*, p. 31; Johnson and Kwak, *13 Bankers*, pp. 35–37.

79. Alan S. Binder, *After the Music Stopped: The Financial Crisis, the Response, and the Work Ahead* (New York: Penguin, 2013), p. 29.

80. Michel G. Crouhy, Robert A. Jarrow, and Stuart M. Turnbull, "The Subprime Credit Crisis of 2007," *Journal of Derivatives* 16, no. 1 (Fall 2008), pp. 84–87; Robert

Shiller, *The Subprime Solution: How Today's Global Financial Crisis Happened, and What to Do about It* (Princeton, NJ: Princeton University Press, 2008), pp. 39–47; Roy E. Allen, *Financial Crises and Recession in the Global Economy*, 3rd ed. (Northampton, MA: Edward Elgar, 2009), pp. 113–114.

81. See Andrew Ross Sorkin, *Too Big to Fail* (New York: Penguin, 2010).
82. Johnson and Kwak, "Policy Advice and Actions During the Asian and Global Financial Crises," pp. 158–175.
83. Steven J. Markovich, "The Dodd-Frank Act," *Council on Foreign Relations*, July 23, 2012, p. 1.
84. Alejandro Komai and Gary Richardson, "A Brief History of Regulations Regarding Financial Markets in the United States: 1789 to 2009," NBER Working Paper 17443, September 2011, p. 19.
85. Johnson and Kwak, "Policy Advice and Actions During the Asian and Global Financial Crises," p. 174.
86. Ivan T. Berend, *Europe in Crisis: Bolt from the Blue?* (New York: Routledge, 2013), pp. 22–28; Philippe Legrain, *European Spring: Why Our Economies and Politics Are in a Mess* (New York: CB Books, 2014), pp. 14–15.
87. Susanne Lutz and Matthias Kranke, "The European Rescue of the Washington Consensus? EU and IMF Lending to Central and Eastern European Countries," *Review of International Political Economy*, February 22, 2013, pp. 3–5.
88. Quoted in Peter Spiegel and Kerin Hope, "EU's Olli Rehn Lashes Out at IMF Criticism of Greek Bailout," *Financial Times*, June 7, 2013.
89. Mark Blyth, *Austerity: The History of a Dangerous Idea* (New York: Oxford University Press, 2013), p. 2.
90. Donald Moggridge, ed., *The Collected Writings of John Maynard Keynes*, vol. XXI (New York: Cambridge University Press, 1982), p. 390.
91. Paul Krugman, "A Permanent Slump?" *New York Times*, November 18, 2013.
92. Lawrence H. Summers, "Austerity Would Hurt U.S. Jobs and Growth," *Washington Post*, June 2, 2013; Charles Lane, "Austerity and Keynes Can Coexist," *Washington Post*, May 21, 2013.
93. David Stuckler and Sanjay Basu, "How Austerity Kills," *New York Times*, May 13, 2013; Blyth, *Austerity*, pp. 8 and 49–50.
94. Blyth, *Austerity*, pp. 8–10.
95. See James M. Buchanan and Richard E. Wagner, *Democracy in Deficit: The Political Legacy of Lord Keynes* (New York: Academic Press, 1977).
96. Konrad Yakabuski, "Why Hollande's France is the Sick Man of Europe," *Globe and Mail*, November 25, 2013, p. A13.

Global Trade Relations

Trade relations have aroused strong positive and negative emotions from the earliest times. Whereas proposals linking free trade with world peace can be traced back to the seventeenth century, trade conflicts have been common since the Middle Ages. The conflicts are often limited in scope, but sometimes escalate and become "trade wars."[1] Societal groups often have strongly-held views about trade. For example, internationalist firms that depend on exports, imports, and multinational production pressure for trade liberalization agreements; but domestically oriented firms threatened by import competition may oppose these agreements.[2] Trade is a contentious issue because interest groups and the broader public view their welfare as being more affected by trade policy than by monetary, investment, or financial policy. Thus, business, labor, agricultural, consumer, environmental, and cultural groups try to influence government trade policies.

The forces of globalization have had a major effect on trade relations. From 1950 to 1973, world economic output (or GDP) grew at an average annual rate of 5.1 percent while trade increased on average by 8.2 percent. From 1980 to 2011, world trade grew on average almost twice as fast as world economic output.[3] The 2008 global financial crisis precipitated "drops in global production and trade, first in the developed economies and then in developing countries."[4] However, the rise of trade protectionism in response to the 2008 crisis was quite muted, and not at all comparable to the protectionist surge in response to the Great Depression of the 1930s.[5] In the 1930s there was no global trade organization, whereas today we have the **World Trade Organization (WTO)** and a large number of regional trade organizations that help to stabilize trading relations. Furthermore, multinational corporations (MNCs) today have a strong vested interest in trade liberalization, and **intrafirm trade** within MNCs accounts for about one-third of total world trade. As a former WTO director-general stated, "businesses now trade to invest and invest to trade—to the point where both activities are increasingly part of a single strategy to deliver products across borders."[6] This chapter discusses the postwar global trade regime and the changing role of the North and South in the regime. A major theme relates to the competing pressures for trade liberalization and protectionism.

TRADE THEORY

Liberal theorists view trade as a positive-sum game that provides mutual benefits to states, whereas neomercantilists see trade as more competitive, with each state striving to increase its exports and decrease its imports. Historical materialists view trade as a form of unequal exchange, in which advanced capitalist states in the core export manufactured and high-technology goods, and import raw materials and less processed goods from the periphery. Although liberal trade theory has evolved, the ideas of Adam Smith and David Ricardo are still central to the defense of free trade. Smith argued that the gains from free trade result from **absolute advantage**, in which a state exports goods that it can produce at a lower cost than others, and imports goods that other states can produce at a lower cost. For example, if France produces wine more cheaply than England and England produces cloth more cheaply than France, both states can benefit from specialization and trade. Ricardo's theory of **comparative advantage** is less intuitive and more powerful because it indicates that trade is beneficial even in the absence of absolute advantage. In his *Principles of Political Economy and Taxation*, Ricardo argued that England and Portugal could gain from trading wine for cloth even if Portugal produced *both* goods more cheaply than England.[7] Central to Ricardo's argument is the concept of **opportunity cost**, which refers to the cost of producing less of one product in order to produce more of another product. If Portugal produces wine more efficiently than cloth, it has a lower opportunity cost if it produces more wine and trades it for cloth. If England produces cloth more efficiently than wine, it has a lower opportunity cost if it produces more cloth and trades it for wine. This is the case even if Portugal produces *both* wine and cloth more efficiently than England.

Tables 8.1 and 8.2 use arbitrary figures to demonstrate Ricardo's theory of comparative advantage. Table 8.1 shows the bottles of wine and yards of cloth that England and Portugal produce in one day using the same number of labor hours for wine and cloth production. Ricardo assumed that labor productivity was the only factor determining comparative advantage. As Table 8.1 shows, Portugal produces 16 bottles of wine and 8 yards of cloth, while England produces 3 bottles of wine and 6 yards of cloth. Portugal produces more of both products than England; but Portugal is *relatively* more efficient in wine (16) than cloth (8) production, and England is *relatively* more efficient in cloth (6) than wine (3) production. Table 8.2 shows how many bottles of wine and yards of cloth England and Portugal can produce if each specializes in producing the product with the lowest opportunity cost (wine for Portugal and cloth for England), and engages in trade. As Table 8.2 shows, if England

---

TABLE 8.1

Production of Wine and Cloth in One Day
Without Trade

	Bottles of Wine	Yards of Cloth
England	3	6
Portugal	16	8
Total	19	14

TABLE 8.2

Production of Wine and Cloth in One day
With Specialization and Trade

	Bottles of Wine	Yards of Cloth
England	1 (−2)	10 (+4)
Portugal	20 (+4)	6 (−2)
Total	21	16

---

produces two less bottles of wine, it can produce four more yards of cloth; if Portugal produces two less yards of cloth, it can produce four more bottles of wine. By specializing and engaging in trade, England and Portugal can produce two more bottles of wine (21) and two more yards of cloth (16) using the same number of labor hours. Thus, countries can benefit from specializing according to comparative advantage and engaging in trade.

Although Ricardo provided a powerful argument for free trade, he assumed that comparative advantage results only from differences in labor productivity. In the 1920s, the Swedish liberal economists Eli Heckscher and Bertil Ohlin developed a theory to show that comparative advantage also results from other factors of production such as capital and natural resources. The **Heckscher–Ohlin theory** posits that a state has a comparative advantage in producing goods that involve intensive use of its most abundant factor of production. For example, labor is a less expensive input in a state with an abundant supply of labor and this gives labor-abundant states a cost advantage in producing labor-intensive goods; capital-rich DCs have a comparative advantage in producing capital-intensive goods, and states rich in arable land have a comparative advantage in agriculture. Building on the Heckscher–Ohlin theory, two U.S. economists (Wolfgang Stolper and Paul Samuelson) developed a theory to explain why some domestic groups are protectionist and others are free-trade oriented. According to the **Stolper–Samuelson theory**, trade liberalization benefits abundantly endowed factors of production and hurts poorly endowed factors. For example, if state A has an abundance of labor, workers in A will favor freer trade because A is competitive in producing labor-intensive goods for export. Although workers' wages in A will initially be low because of the abundant labor supply, as A shifts its production toward labor-intensive goods the demand and wages for labor will increase. If state A has a shortage of arable land, farmers in A will favor agricultural protectionism vis-à-vis states where arable land is more abundant. Thus, owners of abundant factors of production in a state support freer trade and owners of scarce factors oppose it. The Stolper–Samuelson theory helps explain why U.S. and Canadian blue-collar labor opposed NAFTA (Mexico has many more less skilled workers) and why French wheat farmers oppose agricultural trade liberalization in the WTO (the United States, Canada, Australia, and Argentina have more land for wheat production).[8]

Although the theory of comparative advantage and its offshoots provide powerful arguments for inter-industry trade, they do not explain the rapid increase of intraindustry and intrafirm trade. For example, the Heckscher–Ohlin assumption that trade is most beneficial between states with different factor endowments does not explain the rapid rise of intraindustry trade among DCs with similar factor endowments. Whereas traditional trade theory assumes that goods are homogeneous, in **intraindustry trade** differentiated products are traded within the same industry group. For example, Germany and Japan produce automobiles and trade with each other because consumers value product differentiation and have product preferences.[9] Liberals theorize that intraindustry trade provides benefits such as economies of scale, the satisfaction of varied consumer tastes, and the production of sophisticated manufactured products. The Stolper–Samuelson theory is also less applicable to intraindustry trade. It is harder to find owners of scarce factors opposing intraindustry trade because DCs often trade products that use similar factor intensities. Thus, trade negotiations have been most successful for manufactured products in which DCs engage in intraindustry trade. Trade barriers are more persistent for agricultural products traded between DCs and LDCs with different factor endowments. Much present-day trade is also intrafirm trade between MNC parent companies and their subsidiaries. Theories of the firm best explain why trade occurs between MNC affiliates (see Chapter 9).

To this point, we have discussed the theories of liberal *economists* in favor of free trade. However, liberal IPE specialists also seek to examine the *political* reasons why states may diverge from free trade policies even if they are beneficial. Liberal IPE theorists view free trade as a *public good* that provides widespread benefits for states. As our discussion of prisoners' dilemma in Chapter 4 shows, however, the decision of rational, self-interested states to become "free riders" may interfere with the provision of free trade as a public good. To gain a strategic advantage in trade, a state may impose import barriers and seek to benefit from the free trade policies of other states in promoting its exports. If every state acts on the basis of individual rationality, all states will end up with a Pareto-deficient outcome in trade (see Chapter 4). Liberals therefore view global hegemons and international organizations such as the World Trade Organization as important in providing free trade as a public good. A global hegemon opens its market to other countries' exports and prevents cheating by coercing other states to abide by trade regime rules and principles. The WTO helps prevent states from becoming free riders by bringing them together on a regular basis. A state that interacts regularly with others is less likely to cheat because the other states have many opportunities to retaliate. The WTO also enforces principles and rules to ensure that cheaters are punished, and collects information on members' policies, increasing transparency or confidence that cheaters will be discovered.[10] This chapter assesses the efforts of the WTO and its predecessor the General Agreement on Tariffs and Trade (GATT) to deal with the collective action problem in trade.

The liberal theories to explain inter-industry, intraindustry, and intra-firm trade are prescriptive as well as descriptive, because they assume that all states benefit from specialization and trade (even if they do not benefit equally). However, neomercantilists and historical materialists do not accept this assumption. Neomercantilists view trade as being closely tied with security as well as economic issues. Under some circumstances this may lead them to support trade liberalization. For example, during the Cold War the United States as global hegemon opened its market to European and Japanese exports to promote capitalism and democracy over Communism. However, neomercantilists also assert that free trade is *not* beneficial if it jeopardizes a state's national security. Dependence on foreign states for imports of strategic goods or basic foodstuffs can become a national security threat, especially if the imports come from unfriendly states. Thus, Article 21 of GATT provides an exception to trade obligations for national security reasons such as the regulation of traffic in arms; and U.S. law permits the president to limit imports for national security purposes.[11] Some neomercantilists also argue that free trade may impede LDC development. Because LDCs are late industrializers, they must limit DC industrial imports until their *infant industries* become more competitive. Looking at the *relative gains* of trade based on comparative advantage, neomercantilists believe that Ricardo's advice to Portugal did not serve its long-range interests. Portugal may have gained some short-term advantages from specializing in wine, but it became less competitive than England in the long term because cloth production was a higher-growth, higher-technology industry. In the neomercantilist view, Portugal should have *created* a comparative advantage for itself in cloth through government assistance, even if its "natural" comparative advantage was in wine. **Strategic trade theory** focuses on a state's creation of comparative advantage, referred to as *competitive advantage*, through industrial targeting. Although efforts to gain a competitive advantage in trade are not new, the growing emphasis on high-technology industries provides "a fertile breeding ground for interventionist policies."[12] Strategic trade theorists argue that interventionist policies can improve a state's economic position, and they point to Japan and the East Asian NIEs as states that mobilize a limited amount of resources to create competitive advantage. However, liberals view the risks of strategic trade policy as outweighing the benefits. When a state employs strategic trade policy to gain a competitive advantage at the expense of others, other states retaliate and everyone is worse off.[13] Despite the liberal warnings, the temptation to engage in strategic trade policy remains strong in an age of global competition.

Historical materialists have stronger objections to free trade than neomercantilists. As discussed in Chapter 5, Raúl Prebisch argued that LDCs in the periphery suffer from declining terms of trade with DCs in the core because of their dependence on agricultural and raw material exports. He advised LDCs to adopt import substitution policies, imposing trade barriers and producing manufactures domestically to satisfy demand previously met by imports. Dependency theorists go further, arguing that DCs either underdevelop LDCs or prevent them from achieving genuine, autonomous development; thus, LDCs should decrease or sever trade ties with the core. In his theory of unequal exchange, Arghiri Emmanuel argues that wages are higher in the core because labor is not internationally mobile and DCs specialize in producing higher value-added goods. The higher wages in DCs create a larger local market for goods, encourage mechanized production, and elevate the prices for DC goods. Thus, North–South trade is an unequal exchange, with LDCs paying more for imports from high-wage DCs than they receive for their exports. Although Emmanuel provides insights on the effects of labor immobility on international prices, he does not consider the effects of different productivity levels between core and peripheral labor or explain why capital does not flow to low-wage areas.[14]

Despite the wide range of theoretical perspectives on trade, most DC economists and international economic organizations have adhered to liberal trade theories.

GLOBAL TRADE RELATIONS BEFORE WORLD WAR II

Throughout history, states have shifted between trade liberalization and protectionism. In the nineteenth century mercantilist trade restrictions gave way to freer trade: Britain lowered its import duties in 1815 and opened its borders to food imports by repealing its Corn Laws in 1846; Britain and France then signed the Cobden–Chevalier Treaty in 1860, which resulted in a network of treaties lowering tariff barriers throughout Europe. However, Britain's declining hegemony, France's defeat in the Franco-Prussian War, and the 1873–96 depression lowered the enthusiasm for free trade; and the outbreak of World War I completely disrupted the European trade treaties.[15] Efforts to remove trade restrictions after World War I were unsuccessful as states reacted to harsh economic conditions by increasing their **tariffs,** or taxes on products that pass through a customs border. Tariffs rose not only in European states recovering from the war but also in the United States, which had become a net creditor nation and the world's largest industrial power. The U.S. Congress increased import duties with the 1922 Fordney–McCumber Tariff, and after the stock market crash Congress passed the 1930 Smoot–Hawley Tariff Act, which increased average ad valorem rates on dutiable imports to 52.8 percent, the highest U.S. tariffs in the twentieth century.[16]

The question arises as to why the United States as the top economic power did not stem the rise of protectionism during the interwar period.

Some hegemonic stability theorists argue that the United States was able but unwilling to become a hegemon until its position became more firmly established after World War II.[17] Others point to Britain's continuing influence and question whether the United States was able to establish an open economic system during the interwar period.[18] Some theorists explain U.S. protectionism in terms of domestic politics. Although the United States was the largest industrial power during the interwar period, U.S. industries feared a renewal of European competition, and U.S. agricultural groups were concerned about lower agricultural prices. The U.S. Constitution gives Congress the sole power to regulate commerce and impose tariffs, and members of Congress were susceptible to protectionist pressures because (unlike the president) they do not have national constituencies. Protectionist producer groups were politically organized in specific industries, whereas consumer groups benefiting from free trade were more diffuse and had little influence. Party politics also played a role in the Smoot–Hawley tariff because the Republicans who were more protectionist than the Democrats had a Senate majority.[19]

The Smoot–Hawley tariff had disastrous results as other states retaliated with their own import barriers: World trade declined from $35 billion in 1929 to $12 billion in 1933, and U.S. exports fell from $488 million to $120 million. To reverse this damage, the U.S. Congress passed the 1934 **Reciprocal Trade Agreements Act** (**RTAA**), which transferred authority to the president to lower tariffs by up to 50 percent in bilateral trade negotiations with other countries. The RTAA for the first time linked U.S. tariff levels to international negotiations instead of having Congress set tariffs on a unilateral, statutory basis.[20] From 1934 to 1945, the United States lowered its tariffs by an average of 44 percent in bilateral trade agreements with 27 countries; but tariffs were so high in the early 1930s that these agreements mainly corrected earlier excesses. The U.S. decision to lower tariffs only in exchange for similar concessions by other states (hence the name *Reciprocal* Trade Agreements Act) also limited the scope of the agreements, and many states refused to lower their tariffs. Thus, protectionism continued to affect trade relations throughout the interwar period.[21]

GATT AND THE POSTWAR GLOBAL TRADE REGIME

To prevent a recurrence of the interwar period protectionism, the United States and Britain began bilateral discussions in 1943 to lay the groundwork for postwar trade negotiations. In 1945, a U.S. State Department document formed the basis for multilateral negotiations that resulted in the 1948 *Havana Charter*, or Charter for an International Trade Organization (ITO). In addition to trade policy, the charter dealt with economic development, full employment, international investment, international commodity arrangements, restrictive business practices, and the functions of an ITO.[22] However, the Havana Charter negotiations were protracted, and 23 states began negotiations to lower tariffs before the charter was ratified; in October 1947, these states signed the **General Agreement on Tariffs and Trade** (**GATT**). It was assumed that GATT would be folded into the ITO when it was formed, but the Havana Charter did not satisfy either U.S. protectionists or free traders. Whereas protectionists feared that the ITO would permit low-cost imports and infringe on U.S. trade policy, free traders believed that the charter's escape clauses and exceptions would hinder trade liberalization. Thus, the U.S. Congress never ratified the Havana Charter, and GATT became an informal, global trade organization by default.[23] Unlike the proposed ITO, GATT did not require ratification by the U.S. Congress because it was simply a trade agreement. Thus, GATT signatories were *contracting parties* rather than members. (We use the term *GATT members* for the sake of brevity.) Whereas the ITO would have been a UN-specialized agency like the IMF and World Bank, GATT never gained specialized agency status; it was mainly a written code of behavior on international trade with more limited legal obligations than the planned ITO.

Despite its informal origins, GATT gradually developed characteristics of an IO; it had committees, working parties, and a small secretariat, and it made decisions that were binding on members. Some analysts even argue that GATT was more effective than the IMF and World Bank because of its informality. Whereas "the strength of a formal arrangement such as the IMF is its rigidity; that of an informal, ideas-based institution such as GATT is its adaptability."[24] GATT's strengths included its negotiations to reduce tariffs and nontariff barriers, and its steadily growing membership. However, GATT's informality also resulted in several weaknesses. First, some trade sectors were largely exempt from GATT regulations. Agriculture was treated as an exception to GATT restrictions on import quotas and export subsidies, and the North imposed quotas on textile imports. Second, GATT was more like a club than a formal organization, and its members could easily waive some regulations. For example, states circumvented the GATT ban on import quotas through **voluntary export restraints,** or pressure on others to "voluntarily" decrease their exports. Third, GATT's dispute settlement procedures often did not resolve trade conflicts. Fourth, U.S. balance-of-trade deficits caused the United States to charge that others were unfair traders. Only by enhancing GATT's authority could the United States be deterred from taking unilateral measures to ensure fair trade. Fifth, as globalization increased, many DCs wanted GATT rules to extend beyond trade in goods to trade in services, intellectual property, and investment.

By the mid-1980s, a number of trade experts therefore warned that GATT had to upgrade its rules and dispute settlement procedures; extend its discipline to agriculture and textiles; and focus on newer areas such as services and intellectual property.[25] Although the Uruguay Round negotiations began with plans to simply upgrade GATT, the decision was made during the round to replace it with the WTO. (GATT continues to exist as the largest trade agreement under the WTO.)

PRINCIPLES OF THE GLOBAL TRADE REGIME

The GATT-based global trade regime marked a critical turning point because it relied on *multilateral* negotiations and the embedded liberal compromise. The major trading nations agreed to liberalize trade, but they also supported safeguards and exemptions to protect countries' social policies and balance of payments.[26] Despite its informal origins, GATT provided the basis for a highly developed global trade regime that helped provide freer trade as a public good and prevent free riding. The following sections discuss the trade regime principles.

Trade Liberalization

In earlier years, GATT promoted the *trade liberalization* principle mainly by lowering *tariffs* (taxes on products passing through customs borders). GATT permitted tariffs, but it lowered them through eight rounds of *multilateral trade negotiations* (*MTNs*), as indicated in Table 8.3. Members negotiated item-by-item tariff reductions in the first five rounds, but these negotiations became too time-consuming as GATT membership increased, and the sixth round—the Kennedy Round—therefore shifted to linear or across-the-board tariff reductions (there was an average 35 percent tariff reduction on all industrial goods).[27] Tariffs are preferable to import quotas because reasonable tariffs permit efficient producers to increase their exports, whereas quotas set an arbitrary limit on imports. Thus, GATT Article 11 called for the "general elimination of quantitative restrictions" or import quotas. However, GATT permitted a number of exceptions to Article 11. For example, GATT members could impose import quotas on agricultural products when they were needed to enforce domestic supply management measures. Viewing trade negotiations as a two-level game (see Chapter 4), domestic groups in DCs often insisted that agriculture be an exception to trade liberalization agreements.[28]

As the first five GATT rounds lowered tariffs, members turned to **nontariff barriers (NTBs)** as an alternative means of protecting their producers. NTBs include a wide array of measures that restrict imports, assist domestic production, and promote exports, and they are often more restrictive, ill-defined, and inequitable than tariffs. NTB negotiations are also more problematic than tariff negotiations, because states tend to view NTBs as adjuncts to their domestic policies and therefore not subject to international regulation.[29] The Kennedy Round had limited NTB negotiations, but the Tokyo Round NTB negotiations were far more extensive and resulted in NTB codes dealing with technical barriers to trade, government procurement, subsidies and countervailing duties, customs valuation, and import licensing. Unlike multilateral agreements, the NTB codes were *plurilateral*; that is, they bound only the signatories because most LDCs were not willing to participate. The Uruguay Round widened the negotiations to include not only trade in goods but also services trade, intellectual property, and trade-related investment measures; and it also began focusing on sensitive areas such as agriculture and textiles. For example, the Uruguay Round agreement called on all members to convert their agricultural NTBs into tariffs (referred to as *tariffication*). However, agricultural tariffs in some countries are still exceedingly high.[30] The effects of globalization on trade were evident in the broader scope of the Uruguay Round and the increased number of participants. Table 8.3 shows that the

---

TABLE 8.3

The Rounds of GATT and WTO Negotiations

Name	Years	Subject Covered	# of Participating Countries
Geneva	1947	Tariffs	23
Annecy	1949	Tariffs	13
Torquay	1951	Tariffs	38
Geneva	1956	Tariffs	26
Dillon	1960–61	Tariffs	26
Kennedy	1964–67	Tariffs and antidumping measures	62
Tokyo	1973–79	Tariffs, nontariff measures, plurilateral agreements	102
Uruguay	1986–93	Tariffs, nontariff measures, rules, services, intellectual property, dispute settlement, trade-related investment, textiles, agriculture, creation of World Trade Organization	123
Doha (WTO)	2001–	Agriculture, services, tariffs, nontariff measures, intellectual property, dispute settlement	153

Source: Adapted from WTO Focus Newsletter no. 30, May 1998, p. 2, and other WTO information. By permission of World Trade Organization.

---

number of participants rose from 23 in the first GATT round (Geneva) to 123 in the eighth round (Uruguay). Table 8.3 also shows that after the Dillon Round, the rounds became more lengthy and complicated. The Uruguay Round involved seven years of difficult negotiations, but it resulted in the establishment of the WTO.

IPE scholars ask *why* trade liberalization continued, despite the decline in U.S. trade hegemony. In 1953, the United States accounted for almost 30 percent of all manufactured exports, but by the late 1970s it accounted for only 13 percent. West Germany had moved into first place with 16 percent, and Japan was close behind the United States with 11 percent. Although NTBs increased during the late 1970s, trade liberalization was *not* as seriously threatened as it had been in the 1920s when Britain's trade hegemony was declining. Indeed, the Tokyo Round (1973–79) reduced industrial tariffs to low levels and developed the NTB codes. Some scholars explain the difference between the 1920s and 1970s in terms of the role the GATT-centered global trade regime played in upholding the trade liberalization principle even as U.S. trade hegemony declined. Others point to domestic politics to explain the differences in the 1920s and 1970s. As discussed, the U.S. Congress has the power to regulate commerce, and in the 1920s it increased tariffs in response to interest group pressures. By the 1970s, however, Congress was transferring its tariff-making authority to the president, who was more insulated from interest group pressures (this transfer began with the 1934 RTAA). Another important domestic factor stems from the forces of globalization. In the 1920s, most industries had few international ties and favored protectionism to limit competition. By the 1970s, "increased economic integration of advanced industrial states into the world economy … altered the domestic politics of trade."[31] More business firms in the 1970s depended on multinational production, exports, imports, and intrafirm trade, and they resisted protectionism despite the decline in U.S. trade hegemony.

Nondiscrimination

GATT's first director-general referred to the *nondiscrimination* principle as "the fundamental cornerstone" of the organization.[32] The nondiscrimination principle has both external (most-favored-nation treatment) and internal (national treatment) aspects. The unconditional **most-favored-nation (MFN) principle** in Article 1 of the General Agreement stipulates that every trade advantage or privilege a GATT member gives to any state must be extended, immediately and unconditionally, to all other GATT members. The equal treatment of imports from different states helps ensure that imports come from the lowest-cost foreign suppliers. GATT permitted several exceptions to MFN treatment; the most important exception was for regional trade agreements (RTAs). Members of RTAs such as the EU and NAFTA abolish tariff barriers among themselves and thus give each other more favorable treatment than they give to other GATT/WTO members. As Chapter 9 discusses, the proliferation of RTAs poses a major threat to the MFN principle.

Whereas MFN treatment prevents discrimination at a country's border, **national treatment** counters internal discrimination. GATT Article 3 requires members to treat foreign products—once they have been imported—at least as favorably as domestic products with regard to internal taxes and regulations. This provision is designed to prevent states from using domestic measures to limit foreign competition as their tariffs and other external trade barriers decline. National treatment has often been the subject of GATT/WTO dispute settlement cases; in 1988, for example, a GATT panel found that the pricing and listing practices of Canadian provincial liquor boards discriminated against foreign wines and were inconsistent with Canada's national treatment obligations.[33]

Reciprocity

The **reciprocity principle** stipulates that a state benefiting from another state's trade concessions should provide roughly equal benefits in return. By ensuring that the exchange of concessions is balanced, reciprocity limits free riding under the unconditional MFN principle. Liberal economists argue that a state gains by liberalizing its trade unilaterally as well as through negotiation.

However, protectionist producers are often well organized and able to mobilize domestic opposition to unilateral trade liberalization. In *reciprocal* trade agreements, by contrast, governments can rely on support from export-oriented domestic industries that expect to gain from the agreements. The reciprocity principle also applies to new WTO members, who obtain the market access benefits resulting from earlier negotiating rounds and are expected to provide reciprocal benefits in return.

In practice, the reciprocity principle ensures that tariff negotiations reflect the interests of the major trading powers. WTO members with the largest domestic markets and highest trade volumes have the most leverage because they have the greatest reciprocal concessions to offer. The United States and the EU (and to a lesser extent, Japan) were the leading powers in GATT because of the reciprocity principle. Thus, the GATT Kennedy Round was not completed until the United States and the EU reached a compromise on key issues, and they initiated agreements in the Tokyo Round before other states became involved in reaching a broader consensus. LDCs had more influence during the Uruguay Round, but even in this case U.S. agreements with the EU and Japan on agriculture were critical to ultimate success. However, some emerging economies are now posing a major challenge to the United States, the EU, and Japan in the WTO. As Table 8.4 shows, in 2013 China was the second largest merchandise exporter after the EU, and South Korea ranked fifth in exports. In terms of merchandise imports, China ranked third after the United States and the EU, and Hong Kong, China ranked fifth. (China and Hong Kong are separate WTO members despite the fact that Hong Kong is now part of China. See discussion of China and the WTO below.) As the largest single-country market for merchandise imports, the United States has considerable influence under the reciprocity principle; but its lower ranking as an exporter has resulted in its large balance-of-trade deficits. Some emerging economies have also been making major gains in commercial services trade. As Table 8.5 shows, in 2013 China and India ranked third and fourth as services trade exporters, and China and Singapore ranked third and fifth as services trade importers. In sum, during the years of GATT the reciprocity principle gave the major DCs the most influence in global trade negotiations. However, since the WTO replaced GATT as the global trade organization in 1995, some emerging economies have gained considerable influence. Despite the gains of some emerging economies, the reciprocity principle continues to limit the ability of many smaller, poorer LDCs to exert influence and protect their interests.[34]

Reciprocity may be either specific or diffuse. **Specific reciprocity** refers to a simultaneous exchange of equivalent benefits or obligations. **Diffuse reciprocity** imposes a more general obligation on the recipient for repayment in the future.[35] Diffuse reciprocity can coexist with *unconditional* MFN treatment. For example, the United States and EU offered more MFN concessions than some smaller states to reach an agreement in the GATT Kennedy Round, and did not expect repayment for these concessions until the Tokyo Round. Specific reciprocity is more like *conditional* MFN treatment, in which state A

TABLE 8.4

Leading World Merchandise Traders (Excluding Intra-EU Trade), 2013 (US$ billions)

Rank	Exporters	Value	Rank	Importers	Value
1	Extra-EU (28)*	2,307	1	United States	2,329
2	China	2,209	2	Extra-EU (28)*	2,235
3	United States	1,580	3	China	1,950
4	Japan	715	4	Japan	833
5	South Korea	560	5	Hong Kong, China	622

* Excludes intra-EU trade

Source: Derived from World Trade Organization Secretariat, *World Trade Report—2014* (Geneva: WTO, 2014), Appendix Table 4, p. 35.
www.wto.org/english/res_e/booksp_e/world_trade_report14_e.pdf

TABLE 8.5

Leading World Commercial Services Trade Exporters and Importers 2013 (US$ billions)

Rank	Exporters	Value	Rank	Importers	Value
1	Extra-EU (28)*	891	1	Extra-EU (28)*	668
2	United States	662	2	United States	432
3	China	205	3	China	329
4	India	151	4	Japan	162
5	Japan	145	5	Singapore	128

* Excludes intra-EU trade

Source: Derived from World Trade Organization Secretariat, *World Trade Report—2014* (Geneva: WTO, 2014), Appendix Table 6, p. 37.
www.wto.org/english/res_e/booksp_e/world_trade_report14_e.pdf

grants concessions to state B *only if* B promptly offers equivalent concessions to A. Neomercantilists concerned with relative gains prefer specific reciprocity, whereas liberals focused on absolute gains accept diffuse reciprocity. Specific reciprocity is less conducive to cooperation because it is difficult to determine whether concessions are strictly equivalent; if states always demanded specific reciprocity it would be impossible to conduct multilateral negotiations. However, the United States responded to its growing balance-of-trade deficits with claims that specific reciprocity is sometimes necessary to prevent others from acting as free riders. In the 1980s, for example, the United States claimed that Japan had hidden trade barriers and demanded agreements that would give it a specified share of the Japanese market in return for access to the U.S. market. However, Japan argued that its trade surpluses resulted from its competitive advantage and not from unfair trading practices.[36]

Safeguards

When GATT/WTO members negotiate reciprocal tariff reductions, these are "bound" tariffs that cannot be unilaterally raised at a later date (there are some exceptions for LDCs). However, the GATT/WTO includes **safeguards** that permit members to *temporarily* raise a duty to limit imports that may harm domestic producers. Safeguards were central to embedded liberalism after World War II, because they allowed states to sign international agreements without jeopardizing domestic stability. Indeed, states would not agree to trade commitments if rigid adherence was necessary in all circumstances. Safeguards permit a state to temporarily increase protectionism without withdrawing entirely from a trade agreement.[37] Three prominent safeguard measures are the safeguards agreement, antidumping duties, and countervailing duties.

Article 19 of the 1947 GATT included a safeguards clause that was replaced by the WTO Agreement on Safeguards in 1995. The GATT safeguards clause permitted a state to raise import barriers in response to "import surges" that could cause *serious* injury to a domestic industry. However, the state had to apply the safeguard action to *all* GATT members in accordance with MFN treatment, and affected states could request compensation and retaliate if compensation was not considered adequate. In view of these stringent requirements, states turned to remedies targeted at specific exporters such as voluntary export restraints and antidumping actions. The WTO safeguards agreement makes it easier to take safeguard actions, but countries are reluctant to invoke it because the WTO has retained two major GATT requirements: First, the state must claim there is *serious* injury to its domestic producers, which is difficult to prove in dispute settlement cases. Second, the import barriers must be imposed on *all* WTO members, which can lead to serious disputes and threats of retaliation. For example, the United States adopted safeguards for certain steel products in 2001, but the EU threatened retaliation and requested that a WTO dispute settlement panel be formed. The panel ruled against the safeguards and the United States withdrew them.

Because it is difficult to adopt safeguards, states have been more inclined to use **antidumping duties** (**ADDs**) and **countervailing duties** (**CVDs**). Whereas safeguards deal with import surges even when other states engage in fair trade, ADDs and CVDs counter allegedly unfair trade practices. **Dumping** occurs when a firm sells products for export at a lower price than it charges in the home market or below the cost of production. The WTO permits a state to impose ADDs if foreign goods are dumped and the dumping causes or threatens material injury to its domestic producers. Whereas ADDs counter private corporate practices, CVDs are a response to government subsidies. The WTO permits state A to impose CVDs if state B provides trade-distorting subsidies that produce or threaten material injury to state A's domestic producers. Unlike safeguard actions, a state imposes ADDs and CVDs in response to *material* injury (which is easier to prove than *serious* injury), and targets only states charged with engaging in unfair trade. A state may impose ADDs and CVDs in response to unfair foreign trade practices, but it may also use them to justify protectionist trade policies. Thus, ADDs and CVDs are highly controversial, and WTO dispute settlement panels often examine these actions. For example, the United States and Canada have had many disputes over Canadian softwood lumber exports. The United States has imposed CVDs, claiming that the fees some Canadian provincial governments charge private firms to harvest trees on public lands constitute a subsidy to Canadian lumber; but Canada disagrees and GATT/WTO dispute settlement panels have offered several judgments on this issue.[38] In sum, safeguards are an essential but controversial GATT/WTO principle, because a state's measures to protect its domestic producers are often viewed by others as an unjustifiable trade barrier.[39]

Development

The failed Havana Charter contained provisions on economic development that did not become part of the 1947 General Agreement. Thus, GATT had little involvement with development issues during the 1940s and 1950s. As more LDCs joined GATT, a "development principle" began to emerge and several new GATT provisions gave LDCs special treatment that diverged from the nondiscrimination and reciprocity principles. However, development remained a subsidiary trade regime principle because the major trading nations agreed to only limited concessions to LDCs.[40] LDCs were more involved in the GATT Uruguay Round than in previous rounds; and the WTO Doha Round which began in 2001 was called the Development Round. As we discuss later in this chapter, the Doha Round has still not been completed, partly because of major North–South divisions. In sum, development continues to be a contested principle in the WTO.

FORMATION OF THE WTO

The trade regime principles were all in flux by the early 1980s, and many GATT achievements were in jeopardy. Although the GATT rounds had lowered tariffs, the liberalization principle was threatened because states were using NTBs that were not even covered by GATT rules. Furthermore, liberalization did not extend to textiles and agriculture, and GATT dispute settlement procedures were inadequate. RTAs that did not adhere to MFN treatment were also posing a threat to the nondiscrimination principle. As for the reciprocity and safeguard principles, the United States and the EC were demanding specific rather than diffuse reciprocity from some trading partners, and countries were resorting to unilateral protectionist actions. LDCs had little involvement with GATT, and most of them refused to sign the Tokyo Round NTB codes. In view of GATT's shortcomings, the United States pressured for a new round of negotiations and the GATT members agreed to launch the Uruguay Round in 1986. Although the negotiators at first focused on extending GATT's jurisdiction, in April 1990 Canada proposed that a formal WTO should replace the informal GATT, and the EC supported this idea.[41] However, U.S. negotiators believed that plans to create a WTO would detract from the Uruguay Round's substantive negotiations and that Congress would oppose the WTO just as it had opposed the ITO in the 1940s. In the end, the United States altered its view, and the WTO replaced GATT in 1995 as the main global trade organization.[42]

In contrast to GATT, the WTO is a formal, legally constituted organization like the IMF and World Bank. GATT has reverted to its original status as an agreement for trade in goods, which the WTO oversees along with three new treaties negotiated during the Uruguay Round: the **General Agreement on Trade in Services** (**GATS**), and the Agreements on **Trade-Related Intellectual Property Rights** (**TRIPs**) and **Trade-Related Investment Measures** (**TRIMs**). GATT is the most important of these agreements because trade in goods is the largest aspect of international trade. The DCs supported the GATS, TRIPs, and TRIMs agreements for several reasons. First, the United States wanted to redress its merchandise trade deficits by extending rules to services trade and intellectual property where it was more competitive. Second, the DCs wanted to regulate services trade which had a 19 percent annual growth rate from 1970 to 1980 whereas merchandise trade grew by only 5.4 percent. Third, DCs would benefit most from the GATS, TRIPs, and TRIMs because they were the major exporters of services, intellectual property, and investment. The DCs had to offer trade-offs to the LDCs so they would accept these new agreements.[43]

The WTO's highest authority is the *Ministerial Conference*, which includes all WTO members and makes decisions under the multilateral trade agreements (see Figure 8.1). Whereas GATT normally met at the ministerial level only to launch or conclude negotiating rounds, the Ministerial Conference meets every two years to provide guidance to the WTO at a higher political level. Between Ministerial Conference meetings, the *General Council* manages WTO affairs and oversees the *Councils for Trade in Goods*, *Trade-Related Aspects of Intellectual Property Rights*, and *Trade in Services* (see Figure 8.1). The General Council also convenes as the Trade Policy Review and Dispute Settlement Bodies when necessary (see Figure 8.1). The *Trade Policy Review Body* reviews WTO members' trade policies to increase transparency and promote trust that agreements are being enforced. The *Dispute Settlement Body* forms panels to investigate complaints and adjudicate trade disputes. A WTO member may invoke the dispute settlement procedures if another member has broken a WTO regulation or reneged on an agreement. Dispute settlement procedures are more binding and timely under the WTO than they were under GATT. Whereas a single member (including a party to a dispute) could block the adoption of a GATT panel report, a consensus of member states is required to block a WTO panel report, a *highly* unlikely occurrence. A WTO member may appeal a dispute settlement decision to the *Appellate Body*, but if the Appellate Body agrees with the panel report, the member must implement the recommendations or provide compensation. If a member fails to implement a report or provide compensation, the Dispute Settlement Body can authorize the complainant to retaliate.[44]

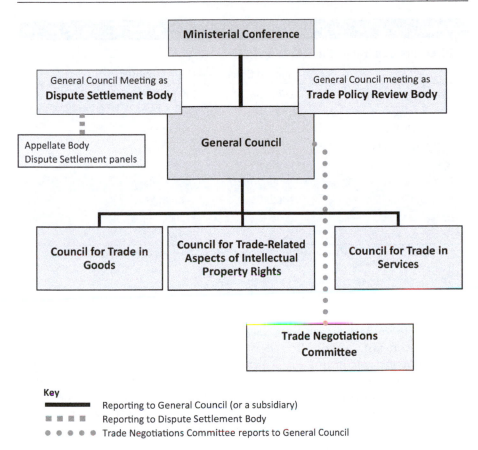

Key

━━━━━━━━ Reporting to General Council (or a subsidiary)

■ ■ ■ ■ Reporting to Dispute Settlement Body

● ● ● ● ● Trade Negotiations Committee reports to General Council

The General Council also meets as the Trade Policy Review Body and Dispute Settlement Body

FIGURE 8.1

Structure of the World Trade Organization

Source: Adapted from the WTO Organization Chart. www.wto.org/english/thewto_e/whatis_e/tif_e/organigram_e.pdf. © World Trade Organization. By permission of the World Trade Organization.

The *director-general* is the chief administrative officer of the GATT/WTO. Unlike the tacit agreement that the World Bank president would be American and the IMF managing director European, there was no agreement for GATT. As Table 8.6 shows, all GATT directors-general from 1948 to 1995 were European. This issue became contentious when the WTO was formed in 1995 for several reasons: the higher profile of the WTO; the tendency for politicians to become WTO directors-general (unlike the case of GATT); greater U.S. assertiveness in response to its declining trade hegemony; increased rivalry among Europe, the United States, and Japan; and the South's unwillingness to accept the North's dominance in the WTO. The United States reluctantly agreed to the selection of Renato Ruggiero (a former Italian trade minister) as the first WTO director-general, but insisted that the next WTO head be non-European.

TABLE 8.6

Directors-General of the GATT[a] and WTO

	Years in Office	Nationality-Country
Eric Wyndham-White	1948–68	Britain
Olivier Long	1968–80	Switzerland
Arthur Dunkel	1980–93	Switzerland
Peter Sutherland	1993–95	Ireland
Renato Ruggiero	1995–99	Italy
Mike Moore	1999–2002	New Zealand
Supachai Panitchpakdi	2002–05	Thailand
Pascal Lamy	2005–13	France
Roberto Azevêdo	2013–	Brazil

[a]The name of GATT's chief administrative officer was changed from *secretary-general to director-general* in 1965.

Source: www.wto.org/english/thewto_e/dg_e/exdgs_e.htm

As Table 8.6 shows, there have been three non-European WTO directors-general since 1999. The current WTO director-general is Roberto Azevêdo from Brazil. In contrast to the IMF and World Bank, the WTO (like GATT) is a one-nation, one-vote institution. Depending on the issue, WTO votes require a simple majority, a special majority of two-thirds or three-quarters, or unanimity. The one-nation, one-vote system gives LDCs less influence than one might expect because most decisions are made by consensus, and trade negotiations do not depend on vote-taking.

THE WTO AND THE GLOBAL TRADE REGIME

The WTO was designed to be more authoritative than GATT, and we will assess its effectiveness by looking at its three main functions: (1) to implement and monitor trade principles and rules; (2) to settle disputes among WTO members; and (3) to conduct multilateral trade negotiations (MTNs).[45] Regarding the first function, the WTO has more authority to implement global trade rules because it is a formal IO comparable in status with the IMF and World Bank. The WTO applies global rules not only to trade in goods (GATT), but also to services trade (GATS) and intellectual property rights (TRIPs). WTO rules also affect a larger and more diverse group of states, because its membership increased to 161 as of April 2015, and it has done more to integrate LDCs and transition economies into the global trade regime. Regarding the second function, members are using the WTO's binding dispute settlement system more often than they used GATT's less-binding dispute settlement system. However, the WTO has encountered major problems with its third function, conducting MTNs. Whereas GATT negotiated eight MTN rounds, the WTO has not even completed negotiating its first round: the Doha Round. Scheduled for completion in January 2005, the Doha Round negotiations faced numerous obstacles and reached an impasse in December 2011. The results of efforts to reach a much more limited Doha Round agreement at the WTO Bali Ministerial in December 2013 are still uncertain.

Some trade specialists argue that the WTO "is not sick" because it is performing two of its three main functions, but that "something is manifestly wrong with the Doha Round."[46] However, others warn that the WTO will become sick if the Doha Round is not successful because "a trading system that does not generate new agreements risks falling backward."[47] The view of some economic liberals is that in trade negotiations "*the bicycle must keep moving*. Forward momentum is essential to avoid backsliding into protectionism and mercantilism."[48] Some critics question this bicycle analogy, pointing out that there has been no major "backsliding" to protectionism, despite the failure to conclude the Doha Round. However, there are strong arguments that the WTO's future cannot be separated from the outcome of its trade negotiations, because without "the promise of further gains from future trade rounds, the Organization would run the risk of sliding into ... irrelevance."[49] In sum, trade experts do not agree on whether the WTO can be an effective organization without completing an MTN round. The following section examines the factors that have blocked completion of the Doha Round.

Many liberals focus on institutional factors in explaining the Doha Round's problems, while neomercantilists and some liberals focus on changing geopolitical and economic events and relationships. Both factors help account for the Doha Round's problems. Institutional factors include WTO membership, the single undertaking, and the trade negotiations agenda: (1) Regarding membership, some argue that the WTO has become too large and diverse to reach a consensus on a broad-ranging MTN agreement. The major trading powers often meet in smaller groups to decide on agreements that they then present to the entire membership for approval. In the past, these smaller groups consisted mainly of like-minded Western countries and Japan; but now these groups include important emerging economies. With the increased size and diversity of participants, the WTO's dependence on consensus decision-making makes it very difficult to achieve agreement on a broad-ranging MTN. (2) The GATT Uruguay Round was the first round to be treated as a **single undertaking**, which meant that countries accepting the final accord had to accept *all* of the agreements. The WTO Doha Round has also been treated as a single undertaking, but it is unrealistic to expect to achieve consensus among the 161 WTO members on all parts of an agreement. (3) As for the trade negotiations agenda, earlier rounds dealt with border measures such as tariffs and with less problematic NTBs. Current negotiations deal with more sensitive behind-the-border measures, and with areas such as agriculture and services that are often subject to strong protectionist forces.

The second factor accounting for the Doha Round's problems is changing geopolitical and economic events and relationships. As discussed, the GATT Kennedy and Tokyo Rounds were not completed until the United States and EU reached an agreement. Although LDCs had more influence in the GATT Uruguay Round, it was also not completed until the United States, the EU, and Japan reached an agreement. The decline of U.S. and EU influence, which was exacerbated by the 2008 global financial crisis, and the growing influence of emerging economies have made it more difficult to reach a consensus among older and newer powers with different world outlooks. Another external factor hampering the Doha Round has been the preoccupation with other issues, ranging from the 2008 global financial crisis, to terrorism, environmental concerns such as global warming, and confrontation between Russia and the West over Ukraine.[50] The following sections focus on growing diversity in the GATT/WTO. After discussing the transition economies and the LDCs, we then examine the challenge that three emerging economies—Brazil, India, and China—are posing to the global trade regime.

THE TRANSITION ECONOMIES AND GLOBAL TRADE RELATIONS

The Soviet Union did not attend the Havana Charter negotiations, and most centrally planned economies (CPEs) did not become GATT members. The General Agreement devoted little attention to state trading and central planning, because it was assumed that GATT members would be free market economies. Indeed, GATT was committed to limiting government actions that interfered with market forces. As Table 8.7 shows, Czechoslovakia was a founding member that remained in GATT even after it became Communist, but its membership was largely inactive. Other Eastern European states (Yugoslavia, Poland, Romania, and Hungary) joined GATT in the 1960s–1970s. GATT admitted these CPEs under special provisions, because they excluded foreign products through administrative controls over prices and purchasing. In the late 1980s–1990s, the membership requirements became more rigorous, and nonmarket economies had to institute specific reforms as a condition for admission. The more stringent requirements stemmed from concerns about the possible admission of China and the Soviet Union (later Russia), the revival of orthodox liberalism, and the creation of the more formal WTO. GATT's problems with its Eastern European members had only a limited effect on the global trade regime; but Chinese and Russian membership could have major consequences. The IMF and World Bank accepted China and Russia as members because they were loan recipients and had little influence in these weighted-voting institutions. However, the major trading nations were concerned that these two states could shift the balance of power in the GATT/WTO.[51] This section briefly discusses Eastern Europe and Russia's path to membership in the GATT/WTO. Later in the chapter we discuss the role of China, India, and Brazil as key emerging economies in the WTO.

The IMF and the Bank ousted Czechoslovakia shortly after it became a nonmarket economy, but it was an inactive GATT member for many years because of GATT's informality. Table 8.7 shows that Yugoslavia, Poland, Romania, and Hungary were able to join GATT in the 1960s–1970s, because of the GATT secretariat's goal of universal membership and the Western

TABLE 8.7

Membership of Transition Economies in the GATT/WTO

1948	Czechoslovakia, China and Cuba (founding members)	1997	Mongolia
1950	Republic of China (Taiwan) withdraws from GATT	1998	Kyrgyz Republic
1966	Yugoslavia	1999	Latvia, Estonia
1967	Poland	2000	Albania, Croatia, Georgia
1971	Romania	2001	Lithuania, Moldova, China
1973	Hungary	2002	Chinese Taipei (Taiwan)
1990	East Germany (via German reunification)	2003	Armenia, Macedonia
1993	Czech Republic, Slovak Republic	2004	Cambodia
1994	Slovenia	2008	Ukraine
1996	Bulgaria	2012	Montenegro, Russian Federation
		2013	Tajikistan

Source: www.wto.org/english/thewto_e/gattmem_e.htm

policy of *differentiation*. This policy sought to contain the Soviet Union by rewarding Eastern European states that adopted more independent policies. After its break with the Soviet bloc in 1948, Yugoslavia opted for economic decentralization, and it became a GATT member in 1966 when it moved from protectionist policies toward the GATT model; this showed that a CPE could participate in GATT under conditions similar to those for a market economy. Unlike Yugoslavia, Poland and Romania applied to GATT when they were not yet moving toward market reform. Tariffs have little influence over the import decisions of CPEs, so they had to commit to increasing their imports in return for GATT membership. When Poland joined GATT in 1967, it agreed to increase its imports from GATT members by 7 percent (by value) per year, and in return it received limited MFN treatment. GATT agreed to classify Romania as an LDC, so it was subject to less rigid requirements. Romania expressed a "firm intention" to increase its imports from GATT members by a specific amount, but this condition was unenforceable. Hungary was able to provide tariff concessions rather than commitments to increase its imports when it joined GATT in 1973, because it had instituted liberal economic reforms under its New Economic Mechanism. Bulgaria's efforts to join GATT failed because it was a close Soviet ally, and its case became enmeshed with the issue of membership for China and Russia. It was not until 1996 that the WTO finally admitted Bulgaria. Despite GATT's admission of Eastern European states, their acceptance was conditional. For example, the accession agreements for Poland, Romania, and Hungary permitted the EC to impose quantitative restrictions on imports from these states; and their trade with the United States was subject to special restrictions under U.S. law. With the breakup of the Soviet bloc, the terms of participation for Eastern Europe were gradually normalized.[52]

In the 1980s, the Soviet Union reacted to its growing economic problems by seeking GATT observer status and quietly exploring possible membership. However, the major trading nations viewed the Soviet economic and political system as incompatible with the global trade regime. After the breakup of the Soviet Union, Russian leaders realized that a transition to market orientation would require integration with the global economy. Thus, Russia lowered trade barriers and applied for GATT membership in 1993; but the negotiations were difficult.[53] Russia's membership in the WTO was initially delayed because of its declining economic conditions. In the first five years after the Soviet Union's collapse, the Russian economy contracted to about half its former size. A second factor delaying membership related to Russia's domestic policies. Russian had conflicting views regarding the possible results of freer trade and the need for structural reform. Furthermore, some powerful private groups feared that WTO accession would increase competition and reduce their protection and profits. A third factor delaying membership was friction with the West over Russia's pricing policies for its energy exports. Whereas privatization was common in the Russian oil sector in the 1990s, President Vladimir Putin has returned the sector back toward fuller state control and has employed energy as a lever to extend Russia's influence in former Soviet Union (FSU) countries such as Ukraine, and in Eastern and Western Europe. As Table 8.7 shows, the WTO admitted a number of FSU states from 1998 to 2008. However, as was the case for China, WTO members imposed more stringent conditions for Russian accession because of its size and importance.[54] After China became a WTO member in 2001, Russia was the largest economy outside the organization. In August 2012, Russia finally joined the WTO.

THE SOUTH AND GLOBAL TRADE ISSUES

DCs were the main participants in postwar trade negotiations, and LDCs were largely uninvolved. Although the Havana Charter had some provisions on LDC issues, most of them were not incorporated into GATT. LDCs were also wary of participating in GATT, because it did not recognize their need for **special and differential treatment** (**SDT**). For many years the South therefore sought special access to DC markets and exemptions from trade regime principles and rules. In the 1980s, however, the South became more actively involved in the liberal economic global trade regime. The following discussion identifies five stages of LDC participation in the regime:

- *1940s to early 1960s.* LDCs had limited involvement in GATT.
- *1960s to early 1970s.* LDCs increased their GATT membership and sought special treatment.
- *1970s to 1980.* North–South confrontation increased, and LDCs demanded a *New International Economic Order* (*NIEO*).

- *1980s to 1995.* LDCs were more willing to accept GATT's liberal economic principles.
- *1995 to the present.* LDCs were disillusioned with the Uruguay Round and demand changes in the Doha Round.

1940s to Early 1960s: Limited LDC Involvement

LDCs were less involved in the global trade regime during the early postwar years because of their limited numbers (many were still colonies), their protectionist trade policies, and GATT's inattention to development issues. Raúl Prebisch, an Argentinian economist, argued that LDCs could not achieve high economic growth rates by exporting primary products and importing industrial goods.[55] LDCs therefore adopted protectionist *import substitution industrialization (ISI)* policies in the 1950s to replace industrial imports with domestic production (see Chapter 11). Thus, the LDCs did not participate actively in GATT, and GATT devoted little attention to them.[56]

1960s to Early 1970s: Growing Pressures for Special Treatment

The ISI policies resulted in serious problems, including decreased exports, dependence on intermediate imports for the production of industrial goods, and balance-of-payments deficits (see Chapter 11). Thus, some LDCs became more outward-looking and demanded special treatment to promote their exports. As their numbers increased with decolonization, LDCs were also better able to press their demands. In 1961, the UN General Assembly declared that the 1960s would be the UN Development Decade; in 1963 the South established the G77; and in 1964 UNCTAD was formed. UNCTAD never posed a serious challenge to GATT as the global trade organization, but it introduced a number of influential *ideas* regarding the role of LDCs in the global trade regime. For example, UNCTAD provided analyses of the South's involvement in trade issues, and an understanding reached in UNCTAD led to the introduction of a **generalized system of preferences (GSP)** for LDCs (see discussion below). In 1965 GATT members added a new Part IV to the General Agreement calling for special treatment for LDCs. Part IV only *recommended* that DCs reduce their import barriers to LDCs, and the North in fact raised its barriers for some LDC exports. For example, the North violated GATT Article 11's ban on import quotas and imposed "voluntary" restraints on the South's textile and clothing exports. A 1961 Short-Term Arrangement on Cotton Textiles was followed by several Long-Term Arrangements and Multi-Fiber Arrangements (MFAs).[57]

The South gained a more concrete concession in 1971 when the North established the GSP for LDCs through a 10-year renewable waiver from the MFN clause. The GSP refers to the preferential lowering of DC tariffs for certain LDC imports. Although some LDCs have benefited from these preferences, the North refused to accept a legal obligation to provide preferences or to bind itself to an international GSP plan. Instead, each DC established its own GSP, limited the amount of imports that could enter at lower duties, excluded sensitive products such as textiles, and reduced or eliminated preferences for LDCs that were especially successful in increasing their exports. In view of the complexities of GSP schemes, more competitive LDCs have benefited most, and the GSP has offered very few benefits to poorer LDCs. One study found that Hong Kong, South Korea, and Taiwan accounted for 44 percent of the total gains from GSP tariff reductions.[58]

1970s to 1980: Increased North–South Confrontation

OPEC's success in raising oil prices in 1973 encouraged LDCs in the UN to call for a *New International Economic Order (NIEO)*, in which the South would gain sovereignty over its natural resources, more control over foreign investment, more development assistance, greater influence in the international economic organizations, and higher prices for commodity exports. The North agreed to negotiate these demands because of its concerns about high oil prices, and the UN passed some NIEO-related resolutions.[59] However, most of these resolutions were not implemented, largely because the 1980s foreign debt crisis decreased the South's ability to influence the North. While the South was confronting the North in the UN, it participated in the 1973–1979 GATT Tokyo Round. One result of the Tokyo Round was the *enabling clause*, which "established for the first time in trade relations … a permanent legal basis for preferences" for LDCs.[60] The clause gave permanent legal authorization for the GSP and for preferential RTAs among LDCs. Although the North agreed to the enabling clause, it insisted on a "graduation" principle for states that made notable progress in development. More advanced LDCs (e.g., South Korea, Taiwan, and Brazil) whose exports threatened DC producers would have to give up special treatment and accept greater GATT discipline.[61] As discussed, most LDCs refused to participate in the Tokyo Round NTB codes for government procurement, subsidies, dumping, technical barriers to trade, and import licensing; but the South would become much more involved in GATT in the 1980s.

1980s to 1995: More LDC Participation in GATT

LDCs initially opposed the idea of GATT negotiations in the 1980s because of global trade inequities and DC efforts to include services, intellectual property, and investment in the negotiations. However, their opposition softened when the North agreed to include issues of interest to them such as trade in textiles and agriculture. Unlike earlier periods, LDCs liberalized their trade policies during the 1980s and actively participated in the Uruguay Round. LDCs were also more willing to accept the reciprocity principle, and they agreed to treat the round as a *single undertaking*: Acceptance of the Uruguay Round accord meant acceptance of *all* its agreements. The single undertaking was a marked contrast to the Tokyo Round's plurilateral NTB codes, in which most LDCs did not participate.[62] Although LDCs continued receiving some SDT during the Uruguay Round, they accepted "a dilution of special and differential treatment in exchange for better market access and strengthened rules."[63] LDCs also functioned less as a bloc in the Uruguay Round and joined several North–South coalitions such as the **Cairns Group** of agricultural exporters that first met in Cairns, Australia, in 1986. The Cairns Group added a powerful new voice, ensuring that GATT—and the EC, the United States, and Japan—would have to deal with agriculture. The founding members of the Cairns Group included eight LDCs, three DCs (Australia, Canada, and New Zealand), and an Eastern European country (Hungary).[64]

Liberals and historical materialists cite different reasons for the South's policy shift. According to liberals, LDCs shifted toward liberal economic policies for several reasons: GSP tariff preferences for the South were eroding because tariffs declined with each GATT round; the North viewed LDCs as free riders receiving special treatment and therefore marginalized them in trade negotiations; and LDCs recognized the failure of inward-looking ISI policies and began to emulate the successful East Asian export-led growth strategies (see Chapter 11).[65] Historical materialists by contrast argue that LDCs were *forced* to alter their policies. The IMF and World Bank provided structural adjustment loans to LDCs during the 1980s foreign debt crisis, on the condition that they decrease government spending, liberalize trade, and privatize their economies (see Chapter 7). Thus, one critic argues that "the current rush toward free trade follows on the heels of 10 years of structural adjustment, a logical 'next step' in the overhaul of the global economy."[66]

1995 to the Present: LDC Disillusionment with the Uruguay Round and Demands in the Doha Round

Theorists also differ regarding the Uruguay Round's effects on the South. Many liberals agree that LDCs gained benefits from agreements in textiles and agriculture, flexibility in fulfilling their commitments, longer transition times to implement agreements, technical assistance from the North, and above all from liberalizing their trade policies. However, orthodox liberals clearly state that the Uruguay Round benefited the South more than the North, whereas interventionist liberals often point to the Round's shortcomings for the South. Historical materialists and some interventionist liberals argue that the South gave up more than it received in the Uruguay Round. The South in fact received much less than it had expected. Although the Uruguay Round provided some "fairly significant benefits" to LDCs, they realized belatedly "that they had accepted fairly weak commitments in agriculture and textiles while making substantially stronger ones, especially in ... intellectual property."[67] Many LDCs depend on agricultural exports and wanted significant cutbacks in the North's support for their farmers, but the Uruguay Round did little to reduce DC agricultural subsidies and trade barriers.

In view of the South's disillusionment with the GATT Uruguay Round, it was very reluctant to agree to a new MTN round under the WTO. The North recognized that the South was dissatisfied with the Uruguay Round, and that promising better results for LDCs was necessary to get their support for a new MTN round. Thus, the WTO Doha Round was called the **Doha Development**

Agenda (**DDA**), and "it promised special attention to the concerns of the Least Developed Countries" (LLDCs).[68] As discussed, however, the increasing size and diversity of the WTO membership has to this point precluded a Doha Round agreement. DCs, emerging economies, and LLDCs have a range of disparate expectations in the negotiations. The Doha Round is still not completed, despite its scheduled completion date of January 2005. However, after 10 years of stalemate, an agreement on some of the Doha Round issues was finally reached at the WTO's ninth ministerial conference in Bali in December 2013. Although the agreement is much less ambitious than the original DDA agenda, many consider it to be a major breakthrough. The Bali agreement deals mainly with three areas: trade facilitation, which is mainly of interest to the DCs; food security; and a package of measures for LLDCs such as duty-free and quota-free market access for most products from LLDCs. It is impossible to discuss here the detailed results of the Bali agreement. We simply note that trade and development specialists disagree on whether the agreement is a major gain for the South. Some analysts assert that "it is business as usual because the Bali package will be of disproportionally greater value to the industrial states than to their developing and least developed counterparts."[69] Other analysts by contrast contend that

> it would be wrong to dismiss the Bali Package as an aggregate loss to the world's poor ... the agreement has breathed new life into the [Doha] Round, retained and reinforced the promise of development as envisioned by the DDA, and has bolstered the credibility of the multi-lateral trading system.[70]

The effects of the Bali agreement on the South and the ultimate success or failure of the Doha Round remain to be seen. One of the major problems in reaching a final Doha Round agreement is the growing diversity of the South. For example, the United States will most likely "press for some members, especially China, to 'graduate' from special and differential treatment."[71] The next section deals with the growing influence of three major emerging economies in global trade relations: China, India, and Brazil.

The Emerging Economies: China, India, and Brazil

China, India, and Brazil stand out among LDCs in the challenge they present to DC dominance in the global trade regime. By 2013, the combined GDP of these three LDCs was "about equal to the combined GDP of the long-standing industrial powers of the North—Canada, France, Germany, Italy, the United Kingdom, and the United States."[72] China, India, and Brazil are highly atypical of most LDCs in terms of global economic power and influence, but they have the capacity to represent the interests of the South, and this has been evident in the WTO Doha Round. China is clearly the most economically important of these three LDCs. Its GDP is much larger, and its exports account for about 10 percent of global trade, compared with only 2 and 1 percent for India and Brazil, respectively. However, "Brazil and India have assumed a more aggressive and activist role in WTO negotiations than China."[73] In view of China's greater economic importance, we begin with a discussion of its role in the WTO and then draw comparisons with India and Brazil.

China followed autarkic policies in the 1960s during the Cultural Revolution, but in the 1970s it occupied the "China seat" in the UN (which Taiwan had held) and expanded commercial contacts with the West. In 1986 China indicated that it wanted to "rejoin" GATT, but its accession to the GATT/WTO was a protracted affair. The delay stemmed partly from China's ambivalence. As a member, China would have to submit to GATT rules and open its market, and it already received *de facto* MFN treatment from most states. Although the U.S. Congress held an annual vote on this issue, it had renewed China's MFN status every year. However, China decided that GATT membership would consolidate its liberalization measures and give it legal access to export markets and the GATT dispute settlement system. China had been a founding member of GATT in 1948, and it wanted to simply renew its membership. In 1950, the Chiang Kai-shek government had sent a cable from Taiwan where it had fled withdrawing China from GATT membership, but China argued this had no legal effect because Chiang Kai-shek was no longer leading the Chinese government. However, China had not abided by GATT obligations for 35 years, and it eventually had to agree to negotiate as a new member.[74]

China was never admitted to GATT, and it did not join the WTO until December 2001. Several issues were central to China's accession negotiations. First was the requirement that China liberalize its economy. Although China had introduced a number of market reforms, government intervention continued to produce major trade distortions. The United States strongly criticized these distortions because of its growing trade deficit with China. Others also argued that China's trade policies were not based on comparative advantage, and the WTO refused to accord China the same terms as it gave to market economies. A second issue was China's status as an LDC. China wanted special treatment given to LDCs at similar levels of economic development, including protection for its infant industries, the GSP, and longer transition times to implement WTO agreements. However, many WTO members argued that China should meet the same reciprocity conditions as DCs because of its size and status as a world exporter. The WTO refused to treat China as a "normal" LDC, but permitted it to phase-in reforms in some areas as a transition economy.[75] A third issue was China's past record in implementing agreements. In 1992, for example, the United States and China had agreed to improve protection of intellectual property. Despite this agreement, pirated intellectual property continued to be readily available in major Chinese cities.[76] After years of negotiation on these issues, China finally joined the WTO in December 2001. China does not accept Taiwan's sovereignty, but it agreed to Taiwan's admission to the WTO in January 2002 as "Chinese Taipei." Although most WTO members are sovereign states, the only requirement is that a member must be a separate customs territory with its own commercial policy. In addition to Chinese Taipei, Hong Kong and Macao continue to be separate members of the WTO.[77]

Whereas China did not join the WTO until 2001, India and Brazil were original members of GATT, dating back to 1947. Thus, India and Brazil have a long history of activism in the GATT and WTO as recognized leaders in the South. Although India and Brazil participated in GATT's so-called "Green Room" meetings along with other major economies, the North clearly dominated global trade negotiations until the Doha Round. The *Quadrilateral Group* or *Quad*, which included the United States, the EU, Japan, and Canada, was formed in 1981–82 and guided the negotiations in the GATT Uruguay Round.[78] In the Doha Round, however, the Quad has been displaced because of the growing influence of emerging economies in the WTO. While India and Brazil have continued their long history of trade activism in the Doha Round, "China has only recently shifted from being a low-key actor in the Doha Round negotiations to taking a firmer stand" on behalf of the South.[79]

Unlike China, India and Brazil cannot rely on their own economic power to exert influence, and coalition-building with other LDCs has been an important strategy for both countries. Despite differences in their negotiating positions, India and Brazil realized that an alliance was necessary to achieve their objectives. Thus, they have jointly led coalitions ensuring that such issues as DC agricultural subsidies and market access, and special safeguards for LDCs, would be a central part of the negotiations. Brazil has uncovered major inconsistencies between WTO rules and U.S. and EU agricultural policies; and India has actively promoted *developmental multilateralism*, which seeks to foster economic growth through trade principles and rules that take account of historical and cultural sensitivities. Whereas India and Brazil have required coalition behavior to exert more influence in the WTO's inner circle, China can depend on its own rising economic power to exert influence. However, China has also been less proactive than India and Brazil in pushing its trade agenda because other countries view its rapid growth in exports, and the size and growth of its economy, as a competitive threat to their own trade interests. China has joined in several LDC coalitions because it sees the DCs as posing the greatest obstacle to its trade objectives. In sum, the rising influence of China, India, and Brazil has ensured that they and their coalition partners can prevent the successful completion of the Doha Round if it does not serve the interests of the South as well as the North.[80]

CIVIL SOCIETY AND GLOBAL TRADE RELATIONS

Civil society groups in earlier years had little involvement with GATT because it focused mainly on lowering tariffs. However, this changed in the 1990s when the GATT/WTO became more involved with behind-the-border issues that had a greater impact on society. Civil society groups protested against the WTO even before it began operations, but the protests reached new levels when about 50,000 protesters demonstrated at the 1999 WTO ministerial in Seattle. Whereas citizens can hold their national governments to account for the policies they follow, to whom is the WTO accountable? Global trade governance seems far removed from accountable government, and this results in a "democratic deficit" according to civil society groups. In response to NGO pressure, the WTO has adopted some policies to increase transparency; for example, it provides more information on its website, makes derestricted documents available to the public more promptly, and permits accredited NGOs to attend the WTO ministerial meetings. However, NGOs are excluded from almost all meetings of the WTO bodies such as the Governing Council, committees, and working parties. Formally, WTO policy-making operates according to a *club model*, in which only government officials and political leaders have the authority to make decisions. WTO agreements establish formal rights and obligations only for member governments, and WTO dispute settlement is formally open only to states. The club model rests on the neomercantilist view that the WTO functions best "when governments can speak clearly to each other without a cacophony of other voices."[81] Despite the formal limitation to governments, WTO policy-making in fact operates according to an *adaptive club model*, in which governments regularly consult with private business groups. For example, although states are the only formal participants in WTO dispute settlement, trade ministries often lack the time, expertise, and resources to gather information for WTO investigations. Thus, MNCs give governments informal advice on legal matters, and assistance in preparing written submissions to dispute settlement panels. In a U.S.–Japanese dispute over the photographic film industry, Kodak performed these functions for the U.S. Trade Representative (USTR) office while Fuji assisted the Japanese government. NGOs have argued that a *multistakeholder model*, in which *all* stakeholders have a role in the policy process, would be more democratic; this would provide alternative sources of advice and would decrease alienation from the WTO. Opponents of a multistakeholder model argue that NGOs can already participate at the domestic level, that they do not represent the national interest, and that many NGOs oppose trade liberalization. It is unlikely that the WTO will accept the multistakeholder model, because many member governments do not want their NGOs to participate independently.[82]

NGOs have had an effect on WTO operations in some areas. For example, NGOs argued that the WTO TRIPs agreement was limiting access to affordable medicines to treat HIV/AIDS, tuberculosis, and malaria in LDCs. As a result, the Doha Declaration stated that TRIPs should not prevent countries from "protecting public health and promoting access to essential medicines."[83] Some NGOs have also developed innovative strategies such as the fair trade movement to alter global trade relations in general. **Fair trade** is a trading partnership that contributes to greater equity and sustainable development by securing more rights and better trading conditions for marginalized workers, especially in the South.[84] In the 1960s, the movement focused on the unequal trade relations facing the world's poor and branched out from handicrafts to food commodities such as coffee, tea, and cocoa. Alternative trading organizations such as Oxfam and Twin Trading, and cooperatives such as Equal Exchange, carry out fair trade, but marketing success also depends on the willingness of large-scale retailers and corporations to bring fair trade to the mainstream public. Critics warn that the expansion of fair trade as a marketing device is threatening fair trade as a social movement.[85]

TRADE AND THE ENVIRONMENT

Debates over trade and the environment are often framed by competing theoretical points of view. Orthodox liberals believe that free trade based on comparative advantage will have positive effects on the environment for several reasons. As wealth and prosperity increase, people will have the incentive and ability to improve the environment; states will be able to consume more goods with fewer resources; and DCs will disperse cleaner technologies to LDCs. Orthodox liberals see efforts to inject the environment into trade discussions as interference with the market and an excuse for protectionism. For example, they oppose the use of the "precautionary principle" in trade negotiations, which enables states to limit imports that pose a possible health risk in cases of scientific uncertainty. The EU has used the precautionary principle to limit imports of beef with certain hormones and genetically modified foods from the United States and Canada. Interventionist liberals also favor market-based policies, but view some environmental controls as necessary when markets function imperfectly; for example, governments should address the problems of trade in hazardous wastes, dangerous chemicals, and endangered species. Institutional liberals often accept the WTO's involvement with environmental issues, because the environment as well as trade requires a degree of global governance. Some interventionist and institutional liberals accept the limited use of the precautionary principle, but warn that states could use it for protectionist purposes.

The greens (discussed in Chapter 5) see freer trade as a *cause* of global environmental problems for a number of reasons. First, global trade has transportation and environmental costs because manufacturing takes place far from the point of consumption. Second, freer trade imposes a burden on poorer states with serious environmental and social problems. Whereas LDCs produce the most polluting goods that depend on the unsustainable use of local natural resources, DCs benefit from importing these products. Third, freer trade contributes to the growth of consumption, which puts pressure on the sustainability of the planet. Fourth, freer trade causes states to lower their environmental standards to become more cost-competitive; this leads to a "race to the bottom." Thus, the greens advise states and global institutions to restrict trade when necessary to achieve environmental goals. Whereas liberals prefer voluntary environmental agreements, the greens favor trade sanctions to induce states to adhere to environmental standards. The greens also strongly support the precautionary principle.[86]

The GATT/WTO gives priority to trade over environmental goals, but there has been some change over time. Environmental protection was not a major issue in the 1940s, and GATT did not even explicitly refer to the "environment."[87] GATT Article 20 permits exceptions to GATT rules "to protect human, animal or plant life or health," and for "conservation of exhaustible natural resources." However, such exceptions should be avoided if other measures are available that do not restrict trade. Many environmental problems such as global warming or dumping at sea also do not qualify for GATT exceptions because they are not included in Article 20. The WTO treats the environment as a more prominent issue. For example, the WTO's objectives include "sustainable development" and "seeking to protect and preserve the environment," and it sponsors a Public Forum with civil society and private sector participants in which environmental concerns are an important focus. The WTO focuses on trade and the environment through two main routes. First, the WTO's Committee on Trade and Environment (CTE) tries to reach a consensus among WTO members on environmental issues. Second, environmental issues have been prominent in some WTO dispute settlement cases. Because the CTE has been unable to forge a consensus, "the relationship between trade and environment in the WTO is, in effect, being created through disputes."[88]

The GATT/WTO has had some important environmental dispute settlement cases. One of the most prominent was the tuna–dolphin case in the early 1990s. Mexico complained that the United States refused to import its tuna because of claims that Mexico's netting practices were harming dolphins, and the GATT panel decided against the United States for two reasons. First, the national treatment obligation and GATT Article 20 indicate that states can only limit trade because of the material composition of the products (what is produced), and not because of the production and processing methods (how they are produced). The United States had not shown that the quality of Mexican tuna was inferior, and it was only objecting to the production and processing method (which it claimed was harming dolphins). Second, the GATT/WTO does not permit a state to use extraterritorial measures to protect natural resources outside its borders, and the United States was trying to impose its domestic measures on Mexico. Prominent WTO environmental disputes have been the U.S. gasoline imports case, the shrimp–sea turtle case, the EU hormone-treated beef case, the French asbestos case, and the EU genetically modified foods case. In only one of these cases did the dispute settlement panel clearly give priority to the environment over trade: The WTO panel and Appellate Body decided that France could prevent imports of Canadian asbestos on health and safety grounds.[89] (The decision in the shrimp–sea turtle case was a partial victory for environmentalists.)

Predictably, reactions to the WTO dispute settlement cases vary in accordance with the views of the observer. Whereas orthodox liberals believe that the market should always take priority over the environment in dispute settlement cases, institutional liberals see WTO dispute settlement as ushering in "an important period of reform" in "the interplay of trade and the environment."[90] Institutional liberals also argue that the judgments in dispute settlement cases have gradually shifted toward more recognition of the environment, and that Appellate Body decisions have "convinced many environmentalists that legitimate environmental measures would be permitted by the WTO."[91] Green theorists by contrast argue that when free trade and environmental regulation "come into conflict, the GATT/WTO dispute settlement system always found in favor of trade, and against national environmental regulation," and that the dispute settlement panelists are "never environmentalists."[92] Thus, many green theorists see the WTO as unreformable and would like to replace it with a more environmentally friendly organization.

Considering IPE Theory and Practice

Liberals view free trade as a collective or public good that provides widespread benefits for states. A global hegemon such as the United States and international organizations such as the GATT/WTO have upheld trade principles and rules to avoid collective action problems such as free riders in providing this public good. As a result, GATT oversaw eight rounds of multilateral trade negotiations which lowered tariff barriers and began to deal with NTBs. The Uruguay Round was especially important, leading to the creation of the WTO and the extension of international rules beyond trade in goods to include services trade (GATS), intellectual property rights (TRIPs), and investment measures (TRIMs). However, the inexorable growth of trade has also been marked by resistance and conflict, and there is still no Doha Round agreement. This section discusses the competing theoretical views regarding the problems with the Doha Round.

Neomercantilists attribute the Doha Round problems to the growing North–South struggle, in which the South seeks more wealth and power in the global trade regime. The balance of power in trade is shifting from "a bipolar system driven by the United States and Europe—to a multipolar one," in which emerging economies such as China, India, and Brazil have growing influence.[93] The United States, Europe, and Japan have been reluctant to accept this change in geopolitical power relationships, and China, India, and Brazil have been equally adamant in demanding change. As U.S. trade hegemony has declined, it has had fewer "options in providing leadership in the trading system. Yet, this lack of leadership has not been replaced by any efforts on the part of other major players."[94] Neomercantilists also note that this is still a world of states looking after their national interest and that trade negotiations are now more complicated with 161 diverse WTO members.

Most liberals do not view the problems with the Doha Round as irreparable, because the WTO continues to effectively uphold trade principles and rules and provide a venue for dispute settlement. However, liberals who believe that there will be a reversion to protectionism if the "bicycle" does not keep moving view the failure to complete the round as a serious problem. The 2008 global financial crisis is yet another major setback, because countries are often under the illusion that protectionism will help them recover from financial crises. Many states are also signing regional free trade agreements as a result of the Doha Round problems. As we discuss in Chapter 9, many liberals view RTAs as a "second-best option" after global free trade. However, some liberals warn that RTAs are a divisive force; Jagdish Bhagwati, for example, refers to preferential trade agreements as "termites in the trading system."[95] Liberal pluralists view the Doha Round negotiations as a "two-level game," in which delegates negotiate not only with each other but with their own domestic groups. The Doha Round is dealing with many behind-the-border barriers in areas such as agriculture, where protectionist groups have considerable influence.

Historical materialists welcome the breakdown of the Doha Round, because the WTO trade principles and rules benefit DCs and private corporations at the expense of LDCs and workers. For example, the WTO dispute settlement system only protects the rights of the strong. The high costs of litigation preclude the use of the system by many LDCs, and trade retaliation, which is the only means of enforcing a finding, is of little use to an LDC in a dispute with a more powerful DC.[96] The TRIPs agreement is another example of the differing views of liberals and historical materialists. Liberals argue that individuals have little incentive to engage in research and development if they do not have sufficient patent protection. Historical materialists by contrast assert that more than 80 percent of patents in the South are owned by foreigners, mainly by MNCs in the North. Thus, the TRIPs agreement limits and distorts trade, hinders the transfer of technology to the South, and transfers resources from the South to the North. Some critical theorists argue that the WTO must become a broader, more democratic organization that addresses concerns of labor, the environment, civil society groups, and LDCs. Others believe that the WTO is incapable of change, and that it should be abolished.

A complicating factor in the WTO is that the global trade principles sometimes collide. For example, it is difficult to reconcile the reciprocity principle with the special and differential treatment (SDT) principle. Many interventionist liberals and historical materialists argue that LDCs require SDT until their infant industries become more established and they become more competitive with the DCs. Orthodox liberals by contrast argue that SDT violates the reciprocity principle and enables LDCs to avoid liberalizing their trade policies. Some liberal theorists have adopted a more nuanced position, suggesting that SDT can be reconciled with reciprocity if LDCs are expected to liberalize their trade, but are given more time than DCs to meet their commitments. Furthermore, emerging economies that have grown rapidly such as China should "graduate" and no longer be SDT recipients.[97]

The breakdown of the Doha Round and the divergent views of theorists demonstrate that trade is one of the most contentious areas of IPE. Chapter 9 deals with regional trade agreements, which are of growing importance.

QUESTIONS

1. How has liberal trade theory evolved over time? (Discuss the theories of absolute and comparative advantage, and the Heckscher–Ohlin and Stolper–Samuelson theories.) How do the neomercantilist concepts of competitive advantage and strategic trade theory differ from the liberal concept of comparative advantage?
2. Is the GATT/WTO most-favored-nation principle compatible with specific reciprocity, diffuse reciprocity, and the development principle? Explain.

3. Why are safeguards an essential part of most trade agreements? What are CVDs and ADDs, and what must a country demonstrate to impose them? Why are CVDs and ADDs so controversial?

4. What are the similarities and differences between GATT and the WTO? How successful has the WTO been in global trade governance? What are the competing explanations for the Doha Round problems, and which explanations do you think are the most plausible?

5. How has the South's role in the GATT/WTO changed over time? Why did LDCs become more actively involved in the GATT Uruguay Round, and what has been their position in the Doha Round?

6. In what ways are China, India, and Brazil posing a challenge to DC dominance in the global trade regime?

7. How much priority have GATT and the WTO given to the environment? Is free trade compatible with protection of the environment?

8. What is the relationship between civil society groups and the GATT/WTO, and how has this relationship changed over time?

KEY TERMS

absolute advantage
antidumping duties
Cairns Group
comparative advantage
countervailing duties
diffuse reciprocity
Doha Development
  Agenda
dumping
fair trade
General Agreement on
  Tariffs and Trade
General Agreement on
  Trade in Services

generalized system of
  preferences
Heckscher–Ohlin theory
intrafirm trade
intraindustry trade
most-favored-nation
  principle
national treatment
nontariff barriers
opportunity cost
Reciprocal Trade
  Agreements Act
reciprocity principle
safeguards

single undertaking
special and differential
  treatment
specific reciprocity
Stolper–Samuelson theory
strategic trade theory
tariffs
Trade-Related Intellectual
  Property Rights
Trade-Related Investment
  Measures
voluntary export
  restraints
World Trade Organization

FURTHER READING

Comprehensive studies of the GATT/WTO from a liberal institutional perspective include Kent Jones, *Reconstructing the World Trade Organization for the 21st Century* (New York: Oxford University Press, 2015); and Bernard M. Hoekman and Michel M. Kostecki, *The Political Economy of the World Trading System: The WTO and Beyond*, 3rd ed. (New York: Oxford University Press, 2009). A study from a neomercantilist perspective is Laura D'Andrea Tyson, *Who's Bashing Whom? Trade Conflict in High-Technology Industries* (Washington, DC: Institute for International Economics, 1992). A study from a critical perspective is Fatoumata Jawara and Aileen Kwa, *Behind the Scenes at the WTO: The Real World of International Trade Negotiations* (New York: Zed Books, 2003).

Recommended studies on the WTO also include articles on WTO structural issues in the journal *World Trade Review* 14, no. 1 (January 2015); Rorden Wilkinson, *What's Wrong with the WTO and How to Fix It* (Malden, MA: Polity, 2014); and Amrita

Narlikar, Martin Daunton, and Robert M. Stern, eds., *The Oxford Handbook on the World Trade Organization* (New York: Oxford University Press, 2012). On the formal and informal institutions in the global trade regime see Theodore H. Cohn, *Governing Global Trade: International Institutions in Conflict and Convergence* (Burlington, VT: Ashgate, 2002).

On domestic politics and international trade, see Oluf Langhelle, ed., *International Trade and Domestic Politics* (New York: Routledge, 2014); and Ronald Rogowski, *Commerce and Coalitions: How Trade Affects Domestic Political Alignments* (Princeton, NJ: Princeton University Press, 1989).

Studies of North–South trade relations and the emerging economies include Kristen Hopewell, "Different Paths to Power: The Rise of Brazil, India and China at the World Trade Organization," *Review of International Political Economy* 22, no. 2 (2015), pp. 211–238; WTO, *World Trade Report 2014: Trade and Development* (Geneva: WTO, 2014); Michael Pettis, *The Great Rebalancing* (Princeton, NJ: Princeton University Press, 2013); and Sonia E. Rolland, *Development at the World Trade Organization* (New York: Oxford University Press, 2012).

On the GATT/WTO and the environment, see Jennifer Clapp and Peter Dauvergne, *Paths to a Green World: The Political Economy of the Global Environment*, 2nd ed. (Cambridge, MA: MIT Press, 2011), ch. 5; Gary Sampson and John Whalley, eds., *The WTO, Trade and the Environment* (Northampton, MA: Edward Elgar, 2005); and Daniel C. Esty, *Greening the GATT: Trade, Environment, and the Future* (Washington, DC: Institute for International Economics, 1994).

NOTES

1. John A. C. Conybeare, *Trade Wars: The Theory and Practice of International Commercial Rivalry* (New York: Columbia University Press, 1987).
2. Helen V. Milner, *Resisting Protectionism: Global Industries and the Politics of International Trade* (Princeton, NJ: Princeton University Press, 1988), pp. 290–291.
3. World Trade Organization, *World Trade Report—2008* (Geneva: WTO, 2008), p. 15; WTO, *World Trade Report—2013* (Geneva: WTO, 2013), p. 5.
4. WTO, *World Trade Report—2009* (Geneva: WTO, 2009), p. 2.
5. WTO, *World Trade Report— 2014* (Geneva: WTO, 2014), p. 13.
6. Renato Ruggiero, "Charting the Trade Routes of the Future: Towards a Borderless Economy," September 29, 1997, *WTO Press Release*, Geneva, Press/77, p. 4.
7. David Ricardo, *The Principles of Political Economy and Taxation* (Homewood, IL: Irwin, 1963).
8. Wolfgang F. Stolper and Paul A. Samuelson, "Protection and Real Wages," *Review of Economic Studies* 9, no. 1 (November 1941), pp. 58–73; Ronald Rogowski, *Commerce and Coalitions: How Trade Affects Domestic Political Alignments* (Princeton, NJ: Princeton University Press, 1989).
9. Elhanan Helpman and Paul R. Krugman, *Market Structure and Foreign Trade: Increasing Returns, Imperfect Competition, and the International Economy* (Cambridge, MA: MIT Press, 1985), p. 3; Robert Gilpin with Jean M. Gilpin, *The Political Economy of International Relations* (Princeton, NJ: Princeton University Press, 1987), pp. 175–178.
10. Robert O. Keohane, "Neoliberal Institutionalism: A Perspective on World Politics," in Robert O. Keohane, ed., *International Institutions and State Power: Essays in International Relations Theory* (Boulder, CO: Westview Press, 1989), pp. 1–20.

11. John H. Jackson, *The World Trading System: Law and Policy of International Economic Relations*, 2nd ed. (Cambridge, MA: MIT Press, 1997), pp. 229–232.

12. Laura D'Andrea Tyson, *Who's Bashing Whom? Trade Conflict in High-Technology Industries* (Washington, DC: Institute for International Economics, 1992), p. 4.

13. Klaus Stegemann, "Policy Rivalry Among Industrial States: What Can We Learn from Models of Strategic Trade Policy?" *International Organization* 43, no. 1 (Winter 1989), p. 99.

14. Arghiri Emmanuel, *Unequal Exchange: A Study of the Imperialism of Trade* (New York: Monthly Review Press, 1972); Anthony Brewer, *Marxist Theories of Imperialism: A Critical Survey*, 2nd ed. (New York: Routledge, 1990), pp. 200–224.

15. Edward John Ray, "Changing Patterns of Protectionism: The Fall in Tariffs and the Rise in Non-Tariff Barriers," *Northwestern Journal of International Law & Business* 8 (1987), pp. 294–295.

16. Robert A. Pastor, *Congress and the Politics of U.S. Foreign Economic Policy, 1929–1976* (Berkeley, CA: University of California Press, 1980), p. 78.

17. Charles P. Kindleberger, *The World in Depression 1929–1939* (Berkeley, CA: University of California Press, 1973), pp. 291–307.

18. Stephen D. Krasner, "State Power and the Structure of International Trade," *World Politics* 28, no. 3 (April 1976), p. 338.

19. E. E. Schattschneider, *Politics, Pressures and the Tariff: A Study of Free Private Enterprise in Pressure Politics, as Shown in the 1929–1930 Revision of the Tariff* (Hamden, CT: Archon Books, 1963); Pastor, *Congress and the Politics of U.S. Foreign Economic Policy*, pp. 80–84.

20. I. M. Destler, *American Trade Politics*, 2nd ed. (Washington, DC: Institute for International Economics and Twentieth Century Fund, 1992), pp. 14–15; Gilbert R. Winham, *The Evolution of International Trade Agreements* (Toronto: University of Toronto Press, 1992), p. 19.

21. John W. Evans, *The Kennedy Round in American Trade Policy: The Twilight of the GATT?* (Cambridge, MA: Harvard University Press, 1971), pp. 5–7.

22. Robert E. Hudec, *The GATT Legal System and World Trade Diplomacy* (New York: Praeger, 1975), pp. 7–18; Simon Reisman, "The Birth of a World Trading System: ITO and GATT," in Orin Kirshner, ed., *The Bretton Woods–GATT System: Retrospect and Prospect After Fifty Years* (Armonk, NY: Sharpe, 1996), pp. 83–85.

23. William Diebold, Jr., "The End of the I.T.O.," *Essays in International Finance* no. 16 (Princeton, NJ: International Finance Section, Department of Economics and Social Institutions, Princeton University, October 1952), p. 2; Richard N. Gardner, *Sterling-Dollar Diplomacy in Current Perspective: The Origins and Prospects of Our International Economic Order*, expanded ed. (New York: Columbia University Press, 1980), pp. 348–380.

24. Barry Eichengreen and Peter B. Kenen, "Managing the World Economy Under the Bretton Woods System: An Overview," in Peter B. Kenen, ed., *Managing the World Economy: Fifty Years After Bretton Woods* (Washington, DC: Institute for International Economics, 1994), p. 7.

25. Bernard M. Hoekman and Michel M. Kostecki, *The Political Economy of the World Trading System: From GATT to WTO*, 2nd ed. (New York: Oxford University Press, 2001), pp. 1–3.

26. John Gerard Ruggie, "International Regimes, Transactions, and Change: Embedded Liberalism in the Postwar Economic Order," in Stephen D. Krasner, ed., *International Regimes* (Ithaca, NY: Cornell University Press, 1983), p. 212.

27. Item-by-item negotiations continued during the Kennedy Round for agricultural goods and some other sensitive products. Hoekman and Kostecki, *The Political Economy of the World Trading System*, pp. 127–129.

28. Jock A. Finlayson and Mark W. Zacher, "The GATT and the Regulation of Trade Barriers: Regime Dynamics and Functions," in Stephen D. Krasner, ed., *International Regimes* (Ithaca, NY: Cornell University Press, 1983), pp. 282–286; William P. Avery, ed., *World Agriculture and the GATT* (Boulder, CO: Lynne Rienner, 1993).

29. Theodore H. Cohn, *The International Politics of Agricultural Trade: Canadian–American Relations in a Global Agricultural Context* (Vancouver: University of British Columbia Press, 1990), pp. 141–142.

30. Ernest H. Preeg, "The Uruguay Round Negotiations and the Creation of the WTO," in Amrita Narlikar, Martin Daunton, and Robert M. Stern, eds., *The Oxford Handbook on the World Trade Organization* (New York: Oxford University Press, 2012), pp. 133–136.

31. Milner, *Resisting Protectionism*, p. 290.

32. Eric Wyndham-White, "Negotiations in Prospect," in C. Fred Bergsten, ed., *Toward a New World Trade Policy: The Maidenhead Papers* (Lanham, MD: Lexington Books, 1975), p. 322.

33. Winham, *The Evolution of International Trade Agreements*, pp. 46–48; Hoekman and Kostecki, *The Political Economy of the World Trading System*, pp. 29–31.

34. Finlayson and Zacher, "The GATT and the Regulation of Trade Barriers," pp. 286–290; Gilbert Winham, *International Trade and the Tokyo Round Negotiations* (Princeton, NJ: Princeton University Press, 1986), pp. 172–175.

35. Robert O. Keohane, "Reciprocity in International Relations," *International Organization* 40, no. 1 (Winter 1986), p. 4.

36. Carolyn Rhodes, "Reciprocity in Trade: The Utility of a Bargaining Strategy," *International Organization* 43, no. 2 (Spring 1989), p. 276.

37. B. Peter Rosendorff and Helen V. Milner, "The Optimal Design of International Trade Institutions: Uncertainty and Escape," *International Organization* 55, no. 4 (Autumn 2001), pp. 829–857.

38. Gilbert Gagné and François Roch, "The US-Canada Softwood Lumber Dispute and the WTO Definition of Subsidy," *World Trade Review* 7, no. 3 (2008), pp. 547–572.

39. John H. Barton, Judith L. Goldstein, Timothy E. Josling, and Richard H. Steinberg, *The Evolution of the Trade Regime: Politics, Law, and the Economics of the GATT and the WTO* (Princeton, NJ: Princeton University Press, 2006), pp. 109–118; Bernard M. Hoekman and Petros C. Mavroidis, *The World Trade Organization: Law, Economics, and Politics* (New York: Routledge, 2007), pp. 48–51.

40. Finlayson and Zacher, "The GATT and the Regulation of Trade Barriers," pp. 293–296.

41. Minister for International Trade, "Canada Proposes Strategy for Creation of a World Trade Organization," *News Release* no. 077, External Affairs and International Trade Canada, April 11, 1990.

42. John Croome, *Reshaping the World Trading System: A History of the Uruguay Round* (Geneva: WTO, 1995), pp. 271–274, 358–361; Ernest H. Preeg, *Traders in a Brave New World: The Uruguay Round and the Future of the International Trading System* (Chicago, IL: University of Chicago Press, 1995), pp. 113–126.

43. Theodore H. Cohn, *Governing Global Trade: International Institutions in Conflict and Convergence* (Burlington, VT: Ashgate, 2002), pp. 142–146.

44. Hoekman and Kostecki, *The Political Economy of the World Trading System*, pp. 74–98.
45. Kent Jones, *Reconstructing the World Trade Organization for the 21st Century* (New York: Oxford University Press, 2015), p. 3.
46. Robert Wolfe, "First Diagnose, Then Treat: What Ails the Doha Round?" *World Trade Review* 14, no. 1 (January 2015), pp. 7–8.
47. Jones, *Reconstructing the World Trade Organization*, p. 3.
48. C. Fred Bergsten, "Fifty Years of Trade Policy: The Policy Lessons," *World Economy* 24, no. 1 (January 2001), p. 1.
49. Rorden Wilkinson, "Of Butchery and Bicycles: The WTO and the 'Death' of the Doha Development Agenda," *Political Quarterly* 83, no. 2 (April–June 2012), pp. 397–399.
50. Jones, *Reconstructing the World Trade Organization*, pp. 5–9; Wolfe, "First Diagnose, Then Treat," pp. 9–20.
51. John H. Jackson, *The World Trading System: Law and Policy of International Economic Relations* (Cambridge, MA: MIT Press, 1989), pp. 283–286.
52. Leah A. Haus, *Globalizing the GATT: The Soviet Union's Successor States, Eastern Europe, and the International Trading System* (Washington, DC: Brookings Institution, 1992); Jozef M. van Brabant, *The Planned Economies and International Economic Organizations* (New York: Cambridge University Press, 1991), pp. 199–201.
53. Harry G. Broadman, "Global Economic Integration: Prospects for WTO Accession and Continued Russian Reforms," *Washington Quarterly* 27, no. 2 (Spring 2004), pp. 79–81.
54. David A. Dyker, "Russian Accession to the WTO—Why Such a Long and Difficult Road?" *Post-Communist Economies* 16, no. 1 (March 2004), pp. 3–20.
55. Raúl Prebisch, "The Economic Development of Latin America and Its Principal Problems," *Economic Bulletin for Latin America* 7, no. 1 (February 1962), pp. 1–59.
56. Robert E. Hudec, *Developing Countries in the GATT Legal System* (Brookfield, VT: Gower, 1987), pp. 23–24.
57. Marc Williams, *Third World Cooperation: The Group of 77 in UNCTAD* (London: Pinter, 1991), pp. 89–90; Vinod K. Aggarwal, *Liberal Protectionism: The International Politics of Organized Textile Trade* (Berkeley, CA: University of California Press, 1985), p. 8.
58. Anne O. Krueger, *Trade Policies and Developing Nations* (Washington, DC: Brookings Institution, 1995), p. 41.
59. Jeffrey A. Hart, *The New International Economic Order: Conflict and Cooperation in North–South Economic Relations, 1974–77* (New York: St. Martin's Press, 1983).
60. Olivier Long, *Law and Its Limitations in the GATT Multilateral Trade System* (Dordrecht, The Netherlands: Nijhoff, 1985), p. 101.
61. Hudec, *Developing Countries in the GATT Legal System*, pp. 70–91.
62. Robert Wolfe, "Global Trade as a Single Undertaking: The Role of Ministers in the WTO," *International Journal* 51, no. 4 (Autumn 1996), pp. 690–709.
63. Quoted in Mari Pangestu, "Special and Differential Treatment in the Millennium: Special for Whom and How Different?" *World Economy* 23, no. 9 (September 2000), p. 1291.
64. Colleen Hamilton and John Whalley, "Coalitions in the Uruguay Round," *Weltwirtschaftliches Archiv* 125, no. 3 (1989), pp. 547–561; Richard A.

Higgott and Andrew Fenton Cooper, "Middle Power Leadership and Coalition Building: Australia, the Cairns Group, and the Uruguay Round of Trade Negotiations," *International Organization* 44, no. 4 (Autumn 1990), pp. 589–632.

65. John Whalley, "Recent Trade Liberalisation in the Developing World: What Is Behind It and Where Is It Headed?" in David Greenaway, Robert C. Hine, Anthony P. O'Brien, and Robert J. Thornton, eds., *Global Protectionism* (London: Macmillan, 1991), pp. 225–253.

66. John Gershman, "The Free Trade Connection," in Kevin Danaher, ed., *Fifty Years Is Enough: The Case Against the World Bank and the International Monetary Fund* (Boston, MA: South End Press, 1994), p. 24.

67. Jayashree Watal, "Developing Countries' Interests in a 'Development Round,'" in Jeffrey J. Schott, ed., *The WTO After Seattle* (Washington, DC: Institute for International Economics, 2000), pp. 71–72; Chakravarthi Raghavan, *Recolonization: GATT, the Uruguay Round and the Third World* (London: Zed Books, 1990).

68. Amrita Narlikar and Shishir Priyadarshi, "Empowering the Poor? The Successes and Limitations of the Bali Package for the LDCs," *Third World Quarterly* 35, no. 6 (September 2014), p. 1051.

69. Rorden Wilkinson, Erin Hannah, and James Scott, "The WTO in Bali: What MC9 Means for the Doha Development Agenda and Why It Matters," *Third World Quarterly* 35, no. 6 (September 2014), p. 1032.

70. Narlikar and Priyadarshi, "Empowering the Poor?" pp. 1056 and 1061–1062.

71. Wilkinson, Hannah, and Scott, "The WTO in Bali," p. 1046.

72. UNDP, *Human Development Report 2013* (New York: UN, 2013), pp. 12–13.

73. Kristen Hopewell, "Different Paths to Power: The Rise of Brazil, India and China at the World Trade Organization," *Review of International Political Economy* 22, no. 2 (2015), p. 311; Ramesh Thakur, "How Representative Are BRICS?" *Third World Quarterly* 35, no. 10 (December 2014), pp. 1794–1799.

74. Chung-Chou Li, "Resumption of China's GATT Membership," *Journal of World Trade Law* 21, no. 4 (1987), pp. 26–30.

75. Paul D. McKenzie, "China's Application to the GATT: State Trading and the Problem of Market Access," *Journal of World Trade* 24, no. 5 (October 1990), pp. 144–145; Harold K. Jacobson and Michel Oksenberg, *China's Participation in the IMF, the World Bank, and GATT: Toward a Global Economic Order* (Ann Arbor, MI: University of Michigan Press, 1990), pp. 83–92.

76. Greg Mastel, "China and the World Trade Organization: Moving Forward Without Sliding Back," *Law and Policy in International Business* 31, no. 3 (Spring 2000), pp. 988–991.

77. Zeng Huaqun, "One China, Four WTO Memberships: Legal Grounds, Relations and Significance," *Journal of World Investment and Trade* 8, no. 5 (October 2007), pp. 671–690.

78. For a detailed discussion of the Quad see Theodore H. Cohn, *Governing Global Trade* (Burlington, VT: Ashgate, 2002).

79. Brendan Vickers, "The Role of the BRICS in the WTO: System-Supporters or Change Agents in Multilateral Trade?" in Amrita Narlikar, Martin Daunton and Robert M. Stern, eds., *The Oxford Handbook of the World Trade Organization* (New York: Oxford University Press, 2012), p. 261.

80. Hopewell, "Different Paths to Power," pp. 311–338; Charalampos Efstathopoulos and Dominic Kelly, "India, Developmental Multilateralism and the Doha Ministerial Conference," *Third World Quarterly* 35, no. 6 (2014), pp. 1066–1081.

81. Daniel C. Esty, "Non-Governmental Organizations at the World Trade Organization: Cooperation, Competition, or Exclusion," *Journal of International Economic Law* 1, no. 1 (March 1998), p. 140.

82. The terminology in this section is taken from Brian Hocking, "Changing the Terms of Trade Policy Making: From the 'Club' to the 'Multistakeholder' Model," *World Trade Review* 3, no. 1 (2004), pp. 3–26.

83. Jens Steffek, "Awkward Partners: NGOs and Social Movements at the WTO," in Amrita Narlikar, Martin Daunton, and Robert M. Stern, eds., *The Oxford Handbook on the World Trade Organization* (New York: Oxford University Press, 2012), p. 314.

84. Laura T. Raynolds and Michael A. Long, "Fair/Alternative Trade: Historical and Empirical Dimensions," in Laura T. Raynolds, Douglas L. Murray, and John Wilkinson, eds., *Fair Trade: The Challenges of Transforming Globalization* (New York: Routledge, 2007), pp. 17–18.

85. Laura T. Raynolds, Douglas L. Murray, and John Wilkinson, eds., *Fair Trade: The Challenges of Transforming Globalization* (New York: Routledge, 2007), chs. 1, 2, and 13; Anil Hira and Jared Ferrie, "Fair Trade: Three Key Challenges for Reaching the Mainstream," *Journal of Business Ethics* 63 (2006), pp. 107–118.

86. Jennifer Clapp and Peter Dauvergne, *Paths to a Green World: The Political Economy of the Global Environment*, 2nd ed. (Cambridge, MA: MIT Press, 2011), pp. 127–143; Daniel C. Esty, *Greening the GATT: Trade, Environment, and the Future* (Washington, DC: Institute for International Economics, 1994), pp. 35–41; Steven Bernstein, *The Compromise of Liberal Environmentalism* (New York: Columbia University Press, 2001), pp. 229–232.

87. Esty, *Greening the GATT*, p. 9.

88. Sabrina Shaw and Risa Schwartz, "Trade and Environment in the WTO: State of Play," *Journal of World Trade* 36, no. 1 (2002), p. 129.

89. Clapp and Dauvergne, *Paths to a Green World*, pp. 146–151.

90. Steve Charnovitz, "The WTO's Environmental Progress," *Journal of International Economic Law* 10, no. 3 (September 2007), p. 685.

91. Charnovitz, "The WTO's Environmental Progress," p. 695.

92. Richard Peet, *Unholy Trinity: The IMF, World Bank and WTO* (New York: Zed Books, 2003), pp. 182–183.

93. Debra P. Steger, "The Culture of the WTO: Why It Needs to Change," *Journal of International Economic Law* 10, no. 3 (September 2007), p. 487.

94. Vinod Aggarwal, "Reluctance to Lead: U.S. Trade Policy in Flux," *Business and Politics* 11, no. 3 (2009), p. 18.

95. Jagdish Bhagwati, *Termites in the Trading System: How Preferential Agreements Undermine Free Trade* (New York: Oxford University Press, 2008).

96. Fatoumata Jawara and Aileen Kwa, *Behind the Scenes at the WTO: The Real World of International Trade Negotiations* (New York: Zed Books, 2003), pp. 302–303.

97. Paola Conconi and Caro Perroni, "Special and Differential Treatment of Developing Countries in the WTO," *World Trade Review* 14, no. 1 (January 2015), pp. 67–86.

Regionalism and the Global Trade Regime

The major trading nations supported multilateral trade liberalization when they signed the General Agreement on Tariffs and Trade (GATT) in 1947, but regionalism also emerged as a significant force with the creation of a number of *regional trade agreements* (*RTAs*). Traditionally, neighboring states have formed RTAs such as the European Community and the Central American Common Market. In more recent years, however, countries in distant locations have also joined in trade liberalization agreements. Indeed, about one-half of RTAs currently in force include countries from different regions.[1] Some analysts therefore use the term *preferential trade agreements* (*PTAs*) rather than RTAs. However, we use the more commonly recognized term RTAs to describe these agreements. In recent years there has been a surge in the growth of RTAs, partly because of the difficulties in reaching a WTO Doha Round agreement. Indeed, the value of intra-RTA trade increased from about 28 percent of world trade in 1990 to 50 percent of world trade in 2008.[2] This chapter addresses the issue as to whether these RTAs are likely to be "stepping stones" or "obstacles" to global free trade. The first part of this chapter examines why RTAs are formed and how they affect the global trade regime; the second part focuses on some specific RTAs. RTAs exist at different stages or levels of integration (see Figure 9.1):

1. **Free trade area (FTA).** Member states eliminate tariffs and other restrictions on substantially all trade with each other, but each member can retain its own trade policies toward nonmember states. Thus, an FTA poses less of a threat to national sovereignty and is more acceptable to states with politically sensitive relationships. More than 90 percent of RTAs are FTAs. The **North American Free Trade Agreement (NAFTA)** and the *Association of Southeast Asian Nations* or *ASEAN Free Trade Area (AFTA)* are examples.

	Free trade area (FTA)	Customs union (CU)	Common market	Economic union	Political union
Removal of tariffs among members	X	X	X	X	X
Common external tariff		X	X	X	X
Free movement of labor and capital			X	X	X
Harmonized economic policies				X	X
Political unification					X

FIGURE 9.1
Stages of Regional Economic Integration

2. **Customs union (CU).** A CU has the characteristics of an FTA *plus* a *common external tariff* (CET) toward outside states. A CU has institutions to administer the CET, and the members have less ability to make independent decisions. When six states (France, West Germany, Italy, Belgium, the Netherlands, and Luxembourg) formed the **European Community (EC)** as a CU in 1957, Britain was not included because it wanted to retain its Commonwealth preference system. To join the EC, Britain would have to raise its tariffs with Commonwealth countries to the same levels as the CET. Instead, Britain formed the **European Free Trade Association (EFTA)** with Austria, Denmark, Norway, Portugal, Sweden, and Switzerland in 1960 and retained its Commonwealth preferences. However, Britain's trade with EC members gradually increased, and in 1973 it joined the EC and phased out its Commonwealth preferences. There are only a small number of CUs, and the **European Union (EU)** is the most important of them. (We use the term EC from 1957 to 1992, and EU after 1992 to reflect the name change in 1993.)
3. **Common market.** A common market has the characteristics of a CU *plus* the free mobility of factors of production (labor and capital) among members. The increased labor mobility induces members to establish similar health, safety, educational, and social security standards so that no country's workers have a competitive advantage. Successful common markets are rare because they require high levels of integration; the EU is a common market.
4. **Economic union.** An economic union has the characteristics of a common market, and it harmonizes members' industrial, regional, transport, fiscal, and monetary policies. A full economic union includes a monetary union with a common currency. As discussed, 19 of the 28 EU members have adopted the euro as their common currency.
5. **Political union.** A political union has the characteristics of an economic union and also harmonizes members' foreign and defense policies. A fully developed political union is more like a federal political system than an agreement among sovereign states.

It is important to note that these stages of integration are models that do not fully describe reality. NAFTA, for example, is an FTA (stage 1); but its provisions also require more openness toward foreign investment identified with stage 3 (a common market). Furthermore, some RTAs in the South described as CUs and common markets have not actually reached those levels. Although these stages are only models, they provide general guidance to the process by which states become more integrated.

REGIONALISM AND THE IPE THEORETICAL PERSPECTIVES

In some cases multilateralism and regionalism are competing approaches to trade. Whereas multilateralism contributes to global trade liberalization, regionalism may divide the world into competing trade blocs. However, "open regionalism" can break down national trade barriers and serve as a stepping stone rather than an obstacle to global free trade. RTAs following open regionalism abolish barriers on substantially all trade within the RTA and lower trade barriers to outsiders. MNCs often use open regionalism and multilateralism as complementary strategies to promote market forces and increase their competitiveness in the global economy.

Liberal economists see multilateralism as the best route to freer trade because it breaks down regional as well as national barriers. Some liberals who are highly committed to multilateralism focus on "the damage" RTAs "impose on the multilateral trading system."[3] For example, they view the recent trend toward forming numerous bilateral FTAs as producing overlapping FTAs that undermine "transparency and predictability in international trade relations."[4] Other liberals take a more nuanced approach. They consider closed RTAs as a threat to global free trade, but they support open RTAs as a "second-best" route to trade liberalization when global trade negotiations fail. Although they acknowledge that open regionalism may harm some groups such as displaced workers, they believe that the efficiency gains outweigh the costs incurred. They do not view power disparities as a problem for smaller states in RTAs because they assume that all states benefit from open RTAs. Indeed, they argue that small states benefit more than large states because of economies of scale and increased demand for their exports. Neomercantilists and historical materialists by contrast believe that RTAs have important distributional effects, with some states benefiting at the expense of others. Neomercantilists argue that larger RTA members expect "side payments" from smaller members that exceed any economic benefits the smaller members receive from gains in market access and economies of scale. For example, Canada and Mexico sought free trade with the United States to gain more assured access to the large U.S. market. The United States, however, expected side payments in foreign investment, services trade, and access to natural resources—especially energy.[5] Thus, neomercantilists expect the distribution of benefits in RTAs to reflect the asymmetries of power, wealth, and technology among member states. Historical materialists see MNCs and transnational capital as the main beneficiaries of RTAs, and the working class and poorest states as the main losers. MNCs locate their production in states with the lowest wages, environmental standards, and taxes and export freely to other states in the RTA.

This chapter discusses the relationship between regionalism and globalization, the historical development of RTAs, the reasons states form RTAs, the relationship between the WTO and RTAs, and prominent examples of RTAs.

REGIONALISM AND GLOBALIZATION

Regionalism is a difficult term to define because it connotes both geographic proximity and a sense of cultural, economic, political, and organizational cohesiveness.[6] To compound the confusion, many FTAs today are cross-regional, and the WTO includes these in its list of RTAs. For example, the EU has bilateral FTAs with Mexico, Chile, and South Africa; and the United States has bilateral FTAs with Singapore, Chile, Israel, and Jordan. As discussed, some scholars argue that the term *preferential trade agreements* better captures these agreements among states in different geographic regions.[7] However, we use "RTAs" for cross-regional as well as regional agreements because it is the preferred term of the WTO. We also discuss the fact that some countries have strong regional economic ties that are not associated with formal agreements.

In some respects, globalization limits the growth of regionalism. As interdependence increases, financial crises, trade wars, and environmental degradation require management at the global level. The WTO, IMF, and World Bank are better equipped than regional organizations to deal with these problems. Globalization also promotes linkages among regions as well as states, and in this sense it can undermine regional cohesiveness. However, globalization may also stimulate the growth of regionalism. States often rely on institutions above the national level to deal with global interdependence issues, but IOs with large, diverse memberships may be unable to identify common interests and sanction defectors.[8] Thus, regional institutions composed of like-minded states may be more effective than larger multilateral institutions in dealing with cross-national problems. Globalization also contributes to increased competition, and states and MNCs can often improve their global competitiveness by organizing regionally. For example, European MNCs have improved their global competitiveness by using the EU as a regional platform, and U.S. MNCs have benefited from the existence of NAFTA. Furthermore, globalization is associated with neoliberalism, which favors a shift in authority from the state to the market. Market pressures weaken state barriers and contribute to the growth of private and public linkages at both the regional and global levels. Thus, regionalism and globalization can be both conflictual and complementary.[9]

A HISTORICAL OVERVIEW OF RTAs

RTA proposals extend back to at least the seventeenth century, and some agreements resulted in political as well as commercial unions. Examples of early integration efforts were an 1826 CU between England and Ireland; an 1833 treaty establishing a Zollverein or CU among German states; and an 1854 Canada–U.S. Reciprocity Treaty removing all tariffs on natural products. Examples in the South included a 1910 South African Customs Union among the Union of South Africa, Bechuanaland, Basutoland, and Swaziland; and a 1917 CU among the British colonies of Kenya, Uganda, and Tanganyika.[10] Regional integration in its modern form developed after World War II with the creation of the EC. This chapter deals with the two major waves of regionalism during the postwar period.

The First Wave of Regionalism

In 1949 the Soviet Union signed a treaty with Bulgaria, Czechoslovakia, Hungary, Poland, and Romania establishing the *Council for Mutual Economic Assistance (CMEA)*. Although CMEA members engaged in technical cooperation and joint planning, state-centered central planning precluded any moves toward regional economic integration.[11] Thus, most writers view the first wave of regionalism as beginning with the formation of the EC in 1957 and EFTA in 1960.[12] Regionalism then spread to Latin America and Africa during the 1960s. However, RTAs in the South were designed mainly to provide larger markets and economies of scale for LDC production of industrial goods through import substitution policies. The first wave of regionalism was largely unsuccessful outside Europe, because the South's attempts to promote import substitution at the regional level led to numerous problems. Only a limited number of industries were willing to locate in Southern RTAs, and they were concentrated in the larger, more advanced LDCs. This unequal distribution of benefits led to disputes among member states; in the East African Common Services Union, for example, Tanzania and Uganda were resentful that most industries located in Kenya. Some Southern RTAs tried to allocate industries among members by bureaucratic means, but this led to economic inefficiencies and further conflict.

RTAs in the first wave (the 1950s to 1960s) also had some other characteristics. First, they were *plurilateral* rather than bilateral; that is, they were formed among at least three states. Second, all RTA members were from the same geographic region. Third, the RTAs were either among DCs (North–North) or among LDCs (South–South). For example, six European states formed the EC, and four Central American states formed the Central American Common Market. Fourth, the United States as global hegemon firmly supported multilateral trade, generally opposed RTAs, and would not join them. The United States made an exception in supporting the EC to promote an economically strong Western Europe in the Cold War struggle with the Soviet Union.[13]

The Second Wave of Regionalism

The second wave of regionalism, which began in the 1980s, is much more widespread and durable than the first wave. The most notable part of the second wave has been the proliferation of RTAs since the creation of the WTO. GATT/WTO members are to notify the organization of all RTAs in which they participate. Notifications refer to both the creation of new RTAs and the accession of new states to an RTA (e.g., the 2007 accession of Romania and Bulgaria to the EU). From 1948 to 1994 the GATT received 124 notifications of RTAs covering trade in goods, and from 1995 to 2015 the WTO received over 400 additional notifications of RTAs covering trade in goods or services.[14] Furthermore, a number of RTAs today have not been notified to the WTO.[15] Many states view RTAs as the centerpiece of their commercial policy, and for some WTO members preferential trade now accounts for more than 90 percent of their total trade.[16]

What accounts for the importance of the second wave? First, the EU has broadened and deepened the integration process. Table 9.1 shows that there were 28 EU members in 2015; 19 of these members (with a superscript a) have adopted the euro as a common currency. Second, the United States reversed its policy and has formed FTAs with a growing number of countries. Third,

TABLE 9.1

Expanding Membership of the European Union

Member Year	Members	Population % Added	GDP[b] (PPP)[c] % Addition	GDP per Capita as % of EU Average
1957	France[a], West Germany, Italy[a], Belgium[a], Netherlands[a], Luxembourg[a]	100	N/A	100
1973	United Kingdom, Denmark, Ireland[a]	33.4	31.9	96.4
1981	Greece[a]	3.7	1.8	48.4
1986	Spain[a], Portugal[a]	17.8	11.0	62.2
1990	Germany unified[a]	5.9	3.8	
1995	Austria[a], Finland[a], Sweden	6.3	6.5	103.5
2004	Cyprus[a], Czech Republic, Estonia[a], Hungary, Latvia[a], Lithuania[a], Malta[a], Poland, Slovakia[a], Slovenia[a]	19.6	8.9	45.4
2007	Bulgaria, Romania	6.5	2.0	17.7
2013	Croatia	0.8	0.7	38.8

[a] euro zone members, [b] gross domestic product, [c] purchasing power parity

Sources: The World Bank—GDP per Capital (current US$).
Eurostat—Tables, Graphs, and Maps—Population by Country by Year 2003–2014.
http://data.worldbank.org/indicator/NY.GDP.PCAP.CD/countries?page=1
http://ec.europa.eu/eurostat/tgm/refreshTableAction.do?tab=table&plugin=1
&pcode=tps00001&language=en

NAFTA was the first reciprocal RTA between DCs (the United States and Canada) and an LDC (Mexico). This marked a change from the RTAs in the first wave which were only North–North or South–South. Fourth, the second wave is marked by a proliferation of bilateral RTAs, unlike the plurilateral RTAs of the first wave. Fifth, many bilateral RTAs are between states that are not in the same geographic region. Sixth, LDCs are joining in a growing number of RTAs, which are no longer based on import substitution policies and are more open to global market forces. Finally, there are attempts to form larger cross-regional RTAs such as the *Trans-Pacific Partnership* agreement.[17]

EXPLANATIONS FOR THE RISE OF REGIONAL INTEGRATION

Neomercantilists, liberals, and historical materialists emphasize different factors in explaining the rise of regional integration. Whereas neomercantilists look to security and power relationships, liberals focus on the growth of interdependence, and historical materialists emphasize the role of transnational capital.

Neomercantilist Explanations

Some neomercantilists see regional integration as a response to security and power relationships. For example, the U.S.–Soviet bipolar system after World War II helped spark European integration for several reasons. First, most EC members were also members of the NATO alliance, and "tariff cuts are more likely between allies than between states belonging to different military coalitions."[18] Second, the U.S. and Soviet superpowers assumed the main security responsibilities under the bipolar system, and this enabled Western Europe to focus on regional economic integration.[19] Third, the emergence of the United States and Soviet Union as superpowers gave Europeans an incentive to form the EC. With European states facing the loss of their colonies, integration was necessary if they were to retain some influence in the bipolar world. Fourth, although the United States generally opposed RTAs during the 1950s–1960s, it supported the EC because Western Europe's economic recovery was viewed as essential to meeting the Soviet security threat. Indeed, U.S. insistence that Europeans jointly administer U.S. Marshall Plan aid resulted in the formation of the **Organization for European Economic Cooperation (OEEC)** in 1948. The OEEC also oversaw moves toward the convertibility of European currencies and the integration of West Germany in Western Europe; this laid the foundations for the formation of the EC.[20]

When the Soviet Union collapsed and the Cold War ended in the early 1990s, the neomercantilist John Mearsheimer argued that the EU would no longer be necessary to counter the Soviet threat. Thus, EU integration would decline and each EU member would begin to focus on its relative gains vis-à-vis the other members. However, the formation of the euro zone and the expansion of the EU to 28 members indicated that other factors also had to be considered (see discussion in this chapter).[21] Furthermore, neomercantilists looking at some other states and regions in the 1980s–1990s predicted that regional integration would increase. After World War II, the United States as global hegemon used its power and resources to support the GATT-based multilateral trade regime. As U.S. economic hegemony declined, it was less willing to continue providing this support, and it sought to regain its economic leverage by joining RTAs such as NAFTA. U.S. participation in RTAs was a major factor contributing to the rise of regional integration in the second wave.[22] Some neomercantilists also point to security considerations in explaining the formation of some North–South bilateral FTAs. For example, Singapore and South Korea sought bilateral FTAs with the United States partly to maintain a continued U.S. presence in East Asia as a counterbalance to China, Japan, and North Korea.[23]

Liberal Explanations

Liberals have been the main contributors to regional integration theory. We discuss liberal theory on the deepening of integration from an FTA to a CU, common market, and economic union in the section of this chapter on Europe. Liberal views concerning the reasons states form RTAs include the following:

- Global and regional institutions are created to support a liberal economic order. Liberalism in the postwar era was closely linked with the creation of the IMF, World Bank, GATT, and RTAs.
- RTAs are created to promote regional peace. For example, France, West Germany, Italy, the Netherlands, Belgium, and Luxembourg formed the **European Coal and Steel Community (ECSC)** in 1951 to integrate France and West Germany's coal and steel resources and prevent them from renewing their age-old conflicts. (The six ECSC members formed the EC in 1957.) These views draw on David Mitrany's theory of functionalism, which states that "international economic and social cooperation is a major prerequisite for the ultimate solution of political conflicts and the elimination of war."[24]
- RTAs are formed to provide a larger market for members' goods. The EC agreement was based partly on an understanding that it would provide a regional market for France's agricultural goods and West Germany's industrial products. A major attraction of NAFTA for the two smaller partners (Canada and Mexico) was free trade access to the much larger U.S. market for their exports.
- RTAs are formed to increase foreign investment. For example, Mexico joined NAFTA partly to attract more foreign investment from the United States; and the United States supported NAFTA partly to liberalize regional foreign investment flows.
- RTA negotiations are often a more achievable route to freer trade than GATT/WTO negotiations because they involve smaller groups of

like-minded states. Thus, the number of RTAs increased rapidly as a result of problems with the Uruguay and Doha Rounds. Furthermore, states may seek RTAs to provide a positive demonstration effect for the GATT/WTO; for example, the 1988 Canada–U.S. Free Trade Agreement (CUSFTA) included provisions on trade in services and agriculture before GATT addressed these issues.[25]

■ RTAs are formed because of pressure from domestic groups. With globalization, many private firms have become more dependent on trade and have shifted their operations from the national to the multinational level. These internationalist firms pressure for regional as well as global trade agreements. Regionalism improves the competitiveness of international firms, because they benefit from "the larger regional markets as their base rather than just the home market."[26]

■ RTAs are formed as part of a "two-level game," in which political leaders use the RTA regulations to bring about domestic changes. For example, Canada sought the CUSFTA partly because "more open borders would expose Canadian firms to greater international competition and encourage them to restructure and modernize."[27]

Historical Materialist Explanations

Historical materialists, like liberals, see MNCs as having a central role in the creation of RTAs. Unlike liberals, however, historical materialists believe that RTAs permit MNCs to locate their production facilities in states with the lowest taxes, wages, and environmental standards and then export freely within the RTA. Whereas the capitalist class benefits from the growth of regionalism, domestic labor suffers because capital can move more easily to low-wage regions and states. Historical materialists also attribute the development of RTAs to the desire of powerful states to seek regional hegemony. As its global economic hegemony declined, the United States sought to recoup its losses by establishing its hegemony more firmly on a regional basis. Thus, some critics charge that NAFTA was "designed to fit Canada and Mexico into the American model of development, on terms amenable to American corporations."[28]

THE GATT/WTO AND RTAs

The United States as the postwar global hegemon opposed preferential agreements that would interfere with an open multilateral trade regime. However, Britain wanted to preserve its discriminatory imperial preferences, and a number of states wanted to establish RTAs. The U.S. views largely prevailed, and GATT Article 1 calls for unconditional MFN treatment. However, **GATT Article 24** permits countries to form FTAs and CUs that do not adhere to MFN treatment, as long as these agreements meet specific conditions.[29] Article 24's acceptance of CUs and FTAs stems from the liberal view that open RTAs offer a second-best route to freer trade; thus, Article 24 seeks to ensure that the

RTAs are more trade-creating than trade-diverting. Before discussing Article 24, it is necessary to describe the ways in which RTAs are trade-creating and trade-diverting.

Trade Diversion

RTAs can be trade-diverting because the elimination of intraregional trade barriers shifts some imports from more efficient outside suppliers to less efficient regional suppliers. Furthermore, the freeing of trade within an RTA increases competition in member countries' markets. Inefficient industries may lobby for increased external trade barriers to shift the adjustment burden onto countries outside the RTA. Thus, trade diversion can result when RTAs raise protectionist barriers against outsiders. Investment diversion may also occur when MNCs put branch plants inside an RTA to take advantage of the tariff-free zone instead of producing in the least-cost location and shipping goods to the region.

A CU is more trade-diverting in some respects than an FTA. Even if external tariffs do not increase when a CU is formed, protectionism may increase if the CU imposes antidumping and countervailing duties in response to pressure from import-competing industries. These duties limit imports to the entire CU area because of the common external tariff. Antidumping and countervailing duties pose less of a problem for outsiders in an FTA because each FTA member levies its own tariffs, and industries cannot pressure for area-wide protection. However, FTAs are more trade-diverting than CUs in terms of **rules of origin**, because each FTA member has its own external tariffs. FTAs require rules of origin to prevent importers from bringing goods in through the lowest duty member and then shipping them duty-free to other FTA members. The rules of origin determine whether products have undergone enough processing within the FTA to qualify for the trade preferences. It is difficult to formulate these rules because many goods are manufactured with components from a number of countries. Domestic firms often pressure FTAs for stiffer rules of origin which are more protectionist against outsiders. Rules of origin are a less significant issue for CUs because of the common external tariff.[30] Trade diversion depends on external as well as internal factors. When an RTA is formed, nonmember states have an incentive to establish their own RTAs to "better defend themselves against the discriminatory effects of other regional groups."[31] Furthermore, regional trade blocs such as the EU become larger when pressure from nonmember firms triggers "membership requests from countries that were previously happy to be nonmembers."[32] This proliferation of regionalism fragments the global trade regime.

Trade Creation

The main source of trade creation is the increased trade among RTA members, which shifts demand from less efficient domestic suppliers to more efficient regional suppliers. When firms within the region become more competitive as a result of the RTA, they are also more likely to support global as well as regional free trade. Furthermore, RTAs often achieve a deeper level of integration than multilateral trade agreements because negotiations occur among a smaller number of like-minded partners. RTAs may therefore have a positive demonstration effect on multilateral trade negotiations. For example, the inclusion of agriculture, services, and intellectual property in the NAFTA provided a stimulus for negotiating these issues in the GATT Uruguay Round.

GATT Article 24 and RTAs

GATT Article 24 seeks to ensure that RTAs result in more trade creation than trade diversion. To increase trade creation, Article 24 stipulates that FTAs and CUs are to eliminate tariffs on "substantially all" trade among the members within a "reasonable" time period. (GATT granted waivers from the substantially all trade requirement for the ECSC in 1952 and the Canada–U.S. Auto Pact in 1965.) This requirement limits preferential agreements with only partial trade liberalization such as those that contributed to protectionism during the 1930s. RTAs that remove all internal trade barriers are more likely to serve as stepping stones to multilateral free trade. To decrease trade diversion, Article 24 stipulates that an RTA should not raise tariffs on the average to countries outside the agreement. Whereas individual members of an FTA are not to raise their average level of duties, the common external tariff of a CU may not "on the whole" be higher than the member states' duties before the CU was established. These provisions are designed to limit reductions in imports from nonmembers as a result of the RTA.[33] However, GATT Article 24 has been more effective in theory than in practice.

The Effectiveness of GATT Article 24

When countries formed an RTA, GATT established a working party to determine whether it met the Article 24 conditions; but these working parties had only limited influence. GATT's regulations for RTAs were drafted with smaller agreements in mind, such as the Benelux customs union negotiated by Belgium, the Netherlands, and Luxembourg in 1944. In 1957 the EC members were unwilling to wait for GATT approval before proceeding with economic integration because of the size and importance of the EC. Negotiating the Treaty of Rome had been a difficult process, and EC members would not readjust the treaty to satisfy GATT.[34] In the end, GATT acceded to the EC demands and never finished examining the Treaty of Rome, even though it had reached no consensus on the treaty's consistency with Article 24. GATT's acquiescence in this case limited its authority over subsequent RTAs, and its working parties could do little to change RTAs after member states had negotiated them. Whereas GATT was notified about early agreements such as the EC before they entered into force, some later agreements such as NAFTA entered into force before a working party was even formed to examine them.[35]

It is not surprising that GATT had little influence over RTAs after they were negotiated. Governments had already engaged in extensive bargaining and were reluctant to reopen negotiations in response to outside criticism. GATT working parties could only try to embarrass RTA members with allegations of noncompliance and encourage them to comply with the guidelines in the future. However, GATT did influence decision-making at earlier stages by setting broad parameters for conducting the regional negotiations. For example, the diplomats negotiating RTAs often operated

> under instructions to make maximum efforts to comply with GATT rules, and the actual results of these negotiations testify that a quite important degree of GATT compliance was achieved. Except for agriculture ... and except for the EC's relationship with former colonies, the ... developed-country agreements ... were essentially GATT-conforming. To be sure, GATT was unable to do anything further once the agreements were signed and deposited in Geneva.[36]

Some analysts note that GATT was less effective because Article 24 requirements that RTAs should cover "substantially all" trade, not be more restrictive "on average" to outsiders, and be implemented in a "reasonable length of time" are ambiguous. In view of the imprecise wording, working parties were reluctant to give RTAs unqualified approval. By 1994, only 6 of 69 working parties had reached a consensus that particular RTAs conformed to Article 24, and only 2 of these 6 RTAs are still operative. In most cases, working parties simply noted that members had divergent views regarding the RTA's conformity with GATT. However, GATT never explicitly concluded that an RTA did *not* meet the legal requirements![37] To improve the regulation of RTAs, the GATT Uruguay Round agreement included an Understanding on the Interpretation of Article 24 and a GATS article on regional trade in services (Article 5). Furthermore, the WTO replaced the working parties with a single *Committee on Regional Trade Agreements* (*CRTA*) to determine whether RTAs conform with the WTO.[38] Although the Uruguay Round and CRTA have dealt with some GATT Article 24 shortcomings, many problems remain. For example, divisions persist on the interpretation of the "substantially all trade" requirement (many RTAs exclude agriculture), and the Uruguay Round negotiators did not decide how to deal with restrictive rules of origin in FTAs. In 2006 a negotiating group agreed on a mechanism to ensure that the WTO receives early notification of new RTAs; but this mechanism may not become permanent because of the breakdown of the Doha Round.

Special Treatment for LDCs

Although GATT Article 24 was to apply to all RTAs, LDCs receive special treatment. This is evident from the GATT/WTO's treatment of RTAs among LDCs and from its response to the EU association agreements with LDCs.

RTAs among LDCs   The GATT/WTO takes a more lenient approach to RTAs among LDCs. For example, GATT accepted the formation of the Latin American Free Trade Association in 1960, even though it "did not even approach the requirements of total integration."[39] After Part IV on trade and development was added to GATT in 1965, LDCs sometimes invoked it to justify forming RTAs that did not meet Article 24's requirement to include substantially all trade. When the 1979 enabling clause was enacted, it became the main legal basis for LDCs forming questionable RTAs. The enabling clause permits LDCs to form RTAs that include a limited range of products and decrease rather than eliminate tariffs. RTAs are eligible for special treatment under the enabling clause if they do not include any DC members. For example, *Mercosur* (discussed later) was notified to GATT under the enabling clause, not Article 24.[40] Despite the GATT/WTO's permissiveness, recent LDC moves toward freer trade have inevitably affected their RTAs. The negative experience of LDCs with protectionist import substitution policies, and IMF and World Bank pressure on LDC debtors to liberalize their trade policies, have caused RTAs among LDCs to become more outward looking.

EU Association Agreements with LDCs   As discussed in Chapter 8, DCs unilaterally established a generalized system of preferences (GSP) for LDCs. EU association agreements with LDCs by contrast are jointly negotiated preferential agreements. When the EC was formed in 1957, the Treaty of Rome provided associate status to France's African Overseas Territories.[41] The EC's enlargement when Britain, Denmark, and Ireland joined in 1973 (see Table 9.1) necessitated a change because of Britain's relationship with Commonwealth LDCs. In 1975, the nine EC members concluded the first **Lomé Convention** (Lomé I) with 46 African, Caribbean, and Pacific (ACP) countries; three more Lomé Conventions followed in 1979, 1984, and 1989 (eventually with 71 ACP states). The Lomé Conventions offered preferential access for ACP goods to the EC market without requiring reciprocity. Critics argued that the Lomé system was not a genuine FTA because it was nonreciprocal; GATT Article 24 provides an exception to MFN treatment only for RTAs that follow the reciprocity principle. Furthermore, the 1979 enabling clause permits DCs to provide trade preferences only if they are offered to *all* LDCs. The enabling clause does not sanction EU discrimination in favor of its ex-colonies at the expense of other LDCs.

The EU argued that the nonreciprocal association agreements were justified because they contributed to LDC economic development; but external events increased the pressures for change. In 1994 Mexico formed the NAFTA with the United States and Canada, showing that LDCs could join in reciprocal FTAs with DCs.[42] Analysts also began to question the value of the Lomé Conventions to the ACP states, because their share of the EU market fell from 6.7 percent in 1976 to 3 percent in 1998; more than 60 percent of the ACP exports were concentrated in only 10 primary products. Historical materialists described EU nonreciprocal preferences "as a form of neocolonialism that perpetuates the production of … products not compatible" with the long-term interests of the ACP states.[43] Thus, the EU and ACP states negotiated the more WTO-compatible **Cotonou Agreement** (or *New Partnership Agreement*) in 2000. This agreement stipulates that, beginning in 2008, ACP–EU reciprocal "economic partnership" agreements will gradually replace the nonreciprocal preferences over a 10- to 12-year period. Although supporters of the Cotonou Agreement believe that the ACP states will benefit by liberalizing their trade policies, critics argue that EU–ACP nonreciprocal relations must continue because the ACPs have a lower level of development.[44]

The following sections focus on the EU, NAFTA, Mercosur, and two attempts to form large cross-regional RTAs in view of the protracted Doha Round negotiations: the Trans-Pacific Partnership and the Trans-Atlantic Trade and Investment Partnership.

THE EUROPEAN UNION

Europe has led the way in postwar regional integration, with European states as parties to 76 of the 109 RTAs formed from 1948 to 1994.[45] In 1951, six states (Belgium, France, West Germany, Italy, Luxembourg, and the Netherlands) formed the ECSC and then established the EC and the *European Atomic Energy Community (Euratom)* in 1957 (see Table 9.2). In 1959, seven states (Austria, Britain, Denmark, Norway, Portugal, Sweden, and Switzerland) formed the EFTA instead of joining the EC, because the EC's customs union threatened Britain's Commonwealth preference system and the nonaligned policies of states such as Sweden and Switzerland. In 1993 the EC's name was changed to the EU to symbolize the extension of the community from trade and economic matters to a much broader range of activities under the Maastricht Treaty.

TABLE 9.2

The Deepening of European Integration

Year	Event	Description
1951	European Coal and Steel Community (ECSC)	• 6 states integrate their coal and steel resources
1957	Treaty of Rome	• Establishes the European Economic Community (EC) and Euratom
1986	Single European Act (SEA)	• To free the movement of goods, services, and labor • Commitment to form a monetary union (EMU)
1992	Maastricht Treaty (or Treaty on European Union)	• Commitment to form a monetary union, and common foreign, security, and social policies • Renames the EC the European Union (EU)
1999	Creation of the euro	• 11 EU states adopt the euro as a common currency. The euro zone members increase to 19 by 2015
2009	Lisbon Treaty	• Establishes an EU high representative • Gives new powers to European Commission, Parliament, and Court of Justice • Removes national vetoes in some areas • Redistributes voting weights among member states

Thus, the term "EC" is used when discussing events from 1957 to 1992, and "EU" is used for events from 1993 to the present.

As discussed, the EU is an economic union, and 19 of the 28 members have discarded their national currencies and adopted the euro (see Table 9.1). The EU's institutional structure differentiates it from RTAs at lower levels of integration. The *European Commission* represents general EU interests rather than those of individual member states, and the powers of the *European Court of Justice (ECJ)* are greater than those of other international courts. The EU is therefore a "supranational" organization that operates above the level of the nation-state in some areas. However, the *Council of Ministers* (or *Council of the European Union*) is the most powerful EU institution in day-to-day politics. The fact that the Council of Ministers is composed of foreign ministers representing their governments is a reminder that the EU (despite its supranationality) is still beholden to its member states. Other important institutions of the EU are the *European Parliament* and *European Council* (of Heads of State and Government). In sum, the EU's unique institutional structure gives it more authority than other IOs, but the EU remains subject to a considerable amount of control by its member states.[46]

The Deepening of European Integration

European integration has been an uneven process, sometimes marked by obstacles and conflict, and other times by optimism and growth. For example, the EC began its operations with considerable enthusiasm in 1957, but the 1970s were marked by "Eurosclerosis" (i.e., stagnation) and a loss of faith in the EC's vitality. Divisions within the EC as a result of differential taxation, border inspections, domestic subsidies, and limits to market access were a major source of the problem. Thus, the EC sought to create a unified European market with more competitive firms based on specialization and economies of scale. The 1986 *Single European Act (SEA)* was designed to abolish nontariff barriers, liberalize trade in services, and facilitate the movement of capital and labor by 1992, and it also included a commitment to form an **economic and monetary union (EMU)**. Monetary union was to occur in a three-stage process, and negotiations resulted in the Treaty on European Union or **Maastricht Treaty** in 1992 (see Table 9.2).

The Maastricht Treaty changed the name of the EC to the EU because the economic pillar—the EC—was joined by two new pillars: for a common foreign and security policy, and for a common social policy. Whereas supranational decision-making is sometimes used for the EC, intergovernmental decision-making is the norm for foreign/security and social policy. The Maastricht Treaty also outlined a timetable for setting up the EMU, criteria for joining the EMU (e.g., a budget deficit of less than 3 percent of GDP, and public debt of no more than 60 percent of GDP), and functions the EMU would perform (e.g., the role of the European Central Bank).[47] As discussed in Chapter 6, 11 EU members formed the euro zone in 1999 and agreed to adopt the euro in place of their national currencies. Eight more EU members joined later, and the euro zone now has 19 members. The European sovereign debt crisis has resulted in serious problems for the euro zone, and for the EU in general. A major source of the problem has been the decision to establish a monetary union without political or at least fiscal unity among those countries adopting the euro. The transfer of tax authority to the EU continues to be limited, exemplifying "the failure of political and fiscal integration."[48]

Another aspect of the deepening of European integration relates to cross-border migration. The **Schengen Agreement** calling for the gradual abolition of border checks between countries was originally signed in 1985 by France, Germany, Belgium, the Netherlands, and Luxembourg outside the auspices of the EU. The agreement was incorporated into the EU framework as part of the 1997 Amsterdam Treaty, and today the Schengen Agreement has 26 member countries. Twenty-two of the Schengen members are EU countries, and four members are not in the EU: Iceland, Liechtenstein, Norway, and Switzerland. Two EU members—the United Kingdom and Ireland—have opted out of joining the Schengen Agreement. The United Kingdom wants to control its own borders, and Ireland has given priority to its Common Travel Area with the United Kingdom over free travel within the Schengen area. Four other EU members—Bulgaria, Croatia, Cyprus, and Romania—should soon be joining the Schengen Agreement. The "Arab Spring" uprisings began to create problems in the Schengen area when France shut its borders to trains carrying African migrants from Italy in April 2011, and the problems increased with the large movement of migrants from Syria, Iraq, and elsewhere to Europe in 2015. Many of the migrants are refugees seeking to escape areas of serious conflict, and major disagreements among EU countries as to how to deal with this issue raise questions about the viability of the Schengen Agreement over the long term (see Chapter 12). In sum, European integration has deepened over the years. However, problems within the euro zone, the Schengen area, and a promised upcoming referendum in Britain on its membership in the EU pose major challenges for the future of the integration project.

The Widening of European Integration

As Table 9.1 shows, the EU expanded from 6 to 28 members in several enlargements. Whereas the deepening of integration has often been a response to economic conditions, the recent widening was "thrust on the EU by the failure of communism in Europe."[49] This section focuses on the accession of Central and Eastern European countries (CEECs) to the EU.

When the EC was formed in 1957, the Soviet Union insisted that the Council for Mutual Economic Assistance (CMEA) be the vehicle for EC economic contacts with Eastern Europe. However, the EC preferred to negotiate bilateral agreements with Eastern European states and some of them broke ranks with the Soviet position. For example, the EC granted the GSP to Romania in 1972, and signed a trade and cooperation agreement with Romania in 1980. As economic conditions in the East worsened, the Soviets softened their position on economic linkages with the West; thus, a 1988 EC–CMEA agreement sanctioned EC negotiations with individual Eastern European states. After the breakup of the Soviet bloc, the EU negotiated a number of "Europe agreements" with Eastern European states. However, the EU offered them only limited trade concessions, and they began to apply for full EU membership.[50]

The wide disparity in economic development between most EU members and the CEECs posed an obstacle to their admission. Ten CEECs that signed Europe agreements with the EU had only one-fourth of the purchasing power of the EU average, and about 20 percent of their workers had agricultural jobs compared with only 6 percent of EU workers.[51] Thus, an EU Commission report warned that admission of the CEECs would cause migration to Western Europe, an eastward movement of firms because of lower labor costs in Eastern Europe, and a sharp increase in the population eligible for EU social and economic development funds. However, official EU statements described enlargement as "a political necessity and a historic opportunity."[52] Both the CEECs and the EU saw some advantages from enlargement. The CEECs felt that EU and NATO membership would give them security vis-à-vis Russia and that access to EU capital, technology, and markets would help close the economic gap with the West. EU members believed that stable CEECs would provide a buffer against political instability, the CEECs would provide the EU with cheaper workers and investment opportunities, and enlargement would enhance the EU's external influence.

Ten CEECs were admitted to the EU in May 2004. As Table 9.1 shows, the per capita GDP of these 10 countries was only 45.4 percent of the EU average. Although these CEECs added 19.6 percent to the EU population, they added only 8.9 percent to the EU's GDP. Table 9.1 shows that the per capita GDP of Bulgaria and Romania were only 17.7 percent of the EU average when they joined in 2007 and that Croatia's per capita GDP was only 38.8 percent of the EU average when it joined in 2013. Widening need not hinder the deepening of integration, and sometimes they occur together. However, the large number of states involved in the CEEC enlargements and their lower level of economic development contributed to a diversity of interests that was "harder to contain within a single framework."[53] Many European leaders believed that the EU enlargement necessitated major institutional reforms. To this end, a Convention in Brussels produced a draft Constitution for Europe that was signed in October 2004. This Constitutional Treaty did not receive final approval from voters in several states, but a less ambitious *Lisbon Treaty* did receive final acceptance in 2009. The provisions of the Lisbon Treaty are designed to facilitate internal and external policy-making by the EU with its enlarged membership. As Table 9.2 shows, the Lisbon Treaty establishes a new high representative position to give the EU more influence in international forums; gives new powers to the European Commission, Parliament, and Court of Justice; removes national vetoes in some areas; and redistributes voting power among the member states.

Despite the approval of the Lisbon Treaty, many uncertainties remain. First, the treaty is complex and difficult to read, and its effects remain to be seen. Second, Ireland was the only EU country to hold a referendum on the treaty. EU leaders in other states circumvented ambivalent attitudes by arguing that there was no need for referenda because Lisbon simply amended earlier treaties. Third, both the deepening and widening of EU integration have been deeply shaken by "the internal crisis over the euro."[54] As discussed, the EU sovereign debt crisis has widened divisions among member states and raised questions about the future of the euro zone. The economic problems have contributed to strong populist fears that the migration of labor from poorer to richer EU states is contributing to unemployment problems and adding to pressure on social welfare systems. As for external pressures, shortly after Croatia joined the EU in 2013, Russia took actions to prevent Armenia and Ukraine from signing EU association agreements; and the EU has had difficulty in responding to Russia's strong pressures on Ukraine. Whereas the EU views Russia's actions as aggression, Russia argues that it is defending its own vital interests. It remains to be seen whether "Russian pressure in the east" will drive EU members "together or apart."[55] Adding to the external pressures, the large influx of migrants into Europe is putting new strains on the Schengen Agreement.

Theoretical Perspectives and the EU

Scholars have applied a wide range of theories to European integration. For example, one book divides the theoretical approaches into three parts: those that explain European integration, analyze European governance, and construct the EU.[56] We focus on three of the main theoretical approaches: **neofunctionalism, liberal intergovernmentalism,** and **constructivism.** We then discuss a general criticism of the theories and refer to the theory of *plutocratic delegation.*

Neofunctionalism Theorists often ask why European states have pooled substantial elements of their sovereignty in the EU. Neofunctionalism describes integration in one economic sector as creating pressures for further integration. For example, the six ECSC members found that integrating their coal and steel resources would have more benefits if they also integrated their transportation systems for moving the coal and steel. Thus, regional integration has an expansive logic, in which integration in one economic sector creates pressures for *spillover* into related sectors. Spillover can also contribute to the deepening of integration from an FTA to a CU, common market, and economic union. Whereas functionalists see spillover as an automatic process, neofunctionalists see political activism by interest-driven actors as also necessary. First, integration in one sector engenders increased transactions and new organizations representing business, labor, and consumer interests at the regional level. These regional interests exert political pressure for deeper integration. Second, the supranational bureaucracy (the European Commission in the EU) has a vested interest in expanding its authority through deepening integration over a wider range of sectors. Thus, Ernst Haas describes integration as "the process whereby political actors in several distinct national settings are persuaded to shift their loyalties, expectations and political activities toward a new center, whose institutions possess or demand jurisdiction over the pre-existing national states."[57]

Neofunctionalism had considerable influence on the study of regional integration, but its influence varied over the years. The expansion of integration from the ECSC to the EC seemed to support neofunctionalism, but problems such as Eurosclerosis in the 1970s raised questions about the expansive logic of the theory. Neofunctionalist ideas such as "spillover" had somewhat of a revival in the 1990s with the SEA, the Maastricht Treaty, and the creation of the EMU, but the newer neofunctionalists viewed it as a less ambitious theory that only explained some aspects of the integration process. Few scholars call themselves neofunctionalists today because the theory has been subject to numerous criticisms. First, the tortuous path of European integration demonstrates conflicting pressures for integration and diversity, and there is no certainty that spillover will occur. Second, neofunctionalists tended to ignore the fact that the average citizen has been more skeptical of European integration than the elites. Contrary to what Haas predicted, citizens have *not* shifted their "loyalties, expectations and political activities toward a new center." Third, critics argue that the member states, rather than interest groups and the EU institutions, have the main power in the EU. States resist further integration when it does not serve their national objectives.[58]

Liberal Intergovernmentalism   Whereas neofunctionalists focus on societal interests and supranational institutions, liberal intergovernmentalists assert that member states (central governments) remain free to choose how the EU functions. Andrew Moravcsik is the founder of liberal intergovernmentalism, which is "liberal" in its view of governments as bringing together domestic interest groups within a state, and "intergovernmentalist" in its emphasis on the central role of states (which also shows the influence of neomercantilism). Moravcsik argues that the EU rests on a series of bargains between member states, which are self-interested and rational in pursuing outcomes that serve their economic interests. Major policy decisions reflect the preferences of national governments rather than supranational institutions, and each state's preferences reflect the balance of its domestic economic interests. Conflict may arise between states with different preferences, and the status quo changes only when the largest states accept compromise agreements. Intergovernmentalists seek to explain how national interests are reconciled in intergovernmental bargains, and they see the EU as occupying "a permanent position at the heart of the European landscape" only because of decisions by member states.[59] European integration is reversible, because member states support the EU supranational institutions as a means of enforcing intergovernmental bargains. Whereas neofunctionalists are criticized for underemphasizing the role of governments, liberal intergovernmentalists are criticized for overemphasizing their role. Moravcsik focuses on a series of "grand bargains" between governments, but devotes less attention to the EU's day-to-day politics. Because governments cannot monitor daily activities, institutions such as the EU Commission have considerable discretion in making decisions. Furthermore, neofunctional theorists argue that state bargains may have "unintended consequences" in giving more discretion than states anticipate to supranational institutions.

Constructivism Neofunctionalists and liberal intergovernmentalists emphasize the role of material factors such as interests in the integration process.
Constructivists by contrast focus on the role of ideas, norms, and identity. In
studying European integration, we need to understand not only the EU's interactions with member states and interest groups, but also the effects of national
self-image, identity, and views of the integration process. For example, compliance with EU principles and rules often depends less on EU sanctions and
rewards than on whether a country sees itself as law-abiding. Some EU states
are noted for implementing EU laws even when there is strong domestic opposition to them. Compliance with EU rules also depends on the development of
a European identity within societies, and this can only occur if there is some
compatibility between the EU and the core elements of national identity. Furthermore, assessments of the integration process require some understanding
of the developing European identity. If various European groups do not view
some states such as Turkey as being "European," they might oppose their joining the EU even if they meet the objective criteria for membership. Although
constructivists correctly alert us to the importance of ideas, norms, and identities, critics argue that they have not yet developed shared theoretical principles
and research strategies for studying the integration process.[60]

Criticisms of the Theoretical Perspectives Despite the richness and diversity
of European integration theory, two general criticisms can be made. First, the
disruptive effects of the European sovereign debt crisis point to the fact that
"overviews of EU theories barely touch upon the issue of disintegration, if at
all."[61] Integration theories do examine reversals. For example, neofunctionalists refer to *spillback* as well as spillover, when states withdraw from a specific set of obligations; and liberal intergovernmentalists point to situations in
which member states become less willing to support compromise solutions.
However, Hans Vollaard notes that disintegration is not simply integration
in reverse. Disintegration may result not only in a reversion from EU authority back to nation-states, but to some other formation such as subnational
regions. Thus, theorizing on disintegration as well as integration is necessary.
A second criticism is that integration theory has been so fixated on the EU that
it has not focused sufficiently on forms of governance other than intergovernmentalism and supranationalism. For example, a study by Kathleen Hancock focuses on **plutocracy**, in which "smaller member states delegate policy
making to the wealthiest state in the integration accord."[62] Whereas supranational institutions have a significant role in the EU, in plutocratic integration
that role is performed by the wealthiest state. States formed customs unions
using plutocratic structures in the nineteenth century in Prussia and elsewhere.
More recently, the Eurasian Customs Union formed by Russia, Belarus, and
Kazakhstan in 2007, which became the **Eurasian Economic Union** in 2015
(also including Armenia and Kyrgyzstan), has some characteristics of a plutocracy. The interesting question is why some smaller states have been more willing to opt for plutocratic integration with Russia than others. Whereas Belarus
and Kazakhstan joined with Russia at an early stage, Ukrainians were deeply

divided over this issue, and opted against joining. The result has been conflict between Russia and the West over Ukraine, and less credibility for the Eurasian Economic Union without Ukraine as a member. The important point is that integration theorists should not limit their vision only to the EU in formulating their theories.

THE NORTH AMERICAN FREE TRADE AGREEMENT

Regionalism in the Western Hemisphere is more heterogeneous than in Europe. Efforts to form a Free Trade Area of the Americas for the entire hemisphere failed, and the most important RTAs are NAFTA and Mercosur. As discussed, the United States would not participate in comprehensive RTAs from the 1940s to the early 1970s, and it focused instead on GATT-based multilateral trade. However, a reversal of U.S. policies combined with greater openness to free trade in Canada and Mexico resulted in the **Canada–U.S. Free Trade Agreement (CUSFTA)** in 1988 and the North American Free Trade Agreement (NAFTA) in 1994.

The Formation of NAFTA

A noted Canadian historian has observed that one economic issue in Canada "comes close to rivalling the linguistic and race question for both longevity and vehemence, and this is, of course, the question of free trade with the United States."[63] In 1854, the two countries concluded a Reciprocity Treaty providing for free trade in natural products such as grains, meat, dairy products, and fish. However, the United States abrogated the treaty in 1866 because of its negative trade balance with Canada, increased Canadian duties on U.S. manufactures, and the British role in the U.S. Civil War. Efforts to revive free trade in 1911 and 1948 were unsuccessful, but the 1965 Canada–U.S. Auto Agreement provided for free trade in automobiles and parts (GATT provided a waiver from the Article 24 provision that FTAs should cover substantially all trade). In 1988 the two states established a comprehensive FTA, the CUSFTA; when Mexico, the United States, and Canada signed NAFTA in 1992, it superseded CUSFTA.

The question arises as to why these FTAs were formed after so many years. The United States reversed its policy on RTAs with the 1974 U.S. Trade Act, which permitted the president to "initiate negotiations for a trade agreement with Canada to establish a free trade area."[64] However, Canadian and Mexican requests initiated the negotiations for CUSFTA and NAFTA. Both countries had become more dependent on trade with the United States and cross-border production with U.S. companies, and they viewed freer trade as a means of increasing their competitiveness. When the United States responded to its balance-of-payments deficits in the mid-1980s with increased protectionism, Canada viewed an FTA as necessary to gain more assured access to the U.S. market. Mexico was concerned about Canada's favored position as a U.S. trader in the Canada–U.S. FTA, and as an LDC Mexico viewed an FTA as essential for attracting more U.S. foreign investment. The United States as a major economic power was more concerned about global trade linkages, and it concluded the CUSFTA and NAFTA largely because of frustration with the slow pace of the GATT Uruguay Round. Negotiating RTAs, in the U.S. view, would induce the EU and Japan to offer concessions in the GATT negotiations. Regionalism also tends to breed more regionalism, and the EU's enlargement gave the United States another reason to join RTAs. Furthermore, the United States became less committed to multilateralism as the sole option as its trade hegemony declined. The United States also wanted Canada and Mexico to ease their regulations on foreign investment and natural resources, and it was willing to open its market to Canadian and Mexican goods in return. Cross-border intraindustry trade and gains from economies of scale also induced producers in key sectors such as computers, automobiles, electronics, and machinery to pressure for an RTA.[65]

NAFTA as a Free Trade Agreement

Unlike the EU, NAFTA has remained a free trade agreement. All three countries have been skeptical of EU-type supranational institutions that would impinge on national sovereignty, and the U.S. Congress has resisted agreements that interfere with U.S. trade policy. However, Mexico and Canada as the two smaller NAFTA members realized that some integration was necessary to protect their interests, even if it infringed on their sovereignty. For example, Canada views U.S. antidumping and countervailing duty laws as protectionist, and favors either their elimination among NAFTA members or a common code to define which subsidies are permissible. However, the United States sees the use of ADDs and CVDs as its sovereign prerogative, and NAFTA dispute settlement panels can only decide whether a country's decision to levy a CVD is made in accordance with its own law; the panels cannot assess the fairness of each country's laws. When Vicente Fox became Mexico's president in 2000, he proposed that NAFTA extend to the free movement of labor as well as goods and services, and that a development fund be established to upgrade North American infrastructure. However, the United States and Canada did not support these proposals, and the NAFTA approach depends on the market to facilitate integration and decrease inequalities.[66] Although NAFTA includes some innovative features in services, agricultural trade, investment, and dispute settlement, it remains an FTA with a minimal degree of institutionalization.

How successful has NAFTA been as an FTA? NAFTA was contentious from the time it was formed, with supporters overestimating its possible benefits, and opponents overestimating its drawbacks. Thus, authors of a 2014 assessment write that "in truth the claims on both sides of the NAFTA issue 20 years ago were overblown."[67] The contentiousness over NAFTA has continued into the present, and NAFTA is being invoked by both sides in the current debate over whether the United States should participate in a much larger *Trade-Pacific Partnership* (TPP) agreement (the TPP is discussed later). The controversy over NAFTA in all three member countries is reflected in divisions among and within the IPE theoretical perspectives.

Liberalism Liberal economists often see NAFTA as an open FTA that serves as a stepping stone to multilateral free trade. NAFTA had a positive demonstration effect on the WTO in services trade, investment, and intellectual property rights, and it goes beyond the WTO in these areas. For example, NAFTA follows a "negative list" approach to national treatment for trade in services, which puts the onus on each member to list the services it wants to exclude from national treatment; all services a country does not list are automatically included. The General Agreement on Trade in Services (GATS), by contrast, takes a "positive list" approach; that is, national treatment applies only to sectors included in a member's list of commitments. Although liberals acknowledge that NAFTA has produced both winners and losers, they believe that the rewards greatly exceed the costs, and they place particular emphasis on private enterprise.[68] For example, the U.S. Department of Commerce finds "overwhelming evidence across the United States that NAFTA-related trade and investment liberalization has allowed U.S. firms to maximize efficiencies, remain globally competitive, and increase sales and exports as a result."[69] Liberals also point to the positive effects of NAFTA on foreign investment, noting that "in 1993, Mexico's inward stock of FDI was just $52 billion, about 7 percent of GDP. By 2012, the stock reached $315 billion, some 27 percent of GDP."[70] Overall, liberals laud NAFTA for increasing interdependence among the three countries.

Despite this generally positive assessment, liberals also point to NAFTA problems. For example, liberals criticize restrictions that continue to limit trade and investment. One study notes that "while CUSFTA and NAFTA both contained services chapters ... regulatory barriers to cross-border trade in services were not much reduced."[71] Liberals also consider rules of origin to be a protectionist device in FTAs and they note that NAFTA has highly restrictive rules of origin for automobiles, textiles and apparel, and color televisions. Recognizing that interdependence requires more policy coordination, many liberals favor a deepening of integration; for example, some liberals propose that NAFTA should become a customs union.[72] Differences, of course, exist among liberals. *Orthodox liberals* often praise NAFTA for its market orientation and for being the first North–South FTA that does not give special treatment to LDC members (Mexico). *Interventionist liberals* by contrast argue that some measures should be taken to deal with the wide disparity between incomes, wages, and standards in NAFTA; and *institutional liberals* call for more institutions to address NAFTA's internal and external shortcomings. Orthodox liberals also view NAFTA's environmental and labor side agreements as nontrade issues that can be used to impose protectionist trade barriers, whereas interventionist liberals see these agreements as necessary to correct market imperfections. Finally, some liberals such as Jagdish Bhagwati are more critical of the proliferation of RTAs than others. Despite these differences, most liberals generally favor NAFTA as an open RTA. For example, one liberal study concludes that "NAFTA remains vital to maintaining trade and investment in the three countries and helps anchor the economic health of the North American marketplace."[73]

Neomercantilism Neomercantilists emphasize NAFTA's asymmetries in power and levels of economic development. They reject the liberal view that smaller states often benefit from FTAs more than larger states because of increased exports and economies of scale. As the larger partner, the United States expects its benefits from free trade to outweigh those of the smaller partners. For example, Canada sought free trade with the United States to gain more assured access to the U.S. market; but the United States expected side payments in return such as less regulation of U.S. foreign investment, greater U.S. access to Canadian energy, and a services trade agreement. The United States also expected Mexico to grant access to its market for U.S. agricultural goods and to give up claims as an LDC to special treatment. Neomercantilists also see NAFTA as a threat to national sovereignty. For example, they are highly critical of NAFTA's Chapter 11, which gives private investors access to binding international arbitration in disputes over a host government's investment measures. (This contrasts with WTO dispute settlement cases where only states are directly involved in dispute settlement.) Chapter 11 has resulted in some high-profile investor suits against government efforts to implement environmental and health regulations. Whereas liberals view NAFTA's Chapter 11 as an innovative mechanism that permits foreign enterprises to prevent states from discriminating against them, neomercantilists see it as "a vehicle for investors to harass governments whose policies they dislike."[74] Neomercantilists also argue that the benefits of NAFTA are over-rated, because RTAs are "no substitute for a coherent national development strategy."[75]

Historical Materialism Historical materialists argue that NAFTA is shifting power to the capitalist class and against labor groups. For example, NAFTA enables MNCs to avoid labor and environmental standards in Canada and the United States by relocating production in Mexico. As capital leaves the United States and Canada, wages and employment in these countries decline. Some historical materialists use the terms *core* and *periphery* to designate social position and class rather than geographic location, arguing that NAFTA has relegated many U.S. and Canadian workers to peripheral status. For example, one study concludes that Mexico's emergence as a clothing exporter "to the United States as a result of NAFTA has been accompanied by dramatic growth of garment maquiladora employment south of the border and a dramatic decline in the garment industry north of the border, especially among manual, direct production workers."[76] The losses for U.S. and Canadian workers, according to historical materialists, do not result in comparable gains for Mexican workers. For example, NAFTA is destroying the livelihoods of Mexican peasants because U.S. corn, which benefits from government subsidies, is being freely exported to Mexico. Historical materialists therefore argue that NAFTA is increasing poverty and inequality between the rich and poor in all three states. A 2014 study concludes that NAFTA has "contributed to mass job losses, soaring income inequality, agricultural instability, corporate attacks on domestic health and environmental safeguards, and mass displacement and volatility in Mexico."[77] Some Gramscian theorists assert that a coalition of labor, environmental, consumer, and women's groups should form a counterhegemonic bloc against the domination of corporate capital in NAFTA. This bloc would replace the corporate view of liberalization in North America with a more democratic, participatory model.[78]

Environmentalism   NAFTA was the first significant trade agreement to include an environmental side agreement and establish institutions for monitoring and finance. During the NAFTA negotiations, there were serious disagreements over the environmental provisions. The greens such as Greenpeace, Public Citizen, and the Sierra Club argued that the NAFTA provisions favored corporate interests and trade liberalization over environmental concerns. For example, they charged that NAFTA's Chapter 11 opened a new legal channel for private investors to contest a state's environmental policies, and they dismissed the environmental side agreement as ineffective and unenforceable. In contrast, some business groups argued that the environmental side agreement would interfere with free trade and result in costly new regulations. Liberal environmental groups such as the World Wildlife Fund, Environmental Defense, and the National Resources Defense Council took a position between these extremes. Although they wanted the side agreement to put more emphasis on the upward harmonization of environmental standards, they favored trade liberalization and generally supported the efforts to include environmental provisions in NAFTA.

The NAFTA environmental provisions in fact have been mixed but in need of improvement. One study concludes that "Mexico's environmental laws have improved since NAFTA came into force," but that "Canada's post-NAFTA record has been less impressive."[79] Another study by contrast argues that Mexico's governments have lacked commitment to environmental protection in the post-NAFTA era, and spending and inspection levels have declined. Whereas many greens see NAFTA as beyond repair, interventionist liberals believe that the NAFTA environmental provisions can be upgraded by adopting stronger provisions. For example, some interventionists argue that the environmental provisions should be subjected to the same enforcement and dispute resolution provisions as the commercial parts of NAFTA.[80] In the view of two noted liberals,

> it makes more sense to tackle the shortcomings than to lament the existence of an FTA, as many environmentalists do, or to overlook the problems, as a very few diehard free trade advocates might. With the necessary tuning, NAFTA can become a trade agreement that both environmentalists and free traders appreciate.[81]

In sum, NAFTA remains highly contentious in all three member states. A major problem is that NAFTA supporters and opponents focus on different aspects of the agreement. Whereas supporters laud NAFTA "for enhancing economic linkages between countries, creating more efficient production processes [and] increasing the availability of lower-priced consumer goods," opponents blame NAFTA "for disappointing employment trends, a decline in U.S. wages, and for not having done enough to improve labor standards and environmental conditions."[82]

MERCOSUR

RTAs in Latin America during the 1960s–1970s were inward-looking, but there was a revival of Latin American regionalism in the mid-1980s on a more open basis. The largest of these newer RTAs is **Mercosur**, or the *Common Market of the Southern Cone*. In 1991 Argentina, Brazil, Paraguay, and Uruguay signed the Treaty of Asunción (TOA) to establish Mercosur, and Venezuela joined as a full member in 2012. The TOA timetable included the formation of an FTA from 1991 to 1994, a CU in 1995, and eventually a common market; this schedule was unusual for Latin America, where most integration plans included only vague promises. Mercosur's significance also stemmed from the importance of its two largest members, Brazil and Argentina. Many observers were skeptical about Mercosur because of Latin America's history of inward-looking development policies and the long-term enmity between Brazil and Argentina. However, most Latin American LDCs were active participants in the GATT Uruguay Round, and the Argentine and Brazilian presidents supported integration because of their neoliberal economic strategies and their belief that integration would strengthen their position vis-à-vis the United States and the EU.[83]

The integration process was quite dynamic from 1991 to 1995 as tariffs were gradually eliminated and some business firms began to organize their production and sales on a regional basis. However, Brazil and Argentina introduced new tariffs and NTBs after 1995, and intra-Mercosur exports as a share of total exports declined. During the 1990s regional trade had risen from 10 to 25 percent of total trade, but from 1999 to 2003 it fell back to about 10 percent. From 1999 to 2002 the devaluation of the Brazilian currency and the subsequent crisis in Argentina put Mercosur in serious jeopardy. Beginning in 2003, the member states have taken steps to revive Mercosur with political and social as well as economic agreements. For example, a Mercosur Parliament (which only makes political recommendations) was formed in 2005. However, political and economic problems remain; one example was the suspension of Paraguay from Mercosur in June 2012. Although most merchandise trade within Mercosur is now duty-free, rules do not extend to services trade, government purchases, and many NTBs and administrative barriers. Mercosur has also not yet established a CU with a common external tariff. To maintain a CET, no member state can negotiate bilaterally with outside states.[84]

International, regional, and national factors account for Mercosur's problems. First, Mercosur members as LDCs are highly vulnerable to international developments. For example, the Mexican and East Asian financial crises in the 1990s contributed to the loss of markets for Latin American exports and a marked decrease in the prices of primary commodities. Second, in 2005 intra-Mercosur trade accounted for only 13 percent of the members' total trade. Only about 10 percent of Brazil's trade was with other Mercosur members in 2012. The dependence on trade with external actors such as the United States and the EU limits Mercosur's importance. Third, there is a high level of asymmetry, with Brazil accounting for about 70 percent of Mercosur's GDP. To ensure that Mercosur does not infringe on its sovereignty, Brazil has opposed a strong dispute-settlement body.[85] Fourth, Mercosur has done little to harmonize the members' macroeconomic policies. In 1991 Argentina pegged its peso to the U.S. dollar, whereas Brazil adjusted its exchange rate. After Brazil devalued its currency in 1999, Argentina's trade balance with Brazil sharply deteriorated and many companies moved from Argentina to Brazil. By 2001, Argentina had a massive foreign debt and defaulted on its loans partly because its peso was pegged to the U.S. dollar. This provided the setting for the 1999 to 2002 crisis in Mercosur.[86]

Neomercantilists see Mercosur as contributing to security as well as economic ties; Argentina and Brazil have upgraded their military cooperation, with joint military exercises and annual meetings between their joint chiefs of staff. Neomercantilists also argue that Mercosur strengthens its members' bargaining power vis-à-vis the United States and the EU. Liberals favor widening the scope of Mercosur's trade liberalization and predict that domestic business groups will continue to see Mercosur as a means of attracting foreign investment. Historical materialists argue that Mercosur resulted from IMF pressure on Latin Americans to liberalize their policies and that Mercosur incorporates its members "within the world capitalist system while preserving their subordinate status in the system."[87] Constructivists have asked whether efforts to extend Mercosur to social and political areas since 2003 have helped in establishing a feeling of collective identity. It remains to be seen how the balance between the forces of regionalism and nationalism affects the future of Mercosur as an RTA.

THE TRANS-PACIFIC PARTNERSHIP

Difficulties with completing the WTO Doha Round, and with the "spaghetti-bowl" of smaller bilateral FTAs that often have conflicting provisions, have sparked an effort to negotiate several mega-regional agreements. The proposed *Trans-Pacific Partnership (TPP)* may be the most ambitious of these agreements. The TPP negotiations officially began in March 2010, and 12 countries have participated: Australia, Brunei, Canada, Chile, Japan, Malaysia, Mexico, New Zealand, Peru, Singapore, the United States, and Vietnam. The negotiators finally reached an agreement on October 5, 2015, but the details of the agreement are still to be finalized, and the TPP must then be ratified by the legislatures in the 12 participating countries. The TPP's importance stems from the fact that it would have no exclusions from trade liberalization and could serve as a major stepping stone to global trade liberalization. Thus, one analyst indicates that it could be "a game changer" in international trade.[88] The TPP's importance also relates to the greater centrality of the Asia–Pacific region which has a growing array of supply-chain networks for production, intermediate goods trade, and assembly of products. *Supply chains* include all the companies involved in manufacturing, assembling, delivering, and selling products. Optimal supply chains can significantly lower costs for a company.[89]

The TPP negotiations involve the type of trade agenda that the United States has been unable to achieve in the WTO. Leading this regional effort could also help the United States regain the initiative in global trade policy and provide a counterweight to China's growing influence in Asia. However, the TPP is highly controversial in the United States, and it was difficult for the Obama administration to win *trade promotion authority (TPA)*, also called *fast-track authority*, to continue negotiating the TPP. TPA rules were first set out in the 1974 U.S. Trade Act: If Congress grants TPA, it can only accept or reject trade agreements without amending them; TPA is granted for a specific time period, not for a specific trade deal; and TPA sets mandatory deadlines and a limit on debate in Congress. Without TPA, a TPP agreement would be subject to re-negotiations and delays in ratification in the U.S. Congress.[90] Many Democrats and labor union leaders have opposed the TPP, arguing that it mainly serves the agenda of MNCs, and the White House had to spend months garnering support for TPA to continue the negotiations. In June 2015 the Republican-controlled Senate finally passed the TPA or fast-track legislation, and this was a significant victory for the Obama administration. Congress can still reject the final TPP agreement, but the TPA legislation prevents it from amending the agreement. It is uncertain that the TPP will be ratified by Congress at the time of this writing, because the agreement was reached in Obama's final year in office, and populist anti-free trade sentiment was higher in the lead-up to the U.S. presidential election.

Ratification of the TPP agreement faces a number of other obstacles. First, the TPP goes far beyond a traditional trade agreement and involves highly sensitive sectors and behind-the-border trade rules. There are North–South divisions on services, environment, and labor issues, and disagreements among both DCs and LDCs on intellectual property and agricultural agreements. Second, other major negotiators could limit the success of the TPP negotiations. It took Japan over two years to decide to join the TPP negotiations in November 2010, and it is the "debate dividing the nation into two."[91] To induce Japan to support the TPP, the United States agreed to the idea that cars from TPP members could be sold duty-free in North America with only 45 percent content from the NAFTA countries, and auto parts could enter duty-free with only 30 percent content. Under current NAFTA rules, auto parts can move duty-free in North America only if at least 60 percent of the content is from the three countries, and cars must have at least 62.5 percent North American content. The U.S.–Japan agreement would permit Japan to assemble cars with a much higher percent of auto parts from China and Southeast Asia and export them duty-free to North America. The United States assured Japan that it could convince its NAFTA partners to support this agreement, but Canada and Mexico strongly opposed it. The negotiations resulted in a TPP agreement that requires more North American content than Japan wanted, but less than that desired by Canada and Mexico. One reason Mexico and Canada joined the TPP negotiations was to protect their NAFTA benefits and ensure that they would receive trade concessions the United States offered to other TPP countries. However, the two smaller NAFTA partners are now concerned that the TPP will provide them with fewer benefits than NAFTA. Whereas Canada and Mexico as smaller countries focus more on North America, the United States is more fixated on its global trade, investment, and security interests.

From a U.S. perspective, failure to negotiate a TPP could have major implications for its economic influence in Asia, partly because there is an alternative agreement under negotiation. In May 2013 a *Regional Comprehensive Economic Partnership (RCEP)* was announced, which involves the **Association of Southeast Asian Nations (ASEAN)** and six other countries in the region: China, South Korea, Japan, India, Australia and New Zealand. (ASEAN has 10 members: Brunei Darussalam, Cambodia, Indonesia, Laos, Malaysia, Myanmar, Philippines, Singapore, Thailand, and Vietnam.) The proposed RCEP would be much less ambitious than the TPP in terms of scope and depth of liberalization. Most importantly, the RCEP would marginalize the United States; hence the importance of the TPP for a continued strong U.S. economic presence in East Asia. Thus, one analyst asserts that "choosing between the TPP and RCEP will ... force governments to signal their geopolitical allegiances between the two great powers in the region."[92]

Another mega-regional trade negotiation, which is at an early stage, is the U.S.–EU *Transatlantic Trade and Investment Partnership (TTIP)* negotiation which began in July 2013. In view of the 2008 global financial crisis and the European sovereign debt crisis, both partners viewed a new trade agreement as a way to revitalize their economies. The United States and the EU have the largest bilateral commercial relationship in the global economy, and a successful TTIP negotiation could have a major effect on the future course of global trade negotiations in such areas as liberalizing services trade and reducing regulatory barriers.[93] In sum, the outcome of mega-regional negotiations for a TPP, RCEP, and TTIP could have a major effect, not only on the possibilities for further multilateral trade liberalization, but also on U.S.–Chinese geopolitical rivalry.

Considering IPE Theory and Practice

During the postwar period there have been two major waves of regionalism, the first in the 1950s and 1960s, and the second since the mid-1980s. Globalization has provided a stimulus to the second wave, which has been more enduring. A contentious issue among economic liberals in the current wave is whether RTAs serve as stepping stones or obstacles to global free trade; thus, some major debates in IPE are among theorists within the same perspective. Liberals generally agree that multilateralism is the best route to trade liberalization and that open RTAs are a second-best option because they divert some imports from more efficient outside suppliers to less efficient regional suppliers. However, some liberals see RTAs today as a serious threat to an open multilateral trade regime, whereas others believe that RTAs can coexist beneficially with multilateralism.

A notable theorist taking the first position is Jagdish Bhagwati, who describes RTAs as "termites" that are "eating away at the multilateral trading system."[94] Bhagwati prefers the term *preferential trade agreements* (*PTAs*) to *free trade agreements* (*FTAs*), because it highlights the discriminatory nature of these trade arrangements. Bhagwati and others in the first group present several arguments to show that RTAs pose a threat to the global trade regime: RTAs are discriminatory and therefore incompatible with MFN treatment, a basic trade regime principle; LDCs have a special exemption for RTAs under the enabling clause, which allows them to engage in discrimination without any discipline; the recent proliferation of bilateral FTAs is bringing chaos to the global trade regime, with different rules and tariff rates for each FTA; RTAs are creating a "spaghetti-bowl" of different rules and procedures; FTA rules of origin are often used as a disguised form of protectionism; many bilateral FTAs between rich and poor countries permit "the exercise of virtually unconstrained political and economic power by the United States and EU to secure concessions";[95] and RTAs divert valuable resources away from multilateral negotiations such as the Doha Round. The second group of liberals agree that RTAs can create problems such as trade diversion. However, they see some plurilateral FTAs such as NAFTA as more trade-creating than diverting, and they believe that trade regionalism can coexist with global trade liberalization. When NAFTA was formed, Gary Clyde Hufbauer and Jeffrey J. Schott predicted (in 1993) that "on balance ... the trade created by growth in the NAFTA region should more than offset the trade diverted in particular sectors."[96] In a 2005 study, Hufbauer and Schott referred to empirical studies which "on balance ... find that NAFTA tends to promote trade creation more than trade diversion." Although the authors criticize NAFTA for its restrictive rules of origin, they rate the agreement as a "success."[97] Liberals in the second group also support the proposed TPP, which they view as a possible stepping stone to global trade liberalization. Arguments of theorists in the second group include the following: FTAs contribute to economies of scale and a division of labor based on comparative advantage; trade creation is likely to be greater than trade diversion if the FTA members are already major trading partners; RTAs allow members to overcome regional disagreements, which helps reduce the complexity of the WTO negotiations; and by promoting deeper integration at the regional level, RTAs can lead the way for multilateral trade negotiations. For example, NAFTA liberalized trade in services and agriculture before the GATT/WTO.[98]

Although liberal theorists often base their findings on empirical studies, "different studies come out with different trade effects for the same RTAs. This is due to the use of different estimation methods, different databases and time periods to measure these trade effects."[99] In the first group, Bhagwati uses historical analysis to show that political factors resulted in the exceptions the GATT/WTO provides to RTAs, and he views these exceptions as mainly trade-diverting. In the second group, many analysts focus on specific RTAs for which they have a strong affinity. For example, Hufbauer and Schott want NAFTA to establish a common external tariff, strengthen its institutions, and promote closer monetary cooperation. Thus, the diversity of findings does not result only from different methodologies; nonmaterial factors such as the assumptions and values of the theorists also affect their findings.

Chapters 8 and 9 have focused on trade, but the relationship between trade and investment is extremely close; for example, RTAs affect regional production, intraindustry specialization, and the location of firms. A former WTO director-general notes that "businesses now trade to invest and invest to trade—to the point where both activities are increasingly part of a single strategy to deliver products across borders."[100] The next chapter deals with the issue of MNCs and foreign investment.

QUESTIONS

1. What are the differences between a free trade area, CU, common market, and economic union? Do any RTAs fit completely within one of these models of integration?
2. How do neomercantilists, liberals, and historical materialists explain the rise of regional integration?
3. In what ways can RTAs be trade-diverting and trade-creating? Do you think that RTAs are stepping stones or obstacles to global trade liberalization, and why do you think liberal theorists cannot agree on this issue?
4. What conditions does GATT Article 24 impose on RTAs? How successful has the GATT/WTO been in regulating RTAs?
5. In what ways do LDCs receive special treatment as members and associate members of RTAs? Does Mexico receive special treatment in NAFTA?
6. In what ways is the EU a unique RTA? What are the neofunctionalist, liberal intergovernmentalist, and constructivist theoretical approaches to economic integration, and why are they applied mainly to Europe? What is plutocratic theory (or plutocracy)? How does it differ from the major theoretical approaches to European integration?
7. What are some of the problems confronting NAFTA today? What are the liberal, neomercantilist, historical materialist, and environmentalist views of NAFTA? What are the TPP negotiations, and are they likely to have an effect on NAFTA?
8. What special problems do FTAs among LDCs such as Mercosur have in achieving regional integration? In what ways are politics and economics intertwined in Mercosur?

KEY TERMS

Association of Southeast Asian Nations
Canada–U.S. Free Trade Agreement
common market

Cotonou Agreement
customs union
economic and monetary union economic union
Eurasian Economic Union

European Coal and Steel Community
European Community
European Free Trade Association

European Union
free trade area
GATT Article 24
liberal
  intergovernmentalism
Lomé Convention

Maastricht Treaty
Mercosur
neofunctionalism
North American
  Free Trade
  Agreement
Organization for

European Economic
  Cooperation
plutocracy
political union
rules of origin
Schengen Agreement

FURTHER READING

On the relationship between regionalism and globalization, see Louise Eva Mossner, "The WTO and Regional Trade: A Family Business?" *World Trade Review* 13, no. 4 (October 2014), pp. 633–649; Pravin Krishna, "Preferential Trade Agreements and the World Trade System," and "comments," in Robert C. Feenstra and Alan M. Taylor, eds., *Globalization in an Age of Crisis* (Chicago, IL: University of Chicago Press, 2014), pp. 131–164; David A. Lynch, *Trade and Globalization: An Introduction to Regional Trade Agreements* (New York: Rowman & Littlefield, 2010); and Rick Fawn, ed., *Globalising the Regional, Regionalising the Global* (New York: Cambridge University Press, 2009). Jagdish Bhagwati strongly criticizes RTAs from a liberal perspective in *Termites in the Trading System: How Preferential Agreements Undermine Free Trade* (New York: Oxford University Press, 2008).

General studies of the EU include Roger Bootle, *The Trouble with Europe* (Boston: Nicholas Brealey, 2014); and Erik Jones, Anand Menon, and Stephen Weatherill, eds., *The Oxford Handbook of the European Union* (New York: Oxford University Press, 2012). On the deepening of European integration and the EMU, see Martin Heipertz and Amy Verdun, *Ruling Europe: The Politics of the Stability and Growth Pact* (New York: Cambridge University Press, 2010). On the widening of European Integration, see Heather Grabbe, "Six Lessons of Enlargement Ten Years On," *Journal of Common Market Studies* 52, Issue Supplement (September 2014), pp. 40–56. On regional integration theory, see Antje Wiener and Thomas Diez, *European Integration Theory*, 2nd ed. (New York: Oxford University Press, 2009); Ben Rosamond, *Theories of European Integration* (New York: St. Martin's Press, 2000); and Kathleen J. Hancock, *Regional Integration: Choosing Plutocracy* (New York: Palgrave Macmillan, 2009).

On integration in the Western Hemisphere see Gary Clyde Hufbauer, Cathleen Cimino, and Tyler Moran, "NAFTA at 20: Misleading Charges and Positive Achievements," Peterson Institute of International Economics, no. PB14–13, May 2014; Robert A. Pastor, *The North American Idea* (New York: Oxford University Press, 2011); Joseph A. McKinney and H. Stephen Gardner, eds., *Economic Integration in the Americas* (New York: Routledge, 2008); and Isabel Studer and Carol Wise, eds., *Requiem or Revival? The Promise of North American Integration* (Washington, DC: Brookings Institution, 2007). An assessment of NAFTA from a liberal perspective is Gary C. Hufbauer and Jeffrey J. Schott, *NAFTA Revisited: Achievements and Challenges* (Washington, DC: Institute for International Economics, 2005); from a critical perspective see Isidro Morales, *Post-NAFTA North America: Reshaping the Economic and Political Governance of a Changing Region* (New York: Palgrave Macmillan, 2008). On Mercosur, see Sergio Caballero Santos, "Identity in Mercosur: Regionalism and Nationalism," *Global Governance* 21 (2015), pp. 43–59; Gian Luca Gardini, *The Origins of Mercosur* (New York: Palgrave Macmillan, 2010); and

Rafael A. Porrata-Doria, Jr., *MERCOSUR—The Common Market of the Southern Cone* (Durham, NC: Carolina Academic Press, 2005).
On the proposed TPP see Amitendu Palit, *The Trans-Pacific Partnership, China and India* (New York: Routledge, 2014); C. L. Lim, Deborah K. Elms, and Patrick Low, *The Trans-Pacific Partnership* (New York: Cambridge University Press, 2012); and Peter A. Petri, Michael G. Plummer, and Fan Zhai, *The Trans-Pacific Partnership and Asia-Pacific Integration* (Washington, DC: Peterson Institute for International Economics, 2012).

NOTES

1. WTO, *World Trade Report—2011* (Geneva: WTO, 2011), p. 58.
2. Pravin Krishna, "Preferential Trade Agreements and the World Trade System," in Robert C. Feenstra and Alan M. Taylor, eds., *Globalization in an Age of Crisis* (Chicago, IL: University of Chicago Press, 2014), p. 135.
3. Jagdish Bhagwati, *Termites in the Trading System: How Preferential Agreements Undermine Free Trade* (New York: Oxford University Press, 2008), p. 88.
4. Jo-Ann Crawford and Robert V. Fiorentino, "The Changing Landscape of Regional Trade Agreements," Discussion Paper 8 (Geneva: WTO Secretariat Staff, 2005), p. 1.
5. Gerald K. Helleiner, "Considering U.S.–Mexico Free Trade," in Ricardo Grinspun and Maxwell A. Cameron, eds., *The Political Economy of North American Free Trade* (Montreal: McGill-Queen's University Press, 1993), pp. 50–51.
6. Andrew Hurrell, "Explaining the Resurgence of Regionalism in World Politics," *Review of International Studies* 21 (1995), p. 333.
7. See Bhagwati, *Termites in the Trading System.*
8. Mancur Olson, *The Logic of Collective Action: Public Goods and the Theory of Groups* (Cambridge, MA: Harvard University Press, 1965).
9. Hurrell, "Explaining the Resurgence of Regionalism in World Politics," pp. 345–347.
10. Fritz Machlup, *A History of Thought on Economic Integration* (New York: Columbia University Press, 1977).
11. Michael Kaser, *Comecon: Integration Problems of the Planned Economies* (London: Oxford University Press, 1965).
12. The European Economic Community's name was changed, first to the European Community, and then to the European Union.
13. Jagdish Bhagwati, "Regionalism and Multilateralism: An Overview," in Jaime de Melo and Arvind Panagariya, eds., *New Dimensions in Regional Integration* (New York: Cambridge University Press, 1993), pp. 28–29.
14. WTO, "Regional Trade Agreements: Facts and Figures," www.wto.org/english/tratop_e/region_e/regfac_e.htm (accessed May 31, 2015).
15. See Shintaro Hamanaka, "Study of Non-Notified Trade Agreements to the World Trade Organization: The Case of Asia and Pacific Region," Asian Development Bank Working Paper Series on Regional Integration, no. 132, May 2014.
16. World Trade Organization, *Understanding the WTO*, 3rd ed. rev. (Geneva: WTO, October 2005), pp. 67–68.
17. Bhagwati, "Regionalism and Multilateralism," pp. 29–31.
18. Joanne Gowa, "Bipolarity, Multipolarity, and Free Trade," *American Political Science Review* 83, no. 4 (December 1989), p. 1248.

19. Kenneth N. Waltz, *Theory of International Politics* (Reading, MA: Addison-Wesley, 1979), p. 70.
20. In 1960 the OEEC became the OECD, which also includes non-Europeans. Theodore H. Cohn, *Governing Global Trade: International Institutions in Conflict and Convergence* (Burlington, VT: Ashgate, 2002), pp. 37–41.
21. John J. Mearsheimer, "Back to the Future: Instability in Europe After the Cold War," *International Security* 15, no. 1 (1990), pp. 5–56; Mark A. Pollack, "International Relations Theory and European Integration," *Journal of Common Market Studies* 39, no. 2 (June 2001), pp. 222–223.
22. Hurrell, "Explaining the Resurgence of Regionalism in World Politics," pp. 341–342; Gowa, "Bipolarity, Multipolarity, and Free Trade", pp. 1245–1256.
23. Bhagwati, *Termites in the Trading System*, p. 44.
24. Inis L. Claude, Jr., *Swords into Plowshares: The Problems and Progress of International Organization*, 4th ed. (New York: Random House, 1971), p. 379; David Mitrany, *A Working Peace System* (Chicago, IL: Quadrangle Books, 1966).
25. Bernard M. Hoekman and Michel M. Kostecki, *The Political Economy of the World Trading System: The WTO and Beyond*, 2nd ed. (New York: Oxford University Press, 2001), pp. 347–352.
26. Marc L. Busch and Helen V. Milner, "The Future of the International Trading System: International Firms, Regionalism, and Domestic Politics," in Richard Stubbs and Geoffrey R. D. Underhill, eds., *Political Economy and the Changing Global Order* (Toronto: McClelland & Stewart, 1994), p. 270.
27. Michael Hart, *A North American Free Trade Agreement: The Strategic Implications for Canada* (Halifax, NS: Institute for Research on Public Policy, 1990), pp. 45–46.
28. Duncan Cameron, "Introduction," in Duncan Cameron and Mel Watkins, eds., *Canada Under Free Trade* (Toronto: Lorimer, 1993), p. xxi.
29. GATT, *Text of the General Agreement* (Geneva: GATT, July 1986), Article 24.
30. Hoekman and Kostecki, *The Political Economy of the World Trading System*, pp. 350–363; Robert Z. Lawrence, *Regionalism, Multilateralism, and Deeper Integration* (Washington, DC: Brookings Institution, 1996), pp. 41–42.
31. Gardner Patterson, *Discrimination in International Trade: The Policy Issues: 1945–1965* (Princeton, NJ: Princeton University Press, 1966), pp. 146–147.
32. Richard E. Baldwin, "A Domino Theory of Regionalism," in Richard Baldwin, Pertti Haaparanta, and Jaakko Kiander, eds., *Expanding Membership of the European Union* (New York: Cambridge University Press, 1995), p. 45.
33. Bhagwati, "Regionalism and Multilateralism," pp. 25–26; World Trade Organization Secretariat, *Regionalism and the World Trading System* (Geneva: WTO, April 1995), p. 7.
34. Robert E. Hudec, *The GATT Legal System and World Trade Diplomacy* (New York: Praeger, 1975), pp. 195–196; J. Michael Finger, "GATT's Influence on Regional Arrangements," in Jaime de Melo and Arvind Panagariya, eds., *New Dimensions in Regional Integration* (New York: Cambridge University Press, 1993), pp. 136–137.
35. WTO Secretariat, *Regionalism and the World Trading System*, pp. 12–13.
36. Robert E. Hudec, "Discussion," in Jaime de Melo and Arvind Panagariya, eds., *New Dimensions in Regional Integration* (New York: Cambridge University Press, 1993), p. 152.
37. WTO Secretariat, *Regionalism and the World Trading System*, pp. 16–17; Gary C. Hufbauer and Jeffrey J. Schott, *NAFTA: An Assessment*, rev. ed. (Washington, DC: Institute for International Economics, 1993), p. 112.

38. WTO, *The Results of the Uruguay Round of Multilateral Trade Negotiations—The Legal Texts* (Geneva: WTO, 1994), pp. 31–34, 331–332.
39. Hudec, *The GATT Legal System and World Trade Diplomacy*, pp. 205–206.
40. Olivier Long, *Law and Its Limitations in the GATT Multilateral Trade System* (Dordrecht, The Netherlands: Nijhoff, 1985), p. 101; Sam Laird, "Regional Trade Agreements: Dangerous Liaisons?" *World Economy* 22, no. 9 (1999), p. 1196.
41. Martin Holland, *The European Union and the Third World* (London: Palgrave, 2002), pp. 25–32.
42. Matthew McQueen, "ACP-EU Trade Cooperation after 2000: An Assessment of Reciprocal Trade Preferences," *Journal of Modern African Studies* 36, no. 4 (1998), p. 669; Richard Gibb, "Post-Lomé: The European Union and the South," *Third World Quarterly* 21, no. 3 (2000), pp. 457–467.
43. Bonapas F. Onguglo, "Developing Countries and Trade Preferences," in Rodriguez Mendoza, Patrick Low, and Barbara Kotschwar, eds., *Trade Rules in the Making: Challenges in Regional and Multilateral Negotiations* (Washington, DC: Brookings Institution, 1999), p. 119.
44. Francis A. S. T. Matambalya and Susanna Wolf, "The Cotonou Agreement and the Challenges of Making the New EU-ACP Trade Regime WTO Compatible," *Journal of World Trade* 35, no. 1 (2001), pp. 123–144.
45. WTO Secretariat, *Regionalism and the World Trading System*, pp. 27–29.
46. On the EU institutions see Helen Wallace, Mark A. Pollack, and Alasdair R. Young, eds., *Policy-Making in the European Union*, 6th ed. (New York: Oxford University Press, 2010), pp. 69–104.
47. Birol A. Yeşilada and David M. Wood, *The Emerging European Union*, 5th ed. (New York: Longman, 2010), chs. 4 and 9.
48. Fabio Wasserfallen, "Political and Economic Integration in the EU: The Case of Failed Tax Harmonization," *Journal of Common Market Studies* 52, no. 2 (2014), p. 420.
49. Thomas C. Fischer, *The United States, the European Union, and the "Globalization" of World Trade* (Westport, CT: Quorum Books, 2000), p. 136.
50. Enzo R. Grilli, *The European Community and the Developing Countries* (New York: Cambridge University Press, 1993), pp. 7–8, 296–316.
51. Erik Faucompret and Jozef Konings, "The Integration of Central and Eastern Europe in the European Union," *Journal of World Trade* 33, no. 6 (December 1999), pp. 121–127; Pier C. Padoan, "The Changing European Political Economy," in Richard Stubbs and Geoffrey R. D. Underhill, eds., *Political Economy and the Changing Global Order* (Toronto: McClelland & Stewart, 1994), pp. 340–342.
52. Quoted in "Arguments for Enlargement," *The Economist*, August 3, 1996, p. 41.
53. "A Divided Union," in "A Survey of the European Union," *Economist*, September 25, 2004, p. 4; Amy Verdun and Osvaldo Croci, eds., *Institutional and Policy-Making Challenges to the European Union in the Wake of Eastern Enlargement* (Manchester, UK: Manchester University Press, 2004).
54. Heather Grabbe, "Six Lessons of Enlargement Ten Years On: The EU's Transformative Power in Retrospect and Prospect," *Journal of Common Market Studies* 52, Annual Review (2014), p. 41.
55. Grabbe, "Six Lessons of Enlargement Ten Years On," p. 54.
56. See Antje Wiener and Thomas Diez, eds., *European Integration Theory*, 2nd ed. (New York: Oxford University Press, 2009), p. 11.
57. Ernst Haas, *The Uniting of Europe: Political, Social and Economical Forces 1950–1957* (London: Stevens & Sons, 1958), p. 16.

58. Ben Rosamond, *Theories of European Integration* (New York: St. Martin's Press, 2000), pp. 50–73.

59. Andrew Moravcsik, *The Choice for Europe: Social Purpose and State Power from Messina to Maastricht* (Ithaca, NY: Cornell University Press, 1998), p. 501.

60. Clive Archer, *The European Union* (New York: Routledge, 2008), pp. 8–17; Young J. Choi and James A. Caporaso, "Comparative Regional Integration," in Walter Carlsnaes, Thomas Risse, and Beth A. Simmons, eds., *Handbook of International Relations* (Thousand Oaks, CA: SAGE, 2002), pp. 485–491.

61. Hans Vollaard, "Explaining European Disintegration," *Journal of Common Market Studies* 52, no. 5 (September 2014), p. 1143.

62. Kathleen J. Hancock, *Regional Integration: Choosing Plutocracy* (New York: Palgrave Macmillan, 2009), p. 31.

63. Jack L. Granatstein, "Free Trade Between Canada and the United States," in Dennis Stairs and Gilbert R. Winham, eds., *The Politics of Canada's Economic Relationship with the United States*, vol. 29, Royal Commission on the Economic Union and Development Prospect for Canada (Toronto: University of Toronto Press, 1985), p. 11.

64. "U.S. Trade Act of 1974, as amended (Public Law 93-618)," Title VI, section 612, in *Legislation on Foreign Relations Through 1989* (Washington, DC: U.S. Government Printing Office, 1990), p. 456.

65. John Whalley, "Regional Trade Arrangements in North America: CUSTA and NAFTA," in Jaime de Melo and Arvind Panagariya, eds., *New Dimensions in Regional Integration* (New York: Cambridge University Press, 1993), pp. 352–353; Carol Wise, "Unfulfilled Promise: Economic Convergence under NAFTA," in Isabel Studer and Carol Wise, eds., *Requiem or Revival? The Promise of North American Integration* (Washington, DC: Brookings Institution, 2007), p. 28.

66. Isabel Studer, "Obstacles to Integration: NAFTA's Institutional Weaknesses," in Isabel Studer and Carol Wise, eds., *Requiem or Revival? The Promise of North American Integration* (Washington, DC: Brookings Institution, 2007), pp. 53–58.

67. Gary Clyde Hufbauer, Cathleen Cimino, and Tyler Moran, "NAFTA at 20: Misleading Charges and Positive Achievements," Peterson Institute for International Economics, no. PB14-13, May 2014, p. 1.

68. Bernard Hoekman and Pierre Sauvé, "Liberalizing Trade in Services," *World Bank Discussion Papers*, no. 243 (Washington, DC: World Bank, 1994).

69. U.S. Department of Commerce, International Trade Administration, "NAFTA 20 Years Later," n.d.

70. Hufbauer, Cimino, and Moran, "NAFTA at 20," p. 16.

71. Hufbauer, Cimino, and Moran, "NAFTA at 20," p. 16.

72. Jeffrey J. Schott, "Trade Negotiations Among NAFTA Partners: The Future of North American Economic Integration," in Isabel Studer and Carol Wise, eds., *Requiem or Revival? The Promise of North American Integration* (Washington, DC: Brookings Institution, 2007), p. 86.

73. Alan S. Alexandroff, Gary C. Hufbauer, and Krista Lucenti, "Still Amigos: A Fresh Canada-US Approach to Reviving NAFTA," C.D. Howe Institute, The Border Papers, no. 274, September 2008, p. 1.

74. Jon R. Johnson, *The North American Free Trade Agreement—A Comprehensive Guide* (Aurora, Ont.: Canada Law Book, 1994), p. 512.

75. Pardee Center Task Force Report, *The Future of North American Policy: Lessons from NAFTA*, Boston University, November 2009, p. 5.

76. David Spener and Randy Capps, "North American Free Trade and Changes in the Nativity of the Garment Industry Workforce in the United States," *International Journal of Urban and Regional Research* 25, no. 2 (June 2001), p. 320.

77. Public Citizen's Global Trade Watch, "NAFTA's 20-Year Legacy and the Fate of the Trans-Pacific Partnership," February 2014, p. 26.

78. Mark E. Rupert, "(Re) Politicizing the Global Economy: Liberal Common Sense and Ideological Struggle in the US NAFTA Debate," *Review of International Political Economy* 2, no. 4 (Autumn 1995), pp. 679–681.

79. Jennifer Clapp and Peter Dauvergne, *Paths to a Green World*, 2nd ed. (Cambridge, MA: MIT Press, 2011), p. 158.

80. Kevin P. Gallagher, "NAFTA and the Environment: Lessons from Mexico and Beyond," in Pardee Center Task Force Report, *The Future of North American Policy*, pp. 61–69.

81. Gary C. Hufbauer and Jeffrey J. Schott, *NAFTA Revisited: Achievements and Challenges* (Washington, DC: Institute for International Economics, 2005), p. 183; Hufbauer and Schott, *NAFTA: An Assessment*, pp. 157–163; Jennifer Clapp and Peter Dauvergne, *Paths to a Green World: The Political Economy of the Global Environment* (Cambridge, MA: MIT Press, 2005), pp. 151–152.

82. M. Angeles Villarreal and Ian F. Fergusson, "The North American Free Trade Agreement," Congressional Research Service Report, April 16, 2015, p. 1.

83. Jeffrey Cason, "On the Road to Southern Cone Economic Integration," *Journal of Interamerican Studies and World Affairs* 42, no. 1 (2000), pp. 23–28.

84. Sergio Caballero Santos, "Identity in Mercosur: Regionalism and Nationalism," *Global Governance* 21 (2015), pp. 47–50; Mario E. Carranza, "Can Mercosur Survive? Domestic and International Constraints on Mercosur," *Latin American Politics and Society* 45, no. 2 (Summer 2003), p. 94.

85. Rafael A. Porrata-Doria, Jr., *MERCOSUR—The Common Market of the Southern Cone* (Durham, NC: Carolina Academic Press, 2005), p. 41.

86. Sebastian Krapohl, "Financial Crises as Catalysts for Regional Cooperation? Chances and Obstacles for Financial Integration in ASEA+3, Mercosur and the Eurozone," *Contemporary Politics* 21, no. 2 (2015), p. 169; Michael Mecham, "Mercosur: A Failing Development Project?" *International Affairs* 79, no. 2 (March 2003), pp. 377–379.

87. Donald G. Richards, "Dependent Development and Regional Integration: A Critical Examination of the Southern Cone Common Market," *Latin American Perspectives* 24, no. 6 (November 1997), p. 133.

88. Bryan Mercurio, "The Trans-Pacific Partnership: Suddenly a 'Game-Changer'," *World Economy* 37, no. 11 (November 2014), pp. 1558–1574.

89. Kent Jones, *Reconstructing the World Trade Organization for the 21st Century* (New York: Oxford University Press, 2015), pp. 169–171.

90. Paola Conconi, Giovanni Facchini, and Marizio Zanardi, "Fast-Track Authority and International Trade Negotiations," *American Economic Journal* 4, no. 3 (August 2012), pp. 146–189.

91. Megumi Naoi and Shujiro Urata, "Free Trade Agreements and Domestic Politics: The Case of the Trans-Pacific Partnership Agreement," *Asian Economic Policy Review* 8 (2013), p. 326; William A. Kerr, "Negotiating in Disequilibrium: Can a Trans-Pacific Partnership Be Achieved as Potential Partners Proliferate?" *The Estey Centre Journal of International Law and Trade Policy* 14, no. 2 (2013), pp. 1–12.

92. Jeffrey D. Wilson, "Mega-Regional Trade Deals in the Asia-Pacific: Choosing Between the TPP and RCEP?" *Journal of Contemporary Asia* 45, no. 2 (2015),

p. 352; Mireya Solis, "The Trans-Pacific Partnership: Can the United States Lead the Way in Asia-Pacific Integration?" *Pacific Focus* 27, no. 3 (December 2012), p. 319.

93. Ashley J. Tellis, "The Geopolitics of the TTIP and the TPP," *Adelphi Series* 54, no. 450 (March 2, 2015), pp. 93–120; Jones, *Reconstructing the World Trade Organization*, pp. 180–183.

94. Bhagwati, *Termites in the Trading System*, pp. xii and 18.

95. Frederick M. Abbott, "A New Dominant Trade Species Emerges: Is Bilateralism a Threat?" *Journal of International Economic Law* 10, no. 3 (September 2007), p. 583.

96. Hufbauer and Schott, *NAFTA: An Assessment*, p. 113.

97. Hufbauer and Schott, *NAFTA Revisited*, p. 24.

98. Paul Wonnacott and Mark Lutz, "Is There a Case for Free Trade Areas?" in Jeffrey J. Schott, ed., *Free Trade Areas and U.S. Trade Policy* (Washington, DC: Institute for International Economics, 1989), pp. 69–72; Matthew Schaefer, "Ensuring That Regional Trade Agreements Complement the WTO System: US Unilateralism a Supplement to WTO Initiatives?" *Journal of International Economic Law* 10, no. 3 (September 2007), pp. 585–603.

99. Helen Cabalu and Cristina Alfonso, "Does AFTA Create or Divert Trade?" *Global Economy Journal* 7, no. 4 (2007), p. 3.

100. Renato Ruggiero, Director-General of the World Trade Organization, "Charting the Trade Routes of the Future: Towards a Borderless Economy," address to the International Industrial Conference, San Francisco, September 29, 1997, *World Trade Organization Press Release* (Geneva: Press/77), p. 4.

Multinational Corporations and Global Production

The largest **multinational corporations** (**MNCs**) are in many respects the main agents of globalization. They produce and distribute goods and services across national borders; plan their operations on a global scale; and spread ideas, tastes, and technology throughout the world. MNCs are firms that own assets and conduct business activities in more than one country. MNC parent firms in *home* countries acquire foreign assets by investing in affiliate or subsidiary firms in *host* countries. This is **foreign direct investment** (**FDI**), which involves management rights and control. **Portfolio investment,** by contrast, is investment without control; it involves the purchase of bonds, money market instruments, or stocks simply to realize a financial return. The growing importance of FDI testifies to the role of MNCs as agents of globalization. **FDI flows,** or the value of FDI in a single year, have generally increased, but sometimes they decline because of international developments. For example, global FDI inflows declined from $1.47 trillion in 2013 to $1.23 trillion in 2014 because investors reacted cautiously to a fragile global economy and increased geopolitical risks. **FDI stock** refers to the net accumulated value of FDI resulting from past flows. In 2014, for example, global inward FDI stock was valued at $26.0 trillion. Foreign affiliates of MNCs employed about 75 million people in 2014, and more than one-third of world trade occurs as *intra-firm trade* (international trade between a parent firm and its affiliates). International production is also fairly concentrated. Although the world's 100 largest MNCs represent only about 0.13 percent of the total number of MNCs, in 2011 they accounted for 9.3 percent of the foreign assets, 21 percent of the foreign sales, and 14.4 percent of the employment of all MNCs. However, smaller companies are finding it easier to become MNCs because of advances in information and communication technologies.[1] As discussed, FDI flows have declined in some years, and the IMF reported in 2015 that "Private fixed investment in advanced economies contracted sharply during the global financial crisis and there has been little recovery since."[2] MNCs can also decline. For example, no one predicted that General Motors would fall to the level it did during the global financial crisis. One-third of the corporations in the Fortune 500 list of the largest U.S. corporations in 1980 were no longer on the list in 1990 because of decline, acquisition, or bankruptcy. Despite these reversals, FDI inflows have generally grown much faster than trade or income. From 1985 to 1999, the growth rates of global GDP, exports, and FDI inflows were 2.5, 5.6, and 17.7 percent, respectively.[3] The growing importance of MNCs has caused some analysts to argue that the critical problem in IPE today "is the tension between states and multinationals, not states and markets."[4] However, MNCs receive less attention because most IR scholars focus on relations among governments. Limited amounts of reliable data also hinder efforts to study MNCs, because they are reluctant to provide information and adept at obscuring their activities. This problem is compounded by the fact that IOs regulate monetary, trade, and development activities but not foreign investment. Furthermore, MNCs evoke strong positive and negative reactions; in debates about MNCs it is common for "anecdote to replace data" and "the witty phrase to replace analysis."[5]

In this age of globalization, liberals often view MNCs and private banks as "the major weavers of the world economy."[6] Liberals also believe that FDI stimulates innovation, competition, economic growth, and employment, and that MNCs provide countries with capital, technology, managerial skills, and marketing networks. Historical materialists also refer to the growing power of MNCs, but they see corporate managers as a transnational class that maintains and defends the capitalist system. They also view MNCs as predatory monopolists that overcharge for their goods and services, limit the flow of technology, create dependency relationships with LDC host countries, and impose downward pressures on labor and environmental standards. Neomercantilists are more inclined to downgrade the political importance of MNCs; they see the most powerful states as having considerable control over their MNCs, and MNCs as retaining close ties with their home governments.[7]

DEFINITIONS AND TERMINOLOGY

An MNC is usually defined as a firm that acquires ownership and control of affiliates in at least two countries. However, the question arises as to what constitutes "control." The U.S. Department of Commerce and IOs such as the IMF and OECD set a minimum of 10 percent equity ownership for a firm to exercise control. However, the 10 percent figure does not *necessarily* confer control. If equity is widely distributed among many shareholders, 10 percent may be sufficient, but if there are a small number of large shareholders a much higher percent of the shares may be necessary to exert control. The important point is that a shareholder can exercise control without holding a majority of shares. Foreign affiliates may be minority-owned (10–50 percent of equity), majority-owned (more than 50 but less than 100 percent), or wholly owned (100 percent) subsidiaries. It is also important to note that equity ownership alone is not sufficient to exert control. The firm must also have the technological and organizational skills to "plan, organize, coordinate and control production" in other countries.[8] A firm can undertake FDI in a host country in two forms: **greenfield investment,** or the creation of new facilities and productive assets by foreigners; and *mergers and acquisitions (M&As)*, or the purchase of stocks in an existing firm with the purpose of participating in its management. In a *cross-border merger*, the assets and operations of two firms belonging to different countries are combined to establish a new legal entity. In an *acquisition*, a local firm becomes an affiliate or subsidiary of a foreign firm. During the past decade, most growth in international production has occurred through M&As rather than greenfield investment, and acquisitions are much more common than mergers.[9]

Differences exist not only over definitions but also over the use of the term *MNC*. The United Nations and a number of scholars prefer the term *transnational* to *multinational* because the ownership and control of most firms is not really multinational; a firm normally extends its operations from a single home country across national frontiers. Most MNCs are in fact *ethnocentric* or home-country-oriented, with directives flowing from the headquarters to the affiliates and much of the MNC's R&D located in the home country. However, a small but growing number of MNCs are *geocentric* or *stateless*; they adopt a worldwide approach and are not closely tied to a single state. Strategic alliances among MNCs from different states further complicate the task of associating an MNC with a home government; they may take the form of production-sharing agreements, or collaborative research and networking arrangements. Finally, MNCs sometimes gain entry into a foreign country by agreeing to form *joint ventures* with local firms; joint ventures are increasingly common in LDCs and transition economies. This text uses the term *MNC* simply to signify that a firm has ongoing managerial and productive activities in more than one country.[10]

WHY DO FIRMS BECOME MNCS?

John Dunning developed a seminal theory that firms engage in FDI for reasons of ownership, location, and internalization, and the following discussion draws partly on his ideas.[11] To understand why firms become MNCs, we must distinguish between horizontal and vertical integration. A *horizontally integrated MNC* extends its operations abroad by producing the same product or product line in its foreign affiliates. Firms engage in **horizontal integration** to defend or increase their market share. Although a firm's exports from the home country may initially meet the foreign demand for products and services, the firm may have to set up a subsidiary to compete with new local suppliers. The MNC can compete more effectively with local firms through its subsidiaries because they have lower transportation costs and become more aware of the market's special characteristics; and labor costs are lower if a DC firm produces directly in LDC markets. Firms also engage in horizontal integration because of foreign government policies. When a government's tariffs and NTBs limit exports from a firm's home country, it may establish foreign operations to get behind the trade barriers. For example, Honda began to produce automobiles in the United States when the U.S. government imposed voluntary export restraints on Japanese auto imports in the 1980s. National and subnational governments also provide investment incentives to encourage firms to locate production facilities in their territories.[12]

A *vertically integrated MNC* geographically separates the different stages of production, with the outputs of some affiliates serving as inputs to other affiliates. Firms engage in **vertical integration** to gain the benefits of comparative advantage in the production process. For example, an electronics firm can lower production costs by locating assembly operations in low-wage LDCs, chip production in an NIE such as Singapore, and high-end R&D operations in California. Vertically integrated MNCs can also gain control of uncertain transactions at various stages of the production process by *internalizing* them within the firm. Firms opt for *backward integration* when raw materials and other production inputs they require are not readily available or have high transaction costs. Examples of backward integration include steel firm investments in iron ore operations, oil company investments in the extraction of crude oil, and rubber manufacturer investments in natural rubber plantations. Backward integration also enables MNCs to gain control over the quality of inputs. For example, three vertically integrated MNCs accounted for 60 percent of the banana export trade during the 1980s, because bananas are highly perishable and require specific handling and ripening conditions. MNCs also engage in *forward vertical integration* to reduce uncertainty and transaction costs, and to ensure the quality of goods and services that reach the consumer.[13] Another reason firms engage in vertical integration is to limit competition. When a small number of MNCs control the raw materials for an industry, they can impose stiff barriers to the entry of new rival firms. MNCs also engage in vertical integration to limit government scrutiny of their activities. For example, MNCs sometimes manipulate their **transfer prices** (the prices an MNC's affiliates charge for the *internal* sales of goods and services) without detection by governments. Transfer prices help an MNC efficiently manage its internal operations and monitor the performance of its affiliates; but they can also enable an MNC to shift its reported profits from high-tax to low-tax countries (and thus avoid paying some taxes) by raising or lowering the prices charged by each affiliate. In 1993 the U.S. Internal Revenue Service ruled that Nissan Motor Company used transfer prices to underreport its U.S. income, and Nissan had to pay the United States about $150 million.[14]

Firms that become MNCs must have the ability as well as incentive to make the transition. Innovations in communications, transportation, and technology have enabled firms to internationalize, and they are more successful if they can "think globally" and "act locally." On the one hand, large MNCs have advantages such as economies of scale, brand-name reputation, and access to global financing and inputs such as raw materials. On the other hand, MNCs operate in a world of states in which they must adhere to national laws and cater to the demands of local consumers.[15]

THE HISTORICAL DEVELOPMENT OF FDI

Although the rapid expansion of MNCs is a post-World War II phenomenon, some scholars trace the origin of MNCs to the transborder business operations of medieval banks in fifteenth-century Florence. During the sixteenth to eighteenth centuries, international trading companies such as the English, Dutch, and French East India Companies and the Hudson's Bay Company also coordinated cross-border business activities. In the nineteenth century, firms that are commonly considered to be MNCs were investing in a number of countries; thousands of these MNCs existed by the time of World War II.[16] A number of factors have affected the growth—and sometimes the contraction—of MNC activity:

- MNC activity increases when advances in communications, transportation, and technology facilitate MNC control over foreign operations.
- Rapid economic growth often stimulates MNC expansion, whereas depressed economic conditions have the opposite effect.
- MNC expansion depends on national and international rules and events. For example, the rules protecting private property encouraged FDI, whereas major wars had a depressing effect on FDI.
- Capital liberalization leads to increased FDI; capital and exchange controls discourage FDI.
- FDI often contracts in response to financial crises, but it may expand in response to trade protectionism because MNCs shift production abroad to circumvent trade barriers.

The following discussion focuses on three periods: pre-World War II, the mid-1940s to mid-1980s, and 1990 to the present.

The Pre-World War II Period

According to earlier studies, *portfolio* investment accounted for most of the long-term capital flows during the nineteenth and early twentieth centuries. However, economists upgraded their estimate of foreign *direct* investment flows after refining their definitions. Thus, some studies indicate that FDI accounted for up to 45 percent of British foreign investment in 1913 and 1914.[17] As the first country to industrialize, Britain was the main force behind FDI growth during the nineteenth century. Although there were no government guarantees or international institutions to provide safeguards, investments were fairly secure for several reasons: Economic risk was lower under the pre-World War I gold standard because currencies were convertible and exchange rates were fairly stable; political risk was lower because a large share of European investment was in colonial territories operating under home country rules; there were no major restrictions on capital flows; and wars were limited in scope. The nineteenth century was also a period of rapid advances in rail and sea transport and communications, which facilitated the expansion of FDI. Although FDI continued to increase in the twentieth century, there was an investment downturn after World War I because of global economic and political instability. For example, a number of countries imposed restrictions on inward FDI, the Soviet Union nationalized foreign property, and the gold exchange standard was suspended. FDI contracted further during the Great Depression and World War II, and MNCs accounted for a smaller share of world economic activity in 1949 than in 1929. It was not until after World War II that the vigorous growth of MNCs and FDI would resume.[18]

The Mid-1940s to Mid-1980s

The United States overtook Britain as the leading source of FDI after World War II. As Table 10.1 shows, U.S. firms accounted for 47.1 percent of outward FDI stock in 1960, compared with Britain's 18.3 percent. FDI expanded rapidly under U.S. leadership because the North had sustained economic growth from 1950 to 1973; there were major improvements in international transportation and communications; and most DCs relaxed their controls over FDI after their currencies became convertible. (A notable exception was Japan, which continued to restrict foreign investment.) Since the late 1960s, the U.S. share of outward FDI has declined steadily, partly because of Japan and Germany's rapid economic growth as they recovered from the war. Thus, Table 10.1 shows that the U.S. share of outward FDI stock fell from 47.1 percent in 1960 to 32.3 percent in 1985, whereas Japan's share rose from 0.7 to 6.0 percent, and West Germany's share rose from 1.2 to 8.1 percent. Table 10.1 also shows that DCs were the source of most outward FDI stock: 99 percent in 1960 and 90 percent in 1985. However, MNCs based in the South increased their share of outward FDI stock from only 1 percent in 1960 to 10 percent in 1985. Most of this FDI came from Asian and Latin American LDCs and OPEC countries. The five largest LDC sources of outward FDI stock in 1985 were Brazil, South Africa, Argentina, Singapore, and Hong Kong.[19]

Table 10.2 shows that the DCs were also the largest recipients of FDI, accounting for 58.6 percent of inward FDI stock in 1985. Whereas the U.S. share of outward FDI stock was declining, its share of inward FDI stock increased from 12 percent in 1980 to 19 percent in 1985. Japan was the only DC with an extremely low share of inward FDI stock, at 0.5 percent in 1985, because of its governmental, societal, and cultural investment barriers. The South had received over 60 percent of total FDI before World War II, but this figure fell after the war because of LDC demands for more control over their natural resources, the 1980s foreign debt crisis, a gradual shift in FDI from primary products to manufacturing, and an increase in technology-related investment in the North. Among the LDCs, the most prosperous states received the most FDI. Thus, Table 10.2 shows that the share of FDI stock directed to Africa, which has many LLDCs, declined from 4.6 percent in 1980 to 3.5 percent in 1985. Asian and Latin American LDCs, by contrast, received 30 and 8.2 percent of total inward FDI stock in 1985. The five largest LDC recipients of inward FDI stock in 1985 were Hong Kong, Brazil, Indonesia, Saudi Arabia,

TABLE 10.1

Outward FDI Stock (U.S.$ billions)

	1960 Value	1960 %	1975 Value	1975 %	1985 Value	1985 %	1990 Value	1990 %	2000 Value	2000 %	2014 Value	2014 %
United States	31.9	47.1	124.2	44.0	238.4	32.3	731.8	32.5	2,694.0	36.9	6,318.6	24.4
Japan	0.5	0.7	15.9	5.7	44	6.0	201.4	8.9	278.4	3.8	1,193.1	4.6
Germany[a]	0.8	1.2	18.4	6.5	59.9	8.1	308.7	13.7	541.9	7.4	1,583.3	6.1
United Kingdom	12.4	18.3	37	13.1	100.3	13.6	229.3	10.2	923.4	12.7	1,584.1	6.1
France	4.1	6.1	10.6	3.8	37.8	5.1	119.9	5.3	365.9	5.0	1,279.1	4.9
Italy	1.1	1.6	2	3.3	16.6	2.2	60.2	2.7	170.0	2.3	548.4	2.1
Canada	2.5	3.7	3.5	10.4	43.1	5.8	84.8	3.8	237.6	3.3	714.5	2.8
Total G7[b]	53.3	78.7	219.8	77.9	540.1	73.1	1,736.1	77.0	5,211.2	71.4	13,221.0	51.1
Total DCs[c]	67	99.0	275.4	97.7	664.9	90.0	2,114.5	93.8	6,535.7	89.6	20,554.8	79.4
World Total	67.7	100	282	100	738.8	100	2,253.9	100	7,298.2	100	25,874.8	100

[a] The 1960 to 1985 data are for West Germany; [b] G7 = Group of Seven; [c] DCs = developed countries

Sources: Transnational Corporations in World Development: Trends and Prospects (New York: UN, 1988), Table 1.2, p. 24 (1960 and 1975 data); UNCTAD, *World Investment Report 2004* (New York: UN, 2004), Annex Table B.4, p. 382 (1985 data); UNCTAD, *World Investment Report 2015* (New York: UN, 2014), Annex Table 2, pp. A7–A10 (1990, 2000, and 2014 data); http://unctad.org/en/PublicationsLibrary/wir2015_en.pdf

TABLE 10.2

Inward FDI Stock (U.S.$ billions)

	1980		1985		1990		2000		2014	
	Value	%	Value	%	Value	%	Value	%	Value	%
DCs[a]	390.7	56.4	569.7	58.6	1,687.6	76.8	5,476.6	76.0	17,003.8	65.3
United States	83.0	12.0	184.6	19.0	539.6	24.6	2,783.2	38.6	5,409.9	20.8
Japan	3.3	0.4	4.7	0.5	9.8	0.4	50.3	0.7	170.6	0.7
Germany[c]	36.6	5.2	36.9	3.8	226.5	10.3	271.6	3.8	743.5	2.9
United Kingdom	63.0	9.1	64.0	6.6	203.9	9.3	463.1	6.4	1662.9	6.4
France	25.9	3.7	36.7	3.8	104.3	4.7	184.2	2.6	729.1	2.8
Italy	8.9	1.3	19.0	2.9	60.0	2.7	122.5	1.7	373.7	1.4
Canada	54.2	7.8	64.7	6.7	112.8	5.1	212.7	3.0	631.3	2.4
LDCs[b]	302.0	43.6	402.5	41.4	510.1	23.2	1,669.8	23.2	8,310.0	31.9
Africa	32.0	4.6	33.8	3.5	60.7	2.8	153.7	2.1	709.2	2.7
Asia	218.3	31.5	287.3	30.0	342.2	15.6	1,055.1	14.6	5,707.3	21.9
Latin America and Caribbean	50.4	7.3	80.1	8.2	107.2	4.9	461.0	6.4	1,893.5	7.3
World Total	692.7	100.0	972.2	100.0	2,197.8	100.0	7,202.3	100.0	26,038.8	100.0

[a] DCs = developed countries; [b] LDCs = less developed countries; [c] 1980 and 1985 data are for West Germany.

Sources: UNCTAD, *World Investment Report 2004* (New York: UN, 2004), Annex Table B.3, pp. 376–380 (1980 and 1985 data); UNCTAD, *World Investment Report 2014* (New York: UN, 2014), Annex Table 2, pp. A7–A10 (1990, 2000, and 2014 data); http://unctad.org/en/ PublicationsLibrary/wir2014_en.pdf

and Mexico. Eastern Europe and the Soviet Union received almost no FDI from 1975 to 1985.[20] Thus, DCs were directing most of the FDI in the mid-1980s to each other, and many LDCs were marginalized.

1990 to the Present

FDI flows declined during the 2008 global financial crisis because of decreased access to finance, negative market prospects, and risk aversion by investors. However, global FDI flows *on average* have increased dramatically since the 1990s. Even in 2008 and 2009 the internationalization of production continued, because the decline in MNC sales was more limited than the contraction of the global economy. Thus, Table 10.3 shows that inward and outward FDI stock as a share of the GDPs of DCs increased from 8.9 and 11.2 percent in 1990 to 36.4 and 47.1 percent in 2013. A number of factors account for the rapid

TABLE 10.3

Share of Inward and Outward FDI Stock as a Percent of GDP[a]

	1990	1995	2000	2005	2010	2013
DCs[b]						
Inward	8.9	11.0	22.4	25.1	31.7	36.4
Outward	11.2	14.7	28.0	31.9	42.3	47.1
United States						
Inward	9.4	13.7	26.9	21.4	22.7	29.4
Outward	12.7	18.5	26.0	27.6	31.9	37.8
Japan						
Inward	0.3	0.6	1.1	2.2	3.9	3.5
Outward	6.5	4.5	5.9	8.5	15.1	20.3
Germany						
Inward	6.5	6.6	14.4	17.2	21.7	23.4
Outward	8.8	10.6	28.7	33.5	44.3	47.0
U.K.						
Inward	20.1	17.3	31.0	36.7	49.5	63.3
Outward	22.6	26.3	61.8	52.4	71.3	74.3
France						
Inward	7.9	15.1	29.4	41.5	38.5	39.5
Outward	9.0	24.2	69.7	57.6	59.0	59.8
Italy						
Inward	5.3	5.8	11.1	13.3	16.0	19.5
Outward	5.3	9.4	15.4	13.7	23.8	28.9
Canada						
Inward	19.4	20.9	28.8	29.3	36.7	35.3
Outward	14.6	20.0	32.1	33.4	39.4	40.1

[a] GDP = gross domestic product; [b] DCs = developed countries.

Source: http://unctad.org/en/Pages/DIAE/World%20Investment%20Report/Annex-Tables.aspx.

growth of FDI. First, the emergence of neoliberalism with deregulation, privatization, and an end to restrictions on capital flows gave MNCs more freedom to expand their activities. Second, the breakup of the Soviet bloc opened up large new areas for FDI as the transition economies instituted market reforms, and China also became a major FDI recipient. Third, the protracted Uruguay and Doha Rounds of multilateral trade negotiations, combined with the use of NTBs, caused many MNCs to extend their activities abroad to circumvent trade barriers. Finally, significant advances in information and transportation technologies enabled MNCs to extend their global network.[21]

Although the DCs have the most outward FDI stock, their predominance has declined, and there have been some other notable changes. First, the United States lost its dominant position as a source of FDI. As Table 10.1 shows, the U.S. share of outward FDI stock fell from 44 percent in 1975 to 24.4 percent in 2014. Second, there were erratic changes in Japan's share of outward FDI. As Table 10.1 shows, Japan's share of outward FDI stock rose from 6 percent in 1985 to 8.9 percent in 1990. A strong Japanese yen as a result of the 1985 Plaza accord, combined with voluntary export restraints on Japanese goods, forced Japanese firms to invest and produce more abroad.[22] However, Japan's share of outward FDI stock fell back to 4.6 percent in 2014. Persistent economic recession and the financial problems of major Japanese banks led to changes in the corporate strategies of many Japanese MNCs, which made it difficult to expand abroad.[23] Table 10.3 shows that Japan's outward FDI stock accounted for 20.3 percent of its GDP in 2013, the lowest share of any G7 country. Third, as Table 10.1 shows, the DC share of outward FDI stock fell from 93.8 percent in 1990 to 79.4 percent in 2014. The 2008 financial crisis was a major factor contributing to an increase in the LDC and transition economy shares of outward FDI; this is especially evident from the data on yearly FDI outflows. Whereas LDCs and transition economies accounted for about 12 percent of global FDI outflows in 2000, their share rose to 39 percent in 2013. As Table 10.4 shows, four emerging economies ranked among the 10 largest sources of FDI outflows in 2014: Hong Kong, China; China; Russian Federation; and Singapore.[24]

There have also been some notable changes in inward FDI stock since 1990. First, Table 10.2 shows that the U.S. share of inward FDI stock steadily increased from 12 percent in 1980 to 38.6 percent in 2000. However, the U.S. share declined to 20.8 percent in 2014; this is concerning because inward FDI has become important for future U.S. prosperity. Several factors help to explain the recent downward trend: Some other countries give more incentives to MNCs to engage in offshore production; U.S. corporate taxes are higher than taxes in some other locations; and emerging economies such as China and Brazil have drawn increasing amounts of inward FDI away from the United States and other DCs. Second, Canada is the only G7 country whose share of inward FDI stock fell in all of the years listed in Table 10.2; overall, the Canadian share fell from 7.8 percent in 1980 to 2.4 percent in 2014. The U.S. share of Canada's inward FDI has declined from about 80 percent in 1980 to 60 percent, largely because of CUSFTA and NAFTA. Before free trade, U.S. MNCs often located inside Canada to avoid paying tariffs; but under NAFTA, a U.S. firm

TABLE 10.4

Foreign Direct Investment (FDI): Top 20 Host and Home Economies 2014 (billions of US dollars)

Inflows—Host			Outflows—Home		
Rank	$	Country	Rank	$	Country
1	128.5	China	1	336.9	United States
2	103.2	Hong Kong, China	2	142.7	Hong Kong, China
3	92.4	United States	3	116.0	China
4	72.2	United Kingdom	4	113.6	Japan
5	67.5	Singapore	5	112.2	Germany
6	62.5	Brazil	6	56.4	Russian Federation
7	53.9	Canada	7	52.6	Canada
8	51.8	Australia	8	42.9	France
9	34.4	India	9	40.8	Netherlands
10	30.2	Netherlands	10	40.7	Singapore
11	22.9	Chile	11	31.8	Ireland
12	22.9	Spain	12	30.7	Spain
13	22.8	Mexico	13	30.6	Korea
14	22.6	Indonesia	14	23.4	Italy
15	21.9	Switzerland	15	19.2	Norway
16	21.0	Russian Federation	16	16.8	Switzerland
17	18.6	Finland	17	16.4	Malaysia
18	16.0	Colombia	18	13.1	Kuwait
19	15.2	France	19	13.0	Chile
20	13.9	Poland	20	12.7	Taiwan

Sources: United Nations Conference on Trade and Development UNCRAD, World Investment Report 2015, Figure 1.3 FDI Inflows: top 20 host economies, and Figure 1.8 FDI outflows: top 20 home economies. http://unctad.org/en/PublicationsLibrary/wir2015_en.pdf

can produce in the United States or Mexico and freely export to Canada. Most importantly, there has been a major shift in the North American auto industry away from Canada and toward Mexico. Lower wages in Mexico and shifts in the auto industry toward the southern United States are two of the factors in this change. Canada has not attracted more FDI from non-U.S. sources because of problems with productivity, labor costs, and taxes.[25] Third, Japan continues to lack openness to inward FDI. Table 10.2 shows that Japan accounted for only 0.7 percent of inward FDI stock in 2014. Table 10.3 shows that inward FDI stock accounted for only 3.5 percent of Japan's GDP in 2013, well below the figures for the other G7 countries. Fourth, the DC share of inward FDI stock has declined, and the LDC share has increased, especially since the 2008 global financial crisis. Table 10.2 shows that the DC share of inward FDI stock fell from 76.8 percent in 1990 to 65.3 percent in 2014, whereas the LDC share rose from 23.2 to 31.9 percent during the same period. The (yearly) FDI inflow figures show the shift toward emerging economies much more clearly than the (cumulative) FDI stock figures. Table 10.4 shows that China replaced the United States as the top host economy for FDI inflows in 2014; Hong Kong, China placed second; and the United States placed third. Hong Kong serves as an important conduit for FDI to other parts of China and Asia. Table 10.4 also shows that four of the top six host economies for FDI inflows in 2014 were emerging economies: China, Hong Kong, Singapore, and Brazil. China and India are major candidates for inward FDI because they offer MNCs a huge supply of cheap labor, their workforces are becoming more educated and technologically skilled, and, in terms of numbers, they are the two largest consumer markets in the world.[26] In contrast to the large emerging economies, most Sub-Saharan African LDCs have been marginalized. Table 10.2 shows that Africa accounted for only 2.7 percent of inward FDI stock in 2014, compared with 21.9 percent for Asia and 7.3 percent for Latin America. East and Southeast Asia constitute the largest recipient region for FDI inflows in the world.

Another significant change is the increased importance of state-owned MNCs. Although state-owned MNCs comprise less than 1 percent of all MNCs, they account for over 11 percent of global FDI flows. A number of European countries and emerging economies are home to state-owned MNCs, some of which are among the largest MNCs in the world. State-owned MNCs have raised concerns in host countries about a level playing field and national security issues because of their government linkages. Another possible source of FDI is **sovereign wealth funds** (SWFs), which are "government investment funds, funded by foreign currency reserves but managed separately from official currency reserves."[27] The rapid growth of SWFs signifies a partial return to state capitalism after decades of privatization in the West. SWFs have existed at least since the 1950s, but they have grown dramatically in recent years because of financial globalization, imbalances in the global financial system, and the large surpluses of some states due to oil revenues. SWFs managed more than $7 trillion of assets in 2014, but they invested only $16 billion in FDI.[28]

The following sections examine the effects of MNCs on home and host states. Most of the discussion of host state–MNC relations is devoted to the LDCs, and much of the discussion of home state–MNC relations focuses on the advanced industrial states. However, China and some other emerging economies are also becoming important home states.

MNC–HOST COUNTRY RELATIONS: DETERMINANTS AND EFFECTS OF FDI

It is not always clear as to why firms direct FDI to one host state rather than another. For example, analysts disagree as to whether MNCs are more likely to invest in LDCs with democratic or authoritarian governments. Some analysts assume that democratic LDCs attract more FDI, because democratic institutions impose constraints on governments that decrease political risks and preserve MNCs' private property rights. Others assume that authoritarian LDCs attract more FDI, because autocratic leaders can repress labor unions, drive down wages, and shield MNCs from popular pressures for environmental controls. The results of empirical studies on this issue are inconclusive. For example, one study found that "regime type ... seems to have little impact on foreign investors"; a second study found that "empirically the results prove rather conclusive—democracies attract more FDI"; and a third study found that "in fifteen Latin American countries for the period of 1981 to 1996 ... abuse of civil liberties and political rights ... had a positive and statistically significant effect on inflows of U.S. FDI."[29] A major problem is that authors use different measures of democracy; whereas some focus on holding elections, others emphasize the rights of workers and peasants, freedom of the press, or economic rights and privileges. Thus, more research is needed to determine which types of countries attract FDI. Scholars also differ on the *effects* of FDI on host states. Orthodox liberals argue that MNCs contribute to LDC development by providing external capital, new technologies, and modern ideas that replace traditional social values. States have different factor endowments, and foreign investment goes to areas where it is most needed or in shortest supply. Thus, inward FDI compensates for inadequate local savings, export earnings, and foreign aid; tax revenues from MNC profits supplement local taxes; and MNCs fill LDC needs for imported technology. Although liberals acknowledge that a strong MNC presence may initially result in more income inequality, they attribute this to the positive effect of MNCs on income growth in general. This inequality is a temporary price to be paid for economic success, and the market will bring about more convergence of incomes over the long term.[30]

The first major challenge to orthodox liberal views came from two economists, Stephen Hymer (a Marxist) and Charles Kindleberger (a liberal). They argued that FDI cannot simply be equated with the movement of capital from home to host countries, because MNCs often finance their FDI by borrowing funds in the host countries. Although FDI supporters view free markets as promoting open competition, Hymer and Kindleberger noted that MNCs gain competitiveness by creating an oligopoly. For example, an MNC can raise barriers to the entry of other firms through its use of new technologies, economies of scale, and privileged access to global finance. Thus, Hymer wrote that "the industries in which there is much foreign investment tend to be concentrated industries, while the industries in which there is little or no foreign investment tend to be unconcentrated."[31] Drawing on Hymer's ideas, dependency theorists argue that MNCs appropriate local capital rather than bringing in new capital, prevent local firms from participating in the dynamic sectors of the economy, increase income inequalities in the host country, and use capital-intensive technologies that contribute to unemployment. They also assert that MNCs undermine host countries by co-opting local elites, imposing political and economic pressure (often with help from the home country), and altering consumer tastes and habits. Although Latin American and East Asian NIEs are industrializing, MNCs prevent these states from achieving genuine autonomous development; for example, one study claims that MNCs in Brazil keep "the innovative side of their businesses as close to home as possible" and ensure that "the industrialization of the periphery will remain partial."[32]

A number of studies indicate that MNC effects on host states are neither as positive nor as negative as neoliberal and dependency theorists maintain, and that a host state's options vary under different circumstances. For example, one factor affecting a host state's options is the amount of competition among investors; a host state has greater leverage if it has more investors to choose from. Although states have become more dependent on foreign investment, the diversity of investment sources has increased because U.S. MNCs have become less dominant and there are more European, Japanese, and Southern MNCs. Raymond Vernon's **obsolescing bargain model (OBM)** highlights another factor that can cause changes in a host state's relations with MNCs. A host state has a weak bargaining position before an MNC invests in it because the MNC can pursue other options and the host state must offer incentives to attract the initial investment. The MNC's bargaining power stems from its sophisticated technology, brand-name identification, access to capital, product diversity, and ability to promote exports. After the investment is made, however, the host state has more bargaining leverage because the MNC commits itself to some immobile resources. The host state can treat these resources as a "hostage," and it gains bargaining, technological, and managerial skills through spin-offs from the foreign investment. Thus, the host state may be able to renegotiate the original bargain and gain more favorable terms from the MNC.[33]

Three factors—fixed investments, new technologies, and brand-name identification—help determine whether an industry will be subject to the OBM. Regarding the first factor, the OBM is more applicable to projects that require large fixed investments. Although such projects initially give foreign investors considerable leverage, later the fixed investments can become hostage to the host state. MNCs with smaller fixed investments can more easily withdraw from the host state. A second factor is the type of technology used; MNCs using sophisticated technologies that are unavailable to the host state may be less vulnerable to aggressive host state policies at a later date. A third factor is the importance of product differentiation through advertising. When a firm's sales depend on brand identification and consumer loyalty, it is in a stronger position vis-à-vis the host state.[34] MNCs can employ various strategies to offset the risks of the OBM. They can decrease their vulnerability to host state pressures by vertical integration, because each host state will be involved in only part of the production process. MNCs can also decrease their vulnerability by establishing alliances with the local private sector in joint ventures. When MNCs become more firmly established in host states, they can gain political and economic support by creating linkages with local suppliers, distributors, and consumers. State-to-state interactions can also affect MNC–host state relations, and "first-tier bargaining" between the host and home states can give MNCs more influence in "second-tier" bargaining with host states.[35] For example, DC home states have induced LDC host states to liberalize their policies toward FDI through bilateral investment agreements (discussed later in this chapter) and conditions attached to IMF and World Bank structural adjustment loans.

Foreign investment in the oil industry is one example of how the OBM is more applicable in some periods than in others. There was strong evidence for the OBM in the 1970s and early 1980s when control over oil produced for the world market gradually shifted from the international oil companies to the LDC producers. From the mid-1980s, however, the international oil companies began to regain their leverage over LDC producers as oil prices declined; the oil companies found alternative investment options; and British Prime Minister Thatcher and U.S. President Reagan called for economic liberalization, privatization, and deregulation. Expropriation and nationalization in the natural resource industries declined sharply in the 1980s and 1990s, and a number of scholars concluded that the OBM had "outlived its usefulness."[36] However, there was a resurgence of resource nationalism when rising oil prices gave oil-exporting LDCs increased bargaining power, and the OBM regained some of its importance in explaining MNC–host state relations. In sum, theoretical models such as the OBM are more relevant in some periods than in others.

HOST COUNTRY POLICIES TOWARD MNCS

Host state policies toward MNCs vary widely, ranging from nationalization to efforts to attract MNCs with concessions and incentives; and many states have an "attraction-aversion dilemma" vis-à-vis FDI. For example, governments may welcome FDI in some sectors while limiting or blocking it in others (e.g., in defense or cultural industries). States may also try to impose obligations such as performance requirements on MNCs to maximize the benefits of FDI. Some federal governments follow restrictive policies toward foreign investment, while their subnational governments (e.g., states, provinces, or cities) compete with one another to attract FDI. Although countries seek the capital, technology, and organizational skills of MNCs, they may try to preserve large segments of the domestic market for local firms. The issue becomes even more complicated when a country's positive statements about FDI differ from the experiences of foreign investors.[37] The following sections discuss host state policies in the South and the North.

The South

The South imposed very few restrictions on MNCs before World War I. Colonial territories were open to investment from the imperial powers, and independent Latin American LDCs generally accepted the liberal view that foreign investment would further their economic development. Russia's nationalization of its oil industry after the 1917 revolution had an impact on LDC attitudes, with some shifting to more nationalist policies during the interwar period. However, the South's adoption of restrictive policies was more notable after World War II. In extreme cases, Communist regimes in China, North Korea, North Vietnam, and Cuba nationalized Western assets. In other cases, many newly independent states sought limits on FDI to preserve their national sovereignty. FDI often bred hostility because it involved foreign control over LDCs' natural resources and public utilities, and was associated with former colonial powers. However, LDCs had limited ability to capture a greater share of FDI benefits because they lacked experience in dealing with MNCs and had few sources of external finance. From 1946 to 1959, U.S. MNCs accounted for more than two-thirds of all new foreign-owned subsidiaries in the South.[38]

In the 1960s–1970s, LDCs were more activist and had more leverage for several reasons. The growing number of non-U.S. MNCs gave LDCs alternative sources of finance; FDI was often in natural resources, which were subject to the obsolescing bargain; OPEC's success in raising oil prices encouraged LDC activism vis-à-vis MNCs in general; dependency theorists encouraged the South to exert more pressure on MNCs; and LDCs increased their managerial, administrative, and technical abilities to regulate MNC behavior. Thus, nationalization of foreign firms became widespread in the petroleum and mining industries. LDCs also posed a major challenge to liberal economic views of FDI in the United Nations. In the 1950s–1960s, the liberal approach to FDI had emphasized national treatment, compensation to MNCs for any infringement of their privileges, and the right of MNCs to seek support from their home countries. By the late 1960s, however, LDCs were pressuring for agreements to restrict the rights of MNCs, permit discrimination in favor of domestic firms, and give host state institutions authority to resolve investment disputes. OPEC's success in raising oil prices in 1973 gave the LDCs more influence, and the UN General Assembly passed resolutions on FDI despite the North's objections, such as the 1974 NIEO Declaration calling on host states to unilaterally apply rules to resident MNCs. However, these resolutions were largely symbolic, and the UN failed to reach an agreement on a comprehensive code of conduct for MNCs (discussed later in this chapter).[39]

By the early 1980s, the South adopted a more conciliatory position for several reasons:

- The rise of neoliberalism under Reagan and Thatcher affected the policies of many LDCs as well as DCs.
- LDC experience with nationalizing natural resource industries was disappointing because of declining productivity, failure to introduce new technologies, and continued dependence on MNCs for marketing products.
- LDC militancy caused MNCs to shift some of their investments from the South to DCs with natural resources such as Australia, Canada, and the United States.
- The 1980s foreign debt crisis led to cutbacks in bank loans to LDCs, and the South's fear of exploitation by MNCs was replaced by concern that its inward FDI was declining.

Many LDCs therefore adopted more open policies toward MNCs during the 1980s; for example, Mexico liberalized its policies and supported the NAFTA provisions for freer foreign investment flows. The most significant change was in the policies of transition economies, especially China. Although China was largely closed to FDI from the 1950s to 1970s, it became more welcoming to FDI in the late 1970s and even granted foreign investors special treatment not available to domestic firms.[40] As Table 10.4 shows, China became the largest host country for FDI inflows in 2014. Although LDCs adopted more welcoming policies, some governments imposed local content and export requirements on MNCs and pressured them to enter into joint ventures with local firms. The East Asian NIEs, for example, welcomed investment but attached a number of conditions to inward FDI. However, most LDCs, transition economies, and DCs are currently seeking to attract FDI. According to UNCTAD, 37 economies adopted 63 policy measures affecting foreign investment in 2014. Forty-seven of these measures involved liberalization, promotion, and facilitation of investment, while only nine introduced new investment restrictions or regulations. (The restrictions were related to strategic sectors, national security issues, and land ownership.) For example, most new LDC measures reduce restrictions on foreign entry and offer incentives such as lower taxes to promote investment in priority industries. FDI is the largest source of external finance for LDCs, and during financial crises FDI has been more stable than other capital flows. Whereas investment ratings and short-term financial considerations influence access to bank lending and portfolio investment, FDI responds more to underlying economic fundamentals.[41] Despite the general LDC trend toward welcoming FDI, exceptions exist in certain sectors and geographic regions. For example, some Latin American countries nationalized strategic industries, especially extractive industries. In Venezuela, the national oil company Petróleos de Venezuela S.A. took over the operations of the gas company Exterran (the United States); in Bolivia, the government completed the nationalization of the oil and natural gas industry; and in Ecuador, increased taxes on windfall profits on oil generated friction with some foreign companies.[42]

It is important to note that the poorest LDCs find it difficult to attract FDI even when they liberalize their investment policies. For example, most Sub-Saharan African LDCs adopted policies to encourage FDI, partly under pressure from IMF and World Bank structural adjustment loans (see Chapter 7). However, low economic growth rates, civil conflicts, political crises, and high indebtedness levels have adversely affected their FDI inflows. As Table 10.2 shows, Africa's share of inward FDI stock was only 2.7 percent in 2014, compared with much higher shares for Asia and Latin America.

The North

MNC investments have on average focused more on natural resources and lower technology manufacturing in the South, and on higher technology production in the North. MNCs also loom larger in LDC than DC economies, and DCs are more often major home as well as host countries for FDI; thus they are reluctant to restrict incoming FDI. Despite these differences, DC policies have also shifted over time.

The United States, Western Europe, and Canada imposed very few controls on foreign firms during the nineteenth century, largely because of liberal attitudes fostered by British hegemony. Western Europe followed more open policies than the United States toward FDI after World War I, but their positions reversed after World War II when the United States emerged as the global hegemon. Indeed, the Europeans adopted more restrictive policies in the 1960s because of concerns about the dominance of American MNCs. In his book *The American Challenge*, the French writer Jean-Jacques Servan-Schreiber warned that U.S. MNCs in Europe were the world's third largest economy after the United States and Europe, and he called on Europe to reform its educational, industrial, and social policies, and focus on establishing its own MNCs.[43] In response, European governments promoted national champions in key industries by subsidizing research, encouraging mergers, and increasing procurement from national firms; and they demanded that foreign MNCs contribute to job creation and export promotion. France in particular screened inward FDI and rejected more FDI proposals than other European states. Canada also began a screening process in the 1970s because 50 percent of its manufacturing output and 70 percent of its oil production were foreign-controlled. Inward FDI accounted for 20.4 percent of Canada's GDP in 1980, compared with only 11.8 percent for the United Kingdom, 3.8 percent for France, 3 percent for the United States, and 0.3 percent for Japan. In 1974 Canada created a Foreign Investment Review Agency (FIRA) to determine whether foreign takeovers were of "significant benefit" to the country, and in 1980 it developed a National Energy Program (NEP) to increase Canadian ownership in the oil and gas industry. These policies produced major tensions with the United States.[44] However, Japan had the most interventionist DC policy. As Table 10.2 shows, Japan accounted for only 0.4 percent of total inward FDI stock in 1980, compared with 12 percent for the United States and 9.1 percent for the United Kingdom. Japan's low level of inward FDI resulted partly from the difficulty Western MNCs had in adapting to its cultural and linguistic differences, but its investment restrictions also played a critical role. Dating back to the sixteenth century, Japan's international economic controls resulted from fear of foreign intervention and pride in its distinct economy and society. During the 1930s, Japan developed policies to extract benefits from foreign investment, such as access to capital and technology, while avoiding the drawbacks of foreign control; and after World War II Japan continued to restrict FDI inflows.[45]

In contrast to the restrictions of the 1970s, most DCs began to seek FDI in the mid-1980s for several reasons. First, FDI restrictions seemed less legitimate because of the phasing out of global capital controls and the reemergence of orthodox liberalism. Second, states viewed FDI as a remedy for increased global competitiveness and unemployment. The average unemployment rate in OECD countries rose from 3.3 percent in 1973 to 8.6 percent in 1983, and governments valued the jobs FDI could provide. DCs also began to view inward FDI as a means of enhancing their competitiveness, and they offered financial incentives and tax concessions to attract MNCs. A third factor was the change in the country composition of FDI. As other DCs joined the United

States as important home countries for FDI, they favored fewer restrictions on MNCs. For example, the EC was ambivalent about a 1981 U.S. proposal that GATT should compile an inventory of host countries' trade-related investment measures; but after European MNCs increased their outward FDI, they favored greater discipline over host countries and supported the U.S. position in the GATT Uruguay Round.[46] Japan also felt pressure to ease its inward FDI restrictions as its outward investment increased, and it had removed most legal obstacles to inward FDI by the 1980s. However, intangible barriers continue to limit the role of foreign firms in Japan. Foreign M&As are less common in Japan because shareholders with ties to the firms' management and members of *keiretsu* (groups with extensive cross-shareholdings) hold most of the stock in Japanese firms. For example, of the 584 M&As involving Japan in 1992, 165 were Japanese firms acquiring other Japanese firms, 165 were Japanese firms acquiring foreign firms, and only 32 were foreign firms acquiring Japanese firms. It is also difficult to develop new FDI projects because of the costs and complexities of doing business in Japan, exclusionary business practices of the *keiretsu*, and bureaucratic practices that discriminate against foreign firms. Japan is adopting policies to encourage more openness, and foreign takeovers of Japanese firms are increasing. However, Table 10.3 shows that inward FDI accounted for only 3.5 percent of Japan's GDP in 2013; this was well below the 36.4 percent average figure for all DCs.[47]

A fourth reason for more open investment policies was the pressure imposed by the United States. Canada and Mexico as U.S. neighbors felt this pressure most strongly. For example, the Canadian Liberal government loosened the controls on inward FDI it had instituted through FIRA and the NEP because of U.S. protests and a U.S. challenge in GATT. The Progressive Conservative government elected in 1984 then rescinded the NEP and replaced FIRA with Investment Canada, which did more to encourage than to review inward FDI. Subsequently, the CUSFTA and NAFTA led to further liberalization of Canadian (and Mexican) foreign investment regulations. Canada's position on inward FDI was also changing because it was becoming a more important *source* of FDI. As Table 10.3 shows, in 2013 Canada's outward FDI stock accounted for a higher percentage of its GDP (40.1 percent) than its inward FDI stock (35.3 percent).[48]

As the main advocate of open investment policies, it is ironic that the United States began to adopt some restrictive policies in the 1980s–1990s. This policy shift resulted from the relative decline of its economic hegemony and its increased role as a host country for FDI. U.S. inward FDI stock accounted for only 3 percent of GDP in 1980 and 4.4 percent in 1985. However, Table 10.3 shows that U.S. inward FDI rose to 13.7 percent of GDP in 1995 and to 29.4 percent in 2013. Some Congressional leaders warned that foreign investors were acquiring U.S. high-technology firms and that the U.S. military was depending more on foreign-controlled suppliers. Thus, U.S. policies became more interventionist with a number of proposed and actual legislative changes. Most important was the Exon-Florio amendment to the 1988 Omnibus Trade and Competitiveness Act, which enables the president to block foreign mergers or acquisitions of U.S. firms that pose a possible danger to national security. The authority to implement Exon-Florio rests with an interagency *Committee on Foreign Investment in the United States (CFIUS)*. The U.S. president and CFIUS have blocked only two investments—in the 1990s and in 2012. However, the CFIUS review process has discouraged some investors and delayed some investments. In 2012, a number of U.S. members of Congress expressed concerns about the security and economic implications of the growing number of investments by Chinese firms. Despite the Exon-Florio amendment, the United States continues to support liberal foreign investment policies in international forums. For example, the United States was the main force behind the TRIMs negotiations in the GATT Uruguay Round and negotiations for a Multilateral Agreement on Investment in the OECD. The North in general supports liberalization, and most DC policies in recent years have been investment-friendly.[49]

MNC–HOME COUNTRY RELATIONS

The number of major home countries for MNCs has always been small. Western Europe was the source of about 80 percent of FDI before World War I, and Britain accounted for the largest share. The United States, Britain, and the Netherlands accounted for 65–75 percent of outward FDI stock between World War I and 1980. Although the sources of FDI became more diverse after 1980, six DCs accounted for about 75 percent of the total in the early 1990s— the United States, Britain, Germany, France, Japan, and the Netherlands. As discussed, the DCs' predominance has declined since the 1990s. As Table 10.4 shows, China, Hong Kong, China, the Russian Federation, and Singapore were among the top 10 sources of FDI outflows in 2014; and the total value of outward FDI stock from the LDCs and transition economies reached $5.3 trillion in 2014.[50] However, Table 10.1 shows that DCs still accounted for 79.4 percent of outward FDI stock in 2014. This discussion of FDI–home country relations therefore focuses mainly on the North.

The effects of FDI on a home country depend on the characteristics of both the home country and its MNCs. This section begins with a discussion of home country policies toward MNCs. It then examines two contentious questions in regard to MNC–home country relations: (1) What are the costs and benefits of FDI for labor groups in the home country? and (2) What is the relationship between the competitiveness of a home country and the competitiveness of its MNCs?

Home Country Policies Toward MNCs

Home countries normally view outward FDI as an indication of economic and political strength and as beneficial to their competitiveness. Thus, they usually give their MNCs favored treatment and try to protect them from hostile actions by foreigners, especially when the MNCs operate in strategic industries. However, governments sometimes associate outward FDI with a decrease in home country exports, a decline in the country's industrial base, and losses in domestic employment. In such circumstances, home countries may try to stem the flow of outward FDI. Some governments also view their MNCs as tools of foreign policy and may attempt to monitor, control, or restrain their outward FDI in the interests of the home economy.

The Pre-World War II Period   During the nineteenth and early twentieth centuries, home countries supported their corporations and protected them vis-à-vis foreigners. For example, European states sometimes intervened militarily during the colonial period to ensure that their companies developed and prospered. During the interwar years, European home countries provided subsidies and other assistance to support airlines, shipping firms, and oil companies that were closely tied to their strategic interests. In the 1930s, the Japanese army occupied Chinese plants and gave Japanese companies control over their management. The United States also was sometimes willing to support its companies' interests in Latin America with military force. However, governments at times took actions to limit outward FDI; for example, the Nazi government in Germany had to approve all new FDI, and it only rarely gave its approval. Although the U.S. government was concerned that outward FDI could transfer technology and employment to foreign countries, it adopted no policies to restrict FDI outflows before World War II.[51]

Early Postwar Period   In the 1950s to 1970s, the United States as the hegemonic power both protected its MNCs and pressured them for political and economic reasons. For example, in 1962 the U.S. Congress passed the Hickenlooper Amendment, which threatened to withhold development assistance from LDCs that nationalized American MNC affiliates without providing adequate compensation. The United States also viewed its MNCs as tools of foreign policy. For example, the U.S. government used its Trading with the Enemy Act and Foreign Assets Control Legislation in the 1960s–1970s to limit the trade of U.S. subsidiaries with China, Cuba, North Vietnam, and North Korea. Host governments for U.S. subsidiaries in Canada, Europe, and Latin America considered these policies an infringement of their sovereignty, and they often adopted laws to counter the U.S. legislation. The United States also tried to control corporate behavior in response to its growing balance-of-payments deficits. In the 1960s, the government called on U.S. MNCs to limit capital outflows to their foreign affiliates; in the 1970s, the government created the Domestic International Sales Corporation (DISC) program, which provided tax incentives to encourage MNCs to export from the United States instead of from abroad.[52]

Although European governments recovering from World War II were concerned that outward FDI would adversely affect their balance of payments, they did little to either encourage or limit outward FDI in the 1950s–1960s. Japan was the only major economy that systematically restricted outward FDI for about two decades after World War II. To keep scarce capital at home for postwar reconstruction, Japan scrutinized FDI projects and approved only those that would increase exports, provide access to raw materials, and pose no threat to Japanese producers. Thus, Table 10.1 shows that Japan accounted for only 0.7 percent of outward FDI stock in 1960. Japan did not begin to liberalize its policies on outward FDI until the late 1960s, when its balance-of-trade surpluses were rapidly increasing.

The 1980s to the Present Although the United States eased its limits on economic transactions with Communist countries as the Cold War declined, it sometimes acted in response to international events. In the early 1980s, for example, Western Europe and the Soviet Union agreed to construct a natural gas pipeline; Western European firms were to provide equipment for the pipeline's construction in return for future deliveries of Soviet natural gas. After Poland declared martial law in December 1981, the United States retaliated against the Soviet Union by imposing an embargo on materials produced by U.S. companies that were to be used in constructing the pipeline. The United States not only prohibited subsidiaries of U.S. MNCs from exporting equipment and technology to the Soviet Union, but also ordered *foreign* companies not to export goods produced with technology acquired under licensing agreements with U.S. companies. The Reagan administration's opposition to the pipeline stemmed from concerns that Western Europe would become dependent on Soviet gas exports, and that these exports would strengthen the Soviet economy. However, planning for the pipeline was at an advanced stage, and Britain, France, West Germany, and Italy ordered their resident firms to ignore the U.S. restrictions and provide the goods and technology to the Soviet Union. A number of firms, such as Dresser-France (a U.S. subsidiary) and licensees of General Electric in Britain, Italy, and West Germany, complied with the European orders. Although the United States imposed penalties on these firms, the Europeans did not back down; eventually the U.S. sanctions were removed and the European sales proceeded.[53] After the breakup of the Soviet Union, U.S. extraterritorial actions were aimed mainly at Cuba. For example, the 1996 Helms–Burton Act strengthened the U.S. trade embargo on Cuba. The Act extended prohibitions on trade to companies doing business with Cuba and penalized *foreign* companies for doing business in Cuba if they used property that Cuba had nationalized from U.S. companies. Although the United States is re-establishing diplomatic ties with Cuba, only an act of Congress will fully end the trade embargo.[54]

Other home countries have been less inclined than the United States to take such blatant political actions to control MNC behavior. However, Japan and Western Europe have established close linkages with their MNCs to achieve common *economic* objectives, whereas the United States has maintained more of an arm's length relationship between business and government (the U.S. defense and oil industries are notable exceptions). Neomercantilists argue that the United States should counter the actions of Japan and Europe by developing an industrial policy to support U.S. MNCs, especially in high-technology areas; this would involve assessing competitive trends in high-technology industries and shifting federal R&D funds from military uses to dual-use and economic areas. The United States has pursued some limited industrial policy initiuals, but not to the same extent as Japan and some European countries. Liberals oppose industrial policy measures and support dependence on the market and on the lowest-cost suppliers, regardless of their nationality.[55] As discussed, the growth of state-owned MNCs is another type of linkage between home countries and their corporations; they now account for more than 11 percent of FDI flows.

The Effects of MNCs on Labor Groups in Home Countries

A major controversy regarding MNCs and home countries relates to the effect of foreign production on exports and jobs. The debate began in the 1970s when the American Federation of Labor–Congress of Industrial Organizations (AFL-CIO) reversed its liberal trade policy and called for limits on imports and on FDI by American firms. In the early 1990s, U.S. labor groups opposed NAFTA because of concerns that MNCs would shift their operations to Mexico. The AFL-CIO and other U.S. labor groups assume that workers in the home country are likely to lose their jobs when a U.S. firm switches from exporting to serving foreign markets through subsidiaries. The outsourcing of service and clerical jobs to India by MNCs became a major issue in Senator John Kerry's 2004 presidential election campaign. Other DCs have also been concerned about FDI and job losses. For example, a 1993 report to the French Senate argued that outward FDI was a major cause of unemployment among factory workers; Japanese policy-makers warned that unemployment resulted from the relocation of plants to other Asian countries; and Germany was concerned about the employment effects of industries relocating in Eastern Europe.[56]

Liberals generally dismiss these concerns, arguing that U.S. FDI "tends … to create rather than destroy U.S. job opportunities in high-wage, export-oriented industries."[57] Although some home country jobs are lost, outward FDI "creates others, and the jobs thus gained tend to pay higher wages than the jobs lost."[58] Thus, liberals present evidence that MNCs have a better record than domestic firms in job creation, worker salaries, export performance, and technological innovations in the home country. Liberals also reject the idea that home country workers suffer because MNCs transfer activities to LDC subsidiaries with lower wages and standards. For example, one liberal study argues that investment by U.S. firms in Mexico as a result of NAFTA "creates U.S. jobs, both in the short run, by boosting U.S. exports of capital goods, and in the long run, by establishing channels for the export of U.S. intermediate components, replacement parts, and associated goods and services."[59] Neomercantilists and historical materialists by contrast emphasize the negative effects of outward FDI on employment stemming from export substitution and intrafirm imports. *Export substitution* occurs when production of a subsidiary in country B substitutes for exports from the parent firm in country A, or when exports from the subsidiary in B to a third country (C) substitute for goods and services that A formerly exported to C. *Intrafirm imports* are goods and services that the home country imports from foreign affiliates of a parent firm. Neomercantilists argue that export substitution and intrafirm imports reduce production and employment in the home country, and historical materialists add that the mobility of capital and MNCs puts immobile workers at a disadvantage. The constant threat that MNCs will outsource jobs to subsidiaries in low-wage countries forces workers in the home country to accept lower salaries, health benefits, pensions, and job security. MNCs from this perspective benefit both by exploiting low-cost labor in LDC host countries and by reducing labor costs in DC home countries. Critical theorists reject the liberal view that home country workers will be compensated for the loss of manufacturing jobs with the growth of skilled service positions by arguing that MNCs are now even exporting more skilled positions to lower-salary locations.[60]

Despite numerous studies on MNCs, it is difficult to find unequivocal evidence supporting one side or the other on this issue. A major problem is that researchers cannot know whether a specific firm's exports would have been maintained if it had *not* established foreign subsidiaries. Firms that establish foreign affiliates are often more competitive, and workers in a less competitive firm may lose jobs whether at home or abroad. Creation of foreign production facilities can also be both job-displacing and job-creating for workers in the home country, depending on whether an MNC is able to expand and diversify its production facilities. With all the variables involved, it may be easier to determine the impact of FDI on specific jobs in specific firms than to provide a broader view of the impact on aggregate employment and exports. Finally, most analysts would agree that FDI in LDCs is more likely to adversely affect less skilled workers in DC home countries. The "fairness" of this situation depends not only on our economic views but also on our political and social views. Thus, the controversy over the effects of FDI on home country workers shows no signs of abating.[61]

Competitiveness and Home Country–MNC Relations

Another contentious issue involves the relationship between a state's competitiveness and the competitiveness of its MNCs. Neomercantilists argue that a state's MNCs have a major impact on its competitiveness because its "standard of living in the long term depends on its ability to attain a high and rising level of productivity in the industries in which its firms compete."[62] For example, Canada has a good standard of living despite the high degree of foreign ownership in its manufacturing industry; but it can never have the highest standard because the best jobs and R&D are in the home country.[63] Liberals by contrast argue that MNCs seek profitable opportunities around the world and "are becoming disconnected from their home nations."[64] They see U.S. competitiveness as depending more on U.S. workers' education and skills than on U.S. corporate ownership; if Americans have the requisite training, foreign MNCs will employ them. According to U.S. Senator Lamar Alexander, the American auto industry was not limited to "the Big Three companies in Detroit. Now the definition is any company that makes a substantial number of cars and trucks in the U.S. and has a big payroll here, pays big taxes here and buys supplies here."[65] Some liberals go even further and assert that we are entering a "borderless world" in which a corporation's nationality no longer makes a difference.[66] An analyst's position on competitiveness affects their policy prescriptions. Whereas neomercantilists argue that governments should pursue industrial policies to promote their own MNCs in high-technology areas, interventionist liberals believe that governments should focus on upgrading workers' skills so that MNCs of any nationality will want to do business, invest, and pay taxes there.

Interventionist liberals point to China as a country that has reaped enormous benefits from foreign MNCs because of its large population, its booming market, its low production costs, and its reasonably skilled, hard-working, and low-wage workers. China's surging exports have been "one of the great economic success stories in the modern era," and foreign MNCs have had a major role in this export success.[67] Whereas wholly and partially owned foreign subsidiaries accounted for less than 6 percent of China's exports in 1986, this figure climbed to about 55 percent in 2004. Foreign subsidiaries also accounted for 81 percent of China's exports of technology-intensive goods in 2000 and for more than 90 percent of China's exports of electronic circuits and mobile phones. Foreign MNCs have used China as an export platform, from which they send goods around the world.[68]

As liberals note, there is also evidence that large MNCs are becoming more global in their operations and less closely tied to their home countries. For example, the sales of foreign affiliates of U.S. firms were four times greater than U.S. merchandise exports between 1988 and 1990; U.S. foreign affiliates accounted for 43 percent of their parent companies' total profits in 1990; and U.S. firms increased their foreign R&D spending by 33 percent, compared with an increase of only 6 percent in the United States from 1986 to 1988. National boundaries are also becoming blurred as some MNCs spread their head office functions and list their shares in several countries' stock exchanges. For example, Shell and Unilever have headquarters in Britain and the Netherlands, and Astra-Zeneca has its headquarters in one state and conducts most of its R&D in another state. Asea Brown Boveri was formed from a merger of Sweden's ASEA and Switzerland's Brown Boveri; moved its headquarters from Stockholm to Zurich; has Swiss, German, and Swedish managers; and does its business in English. The increase of cross-border M&As and cross-holding of shares also make it difficult to determine an MNC's nationality, and integrated production systems make it difficult to determine a product's origins. MNCs can insulate themselves from national policies and conditions by sourcing inputs, information, and personnel from around the world. For example, an automobile manufactured by Ford may be assembled in Britain with inputs from all over Europe, designs produced in the United States, and stages of processing in various locations. In this age of globalization, liberals argue that the highest priority should be "to provide competitive conditions for businesses in general in the country rather than only for the country's firms in particular."[69]

Despite the blurring of nationalities, neomercantilists note that *most* MNCs are home country-oriented and that a state's competitiveness is linked with the competitiveness of its MNCs. R&D is a major factor promoting competitiveness, and MNCs tend to keep much of their R&D activity at home. In 1984, for example, the ratio of R&D to sales for industrial machinery and equipment firms in Canada was only 40 percent of the U.S. ratio, and this difference resulted largely from the extensive foreign ownership in Canadian industry. Although U.S. MNCs invest more than Japanese MNCs in R&D abroad, even U.S. companies spent only 8.6 percent of their R&D funding in foreign countries in 1988.[70] R&D funding is essential for developing new technologies, and the control of high-technology industries can affect a country's national security. Despite China's success as an export platform for foreign MNCs, "its reliance on stitching and welding together products that are imagined, invented and designed by others" means that it sometimes has to pay large amounts in licensing fees and patent royalties to foreigners. Much of Apple's iPhone is made in China, but only a small share of the profits from the sale of iPhones stays in China.[71]

Although a state's competitiveness is tied to the competitiveness of its firms, there are important national differences. For example, U.S. MNCs tend to favor their home country less than Japanese and German MNCs. Studies show that U.S. MNCs are more interested in the financial returns on investments, whereas Japanese MNCs emphasize market share; U.S. MNCs are more willing to invest in overseas R&D than Japanese MNCs; and German and Japanese MNCs emphasize exporting from the home country more than U.S. MNCs. Thus, Robert Reich's question as to whether "our MNCs" look after "our national interests" may be more relevant for U.S. MNCs than for Japanese and German MNCs.[72]

A REGIME FOR FDI: WHAT IS TO BE REGULATED?

Despite the global influence of MNCs, the principles, norms, and rules for foreign investment are more rudimentary than those for trade and monetary relations; and no IO has a role in a foreign investment regime comparable to the WTO's role in the global trade regime. Most government policies on MNCs are formulated at the national level, but the transnational nature of MNCs makes these policies inadequate. The main obstacle to forming a foreign investment regime is the lack of consensus on what should be regulated—the MNC, the host state, or the home state. The prominent role of private actors (MNCs and multinational banks) as sources of investment capital also makes international regulation a difficult and contentious issue. According to orthodox liberals, investment agreements should regulate host state behavior and provide maximum protection against nationalization, performance requirements, and other impediments to MNC operations. Home countries should also be able to intervene on behalf of their MNCs to counter host country actions that inhibit investment flows. Neomercantilists and historical materialists, by contrast, view host country restrictions on foreign investment as perfectly legitimate. Neomercantilists see state intervention as necessary to ensure that FDI does not conflict with the national interest and national security, and historical materialists believe that investment agreements should regulate MNCs rather than host states.

The United States as the global hegemon provided much of the foreign investment regulation in the 1950s–1960s. U.S. policy sought to protect FDI flows against host country actions such as nationalization and to ensure that MNC behavior did not conflict with the West's Cold War objectives. European states concluded **bilateral investment treaties** (**BITs**) in the 1960s to protect their investments in LDCs. In the 1970s, attention shifted to developing international regulations for FDI, and some economists called for the creation of "a General Agreement for the International Corporation" like the GATT for trade.[73] In a widely quoted study, Raymond Vernon argued that "global corporations must be regulated to restore sovereignty to government" because the MNC is "not accountable to any public authority that matches it in geographical reach."[74] Some DCs such as France and Canada began to screen foreign investment to limit the influence of U.S. MNCs. However, the South took the main initiative in the 1970s, pressuring for UN regulation of MNCs rather than host states. As a result, the UN set up a Commission on Transnational Corporations in 1974 with a mandate to develop a binding Code of Conduct for MNCs. To counter the UN emphasis on regulating only MNCs, the OECD's 1976 Declaration and Decisions on International Investment and Multinational Enterprises included guidelines for the behavior of both MNCs and host states.[75]

By the late 1970s, it was evident that the North would not agree to the South's demands for a UN Code of Conduct for MNCs, and several factors contributed to a shift back to controlling the behavior of host states. For example, the South's share of inward FDI was declining because of the 1980s foreign debt crisis, concerns about LDC political and economic stability, and the emphasis on high-technology investment in the North. LDCs followed less interventionist policies toward MNCs as their needs for capital increased, and the North was able to begin forging a consensus that host state (not MNC) behavior should be regulated. Before examining the multilateral efforts to regulate foreign investment, the next section provides some background on BITs.

BILATERAL INVESTMENT TREATIES

Bilateral treaties to protect and promote foreign investment have a long history. In the eighteenth century, the United States, Japan, and some European states concluded bilateral treaties dealing with investment, trade, maritime, and consular relations. When the GATT multilateral trade regime was formed, countries began to conclude separate BITs. After the first BIT between Germany and Pakistan was signed in 1959, BITs became the main instrument for managing investment relations between DCs and LDCs. BITs give priority to protecting FDI and MNCs. They call on host states to provide national treatment to MNC subsidiaries (i.e., they must be treated as least as favorably as domestic firms); give MNCs the right to repatriate profits; and call for "fair" compensation for MNCs in cases of expropriation. Over time BITs also developed investor-state dispute settlement (ISDS) provisions that give investors access to dispute settlement procedures against a foreign government.[76]

The South has viewed BITs with the North as one-sided because they obligate the host state to protect foreign investment without corresponding obligations on the MNC. However, many LDCs have signed BITs because they assume this is necessary to attract foreign investment. The 1980s foreign debt crisis resulted in a sharp reduction in commercial bank loans, and LDC debtors became more dependent on foreign investment for development finance. Thus, the total number of BITs increased from 167 in the late 1970s to 385 in 1989. With the fall of the Berlin Wall in 1989 and the breakup of the Soviet Union, BITs were signed at a much more rapid pace in the 1990s with transition economies as well as LDCs; and as more LDCs became home countries for MNCs, BITs were signed between LDCs. DCs, LDCs, and transition economies all viewed participation in BITs as essential in the competition for foreign investment. Thus, the number of BITs increased to 2,676 in 2008.[77]

After 2008 the pace of forming new BITs slowed down, because several changes revealed their shortcomings. First, the 2008 global financial crisis pointed to the need for regulatory reform. The large number of BITs were a major problem because they resulted in "a wide range of non-uniform and inconsistent arrangements that could become increasingly inefficient, complex, and non-transparent."[78] Second, the increase of ISDS cases from 326 in 2008 to 608 in 2014 caused conflict between those who favor the right of investors to sue the state for compensation, and those who oppose new restrictions on the regulatory activities of the state. Since a global investment agreement has proved to be elusive, a number of states are looking to regional investment agreements as a "second-best solution." A smaller number of regional investment agreements would permit some rationalization of the conflicting provisions in the numerous BITs. However, BITs continue to play an important role. In 2013 there were 3,236 international investment agreements, and 2,902 of these were BITs.[79] The following sections focus on efforts to establish more uniform regulations in the United Nations, the EU, NAFTA, the GATT/ WTO, and the OECD.

THE UNITED NATIONS

As discussed, concerns were raised about the effects of MNCs on the national sovereignty of host states in the 1960s–1970s. A high-profile case involving the International Telephone and Telegraph Corporation (ITT) and Chile brought the issue of regulating MNCs to UN attention. ITT was determined to protect its interests in the communications sector in Chile, and after the 1970 presidential election it allegedly plotted with the U.S. Central Intelligence Agency (CIA) to overthrow the socialist government of Salvador Allende. When ITT's actions became public in 1972 through published documents of a syndicated columnist, a U.S. Senate subcommittee investigated the case and released a report on *The International Telephone and Telegraph Company and Chile*. The UN secretary-general also responded to the ITT case by appointing a Group of Eminent Persons to examine the impact of MNCs. In 1974 the UN group's report condemned "subversive political intervention" by MNCs such as ITT in Chile, and called for the development of a code of conduct for governments and MNCs.[80] The UN then established a *Commission on Transnational Corporations* to develop the code of conduct and a comprehensive information system on MNC activities, and a *UN Center on Transnational Corporations (UNCTC)* to serve as its secretariat. An intergovernmental working group began preparing a draft code of conduct and submitted its report to the commission in 1982, but a long period of negotiations followed because of fundamental disagreements among UN members. For example, there was no consensus on whether the code should be a set of voluntary guidelines or have the force of law. Most LDCs and socialist states supported the draft code because it sought to prevent MNC tax evasion, restrictive business practices, and transfer pricing. The DCs as leading home states for MNCs, by contrast, argued that the draft code did not deal with host state treatment of MNCs. After years of sporadic negotiations, the UN abandoned its efforts to form a consensus on a code of conduct for MNCs in 1992. As a result, the UNCTC was dissolved in 1993 and replaced by a less proactive Division on Transnational Corporations and Investment under UNCTAD auspices.[81]

UNCTAD has developed expertise on foreign investment issues, and its annual *World Investment Reports* and *Trade and Development Reports* are highly regarded. However, UN efforts since 1993 have been limited to promoting *voluntary* standards of behavior for MNCs. At the 1999 World Economic Forum in Davos, UN secretary-general Kofi Annan invited MNCs to join a UN-led partnership mission called the **Global Compact**. The compact comprises 10 principles on human rights, labor standards, the environment, and anticorruption that are designed to promote responsible global capitalism. The compact has continued to gain support, and hundreds of companies and organizations ranging from business, labor, and civil society groups to cities and even stock exchanges have signed on to it. Unlike a regulatory code of conduct, the Global Compact is voluntary and depends on a self-reporting system. Critics argue that MNCs may endorse the compact to gain publicity, but that they are often slow in implementing the 10 principles. The UN's Global Compact Office has responded by generating a "grey list" with names of companies that signed on but did not report on what they were doing to comply with the compact's terms. However, the efficacy of this "moral suasion" approach is uncertain, and only "time will tell whether these changes will influence corporate conduct in the long term."[82]

REGIONAL APPROACHES: THE EU AND NAFTA

Regional trade agreements often include investment as well as trade provisions, partly because of the failure of multilateral institutions to develop a strong foreign investment regime; this section focuses on two important examples: the EU and NAFTA. As a common market, the EU provides for the free movement of capital and protection of FDI among the member states. Thus, the European

Commission has legal authority to monitor and regulate MNC activities to ensure that there is a "level playing field." The EU has also been concerned that European MNCs are not large enough to compete with American and Japanese MNCs, and its policy toward MNCs is "two-edged, encouraging multinational activity in a transnational European market, while seeking to remedy the concerns caused by this activity by specific binding measures of containment."[83] In view of the high level of EU integration, NAFTA's method of dealing with FDI is more likely than the EU's to serve as a model for future efforts to develop a multilateral foreign investment regime.

The investment provisions in NAFTA's Chapter 11 have created considerable controversy. Chapter 11 marked the first time that a regional FTA "provided a full set of legal rights and protections to foreign direct investors (from other member countries)."[84] However, the Chapter 11 provisions were not really new, because they "carry forward on a trilateral basis all of the key provisions of U.S. bilateral investment treaties."[85] For example, NAFTA commits its three members to provide MFN and national treatment to foreign investors; to ban all new export performance, local content, and technology transfer requirements; and to phase out most existing performance requirements within 10 years. NAFTA also commits governments to compensate investors in case of expropriation, which it defines in very broad terms. Most liberal economists believe that "open investment policies should be the norm," with limited exceptions for issues such as national security.[86] Liberals applaud NAFTA for its significant advances in freeing investment flows, but criticize the sectoral exceptions that prevent NAFTA from completely liberalizing North American investment. For example, the United States excludes its maritime industry, Canada exempts its cultural industries, and Mexico excludes its energy and rail sectors. Neomercantilists and critical theorists, by contrast, view the NAFTA investment provisions as threatening national sovereignty and the ability of environmental and labor groups to protect their interests. In the view of critical theorists, the NAFTA rules increase capital mobility and give the capitalist class greater leverage vis-à-vis labor. MNCs can transfer their operations from the United States and Canada to Mexico to benefit from lower labor costs and environmental standards, contributing to a competitive "race to the bottom."[87] Neomercantilists argue that NAFTA's limits on the use of *performance requirements* (e.g., committing MNCs to export goods produced in the host country, and to purchase local goods and services) prevent host countries from gaining positive spinoffs from foreign investment and from furthering their national objectives.[88]

The most controversial aspect of NAFTA's Chapter 11 is its ISDS provisions, which permit private investors to obtain relief directly from governments for alleged NAFTA violations. Chapter 11 stipulates that a private investor from a NAFTA state can compel another NAFTA government to participate in binding arbitration to determine whether the investor has incurred financial losses because the government breached its obligations. Whereas BITs have included ISDS arbitration for many years, the WTO only gives governments "standing" in dispute settlement cases, and investors must be represented by governments in settling their claims. Liberals praise the ISDS procedures for "distancing investment disputes from the political arena. An investor who feels that it has suffered damage ... by a NAFTA country can pursue its claim without having to involve its government." Neomercantilists by contrast argue that ISDS enables "investors to harass governments whose policies they dislike."[89] By giving MNCs legal standing in investment disputes with governments, NAFTA poses a direct threat to national sovereignty. Environmentalists criticize the fact that many Chapter 11 investor complaints have challenged governments' antipollution and public health policies. Many early supporters of Chapter 11 assumed that it would prevent the Mexican government from over-regulating U.S. and Canadian business; but the U.S. and Canadian governments are being challenged in a growing number of investment disputes. All three NAFTA governments therefore want to ensure that the protection of investors' rights "does not threaten the ability of governments to regulate in the public interest."[90] Despite these concerns, ISDS provisions are involved in negotiations for mega-regional agreements such as the TPP, the TTIP (between the United States and EU), and the *Comprehensive Economic and Trade Agreement* between the EU and Canada. According to UNCTAD, ISDS is "arguably the most controversial issue in international investment policymaking."[91]

THE GATT/WTO TO THE OECD AND BACK TO THE WTO

The WTO is a natural institution to deal with FDI because of the close relationship between foreign investment and trade. However, FDI is the "neglected twin" of trade because it has been less subject to multilateral regulation.[92] The proposed International Trade Organization (ITO) of the 1940s contained some controversial FDI-related topics, and this was a major factor in the U.S. rejection of the Havana Charter. GATT did not deal with investment until the Trade-Related Investment Measures (TRIMs) agreement was negotiated in the Uruguay Round and incorporated into the WTO (see Chapter 8). Although the TRIMs is an important beginning in recognizing the relationship between trade and investment, it is largely symbolic because many LDCs are reluctant to accept limits on their investment policies. TRIMs does not impose major new restraints on government actions; it only bans some investment-related measures that are inconsistent with GATT/WTO provisions. The General Agreement on Trade in Services (GATS) and Trade-Related Intellectual Property Rights (TRIPs) agreement also contain some investment provisions, but the WTO does not provide a comprehensive body of rules for FDI; they are scattered throughout the agreement.

In 1995 the DCs began investment negotiations in the OECD rather than the WTO. The OECD seemed to be a natural venue for negotiating a *Multilateral Agreement on Investment (MAI)* because OECD countries accounted for a large share of FDI inflows and outflows. The OECD also had long-term experience with investment issues: In 1961 it adopted two codes to liberalize capital flows; in 1976 it issued a Declaration on International Investment and Multinational Enterprises; and its ideas had a major influence on the BITs.[93] The United States wanted a comprehensive and binding MAI, and it was frustrated that LDCs had opposed even the limited TRIMs agreement in the GATT negotiations. Since most OECD members are capital exporters, the United States wanted the MAI negotiations to be in the OECD. However, the EU Commission preferred to negotiate in the WTO because the agreement would bind non-OECD countries which were a growing destination for FDI. Canada also favored the WTO as a venue because NAFTA already dealt with its most important investment relationship (the United States), and it wanted an MAI to benefit Canadian MNCs in the South. Despite these differences, the MAI negotiations began in the OECD for several reasons: Many LDCs in the WTO opposed investment negotiations, and some EU members wanted to negotiate for themselves in the OECD rather than having the EU Commission negotiate for them in the WTO. (The EU Commission represents EU members in the WTO, but EU members represent themselves in the OECD.) To allay concerns about the exclusivity of the MAI negotiations, the OECD indicated that nonmember states would be consulted.[94]

The OECD negotiations addressed three major issues: protection for foreign investors, liberalization of investment, and dispute settlement procedures. The investment protection talks focused on compensation for expropriation of property, freedom of investors to transfer profits out of host countries, and equitable treatment for foreign investors. The investment liberalization talks focused on host country obligations to limit performance requirements and provide MFN and national treatment to foreign investors. The dispute settlement talks focused on the submission of complaints by investors as well as states for binding international arbitration. Although the BITs and NAFTA already dealt with these issues, the MAI would be multilateral and more comprehensive than previous agreements. Despite early progress in the talks, the negotiating group requested a one-year extension of its mandate in May 1997 because of significant national differences. For example, France and Canada wanted to exempt culture from the agreement to protect their arts and media sectors; the EU and Canada resented the U.S. Helms–Burton law that could be used to sanction foreign companies for investing in Cuba, Iran, and Libya; and there was no consensus on the inclusion of environmental and labor measures. These differences gave civil society groups and LDCs the opportunity to organize opposition to an agreement. Although LDCs had become more open to foreign investment after the 1982 foreign debt crisis, they resented being excluded from the OECD negotiations and feared that an MAI would limit host government policies. Indeed, most OECD members seemed "to agree that an MAI should not impose any obligations on firms but that it should be binding on governments."[95] This position stemmed from opposition to the South's efforts to develop a UN code of conduct for MNCs and from growing neoliberal support for free foreign investment and capital flows. In the South's view, by contrast, the 1990s Asian financial crisis demonstrated the need for regulation of foreign investment and capital flows (see Chapter 7).[96]

A coalition of NGOs launched the most effective opposition, arguing that an MAI would threaten human rights, labor and environmental standards, and LDC development. They warned that an MAI would result in a race to the bottom, with countries lowering their labor and environmental standards to attract foreign investment. A crucial turning point occurred when Ralph Nader's consumer advocacy group acquired a draft copy of the MAI and put it on the Internet. Gramscian theorists would argue that the NGOs organized a counterhegemony, using the Internet "with incredible effectiveness to derail a planned ... pact designed to increase globalization."[97] OECD divisions also grew when France forced a suspension of the MAI negotiations in 1998 because of concerns about the threat to its culture and national sovereignty. The failed MAI negotiations show that the OECD is better at providing advice and analysis and concluding non-binding accords than at negotiating binding agreements on sensitive issues.

Even before the MAI talks collapsed, the EU and Japan tried to revive the investment issue at the WTO's first Ministerial meeting in 1996 when they pressured for negotiation of the so-called Singapore issues: trade facilitation, competition policy, government procurement, and investment. However, the South strongly opposed negotiating these issues, and the impasse was eventually resolved by the decision that only one of the Singapore issues (trade facilitation) would be negotiated in the Doha Round. Any current work the WTO does on investment will therefore be separate from the multilateral trade negotiations.[98] A major obstacle to WTO negotiations is the wide North–South divergence on whether an MAI should regulate the behavior of MNCs, host states, or home states. With the WTO's failure to regulate foreign investment, the OECD has again moved in to fill the gap. Instead of trying to revive the contentious MAI talks, the OECD has focused on its traditional activities of identifying investment barriers so that peer pressure can be exerted on states. In 2006, the OECD released a comprehensive *Policy Framework for Investment*, identifying policies that states can adopt to attract foreign investment.[99] Despite the OECD's continuing efforts to liberalize investment, governments have not established a multilateral foreign investment regime with effective regulations and procedures. As a result, states are looking to BITs and regional investment agreements as an alternative. At the multilateral level, private actors are having a greater role in regard to FDI issues.

PRIVATE ACTORS

In view of the lack of multilateral mechanisms to regulate MNCs, private actors have become involved with promoting **corporate social responsibility (CSR)**. NGOs representing consumer, environmental, and religious groups have pressured MNCs to engage in socially responsible behavior, and MNCs have been open to some voluntary self-regulation. This section discusses the role of NGOs and civil society groups, and the "Considering IPE Theory and Practice" section that follows examines the CSR concept from different theoretical perspectives.

As discussed in Chapter 2, NGOs and civil society groups may be conformist, reformist, or rejectionist.[100] Conformists largely endorse MNC behavior and do not favor restrictions on their activities, reformists believe that MNCs can and should be reformed with some regulation, and rejectionists argue that MNCs are not reformable. NGO reformists want to promote responsible MNC behavior without engaging in ideological confrontation. For example, reformist environmental strategies include NGO campaigns to purchase products from ecologically minded firms, partnerships between NGOs and business firms to make production methods more environmentally responsible, and codes of conduct that call on MNCs to voluntarily engage in socially conscious behavior.[101] Rejectionist NGOs seek to expose and punish irresponsible corporate behavior and are less willing to engage in dialogue. Their strategies include consumer boycotts to publicly expose and punish environmental abuses, monitors to track and disseminate information about MNCs' destructive activities, and counter-information to refute MNC claims. Some rejectionists aim to develop a counterhegemony to "confront the hegemonic formation of globalization," which includes MNCs.[102] Some NGOs employ both reformist and rejectionist strategies. For example, Greenpeace worked with companies to develop ozone-friendly refrigerators at the same time as it was encouraging consumers to boycott Shell Oil Company over its alleged involvement with state suppression in Nigeria. In efforts to avoid negative NGO campaigns and government regulations, many MNCs have developed their own regulatory frameworks and have collaborated with reformist NGOs. Instead of binding commitments, business firms and associations have supported voluntary agreements as an alternative. Thus, the International Chamber of Commerce endorsed 16 principles on the environment known as the *Business Charter on Sustainable Development* before the 1992 UN Conference on Environment and Development in Rio de Janeiro, Brazil.

The question arises as to how effective NGOs have been in altering MNC behavior. MNCs have different levels of vulnerability to NGO strategies. For example, oil companies are less vulnerable to NGO pressure because governments depend on MNCs' access to oil technology, expertise, and distribution networks. NGOs also have limited monitoring capabilities; although they direct their campaigns and protests at certain high-profile companies, they permit other companies to be free riders. Overall, MNCs have not changed significantly as a result of NGO activities, and NGO pressure does not substitute for adequate multilateral regulation.

Considering IPE Theory and Practice

As discussed, liberals, neomercantilists, and critical theorists have widely divergent views of MNCs. Liberals see MNCs as positive agents of change that contribute to efficiency and stimulate innovation, economic growth, and employment. Neomercantilists believe that host states should be able to impose performance requirements and other regulations on MNCs to promote industrial development and protect the national interest. Critical theorists argue that MNCs overcharge for their goods and services, create dependency relationships with LDC host states, and pose a threat to labor groups and the environment in home as well as host states. This section examines competing theoretical views of corporate social responsibility. Three common definitions of CSR are: a corporation's responsibility to "operate ethically and in accordance with its legal obligations and to strive to minimize any adverse effects of its operations and activities on the environment, society and human health"; "actions that appear to further some social good, beyond the interests of the firm and that which is required by law"; and "the contribution that a company makes in society through its core business activities, its social investment and philanthropy programs, and its engagement in public policy."[103]

The first definition describes CSR as operating ethically but also in accordance with the law, the second describes CSR as going beyond obeying the law, and the third does not even mention the law. CSR can mean different things to researchers and practitioners, and to companies, NGOs, consumers, and governments; it may include such activities as corporate governance, philanthropy, environmental management, labor rights, community development, and animal rights. Some orthodox liberals have rejected CSR as irrelevant to MNCs and their basic objectives. For example, Milton Friedman asserted that there is "one and only one social responsibility of business—to use its resources and engage in activities designed to increase its profits so long as it ... engages in open and free competition, without deception or fraud."[104] However, orthodox liberals today find it more difficult to dismiss CSR than Friedman did in 1962 when he wrote this passage, because many private and public groups now support CSR. Thus, many neoliberals (including MNC and industry representatives) now give credence to CSR, but they believe it should be voluntary rather than regulated; regulation would stifle innovation and national competitiveness. Regulation is also unnecessary because MNCs are aware of the financial benefits in being socially responsible. Peer pressure alone will cause MNCs to develop CSR policies and collectively increase standards.

Critical theorists by contrast view CSR as a contradiction in terms, because the MNC "remains ... a legally designated 'person' designed to valorize self-interest and invalidate moral concern." The corporate ideal from this perspective "compels executives to prioritize the interests of their companies and shareholders above all others and forbids them from being socially responsible—at least genuinely so."[105] These critical theorists basically agree with neoliberals such as Friedman that CSR has little or no relevance for MNCs, but unlike the neoliberals they view this in highly negative terms. Whereas some critical theorists reject the idea that MNCs can be socially responsible, others argue that CSR can only have meaning if it is subject to mandatory regulation; a voluntary approach will not lead to responsible corporate behavior. For example, one NGO has argued that "the image of multinational companies working hard to make the world a better place is often just that—an image ... What's needed are new laws to make businesses responsible for protecting human rights and the environment."[106]

In between the more extreme orthodox liberal and critical views are a wide range of interventionist liberals who see CSR as a viable concept that should depend on a combination of government regulation and voluntary involvement. For example, Jagdish Bhagwati argues that "in the main, voluntary codes must characterize what corporations should do ... and mandatory codes must address what they should not do."[107] MNC self-regulation can supplement but not substitute for government regulation. However, government regulation cannot resolve all CSR issues because the law has many gray areas. MNCs should therefore be expected to follow the spirit as well as the letter of the law. When legal standards are unclear or difficult to enforce, corporate culture or pressure from consumer groups and NGOs may be important. Interventionist liberals believe that MNCs will engage in CSR for various reasons. Companies often view CSR as part of good financial management, because unethical firms tend to be unsustainable in the long term; and CSR can both contribute to society and increase the profitability of participating firms. Some interventionist liberals use the term "strategic CSR" to refer to "good works that are also good for business."[108]

In sum, there is a wide divergence of theoretical views on CSR and on other aspects of MNCs. It is difficult to do good empirical research in this area because of the private nature of MNCs, and because many researchers have strongly held views. As one analyst states, "one of the very few generalizations that accurately characterize FDI and MNCs is that their benefits have been exaggerated by advocates and their harm has been exaggerated by critics."[109] The next chapter addresses another subject on which there is a diversity of strongly held views: international development.

QUESTIONS

1. How would you compare the foreign investment regime with the global trade and monetary regimes? How and why do liberals, neomercantilists, and historical materialists differ in their views of what should be regulated in a foreign investment regime?
2. Do liberals, neomercantilists, and historical materialists believe that the nationality of an MNC makes a difference? Do you think that the competitiveness of a country is closely tied with the competitiveness of its MNCs?
3. What are horizontal and vertical integration? Why does a business firm choose to become horizontally integrated? Why does a firm choose to become vertically integrated?
4. In what ways have the major host and home countries for FDI changed over time? Have there been changes in the position of the South vis-à-vis the North in FDI? Is it possible to generalize about "the South"?
5. What are some of the major effects of MNCs on home and host states? Do you think that the effects have on the average been more positive or negative?
6. What is the role of BITs, NAFTA, the United Nations, the WTO, and the OECD in regulating FDI? Why did the DCs decide to negotiate an MAI in the OECD, and was this a wise decision?
7. What is the obsolescing bargain model? Does the OBM have more validity in some areas and periods of time than in others?

8. Have NGOs had an impact on the behavior of MNCs? What is CSR, and what are the competing theoretical views regarding the value of the concept?

KEY TERMS

bilateral investment
  treaties
corporate social
  responsibility
FDI flows
FDI stock
foreign direct investment

Global Compact
greenfield investment
horizontal integration
investor-state dispute
  settlement
multinational
  corporations

obsolescing bargain
  model
portfolio investment
sovereign wealth
  funds
transfer prices
vertical integration

FURTHER READING

On theories of MNCs see Grazia Ietto-Gillies, *Transnational Corporations and International Production*, 2nd ed. (Northampton, MA: Edward Elgar, 2012); and Mats Forsgren, *Theories of the Multinational Firm: A Multidimensional Creature in the Global Economy* (Northampton, MA: Edward Elgar, 2008). General studies of MNCs include Richard Phillips, "The Firm, the Corporation and Contemporary Capitalism," in Ronen Palan, ed., *Global Political Economy: Contemporary Theories*, 2nd ed. (New York: Routledge, 2013), pp. 29–45; Stephen D. Cohen, *Multinational Corporations and Foreign Direct Investment: Avoiding Simplicity, Embracing Complexity* (New York: Oxford University Press, 2007); Nathan M. Jensen, *Nation-States and the Multinational Corporation: A Political Economy of Foreign Direct Investment* (Princeton, NJ: Princeton University Press, 2006); and Geoffrey Jones, *Multinationals and Global Capitalism: From the Nineteenth to the Twenty-First Century* (New York: Oxford University Press, 2005).

Neomercantilist studies of MNCs include Rawi Abdelal, "The Multinational Firm and Geopolitics: Europe, Russian Energy, and Power," *Business and Politics* 17, no. 3 (2015), pp. 553–576; and Paul N. Doremus, William W. Keller, Louis W. Pauly, and Simon Reich, *The Myth of the Global Corporation* (Princeton, NJ: Princeton University Press, 1998). Studies that discuss MNCs in positive terms are Jagdish Bhagwati, *In Defense of Globalization* (New York: Oxford University Press, 2004), ch. 12; and Edward M. Graham, *Fighting the Wrong Enemy—Antiglobal Activists and Multinational Enterprises* (Washington, DC: Institute for International Economics, 2000). Strong critiques of MNCs include James Petras and Henry Veltmeyer, *Multinationals on Trial: Foreign Investment Matters* (Burlington, VT: Ashgate, 2007); and Joel Bakan, *The Corporation: The Pathological Pursuit of Profit and Power* (New York: Penguin, 2004).

On corporate social responsibility see Samuel O. Idowu et al., eds., *Corporate Social Responsibility and Governance: Theory and Practice* (New York: Springer, 2015); Kernaghan Webb, "Multi-Level Corporate Responsibility and the Mining Sector: Learning from the Canadian Experience in Latin America," *Business and Politics* 14, no. 3 (October 2012), pp. 1–42; and Jennifer A. Zerk, *Multinationals and Corporate Social Responsibility: Limitations and Opportunities in International Law* (New York: Cambridge University Press, 2006).

On public policy and the regulation of FDI see Hugh Compston, "The Network of Global Corporate Control: Implications for Public Policy," *Business and Politics* 15,

no. 3 (2013), pp. 357–379; Tagi Sagafi-nejad with John H. Dunning, *The UN and Transnational Corporations: From Code of Conduct to Global Compact* (Bloomington, IN: Indiana University Press, 2008); and Russell Alan Williams, "The OECD and Foreign Investment Rules: The Global Promotion of Liberalization," in Rianne Mahon and Stephen McBride, eds., *The OECD and Transnational Governance* (Vancouver: University of British Columbia Press, 2008), pp. 117–133.
On emerging economies as host and home countries for FDI, see Claes-Goran Alvstam, Harald Dolles, and Patrik Strom, eds., *Asian Inward and Outward FDI* (New York: Palgrave Macmillan, 2014); Karl P. Sauvant, ed., *The Rise of Transnational Corporations from Emerging Markets: Threat or Opportunity?* (Northampton, MA: Edward Elgar, 2008); and H. S. Kehal, *Foreign Investment in Rapidly Growing Countries: The Chinese and Indian Experiences* (New York: Palgrave Macmillan, 2005).

NOTES

1. UN Conference on Trade and Development (UNCTAD), *World Investment Report 2015* (New York: United Nations, 2015), overview and ch. 1; UNCTAD, *World Investment Report 2013* (New York: United Nations, 2013), overview and ch. 1; Grazia Ietto-Gillies, *Transnational Corporations and International Production* (Northampton, MA: Edward Elgar, 2012), pp. 7–16.
2. International Monetary Fund, *World Economic Outlook*, April 2015 (Washington, DC: IMF, 2015), p. 111.
3. Stephen D. Cohen, *Multinational Corporations and Foreign Direct Investment: Avoiding Simplicity, Embracing Complexity* (New York: Oxford University Press, 2007), p. 23; Giorgio B. Navaretti and Anthony J. Venables, *Multinational Firms in the World Economy* (Princeton, NJ: Princeton University Press, 2004), p. 3.
4. Lorraine Eden, "Bringing the Firm Back In: Multinationals in International Political Economy," in Lorraine Eden and Evan H. Potter, eds., *Multinationals in the Global Political Economy* (New York: St. Martin's Press, 1993), p. 26.
5. Ethan B. Kapstein, "We Are US: The Myth of the Multinational," *The National Interest* (Winter 1991–1992), p. 55.
6. DeAnne Julius, "International Direct Investment: Strengthening the Policy Regime," in Peter B. Kenen, ed., *Managing the World Economy: Fifty Years After Bretton Woods* (Washington, DC: Institute of International Economics, 1994), p. 269.
7. Nathan M. Jensen, *Nation-States and the Multinational Corporation: A Political Economy of Foreign Direct Investment* (Princeton, NJ: Princeton University Press, 2006), pp. 28–34.
8. Ietto-Gillies, *Transnational Corporations and International Production*, p.11; Edward M. Graham and Paul R. Krugman, *Foreign Direct Investment in the United States*, 3rd ed. (Washington, DC: Institute for International Economics, 1995), pp. 9–11; Geoffrey Jones, *The Evolution of International Business: An Introduction* (London: Routledge, 1996), pp. 4–6.
9. UNCTAD, *World Investment Report 2000* (New York: UN, 2000), pp. 99–136; Grazia Ietto-Gillies, *Transnational Corporations and International Production: Concepts, Theories and Effects* (Northampton, MA: Edward Elgar, 2005), pp. 11–31; Geoffrey Jones, *Multinationals and Global Capitalism: From the*

Nineteenth to the Twenty-First Century (New York: Oxford University Press, 2005), pp. 4–14.

10. Howard V. Perlmutter, "The Tortuous Evolution of the Multinational Corporation," *Columbia Journal of World Business* 4, no. 1 (January–February 1969), p. 11.

11. See John H. Dunning's *Explaining International Production* (Boston, MA: Unwin Hyman, 1988); and *Multinational Enterprises and the Global Economy* (Reading, MA: Addison-Wesley, 1993).

12. Keith Head and John Ries, "Exporting and FDI as Alternative Strategies," *Oxford Review of Economic Policy* 20, no. 2 (2004), pp. 409–423.

13. Jean-François Hennart, "The Transaction Cost Theory of the Multinational Enterprise," in Christos N. Pitelis and Roger Sugden, eds., *The Nature of the Transnational Firm* (London: Routledge, 1991), pp. 143–151.

14. Graham and Krugman, *Foreign Direct Investment in the United States*, p. 83.

15. Lorraine Eden, "Thinking Globally—Acting Locally: Multinationals in the Global Political Economy," in Lorraine Eden and Evan H. Potter, eds., *Multinationals in the Global Political Economy* (New York: St. Martin's Press, 1993), pp. 1–2.

16. Alfred D. Chandler, Jr., and Bruce Mazlish, eds., *Leviathans: Multinational Corporations and the New Global History* (New York: Cambridge University Press, 2005).

17. Peter Svedberg, "The Portfolio-Direct Composition of Private Foreign Investment in 1914 Revisited," *The Economic Journal* 88 (December 1978), pp. 763–777; Thomas A. B. Corley, "Britain's Overseas Investments in 1914 Revisited," *Business History* 36, no. 1 (January 1994), pp. 71–88.

18. Edward M. Graham, *Global Corporations and National Governments* (Washington, DC: Institute for International Economics, 1996), pp. 25–26, 136–140.

19. UNCTAD, *World Investment Report 2004* (New York: UN, 2004), pp. 382–385.

20. UNCTAD, *World Investment Report 2004*, pp. 376–380.

21. UNCTAD, *World Investment Report 2010* (New York: UN, 2010), pp. xvii–xviii.

22. Dennis J. Encarnation, *Rivals Beyond Trade: America Versus Japan in Global Competition* (Ithaca, NY: Cornell University Press, 1992), p. 5; Kiyoshi Kojima, *Direct Foreign Investment: A Japanese Model of Multinational Business Operations* (New York: Praeger, 1978), pp. 1–18.

23. UNCTAD, *World Investment Report 1999* (New York: UN, 1999), p. 42.

24. UNCTAD, *World Investment Report 2014* (New York: UN, 2014), pp. xiv–xv; UNCTAD, *World Investment Report 2015*, pp. 5–8; Andrea Goldstein, *Multinational Companies from Emerging Economies: Composition, Conceptualization and Direction in the Global Economy* (New York: Palgrave Macmillan, 2007), pp. 11–12.

25. Greg Keenan, "Mexico Shifts into Overdrive," *Globe and Mail*, February 14, 2015, pp. B1 and B6–7.

26. Cohen, *Multinational Corporations and Foreign Direct Investment*, pp. 161–164; Harbhajan S. Kehal, ed., *Foreign Investment in Rapidly Growing Countries: The Chinese and Indian Experiences* (New York: Palgrave Macmillan, 2005).

27. Lee Hudson Teslik, "Sovereign Wealth Funds," Council on Foreign Relations Backgrounder, January 18, 2008, www.cfr.org/publication/15251.

28. UNCTAD, *World Investment Reports 2013, 2014*, and *2015*, overview and ch. 1.

29. Glen Biglaiser and Karl DeRouen, Jr., "Economic Reforms and Inflows of Foreign Direct Investment in Latin America," *Latin American Research Review* 41, no. 1 (February 2006), p. 69; Jensen, *Nation-States and the Multinational*

Corporation, p. 225; John P. Tuman, "Regime Type, Rights, and Foreign Direct Investment in Latin America: A Brief Comment," *Latin American Research Review* 41, no. 2 (June 2006), p. 184.

30. Grazia Ietto-Gillies, *International Production: Trends, Theories, Effects* (Cambridge, MA: Blackwell, 1992), pp. 78–84.

31. Stephen H. Hymer, *The International Operations of National Firms: A Study of Direct Foreign Investment* (Cambridge, MA: MIT Press, 1976), p. 100.

32. Peter Evans, *Dependent Development: The Alliance of Multinational, State, and Local Capital in Brazil* (Princeton, NJ: Princeton University Press, 1979), p. 37.

33. Raymond Vernon, *Sovereignty at Bay: The Multinational Spread of U.S. Enterprises* (New York: Basic Books, 1971), pp. 46–59; Ravi Ramamurti, "The Obsolescing 'Bargaining Model'? MNC-Host Developing Country Relations Revisited," *Journal of International Business Studies* 32, no. 1 (2001), p. 25.

34. Stephen J. Kobrin, "Testing the Bargaining Hypothesis in the Manufacturing Sector in Developing Countries," *International Organization* 41, no. 4 (Autumn 1987), pp. 609–638.

35. Ramamurti, "The Obsolescing 'Bargaining Model'? MNC-Host Developing Country Relations Revisited," p. 23.

36. Vlado Vivoda, "Resource Nationalism, Bargaining and the International Oil Companies: Challenges and Change in the New Millennium," *New Political Economy* 14, no. 4 (December 2009), p. 519.

37. William A. Stoever, "Attempting to Resolve the Attraction–Aversion Dilemma: A Study of FDI Policy in the Republic of Korea," *Transnational Corporations* 11, no. 1 (April 2002), pp. 49–76.

38. Jones, *The Evolution of International Business*, pp. 288–291.

39. Stephen J. Kobrin, "Expropriation as an Attempt to Control Foreign Firms in LDCs: Trends from 1960 to 1979," *International Studies Quarterly* 28, no. 3 (September 1984), pp. 337–342; Stephen D. Krasner, *Structural Conflict: The Third World Against Global Liberalism* (Berkeley, CA: University of California Press, 1985), pp. 176–195.

40. Kobrin, "Expropriation as an Attempt to Control Foreign Firms in LDCs," p. 338; Graham, *Global Corporations and National Governments*, pp. 17–20.

41. UNCTAD, *World Investment Report 2015*, p. 102; UNCTAD, *World Investment Report 2000*, pp. 6, 7, 17–18.

42. UNCTAD, *World Investment Report 2009* (New York: UN, 2009), pp. 70–71.

43. Jean-Jacques Servan-Schreiber, *The American Challenge*, trans. Ronald Steel (New York: Atheneum, 1979); Tagi Sagafi-nejad with John H. Dunning, *The UN and Transnational Corporations* (Bloomington, IN: Indiana University Press, 2008), pp. 43–44.

44. Stephen Clarkson, *Canada and the Reagan Challenge: Crisis and Adjustment, 1981–85*, updated ed. (Toronto: James Lorimer & Company, 1985), pp. 3–113; Barbara Jenkins, *The Paradox of Continental Production: National Investment Policies in North America* (Ithaca, NY: Cornell University Press, 1992), pp. 113–117; UNCTAD, *World Investment Report 2003* (New York: UN, 2003), Annex Table B6, pp. 278–279.

45. Mark Mason, *American Multinationals and Japan: The Political Economy of Japanese Capital Controls, 1899–1980* (Cambridge, MA: Council on East Asian Studies, Harvard University, 1992), pp. 243–247; UNCTAD, *World Investment Report 2003*, Annex Table B6, pp. 278–279.

46. Jones, *The Evolution of International Business*, pp. 280–281; A. E. Safarian, "Host Country Policies Towards Foreign Direct Investment in the 1950s and 1990s," *Transnational Corporations* 8, no. 2 (August 1999), p. 105.

47. Paul N. Doremus, William W. Keller, Louis W. Pauly, and Simon Reich, *The Myth of the Global Corporation* (Princeton, NJ: Princeton University Press, 1998), pp. 77–78; C. Fred Bergsten and Marcus Noland, *Reconcilable Differences? United States–Japan Economic Conflict* (Washington, DC: Institute for International Economics, 1993), pp. 79–82.

48. Jenkins, *The Paradox of Continental Production*, pp. 117–121; Clarkson, *Canada and the Reagan Challenge*, pp. 83–113.

49. James K. Jackson, "The Exon-Florio National Security Test for Foreign Investment," U.S. Congressional Research Service, March 29, 2013; Graham and Krugman, *Foreign Direct Investment in the United States*, pp. 126–132.

50. UNCTAD, *World Investment Report 2015*, Annex Table 2, pp. A7–A10.

51. UNCTC, *Transnational Corporations in World Development—Trends and Prospects* (New York: United Nations, 1988), p. 240; Jones, *The Evolution of International Business*, pp. 219–220.

52. Robert T. Kudrle, "The Several Faces of the Multinational Corporation: Political Reaction and Policy Response," in W. Ladd Hollist and F. LaMond Tullis, eds., *An International Political Economy* (Boulder, CO: Westview Press, 1985), pp. 176–177.

53. Gary C. Hufbauer and Jeffrey J. Schott, "The Soviet-European Gas Pipeline: A Case of Failed Sanctions," in Theodore H. Moran, ed., *Multinational Corporations: The Political Economy of Foreign Direct Investment* (Lexington, MA: Heath, 1985), pp. 219–245.

54. "Biter Bitten: The Helms-Burton Law," *The Economist*, June 8, 1996, p. 45; Eric Zolov, "Let's Revisit Helms-Burton," January 16, 2015, www.huffingtonpost.com/eric-zolov/lets-revisit-helmsburton_b_6488476.html.

55. Robert B. Reich, "Who Is Us?" *Harvard Business Review* 90, no. 1 (January–February 1990), pp. 59–60; Vernon, *Sovereignty at Bay*, pp. 214–215; Laura D'Andrea Tyson, *Who's Bashing Whom? Trade Conflict in High-Technology Industries* (Washington, DC: Institute for International Economics, 1992), pp. 289–295.

56. Cohen, *Multinational Corporations and Foreign Direct Investment*, pp. 217–218; Jamuna P. Agarwal, "Effect of Foreign Direct Investment on Employment in Home Countries," *Transnational Corporations* 6, no. 2 (August 1997), pp. 1–2; Louise Amoore, "Making the Modern Multinational," in Christopher May, ed., *Global Corporate Power* (Boulder, CO: Lynne Rienner, 2006), p. 59.

57. Edward M. Graham, *Fighting the Wrong Enemy—Antiglobal Activists and Multinational Enterprises* (Washington, DC: Institute for International Economics, 2000), p. 83.

58. Graham, *Fighting the Wrong Enemy*, p. 83.

59. Gary C. Hufbauer and Jeffrey J. Schott, *NAFTA: An Assessment*, rev. ed. (Washington, DC: Institute for International Economics, 1993), p. 19.

60. Agarwal, "Effect of Foreign Direct Investment on Employment in Home Countries," pp. 3–4; James Petras and Henry Veltmeyer, *Multinationals on Trial: Foreign Investment Matters* (Burlington, VT: Ashgate, 2007), pp. 116–118.

61. Cohen, *Multinational Corporations and Foreign Direct Investment*, pp. 217–222.

62. Michael E. Porter, *The Competitive Advantage of Nations* (New York: Free Press, 1990), p. 2; Laura D'Andrea Tyson, "They Are Not Us: Why American Ownership Still Matters," *The American Prospect* 4 (Winter 1991), pp. 37–49.

63. Lester Thurow, *Head to Head: The Coming Economic Battle Among Japan, Europe, and America* (New York: Morrow, 1992), p. 201.

64. Robert B. Reich, *The Work of Nations: Preparing Ourselves for 21st-Century Capitalism* (New York: Vintage Books, 1991), p. 8.

65. Sholnn Freeman, "Detroit Waves Flag That No Longer Flies: Congress Embraces Jobs, Growth Created by Foreign Carmakers," *Washington Post*, August 19, 2006, p. A01.

66. Kenichi Ohmae, *The Borderless World: Power and Strategy in the Interlinked Economy* (New York: HarperPerennial, 1991), p. 10.

67. Cohen, *Multinational Corporations and Foreign Direct Investment*, p. 207.

68. Cohen, *Multinational Corporations and Foreign Direct Investment*, p. 207.

69. UNCTAD, *World Investment Report 2000*, pp. 20–21; Robert B. Reich, "Who Do We Think They Are?" *The American Prospect* 4 (Winter 1991), p. 51.

70. Fred Lazar, "Corporate Strategies: The Costs and Benefits of Going Global," in Robert Boyer and Daniel Drache, eds., *States Against Markets: The Limits of Globalization* (London: Routledge, 1996), p. 285; Louis W. Pauly and Simon Reich, "National Structures and Multinational Corporate Behavior: Enduring Differences in the Age of Globalization," *International Organization* 51, no. 1 (Winter 1997), p. 13.

71. John Pomfret, "Beijing Tries to Push Beyond 'Made in China' Status to Find Name-Brand Innovation," *Washington Post*, May 25, 2010.

72. Reich, "Who Is Us?" pp. 59–60; Pauly and Reich, "National Structures and Multinational Corporate Behavior," pp. 1–30.

73. Paul M. Goldberg and Charles P. Kindleberger, "Toward a GATT for Investment: A Proposal for Supervision of the International Corporation," *Law and Policy in International Business* 2 (Summer 1970), pp. 295–325.

74. Vernon, *Sovereignty at Bay*, p. 249.

75. OECD, *International Investment and Multinational Enterprises: Review of the 1976 Declaration and Decisions* (Paris: Organization for Economic Cooperation and Development, 1979).

76. UNCTAD, *Bilateral Investment Treaties in the Mid-1990s* (New York and Geneva: United Nations, 1998).

77. UNCTAD, *World Investment Report 2003*, p. 89; UNCTAD, *World Investment Report 2008* (New York: UN, 2008), p. 32; UNCTAD, *World Investment Report 2015*, pp. 121–123.

78. Sherif H. Seid, *Global Regulation of Foreign Direct Investment* (Burlington, VT: Ashgate, 2002), p. 55; UNCTAD, *World Investment Report 2009*, pp. 32–33.

79. UNCTAD, *World Investment Report 2015*, pp. 124–125; UNCTAD, *World Investment Report 2014*, p. 114.

80. UN, "Report of the Group of Eminent Persons to Study the Impact of Multinational Corporations on Development and on International Relations," in George Modelski, ed., *Transnational Corporations and World Order* (San Francisco, CA: W.H. Freeman, 1979), pp. 323, 330.

81. UNCTC, *The United Nations Code of Conduct on Transnational Corporations* (New York: United Nations, September 1986), pp. 1–6; R. Alan Hedley, "Transnational Corporations and Their Regulation: Issues and Strategies," *International Journal of Comparative Sociology* 40, no. 2 (May 1999), pp. 218–221.

82. Sagafi-nejad, *The UN and Transnational Corporations*, pp. 195–198.

83. John Robinson, *Multinationals and Political Control* (New York: St. Martin's Press, 1983), p. 44.

84. Cohen, *Multinational Corporations and Foreign Direct Investment*, p. 267.

85. Jon R. Johnson, *The North American Free Trade Agreement—A Comprehensive Guide* (Aurora: Canada Law Book, 1994), p. 275.

86. Graham, *Global Corporations and National Governments*, p. 47.

87. Fred Lazar, "Investment in the NAFTA: Just Cause for Walking Away," *Journal of World Trade* 27, no. 5 (October 1993), pp. 28–29.

88. Gilbert Gagné and Jean-Frédéric Morin, "The Evolving American Policy on Investment Protection: Evidence from Recent FTAs and the 2004 Model BIT," *Journal of International Economic Law* 9, no. 2 (May 2006).

89. Johnson, *The North American Free Trade Agreement*, p. 512.

90. Gagné and Morin, "The Evolving American Policy on Investment Protection," p. 358; Cohen, *Multinational Corporations and Foreign Direct Investment*, pp. 266–272.

91. UNCTAD, *World Investment Report 2014*, p. 126.

92. De A. Julius, *Foreign Investment: The Neglected Twin of Trade*, Occasional Papers no. 33 (Washington, DC: Group of Thirty, 1991).

93. Russell Alan Williams, "The OECD and Investment Rules: The Global Promotion of Liberalization," in Rianne Mahon and Stephen McBride, eds., *The OECD and Transnational Governance* (Vancouver: University of British Columbia Press, 2008), pp. 117–125.

94. Elizabeth Smythe, "Your Place or Mine? States, International Organizations and the Negotiation of Investment Rules," *Transnational Corporations* 7, no. 3 (December 1998), pp. 85–120.

95. Edward M. Graham and Pierre Sauvé, "Toward a Rules-Based Regime for Investment: Issues and Challenges," in Pierre Sauvé and Daniel Schwanen, eds., *Investment Rules for the Global Economy* (Toronto: C.D. Howe Institute, 1996), p. 135.

96. Elizabeth Smythe, "The Multilateral Agreement on Investment: A Charter of Rights for Global Investors or Just Another Agreement?" in Fen O. Hampson and Maureen A. Molot, eds., *Canada Among Nations 1998: Leadership and Dialogue* (Toronto: Oxford University Press, 1998), pp. 239–277.

97. Peter Morton, "MAI Gets Tangled in Web," *The Financial Post*, October 22, 1998, p. 3.

98. Pierre Sauvé, "Multilateral Rules on Investment: Is Forward Movement Possible?" *Journal of International Economic Law* 9, no. 2 (2006), pp. 326–327.

99. Williams, "The OECD and Investment Rules," pp. 128–131.

100. Jan A. Scholte with Robert O'Brien and Marc Williams, "The WTO and Civil Society," *Journal of World Trade* 33, no. 1 (1999), pp. 112–116.

101. Peter Newell, "Environmental NGOs, TNCs, and the Question of Governance," in Dimitris Stevis and Valerie J. Assetto, eds., *The International Political Economy of the Environment: Critical Perspectives* (Boulder, CO: Lynne Rienner, 2001), pp. 85–107.

102. Robert W. Cox, "Civil Society at the Turn of the Millennium: Prospects for an Alternative World Order," *Review of International Studies* 25 (1999), p. 26.

103. Jennifer A. Zerk, *Multinationals and Corporate Social Responsibility: Limitations and Opportunities in International Law* (New York: Cambridge University Press, 2006), pp. 31–32; Abagail McWilliams and Donald Siegel, "Corporate Social Responsibility: A Theory of the Firm Perspective," *Academy of Management Review* 26, no. 1 (January 2001), p. 117; World Economic Forum (WEF), "Follow-up Questionnaire on the World Economic Forum CEO States,"

www.weforum.org/pdf/GCCI/GCCI_CEO_Questionnaire.pdf. (The WEF's "global corporate citizenship" is often used interchangeably with CSR.)

104. Milton Friedman with Rose D. Friedman, *Capitalism and Freedom* (Chicago, IL: University of Chicago Press, 1962), p. 133.

105. Joel Bakan, *The Corporation: The Pathological Pursuit of Profit and Power* (New York: Penguin, 2004), pp. 28, 35.

106. Quoted in Kenneth M. Amaeshi and Bongo Adi, "Reconstructing the Corporate Social Responsibility Construct in *Utlish*," *Business Ethics* 16, no. 1 (January 2007), p. 13.

107. Jagdish Bhagwati, *In Defense of Globalization* (New York: Oxford University Press, 2004), p. 191.

108. Geoffrey P. Lantos, "The Boundaries of Strategic Corporate Social Responsibility," *Journal of Consumer Marketing* 18, no. 7 (2001), p. 595.

109. Cohen, *Multinational Corporations and Foreign Direct Investment*, p. 16.

International Development

The Bretton Woods institutions have been credited with contributing "to almost unprecedented global economic growth."[1] However, a large percentage of people in the South have received little benefit from this growth. According to the 2014 *Human Development Report*, about 1.2 billion people live on less than $1.25 (U.S.) a day and 2.7 billion live on less than $2.50 a day. Some risks such as those associated with the environment and climate change seem to be increasing, and 98 percent of those killed by natural disasters are from LDCs. There are also striking inequalities, both among and within countries. Whereas the poorest two-thirds of the world's population receive less than 13 percent of world income, the richest 1 percent receive almost 15 percent. Beyond income, the richest 1 percent own about half of the world's wealth. Income inequality within many countries is increasing (see Chapter 2).[2]

Despite the prevalence of poverty in the South, there are major differences in per capita income of these countries. As Table 11.1 shows, the East Asian and Latin American NIEs, and OPEC states tend to be middle- to high-income economies. For example, in 2014 Singapore and Hong Kong, China had per capita GNIs (at purchasing power parity rates) of $80,270 and $56,570; OPEC members Qatar and Kuwait had per capita GNIs of $139,760 and $82,210; and Chile and Mexico had per capita GNIs of $21,580 and $16,500. In stark contrast, Table 11.1 shows that poorer African and Asian states such as Congo, DR (Democratic Republic), Liberia, Nepal, and Tajikistan had per capita GNIs of $650, $700, $2,420, and $2,660, respectively. The poorest LDC region is Sub-Saharan Africa, with 40 percent of its workers still living in households earning less than $1.25 a day per person.[3] In addition to their higher incomes, Table 2.3 in Chapter 2 shows that East Asia and Latin America rank higher than other LDC regions on human development indicators. For example, life expectancy in 2013 was 74.9 and 74.0 years for Latin America

TABLE 11.1

GNI[a] per Capita (PPP[b] U.S.$), Southern Economies, 2014

Higher and Middle-Income

East Asian NIEs		OPEC Members		Latin American NIEs	
Singapore	$80,270	Qatar	$139,760	Chile	$21,580
HongKong, China	56,570	Kuwait	[c]82,210	Mexico	16,500
South Korea	34,620	Saudi Arabia	[c]51,320	Brazil	15,590

Low-Income

	Africa		Asia	
	Malawi	$790	Bangladesh	$3,330
	Burundi	770	Cambodia	3,100
	Liberia	700	Tajikistan	2,660
	Congo, DR	650	Nepal	2,420

[a]GNI = gross national income
[b]PPP = purchasing power parity
[c]2013 figure

Source: World Bank, *World Development Indicators Data Bank*, 2015. http://data.worldbank.org/indicator/NY.GNP.PCAP.PP.CD

and the Caribbean, and East Asia and the Pacific, respectively; life expectancy in South Asia and Sub-Saharan Africa, by contrast, was 67.2 and 56.8 years.

The various LDC regions also have different rates of development. As discussed in Chapter 7, the 1980s foreign debt crisis had differential effects on development in the South. Whereas Sub-Saharan Africa, and Latin America and the Caribbean had *negative* economic growth rates of –1.2 and –0.4 percent from 1980 to 1989, East Asia had a *positive* economic growth rate of 6.2 percent during this period. More recently, rapid economic growth in China and, to a lesser extent, India is evident from overall poverty figures. For example, from 1981 to 2001 the number of people living on less than $1 (U.S.) per day fell from 634 million to 212 million in China and from 382 million to 359 million in India. However the number living on less than $1 per day *increased* by almost 90 million in Sub-Saharan Africa from 1990 to 2001, and by more than 14 million in Europe and Central Asia from 1981 to 2001. In Sub-Saharan Africa a major factor was the high incidence of HIV/AIDS; in Europe and Central Asia there was economic disruption after the breakup of the Soviet bloc and Soviet Union.[4]

Despite these regional differences, the South in general lacks wealth and power vis-à-vis the North. Although LDCs look to the North for trade, foreign investment, development assistance, and technology transfers, they fear that these linkages increase their dependence on the North. The OECD countries and the KIEOs (the IMF, World Bank, and WTO) have helped the South gain access to external finance and export markets; but the LDCs believe that some KIEO policies inhibit their development efforts, and they resent the North's dominance in these organizations. This chapter assesses the economic development strategies LDCs have adopted over time, including import substitution, socialism, and export-led growth. With the revival of orthodox liberalism, LDCs have shifted to more open economic policies. However, current development policies fall short in dealing with income inequality in the world, in giving LDCs more "ownership" of their development policies, and in ensuring that development is sustainable (e.g., in preserving the environment). Later in this chapter we discuss how China in particular, but also Brazil, South Africa, Saudi Arabia, and Kuwait, are providing alternative sources of funding to LDCs that could challenge the dominance of the IMF and World Bank. As background for examining the LDC economic development strategies, this chapter first discusses the IPE theoretical perspectives; the role of official development assistance (ODA); and the role of the World Bank, which has "a unique position as a generator of ideas about economic development."[5]

IPE PERSPECTIVES AND NORTH–SOUTH RELATIONS

This section briefly summarizes the main tenets of the IPE perspectives as they relate to North–South relations. (For a more detailed discussion, see Chapters 3–5.) Neomercantilists focus on the issues of power and influence, and they tend to ignore the economic interests of poorer countries in the South. In the neomercantilist view, "Third World states want power and control as much as wealth," and it is only when LDCs pose a challenge to the North's dominance that most neomercantilists take notice.[6] In the 1970s neomercantilist scholars looked at OPEC's increased leverage in raising oil prices and at LDC efforts to gain more power and wealth through an NIEO; in the 1980s and 1990s, neomercantilists focused on the challenge East Asia's developmental state model posed to the North; and today neomercantilists are more interested in emerging powers such as China, India, and Brazil. Despite the inattention of neomercantilists to poverty in the South, neomercantilist *ideas* have had considerable influence on LDC policies. For example, Alexander Hamilton and Friedrich List argued that late industrializers (the United States and Germany at the time) required more government involvement if they were to "catch up" with Britain—the leading state. Drawing on these ideas, LDC development strategies such as import substitution and export-led growth call for a larger role for the state in promoting development.

LDC economic problems in the liberal view stem more from inefficient domestic policies than from their dependent position in the global economy. Indeed, liberals often see North–South interdependence as providing even more benefits for the South than for the North. LDCs that follow open economic policies and increase linkages with the North are more likely to achieve successful development. Although all liberals encourage LDCs to follow open, market-oriented policies, interventionist liberals recognize that North–South inequalities can put LDCs at a disadvantage. Whereas orthodox liberals emphasize equal treatment and reciprocity, interventionist liberals call on the North to consider the special needs of the South. However, interventionist liberals believe that the necessary changes can occur within the capitalist order, and they share the faith of other liberals in private enterprise and the market.

As historical materialists, dependency theorists reject the liberal view that LDC economic problems result from inefficient domestic policies. Instead, they see capitalist states in the core of the global economy as either "underdeveloping" LDCs in the periphery or preventing them from attaining genuine, autonomous development. Elites in the South (the "comprador" class) collaborate with capitalists in the North to reinforce this pattern of LDC dependency. World-systems theorists introduced a third category of countries, the semiperiphery, to explain the fact that some LDCs such as East Asian and Latin American NIEs were industrializing. Countries may move upward from the periphery to the semiperiphery or even the core, but this only rarely occurs. Whereas some historical materialists call for a redistribution of resources from the core to the periphery, others believe that the core will never willingly transfer resources; thus, they call for a social revolution in the South and/or for severing contacts with the North. In the Gramscian view, disadvantaged groups should develop a counterhegemony.

OFFICIAL DEVELOPMENT ASSISTANCE

Development assistance or **foreign aid** refers to grants, loans, or technical assistance that donors provide to recipients on concessional rather than commercial terms. **Concessional loans** (or *soft loans*) have lower interest rates, longer grace periods, and longer repayment periods than *commercial loans* (or *hard loans*). Private actors such as NGOs and foundations (such as the Bill and Melinda Gates Foundation) provide some valuable foreign aid, but by far the largest share of aid is **official development assistance (ODA)** provided by governments. To qualify as ODA, a loan must have a *grant element* of at least 25 percent. The grant element refers to the loan's financial terms, or the interest rate, maturity period, and grace period (the interval before the first repayment of capital); it ranges from 0 for a loan at 10 percent interest to 100 percent for a grant that requires no repayment. Grants and loans for military purposes are not included in ODA.[7] Scholars have widely divergent views regarding the motivations for aid-giving. Most liberals acknowledge that donors provide ODA partly to gain commercial benefits, but they see this aid as a positive-sum game that can also help recipients achieve economic development. Neomercantilists often see aid as a policy tool that donors developed to influence recipients in the bipolar Cold War, and that they now use to support the war on terrorism. Critical theorists view aid in highly negative terms as perpetuating dependency relations, promoting the South's integration in an unequal global market, and failing to deal with problems such as environmental degradation.[8] In reality, all of these theoretical views have some merit. Donors sometimes provide aid for humanitarian and development reasons, but they also seek to promote their own political and economic interests.

Regardless of the motivation for aid-giving, it is important to ask whether it is *necessary* and *effective* in decreasing poverty and promoting economic development. Critics point out that LDCs acquire much more revenue from private capital flows and merchandise exports. From 1990 to 1996 private international finance to LDCs increased to more than six times ODA flows, and in 2002 two Oxfam staff members wrote that "if developing countries increased their share of world exports by just five percent, this would generate $350 billion—seven times as much as they receive in aid."[9] **Remittances**, the money that migrants earn abroad and send back to their home countries, also surpass ODA flows to middle-income LDCs. The World Bank estimated that remittance flows in 2005 amounted to $250 billion (U.S.).[10] However, private capital, trade, and remittances are adequate substitutes for aid for only *some* LDCs. Most private capital to LDCs goes to China and about 10 other East Asian and Latin American countries, and the poorest LDCs are least likely to benefit from international trade. Thus, aid continues to be important for poorer LDCs and for sectors that receive less private capital such as health and education.[11]

Development analysts continue to disagree as to whether ODA should be increased, reduced, or transformed (these categories are not mutually exclusive).[12] The views of Jeffrey Sachs, William Easterly, and Dambisa Moyo exemplify these differences. Sachs argues that "the extreme poor are caught in a poverty trap" because of "disease, physical isolation, climate stress, environmental degradation, and ... extreme poverty itself," and that their governments "lack the financial means" to extricate themselves.[13] In 2000, the United Nations established eight **Millennium Development Goals (MDGs)** to be achieved by 2015, and Sachs has viewed ODA as a critical factor in reaching those goals. In efforts to halve the proportion of people suffering from extreme poverty and hunger between 1999 and 2015 (the first MDG), Sachs recommended a doubling of aid in 2006 and almost another doubling by 2015. The increased ODA would help "to jump-start the process of capital accumulation, economic growth, and rising household incomes."[14] (We discuss the MDGs later in this chapter.) However, critics such as Easterly and Moyo strongly question the effectiveness of aid-giving. Easterly argues that many LDCs have prospered without large amounts of foreign aid, and that aid does not necessarily promote development. Although "the typical African country received more than 15 percent of its income from foreign donors in the 1990s," this "surge of aid was not successful in reversing or halting the slide in growth of income per capita."[15] Easterly argues that aid can sometimes be useful as part of a piecemeal, bottom-up approach to development; but he criticizes the top-down planning approach of most large development agencies, and he attributes LDC problems more to corruption and bad government than to a lack of foreign aid. Dambisa Moyo, a young economist from Zambia, strongly opposes Sachs's pro-aid position. In Moyo's view "millions in Africa are poorer today because of aid; misery and poverty have not ended but have increased."[16] She argues that aid promotes corruption and detracts from development, and that Africa can benefit more from the financial markets, promotion of exports, and investment from China.

The Sachs–Easterly–Moyo debate shows that some major IPE debates are among scholars within the same theoretical perspective—in this case they are all liberal economists. As with many IPE debates, the reality is somewhere in between. Both Sachs's external constraints (lack of capital) and Easterly's and Moyo's internal constraints (bad governance and corruption) can interfere with development. Although Moyo and Easterly are correct that the results of aid have often been disappointing, the poorest LDCs may have few alternatives. Unlike middle-income LDCs, the least developed countries (LLDCs) often lack competitiveness in trade, and creditworthiness for borrowing on financial markets. Moyo's book was written shortly before the 2008 global financial crisis, and by the time it was published the financial markets were virtually closed to borrowing by most LLDCs. Regardless of the overall merits of foreign aid, the amount provided depends on the aid donors. After briefly discussing the trends, determinants, and effects of aid-giving, this chapter focuses mainly on the development strategies of the LDCs.

Aid is often provided for security and commercial reasons, and the main security issue after World War II was the Cold War. The members of the OECD's **Development Assistance Committee (DAC)** provided almost 90 percent of the aid during this period, and the Soviet Union and its Warsaw Pact allies provided about 10 percent. The DAC, which is the leading international forum for countries that provide development assistance, continues to supply most of the aid today; but China has also become an important aid-giver, especially in Sub-Saharan Africa. Currently the DAC has 29 members; 28 of them are OECD members, and the EU is also a DAC member. It is important to note that some OECD members are not in the DAC, and that some countries joined the OECD before joining the DAC. For example, five more OECD members joined the DAC in 2013: the Czech Republic, Iceland, Poland, the Slovak Republic, and Slovenia. In 1970 the UN resolved that the net ODA of DCs should amount to at least 0.7 percent of their GNIs.[17] However, the ODA of most DCs continues to be well below that objective. Table 11.2 shows the net ODA of DAC members as a percent of their GNIs. As the bottom line in Table 11.2 shows, after an initial decline from 0.52 percent in 1960 to 0.34 percent in 1970, ODA stayed in the 0.3 percent range from 1970 to 1990, but by 2000 the ODA level had fallen to 0.22 percent. Most notable was the decline of U.S. aid from 0.21 percent of its GNI in 1990 to 0.10 percent in 2000. Cold War security concerns were a major motivation for U.S. aid in the 1945–1990 period, and U.S. aid declined along with the collapse of the Soviet Union. Geostrategic security issues, especially the terrorist attack on New York's World Trade Center on September 11, 2001, help to explain a degree of revival of foreign aid since 2001. As Table 11.2 shows, total ODA increased from 0.22 percent in 2000 to 0.30 percent of GNI in 2013, and U.S. aid increased from 0.10 to 0.19 percent of its GNI. Despite the low percent of U.S. aid relative to its GNI, it was the largest DAC donor of net ODA in 2013, followed by the United Kingdom, Germany, Japan, and France.[18] Increased ODA has been part of an effort to combat terrorism, on the theory that poverty can contribute to extremism and violence. Commercial factors have also influenced aid-giving, and they became more important with the return of orthodox liberalism. As ODA declined in the 1980s–1990s, increased foreign investment fueled "the belief that the financing needs of developing countries could be

TABLE 11.2

Net Official Development Assistance of DAC[a] Members as a Percent of GNI[b]

	Member Year	1960	1970	1980	1990	2000	2013*
Australia	1961	0.38	0.59	0.48	0.34	0.27	0.34
Austria	1966	-	0.13	0.23	0.25	0.23	0.28
Belgium	1961	0.88	0.48	0.5	0.46	0.36	0.45
Canada	1961	0.19	0.43	0.43	0.44	0.25	0.27
Czech Republic	2013	-	-	-	-	-	0.11
Denmark	1963	0.09	0.38	0.74	0.94	1.06	0.85
Finland	1975	-	-	0.22	0.63	0.31	0.55
France	1961	1.38	0.65	0.63	0.60	0.30	0.41
Germany	1961	0.31	0.32	0.44	0.42	0.27	0.38
Greece	1999	-	-	-	-	0.20	0.13
Iceland	2013	-	-	-	-	-	0.26
Ireland	1985	-	-	0.16	0.16	0.29	0.45
Italy	1961	0.22	0.16	0.17	0.31	0.13	0.16
Japan	1961	0.24	0.23	0.32	0.31	0.28	0.23
Korea	2010	-	-	-	-	-	0.13
Luxembourg	1992	-	-	-	0.21	0.71	1.00
Netherlands	1961	0.31	0.63	0.97	0.92	0.84	0.67
New Zealand	1973	-	-	0.33	0.23	0.25	0.26
Norway	1962	0.11	0.33	0.87	1.17	0.76	1.07
Poland	2013	-	-	-	-	-	0.1
Portugal	1961	1.45	0.45	-	0.25	0.26	0.23
Slovak Republic	2013	-	-	-	-	-	0.09
Slovenia	2013	-	-	-	-	-	0.13
Spain	1991	-	-	-	0.20	0.22	0.16
Sweden	1965	0.05	0.37	0.78	0.91	0.80	1.02
Switzerland	1968	0.04	0.14	0.24	0.32	0.34	0.47
United Kingdom	1961	0.56	0.37	0.35	0.27	0.32	0.72
United States	1961	0.53	0.31	0.27	0.21	0.10	0.19
Total		0.52	0.34	0.37	0.33	0.22	0.30

[a]DAC = Development Assistance Committee of the OECD
[b]GNI = gross national income
*2013 data is preliminary, from figures reported to April 8, 2014

Source: OECD, Development Co-operation (Paris: OECD, various years).

met by a reliance on the markets."[19] However, private investment cannot substitute for ODA to poor countries because it is speculative and volatile, rarely deals with the environment and other social concerns, and is often directed to LDCs that have higher incomes and/or natural resources. In 2011–2012, DAC members gave 61 percent of their ODA as **bilateral aid** directly to recipients, and 39 percent through multilateral channels. (Donors provide **multilateral aid** through IOs whose policies are collectively determined.) To gain commercial benefits, a donor country often uses **tied aid,** in which it ties a percentage of its bilateral aid to purchases from its producers and employment of its technical experts. Other examples of commercial motives are France's directing its ODA "overwhelmingly to its former colonies" and Japan's directing almost three-quarters of its ODA during 1998–2002 to Asian recipients.[20]

Despite the strategic and commercial motives for aid-giving, ODA also plays an important role in addressing the needs of poorer LDCs for development finance. For example, the increase in ODA from 0.22 percent of GNI in 2000 to 0.30 percent in 2013 (Table 11.2) is partly a result of the UN's MDGs. However, the emphasis donors place on commercial and political-security objectives makes ODA a volatile and unpredictable source of funding for long-term development needs. Although aid has revived somewhat, it is not meeting the UN development goals. The 2002 *Monterrey Consensus* on Financing for Development urged DCs to make concrete efforts to reach the ODA target of 0.7 percent of GNI set by the UN in 1970. As Table 10.2 shows, in 2013 only five donors met the 0.7 percent goal: Denmark, Luxembourg, Norway, Sweden, and the United Kingdom. The ODA of the two largest OECD economies, the United States and Japan, amounted to only 0.19 and 0.23 percent of their GNIs in 2013. Some analysts argue that aid has not in fact revived much since 2000, because some of it has gone for debt relief. It is questionable whether this represents a real addition to ODA, because much of the debt would not have been repaid. As discussed, some analysts also question whether aid contributes to economic development. LDCs would therefore be well advised to devote considerable attention to alternative strategies to promote development. Thus, most of this chapter focuses on LDC development strategies. The next section examines the World Bank, which is a major source of multilateral development finance and also has considerable influence over LDC development strategies.

THE WORLD BANK GROUP

The *World Bank* ("the Bank") has a major effect on LDC development strategies because of its dominant role "as a non-private lender, as a research and idea-generating unit, and as a provider of advice to the Third World."[21] The World Bank is the largest lender of multilateral funds for international development, but it also has influence as a rating agency for others; its lending decisions, data collection, and analyses have a strong influence on bilateral donors, regional development banks, and private investors. The Bank's influence has an important coordinating function because aid-giving is so fragmented today. In 2006 there were about 225 bilateral donor agencies and 242 multilateral agencies.[22] The Bank also contributes to the evolution of ideas, and development debates often focus on support for, or opposition to, World Bank positions. Thus, the Bank forms the core of an *epistemic community* or "a network of professionals with recognized expertise and competence in a particular domain and an authoritative claim to policy-relevant knowledge within that domain or issue-area."[23] Recognized expertise is a source of power in today's knowledge-based world economy, and several factors account for the Bank's influence in generating ideas: The Bank affects the terms on which LDCs gain access to development finance and international capital markets, it has the largest group of development economists and research budget of any development organization, and the global media direct attention to Bank reports.

Located in Washington, DC, the Bank is in fact a **World Bank group** composed of five institutions (see Figure 2.1 in Chapter 2). The first institution, the *International Bank for Reconstruction and Development (IBRD)*, was planned at the 1944 Bretton Woods conference. The DCs established the IMF to deal with monetary and balance of payments issues, and their decision to form the IBRD was "something of an afterthought."[24] The DCs expected the IBRD to give priority to European reconstruction over Southern development, and Harry Dexter White of the U.S. Treasury Department even suggested that the new institution be called the Bank for Reconstruction. Although the negotiators responded to LDC protests by pledging that the IBRD would give "equitable" consideration to reconstruction and development, the first IBRD loans in 1947 went to France, the Netherlands, and Denmark. It was not until the United States established the European Recovery Program or Marshall Plan for Western Europe in 1948 that the IBRD shifted its focus mainly to development.[25]

The Bank, like the IMF, is a weighted voting institution. Each member has a capital subscription (or quota) based on its economic strength, which determines its financial contribution to the Bank and its number of votes. The G5 countries (the United States, Japan, Germany, the United Kingdom, and France) had the most votes in these institutions, and the emerging economies were increasingly dissatisfied with their lack of influence; but there were no significant changes until the 2008 global financial crisis. With the G20's approval, the IBRD won a general increase in its capital in April 2010 in return for a transfer of some voting power from smaller European countries to emerging economies. As a result, China leapfrogged over Germany, France, and the United Kingdom, and now has the third largest number of votes in the IBRD. India's voting power also increased, and it now has the seventh largest number of votes (see Table 11.3). However, the G5 countries continue to have the most votes in the IMF (see Chapter 6), and this has threatened the legitimacy of both the IMF and the IBRD. Members pay only 10 percent of their subscriptions to the IBRD and hold the remaining 90 percent as callable capital if needed to meet the IBRD's financial obligations. The IBRD receives most of its funds for development loans from borrowing on world capital markets. A **capital market** consists of institutions in a country (e.g., the stock exchange, banks, and insurance companies) that match supply with demand for long-term capital. The U.S. bond-rating services give IBRD bonds a triple-A credit rating, because LDCs have a good record in repaying its loans and its members provide financial backing if necessary with their callable capital. To make its bonds attractive to purchasers, the IBRD must pay market interest rates on the funds it borrows, and it therefore charges near-conventional interest rates on loans to LDCs. Since IBRD loans are not concessional, the OECD introduced

TABLE 11.3

International Bank for Reconstruction and Development (IBRD)Top Ten Countries by Voting Power

As of July 6, 2015

Rank	Country	No. of Votes	% of Total
1	United States	358,504	16.14
2	Japan	166,100	7.48
3	China	107,250	4.83
4	Germany	97,230	4.38
5/6	United Kingdom	87,247	3.93
5/6	France	87,247	3.93
7	India	67,696	3.05
8	Saudi Arabia	67,161	3.02
9	Russian Federation	62,809	2.83
10	Canada	59,010	2.66

Source: Data extracted from http://siteresources.worldbank.org/BODINT/Resources/278027-1215524804501/IBRDCountryVotingTable.pdf

the concept of **official development finance (ODF)** for official development loans that have too low a grant element to qualify as ODA. The IBRD's quasi-commercial loans qualify as ODF because the IBRD extends them for development purposes, accompanies the loans with economic and technical advice, and provides better terms than LDCs could obtain from borrowing directly on capital markets (LDCs deemed uncreditworthy cannot even borrow on capital markets).

To be a Bank member, a state must also join the IMF and provide it with detailed economic information. This requirement deterred most Communist states from joining the Bank for many years, even though they wanted to receive Bank loans (see Table 7.3 in Chapter 7). The *Board of Governors* is the main policy-making body in the Bank (and the IMF). Every Bank member has one governor, but each governor's votes are based on the weighted voting system. The governors meet once a year to review the Bank's operations and policies, admit new members, and amend the Articles of Agreement, and they delegate most of their functions to a 24-member *Board of Executive Directors* (or *Executive Board*). The Executive Board, which also has weighted voting, is responsible for approving all Bank loan proposals and developing the Bank's general policies. The G5 countries, China, Saudi Arabia, and Russia have appointed their own executive directors, while coalitions of members elect the other executive directors every two years. Elected executive directors must cast the votes of their entire coalition group as a unit.

The DCs were willing to give the Bank president and staff considerable discretion in daily operations because of the lack of Communist members, the Bank's weighted voting system, and the North's dominant position on the professional staff. The staff also has a degree of autonomy from governments because the IBRD receives most of its funds from financial markets (dependence on financial markets has other costs). The Bank staff also has more autonomy from the Executive Board because the executive directors lack analytical support to monitor the staff's management of complex issues; staff members are career civil servants, whereas executive directors are often rotated; and although the Executive Board can reject a staff loan proposal, only the Bank president can propose a loan. Despite the staff's prerogatives, its autonomy has limits, and the United States and some other DCs have scrutinized Bank actions more closely in recent years (see discussion in this chapter).[26]

The *International Finance Corporation (IFC)* became the second Bank group institution in 1956 (see Figure 2.1 in Chapter 2). Reflecting the Bank group's liberal economic orientation, the IFC is the largest multilateral source of loans and equity financing for private-sector projects in the South. Whereas the IBRD provides loans only to governments or with a government guarantee, the IFC gives loans to private ventures in LDCs without a government guarantee. The IFC is also more sensitive to business risk than the IBRD, because it is expected to make a profit in normal commercial terms. The IFC invests in equity shares of corporations, brings foreign and domestic partners together in joint ventures, and persuades commercial banks to lend to LDCs through joint financing deals. Like the IBRD, the IFC charges near-commercial rates on its loans. In view of the IFC's profits and the high interest rate on its loans, critics question whether the IFC is a money-making or philanthropic institution. However, the IFC describes itself as providing technical, financial, and environmental advice for private-oriented development projects.[27]

The *International Development Association (IDA)*, the third Bank group institution, was formed in 1960 in response to the South's complaints that poorer LDCs could not pay the high interest rates on IBRD loans. The South also opposed the Bank's weighted voting system, and demanded a soft-loan agency in which it would have greater control. The North finally agreed to create the IDA, but insisted that it be under World Bank auspices with a weighted voting system. Although the IDA and IBRD are legally and financially distinct, they share the same staff and their projects must meet the same criteria. The IDA provides soft loans or "credits" to LDC governments with no interest, 10-year grace periods, and 35- to 40-year maturities. (The IDA also provides a small share of its funds as grants to low-income countries in "debt distress."[28]) Unlike IBRD and IFC loans, IDA credits meet the criteria for official development assistance (ODA). LDCs and transition economies are categorized in three groups in terms of eligibility for loans: States with stronger economies such as Argentina, Brazil, Mexico, Malaysia, Thailand, Iran, Egypt, Poland, Russia, and China are only eligible for IBRD loans; states with somewhat weaker economies such as India, Pakistan, Bolivia, and Azerbaijan are eligible for both IBRD and IDA funds; and states with the weakest economies such as Bangladesh, Vietnam, Honduras, Tanzania, Kenya, Ethiopia, and Nigeria are only eligible for IDA credits.[29] The interest-free terms of IDA credits give it no basis for borrowing on capital markets, and it therefore depends on replenishments by governments every three years. Other donors often wait for the United States to pledge funds before making their own pledges, and the U.S. Congress sometimes delays approval of IDA contributions. Orthodox liberal views that LDCs should rely on private capital rather than IDA "handouts" pose a constant threat to its finances.

The other two Bank group institutions—the *International Center for Settlement of Investment Disputes (ICSID)* and the *Multilateral Investment Guarantee Agency (MIGA)*—encourage the flow of private foreign investment to LDCs and transition economies. The ICSID, formed in 1966, provides facilities for conciliation and arbitration of investment disputes. The need for a neutral international forum arose because foreign investors view host country courts as biased, and host countries see home country courts as threatening their sovereignty. The MIGA, formed in 1988, provides guarantees to foreign investors for noncommercial risks, such as currency inconvertibility, expropriation, war, and civil disturbances, and helps LDCs and transition economies inform others of investment opportunities.[30]

The Bank has considerable influence over bilateral as well as multilateral aid. Donor governments consider Bank reports a key source of data and analysis on development issues, and the Bank chairs aid consortia and **consultative groups** which enable DC donors to avoid duplication and coordinate their bilateral aid-giving. However, consultative groups also permit donors to exert collective pressures on a recipient government because only one recipient and its major donors attend each meeting.[31] As the most important multilateral development institution, the Bank also provides a model for the Inter-American, African, and Asian Development Banks and the European Bank for Reconstruction and Development (EBRD). Like the World Bank, these regional banks usually raise funds on international capital markets and lend at near-commercial interest rates; they also have IDA-type soft-loan affiliates that raise funds from government subscriptions. Whereas the World Bank focuses on larger projects and programs, the regional banks support smaller regional development projects.[32]

The United States is the most important Bank member, and there are several indications of its influence. First, it has more votes than any other member. Second, English is the Bank's only working language, reflecting its location in Washington, DC. The U.S. view that a single working language contributes to efficiency contrasts with the view of many other states that cultural and ethnic diversity dictates the need for more than one working language in IOs.[33] Third, the Bank president has always been American. Whereas the U.S. Treasury Department handles most matters related to U.S. involvement in the Bank, the White House nominates Bank presidents.[34] However, U.S. influence has declined in some respects. For example, the share of the Bank's outstanding securities held in the United States has steadily decreased, and U.S. voting power has fallen from about 40 percent of the total to less than 17 percent. There is increasing pressure from the emerging economies to end the tacit agreement that the Bank president is always American and the IMF managing director is always European, and the 2008 global financial crisis has given the emerging economies more influence. For example, many DCs are reducing their IDA contributions because of budgetary shortfalls. Emerging economies such as Brazil and China by contrast have become IDA donors, and the Bank is looking to them for increased contributions.

Although U.S. influence has declined, it continues to be the most important Bank member for several reasons:

- The United States is the only country with sufficient voting power (over 15 percent) to veto amendments to the Bank Articles of Agreement and decisions to increase the Bank's capital.
- Other DCs have been willing to let the United States take "the lead—and the heat—for doing what they wanted anyway," and they do not want to jeopardize relations with the United States.[35] Japan and Europe have been more interested in controlling regional institutions such as the Asian Development Bank and the EBRD.
- The United States has considerable structural or soft power in the Bank, enabling it to induce "other countries to *want* what it wants."[36] This soft power depends on U.S.-based civil society actors such as academics, think tanks, and NGOs with ready access to the Bank in Washington, DC.
- The creation of IDA in 1960 gave the United States more influence than it had over the IBRD. The U.S. threat to withhold IDA replenishments is sometimes explicitly linked with U.S. objections to specific Bank policies.

Despite the influence of the United States and other DCs, the Bank sometimes asserts its autonomy and uses its expertise to influence foreign aid officials in the DCs. Thus, the United States and the Bank have "a complex, evolving relationship that is part symbiosis, part two-way influence, and part struggle over the Bank's autonomy of action."[37] As we discuss later in this chapter, China and other emerging economies are seeking to create alternative IOs in which they will have more influence.

This chapter briefly outlines issues raised by critics and supporters of the Bank. The strongest critics are historical materialists on the left and orthodox liberals on the right. Historical materialists accuse the Bank of enriching the North at the expense of the South, and of bolstering "an international capitalist system that is detrimental to mankind and the environment."[38] Some orthodox liberals, by contrast, see the Bank as interested "in ever-increasing multinational aid" and advise it to "impose a greater check on the staff's tendency to be 'state enthusiasts.'"[39] Defenders of the Bank consider it inevitable that it "should be subjected to severe criticism from the ideologues of both left and right."[40] However, scholars who are not ideologues also criticize the Bank's policies. For example, one recent study criticizes the Bank for espousing a number of development policies and goals that it does not put into practice.[41] As this chapter discusses, the Bank has often disregarded challenges to its liberal free market approach to development, and has been more willing to criticize government failure than market failure. During the 1980s–1990s, the Bank used its *structural adjustment loans (SALs)* to pressure LDCs to adopt orthodox liberal policies. Only recently has the Bank adopted some policies to cushion vulnerable groups and states from unrestrained market pressures. Other criticisms of the Bank range from its patronizing attitude toward the *United Nations Development Program (UNDP)* and the regional development banks; to its highly centralized structure in Washington, DC, with too little staff time spent in the field; and the priority it gives to large project commitments with fast-disbursing loans over project supervision, implementation, and evaluation. In fairness to the Bank, as the largest multilateral development institution it is a target of criticism regardless of its policies. For example, some critics charge that the Bank is too slow to change its policies in response to civil society pressures and LDC requirements. However, when the Bank alters its policies, others charge that it is embracing "the latest fads in development thinking regardless of their substantive merits."[42] The Bank, like other IOs, is also largely a creature of its member states, and its ability to increase loans to the poorest LDCs depends on the North's willingness to provide IDA replenishments. We now turn to a discussion of LDC development strategies.

LDC DEVELOPMENT STRATEGIES

As discussed in Chapter 4, orthodox liberals were advocates of *modernization theory* in the 1950s–1960s. Most modernization theorists advised the South to follow the same path to development that the North had taken. Modernization theorists assumed that free trade and capital movements were beneficial, and some such as Walt Rostow were highly optimistic that LDCs would develop rapidly if they emulated the North.[43] However, Rostow's predictions proved to be overly optimistic, and the decline in the North's demand for imports during the 1930s Great Depression caused world prices for Latin American commodity exports to collapse. Thus, John Maynard Keynes's interventionist liberalism had more appeal to many LDC development economists than orthodox liberalism. Interventionist liberals accepted the idea that LDCs required government involvement in their economies. The apparent success of Soviet central planning in the 1930s also contributed to support for "statism," or a greater role for the state. This skepticism of free trade and emphasis on statism provided the setting for the **import substitution industrialization (ISI)** strategy.[44] The remainder of this chapter focuses on the succession of LDC development strategies since World War II.

IMPORT SUBSTITUTION INDUSTRIALIZATION

The ideas of several major economists influenced Southern development strategies during the early postwar period. Although Keynes focused on government involvement in the North, his ideas contributed to the view that LDC governments should do more to promote economic development. Development strategies also drew on the ideas of Raúl Prebisch and Hans Singer, who rejected the classical liberal view that LDCs should rely on their comparative advantage in primary product exports. In 1950, Prebisch and Singer separately published studies arguing that the North–South income gap was growing because of a long-term decline in the prices of primary products (raw materials and agricultural goods). Whereas the demand for industrial goods such as automobiles and televisions rises as income increases, the same does not apply to primary products. Indeed, the North's demand for raw materials may even decline as technological advances lead to the discovery of substitutes (e.g., synthetic rubber for natural rubber). Thus, LDCs that depend on primary product exports have declining terms of trade. When LDCs increase their primary product production to gain more revenue, the surplus stocks in fact result in lower prices and more poverty. LDCs should therefore decrease their emphasis on primary products and focus on industrialization.[45] Prebisch argued that ISI would permit LDCs to produce manufactured goods that they had previously imported. He used the terms *center* and *periphery*, and his writings formed the core of Latin American structuralism. Prebisch's structuralism was a *precursor* to dependency theory. He was more optimistic than dependency theorists that the South could catch up with the North through protectionism and state-promoted industrialization.[46]

Neomercantilists such as Hamilton and List had supported policies similar to ISI for the United States and Germany as late industrializers, and some LDCs had developed ISI as a short-term response to the Great Depression. However, it was only after World War II that the South adopted ISI as a long-term development strategy. Central to ISI was the argument that LDCs should promote industrial growth through protectionist barriers and subsidies for their infant industries. In the 1950s–1960s LDCs in Latin America, Asia, and Africa followed ISI policies, and import substitution "emerged as the new gospel for Third World industrialization."[47] The World Bank generally supported ISI during the 1950s because it was affected by postwar interventionist liberal views that the state should have an important role in development. The Bank's approach to development placed considerable emphasis on industrialization, which meant ISI in the 1950s, and it provided funding for major infrastructure projects such as transportation, communications, and power projects that LDCs needed to industrialize.[48]

Initially, ISI provided some major gains for the South. For example, Latin America had healthy industrial growth rates in the 1940s–1950s, and India's steel production increased by six times from 1951 to 1966. International conditions were favorable for ISI, because LDCs benefited from prosperity and growth in North America and Western Europe. The "green revolution" also led to the development of high-yielding grains that increased agricultural output in Asian LDCs and masked the fact that ISI promoted industrialization at the expense of agriculture. However, serious problems developed with ISI in the 1960s–1970s. For example, LDCs following ISI were more vulnerable to a global food crisis in the 1970s, when global food stocks fell to their lowest levels in 20 years. The food crisis severely affected the South because many LDCs could not purchase foodstuffs on global markets at inflated prices.[49] The sharp rise in OPEC oil prices in 1973 compounded the problems for LDC food and oil importers. These external stresses exposed a number of weaknesses in ISI. First, the global food crisis pointed to the pitfalls in emphasizing industrialization at the expense of agriculture. The LDC share of world agricultural exports fell from 44 percent in 1955 to 32 percent in 1970, and the decline in revenue exacerbated LDC balance-of-payments deficits. Second, despite its emphasis on promoting self-sufficiency, ISI *increased* the South's dependence on the North. In view of their shortages of capital and foreign exchange, LDCs encouraged inward FDI as part of their ISI policies to promote industrialization. Thus, MNCs established subsidiaries behind the LDC trade barriers, and the U.S. government supported ISI as part of "its vigorous efforts to secure favorable conditions for U.S. foreign direct investment."[50]

ISI's most serious weakness was its inability to promote industrial competitiveness. Although industrialization proceeded well under an easier first stage of ISI, the second stage was more difficult. In the first stage, LDCs replaced nondurable consumer imports such as shoes, household products, and clothing with domestic production. LDCs have a sizable domestic market for these labor-intensive goods, and they do not require much capital investment or advanced technology. However, LDCs had to move to a second stage to maintain high industrial growth rates, replacing imports of intermediate goods (e.g., petrochemicals and steel) and producer and consumer durables (e.g., refrigerators and automobiles) with domestic production. These products are more difficult to produce because they are capital-intensive and depend on economies of scale and higher levels of technology. When LDCs imported technology and inputs to produce these goods, the cost of the imports outweighed any savings from locally producing the final products. ISI also exacerbated income inequalities and unemployment, because the emphasis on capital-intensive production concentrated development in a small segment of the population in industrial enclaves.[51] In response to their balance-of-payments problems, LDCs pursuing second-stage ISI sought external loans, aid, and investment and turned increasingly to trade protectionism. Liberal economists argued that "an import substitution policy tends to be less and less successful the longer it continues";[52] and by the late 1960s, World Bank and IFC "financing of profitable import-substituting industry" was giving way "to a more discriminating policy of industrial financing."[53] Even Prebisch warned that "the proliferation of industries of every kind in a closed market has deprived the Latin American countries of the advantages of specialization and economies of scale."[54] Prebisch hoped that regional trade agreements would provide economies of scale so that Latin American LDCs could continue to industrialize under ISI; but Latin American regionalism during the 1970s was unsuccessful (see Chapter 9).

Many Latin American and South Asian states continued with second-stage ISI during the 1960s–1970s, because protectionist domestic groups posed an obstacle to policy change. However, some LDCs turned to socialist central planning based on the Soviet Union model, and others changed from ISI to export-led growth strategies. The following discussion will show that export-led growth was more successful than ISI and socialist development strategies. However, it is important to note that ISI had a significant role in beginning the industrialization process in some LDCs, and that some LDCs (e.g., China and Taiwan) pursued ISI and export-led growth strategies simultaneously.

SOCIALIST DEVELOPMENT STRATEGIES

During the 1960s, scholars challenged ISI from both the right and the left, and many leftist scholars turned to dependency theory (see Chapter 5). Dependency theorists viewed ISI as too moderate, and argued that LDCs could achieve autonomous development only by becoming socialist and severing linkages with the North. A small number of LDCs including China, North Korea, Cuba, Ethiopia, Mozambique, Tanzania, Vietnam, Laos, Cambodia, and Burma adopted socialist development strategies. Some states followed the Soviet model, and tried to replace market signals with state central planning in allocating resources and setting production targets, wages, and prices. LDCs taking the socialist route often reduced inequities by providing better access to health care and education, improving the status of women, and opening more facilities to the public. However, LDCs (other than China to some extent) lacked the communications and transportation infrastructure for central planning and a well-trained bureaucracy to design and monitor the plans. Like the Soviet Union and Eastern Europe, LDC central planners were also more successful in setting production targets and increasing output than in ensuring the quality of output and the efficient use of resources.

Tanzania's experience with socialism is instructive because it began with high ideals under an internationally respected leader Julius Nyerere. Nyerere issued the Arusha Declaration—a statement of party principles—in early 1967 that called for national self-reliance, state control of the major means of production and exchange, and a development approach with a strong rural focus. To implement this program, Nyerere planned widespread nationalization of private banks, insurance companies, food processors, and export-trading companies. He also wanted to promote rural development by creating self-sufficient socialist villages throughout the country. Bringing the rural population together in large communal villages (*ujamaas*) would provide peasant farmers with access to modern methods, equipment, and basic services; reduce inequality among classes; and increase agricultural productivity.

However, Nyerere's plans were unrealistic and had unintended consequences. For example, when the rural population resisted his plans, the government moved about 11 million people to new villages between 1973 and 1977 through coercion and brutality. This mass disruption caused a rapid decline in food production, and Tanzania had to seek IMF and World Bank loans and large amounts of food aid. Nyerere's plans for nationalization and state control were also unsuccessful. Many state corporations were poorly managed, inefficient, overstaffed, and debt-ridden. The 1973–1974 OPEC oil price increases added further to Tanzania's problems, and by the late 1970s it had a soaring trade deficit and foreign debt. As a socialist state, Tanzania registered major improvements in primary school enrollment, adult literacy rates, sanitation, and life expectancy. However, this progress was financed mainly by foreign aid, primarily from the West. High oil prices, poor weather, low export revenues, and increasing debt service were plaguing the country by 1981. When orthodox liberalism returned with Thatcher and Reagan, Tanzania was still very poor and far from self-reliant. Thus, privatization began to take hold, and Nyerere left the presidency saddened and frustrated. Several other LDCs with socialist policies had similar experiences, and they lost a major source of economic and military support when the Soviet bloc collapsed in the 1980s–1990s. Thus, very few LDCs currently follow socialist strategies, and even holdouts such as Cuba are seeking closer ties with the capitalist world.[55]

EXPORT-LED GROWTH

The East Asian NIEs—South Korea, Taiwan, Singapore, and Hong Kong—adopted **export-led growth** strategies that were much more successful than the socialist and ISI strategies in the 1970s–1980s. In the 1950s Taiwan and South Korea had adopted ISI policies, which resulted in balance-of-payments deficits and did not decrease their dependence on primary commodity exports. Thus, they followed Japan's example in the 1960s and shifted from ISI to an export-oriented policy. While maintaining moderate protection of domestic producers, they promoted industrial exports with tax incentives, export credits, and duty-free imports of inputs required by exporters. Taiwan and South Korea also abandoned minimum wage legislation to encourage increased employment in export-oriented industries. During the early 1980s, Southeast Asian economies such as Malaysia, Indonesia, and Thailand also switched to export-led growth strategies. Thus, Hong Kong, Singapore, South Korea, and Taiwan were "first-tier" Asian NIEs; and Malaysia, Indonesia, and Thailand were "second-tier" NIEs. The change to export-led growth had a dramatic effect on economic performance. For example, South Korea's GDP grew at an average annual rate of more than 8 percent during the 1960s, and its exports rose from $31 million in 1960 to $882 million in 1970. In the 1960s most South Korean and Taiwanese industrial exports required relatively little capital and large amounts of unskilled labor, but industrial wages gradually increased and the two economies began producing more sophisticated industrial goods with highly skilled labor. By the late 1980s, Taiwan and South Korea were the tenth and thirteenth largest world exporters of manufactures, respectively.[56]

The East Asian successes of the 1960s to 1980s are often compared with the experiences of Latin American NIEs—Argentina, Brazil, Chile, and Mexico.[57] Although the Latin Americans provided some incentives for exports in the 1960s, their policies continued to be based mainly on ISI. Thus, the first two columns of Table 11.4 show that the East Asian NIEs had much higher GDP per capita growth rates than the Latin American NIEs. Whereas South Korea's GDP per capita of $747 was well *below* the per capita GDPs of all four Latin American NIEs in 1963, by 1988 its per capita GDP of $4,094 was *above* the Latin American figures. Hong Kong and Singapore's GDPs soared above $11,000 by 1988. The last two columns of Table 11.4 show that export-led growth strategies led to much higher export-to-GDP ratios. Whereas South Korea's export-to-GDP ratio of 2.3 was well below the Latin American figures in 1963, its export-led growth policies resulted in a ratio of 35.4 in 1988, exceeding the Latin American ratios. The 1988 export-to-GDP

TABLE 11.4

GDP[a] per Capita and Export/GDP Ratios

	GDP per Capita		Export/GDP Ratios	
	1963	1988	1963	1988
East Asian NIEs[b]				
Hong Kong	$2,247	$11,952	39.0	51.1
South Korea	747	4,094	2.3	35.4
Singapore	1,777	11,693	124.5	164.2
Taiwan	980	4,607	15.3	51.8
Latin American NIEs				
Argentina	$2,949	$3,474	10.0	10.2
Brazil	1,400	3,424	6.0	9.5
Chile	3,231	3,933	11.6	31.9
Mexico	2,312	3,649	5.1	11.9

[a]GDP = gross domestic product
[b]NIEs = newly industrializing economies
Source: Bela Balassa, *Policy Choices for the 1990s* (London: Macmillan, 1993), pp. 57 and 59.

ratios for Singapore (164.2), Taiwan (51.8), and Hong Kong (51.1) were much higher than the Latin American ratios. There were also striking differences in the composition of exports, with Taiwan, South Korea, and Hong Kong *each* producing more manufactured exports than all of Latin America by the late 1980s.[58]

The East Asian NIEs had a few years of reduced growth during the 1980s foreign debt crisis, but they did not seek debt rescheduling and soon adjusted their economies and resumed rapid growth rates. Their healthy export positions, combined with large infusions of foreign investment (especially from Japan), provided sufficient revenue so they could continue their debt payments without depending on IMF and World Bank loans. The Latin Americans following ISI, by contrast, were more severely affected by the debt crisis and had to seek substantial IMF and World Bank funding.[59] As we will discuss, the East and Southeast Asian economies encountered some problems that became starkly evident in the late 1990s. However, just as ISI had been the "gospel" for LDC industrialization in the 1950s, export-led growth emerged as the new gospel from the 1970s to the early 1990s. Although there was a general consensus that export-led growth was more successful than ISI, scholars disagreed on the reasons for the East Asians' success.

IPE Perspectives and the East Asian Experience

Liberals, neomercantilists, and historical materialists had different explanations for East Asia's success in the 1960s to 1980s. Liberal economists viewed East Asia's export-led growth strategy as "outward-oriented" as opposed to

Latin America's "inward-oriented" ISI. East Asians were open to freer trade and competition because they did not have "the mistrust of markets and private entrepreneurship that motivates large-scale doctoring in other Asian countries and in African and South American countries."[60] Thus, liberals attributed the East Asians' success to their adoption of open market policies. Neomercantilists by contrast attributed East Asia's success to the role of a strong **developmental state** "in engineering economic growth, development and success in these countries."[61] Hamilton and List had argued that late industrializers required state intervention to catch up with more advanced states (see Chapter 3), but it was not until the early 1980s that Chalmers Johnson coined the phrase "developmental state" in regard to Japan and the East Asian NIEs.[62] Neomercantilists attributed several characteristics to East Asian developmental states:

- They guided the market, controlling investment flows, promoting the development of technology, and protecting selected infant industries.
- They identified development as the main objective, encouraging citizens to increase investment rather than consumption and using repression if necessary to enforce their priorities.
- They invested heavily in education to give people the skills to be globally competitive.
- They depended on a highly skilled, technocratic bureaucracy to institute economic reforms.

Although ISI and export-led growth both depended on government intervention, neomercantilists argued that they differed in two respects: (1) The developmental state focused mainly on export industries, whereas ISI focused on industrialization mainly to meet domestic demand; (2) ISI protected all local industries, whereas the developmental state's support was targeted to those industries most likely to succeed.

Unlike liberals and neomercantilists, world-systems theorists believed that the NIEs were not achieving genuine economic development. NIEs were in the semiperiphery, and were simply "more advanced exemplars of dependent development," still dependent on states in the core.[63] Thus, André Gunder Frank argued that NIEs producing end products such as shirts, radios, or automobiles were "increasing their dependent integration into a worldwide division of labor ... in which they are allocated the least remunerative and technologically obsolete contribution."[64] A fourth group of theorists explained East Asia's success in terms of *political culture*, or widely shared social values that affect a state's political economy. The neomercantilist focus on the state was insufficient because "the nature of ... society is important in determining whether or not state policies are effective."[65] For example, Confucian philosophy in Japan, China, and the East Asian NIEs is supportive of an economic development model based on collective values, respect for authority, hard work and enterprise, strong kinship ties in entrepreneurship, and a benevolent state staffed by highly educated individuals. Thus, Confucianism was a key factor explaining East Asia's success in promoting economic development.[66]

Most analysts opted for the neomercantilist model of the strong developmental state as the best explanation for East Asia's rapid economic growth. However, the Asian financial crisis of the late 1990s raised serious questions about all of these models and demonstrated "how rapidly an informed consensus can change."[67]

The Asian Financial Crisis

In 1993 the World Bank issued a report on *The East Asian Miracle* that examined the region's "remarkable record of high and sustained economic growth" from 1965 to 1990, and some analysts began to refer to the East Asian "miracle economies."[68] As discussed, economists could not agree on the reasons for East Asia's success, and the term *miracle* implied that "the phenomenon was beyond purely scientific explanation."[69] By the mid-1990s, however, there were signs of lower earnings, slower export growth, and surplus industrial capacity. For example, problems emerged in Thailand's real estate and financial sector, several large South Korean enterprises or *chaebol* failed, and the Japanese economy continued to stagnate. In 1997 there was a sharp downturn in the value of Thailand's *baht* currency, and in the country's growth and assets. Thailand's problems also spread by contagion to neighboring countries such as Indonesia, Malaysia, South Korea, the Philippines, and Singapore, and the most severely affected economies had to seek IMF and World Bank loans. By 1999 the worst part of the financial crisis was over, and the region began to recover as U.S. and European demand for East Asian exports increased. Although there was growing confidence in the future of East Asian economic growth, the economies were slow to institute some needed economic reforms, and they continued to be vulnerable to changing economic conditions.[70] The following discussion examines the reasons for the East Asian shift from "miracle" to "meltdown" status and the effects of the Asian financial crisis on international development strategies. (Chapter 7 discusses the effects of the Asian financial crisis on the IMF's role and the need for a new international financial architecture.)

During the Asian financial crisis, economists who had tried to explain the rapid East Asian growth "now struggled to explain the 'meltdown.'"[71] Historical materialists had questioned whether the East Asian economies were achieving genuine, autonomous development, and they believed that the financial crisis strengthened their arguments. Although the developmental state contributed to rapid East Asian economic growth in the 1970s–1980s, this growth was dependent on U.S. and Japanese policies. Taiwan and South Korea had special linkages with the United States because of their strategic location vis-à-vis the Soviet Union and China; thus, the United States gave them military and economic aid, opened its market to their exports, and permitted them to follow protectionist policies. East Asian economic growth also stemmed from special linkages with Japan. Japanese colonialism had created the social foundations for East Asia's industrialization, but also the basis for dependency relations. When the Japanese yen increased in value as a result of the 1985 Plaza Agreement (see Chapter 6), Japanese companies invested in East Asian subsidiaries to take advantage of cheaper costs of production. These Japanese investments helped East Asia avoid the worst effects of the 1980s foreign debt crisis that ravaged Latin America and Africa (see Chapter 7).

In the late 1980s, however, East Asia's dependence on the United States and Japan became problematic. The United States responded to its growing balance-of-payments deficits by criticizing others' "unfair" trade practices, and South Korea and Taiwan offered concessions because of fears that the United States would retaliate. With the breakup of the Soviet bloc, the United States was also less willing to supply large amounts of aid to South Korea and Taiwan. East Asia's development was also fragile because of its dependence on Japan. Although East Asian industrial exports to the West were increasing, the goods were often produced by Japanese subsidiaries, designed in Japan, composed of imported Japanese components, and dependent on Japanese technology. For example, when Samsung, a large Korean industrial conglomerate, received government approval to enter the auto industry in 1994, it planned to import the advanced technology it needed from Nissan in Japan.[72] Although the East Asians had trade surpluses with the West, they had growing trade deficits with Japan. The depreciation of the Japanese yen relative to the U.S. dollar in the 1990s put downward pressure on East Asian currencies, many of which were pegged (at least partly) to the U.S. dollar. As Japanese exports became more competitive and Japan's imports from East Asia declined, problems of indebtedness and lack of competitiveness in the region increased. The financial crisis began when Thailand had to float its baht currency in 1997 (the baht had been pegged to a basket of currencies, with the U.S. dollar the most important).[73]

Neomercantilists and liberals viewed the historical materialist contention that East Asians had not achieved genuine, autonomous development as unduly negative. East Asia had largely recovered from the financial crisis by 2000, and there was renewed confidence in economic growth in the region. Even if the East Asian NIEs had not been miracle economies, they *had* developed rapidly, and their economic development has resumed. It is therefore important to discuss the liberal and neomercantilist perspectives. In 1968, Samuel Huntington argued that authoritarian governments provided stability and order in developing societies and that democracy was a luxury to be introduced at a later time.[74] Neomercantilists argued that authoritarian East Asian developmental states oversaw some marked improvements in economic growth and prosperity. Liberals by contrast attributed the Asian financial crisis to this pervasive role of governments and government–business linkages. In their view, the 1990s financial crisis revealed that authoritarian developmental states were not as efficient and immune to political pressure as neomercantilists maintained. For example, close government–business linkages contributed to widespread nepotism, and the operation of banks and access to credit depended more on political connections than on market forces. Thus, lenders and foreign investors expanded credit without sufficient safeguards to risky borrowers, and huge sums were spent for questionable building and real estate projects. These inefficiencies challenged the neomercantilist contention that East Asian authoritarian states promoted development.

Whereas liberals questioned the benefits of developmental states, neomercantilists questioned liberal claims that the East Asians benefited from economic interdependence. Indeed, neomercantilists argued that "deeper financial integration" was a "necessary condition" for the Asian financial crisis.[75] East Asian economies had opened their capital accounts and received a dramatic increase of international capital inflows during the early 1990s. The financial crisis resulted from the vulnerability of these economies to the massive reversal of these capital flows. Deeper financial integration also contributed to a *contagion effect* in which creditors engaged in speculative attacks on currencies, not because of economic fundamentals, but because of the actions of other creditors.[76] Neomercantilists, historical materialists, and some liberals also charged that the liberal economic emphasis on composite statistics such as the growth in GDP and per capita GDP had led to an overestimation of East Asian development in the 1980s and early 1990s. For example, Paul Krugman has argued in reference to the East Asian economies that

> sustained growth in a nation's per capita income can only occur if there is a rise in output *per unit of input*. Mere increases in inputs, without an increase in the efficiency with which those inputs are used—investing in more machinery and infrastructure—must run into diminishing returns; input-driven growth is inevitably limited.[77]

Environmentalists have argued that rapid East and Southeast Asian economic growth is not sustainable in the long term. In Indonesia, logging practices are contributing to deforestation of 2.4 million hectares per year; in the Malaysian state of Sarawak, loggers have removed 30 percent of the forest area in 23 years; and in Vietnam, resources are exported with little concern for social and environmental consequences.[78] As discussed in Chapter 5, *sustainable development* is a policy that "meets the needs of the present without compromising the ability of future generations to meet their own needs."[79]

The export-led growth model has a number of strengths, and the East Asian developmental state outperformed other LDCs according to most economic indicators in the 1970s–1980s. However, the Asian financial crisis demonstrated that the export-led growth strategy also has weaknesses. The IMF, World Bank, and most industrial states strongly supported another development strategy in response to the 1980s foreign debt crisis and the 1990s Asian financial crisis: the orthodox liberal model.

THE REVIVAL OF ORTHODOX LIBERALISM

Two characteristics are critical for a successful developmental state: a highly skilled technocratic bureaucracy and close cooperation among major economic groups such as agriculture, business, and labor. However, most LDCs "lack the highly professional merit-based bureaucracies and the tradition of cooperation between key economic actors that would permit them to replicate the East Asian model."[80] The most important constraint on replicating the developmental state model was the revival of orthodox liberalism. In line with the new liberal orthodoxy, critics charge that the IMF and World Bank viewed "the market rational/market ideological approach" as "the only correct course for development."[81] The shift to the right by British Prime Minister Margaret Thatcher and U.S. President Ronald Reagan in the late 1970s–1980s resulted in a strong attack on statist development strategies in the South. Thus, the Reagan administration, the U.S. Treasury, the Federal Reserve, and the international financial institutions responded to the 1980s foreign debt crisis by supporting what later became known as the *Washington Consensus*. The **Washington Consensus** refers to the belief that "the combination of democratic government, free markets, a dominant private sector and openness to trade is the recipe for prosperity and growth."[82] (This is not what John Williamson meant by the term when he coined it in 1989.[83]) In applying the Washington Consensus to the 1980s foreign debt crisis, the IMF and the Bank provided *structural adjustment loans (SALs)* on the condition that recipients control inflation, decrease government spending, balance their budgets, privatize state-owned enterprises, deregulate financial and labor markets, and liberalize their trade and investment policies.

Structural Adjustment and the Theoretical Perspectives

A number of LDC debtors implemented World Bank and IMF-financed *structural adjustment programs (SAPs)* during the 1980s, and the South became "a laboratory for a huge experiment" in promoting economic development through orthodox liberalism.[84] Studies of the effects of SAPs in Sub-Saharan Africa demonstrate the wide range of views regarding the effects of structural adjustment. For example, one study concluded that "the performance of poor compliers deteriorates over time and is significantly worse than the performance of countries that comply" with the SAP conditions; a second study found that LDCs following World Bank structural adjustment policy conditions most closely "failed to grow as quickly as several less compliant African economies during the same period"; and a third study argued that SAPs "over the past decade are leading to the destruction of the [African] continent … with the failure of the state being an immediate outcome and environmental deterioration being devastating in the long run."[85] This section briefly discusses SAPs and the theoretical perspectives.

Historical materialists believe that SAPs are not "simply an innocuous remedial package for sustained growth and development," but "an almost deliberate scheme for the perpetuation of export dependency … and reproduction of existing conditions of global inequality."[86] SAPs will not alleviate the South's problems because the IMF and World Bank caused the LDC debt problems in the first place. Whereas historical materialists are the harshest critics of structural adjustment, orthodox liberals are the strongest supporters. They believe that SAPs provide the necessary discipline based on the Washington Consensus to deal with LDC debt problems. Interventionist liberals agree with orthodox liberals that SAPs are often necessary to combat domestic inefficiencies and corruption in LDCs; but they are more receptive to state interventionism and believe that the World Bank and IMF should be more sensitive to the effect of SAPs on the poorest groups and states. Neomercantilists view the World Bank and IMF's emphasis on downsizing government through privatization, deregulation, and trade liberalization as misguided because late industrializers *require* government intervention to catch up with the leading powers. Despite these differing perceptions, many analysts would agree that SAPs had serious problems in the 1980s–1990s. After referring to some strengths of the SAPs, a discussion of their problems follows.

Structural Adjustment and Questions About Orthodox Liberalism

The World Bank's SAPs were most effective in middle-income LDCs that export manufactures, such as Brazil, Morocco, the Philippines, South Korea, Thailand, and Uruguay. These states had more developed institutions for implementing policy reforms and better resilience in dealing with disruptions resulting from structural adjustment policies. Thus, liberal studies indicate that SAPs in middle-income LDCs sometimes contributed to lower government deficits, increased export earnings, more financing for private investment, and economic growth and efficiency. However, the effects of SAPs on the poorest LDCs and the poorest groups within LDCs were a more contentious issue. The Bank endorsed liberal economic views that benefits from the efficient allocation of resources under free markets would "trickle down" to the poor. However, critics rejected this view and argued that the poorest groups had to bear the largest share of the adjustment burden. The persistence of poverty in low-income LDCs and the poorest groups within LDCs gave credence to these criticisms and eventually forced the Bank to alter its approach.[87] Critics also charged that the emphasis of SAPs on privatization and deregulation did not address the need for effective LDC governments, and that the Bank's "top-down" approach to structural adjustment precluded local participation in "owning" policies and implementing reforms. The following sections examine these criticisms by focusing on an LDC region (Sub-Saharan Africa) and a group within LDCs (women). We then discuss the World Bank's attempts to address the problems by altering its policies.

Structural Adjustment and Sub-Saharan Africa

Some of the strongest criticisms of structural adjustment relate to its effects on Sub-Saharan Africa ("Africa" in this section). More than two-thirds of African states received SALs in the 1980s, but during that decade per capita growth in Africa contracted at an annual rate of 2.2 percent, external debt tripled, and debt service payments accounted for 25 percent of goods and services exports. Per capita income at the end of the 1980s was lower than it had been in 1960, and government deficits rose from 2 percent in 1980 to more than 6 percent at the end of the decade. Thus, the 1980s have been described as a lost decade for Africa.[88]

Liberal economists argue that SAPs are often blamed for problems caused by general economic deterioration. The World Bank and IMF were simply reacting to the foreign debt crisis, which resulted from inefficient LDC economic policies and global changes such as the 1970s oil crisis. African problems such as political instability, civil wars, and famine are also difficult to resolve, and economic conditions would be even worse without IMF and World Bank SAPs. The Bank and IMF market-led prescriptions are the best strategies for eliciting adjustment and growth, because state-led strategies such as ISI were unsuccessful. However, critics argue that SAPs in Africa put too much emphasis on market-oriented policies and impose the largest costs on the poorest groups and states. IMF and World Bank demands that LDC debtors privatize, deregulate, and downgrade the role of government ignore the fact that the public sector provides a critical source of employment for African LDCs. As government capacity declines, infrastructure such as transportation and communications, and services such as health care and education also suffer.

Furthermore, the emphasis on privatization does not address the fact that private firms do not supply public goods required for development. LDCs rely on government to provide resources for education and other aspects of human capital necessary for industrialization and competitiveness. Critics also oppose the emphasis SAPs put on trade liberalization. Although Latin American and East Asian LDCs reap some benefits from freer trade, there are few benefits for lower-income African and Asian LDCs. Domestic industries in Latin America and East Asia are now more competitive because these states sheltered their industrial producers for lengthy periods. African LDCs, by contrast, are only beginning to industrialize and require protection for their infant industries. Structural adjustment funds for privatization also contributed to corruption in many African states. Some African leaders sold "government assets to political cronies and select businessmen at minimum prices on highly favorable terms."[89]

Structural Adjustment and LDC Women

Another criticism of IMF and World Bank SAPs is that they have disregarded gender issues. Since gender inequality and the exploitation of women are prevalent worldwide, it is not possible for SAPs to be gender-neutral. By disregarding the subsidiary role of women, SAPs reinforce male bias and exacerbate the problems confronting LDC women. The positions of LDC women vary widely because of differences in culture, history, levels of economic development, and types of government. The positions of women in the same society may also differ depending on their social class and ethnicity. Nevertheless, we can generalize about the challenges facing most LDC women:

- In the household, women spend more time than men on unpaid subsistence work such as child care, food production and preparation, health care, and education.
- Outside the home, more women than men work in the informal sector of the economy, with little government regulation. They are often service

providers such as food stall operators, market traders, messengers, and shoe shiners, with earnings well below those in the formal sector.

- In the formal sector, women are often in lower-skilled, lower-wage occupations, and they tend to receive lower salaries than men for doing the same work.
- Women are more concentrated in agriculture and less in industry than men. In Africa, women produce about 90 percent of the food but are less important in the production of export crops.
- Women tend to have lower incomes than men, and households where women are the sole breadwinners are among the poorest groups in LDCs.[90]

World Bank policy prescriptions are based on macroeconomic concepts relevant for the economy as a whole rather than individual firms or households. The Bank gives little attention to the effect of its SAPs on women's work, because much of the time they do unpaid work in the household which does not appear in production statistics. For example, SAPs usually call for cutbacks in government spending, leading to decreased public funding for health, education, and water and sanitation facilities. Much of the burden of health care and education therefore shifts to the household, where women have most of the responsibilities. The World Bank and IMF also often pressure LDCs to lower government deficits by phasing out food subsidies. The higher food costs force women to use cheaper foods that take longer to prepare, such as coarse grain and root crops, and to bake at home rather than purchasing bread. Furthermore, hospitals may cut costs by shifting care to the unpaid economy of the household. Whereas the Bank views government spending cutbacks as a sign of increased efficiency, the costs are simply shifted to the unpaid economy where women do most of the work.[91]

In addition to their increased household work, the need for income "has forced women into the labor force to protect their families' survival."[92] Thus, the share of women in the labor force rose in Asia from 29 percent in 1950 to 33.8 percent in 1985, and in Latin America from 18 to 24.2 percent. Women have often fared poorly in the labor force under SAPs. In Africa, for example, men tend to produce the cash crops for export while women produce the subsistence food crops. Men also market most of the crops produced, and women do not benefit from increased prices because men often keep most of the revenue for themselves.[93] In sum, critics argue that SAPs affect women adversely in their roles as mothers, household managers, and wage earners.

ANOTHER SHIFT IN DEVELOPMENT STRATEGY?

In the late 1980s–1990s, the World Bank became more responsive to criticisms of its SAPs and reassessed its approach to the role of the state in development, the poorest groups and LDCs, and the "top-down" imposition of conditionality based on the Washington Consensus. To determine whether the Bank has in fact shifted its development strategy, we divide its reassessment into three periods: the late 1980s to 1994; 1995 to 2005; and 2005 to the present.

The Late 1980s to 1994

The Bank did not want to veer too far from its market-oriented views, but it began to recognize that the state should have a major role in the least developed countries. In 1989 the Bank therefore "explicitly acknowledged for the first time" that Africa's problems "had political as well as economic roots," and that Africa needed to have better government.[94] The Bank's 1991 *World Development Report* asserted that "governments need to do more in those areas where markets cannot be relied upon" such as health, education, family planning, and poverty alleviation. However, the 1991 report added that state intervention had to be market-conforming to have a positive developmental impact, and that "governments need to do less in those areas where markets work, or can be made to work."[95]

Japan, an important aid donor and foreign investor, viewed the changes in the 1991 report as inadequate and insisted that the Bank give more recognition to East Asia's developmental state model. Japan could not "be expected to fund a set of policies, and an underlying ideology" that denied "its own experience of having been heavily interventionist."[96] As a result, the Bank published a 1993 report on *The East Asian Miracle: Economic Growth and Public Policy* (henceforth, "the report") examining the reasons that East Asia had such "a remarkable record of high and sustained economic growth."[97] Recognizing the value of government intervention in some cases, the report noted that Japanese, Korean, and Taiwanese government policies of allocating credit to high-priority activities "may have been beneficial."[98] (Some observers saw this as a concession to Japan's Ministry of Finance, which financed the report.) However, most of the report questioned the value of government-directed industrial policy, indicated that East Asia's model might not be successful elsewhere, and cautioned that the region's successes should not "be taken as an excuse to postpone needed market-oriented reform."[99] The report also claimed that Malaysia, Thailand, and Indonesia achieved rapid economic growth without an industrial policy and that other LDCs should emulate Southeast Asia. In sum, the Bank's approach to the state's role in development did not change significantly during the early 1990s. Although the report gave more recognition to government involvement in East Asian development, it attributed the region's success mainly to liberal market-friendly policies.

The Bank also began to focus more on the poorest LDCs and most vulnerable groups. The Bank (and the foreign aid community) has gone through several phases of thought on poverty reduction.[100] In the first phase from 1945 to the late 1960s, the Bank financed large infrastructure projects in LDCs to provide transportation and communication facilities, ports, and power projects. Bank officials believed that large transfers of capital and technology would contribute to industrial development, employment, and a reduction of poverty. This is the *trickle-down approach* to development aid, which assumes that prosperity will "eventually trickle down from the top, alleviating the problem of poverty at the bottom."[101] A number of LDCs did in fact achieve rapid economic growth in the 1960s, but the large capital-intensive projects bypassed the neediest and increased income disparities. Bank President Robert McNamara responded by ushering in a second phase in the 1970s with a commitment to reduce poverty through a **basic needs** approach. The Bank developed a limited number of projects that provided health, educational, and family planning services to the poor; focused on women and the LLDCs; and increased lending for agricultural and rural development, low-cost urban housing, and primary and nonformal education. However, the Bank's (partial) shift to basic needs by targeting the poor was more difficult than anticipated, and orthodox liberals argued that the basic needs approach distracted attention from the need to promote economic growth.

Disillusionment with the basic needs approach along with significant global changes in the 1980s—the foreign debt crisis and the return of orthodox liberalism—ushered in a third phase in the Bank's approach to poverty. Like the first phase, the third phase relied on trickle-down theories of poverty reduction; but the third phase put much more emphasis on orthodox liberal reforms. SAPs during the 1980s were conditioned on the implementation of neoliberal policies such as privatization, deregulation, and trade liberalization, and the basic needs of vulnerable groups were largely forgotten. Throughout the 1980s, there was growing pressure on the Bank to consider the distributional effects of structural adjustment. For example, a 1987–1988 United Nations Children's Fund (UNICEF) study entitled *Adjustment with a Human Face* argued that it was necessary to include a "poverty alleviation dimension" in adjustment programs.[102] This pressure eventually resulted in a fourth phase of Bank thinking on poverty, which began in the late 1980s.

The fourth phase was similar to the second phase in which the Bank devoted more attention to basic human needs and poverty reduction. In 1989 the Bank acknowledged that "Sub-Saharan Africa has now witnessed almost a decade of falling per capita incomes and accelerating ecological degradation" and that "special measures" were needed "to alleviate poverty and protect the vulnerable."[103] The Bank devoted its 1990 *World Development Report* to poverty and began to redesign its SAPs to decrease adverse effects on the poor.[104] One indication of the Bank's renewed interest in poverty reduction was its attention to **microfinance**. Microfinance refers to the provision of low-cost, short-term financial services, mainly savings and credit, to poor households that do not have access to traditional financial institutions. In the late 1970s, there was growing recognition that the inaccessibility of financial services prevented the working poor from improving their lives. A number of microfinance institutions were established to lend money to the poor; the best known was the *Grameen Bank*, established by Professor Muhammad Yunus in Bangladesh in 1976. In 1993 the World Bank provided an initial grant of $2 million to support international replication of the Grameen Bank model. Many critical as well as liberal theorists supported microfinance. Whereas critical theorists liked "the 'bottom-up' aspects, attention to community, focus on women, and ... the aim to help the underserved," liberals liked "the prospect of alleviating poverty while providing incentives to work, the nongovernmental leadership, the use of mechanisms disciplined by market forces, and the general suspicion of ongoing subsidization."[105]

However, the Bank has never been fully committed to a poverty focus. In view of its sources of finance, tension continued to exist in the Bank between pressures for neoliberal reforms, and concerns with the state and poverty. In December 1994, the Bank had to confront the shortcomings of its development approach when Mexico had a serious financial crisis. Mexico had implemented an economic strategy based largely on the Bank's neoliberal model and had signed the NAFTA with the United States and Canada. Critics also charged that the Bank was more interested in loan approval than development effectiveness and accountability, lent to corrupt governments such as the Suharto regime in Indonesia, and devoted too little attention to the social and environmental effects of its projects.[106] On the fiftieth anniversary of the Bretton Woods agreements in 1994, NGOs launched a "Fifty Years Is Enough" campaign that strongly criticized the Bank for failing to alleviate poverty and promote sustainable development. At the same time, the Bank faced new challenges to its financial influence. Whereas private capital flows to LDCs increased from $40.9 billion in 1990 to $256 billion in 1997, multilateral and bilateral development assistance declined from 57 to only 15 percent of all net financial flows to LDCs. Thus, the Bank had to alter its approach to development if it was to continue to be an effective development institution.[107]

The Wolfensohn Period: 1995 to 2005

When James Wolfensohn became the new Bank president in June 1995, he "promised to revolutionize the Bank and finish the ... business of internal reform long overdue."[108] To prepare the Bank for the twenty-first century, Wolfensohn first addressed the issues of corruption, HIV/AIDS, the role of women, and the information revolution. The Bank was not supposed to delve into politics, but Wolfensohn argued that corruption had to be a Bank concern because it interfered with development. Despite resistance from many member states, Wolfensohn also increased the Bank's involvement in HIV/AIDs programs. Furthermore, Wolfensohn focused on upgrading the role of women in the Bank's professional staff and in LDCs, and he pressed the Bank staff to take more leadership as a source of information on development ideas. Second, Wolfensohn's appointment of Joseph Stiglitz as senior economist of the Bank signaled a change in the Bank's approach to poverty reduction, the state's role in development, and the top-down imposition of conditionality. Stiglitz, who was formerly chair of the U.S. Council of Economic Advisors, had called for limits to privatization and a stronger state role in development.

In regard to the role of government, the 1997 *World Development Report* argued that state minimalism "is at odds with the evidence of the world's development success stories," and described development as requiring "an effective state, one that plays a catalytic, facilitating role, encouraging and complementing the activities of private businesses and individuals."[109] The 1997 report also indicated that Africa had to "rebuild state effectiveness ... through an overhaul of public institutions, reassertion of the rule of law, and credible checks on abuse of state power."[110] However, there were clearly limits to the Bank's support for statism. Thus, the 1997 report warned against state-dominated development and called for "a contraction of the role of the state" in South Asia, because overregulation was "both a cause and effect of bloated public employment and the surest route to corruption."[111] Regarding poverty, in 1995 the Bank helped create a *Consultative Group to Assist the Poorest*, a multi-donor effort to increase resources for microfinance. The Bank also consulted about 60,000 poor people in more than 50 states for a *Voices of the Poor* study, and the theme of the Bank's 2000–2001 *World Development Report* was "Attacking Poverty."[112]

A third change was Wolfensohn's introduction of a *Comprehensive Development Framework (CDF)*. The CDF took a more holistic approach than structural adjustment, emphasizing the linkages among the economic, social, and institutional aspects of development. Unlike the top-down coercive conditionality of structural adjustment, the CDF was a consultative framework for development finance among the Bank, recipient governments, and civil society. Structural adjustment lending was eventually replaced with the **Poverty Reduction Strategy Papers (PRSPs)** approach, which relies on the consultative methods of the CDF. PRSPs are documents the IMF and World Bank require before considering a country for debt relief. In line with the CDF approach, members prepare the PRSPs through a participatory process involving domestic stakeholders, the IMF, and the World Bank. The PRSPs describe the economic and social policies a country will pursue to promote growth and reduce poverty, along with the country's external financing needs.[113]

Despite the Bank's expressed intentions to move away from the Washington Consensus, there were limitations on the degree to which its policies shifted. First, to satisfy critics, the Bank broadened its objectives to include poverty reduction, governance, democratic development and human rights, women in development, the environment, corruption, and microfinance; these are all positive objectives, but they overloaded the Bank's agenda.[114] Second, global events constrained the Bank's ability to alter its strategies. For example, the 1997 *World Development Report* on the need for an effective state was released shortly before the Asian financial crisis. Orthodox liberals argued that the crisis demonstrated the weakness of East Asia's developmental state model, and Japan's economic problems added weight to their arguments. Third, the Bank (and Wolfensohn as Bank president) was subject to external and internal constraints. Stiglitz asked a development economics professor—Ravi Kanbur—to oversee the writing of the 2000–2001 *World Development Report* on attacking poverty, but the United States, the Bank, and the IMF charged that the draft report de-emphasized economic growth. Some Bank members also viewed the Bank's CDF as "a capitulation to NGOs."[115] Stiglitz and Kanbur eventually left the Bank in response to the complaints of major donors, and critics saw this as further evidence of the Bank's "persistent failure ... as a collective entity, to act in accordance with its ideals."[116] Despite these setbacks, Wolfensohn did much to alter the Bank's priorities, with an emphasis on "building institutions, improving governance, enhancing the voice and participation of the poor, strengthening the rule of law, and stamping out corruption."[117]

2005 to the Present

Paul Wolfowitz became the next Bank president in July 2005, but his tenure was marked by controversy and ended prematurely in 2007. In a deviation from previous custom, President George W. Bush nominated Wolfowitz without consulting with other major Bank members; and Wolfowitz came to the Bank amid protests over his role as a key architect of U.S. military operations in Iraq and Afghanistan. During his tenure, Wolfowitz alienated many Bank staff members by attempting to run the Bank through personal aides and by remaining too closely tied to U.S. policies. He tried to continue Wolfensohn's campaign against corruption in LDCs, but his actions were taken "without sufficient consultation and engagement of the World Bank staff or ... its Board and shareholders."[118] Thus, there was little sympathy for him when he was accused of offering special favors to a Bank employee with whom he had a special relationship, and he was forced to resign. Despite wide calls for an open selection process, the United States wanted to continue appointing the Bank president, and Europeans supported this because they wanted to continue appointing the IMF managing director. In July 2007, Robert Zoellick, a former U.S. trade representative and deputy secretary of state, became the next Bank president.

Zoellick, who had been the U.S. trade representative from 2001 to 2005, was a pragmatist who did much to ease tensions in the Bank after Wolfowitz's departure. He did not have major goals to transform the Bank like Wolfensohn, and he was much more of a team player than Wolfowitz. The 2008 global financial crisis occurred during Zoellick's presidency (from 2005 to 2012), and he was quite effective in crisis management and in re-orienting the Bank to take more notice of the emerging economies. In a 2010 talk, Zoellick stated that "the old world of fireside chats among G-7 leaders is gone. Today's discussion requires a big table to accommodate the key participants, and developing countries must have seats in it."[119] It was during Zoellick's tenure that the Bank received a large increase in its capital to deal with the financial crisis, and in return the voting power in the IBRD of some emerging economies such as China and India was increased (see Table 11.3). Zoellick also increased representation of LDCs in the professional staff, and emphasized that LDCs should play a more active role in setting their own priorities. Zoellick did not try to institute major changes in the Bank's development objectives, but one analyst points out that "the focus on big ideas and new missions is misguided. A major problem in the Bank's history has been its tendency to lurch from one big idea to the next at the behest of changing fads and the inclinations of revolving Presidents."[120] Zoellick opposed the idea that "one-size-fits-all" and indicated that a diversity of development measures were required for LDCs. In July 2012, Jim Yong Kim, a physician with years of experience in public health, succeeded Zoellick as World Bank president. To this point it seems that Kim will continue the pragmatic approach to Bank management followed by Zoellick. Recent *World Development Reports* indicate that the Bank is focusing more on social issues and on disadvantaged groups. For example the themes of the 2012 and 2013 reports were "Gender Equality and Development" and "Jobs." However, past experience indicates that it is more difficult to implement changes in such areas than to express good intentions.

China's Development Strategy

Any discussion of a change in development strategies must include the challenge that China and other emerging economies are posing to the World Bank, the United States, and other DCs. In 2004 Joshua Cooper Ramo coined the term the *Beijing Consensus* as a counterpoint to the Washington Consensus. As discussed, the Washington Consensus emphasized the importance of democratic government, free markets, and a dominant private sector in LDCs. The Beijing Consensus by contrast supports a large state role in development and non-interference in the political and economic practices of other states.[121] The DCs have criticized China for not linking its aid with expectations regarding human rights, good governance, and the environment. However, many LDCs are attracted by China's policy of non-interference, and by the financial assistance China can offer them. Non-traditional sources of aid increased from 8.1 to 30.7 percent of the total from 2000 to 2009, and important non-DAC donors include China, Brazil, Kuwait, Saudi Arabia, and South Africa. Although China is still a relatively small provider of concessional aid, it is a much more significant actor if foreign direct investment (FDI), export credits, and natural resource-backed credits are included. Almost half of China's foreign assistance goes to Africa, and China is Africa's second largest trading partner after the United States. Despite China's policy of non-interference, the conditions it imposes on its loans are often onerous. Many LDCs pay high interest rates on Chinese loans and cede their rights to their natural resources for long periods. For example, China has control over almost 90 percent of Ecuador's oil exports, and Ecuador must use Chinese companies and technologies for a substantial share of its projects.[122]

In a direct challenge to the World Bank and IMF, China has drawn on its foreign exchange reserves of almost 4 trillion dollars to help launch two new development banks in which LDCs will have greater influence. In October 2014, China launched the **Asian Infrastructure Investment Bank** (**AIIB**) with the backing of 20 other countries. The AIIB offers an alternative to the *Asian Development Bank (ADB)* in which Japan and the United States are the main shareholders, and the AIIB will have more funding for large infrastructure projects. Although the United States pressured its allies not to join the AIIB, Britain, South Korea, Australia and others gradually joined, and it now has

57 members. After the World Bank president Jim Yong Kim said he would find innovative ways to work with the AIIB, President Obama reversed U.S. policy and indicated that the AIIB could be positive for Asia if it adopted high standards for lending projects. China also had a major role in launching the **New Development Bank (NDB)** with the other BRICS economies—Brazil, Russia, India, and South Africa. Although the NDB has only five founding members, it will begin with an initial capital of $100 billion, the same as the AIIB. The NDB's five members are in principle equal, but China will contribute $41 billion of the capital; Brazil, India, and Russia will each contribute $18 billion; and South Africa will contribute $5 billion. Brazil, India, and South Africa will borrow from the NDB to finance their infrastructure needs, and as the largest contributor China will have the largest role in decision-making. After some delay in agreeing on where to locate the headquarters, the NDB was finally launched in July 2015 with its headquarters in Shanghai. The AIIB and NDB will provide alternatives to World Bank and IMF funds, and this could alter development strategies.

A Diversity of Views on the UN's Development Goals

Earlier in this chapter we referred to the UN's 2000 *Millennium Development Goals (MDGs)*, to be achieved by 2015. The reaction to the MDGs demonstrates the diversity of views that continues to exist on development. In his 2015 report on the MDGs, UN Secretary-General Ban Ki-moon described them as "the most successful anti-poverty movement in history." The aid critic William Easterly by contrast argues that "the MDGs communicated a very wrong idea about how development happens: technocratic, patronizing and magically free of politics ... It's not about western saviors but homegrown efforts."[123] Data on extreme poverty, childhood deaths, and some other indicators show that the MDGs may have had a positive effect. However, some critics attribute these changes to improvements in a few large emerging economies such as China and India; and others argue that these improvements started before the MDGs were even established. Some even question the setting of quantitative goals, because the view that "quantification automatically creates accountability is an error."[124] However, the fact remains that the MDGs may have accelerated progress in some areas of development. Thus, in September 2015 a UN summit meeting in New York established 17 *sustainable development goals (SDGs)*, as a successor to the MDGs, to be achieved by 2030. Whereas the MDGs focused on the LDCs, the SDGs are more ambitious and apply to all countries. Jeffrey Sachs, who supported the MDGs, believes that the SDGs are "a sensible framework. I'm not saying a new dawn has broken, but at least governments are saying we need to try." Easterly by contrast describes the SDGs as "a mushy collection of platitudes that will fail on every dimension."[125] In sum, after decades of development efforts wide divisions among "the experts" continue. The Theory and Practice section that follows relates these differences to the theoretical perspectives.

Considering IPE Theory and Practice

The postwar period has generally been marked by prosperity and economic growth for DCs of the North, but this has not been the case for the poorer LDCs and peoples in the South. However, the "South" is also increasingly diverse, with emerging economies such as China, India, Brazil, and South Korea posing an increasing challenge to DCs in the North. This chapter examines the strategies LDCs have used to promote their economic development, and discusses the role the World Bank has played in framing debates on these strategies. The discussion of ISI, socialist, export-led growth, and orthodox liberal models provides some basis for drawing conclusions about the most appropriate development strategies.

First, all the development strategies have shortcomings. Development is a difficult and complex process, and the "best" development strategy for one state may not be the best or even feasible for another state. Rostow's claim that an LDC's growth would become self-sustaining when it reached the "takeoff stage" raised false hopes that economic development was a readily achievable and irreversible process.[126] As new development strategies emerge, there is always the danger of raising unrealistic expectations. For example, some analysts argue that "too much is claimed for microfinance, and that expectations are grossly exaggerated."[127] Despite the advantages of microfinance in reaching the poor, it is criticized for encouraging poor households to accept loans they may not be able to service, and for focusing on credit and loans when people have more need for savings and insurance. Microfinance also has limitations in reaching the poor. The 1997 Microcredit Summit in Washington, DC launched a nine-year goal of reaching 100 million of the world's poorest families, but microfinance levels have fallen far short of this goal.

ISI had an important role in extricating some LDCs from overdependence on primary product exports, and in beginning industrialization. In the longer term, however, the industrialization process proved to be limited because ISI was too inward-looking. Export-led growth resulted in rapid growth rates in the East Asian NIEs in the 1960s to 1980s, and China has used this strategy to promote its exports and build up the largest monetary reserves of any state. However, Japan's export-led growth strategy left it too dependent on export markets for promoting growth, and China has also not done enough to build up a large domestic market. China's export-led growth policies have also been a major factor contributing to the trade imbalances in the global economy. In today's interdependent world, it is important to consider the external as well as internal effects of development strategies adopted by large economies. The neoliberal model with its emphasis on open economies recognizes the fact that we live in an interdependent world, and some emerging economies have benefited from this development strategy. However, DCs often promoted this model more to gain access to LDC markets for trade and foreign investment than to promote genuine development. Neoliberalism has often prevented poorer LDCs from protecting their infant industries and providing government services to their population. In sum, no development strategy may be adequate by itself, and LDCs may have to employ a combination of strategies.

Second, whereas liberals emphasize the need for domestic changes to achieve economic growth, historical materialists focus on the need to alter international relations (e.g., dependency). Economic development is in fact a complex process that requires *both* domestic and international changes. Only a small number of LDCs such as the East Asian NIEs and the BRIC economies have been able to meet both the domestic and international requirements for rapid economic development; the 1990s Asian financial crisis also shows that such rapid growth may be subject to setbacks.

Third, the same development strategy is neither feasible nor desirable for all LDCs. Although the East Asian LDCs achieved impressive economic growth rates as developmental states, many LDCs would not be able to emulate their experience. The East Asians' success resulted from a confluence of favorable external and domestic circumstances, such as U.S. and Japanese support and the presence of highly skilled, technocratic government bureaucracies. These characteristics are often lacking in poorer African and Asian LDCs. The return to liberal orthodoxy in the 1980s also prevented many LDCs from following state-led growth policies. IMF and World Bank SAPs pressured LDC debtors to engage in deregulation, privatization, and other measures to downsize the state.

Fourth, negative experiences with IMF and World Bank SAPs have pointed to the pitfalls of neglecting the social, human, and environmental aspects of development. The UNDP *Human Development Reports* show that there is "no automatic link between growth and human development."[128] We should assess development not only in terms of a country's per capita GDP growth, but also in terms of life expectancy, health and sanitation, education, employment, and income, gender, and rural–urban gaps. It is also important to look at the environmental implications of development strategies. For example, critics warned that IMF and World Bank prescriptions such as currency devaluation and trade and investment liberalization would increase unsustainable resource exports and pollution-intensive foreign investment in LDCs.[129] The Bank responded to these criticisms by devoting more attention to the environmental aspects of economic development.

Fifth, an economic development strategy should strike a balance between the state and the market. Whereas ISI emphasizes state intervention and gives too little consideration to market signals, orthodox liberalism disregards the fact that late industrializers require an active role for the state. East Asian governments were adept at using state–market interactions to their advantage, and this enabled them to register some striking economic gains. However, the East Asians also sometimes substituted "political whim … for proper risk assessment for commercial activities," and their failure to provide adequate banking regulations helped precipitate the 1990s financial crisis.[130] The 2008 global financial crisis, by contrast, shows the dangers of overdependence on the self-regulating market. We need to determine the amount and type of government regulation that will ensure economic stability and the proper functioning of market signals.

Sixth, an economic development strategy should take account of North–South differences in wealth and power. The North should be willing to provide the poorer

LDCs with special and differential treatment and give them some room for independent action within the limits of global interdependence.

Finally, the Washington Consensus has *not* become the only broadly accepted approach to economic development today. As discussed, negative experiences with IMF and World Bank SAPs raised awareness that the unrestrained market is not the answer to LDC problems. The Beijing Consensus serves as a counterpoint to the neoliberal Washington Consensus with its greater emphasis on state-guided development, and it has gained currency with LDCs along with the economic rise of China. In sum, the neomercantilist, liberal, and critical perspectives all have something important to say regarding development strategies. Furthermore, there is no single best development strategy for all LDCs. A variety of development strategies will be pursued in the future, as they have been in the past.

QUESTIONS

1. Why do the DCs give official development assistance, and why have ODA levels as a percent of countries' GNIs generally declined over the years? What are the debates regarding the effectiveness of aid-giving?
2. Why has the World Bank group been so important in a development context, and how influential has the United States been in the Bank group?
3. What are the five main institutions of the World Bank group, and what functions do they perform?
4. How would you compare the effectiveness of import substitution, socialism, export-led growth, and neoliberal development strategies?
5. What are structural adjustment loans, and how have they affected LDCs, women, and the poorest groups in LDCs?
6. What is the Washington Consensus? What is the Beijing Consensus, and how does it differ from the Washington Consensus? What form do you think a post-Washington Consensus should take?
7. How has the World Bank tried to change its approach to development, and how successful has it been? What are Poverty Reduction Strategy Papers?
8. In what ways are China and the other BRICS economies posing a challenge to the IMF and World Bank?

KEY TERMS

Asian Infrastructure
  Investment Bank
basic needs
bilateral aid
capital market
concessional loans
consultative groups
Development Assistance
  Committee
developmental state

export-led growth
foreign aid
import substitution
  industrialization
microfinance
Millennium Development
  Goals
multilateral aid
New Development
  Bank

official development
  assistance
official development
  finance
Poverty Reduction
  Strategy Papers
remittances
tied aid
Washington Consensus
World Bank group

FURTHER READING

For general discussion of development theories, issues, and strategies see Jan Nederveen Pieterse, "Trends in Development Theory," in Ronen Palan, ed., *Global Political Economy: Contemporary Theories*, 2nd ed. (New York: Routledge, 2013), pp. 177–192; David Williams, *International Development and Global Politics* (New York: Routledge, 2012); Anthony Payne and Nicola Phillips, *Development* (Malden, MA: Polity, 2010); and John Rapley, *Understanding Development: Theory and Practice in the Third World*, 3rd ed. (Boulder, CO: Lynne Rienner, 2007).

On the diversity of views of the World Bank, see Peter J. Hammer, *Change and Continuity at the World Bank* (Northampton, MA: Edward Elgar, 2013); Liam Clegg, *Controlling the World Bank and the IMF* (New York: Palgrave Macmillan, 2013); David Phillips, *Reforming the World Bank* (New York: Cambridge University Press, 2009); Katherine Marshall, *The World Bank: From Reconstruction to Development to Equity* (New York: Routledge, 2008); Catherine Weaver, *Hypocrisy Trap: The World Bank and the Poverty of Reform* (Princeton, NJ: Princeton University Press, 2008); and Eric Toussaint, *The World Bank: A Critical Primer* (Ann Arbor, MI: Pluto Press, 2008).

On the diversity of approaches to development aid see Susan Engel, "The Not-So-Great Aid Debate," *Third World Quarterly* 35, no. 8 (2014), pp. 1374–1389; Ben Ramalingam, *Aid on the Edge of Chaos* (New York: Oxford University Press, 2013); Dambisa Moyo, *Dead Aid* (New York: Farrar, Straus and Giroux, 2009); William Easterly, *The White Man's Burden* (New York: Penguin, 2006); and Jeffrey D. Sachs, *The End of Poverty: Economic Possibilities of Our Time* (New York: Penguin, 2005).

On China's growing role in international development see Jennifer V. J. Hsu, "China's Development: A New Development Paradigm?" *Third World Quarterly* 36, no. 9 (2015), pp. 1754–1769; Lowell Dittmer and George T. Yu, eds., *China, the Developing World and the New Global Dynamic* (Boulder, CO: Lynne Rienner, 2010); and Dennis Hickey and Baogang Guo, eds., *Dancing with the Dragon* (New York: Rowman and Littlefield, 2010). On South–South cooperation see Paolo de Renzio and Jurek Seifert, "South-South Cooperation and the Future of Development Assistance," *Third World Quarterly* 35, no. 10 (2014), pp. 1860–1875.

On the neomercantilist approach to development strategies, see Atul Kohli, *State-Directed Development* (New York: Cambridge University Press, 2004); and Robert Wade, *Governing the Market: Economic Theory and the Role of Government in East Asian Industrialization* (Princeton, NJ: Princeton University Press, 1990). On the Washington Consensus and its aftermath, see Narcis Serra and Joseph E. Stiglitz, eds., *The Washington Consensus Reconsidered: Towards a New Global Governance* (New York: Oxford University Press, 2008); and Pedro-Pablo Kuczynski and John Williamson, eds., *After the Washington Consensus: Restarting Growth and Reform in Latin America* (Washington, DC: Institute for International Economics, 2003). On the critical perspective see Ha-Joon Chang and Ilene Grabel, *Reclaiming Development* (New York: Zed Books, 2014). On the feminist perspective see Shirin M. Rai, *Gender and the Political Economy of Development* (Malden, MA: Polity, 2002).

NOTES

1. Bretton Woods Commission, *Bretton Woods: Looking to the Future* (Washington, DC: Bretton Woods Committee, 1994), p. B3.

2. United Nations Development Program, *Human Development Report 2014* (New York: UN, 2014), pp. 19–20 and 38–39.
3. UNDP, *Human Development Report 2014*, p. 43.
4. World Bank, *World Development Report 1991* (New York: Oxford University Press, 1991), pp. 2–3; UN Department of Economic and Social Affairs, *The Inequality Predicament: Report on the World Social Situation 2005* (New York: UN, 2005), pp. 50–55, 68–71.
5. Robert Wade, "Japan, the World Bank, and the Art of Paradigm Maintenance: The East Asian Miracle in Political Perspective," *New Left Review* 217 (May/June 1996), p. 5.
6. Stephen D. Krasner, *Structural Conflict: The Third World Against Global Liberalism* (Berkeley, CA: University of California Press, 1985), p. 3.
7. OECD, *Development Co-operation Report 2014* (Paris: Organization for Economic Cooperation and Development, 2014), pp. 420–424.
8. Alberto Alesina and David Dollar, "Who Gives Foreign Aid to Whom and Why?" *Journal of Economic Growth* 5, no. 1 (March 2000), pp. 33–63; Ngaire Woods, "The Shifting Politics of Foreign Aid," *International Affairs* 81, no. 2 (2005), p. 394; Tomohisa Hattori, "Reconceptualizing Foreign Aid," *Review of International Political Economy* 8, no. 4 (Winter 2001), p. 634.
9. Kevin Watkins and Penny Fowler, *Rigged Rules and Double Standards: Trade, Globalization and the Fight Against Poverty* (Boston: Oxfam International, 2002), p. 8.
10. Helen S. Toxopeus and Robert Lensink, "Remittances and Financial Inclusion in Development," in Tony Addison and George Mavrotas, eds., *Development Finance in the Global Economy* (New York: Palgrave Macmillan, 2008), p. 236.
11. Janet Hunt, "Aid and Development," in Damien Kingsbury, Mark McGillivray, John McKay, Janet Hunt, and Matthew Clarke, eds., *International Development: Issues and Challenges* (New York: Palgrave Macmillan, 2008), pp. 92–95.
12. Ben Ramalingam, *Aid on the Edge of Chaos* (New York: Oxford University Press, 2013), p. 360.
13. Jeffrey D. Sachs, *The End of Poverty: Economic Possibilities for Our Time* (New York: Penguin, 2005), p. 19.
14. Sachs, *The End of Poverty*, p. 246.
15. William Easterly, *The White Man's Burden* (New York: Penguin, 2006), p. 45.
16. Dambisa Moyo, *Dead Aid* (New York: Farrar, Straus and Giroux, 2009), p. xix.
17. *Partners in Development—Report of the Commission on International Development* (New York: Praeger, 1969), p. 152.
18. Peter Burnell, "Foreign Aid Resurgent: New Spirit or Old Hangover?" in Tony Addison and George Mavrotas, eds., *Development Finance in the Global Economy* (New York: Palgrave Macmillan, 2008), pp. 24–33; Woods, "The Shifting Politics of Foreign Aid," p. 397; OECD, *Development Co-operation Report 2014*, p. 399.
19. Sylvanus I. Ikhide, "Reforming the International Financial System for Effective Aid Delivery," *World Economy* 27, no. 2 (February 2004), p. 149.
20. Alesina and Dollar, "Who Gives Foreign Aid to Whom and Why?" p. 55; OECD, *Development Co-operation Report 2014*, p. 261; Woods, "The Shifting Politics of Foreign Aid," p. 401; Hunt, "Aid and Development," p. 81.
21. Gustav Ranis, "The World Bank Near the Turn of the Century," in Roy Culpeper, Albert Berry, and Frances Stewart, eds., *Global Development Fifty Years After Bretton Woods* (New York: St. Martin's Press, 1997), p. 73.

22. Ranis, "The World Bank Near the Turn of the Century," p. 73; OECD, *Development Co-operation Report 2009* (Paris: Organization for Economic Cooperation and Development, 2009), p. 29.
23. Peter M. Haas, "Introduction: Epistemic Communities and International Policy Coordination," *International Organization* 46, no. 1 (Winter 1992), p. 3; Wade, "Japan, the World Bank, and the Art of Paradigm Maintenance," p. 5.
24. Barry Eichengreen and Peter B. Kenen, "Managing the World Economy Under the Bretton Woods System: An Overview," in Peter B. Kenen, ed., *Managing the World Economy: Fifty Years After Bretton Woods* (Washington, DC: Institute for International Economics, 1994), p. 6.
25. Edward S. Mason and Robert E. Asher, *The World Bank Since Bretton Woods* (Washington, DC: Brookings Institution, 1973), pp. 52–53; Robert E. Wood, *From Marshall Plan to Debt Crisis: Foreign Aid and Development Choices in the World Economy* (Berkeley, CA: University of California Press, 1986), p. 29. Eric Helleiner points out that LDCs had a more active role at Bretton Woods than is commonly recognized in his book *Forgotten Foundations of Bretton Woods* (Ithaca, NY: Cornell University Press, 2014).
26. Devesh Kapur, "The Changing Anatomy of Governance of the World Bank," in Jonathan R. Pincus and Jeffrey A. Winters, eds., *Reinventing the World Bank* (Ithaca, NY: Cornell University Press, 2002), pp. 54–59.
27. David A, Phillips, *Reforming the World Bank* (New York: Cambridge University Press, 2009), pp. 84–87.
28. A. Geske Dijkstra, *The Impact of International Debt Relief* (New York: Routledge, 2008), pp. 118–119.
29. World Bank, *World Bank Annual Report 2009* (Washington, DC: World Bank, 2009), CD-ROM.
30. Ibrahim F. I. Shihata, *MIGA and Foreign Investment* (Boston, MA: Nijhoff, 1988).
31. Anne O. Krueger, Constantine Michalopoulos, and Vernon W. Ruttan, with Keith Jay, *Aid and Development* (Baltimore, MD: Johns Hopkins University Press, 1989), pp. 106–108.
32. Roy Culpeper, *Titans or Behemoths? The Multilateral Development Banks* (Boulder, CO: Lynne Rienner, 1997).
33. Theodore Cohn, "Developing Countries in the International Civil Service: The Case of the World Bank Group," *International Review of Administrative Sciences* 41, no. 1 (1975), pp. 47–56.
34. Stephen Fidler, "Who's Minding the Bank?" *Foreign Policy* 126 (September/October 2001), p. 41; Miles Kahler, *Leadership Selection in the Major Multilaterals* (Washington, DC: Institute for International Economics, 2001), pp. 42–49.
35. Kapur, "The Changing Anatomy of Governance of the World Bank," pp. 58–64.
36. Joseph S. Nye, Jr., "Soft Power," *Foreign Policy* 80 (Fall 1990), p. 166.
37. William Ascher, "The World Bank and U.S. Control," in Margaret P. Karns and Karen A. Mingst, eds., *The United States and Multilateral Institutions* (Boston, MA: Unwin Hyman, 1990), p. 115.
38. Eric Toussaint, *The World Bank: A Critical Primer* (Ann Arbor, MI: Pluto Press, 2008), p. 244. (Originally published in French.)
39. Peter T. Bauer, *Reality and Rhetoric: Studies in the Economics of Development* (London: Weidenfeld and Nicolson, 1984), p. 70; Kalman Mizsei, "The Role of the Bretton Woods Institutions in the Transforming Economies," in Bretton Woods

Commission, *Bretton Woods: Looking to the Future* (Washington, DC: Bretton Woods Committee, 1994), p. C–103.

40. Robin Broad, "Research, Knowledge, and the Art of 'Paradigm Maintenance': The World Bank's Development Economics Vice-Presidency (DEC)," *Review of International Political Economy* 13, no. 3 (August 2006), pp. 390–393.

41. Catherine Weaver, *Hypocrisy Trap: The World Bank and the Poverty of Reform* (Princeton, NJ: Princeton University Press, 2008), p. 176.

42. Fidler, "Who's Minding the Bank?" p. 45.

43. W. W. Rostow, *The Stages of Economic Growth: A Non-Communist Manifesto* (Cambridge, UK: Cambridge University Press, 1960), pp. 4–92.

44. Anthony Payne and Nicola Phillips, *Development* (Malden, MA: Polity Press, 2010), pp. 62–75.

45. Raúl Prebisch, *The Economic Development of Latin America and Its Principal Problems* (New York: UN Economic Commission for Latin America, 1950), pp. 1–59; Hans W. Singer, "The Distribution of Gains Between Investing and Borrowing Countries," *American Economic Review* 40, no. 2 (May 1950), pp. 473–485.

46. Anil Hira, *Ideas and Economic Policy in Latin America: Regional, National, and Organizational Case Studies* (Westport, CT: Praeger, 1998), ch. 3.

47. Ozay Mehmet, *Westernizing the Third World: The Eurocentricity of Economic Development Theories* (London: Routledge, 1995), p. 78; John Rapley, *Understanding Development: Theory and Practice* (Boulder, CO: Lynne Rienner, 1996), pp. 27–34.

48. Luiz C. B. Pereira, "Development Economics and the World Bank's Identity Crisis," *Review of International Political Economy* 2, no. 2 (Spring 1995), pp. 215–217; Devesh Kapur, John P. Lewis, and Richard Webb, *The World Bank: Its First Half Century*, vol. 1 (Washington, DC: Brookings Institution, 1997), p. 451.

49. Rapley, *Understanding Development*, pp. 27–36; Theodore Cohn, *Canadian Food Aid: Domestic and Foreign Policy Implications* (Denver, CO: University of Denver Graduate School in International Studies, 1979), pp. 25–27.

50. Sylvia Maxfield and James N. Nolt, "Protectionism and the Internationalization of Capital: U.S. Sponsorship of Import Substitution Industrialization in the Philippines, Turkey and Argentina," *International Studies Quarterly* 34, no. 1 (March 1990), p. 50.

51. Anne O. Krueger, *Trade Policies and Developing Nations* (Washington, DC: Brookings Institution, 1995), pp. 3–10, 33–44.

52. Anne O. Krueger, "The Effects of Trade Strategies on Growth," *Finance and Development* 20, no. 2 (June 1983), p. 8.

53. Mason and Asher, *The World Bank Since Bretton Woods*, pp. 378–379.

54. Raúl Prebisch, *Towards a Dynamic Development Policy for Latin America* (New York: United Nations, 1963), p. 71.

55. Martin Meredith, *The Fate of Africa* (New York: Public Affairs, 2005), pp. 249–259; Robert Calderisi, *The Trouble with Africa* (New York: Palgrave Macmillan, 2006), pp. 103–113.

56. John M. Page, "The East Asian Miracle: An Introduction," *World Development* 22, no. 4 (1994), p. 619; Robert Wade, *Governing the Market: Economic Theory and the Role of Government in East Asian Industrialization* (Princeton, NJ: Princeton University Press, 1990), p. 34.

57. Bela Balassa, *Policy Choices for the 1990s* (London: Macmillan, 1993), pp. 56–67;

Anil Hira, *An East Asian Model for Latin American Success* (Burlington, VT: Ashgate, 2007).

58. Wade, *Governing the Market*, p. 34. Singapore has the highest trade to GDP ratio in the world due to its role as a major transhipment hub and to the high share of imported components in its exports.

59. Krueger, *Trade Policies and Developing Nations*, pp. 20–23.

60. Staffan B. Linder, *The Pacific Century: Economic and Political Consequences of Asian-Pacific Dynamism* (Stanford, CA: Stanford University Press, 1986), p. 31; Bela Balassa, ed., *The Newly Industrializing Countries in the World Economy* (New York: Pergamon Press, 1981), pp. 6–24.

61. Ronen Palan and Jason Abbott, with Phil Deans, *State Strategies in the Global Political Economy* (London: Pinter, 1996), p. 78.

62. Chalmers Johnson, "Introduction—The Taiwan Model," in James C. Hsiung et al., eds., *Contemporary Republic of China: The Taiwan Experience 1950–1980* (New York: Praeger, 1981), pp. 9–18; Chalmers Johnson, *MITI and the Japanese Miracle: The Growth of Industrial Policy, 1925–1975* (Stanford, CA: Stanford University Press, 1982).

63. Peter Evans, *Dependent Development: The Alliance of Multinational, State, and Local Capital in Brazil* (Princeton, NJ: Princeton University Press, 1979), p. 33.

64. Quoted in William Nester, "The Development of Japan, Taiwan and South Korea: Ends and Means, Free Trade, Dependency, or Neomercantilism?" *Journal of Developing Societies* 6 (1990), p. 206.

65. Cal Clark and Steve Chan, "MNCs and Developmentalism: Domestic Structure as an Explanation for East Asian Dynamism," in Thomas Risse-Kappen, ed., *Bringing Transnational Relations Back In: Non-State Actors, Domestic Structures and International Institutions* (New York: Cambridge University Press, 1995), p. 125.

66. Lucian W. Pye with Mary W. Pye, *Asian Power and Politics: The Cultural Dimensions of Authority* (Cambridge, MA: Belknap Press, 1985), ch. 3.

67. Christopher Lingle, "What Ever Happened to the 'Asian Century'?" *World Economic Affairs* 2, no. 2 (Spring 1998), p. 32.

68. World Bank, *The East Asian Miracle: Economic Growth and Public Policy* (New York: Oxford University Press, 1993), p. 1.

69. Graham Bird and Alistair Milne, "Miracle to Meltdown: A Pathology of the East Asian Financial Crisis," *Third World Quarterly* 20, no. 2 (1999), p. 421.

70. T. J. Pempel, ed., *The Politics of the Asian Economic Crisis* (Ithaca, NY: Cornell University Press, 1999), p. 1; Stephan Haggard, *The Political Economy of the Asian Financial Crisis* (Washington, DC: Institute for International Economics, 2000), p. 3.

71. Bird and Milne, "Miracle to Meltdown," p. 422.

72. Walter Hatch and Kozo Yamamura, *Asia in Japan's Embrace: Building a Regional Production Alliance* (New York: Cambridge University Press, 1996), p. 37.

73. Walden Bello and Stephanie Rosenfeld, *Dragons in Distress: Asia's Miracle Economies in Crisis* (San Francisco, CA: Institute for Food and Development Policy, 1990), pp. 3–10.

74. Samuel P. Huntington, *Political Order in Changing Societies* (New Haven, CT: Yale University Press, 1968).

75. Haggard, *The Political Economy of the Asian Financial Crisis*, p. 4.

76. Stephan Haggard and Andrew MacIntyre, "The Political Economy of the Asian

Economic Crisis," *Review of International Political Economy* 5, no. 3 (Autumn 1998), p. 405.

77. Paul Krugman, "The Myth of Asia's Miracle," *Foreign Affairs* 73, no. 6 (November/December 1994), p. 67.

78. Walden Bello, "Overview of Current Economic, Strategic and Political Developments in Southeast and South Asia," *Focus Files* (Bangkok, Thailand, October 1997), p. 3.

79. World Commission on Environment and Development, *Our Common Future* (New York: Oxford University Press, 1987), p. 8.

80. Howard Handelman, *The Challenge of Third World Development* (Upper Saddle River, NJ: Prentice Hall, 1996), p. 228.

81. Palan and Abbott, *State Strategies in the Global Political Economy*, p. 99.

82. Christopher L. Gilbert and David Vines, "The World Bank: An Overview of Some Major Issues," in Christopher L. Gilbert and David Vines, eds., *The World Bank: Structure and Policies* (New York: Cambridge University Press, 2000), p. 16.

83. John Williamson, "Democracy and the 'Washington Consensus,'" *World Development* 21, no. 8 (August 1993), pp. 1329–1336.

84. Rapley, *Understanding Development*, p. 76.

85. Farhad Noorbakhsh and Alberto Paloni, "Structural Adjustment and Growth in Sub-Saharan Africa: The Importance of Complying with Conditionality," *Economic Development and Cultural Change* 49, no. 3 (April 2000), pp. 479–509; cited in Bob Milward, "The Heavily Indebted Poor Countries and the Role of Structural Adjustment Policies," in *Developments in Economics: An Annual Review*, vol. 17 (Lancashire, UK: Causeway Press, 2001), p. 38; J. Barry Riddell, "Things Fall Apart Again: Structural Adjustment Programmes in Sub-Saharan Africa," *Journal of Modern African Studies* 30, no. 1 (1992), p. 67.

86. Gloria Thomas-Emeagwali, "Introductory Perspectives: Monetarists, Liberals and Radicals: Contrasting Perspectives on Gender and Structural Adjustment," in Gloria Thomas-Emeagwali, ed., *Women Pay the Price: Structural Adjustment in Africa and the Caribbean* (Trenton, NJ: Africa World Press, 1995), p. 5.

87 James H. Weaver, "What Is Structural Adjustment?" in Daniel M. Schydlowsky, ed., *Structural Adjustment: Retrospect and Prospect* (Westport, CT: Praeger, 1995), pp. 12–13.

88. Meredith, *The Fate of Africa*, p. 375.

89. Meredith, *The Fate of Africa*, p. 374; Rapley, *Understanding Development*, pp. 83–92; Riddell, "Things Fall Apart Again," pp. 53–68.

90. Frances Stewart, "Can Adjustment Programmes Incorporate the Interests of Women?" in Haleh Afshar and Carolyne Dennis, eds., *Women and Adjustment Policies in the Third World* (New York: St. Martin's Press, 1992), pp. 22–24.

91. Diane Elson, "Male Bias in Macro-Economics: The Case of Structural Adjustment," in Diane Elson, ed., *Male Bias in the Development Process* (Manchester, UK: Manchester University Press, 1991), pp. 175–178; Penny Griffin, *Gendering the World Bank* (New York: Palgrave Macmillan, 2009), pp. 119–130.

92. Stewart, "Can Adjustment Programmes Incorporate the Interests of Women?" p. 27.

93. Elson, "Male Bias in Macro-Economics," p. 173; Stewart, "Can Adjustment Programmes Incorporate the Interests of Women?" p. 22.

94. Meredith, *The Fate of Africa*, p. 376.

95. World Bank, *World Development Report 1991*, p. 9.

96. Ben Fine, "Neither the Washington nor the Post-Washington Consensus: An Introduction," in Ben Fine, Costas Lapavitsas, and Jonathan Pincus, eds., *Development Policy in the Twenty-First Century: Beyond the Post-Washington Consensus* (London: Routledge, 2001), p. 12.

97. World Bank, *The East Asian Miracle: Economic Growth and Public Policy* (New York: Oxford University Press, 1993), p. 1.

98. World Bank, *The East Asian Miracle*, p. 274.

99. World Bank, *The East Asian Miracle*, p. 26.

100. Ravi Kanbur and David Vines, "The World Bank and Poverty Reduction: Past, Present and Future," in Christopher L. Gilbert and David Vines, eds., *The World Bank: Structure and Policies* (New York: Cambridge University Press, 2000), pp. 87–107.

101. Mohammed H. Malek, "Towards an Integrated Aid and Development Programme for Europe," in Mohammed H. Malek, ed., *Contemporary Issues in European Development Aid* (Brookfield, VT: Avebury, 1991), p. 142.

102. Giovannia A. Cornia, Richard Jolly, and Frances Stewart, eds., *Adjustment with a Human Face, Vol. 1: Protecting the Vulnerable and Promoting Growth* (Oxford, UK: Clarendon Press, 1987), p. 7.

103. World Bank, *Sub-Saharan Africa: From Crisis to Sustainable Growth, a Long-Term Perspective Study* (Washington, DC: World Bank, 1989), pp. 17, xi. See also Julius O. Ihonvbere, "Economic Crisis, Structural Adjustment and Africa's Future," in Gloria Thomas-Emeagwali, ed., *Women Pay the Price: Structural Adjustment in Africa and the Caribbean* (Trenton, NJ: Africa World Press, 1995), pp. 138–147.

104. See World Bank, *World Development Report 1990, "Poverty"* (New York: Oxford University Press, 1990).

105. Jonathan Morduch, "The Microfinance Promise," *Journal of Economic Literature* 37, no. 4 (December 1999), p. 1570; Paul B. McGuire and John D. Conroy, "The Microfinance Phenomenon," *Asia-Pacific Review* 7, no. 1 (2000), pp. 90–93; Alex Counts, *Small Loans, Big Dreams* (Hoboken, NJ: John Wiley, 2008), pp. 201–206.

106. Bruce Rich, "The World Bank Under James Wolfensohn," in Jonathan R. Pincus and Jeffrey A. Winters, *Reinventing the World Bank* (Ithaca, NY: Cornell University Press, 2002), pp. 27–29.

107. John Pender, "From 'Structural Adjustment' to Comprehensive Development Framework: Conditionality Transformed?" *Third World Quarterly* 22, no. 3 (2001), p. 402.

108. Rich, "The World Bank Under James Wolfensohn," p. 26.

109. World Bank, *World Development Report 1997* (New York: Oxford University Press, 1997), Foreword, p. iii.

110. World Bank, *World Development Report 1997*, p. 14.

111. World Bank, *World Development Report 1997*, p. 14.

112. Kanbur and Vines, "The World Bank and Poverty Reduction," p. 88; McGuire and Conroy, "The Microfinance Phenomenon," p. 93.

113. Katherine Marshall, *The World Bank: From Reconstruction to Development to Equity* (New York: Routledge, 2008).

114. Kapur, "The Changing Anatomy of Governance of the World Bank," p. 69.

115. Fidler, "Who's Minding the Bank?" p. 46; Phillips, *Reforming the World Bank*, p. 134; Robert Wade, "Showdown at the World Bank," *New Left Review* 7 (January/February 2001), p. 132.

116. Weaver, *Hypocrisy Trap*, p. 2.

117. Jessica Einhorn, "Reforming the World Bank: Creative Destruction," *Foreign Affairs* 85, no. 1 (January/February 2006), p. 17.
118. Marshall, *The World Bank*, p. 57; Peter J. Hammer, *Change and Continuity at the World Bank* (Northampton, MA: Edward Elgar, 2013), pp. 135–138.
119. Robert B. Zoellick, "The End of the Third World? Modernizing Multilateralism for a Multipolar World," Woodrow Wilson Center for International Scholars, April 14, 2010, p. 4.
120. Hammer, *Change and Continuity at the World Bank*, p. 158.
121. Joshua Cooper Ramo, *The Beijing Consensus*, The Foreign Policy Centre, London, May 2004, pp. 3–4, http://fpc.org.uk/fsblob/244.pdf.
122. Sophie Harman and David Williams, "International Development in Transition," *International Affairs* 90, no. 4 (July 2014), pp. 935–938.
123. Andrew Jack, "Experts Divided Over Value of UN Sustainable Development Goals," *Financial Times*, September 15, 2015.
124. Martin Sandbu, "Critics Question Success of UN's Millennium Development Goals," *Financial Times*, September 15, 2015.
125. Jack, "Experts Divided Over Value of UN Sustainable Development Goals"; "Breakdown of U.N. Sustainable Development Goals," *New York Times*, September 25, 2015.
126. Walt W. Rostow, *The Stages of Economic Growth: A Non-Communist Manifesto* (Cambridge, UK: Cambridge University Press, 1960).
127. Malcolm Harper, "Some Final Thoughts," in Thomas Dichter and Malcolm Harper, eds., *What's Wrong with Microfinance?* (Bourton, UK: Practical Action Publishing, 2007), p. 257.
128. United Nations Development Program, *Human Development Report 1996* (New York: UNDP, 1996), p. 1.
129. Jennifer Clapp and Peter Dauvergne, *Paths to a Green World: The Political Economy of the Environment* (Cambridge, MA: MIT Press, 2005), pp. 196–210.
130. Lingle, "What Ever Happened to the 'Asian Century'?" p. 33.

Concluding Comments

The global political economy has been reshaped by a series of disruptive events during the last three decades of the twentieth century and the beginning of the twenty-first century. The most notable developments have included the food and oil crises in the 1970s, the foreign debt crisis in the 1980s, the breakup of the Soviet bloc and Soviet Union in the 1980s and 1990s, the Asian financial crisis of the late 1990s, the 2008 global financial crisis, the European sovereign debt crisis, and the migration crisis in various parts of the world. As globalization has increased, economic and political events in one part of the world are having a greater impact on distant areas, and predictions about the future of the global economy have become more hazardous. However, the historical and theoretical focus of this book enables us to speculate about current and possible future changes. Chapter 12 examines contemporary trends in the global political economy in terms of the major themes of this book. The chapter also discusses areas such as energy, the environment, and migration that require more attention by IPE scholars.

Current Trends in the Global Political Economy

This book provides a comprehensive approach to the study of IPE, introducing students to the main theoretical perspectives and substantive issue areas. The neomercantilist, liberal, and critical perspectives have evolved and influenced each other over time, and some theoretical approaches such as hegemonic stability theory and regime theory draw upon more than one of these perspectives. Constructivist, feminist, and environmental theories, and approaches that focus on domestic–international linkages are contributing to further changes in the study of IPE. To help draw linkages between theory and practice, this book focuses on three main themes: globalization, North–North relations, and North–South relations. Whereas the more developed transition economies such as the Czech Republic and Poland have levels of development comparable with some DCs, poorer transition economies such as Moldova and Tajikistan face economic problems comparable with some LDCs. This concluding chapter examines where we are with globalization, North–North relations, and North–South relations, and speculates about the future.

GLOBALIZATION

Globalization is a process that involves the broadening and deepening of interdependence among societies and states throughout the world. *Broadening* refers to the geographic extension of linkages to encompass virtually all major societies and states, and *deepening* refers to the greater frequency and intensity of interactions. This book does *not* adopt an extreme view of globalization that we are entering a "borderless world" where MNCs are losing their national identities and states are losing their distinctiveness.[1] Globalization affects some states and regions more than others; threatens the state's autonomy in some respects, but gives the state some new roles and does not prevent it from making policy choices; and contributes to fragmentation and conflict as well as unity and cooperation. Although states and societies were highly interdependent during the nineteenth and early twentieth centuries, globalization is more encompassing today than it was at any time in the past. Advances in technology, communications, and transportation are facilitating the globalization process as never before; the role of MNCs in generating FDI, trade, and technology is unprecedented; the capitalist economic system is spreading throughout the globe; and international economic organizations are becoming truly universal in membership.

Neomercantilists, liberals, and critical theorists have widely divergent views of globalization. Neomercantilists emphasize the importance of the state and often question whether globalization has significantly increased. Although they acknowledge that interdependence is increasing in some areas, neomercantilists see this as occurring only with the permission or encouragement of the most powerful states. Liberals, by contrast, view globalization as a significant force that is eroding state control, and they see the growth of interdependence as a positive development. Unlike neomercantilists, liberals see technological change, advances in communications and transportation, and other indicators of globalization as being beyond state control. Liberals also argue that domestic and transnational actors such as internationalist firms are a major force behind globalization.[2] Critical theorists, like liberals, see globalization as having a significant impact, but they often view this in negative terms. For example, historical materialists see globalization as having negative consequences for lower classes and poorer states in the periphery. Some Gramscian theorists argue that globalization is leading to the development of a "transnational historic bloc" composed of MNCs, international banks, international economic organizations, and international business groups in the most powerful capitalist states. A crucial element of this historic bloc is the power and mobility of transnational capital, which is putting national groups such as labor unions on the defensive. The only way to counter this historic bloc is to develop a counterhegemony composed of labor, human rights, women's, environmental, consumer, and development groups. This bloc would seek to replace the current corporate view of liberalization with a more democratic, participatory model based on socialism.[3]

Globalization and Triadization

Globalization has in many respects been more akin to "triadization." The integrative processes have been most intense among DCs in three regions: Europe, North America, and East Asia.[4] Emerging economies such as China, India, South Korea, Russia, Brazil, and South Africa are making major inroads into the DCs' dominance; but several of them are within the triad (China and South Korea in East Asia; Russia in Europe as well as North Asia). In 2014, the DCs accounted for 79.4 percent of outward FDI stock and 65.3 percent of inward FDI stock (see Tables 10.1 and 10.2 in Chapter 10). However, FDI *stocks* are cumulative over time, and yearly FDI *flows* shows how the DCs are losing their edge. Table 10.4 shows that China and Hong Kong, China ranked first and second in FDI inflows and second and third in FDI outflows in 2014. The triad also dominates global trade flows. Table 8.4 (Chapter 8) shows that the five largest merchandise exporters and importers in 2013 were all from Europe, North America, and East Asia. Although the triad continues to be important, there are major power shifts occurring within it; U.S. economic hegemony is declining, and some economic power is shifting from North America and Europe to Asia. Conflict within the triad on a wide range of security and economic issues has also increased in recent years.

Problems have also arisen because LDCs and emerging economies both within and outside the three major regions sometimes react negatively to feelings of subordination and marginalization. One example is the case of Latin America. The United States' decreasing emphasis on security issues in the 1980s, and Latin America's turn toward market liberalism and democracy, led to hopes for more cooperative linkages. However, the United States devoted much less attention to Latin America after the September 11, 2001 terrorist attacks. Subsequently, efforts to establish a Free Trade Area of the Americas collapsed, some Latin American states turned against democratic practices and market liberalism, and the question arose as to whether the United States was "losing Latin America."[5] These strained relations have made it easier for China to establish a growing economic presence in the region. Russia has also felt marginalized, particularly by the United States and the EU. As its economy revived with revenues from energy and other commodity exports, Russia adopted more hostile policies toward the West on some issues, and the standoff over Ukraine followed by Western sanctions on Russia have exacerbated relations. As discussed, the BRICS economies are dissatisfied with their subordinate position in the IMF and World Bank, and are moving to establish their own institutions. Another problem area outside the triad is the Middle East and North Africa; there has been continued strife among states in the region, and growing tensions between Islamic and Western practices.[6] Sub-Saharan Africa (henceforth, Africa) has been the most marginalized of the LDC regions. Most of the least developed countries (LLDCs) are African, and Africa's trade and investment flows have been very limited. For example, Africa accounted for only 2.7 percent of inward FDI stock in 2014, compared with 21.9 percent for LDCs in Asia and 7.3 percent for Latin America and the Caribbean (Table 10.2). Thus, triadization has had a negative effect on a number of marginalized areas.

Globalization and the State

Liberals see globalization as causing state authority to leak "away upwards, sideways, and downwards."[7] Internationally, states must share authority with MNCs and international institutions; domestically, central governments must share authority with NGOs and regional and local authorities. For example, globalization has constrained the ability of DCs to continue providing the social welfare benefits that citizens came to expect during the 1950s to 1970s, and neoliberalism has made such social expenditures seem less legitimate. Globalization also limits the state's ability to regulate the national economy.

For example, the massive growth of international capital flows has contributed to exchange rate fluctuations that interfere with the state's ability to promote economic stability. Orthodox liberals view the increased capital flows as a positive development because financial markets impose necessary discipline on states, and capital moves to the most productive locations. Interventionist liberals agree that increased capital flows are beneficial, but caution that states and IOs must adopt regulations to limit the volatility of capital flows. Historical materialists see increased capital mobility as a negative development. If states do not adopt capital-friendly policies, MNCs and international banks can shift their funds to more welcoming locations. Thus, MNCs locate their production facilities in states with the lowest wages, taxes, and environmental standards.

Neomercantilists are more inclined to view reports of the state's decline as "greatly exaggerated."[8] They argue that the increase in global financial flows has occurred with the permission or encouragement of the most powerful states and that these states continue to dictate the terms for such transactions. Some neomercantilists also assert that globalization has "enabling" as well as "constraining" effects on the state. Thus, many states have "increased direct tax yields, maintained or expanded social spending, and devised more complex systems of trade and industrial governance in order to cope with deepening integration."[9] The impressive economic growth rates of some states are closely related to their success in fostering a symbiotic relationship with the competitive marketplace. Although the state must vie with a number of nonstate actors, it continues to be the most important actor in the global economy.

Globalization, Inequality, and Poverty

The World Bank has compiled a large body of statistics on global inequality and poverty, but critics from both the right and the left often take issue with the Bank's methodology. These criticisms show that a researcher's theoretical perspective often affects their methodology and findings. For example, one liberal analyst criticizes the Bank for putting "all the households in the world onto one chart to measure worldwide inequality of incomes," because inequality matters most when people compare their income with others in their society:

> What sense does it make to put a household in Mongolia alongside a household in Chile, one in Bangladesh, another in the United States, and still another in the Congo? These households do not belong to a 'society' in which they compare themselves with the others, and so a measure that includes all of them is practically a meaningless construct.[10]

Another analyst writing from a more critical perspective argues that "deep methodological flaws in the Bank's poverty measurement methodology suggest that its figures may be quite inaccurate and that both the incidence and the trend may be worse than reported." This researcher believes that the UNDP, which found greater increases in poverty than the Bank, has "a more plausible poverty measurement methodology."[11]

Although the statistics are sometimes conflicting, some general trends in inequality are evident in today's globalized world. Income disparities among countries have declined over the last 20 years because emerging economies have grown more rapidly than the DCs. However, many poorer LDCs have not shared in this growth, and inequality has increased *within* many DCs and LDCs. Thus, the richest 1 percent of the world's people receive almost 15 percent of world income, while the poorest two-thirds receive less than 13 percent. Beyond income, the richest 1 percent of the world's people own about half of the world's wealth. The 2014 UN *Human Development Report* predicts that "globalization, technological progress, deregulation of labor markets and misguided macroeconomic policies are likely to create and sustain these large gaps in income and wealth."[12] Thomas Piketty has found that income inequality in the United States today is greater than it is in other DCs, and he attributes the growing income disparity to capital income, inherited wealth, and super-salaries for senior executives.[13] However, income inequality is increasing in many DCs and LDCs today. Despite some progress for women's rights in many countries, gender inequality is also persistent, especially in many LDCs. Gender gaps have not declined in some areas such as women's control over resources, their political voice, and cases of domestic violence. These gender gaps have contributed to large differences in income. For example, average wage differences by gender range from 20 percent in Pakistan and Mozambique to more than 80 percent in Jordan, Cote d'Ivoire, Latvia, and the Slovak Republic.[14]

How do IPE theorists interpret the statistics on inequality? Liberals recognize that globalization may contribute to inequality in the short term, but they believe that efficiency gains can reduce poverty even when inequality increases. Thus, one liberal asserts that "globalization does not appear to exacerbate poverty and may indeed contribute toward its reduction," and another argues that "globalization ... has improved the lot of hundreds of millions of poor people around the world."[15] Although the data on poverty give some support to the liberal view, the findings are ambiguous. For example, the number of people living in extreme poverty (less than $1.25 a day) has declined, but this has resulted mainly from economic growth in China and India. For the group of 48 LLDCs, "the proportion of people living in poverty remained persistently high, with 50.8 percent subsisting on less than US$1.25 per day from 2001–2012."[16] Liberals also argue that globalization will reduce inequality over time. For example, one liberal asserts that "the late-comers to modern economic growth tend to catch up with the early-comers"; and another argues that "the economic gap between South Korea and industrialized countries ... has diminished in part because of global markets."[17] Liberals believe that economies such as North Korea and Myanmar that isolate themselves from global markets will continue to be among the poorest LDCs. Although liberals generally point to the benefits of globalization, interventionist liberals are attuned to the problems stemming from inequality. For example, the 2014 *Human Development Report* indicates that inequality can fuel "social tensions that can lead to civil unrest and political instability," and that "large income disparities can even undermine democratic values, if wealthy individuals influence political agendas."[18]

Neomercantilists and historical materialists believe that there are long-term losers as well as winners from globalization. Historical materialists see globalization as benefiting the most powerful capitalist states and MNCs in the core at the expense of peripheral states and vulnerable societal groups. Neomercantilists argue that the most powerful states have control over the pace and direction of globalization and that they use the globalization process "to reinforce their position and their relative power." Globalization for less powerful states, by contrast, "is a process which is happening to them and to which they must respond."[19] Neomercantilists also assert that the policies of states as well as their positions in the global economy can make a difference. For example, some Asian LDCs such as China, India, Bangladesh, and Vietnam have reduced poverty to some extent while liberalizing their trade and investment policies. Variations among LDCs in the concentration of land ownership, the degree to which production is labor-intensive, and other factors can influence the way in which globalization affects the distribution of wealth. Despite the difference of theoretical views, we have discussed the fact that the persistence of poverty and inequality has contributed to disillusionment with the Washington Consensus.[20]

Globalization and Democracy

Many liberals believe that globalization is promoting democracy throughout the world. They point to the spread of liberal democratic practices such as constitutional guarantees, freedom of speech, open elections, and multi-party systems in southern Europe during the 1970s, Africa and Latin America during the 1980s, and Eastern Europe and the FSU countries during the late 1980s–1990s. However, historical materialists and some interventionist liberals note that the poorest individuals in the South lack employment, education, and health facilities. In both the South and the North, political rights mean little to the poorest individuals who lack housing, employment, and other basic amenities. Furthermore, income inequalities resulting from globalization contribute to disparities in political influence that limit opportunities for democratic policy-making. Critics also argue that globalization is transferring control from democratically accountable governments to MNCs, international banks, and IOs. Whereas national governments are accountable to domestic groups and individuals through periodic elections, international institutions lack such accountability. Thus, some scholars ask whether IOs such as the IMF, World Bank, and WTO are "accountable to those whom they directly affect."[21] Liberal supporters of globalization argue that democratization has occurred in the KIEOs in some important respects. For example, KIEO transparency has increased through the publication of minutes, decisions, and documents, and the KIEOs have upgraded their relations with NGOs. Critics by contrast argue that KIEO accountability has not increased in significant areas, and they refer to the gap between national and international governance as a "democratic deficit."[22]

Globalization and Civil Society

Globalization has contributed to the growth of civil society groups committed to social change. As discussed, there are three types of civil society groups: *Conformists* largely endorse the behavior of the KIEOs and private actors such as MNCs; *reformists* accept the KIEOs and MNCs but believe that they should and can be reformed; and *transformists* or *rejectionists* see the KIEOs and MNCs as unreformable, and want to downsize or abolish them. Reformists rely mainly on cooperative strategies to alter the behavior of the KIEOs and MNCs, whereas rejectionists engage in ideological—and sometimes physical—confrontation. Conformists and reformists are liberals, with reformists favoring embedded liberalism that takes account of the social effects of the market. Rejectionists, like historical materialists, are committed to transforming the capitalist system. Some NGOs employ reformist and rejectionist strategies simultaneously; for example, Greenpeace worked with companies to develop ozone-friendly refrigerators at the same time as it encouraged consumers to boycott Shell Oil because of its alleged involvement with state suppression in Nigeria.[23]

In recent years, reformists and rejectionists have organized protests against the WTO, World Bank, IMF, G8, and G20 as purveyors of globalization. Civil society groups have used some of the trappings of globalization such as the World Wide Web in opposing it. As discussed in Chapter 10, the Web was especially useful to protesters against the proposed MAI because it "facilitates networked sociopolitical relationships in important new ways, it (potentially) increases NGOs' organizational effectiveness and political significance, and it helps to foster more broadly participatory (transnational) political processes."[24] The question arises as to whether a "global civil society" is likely to develop a counterhegemony in opposition to globalization in Gramscian terms.[25] Civil society groups have had considerable influence in certain cases such as the proposed MAI, and some IOs and MNCs have responded to civil society pressures by expanding communication with NGOs. However, it is unlikely that a "global civil society" will establish a counterhegemony for several reasons. First, most civil society groups are conformists (a "silent majority") that are not dissatisfied enough to seek major changes. Many conformists also benefit from the current global order. Second, civil society groups have a diverse range of objectives, and they find it easier to agree on what they are against than on what type of world order they favor. Third, civil society groups seeking change—reformists and rejectionists—have widely divergent views regarding the best tactics to pursue. To gain legitimacy and exert influence on the WTO, reformist civil society actors have sometimes formed professional networks with the establishment, and some reformists have been co-opted in the process. Thus, the reformists' advocacy efforts may increasingly operate "within the dominant trade paradigm" and become "a source of legitimation for efforts to continue the liberalization of global markets."[26] In sum, civil society groups have had some influence in inducing international institutions and MNCs to alter top-down modes of decision-making, but one should not overestimate their ability to organize a unified effort to alter the global political economy.

Globalization and Neglected IPE Issues: Energy, the Environment, and Migration

Most IPE theorists associate globalization with the liberalization of trade, foreign investment, and capital flows. However, it is difficult to separate these explicitly economic processes from the effects of globalization on some IPE issues that have received less attention: energy, the environment, and migration.

Energy   Managing global interdependence in energy is a critical issue for many states today, because of greater volatility of prices in international energy markets, more concern about security of supplies, and the need to find alternative energy sources.[27] However, IPE specialists devoted little attention to energy issues after the early 1980s when concerns over the 1970s OPEC oil price increases subsided. Most IPE researchers to this point have focused on oil, and have not examined the changes in the energy field such as "the adoption of alternative fuels and energy efficiency measures ... the rise of China and other developing countries as major energy consumers, and rising concerns about global warming."[28] Neomercantilists, liberals, and critical theorists have differing views of energy interdependence, which will be evident in new research in this area.[29] Neomercantilists view the state as the most important actor in developing energy policy, and believe that national security should be the primary concern. Energy importers should avoid overdependence on one external energy supplier, because this would pose a threat to their national security. Thus, EU countries today are concerned about overdependence on Russian energy exports, and China has assertively sought to draw upon a wide range of energy suppliers throughout the world. Energy exporters by contrast may use their resources as a means of exerting power and influence. This is evident in Russia's policy of withholding supplies and increasing prices for Ukraine, and in its efforts to prevent many European countries from diversifying their import sources.

Liberals point to the shortcomings of the neomercantilist approach, noting that the state cannot act autonomously in the energy sphere. International oil firms have had significant influence over energy policy, and a range of private economic interests have influenced the forms of regulation of coal, oil, and nuclear energy in a number of countries. In the liberal view the competitive marketplace rather than the state is, and should be, the main factor determining the balance between supply and demand of energy products. With fracking in the United States and elsewhere, oil suppliers have become more diverse, and most oil-exporting states can do little to prevent prices from falling when oil supplies outpace demand. Liberals also point to the interdependence between energy producers and consumers, and argue that international institutions can help them realize their shared interests. One example is the *International Energy Forum*, which has 74 members, including oil-producing countries from OPEC, oil-consuming countries from the

International Energy Agency, and other major countries such as China, India, Russia, and South Africa. However, neomercantilists point out that international energy organizations generally are limited to dialogue and have voluntary guidelines rather than binding commitments. Countries emphasize their policy autonomy in this area because they view energy as a critical element of their national and economic security. Historical materialists "assume that the most powerful states, and by extension, energy companies, markets, and institutions, service the interests of the global elite and of the most dominant states in the international system."[30] However, liberal environmentalists point to our shared needs to conserve energy, produce energy-efficient products, and deal with adverse effects of some energy production such as increased pollution and global warming.

The Environment   IPE specialists have devoted more attention to the environment in recent years, but it still receives too little attention in view of environmental degradation and global warming. Liberals view globalization as a positive force for the environment because it contributes to economic growth which is needed to pay for environmental improvements. Many liberals acknowledge that economic growth may increase environmental problems such as industrial pollution and the cutting of forests in the short term. In the longer term, however, growth is necessary to pay for environmental protection. Thus, one theorist asserts that "the overall historical pattern in industrial countries in the last century has been one of increasing and then decreasing emissions over time."[31] Orthodox liberals believe that such improvements will occur naturally with the functioning of free and open markets; if there are fewer market distortions, we will be less likely to undervalue a natural resource. Interventionist and institutional liberals recognize that globalization has "enhanced our ability to exploit" resources "at a pace faster than our ability to manage them has grown."[32] They therefore favor a greater role for governments and IOs in ensuring that development does not pose major damage to the environment. However, liberals are generally optimistic about solving global environmental problems through cooperation and technological advances. For example, they have lauded the success in reducing the amount of chlorofluorocarbons (CFCs) released into the atmosphere. CFCs were used in refrigerators, aerosols, insulation, and solvents, but scientists discovered that they were depleting the ozone layer which protects us from the sun's harmful ultraviolet rays. The 1987 Montreal Protocol on Substances that Deplete the Ozone Layer and subsequent amendments have resulted in significantly reduced CFC production.[33]

Critical environmental theorists—the greens—argue that globalization is linked with a type of economic growth that results in environmental pollution and overconsumption of natural resources. They cite figures to show that global water consumption, deforestation, and pollutants such as carbon dioxide emissions from automobiles are increasing exponentially. Global inequality results in overconsumption by the wealthy and the relegation of the more polluting forms of production to poorer areas and LDCs. Many greens focus specifically on capitalist globalization, which "undermines the quest for an ecologically and socially sustainable future. The constant threat of international capital flight strips individual governments of important domestic regulatory powers."[34] Unlike liberals, the greens view the success in reducing production of CFCs as an exception, and they argue that capitalist globalization has limited progress on most environmental issues. Neomercantilists are less involved in debates over globalization and the environment because of their preoccupation with security issues. They see the environmental effects of globalization as depending more on the actions of states than on the market and international institutions. The main issue for neomercantilists is whether states establish mechanisms to protect the environment, because states will be unwilling to transfer significant authority to international environmental institutions.

Theorists from each of these perspectives have a point. As the greens point out, globalization-generated economic growth can result in environmental pollution and the overconsumption of resources. However, economic stagnation and poverty also pose environmental risks. Thus, liberals are correct in noting that economic growth can create the wealth necessary for dealing with environmental problems. Neomercantilists are also correct that environmental protection will ultimately depend more on the actions of states than on the market or international institutions. Whether states have the motivation and ability to cooperate to protect the environment is a critical question. States have often proved unwilling to commit to environmental regulations and/or to implement their commitments. A prime example is the 1997 Kyoto Protocol which places limits on greenhouse gas (GHG) emissions. The United States, the largest GHG emitter at the time (it is now China), would not join the agreement. Canada had ratified the agreement, but formally withdrew from it in 2012. Climate change and many other environmental issues are *common property goods*, which are rival but nonexcludable (see Chapter 5). Resources such as the air and water can be depleted (they are rival), but no one owns them (they are not excludable). Common property goods such as climate change mitigation present a collective action problem because decreasing GHG emissions involves opportunity costs for individual states and firms; but we all lose when GHG emissions increase. Garrett Hardin described this as the "tragedy of the commons."[35] As with the case of energy issues, states often balk at the idea of accepting and implementing binding international commitments on environmental issues.

Migration   In today's world there are about 214 million international and 740 million internal migrants. Furthermore, about 74 million people have been forcibly displaced; this includes about 16 million refugees who have crossed international boundaries and 41 million displaced within their own countries. It can be difficult to clearly distinguish between forced and voluntary migration, and between refugees and economic migrants; and analysts disagree in particular cases depending on their theoretical perspectives. For example, there may be greater agreement that migration is forced in cases of outright violence, but is migration totally voluntary if people seek to escape poverty, environmental degradation, or a feeling of personal insecurity?[36] Would-be migrants have become more aware of economic disparities and opportunities abroad through advances in communications, and advances in transportation have made migration more widely accessible. Societal groups and states often support some aspects of globalization that they view as beneficial and oppose other aspects of globalization that pose a real or presumed threat to them. Whereas many states and societal groups support freer trade and capital flows, they are much more resistant to the cross-border movement of people. Perhaps reflecting these preferences, most IPE literature "on the drivers of globalization has focused on trade and financial flows. The third driver—international migration—has until recently received relatively little attention."[37] However, it is no longer possible for IPE scholars or people in general to devote less attention to migration issues, because both forced and voluntary migration are increasing dramatically. Most striking is the increase in forced migration today, with the Office of the UN High Commissioner for Refugees reporting that there were almost 14 million newly displaced people in 2014. Most of these refugees flee from LDCs to other LDCs, with Ethiopia, Iran, Kenya, Pakistan, Jordan, and Turkey taking large numbers. However, migrants are also coming across the Mediterranean Sea to Europe in growing numbers. As is the case with environmental issues, the acceptance of migrants is often a prisoners' dilemma issue, with EU leaders taking very different positions on how many migrants they will accept. (See discussion of the Schengen Agreement in Chapter 9.) Whereas Germany with its economic prosperity and need for more foreign workers has been open to accepting more migrants, less prosperous Eastern European countries such as Hungary, Slovakia, and the Czech Republic have been more resistant to opening their borders. Indeed, the migration crisis is creating a backlash in some European countries, which is strengthening populist, xenophobic political parties. This trend is not limited to DCs. In Malaysia and India, for example, populist opposition to "illegal immigration" has resulted in government crackdowns.

Although states and societal groups regulate cross-border migration because of valid concerns about illegal immigration and terrorism, they also impose limits for more questionable reasons. For example, less skilled DC workers sometimes oppose immigration because of concerns that immigrants are taking away their jobs. These concerns have increased with growing unemployment due to the 2008 global financial crisis and European sovereign debt crisis. There is no conclusive empirical evidence of a linkage between immigration from LDCs on the one hand and increased unemployment among semiskilled and unskilled workers in DCs on the other. Indeed, some analysts argue that migrants often enter low-wage occupations which do not attract the local population, that many migrants are self-employed and create their own jobs, and that migration can stimulate growth and thus reduce unemployment. However, by accepting lower-paying jobs, migrants may thereby push down salaries in general and create other job-related problems for host states. For example, some studies find that "in many receiving states, first- and second-generation immigrant and refugee populations (henceforth called migrants) have higher unemployment rates and earn lower wages than do natives. Migrants' relative underperformance is especially problematic in Western European countries."[38] Discrimination has of course played a role in the unemployment problem, and with immigrant populations growing, this has created a major policy challenge in Europe. Hostility to immigrants is also heightened by groups with less legitimate objectives linked with extreme nationalism, racism, and suspicion of those who are different.

Despite these negative societal attitudes, the politics of immigration is complex, and there are also countervailing tendencies. For example, the market demand for certain types of foreign workers sometimes makes it difficult for political leaders to limit immigration. Countries that ignore these market signals may encounter increasing economic problems. For example, Japan's economic problems in recent years stem partly from its highly restrictive immigration policies. "A rapidly aging populace, and the closing of its doors to immigration and the youthful labor and fresh ideas that can bring" have sapped Japan's economic vitality.[39] Although more immigration would bring economic benefits to many countries today, many IPE scholars who write about globalization do not even discuss migration because "no other issue remains so much under the thrall of states and so resistant to globalizing effects."[40] Nevertheless, as globalization increases, migration pressures will grow along with the pressures for other types of international interactions. The UN predicts that the world's population will reach almost 10 billion by 2050 and 11 billion by 2100.[41] Most of the growth will be in poor, conflict-torn regions of the world, and migrant pressures will increase in Europe and other DCs. Regardless of one's views on this issue, IPE scholars should be devoting more attention to implications of the migration issue for the global economy.

NORTH–NORTH RELATIONS

The second theme of this book relates to the interactions among DCs of the North. International economic management has been mainly a North–North issue because only the DCs have had the wealth and power to manage the global economy. However, some emerging states such as the BRIC economies (Brazil, Russia, India, and China) are posing a major challenge to the North's supremacy. The 2008 global financial crisis has sped up this transition, and the September 2009 decision that the G20 would replace the G8 as the main forum for discussing global economic issues was an indication that the South will have a greater role in the management process. This book discusses two factors contributing to international economic management: hegemony and international institutions.

The Current State of U.S. Hegemony

This book provides a mixed picture of the current state of U.S. hegemony. On the one hand, the United States continues to demonstrate a number of strengths as a global hegemon. With the breakup of the Soviet bloc, the United States has emerged as the unchallenged military power in the world. As long as the threat of violent conflict persists, a state with hegemony in security matters will also have a degree of power over economic areas. However, China is increasing its military expenditures, Russia continues to have formidable military power, and U.S. tensions with both countries could increase. The U.S. dollar continues to be the key international currency, and the United States has the largest economy in the world, the largest market for other countries' exports, and the most votes in the IMF and World Bank. The United States has also had structural or soft power; i.e., it is often able to get "other countries to *want* what it wants."[42] For example, Part III shows that the United States had a central role in setting the agenda for the GATT Uruguay Round negotiations and in guiding DC policies on a range of issues extending from liberalizing capital flows to the foreign debt crisis and international development. However, Part III also provides indications of U.S. hegemonic decline. The U.S. dollar shifted from top-currency to negotiated-currency status in the 1960s, and the United States has had chronic balance-of-trade deficits, serious foreign debt problems, and greater dependence on external capital. U.S. indebtedness has increased greatly as a result of stimulus funding required to deal with the 2008 global financial crisis. Furthermore, U.S. soft power has declined in recent years. Although U.S. military predominance increased with the breakup of the Soviet bloc, even traditional U.S. allies resented its unilateral actions on security issues. These unilateral tendencies increased after the understandable outrage against the September 11, 2001 terrorist attacks on U.S. soil. U.S. president Barack Obama has tried to take a more consultative approach on global issues, but it is evident that U.S. soft power is not what it was in the past. The United States has also diverged from its customary role as a prime supporter of liberalization in some key economic areas such as trade. The lack of U.S. leadership in the WTO Doha Round is a further sign of its hegemonic decline.[43]

In sum, the United States continues to be the largest single-country economic power, but there are uncertainties about the future. The World Economic Forum's 2014–2015 *Global Competitiveness Report* (the "Report") notes that the United States is recovering from the 2008 global financial crisis, and it gives the United States a global competitiveness ranking of third after Switzerland and Singapore; but the Report also expresses some concerns. (The Report defines "competitiveness" as "the set of institutions, policies and factors that determine the level of productivity of a country," and it uses 12 measures to assess a country's competitiveness.) The Report notes that U.S. firms are highly innovative and are supported by an excellent university system that collaborates with business in R&D. The huge size of the domestic U.S. economy and its flexible labor markets are other sources of strength. However, the Report also refers to sources of weakness. The business community and the public show more distrust of the U.S. system of governance, and there is a general perception that the government spends its resources wastefully. The most glaring weakness is in the macroeconomic environment, with the high U.S. public debt and fiscal deficits.[44] The next section discusses whether there are possible competitors to the United States as hegemon.

Is There a Candidate to Replace the United States as Global Hegemon?

In the late 1980s, many analysts focused on Japan's hegemonic prospects, and one scholar wrote that "if any country surpasses the United States as the world's leading economic power, it will be Japan."[45] By the mid-1990s, however, most analysts saw Japan as lacking the military power and ideological appeal of a hegemon and as unwilling to assume the responsibility of global leadership. For a number of years after the 1990s Asian financial crisis, political indecisiveness and inflexible economic and social practices prevented Japan from adopting bold policies to reform the economy. Japan continues to have a major competitive edge in business innovation, high R&D spending, world-class research institutions, and high value-added goods and services. However, Japan also has high budget deficits and public debt, and its aging population and highly restrictive immigration policies compound its economic problems.[46] China overtook Japan as the world's second largest economy in 2010, and it is highly unlikely that Japan will replace the United States as a global hegemon.

Some writers have seen the EU as a possible hegemon, and one economist predicted that "future historians will record that the twenty-first century belonged to the House of Europe."[47] The EU has expanded to include 28 member states, and the associate membership of the ACP (Africa, Caribbean, and Pacific) states gives the EU considerable influence among LDCs. The euro was becoming more important, and some scholars predicted that it could replace the U.S. dollar as the key international currency. The EU was also the largest merchandise exporter and the second largest importer in 2013 (see Table 8.4). However, problems confronting the EU today make it an unlikely hegemon and even raise questions about its future as a cohesive unit. Only 19 of the 28 EU members have replaced their national currencies with the euro, and Britain has refused to join the monetary union. The European sovereign debt crisis is threatening the future of the euro zone, and is highlighting the wide economic disparities within the EU. Six European countries were ranked among the 10 most competitive economies in the 2014–2015 *Global Competitiveness Report*; but Portugal, Italy, Bulgaria, Romania, and Greece had rankings of 36, 49, 54, 59, and 81, respectively. The EU has also been unable to adopt a common approach to the migration crisis facing Europe, and Britain is to have a referendum vote on remaining in the EU before the end of 2017. In sum, a combined effort of the member countries is essential if the EU is to remain "a prominent player in the 21st century."[48]

A third possibility is that India could become a global hegemon. Some economists are optimistic about India's long-term economic prospects for several reasons. First, India has a young and growing workforce, whereas China's demography is less favorable due to its one-child policy and aging population. Second, India's more democratic system has some disadvantages, but in the longer term it could be more resilient than China's authoritarian system. Third, India's more individualistic approach to capitalism may result in more long-term productivity than China's state-directed capitalism. However, India has a long way to go before it could be considered as a possible hegemon for several reasons. First, a third of India's population live in extreme poverty, and many people lack access to health care, quality schooling, and sanitary facilities. Second, India must accelerate growth to improve its living standards, but India's growth has been slowing down since 2011. Third, India's competitiveness ranking has dropped for six consecutive years, and the 2014–2015 *Global Competitiveness Report* ranks India 71st out of 144 economies; this is the lowest ranking among the BRICS economies. Fourth, the business environment and market efficiency are hampered by monopolies, protectionism, and administrative barriers to entry and operation. In sum, India has serious problems to overcome if it is to be considered as a possible hegemon.[49]

A fourth, and the most likely, possibility is that China could become the global hegemon. China has developed and diversified its economy, reduced poverty, and raised the standard of living. China has become the world's largest single-country merchandise exporter and manufacturer, and it has the second largest economy after the United States. China's merchandise trade balance of *plus* $351.8 billion in 2013 was a stark contrast with the U.S. balance of *minus* $701.7 billion (see Table 6.2). Whereas the United States is the world's largest foreign debtor, China's foreign exchange reserves amount to about $4 trillion. China's FDI surpassed Japan's in 2014, and is second only to the United States' FDI. The Chinese renminbi (RMB) is being used much more to settle international trade accounts, and China aims to have its currency included with the U.S. dollar, euro, yen, and pound sterling in the SDR (special drawing rights) basket. The 2014–2015 *Global Competitiveness Report* gave China a ranking of 28, well above that for the other BRICS economies—Russia (53), South Africa (56), Brazil (57), and India (71). China's expanding power goes beyond economic areas, and its official statistics report a double-digit annual increase in its defense budget since 1989. The U.S. Pentagon asserts that these "officially published figures substantially underreport actual expenditures for national defense."[50]

Despite China's impressive changes, as an LDC it is more vulnerable to economic and political instability. Whereas some areas of China are experiencing rapid growth, the western and northeastern regions of the country have widespread poverty. Such inequalities are a source of political instability, and protests have increased. Despite China's strong economic performance, its banking system is quite fragile and access to loans is difficult for many small and medium-sized enterprises. China's capital controls, which greatly limit buying and selling of the RMB for investment purposes, may delay the IMF's decision to include it among the major reserve currencies. China is no longer an inexpensive country for labor-intensive production, and it is losing manufacturing jobs to some poorer countries. It is essential that China rebalances its economy away from investment and toward more domestic consumption. China's state-directed brand of capitalism has contributed to development in important respects, but it could become a drawback as domestic pressures for a more democratic lifestyle increase. Government leaders fear that a more open system could encourage separatism in provinces such as Tibet and Xinjiang. There are also questions whether China has enough soft power to be accepted as a hegemon. China's more assertive policies in territorial disputes with Japan, India, and other Asian countries have created animosity at the regional level. It is very likely that China will overtake the United States as the world's largest economy, but questions remain as to whether it will be able and willing to perform the role of hegemon with the support of other major economies.

The Role of International Institutions

Institutional liberals believe that interdependence and globalization create a need for international institutions "to deal with the ever more complex dilemmas of collective action," and international regimes and organizations have been an important part of IPE.[51] Although the North has had the most influence in these institutions, emerging economies are demanding a greater role. The IMF, World Bank, and GATT/WTO are the keystone international economic organizations (KIEOs). Whereas liberals see them as beneficial organizations that promote economic efficiency and openness, neomercantilists view them as creatures of the most powerful member states, and historical materialists see them as instruments the capitalist core uses to exploit weaker states in the periphery. This section assesses the current and possible future influence of the KIEOs.

The KIEOs have retained important roles in global economic management by altering their functions when necessary. As discussed in Chapter 6, the IMF lost one of its two main functions—looking after the pegged exchange rate system—when the major economic powers shifted to floating exchange rates in 1973. IMF loans also became less essential for middle-income LDCs in the 1970s when private banks recycled large sums of petrodollars to the South. During the 1980s, however, the IMF regained its stature when it took the lead role (along with the United States) in managing the LDC foreign debt crisis. The IMF also provided funding for transition economies after the breakup of the Soviet bloc, and it took the lead responsibility for dealing with the 1990s Asian financial crisis. Although the South resented the intrusive conditions attached to IMF structural adjustment loans, the IMF was secure as long as it retained the confidence of the North. However, the 1990s Asian financial crisis marked another turning point as DC economists and policy-makers began to attack IMF stabilization programs. For example, critics charged that the IMF imposed the same conditions on loans to South Korea as it had imposed on foreign debtors in the 1980s, despite major differences in the two cases. Unlike debtors in the 1980s, South Korea's foreign debt was low and its problems stemmed mainly from a temporary lack of liquidity. LDCs such as Brazil, Argentina, and Indonesia that benefited from surging commodity prices in the early twenty-first century were also able to forgo IMF loans and the strict demands that accompany them. Thus, IMF lending began to fall and some analysts asserted that its influence was declining.

However, the IMF's fortunes revived again when the 2008 global financial crisis led to an acute shortage of capital flows and the G20 decided it should have a central role in dealing with the crisis. The IMF has also been a central part of the troika in dealing with the European sovereign debt crisis (see Chapter 7). Despite its more active role, emerging economies have been increasingly dissatisfied with the IMF because the managing director continues to be European and the G5 DCs continue to have the most votes in the organization. This is posing a threat to the IMF's legitimacy, and the BRICS' New Development Bank and the China-led Asia Infrastructure Investment Bank (AIIB) are designed to provide alternatives to the IMF and World Bank. Most analysts believe that the IMF serves an important function, but that it needs to be refocused.[52] A restructured IMF that gives more influence to the emerging economies, tempers its conditionality requirements for loans, and recognizes the important role of governments as well as the market could continue to have an important role in the future.

The World Bank initially provided long-term loans for European reconstruction and LDC development. When the United States launched the Marshall Plan, the Bank shifted entirely to development. The Bank's importance stems partly from the fact that it is the largest source of multilateral finance for LDC development. The Bank also chairs a number of aid consultative groups where DC donors can coordinate their bilateral aid-giving. However, ODA as a percent of donor countries' GNIs steadily declined from 1960 to 2000 (see Table 11.2) for several reasons: Aid agencies encountered obstacles in promoting economic development; the end of the Cold War removed the security rationale for providing aid; and states cut spending in an increasingly competitive global environment. The United States and other donors were also more reluctant to replenish funding for the Bank group's soft-loan affiliate, the IDA. As Table 11.2 shows, ODA increased to 0.30 percent of GNI in 2013, but this was still well below the 0.52 percent level in 1960. Thus, the Bank's importance depends on much more than its roles as an aid coordinator and as a source of development finance.

The 1980s foreign debt crisis gave the Bank as well as the IMF new functions to perform. However, both the IMF and Bank provided SALs to debtor states, and the IMF rather than the Bank coordinated the response to the crisis. Since the IMF and Bank functions overlapped, questions were raised about whether the Bank was redundant. China is also posing a growing challenge to the Bank's favored position in the development area. China's state-owned development bank now provides more funds for international lending than the Bank, and as discussed, the AIIB and the BRICS' New Development Bank pose new challenges for both the IMF and the Bank. However, the Bank continues to have "a unique position as a generator of ideas about economic development," and it is seeking to adapt to changing times.[53] Unlike the IMF, China now has the third largest number of votes in the IBRD. The Bank is also recognizing the need for government involvement in development, and the need to examine the effect of its policies on disadvantaged groups in LDCs such as women.

Unlike the IMF and World Bank which impose conditions on borrowers, the WTO establishes rules and dispute settlement mechanisms for world trade. The WTO's predecessor, the GATT, became a permanent organization by default when the proposed ITO was not approved, but GATT's informal nature permitted it to be highly adaptable. The GATT initially held negotiations to lower tariffs, but it also began to negotiate NTB reductions in the Kennedy Round, and it expanded these negotiations in the Tokyo Round. The Uruguay Round was the most complex and ambitious GATT negotiation, resulting in agreements not only for trade in goods, but also for services trade, intellectual property, and trade-related investment measures. Most important, the Uruguay Round created the WTO, a formal organization with much wider regulatory functions than the GATT. The WTO moved closer to becoming a universal membership organization when China and Russia joined in 2001 and 2012. However, the WTO has so far failed to conclude its first negotiating round, the Doha Round. Scholars differ on whether the WTO can continue to be an effective multilateral trade organization without completion of the Doha Round, but there is no doubt that the WTO faces some threats to its legitimacy. First, North–South divisions have posed a major obstacle to completion of the Doha Round, and a major question is whether the WTO with its 161 members has become so large and diverse that it is impossible to reach a consensus on contentious issues. Second, the proliferation of regional trade agreements in view of the Doha Round problems is posing a challenge to the WTO-based global trade regime. Although some RTAs such as the EU and NAFTA may serve as stepping stones to global free trade, the proliferation of bilateral FTAs threatens to fragment the global trade regime. If negotiations for much larger RTAs such as the Trans-Pacific Partnership (TPP) and the Trans-Atlantic Trade and Investment Partnership (TTIP) are successful, these agreements could facilitate more global free trade. Third, the WTO has a much stronger dispute settlement system than the GATT, but it is uncertain whether major trading powers such as the United States, the EU, Japan, and China would accept a series of major dispute settlement decisions against them. In sum, the WTO, like the IMF and the Bank, faces serious governance challenges.

NORTH–SOUTH RELATIONS

According to the Population Reference Bureau (PRB), there were about 7.1 billion people in the world in 2013, with 5.9 billion in LDCs and 1.2 billion in DCs. More startling is the PRB's estimate that 97 percent of the world population growth is occurring in LDCs because of high birth rates and young populations. Whereas "virtually all future population growth will be in developing countries, the poorest of these countries will see the greatest percentage increase."[54] Despite the growing population of the South, it has had relatively little influence in making decisions regarding the global political economy. Some emerging economies have impressive economic growth rates and are pressuring for more influence in the world's economic forums. For example, emerging countries such as China, Russia, Kuwait, the United Arab Emirates, and Saudi Arabia have accumulated large foreign reserves and sovereign wealth funds which enhance their influence during periods of capital shortages. Groups of LDCs such as the East Asian NIEs, BRIC economies, and OPEC countries are often viewed as economic "success stories." However, these success stories tend to mask the poverty affecting many LDCs today. About 1.2 billion people live on less than $1.25 (U.S.) a day and 2.7 billion live on less than $2.50 a day; and 98 percent of those killed by natural disasters are from LDCs.[55] The UN has identified 49 LLDCs that have extremely low per capita incomes, literacy rates, and shares of manufacturing; almost all these countries are in Sub-Saharan Africa and South Asia. Poverty also has differential domestic effects in the South, with women and children most severely affected. Furthermore, globalization tends to marginalize the weakest states and societal groups, even as it contributes to growth in many stronger states. The following discussion examines how the concept of development is changing and considers whether there is a "best" path to development.

Changing Concepts of Development

During the 1950s–1960s, economic development was usually equated with the growth of a country's GDP and per capita income. Orthodox liberals argued that Western industrial states with high per capita incomes had achieved successful development, and that LDCs should follow the path set by the North. Orthodox liberals were not concerned about redistributing wealth to the poorest LDCs and groups because benefits from the efficient allocation of resources under free markets would "eventually trickle down from the top, alleviating the problem of poverty at the bottom."[56] Although the South experienced unprecedented economic growth during the 1960s, unemployment, poverty, and the gap between rich and poor were increasing. Many development specialists therefore rejected the orthodox liberal view that growth would trickle down to the poor and supported policies to redistribute income and meet basic human needs for health, education, food, and clean water. From this perspective, GDP and per capita income are not the only important development indicators. Human development indicators such as health and sanitation, literacy rates, education, employment, and gender and rural–urban disparities must also be considered. Thus, the human development approach measures development "through investment in people and not just in machinery, buildings, and other physical assets."[57] Those concerned about environmental degradation have also supported a *sustainable development* concept, which calls for meeting "the needs of the present without compromising the ability of future generations to meet their own needs."[58] The sustainable development concept is controversial because the North did not adopt sustainable policies when it was developing, the North produces more pollutants than the South, and many LDCs feel they cannot afford to divert resources from their immediate development needs to the environment. If the North expects the South to follow environmentally friendly policies, it must compensate the South with financial resources.

Our concept of development can have a major effect on policy-making, so it is essential that we opt for a broad definition for two reasons:

- Experience shows that rapid economic growth does not necessarily enrich people's lives and may increase income gaps and poverty under some circumstances. A broader concept of development includes not only economic growth but also human development, poverty reduction, and environmental protection.
- As interdependence increases, the form of development can have major global implications. For example, the World Bank estimates that more than 2 million people in China die each year from air and water pollution and that this pollution extends far beyond China's boundaries. China and India are the two fastest growing sources of greenhouse gases linked to global warming.[59]

In an age of globalization, we can no longer afford to adopt a development concept limited to economic growth. Thus, the North must assist LDCs that lack the capacity to transfer scarce resources from economic growth to other crucial objectives such as sustainability and the reduction of poverty.

Is There a "Best" Development Strategy?

Chapter 11 discussed several development strategies, including ISI, socialist development, export-led growth, orthodox liberalism, and "bottom-up" strategies such as microfinance. Liberals, neomercantilists, and historical materialists disagree as to which strategy is best, and sometimes they even disagree as to the strategy a state is following. For example, when East Asian economies were growing rapidly under export-led growth in the 1970s–1980s, liberals attributed their success to their outward market orientation; neomercantilists pointed to their strong developmental states that promoted an effective industrial policy; and historical materialists argued that the East Asians were still dependent and not as successful as neomercantilists and liberals assumed. Experience indicates that no single development strategy is always the best and that every strategy has strengths and weaknesses. Furthermore, in view of the diversity in the South, the best strategy for one LDC may not be the best or even a feasible strategy for another LDC. A brief recounting of the strengths and weaknesses of various development strategies will help reinforce these points.

As discussed in Chapter 11, many LDCs adopted ISI as a development strategy during the 1950s–1960s. The easier first stage of ISI resulted in economic growth and industrialization in a number of LDCs. However, Latin American LDCs that continued on to a second stage of ISI had growing problems with balance-of-payments deficits, uncompetitive industries, and dependence on external finance. In response to the problems with ISI, some LDCs adopted more extreme inward-looking policies and followed the Soviet Union's socialist planning model. Some LDCs with central planning increased industrial production, but even the largest of these LDCs—China—lacked competitiveness and was plagued by inefficiencies and low-quality production. Smaller LDCs such as Tanzania, North Korea, Cuba, Ethiopia, Mozambique, and Vietnam were even less effective in instituting central planning. Although these states registered some gains in health care and education and reduced socioeconomic inequalities, socialist central planning in LDCs was largely unsuccessful.

The East Asian NIEs, which followed the Japanese model and turned from import substitution to export-led growth policies in the 1960s, were the most successful in promoting economic growth during the 1960s to 1980s. Although liberals and neomercantilists agreed that other LDCs should learn from the East Asian example, they had different explanations for the East Asians' success. The neomercantilist explanations were probably more accurate: The East Asian NIEs (other than Hong Kong) had strong developmental states that provided extensive guidance to the market, controlled investment flows, promoted the development of technology, and protected selected infant industries. A financial crisis during the 1990s, however, demonstrated that the developmental state was not as efficient and immune to political pressures as was earlier assumed. Thus, the crisis stemmed partly from the failure of governments to develop adequate regulations for banking and other financial institutions. It also became evident that the East Asians had benefited from a unique set of circumstances in which the United States and Japan gave them favored treatment in aid, trade, and foreign investment. When U.S. and Japanese policies changed in the 1990s, the East Asian states were highly vulnerable. Environmentalists also raised questions about the sustainability of rapid economic growth in East Asia, because little action was taken to prevent environmental degradation. In the late 1990s, the East Asian financial crisis resulted in rapid outflows of capital, recessions, banking crises, and lower economic growth rates. Thus, many analysts who had viewed the East Asians as "miracle economies" were now questioning the export-led growth model. As discussed, the East Asians recovered quite rapidly from the 1990s financial crisis and resumed their economic growth rates. However, the export-led growth model as practiced by China today has neomercantilist aspects that can create serious trade imbalances; that is, China's huge export surplus depends on the fact that the United States will have massive trade deficits. Thus, for major economies such as China it is important to consider the external as well as domestic effects of export-led growth policies.

During the 1980s, the debt crisis and IMF and World Bank SALs ushered in yet another Southern development strategy based on neoliberalism (a return to orthodox liberalism). In marked contrast to import substitution and export-led growth, neoliberalism emphasized decreased government spending, privatization, deregulation, and open trade and foreign investment policies. The SALs to middle-income LDCs had some positive effects in reducing government budget deficits, increasing export earnings, and enhancing economic efficiency and growth. However, IMF and World Bank SALs had negative effects on the poorest LDCs in Sub-Saharan Africa and Asia and on vulnerable groups in LDCs such as women and children. Critics argued that structural adjustment programs underestimated the need to involve the state in development and to maintain social, health, and educational programs for vulnerable groups.

However, supporters of neoliberalism asserted that LDCs would benefit from liberalizing their economies and following the path of Western Europe and North America.

In view of the global spread of orthodox liberalism, the question arose as to whether we had reached the "end of history" for Southern development strategies and whether neoliberalism had become the only acceptable path to follow.[60] This was clearly not the case. Even the World Bank has acknowledged that SALs will succeed only if they take account of the need for strong, stable LDC governments and include some distributional goals to assist the poorest and most vulnerable groups. As neomercantilists since Friedrich List have noted, strategies that provide an active role for the government may be necessary for states at earlier stages of development if they are to catch up with the leading states. Three events in the twenty-first century have caused a revival of interest in the value of development strategies that have an important role for the government as well as the market. First was the rapid revival of the East Asian NIEs after the 1990s financial crisis. Despite the problems with depending too heavily on export-led growth, the East Asian developmental state model addresses the need to involve the state as well as the market in the development process. Second, the United States and some other countries reacted to the global financial crisis by depending on governments to stimulate economies with massive increases in public expenditures and tax cuts; some referred to this as an "undeniable shift to Keynes."[61] Third, as discussed in Chapter 11, with the rise of China as a major economic power, the so-called Beijing Consensus which emphasizes a greater state role in development is having a greater effect on the policies of countries in the South.

In sum, we have *not* reached the end of history in terms of development strategies. The best strategy is likely to include neomercantilist and historical materialist as well as liberal characteristics. Moreover, the best strategy for some LDCs may not necessarily be the best strategy for others.

A FINAL WORD ON IPE THEORY AND PRACTICE

This book combines theory and practice in the study of IPE, and devotes considerable attention to the three traditional IPE perspectives of neomercantilism, liberalism, and historical materialism. As Chapters 3–5 show, these perspectives remain relevant because they have not been static; they have interacted with each other and evolved over time. However, the dramatic global changes outlined in this book have revealed a need to supplement the traditional perspectives with "new theoretical categorizations."[62] Thus, we also focus on some theoretical perspectives that are newer to IPE such as constructivism, feminism, and environmentalism. Each perspective has its own strengths and weaknesses, and a familiarity with a range of perspectives is necessary to gain a better understanding of the relationship between IPE theory and practice. IPE theory will of course continue to evolve as it has in the past.

IPE as a university discipline only began to develop in the 1970s, and IPE theorists have made great strides since that time. In focusing on IPE issues, however, these theorists have often ignored security issues, just as security theorists have ignored IPE. It is time that theorists devote more attention to the important linkages between IPE and security issues. The globalization phenomenon points to yet another direction theorists should follow: the development of theories that explore domestic–international interactions. With globalization, the sensitivity and vulnerability of national economies to changes in capital, foreign investment, and trade flows have dramatically increased, and policies that were traditionally considered to be domestic can have a major impact on outsiders. The IPE perspectives have devoted too little attention to domestic–international interactions. This book introduces students to a range of theoretical approaches and applies these theories to substantive IPE issue areas. As an international relations theorist has stated, "to think theoretically one must be constantly ready to be proven wrong."[63] This book shows that all theoretical perspectives have limitations, and that a combination of perspectives is necessary to gain a more complete and accurate view of IPE. It is only through formulating and reformulating our theories that we can address anomalies and increase our understanding of the global political economy.

NOTES

1. Kenichi Ohmae, *The Borderless World: Power and Strategy in the Interlinked Economy* (New York: HarperPerennial, 1990).
2. Helen V. Milner, *Resisting Protectionism: Global Industries and the Politics of International Trade* (Princeton, NJ: Princeton University Press, 1988).
3. Stephen Gill and David Law, "Global Hegemony and the Structural Power of Capital," in Stephen Gill, ed., *Gramsci, Historical Materialism and International Relations* (New York: Cambridge University Press, 1993), pp. 93–124.
4. Riccardo Petrella, "Globalization and Internationalization: The Dynamics of the Emerging World Order," in Richard Boyer and Daniel Drache, eds., *States Against Markets: The Limits of Globalization* (London: Routledge, 1996), pp. 77–78.
5. Peter Hakim, "Is Washington Losing Latin America?" *Foreign Affairs* 85, no. 1 (January/February 2006), pp. 39–53.
6. See Mary A. Tétreault and Robert A. Denemark, eds., *Gods, Guns and Globalization: Religious Radicalism and International Political Economy* (Boulder, CO: Lynne Rienner, 2004).
7. Susan Strange, "The Defective State," *Daedalus* 124 (Spring 1995), p. 56.
8. Shalendra D. Sharma, "The Many Faces of Today's Globalization: A Survey of Recent Literature," *New Global Studies* 2, no. 2 (2008), p. 3.
9. Linda Weiss, "The State-Augmenting Effects of Globalisation," *New Political Economy* 10, no. 3 (September 2005), p. 352.
10. Jagdish Bhagwati, *In Defense of Globalization* (New York: Oxford University Press, 2004), p. 67.
11. Thomas Pogge, "Reframing Economic Security and Justice," in David Held and Anthony McGrew, eds., *Globalization Theory: Approaches and Controversies* (Malden, MA: Polity Press, 2007), pp. 212–213.
12. United Nations Development Program, *Human Development Report 2014* (New York: UNDP, 2014), p. 39.

13. "Q & A: Thomas Piketty on the Wealth Divide," The New York Times Blogs, March 11, 2014; Thomas Piketty, *Capital in the Twenty-First Century* (Cambridge, MA: Belknap Press, 2014), p. 249 and chs. 9–11.
14. World Bank, *World Development Report 2012* (Washington, D.C.: World Bank, 2012), pp. 76–80.
15. Michael W. Doyle, "The Liberal Peace, Democratic Accountability, and the Challenge of Globalization," in David Held and Anthony McGrew, eds., *Globalization Theory: Approaches and Controversies* (Malden, MA: Polity Press, 2007), p. 197; Joseph S. Nye, Jr., "Globalization's Democratic Deficit: How to Make International Institutions More Accountable," *Foreign Affairs* 80, no. 4 (July/August 2001), p. 3.
16. United Nations OHRLLS, *State of the Least Developed Countries 2014* (New York: United Nations, 2014), p. 3.
17. Walt W. Rostow, *Why the Poor Get Richer and the Rich Slow Down* (Austin, TX: University of Texas Press, 1980), p. 259; Nye, "Globalization's Democratic Deficit," p. 3.
18. UNDP, *Human Development Report 2014*, p. 39.
19. Andrew Hurrell and Ngaire Woods, "Globalisation and Inequality," *Millennium* 24, no. 3 (1995), p. 458.
20. Joseph E. Stiglitz, *Making Globalization Work* (New York: W.W. Norton, 2007), pp. 36–37.
21. Ngaire Woods and Amritar Narlikar, "Governance and the Limits of Accountability: The WTO, the IMF, and the World Bank," *International Social Science Journal* 170 (December 2001), p. 569.
22. For differing views on this issue, see Tony Porter, "The Democratic Deficit in the Institutional Arrangements for Regulating Global Finance," *Global Governance* 7 (2001), pp. 427–439; Woods and Narlikar, "Governance and the Limits of Accountability"; and Nye, "Globalization's Democratic Deficit."
23. Jan A. Scholte, "Civil Society and Democracy in Global Governance," *Global Governance* 8 (2002), pp. 281–304.
24. Craig Warkentin and Karen Mingst, "International Institutions, the State, and Global Civil Society in the Age of the World Wide Web," *Global Governance* 6, no. 2 (April–June 2000), p. 240.
25. Robert W. Cox, "Civil Society at the Turn of the Millennium: Prospects for an Alternative World Order," *Review of International Studies* 25 (1999), pp. 3–28.
26. Kristen Hopewell, "Multilateral Trade Governance as Social Field: Global Civil Society and the WTO," *Review of International Political Economy*, July 28, 2015, p. 25.
27. Jeffrey D. Wilson, "Multilateral Organisations and the Limits of International Energy Cooperation," *New Political Economy* 20, no. 1 (2015), pp. 85–86.
28. Llewelyn Hughes and Phillip Y. Lipsey, "The Politics of Energy," *Annual Review of Political Science* 16 (May 2013), p. 451; Kathleen J. Hancock and Vlado Vivoda, "International Political Economy: A Field Born of the OPEC Crisis," *Energy Research & Social Science* 1 (March 2014), p. 206.
29. This section relies on Hancock and Vivoda, "International Political Economy: A Field Born of the OPEC Crisis"; Hughes and Lipsey, "The Politics of Energy"; and Wilson, "Multilateral Organisations and the Limits of International Energy Cooperation."
30. Hancock and Vivoda, "International Political Economy: A Field Born of the OPEC Crisis," p. 208.

31. Robert Mendelsohn, "Globalization and the Environment," in Ernesto Zedillo, ed., *The Future of Globalization: Explorations in the Light of Recent Turbulence* (New York: Routledge, 2008), p. 391.

32. Stiglitz, *Making Globalization Work*, p. 184.

33. Jennifer Clapp and Peter Dauvergne, *Paths to a Green World: The Political Economy of the Global Environment* (Cambridge, MA: MIT Press, 2005), pp. 26–31.

34. Ken Conca, "Beyond the Statist Frame: Environmental Politics in a Global Economy," in Fred P. Gale and R. Michael M'Gonigle, eds., *Nature, Production, Power: Towards an Ecological Political Economy* (Northampton, MA: Edward Elgar, 2000), p. 141.

35. Garrett Hardin, "The Tragedy of the Commons," *Science* 162, no. 3859 (December 1968), pp. 1243–1248; Thomas Bernauer, "Climate Change Politics," *Annual Review of Political Science* 16 (May 2013), pp. 423–424.

36. Sunil S. Amrith, "Currents of Global Migration," *Development and Change* 45, no. 5 (2014), pp. 1134 and 1142–1145.

37. Devesh Kapur, "Political Effects of International Migration," *Annual Review of Political Science* 17 (2014), p. 480.

38. Rafaela M. Dancygier and David D. Laitin, "Immigration into Europe: Economic Discrimination, Violence, and Public Policy," *Annual Review of Political Science* 17 (2014), p. 44.

39. Martin Fackler and Steve Lohr, "U.S. Hears Echo of Japan's Woes," *New York Times*, October 20, 2010.

40. Malcolm Waters, *Globalization* (London: Routledge, 1995), p. 89.

41. Eduardo Porter, "A Migration Juggernaut is Headed for Europe," *New York Times*, September 15, 2015.

42. Joseph S. Nye, Jr., "Soft Power," *Foreign Policy* 80 (Fall 1990), p. 166; Susan Strange, *States and Markets*, 2nd ed. (London: Pinter, 1994), p. 29.

43. On the changing U.S. position on international trade see Theodore H. Cohn, *Governing Global Trade: International Institutions in Conflict and Convergence* (Burlington, VT: Ashgate, 2002).

44. Klaus Schwab, ed., *The Global Competitiveness Report 2014–2015* (Geneva: World Economic Forum, 2014), pp. 4–21.

45. Ronald A. Morse, "Japan's Drive to Pre-Eminence," *Foreign Policy* 69 (Winter 1987–88), pp. 3–21.

46. Schwab, *The Global Competitiveness Report 2014–2015*, pp. 21–22.

47. Lester Thurow, *Head to Head: The Coming Economic Battle Among Japan, Europe, and America* (New York: Morrow, 1992), p. 258.

48. Xavier Sala-i-Martin, Jennifer Blanke, Margareta Drzeniek Hanouz, Thierry Geiger, and Irene Mia, "The Global Competitiveness Index 2010–2011," in Klaus Schwab, ed., *The Global Competitiveness Report 2010–2011* (Geneva: World Economic Forum, 2010), pp. 25–26.

49. Schwab, *The Global Competitiveness Report 2014–2015*, pp. 29–31.

50. Quoted in Akiho Tanaka, "Global and Regional Geo-strategic Implications of China's Emergence," *Asian Economic Policy Review* 1, no. 1 (June 2006), pp. 182–183; Schwab, *The Global Competitiveness Report 2014–2015*, p. 27.

51. Andrew Hurrell, "Hegemony, Liberalism and Global Order: What Space for Would-Be Great Powers?" *International Affairs* 82, no. 1 (2006), p. 6.

52. Martin Feldstein, "Refocusing the IMF," *Foreign Affairs* 77, no. 2 (March/April 1998), pp. 20–33.

53. Robert Wade, "Japan, the World Bank and the Art of Paradigm Maintenance: The East Asian Miracle in Political Perspective," *New Left Review* 217 (May/June 1996), p. 5; Clifford Krauss and Keith Bradsher, "China's Global Ambitions, with Strings Attached," *New York Times*, July 24, 2015.

54. "World Population Data Sheet 2012," Population Reference Bureau, Washington, DC, p. 2; "World Population Data Sheet 2013," Population Reference Bureau, Washington, DC, p. 1.

55. United Nations Development Program, *Human Development Report 2014* (New York: United Nations, 2014), pp. 19–20 and 38–39.

56. Mohammed H. Malek, "Towards an Integrated Aid and Development Programme for Europe," in Mohammed H. Malek, ed., *Contemporary Issues in European Development Aid* (Brookfield, VT: Avebury, 1991), p. 142.

57. Wilfred L. David, *The Conversation of Economic Development: Historical Voices, Interpretations, and Reality* (Armonk, NY: Sharpe, 1997), p. 177.

58. World Commission on Environment and Development, *Our Common Future* (New York: Oxford University Press, 1987), p. 8.

59. Nicholas D. Kristof, "Across Asia, a Pollution Disaster Hovers," *New York Times*, November 28, 1997, pp. A1, A10.

60. See Francis Fukuyama, "The End of History?" *The National Interest* 16 (Summer 1989), pp. 3–18.

61. Chris Giles and Ralph Atkins, "The Undeniable Shift to Keynes," *Financial Times*, December 29, 2008.

62. Thomas J. Biersteker, "Evolving Perspectives on International Political Economy: Twentieth-Century Contexts and Discontinuities," *International Political Science Review* 14, no. 1 (January 1993), p. 27.

63. James N. Rosenau, "Thinking Theory Thoroughly," in James N. Rosenau, *The Scientific Study of Foreign Policy*, rev. ed. (London: Pinter, 1980), p. 30.

GLOSSARY

absolute advantage A country has an absolute advantage in a particular good if it can produce that good at a lower cost than another country. See *comparative advantage*.

absolute gains Emphasizes the gains of each state without concern for the gains of others. See *relative gains*.

antidumping duties (ADDs) Duties a country imposes on imported goods if it determines that the goods are being dumped and that this is causing or threatening material injury to its domestic producers. See *dumping*.

appreciation A market-driven increase in the value or price of a currency. See *depreciation*.

Asian Infrastructure Investment Bank (AIIB) Launched by China in 2014, the AIIB (which now has 57 member countries) will provide funds for large infrastructure projects.

Association of Southeast Asian Nations (ASEAN) Established in 1967, ASEAN currently has 10 Southeast Asian members. The ASEAN Free Trade Area (AFTA) has made some progress toward free trade.

Baker Plan Proposed by U.S. Secretary of the Treasury James A. Baker III in 1985 to deal with the LDC foreign debt crisis, the plan called for rescheduling debt service payments, providing new IMF and World Bank loans, and changing debtor country policies.

balance of payments A summary record of all international economic transactions a country has over a one-year period. The most important components of the balance of payments are the *current account* and the *financial account*.

Bank for International Settlements (BIS) The oldest international financial institution, formed in 1930 to oversee German war reparations. Located in Basel, Switzerland, the BIS is the main forum for cooperation and consultation among central bankers in the OECD countries.

basic needs A poverty reduction approach that focuses on health, education, family planning, rural development, and services to the poor and least developed countries. This approach became prominent in the 1970s and marked a shift from the emphasis on GNP growth in the 1960s.

bilateral aid Aid that flows directly from a donor to a recipient government. The largest share of ODA is bilateral.

bilateral investment treaties (BITs) BITs protect foreign investment. They uphold the MFN and national treatment principles, prohibit host-country performance requirements, and require compensation in cases of nationalization.

Brady Plan Proposed by U.S. Secretary of the Treasury Nicholas Brady in 1988, the plan introduced the idea that debt reduction was necessary for some LDCs with severe and protracted debt problems.

Bretton Woods Conference The July 1944 conference to establish the postwar international economic order. The IMF and World Bank were established at Bretton Woods.

BRIC economies Four countries—Brazil, Russia, India, and China—that are challenging the North's economic dominance.

BRICS economies The BRIC economies plus South Africa.

Cairns Group A group of smaller country agricultural exporters formed in 1986 that has pressured for agricultural trade liberalization in the GATT/WTO.

Canada–U.S. Free Trade Agreement (CUSFTA) Concluded in 1988, CUSFTA resulted from a U.S. decision to participate in RTAs, and from Canada's desire to gain more assured access to the U.S. market. NAFTA replaced CUSFTA in 1994. See *North American Free Trade Agreement*.

capital A factor of production, along with land and labor, that consists of physical assets such as equipment, tools, buildings, and other manufactured goods that can generate income and financial assets.

capital market Consists of institutions in a country (e.g., the stock exchange, banks, and insurance companies) that match supply with demand for long-term capital. (A *money* *market* deals with shorter-term loanable funding.)

central bank   A public authority responsible for managing a country's money supply, and for regulating its financial institutions and markets.

civil society   A wide range of nongovernmental, noncommercial groups that seek to either reinforce or alter existing norms, rules, and social structures.

collective action problem   Occurs when the uncoordinated actions of individuals or states do not produce the best possible outcome for them.

common market   A common market has the characteristics of a customs union *plus* the free mobility of factors of production (capital and labor). See *customs union*.

common property goods   Resources such as air, water, outer space, and fish in nonterritorial waters that are rival (they can be depleted) but not excludable (no one owns them).

comparative advantage   A country has a comparative advantage in producing good X if it can produce X at a *relatively* lower cost than other goods, even if it does not have an absolute advantage in producing any good. See *absolute advantage*.

concessional loans   (or soft loans) Loans with lower interest rates, longer grace periods, and longer repayment periods than commercial or hard loans.

conditionality   IMF conditions on loans that typically include borrowers' agreement to decrease government spending, increase government revenues, and adopt policies that facilitate deregulation and privatization.

constructivism   A theory that examines the role of collectively held (or "intersubjective") ideas in IR. Constructivists believe that reality is socially constructed.

consultative groups   Donors use consultative groups to coordinate their bilateral aid-giving and to exert collective pressure on recipient states.

corporate social responsibility (CSR)   The contributions a corporation may be expected to make to society. Some analysts see CSR as a legal responsibility of MNCs, while others simply view it as desirable behavior.

Cotonou Agreement   An agreement negotiated in 2000 to make the EU's relationship with associate ACP (African,

Caribbean, Pacific) states more compatible with WTO rules. See *Lomé Convention*.

countervailing duties (CVDs)   Duties a country imposes on imported goods if it determines that the goods benefit from trade-distorting subsidies that cause or threaten material injury to its domestic producers.

current account   An item in the balance of payments that records a country's trade in goods and services with foreigners, investment income and payments, and gifts and other transfers paid to and received from foreigners.

customs union (CU)   Member states eliminate tariffs on substantially all trade with each other and develop a common external tariff toward outsiders.

debt crisis   A crisis that occurs when some major debtor states lack sufficient foreign exchange to make the interest and/or principal payments on their debt obligations.

debt reduction agreements   Agreements that allow for a decrease in the overall debt burden; that is, they include some debt forgiveness.

debt rescheduling agreements   Agreements that defer debt service payments and apply longer maturities to the deferred amount.

debt service ratio   The ratio of a country's interest and principal payments on its debt to its export income. It is often used to assess a country's ability to repay its foreign debt.

dependency theory   A development theory that sees the world as hierarchically organized, with capitalist states in the core of the global economy exploiting poorer states in the periphery.

depreciation   A market-driven reduction in the value or price of a currency. See *appreciation*.

devaluation   A reduction in the official rate at which one currency is exchanged for another. When a country devalues its currency, the prices of its imported goods and services rise while its exports become less expensive to foreigners. See *revaluation*.

Development Assistance Committee (DAC)   Part of the OECD, the DAC is the leading international forum for states that provide development assistance.

developmental state   A term coined in the 1980s to describe East Asian NIEs that provided extensive guidance to the market, made development their primary objective, invested heavily in education, and depended on a highly skilled technocratic bureaucracy.

diffuse reciprocity Does not require an immediate response to an action. Instead, it imposes a more general obligation on the recipient for repayment in the future. See *specific reciprocity*.

Doha Development Agenda (DDA) The name given to the WTO Doha Round, because of its promise to give special attention to concerns of the least developed countries.

dumping When a firm sells a product for export at a lower price than it charges in the home market or below the cost of production.

economic and monetary union (EMU) The EMU includes the countries in the EU that have adopted the euro and common monetary policies.

economic union An economic union has the characteristics of a common market, and also harmonizes the industrial, regional, fiscal, and monetary policies of the member states. A full economic union also involves the adoption of a common currency. See *common market*, *customs union*.

economism An overemphasis on the importance of economics.

emerging market economies Developing and transition economies that have achieved rapid growth and have adopted many elements of a free market system.

endogenous growth theory Posits that technological change is not simply the result of fortunate breakthroughs in knowledge exogenous to the factors of production; technological knowledge is an *endogenous* factor of production along with labor and capital that gives DCs advantages over LDCs.

epistemic community A group of professionals with acknowledged expertise and a recognized claim to policy-relevant knowledge in a particular issue area.

Eurasian Economic Union A 2015 agreement for closer economic ties between Russia and Belarus, Kazakhstan, Armenia, and Kyrgyzstan.

eurocurrency market Deals with currencies traded and deposited in banks outside the home country, usually (but not only) in Europe.

European Coal and Steel Community (ECSC) Six Western European states formed the ECSC in 1951 to integrate their coal and steel resources and prevent renewed conflict between France and Germany.

European Community (EC) A regional integration agreement formed in 1957 by six Western European states. EC membership increased to 12 states by 1986, and in 1993 it was superseded by the *European Union*.

European Free Trade Association (EFTA) A free trade agreement formed in 1959 by Britain and six other European states that did not join the EC. Today, the EFTA has four remaining members: Iceland, Liechtenstein, Norway, and Switzerland.

European Union (EU) The EC became the EU in 1993, with plans to complete the creation of a single market by removing the remaining fiscal, nontariff, and technical trade barriers. The EU currently has 28 members.

euro zone The members of the European Union that have adopted the euro as their common currency.

exchange rates The number of units of one currency that can be exchanged for a unit of another currency. See *fixed exchange rates* and *floating exchange rates*.

export-led growth A strategy that emphasizes the production of industrial goods for export. Export-led growth is associated with the economic success of the East Asian NIEs.

external debt The total public and private debt owed to nonresidents by residents of an economy.

fair trade A trading partnership that contributes to greater equity and sustainable development by securing more rights and better conditions for marginalized workers, especially in the South.

FDI flows The value of FDI in a single year.

FDI stock The net accumulated value of FDI resulting from past FDI flows.

feminist theory A wide range of theories that address the problems of patriarchy and the inattention to gender issues in IR and IPE.

financial account A balance-of-payments item that includes all movements of financial capital (foreign direct investment and portfolio investment) into and out of a state.

financial contagion The transmission of a financial shock from one market or country to other interdependent markets or countries.

financial crisis An escalation of financial disturbances, such as a sharp decrease in asset prices, the failure of large financial intermediaries, and disruption in foreign exchange markets.

fiscal policy   Fiscal policy affects the economy through changes in taxes and government spending. For example, a government may deal with a balance-of-payments deficit by lowering government expenditures and raising taxes.

fixed exchange rates   In a fixed-exchange-rate regime, currencies are given official exchange rates, and governments regularly take actions to keep the market rates of their currencies close to the official rates.

floating exchange rates   There are three types of floating: With *free floating*, the market alone determines currency valuations; with *managed floating*, central banks intervene to deal with disruptive conditions; with *manipulative floating*, a government manipulates exchange rates to give it an unfair competitive advantage.

foreign aid   Grants, loans, or technical assistance that donors provide to recipients on concessional terms (normally with a grant element of at least 25 percent). See *concessional loans.*

foreign direct investment (FDI)   Foreign investment that involves some ownership and/or operating control. The foreign residents are usually MNCs. See *portfolio investment.*

free trade area (FTA)   Member states eliminate tariffs on substantially all trade with one another, but each member can follow its own trade policies toward nonmembers.

GATT Article 24   Permits countries to form free trade areas and customs unions as an exception to MFN treatment, but seeks to ensure that they are more trade-creating than trade-diverting.

General Agreement on Tariffs and Trade (GATT)   A provisional treaty that became the global trade organization in 1948 when a planned ITO was not formed. When the WTO was formed in 1995, GATT reverted to its original status as a treaty for trade in goods.

General Agreement on Trade in Services (GATS)   An agreement under the WTO that begins the process of creating principles and rules for policies affecting access to service markets.

generalized system of preferences (GSP)   Under the GSP, individual DCs can waive MFN treatment and give preferential treatment to specific imports from LDCs.

Gini coefficient   Measures the deviation of income distribution in a country from an equal distribution.

Glass–Steagall Act   Also called the U.S. Banking Act of 1933, it was designed to insulate commercial banks from the risky activities of investment banks. The Act was repealed in 1999.

Global Compact   A UN-led voluntary compact with principles on human rights, labor standards, the environment, and anticorruption to promote responsible global capitalism. The UN has invited MNCs to sign the compact.

global financial crisis   Began as a result of a U.S. subprime mortgage crisis. Subprime mortgages were packaged and sold to investors in many countries and this had serious global repercussions. See *financial crisis.*

global governance   Formal and informal arrangements that provide a degree of order and collective action above the state in the absence of a global government. See *governance.*

globalization   Refers to the broadening and deepening of interdependence among people and states throughout the world.

gold exchange standard   A monetary system in which central banks fix the value of their currencies and hold international reserves in gold and foreign exchange (e.g., the Bretton Woods regime).

gold standard   A monetary system in which central banks fix the value of their currencies in terms of gold and hold international reserves in gold. A gold standard regime existed from the 1870s to 1914.

governance   Formal and informal processes and institutions that organize collective action. See *global governance.*

greenfield investment   The creation of new facilities and productive assets by foreigners.

gross domestic product (GDP)   The total value of goods and services produced within a country's borders during a given year. GDP counts income in terms of where it is earned rather than who owns the factors of production.

gross national income (GNI) Virtually identical with the GNP. The GNI measures the income produced by the GNP rather than the value of the product itself.

gross national product (GNP) The total value of goods and services produced by domestically owned factors of production during a given year. GNP counts income according to who owns the factors of production rather than where the income is earned.

Group of Five (G5) The G5 includes the finance ministers and central bank governors of the largest DCs: the United States, Japan, Germany, France, and Britain.

Group of Seven (G7) The G5 plus Italy and Canada.

Group of Eight (G8) The G8 includes the G7 members plus Russia.

Group of 10 (G10) The G10 includes the DCs that established the General Arrangements to Borrow with the IMF in 1962. Eleven countries are now G10 members—the G7 plus the Netherlands, Belgium, Sweden, and Switzerland.

Group of 20 (G20) The G20 finance ministers and central bank governors hold an annual summit to discuss key issues in the global economy, and also meet on extraordinary occasions such as the 2008 global financial crisis. Includes the G8, Australia, Turkey, the EU, and nine LDCs.

Group of 24 (G24) Formed in 1972 to represent LDC interests on monetary issues, the G24 includes eight finance ministers or central bank governors from each of the main LDC regions—Africa, Asia, and Latin America.

Group of 77 (G77) The principal group representing the South's economic interests in negotiations with the North. The G77 derives its name from the 77 LDCs that formed the group in 1964, but it now has 130 members.

hard power Power based on the use of coercion and payments.

Heavily Indebted Poor Countries (HIPC) Initiative A 1996 plan to provide relief for the debt of low-income LDCs to the IMF and World Bank. An *enhanced HIPC initiative* introduced in 1999 more than doubled the amount of debt relief available. See *Multilateral Debt Relief Initiative*.

Heckscher–Ohlin theory Postulates that comparative advantage is determined by the relative abundance and scarcity of factors of production (land, labor, and capital). Capital-rich states should specialize in capital-intensive production, and states with an abundance of cheap labor should specialize in labor-intensive production.

hegemonic stability theory Asserts that a relatively open and stable international economic system is more likely to exist when a hegemonic state is willing and able to lead. See *hegemony*.

hegemony Leadership or dominance in the international system, usually associated with a particular state. Gramscian theorists use the term to connote the "ideas" social groups use to legitimize their authority.

historic bloc A Gramscian term referring to the congruence between state power, ideas, and institutions that guide the society and economy.

historical materialism A critical perspective that is "historical" because it examines structural change over time, and "materialist" because it examines the role of material factors in shaping society.

horizontal integration A horizontally integrated MNC produces the same product or product line in affiliates in different countries. Firms often engage in horizontal integration to defend or increase their market share. See *vertical integration*.

human development index (HDI) The UNDP's measure of human development based on life expectancy at birth, adult literacy rates and school enrollments, and PPP-adjusted per capita GNI.

hyperglobalists Hyperglobalists believe that globalization involves the creation of a "borderless world" in which MNCs lose their national identities, and regional and global markets replace national economies.

import substitution industrialization (ISI) A strategy to replace industrial imports with domestic production through trade protectionism and government support for domestic firms. Many LDCs adopted ISI policies in the 1950s–1960s.

inequality-adjusted HDI (IHDI) Combines a country's average achievements in health, education, and income with the distribution of these achievements among the country's population

infant industries Industries not yet able to compete with established industries in more developed countries.

infrastructure The facilities, equipment, institutions, and installations crucial for the functioning of an economy. Examples include transportation systems, public utilities, law enforcement, education, and research.

institutional liberals Liberals who favor strong international institutions as a supplement to the market.

institutions Persistent and connected sets of rules that prescribe behavior, constrain activity, and shape expectations.

instrumental Marxism Marxists who view government institutions as responding in a passive manner to the interests and pressures of the capitalist class. See *structural Marxism*.

interdependence Mutual dependence in which transactions have costly effects that are reciprocal but not necessarily symmetrical.

International Monetary Fund (IMF) An IO formed in 1944 to uphold the system of pegged exchange rates and to provide short-term loans to countries with balance-of-payments problems. The IMF has had a leading role in dealing with financial crises.

international organizations (IOs) Formal institutional arrangements across national boundaries that facilitate cooperation among members. See *institutions*.

international regimes Institutions in which actors' expectations converge around a set of principles, norms, rules, and decision-making procedures. See *institutions*.

internationalists Internationalists recognize that interdependence is increasing, but they believe that the world is no more "global" than it was in the nineteenth century.

interventionist liberals Liberals who support some government involvement to promote more equality and justice in a free market economy.

intrafirm trade Trade within a firm, often between an MNC and its subsidiaries.

intraindustry trade In intraindustry trade, products are traded within the same industry group.

investor-state dispute settlement (ISDS) provisions Give investors access to dispute settlement procedures against a foreign government.

least developed countries (LLDC) Have low per capita GNIs, weak human assets, and high economic vulnerability.

lender of last resort An institution willing and able to provide unlimited amounts of short-term credit to those with serious financial problems.

leverage The process by which an individual, firm, or bank can use borrowed money to make larger investments than they could with their own financial resources.

liberal intergovernmentalism Describes European integration as resting on a series of bargains among member states, which are self-interested and rational in pursuing outcomes that serve their economic interests.

liquidity The ease with which an asset can be used at a known price in making payments. Cash is the most liquid form of an asset.

Lomé Convention Trade and aid agreements between the EU and 71 ACP (African, Caribbean, and Pacific) countries that have associate status in the EU. In 2000, the Lomé Convention was replaced by the more WTO-compatible *Cotonou Agreement*.

London Clubs Informal groups where the largest private creditor banks hold debt rescheduling negotiations with individual LDC debtor countries. They are also called "bank advisory committees" or "private creditor committees." See *Paris Club*.

Maastricht Treaty A 1992 treaty that renamed the EC the EU, and made commitments to form a monetary union, and common foreign, security, and social policies.

market A coordinating mechanism where sellers and buyers exchange goods, services, and factors of production at prices and output levels determined by supply and demand.

market economy An economy in which the market coordinates individual choices to determine the types of goods and services produced, and the methods of production.

market failure Failure of the market to produce an optimal allocation of resources.

mercantilism A policy of states from the sixteenth to eighteenth centuries to increase their relative power and wealth largely by maintaining a balance-of-trade surplus.

Mercosur The Common Market of the Southern Cone, formed in March 1991 when Argentina, Brazil, Paraguay, and Uruguay agreed to eventually establish a common market.

microfinance The provision of low-cost, short-term financial services, mainly savings and credit, to poor households that do not have access to traditional financial institutions.

Millennium Development Goals (MDGs) In 2000, the UN established eight MDGs to be achieved by 2015.

moderate globalists View the state as a viable actor, but differentiate *international* relations among states from *global* relations that take place without regard to territorial boundaries.

monetary policy Monetary policy influences the economy through changes in the money supply. For example, a central bank may deal with a balance-of-payments deficit by limiting public access to funds for spending purposes.

moral hazard The idea that protection against risk encourages a person, firm, or state to engage in riskier behavior. For example, if a lender of last resort exists, states facing financial crises are more likely to take risks because they can count on the lender to rescue them.

most-favored-nation (MFN) principle Stipulates that every trade advantage or privilege a GATT/WTO member gives to any state must be extended to all other GATT/WTO members. A major exception to MFN treatment is provided for regional trade agreements.

multilateral aid Aid in which donor governments provide funding through international organizations whose policies are collectively determined.

Multilateral Debt Relief Initiative (MDRI) Established by the IMF and World Bank in 2006. Low-income LDCs that have their debts reduced under the enhanced HIPC initiative are eligible to have the rest of their debt to the IMF, World Bank, and African Development Bank canceled under the MDRI. See *Heavily Indebted Poor Countries Initiative*.

multinational corporations (MNCs) Firms that own and control facilities for production, distribution, and marketing in at least two countries. Also referred to as transnational corporations or multinational enterprises.

national treatment A principle that all WTO members should treat foreign products—after they have been imported—as favorably as domestic products with regard to internal taxes and regulations.

neofunctionalism Describes economic integration in one sector as creating pressures for spillover into other sectors. Political activism by interest-driven actors is an essential element of spillover.

neo-Gramscian analysis A non-economistic Marxist theory that draws on the ideas of Antonio Gramsci and Robert Cox.

New Development Bank (NDB) Formed by the BRICS economies, the NDB will provide an alternative to the IMF and World Bank as a source of development funding.

New International Economic Order (NIEO) LDC demands for extensive international economic reform and DC concessions presented to the UN in the 1970s. The North ultimately rejected most of these demands.

newly industrializing economies (NIEs) A small number of rapidly growing and liberalizing economies in East Asia and Latin America that have presented a growing competitive challenge to the North.

nontariff barriers (NTBs) A large array of measures that limit imports, assist domestic production, and promote exports. NTBs are often more restrictive, ill-defined, and inequitable than tariffs.

North American Free Trade Agreement (NAFTA) An FTA formed in 1994 by the United States, Canada, and Mexico. NAFTA's importance stems from U.S. membership, the comprehensive nature of the agreement, and the fact that it was the first reciprocal FTA among DCs and an LDC.

obsolescing bargain model (OBM) Postulates that an MNC loses some bargaining leverage once it invests in a host state because it commits itself to some immobile resources in the host state.

official development assistance (ODA) Foreign aid to LDCs and multilateral institutions from official government agencies. See *foreign aid*.

official development finance (ODF) Official development loans with too low a grant element to qualify as official development assistance (e.g., IBRD loans).

opportunity cost The cost of producing less of one product in order to produce more of another product.

optimum currency area A region that maximizes the benefits of using a common currency. These regions are subject to common economic shocks, have a high degree of labor mobility, and have a tax-transfer system that relocates resources to economically weaker areas.

Organization for Economic Cooperation and Development (OECD) An organization of 34 mainly DCs in Paris, France. It does policy studies on economic and social issues, serves as a forum to discuss members' economic policies, and promotes cooperation, and is sometimes a forum for negotiation or prenegotiation.

Organization for European Economic Cooperation (OEEC) An organization of Western European states formed in 1948 that distributed U.S. Marshall Plan funds and facilitated moves toward currency convertibility and trade liberalization. In 1960, the OEEC was replaced by the OECD.

Organization of Petroleum Exporting Countries (OPEC) An organization of LDC oil exporters formed in 1960 that acts as a resource cartel to manipulate oil supplies and prices.

orthodox liberals Liberals who promote freedom of the market to function with minimal interference from the state.

Pareto-deficient outcome A condition in which all actors would prefer another outcome. See *prisoners' dilemma.*

Pareto-optimal outcome A condition in which no actor can become better off without making someone else worse off. See *prisoners' dilemma.*

Paris Club An informal group of DC creditor governments that meets with individual LDC debtor governments to negotiate debt-rescheduling agreements. See *London Clubs.*

patriarchy A system of society or government in which men hold most of the power.

plutocracy An integration agreement in which smaller members delegate policy-making to the wealthiest member.

political union Has the characteristics of an economic union and also harmonizes members' foreign and defense policies. A political union is more like a federal political system than an agreement among sovereign states.

politicism An overemphasis on the importance of politics.

portfolio investment The purchase of stocks, bonds, and money-market instruments by foreigners to gain a financial return. It does not involve foreign ownership or operating control.

Poverty Reduction Strategy Papers (PRSPs) The IMF and World Bank require PRSPs describing the economic and social policies of an LDC before considering the LDC for debt relief. PRSPs eventually replaced IMF and World Bank structural adjustment programs.

prisoners' dilemma A game that examines situations in which individual rationality induces a state to "cheat" regardless of the actions taken by others. Such actions do not produce the best collective outcome. See *Pareto-optimal outcome* and *Pareto-deficient outcome.*

public goods or *collective goods.* These are *nonexcludable* (all states have access to them) and *nonrival* (a state's use of the good will not decrease the amount available for others).

purchasing power parity The number of units of a country's currency needed to buy the same amount of goods and services in the domestic market as a U.S. dollar can buy in the United States.

rational choice Rational choice analysis assumes that individuals have goals and some freedom of choice and that they take actions they believe will achieve their goals.

Realism A statist IR theoretical perspective that emphasizes power and the national interest.

Reciprocal Trade Agreements Act (RTAA) The 1934 RTAA for the first time linked U.S. tariff levels to international negotiations instead of having Congress set tariffs on a unilateral, statutory basis.

reciprocity principle States that a country benefiting from another country's trade concessions should provide roughly equal benefits in return. See *specific reciprocity, diffuse reciprocity.*

relative gains Emphasizes the effects of gains on the relative power positions of states. See *absolute gains.*

remittances The money that migrants earn abroad and send back to their home countries.

revaluation An increase in the official rate or value at which one currency is exchanged for another. See *devaluation*.

rules of origin Regulations to prevent importers from bringing goods into an FTA through the lowest duty member state then shipping them duty-free to other members.

safeguards The safeguards principle permits WTO members to temporarily raise a duty above the maximum tariff binding to limit imports that may harm domestic producers.

Schengen Agreement An agreement to abolish border checks among 26 countries; 22 of the countries are EU members.

seigniorage The profit and advantages a sovereign power gains from issuing money.

single undertaking A principle that acceptance of an agreement requires acceptance of all its parts. The GATT Uruguay Round Agreement was a single undertaking because it required LDCs to accept all parts of the agreement.

soft power Power based on attraction and co-option.

sovereign wealth funds (SWFs) Government investment funds that are managed separately from official currency reserves. SWFs may hold higher risk assets than official reserves.

special and differential treatment (SDT) Special access given to LDCs for exports to DC markets, and LDC exemptions from some WTO rules.

special drawing rights (SDRs) Artificial international reserves created by the IMF and used among central banks. There have been three SDR allocations, the most recent one in 2009.

specific reciprocity A simultaneous exchange of strictly equivalent benefits or obligations. See *diffuse reciprocity*.

stagflation An economy with inflation, stagnant economic growth, and relatively high unemployment.

state A sovereign, territorial political unit.

Stolper–Samuelson theory Posits that trade liberalization benefits abundantly endowed factors of production and hurts poorly endowed factors of production in a state.

strategic trade theory A neomercantilist theory focusing on a state's creation of competitive advantage through industrial targeting.

structural adjustment loans (SALs) Medium-term balance-of-payments financing the World Bank and IMF provided to LDCs after the 1980s foreign debt crisis. LDC recipients had to agree to institute structural reforms.

structural Marxism Marxists who view the state as relatively autonomous from direct pressure from capitalists, but who believe that the state acts in the long-term interests of the capitalist class.

subprime mortgages Mortgages for borrowers who do not qualify for market interest rates because of income level, credit history, size of the downpayment, and/or employment prospects.

sustainable development A policy focused on environmental conservation that calls for meeting the needs of the present without limiting the ability of future generations to meet their own needs.

tariffs Taxes on products that pass through a customs border. Tariffs are usually imposed on imports, but may also apply to exports.

terms of trade The relative prices of a country's exports and imports. Raúl Prebisch argued that LDCs in the periphery of the global economy had deteriorating terms of trade with DCs in the core.

tied aid Aid that is tied to purchases from the donor country's producers and employment of its technical experts.

Trade-Related Intellectual Property Rights (TRIPs) An agreement under the WTO that establishes minimum standards of protection for copyrights, patents, and other intellectual property, and offers remedies to members to protect these rights.

Trade-Related Investment Measures (TRIMs) A rather weak and narrowly defined agreement under the WTO to impose some discipline over trade-related investment issues.

transfer prices Prices a business firm uses for the internal sale of goods and services among its affiliates. They help an MNC manage its internal operations, but the MNC may manipulate these prices to shift its reported profits.

transnational advocacy networks (TANs) TANs are actors working internationally on an issue, who are linked by shared values and exchanges of information and services. They may include NGOs, social movements, the media, labor unions, consumer groups, religious institutions, intellectuals, and branches of government.

Triffin dilemma   The conflict between the "liquidity" and "confidence" functions of the U.S. dollar as the top currency in the Bretton Woods regime. U.S. balance-of-payments deficits decreased confidence in the U.S. dollar, but there would be a liquidity shortage if the United States reduced its payments deficits.

two-level game theory   Views international relations as a two-level game involving a state's international interactions (level 1) and domestic interactions (level 2).

United Nations Conference on Trade and Development (UNCTAD)   A permanent organ of the UN General Assembly, created in 1964 because of the South's dissatisfaction with GATT. UNCTAD promotes the South's trade and development interests.

variable-sum game   A relationship in which groups may gain or lose together. See *zero-sum game*.

vertical integration   A vertically integrated MNC controls production of goods and services at different stages of the production process, with some affiliates providing inputs to other affiliates. Firms become vertically integrated to avoid uncertainty, reduce transaction costs, and limit competition. See *horizontal integration*.

voluntary export restraints   To circumvent the GATT Article 11 ban on import quotas, a state may pressure other states to "voluntarily" decrease their exports of specific products.

Washington Consensus   Refers to the neoliberal belief that countries can best achieve economic growth through free markets, a dominant private sector, democratic government, and trade liberalization.

World Bank   An international organization formed in 1944 to give long-term loans for postwar reconstruction and development. It is also called the International Bank for Reconstruction and Development (IBRD).

World Bank group   Includes the International Bank for Reconstruction and Development, International Finance Corporation, International Development Association, International Centre for the Settlement of Investment Disputes, and Multilateral Investment Guarantee Agency.

World Economic Forum (WEF)   A private institution where business executives, political leaders, and multilateral institutions discuss global problems. The WEF has an annual meeting and regional summits, and issues publications.

world-systems theory   A theory that views problems in the periphery as stemming from the capitalist world-economy. It introduced the "semiperiphery" concept to explain why some states in the periphery are developing.

World Trade Organization (WTO)   The global trade organization formed in 1995. WTO agreements include the General Agreement on Tariffs and Trade, General Agreement on Trade in Services, the Agreement on Trade-Related Intellectual Property Rights, and the Agreement on Trade-Related Investment Measures.

zero-sum game   A relationship in which one group's gain equals another group's loss. See *variable-sum game*.

INDEX

Page numbers in *italic* refer to figures. Page numbers in **bold** refer to tables.

absolute advantage 81, 216
absolute gains 56, 63, 70, 227
adaptive club model of WTO 243
adjustment measures 136, 146–8
Adjustment with a Human Face
  study 365
agricultural protectionism 58–9
agricultural trade 19
Alexander, Lamar 316
Allende, Salvador 320
The American Challenge (Servan-
  Schreiber) 310
American Federation of
  Labor–Congress of Industrial
  Organizations (AFL-CIO) 315
Annan, Kofi 321
antidumping duties (ADDs) 228–9,
  264, 276
appreciation, defined 140
Argentina, Mercosur and 280–1
Article 24 (GATT) 265–6
Arusha Declaration 353
The Ascent of Money (Ferguson)
  172
Asian Development Bank 27, 369
Asian financial crisis (1990s):
  causes/strategies for 195–6;
  international financial
  architecture and 196–8;
  overview of 194–5; theoretical
  perspectives on 357–9
Asian Infrastructure Investment
  Bank (AIIB) 27, 145, 369–70,
  400
Association of Southeast Asian
  Nations (ASEAN) 283
austerity 95, 116, 160, 205–7
*Austerity: The History of a
  Dangerous Idea* (Blyth) 116
Azevêdo, Roberto 26, **232**, 232

backward integration of MNCs
  296
Baker, James, III 153, 187
Baker Plan **187**, 187–8, 189–90
balance of payments 132–5, **133**
balance-of-payments deficits 22,
  135–9, **137**
balance-of-payments financing
  regime 179–81, **180**
balance-of-payments surplus 135
Bank for International Settlements
  (BIS) 21, 148–9
Banking Act of 1933 (Glass-
  Steagall Act) 199–200
banks: financial bailout for 201;
  leverage and 198–9; regulation
  of 201–2; *see also* commercial
  banks; creditor banks
basic needs approach 365
Beijing Consensus 369, 373, 405
Bernstein, Steven 122
Bhagwati, Jagdish 277, 284
the bhat (Thailand currency) 194

bilateral aid 343, 348
bilateral investment treaties (BITs)
  319–20
Birmingham Summit 30
Blinder, Alan 5
Blyth, Mark 84, 116
Board of Executive Directors,
  IBRD 346–7
Board of Governors, IBRD 346
Brady, Nicholas 188
Brady Plan 188–90
Brazil: inequality of wealth in
  11–12; Mercosur and 280–1;
  role in GATT/WTO 242
Brazil, Russia, India, and China
  (BRIC) economies 26, 372, 395
Brazil, Russia, India, China, and
  South Africa (BRICS) economies
  26, 370, 386, 398
Bretton Woods Conference 17–18,
  22, 39–40, 82, 142
Bretton Woods monetary regime:
  demise of 151; formation of 142;
  international monetary relations
  before 140–1; role of U.S. dollar
  in 146–8; shift to multilateralism
  148–50
Britain 19, 20–1, 61
bubble, defined 200
Buchanan, James 206
burden sharing principle 184
Bush, President George W. 368
Business Charter on Sustainable
  Development 326
business firms, global economy
  and 42–3

Cairns Group of agricultural
  exporters 239
Canada: NAFTA and 275–80;
  policies towards MNCs 310,
  311; TPP and 283
Canada–U.S. Free Trade Agreement
  (CUSFTA) 275
capital 105, 113
capital account 132–5, **133**
capital account convertibility 162
Capital in the Twenty-First Century
  (Piketty) 37
capitalism: environmental
  degradation and 120; historical
  materialism and 104, 121; Lenin
  and 107–8; Marx and 106–7
*Capitalism and Underdevelopment
  in Latin America* (Frank) 109
capitalist world-economy
  111–12
capital market 150, 158, 185–6,
  345–6
Cardoso, Fernando Henrique 109
Central and Eastern European
  countries (CEECs) 270–2
central bank, explanation 134–6
central bank governors 29–31, 149

centrally planned economies
  (CPEs) 39–40, **41–2**, 234–5
Charter for an International Trade
  Organization (Havana Charter)
  221–2
Chile, and ITT 320–1
China: balance of payments data
  for 132–5, **133**; challenging
  US hegemony 10; development
  strategy of 369–70; energy
  neomercantilism of 69; foreign
  MNCs and 317–18; global
  hegemony of 66–7; hegemonic
  prospects of 398–9; IMF/World
  Bank membership of 181–3; the
  renminbi's status 161–2; role in
  GATT/WTO 240–1
civil society organizations (CSOs):
  altering MNC behavior and
  325–6; globalization and 43,
  390–1; trade relations and 242–4
Clapp, Jennifer 120
club goods *120*, 120
Cobden–Chevalier Treaty 19, 220
collateralized debt obligations
  (CDOs) 175
collective action problems 63, 86–8
commercial banks 175, 199–200
commercial (or hard) loans 340
commercial policy 136
Committee on Foreign Investment
  in the United States (CFIUS) 312
Committee on Regional Trade
  Agreements (CRTA) 266
common external tariff (CET) 256
common market 256, *256*
common property goods *120*,
  120–1, 393
Commonwealth of Independent
  States (CIS) 116
The Communist Manifesto (Marx
  & Engels) 103–4, 106
Communist states, relation to
  KIEOs 40
comparative advantage 81, 216–17,
  217
competition states 4
competitive advantage 219
competitiveness 316–17, 396
complex interdependence 86
Comprehensive Development
  Framework (CDF) 367
concentrated protectionist interests
  91
concessional (or soft) loans 340
conditionality, IMF 143
conditionality principle 184
confidence, in Bretton Woods
  regime 146–8
conformist CSOs 43, 390
constructivism 52–4, 114–16, 274
consultative groups 348
Consultative Group to Assist the
  Poorest 367

contagion effect 359
Cooper, Richard 85
cooperation, liberal approach to 86–8, 87
Corn Laws 19, 59, 220
corporate social responsibility (CSR) 325, 326–8
Cotonou Agreement 267–8
Council for Mutual Economic Assistance (CMEA) 40, 192, 259, 270–1
Council of Ministers (Council of the European Union) 269
counterhegemony 113, 279, 325–6, 385
countervailing duties (CVDs) 223, 228–9, 276, 395
Cox, Robert 5, 112–13
creditor banks 175, 184–5
creditor groups, private 184–5
credit transactions 132–5, **133**
crisis prevention 197
crisis resolution 197
critical feminists 116
critical perspectives 6, 103, 121–2
cross-border merger 295
cross-conditionality 193
Cuba, U.S trade sanctions and 314
current account, in balance of payments 132–5, 133
customs union (CU) 155, 256, 256, 274
Czechoslovakia, foreign debt strategy 191

Das Kapital [Capital] (Marx) 106
Dauvergne, Peter 120
debit transactions 132–5, **133**
debt crisis, defined 173
debt reduction agreements 173, 188–9
debt rescheduling agreements 173
debt restructuring agreements 173
debt service ratio 191
declinists 64–7
Defending the National Interest: Raw Materials Investments and U.S. Foreign Policy (Krasner) 56
de Gaulle, President Charles 151
democracy, globalization and 389
Dependency and Development in Latin America (Cardoso & Faletto) 109
dependency theory 108–14, 340
depreciation, defined 140
devaluation 21–2, 140
developed countries (DCs): challenges to dominance of 23, 26; comparison to LDCs 10–12; economic relations between 8–10
developmental multilateralism 242
developmental state model 359–60
Development Assistance Committee (DAC) 342–3, **343**
development principle of GATT/ WTO 229
diffuse free-trade interests 91
diffuse reciprocity 226–7
directors-general, of WTO 231–2, **232**
disintegration theory 274

distributional issues 56, 79
Dodd-Frank Wall Street Reform and Consumer Protection Act 201–2
Doha Round (Doha Development Agenda): breakdown of 232–4, 239–40, 401; theoretical views of 246–7
The Dollar Trap (Prasad) 161–2
domestic-international interactions, liberalism and 90–2, 92
Domestic International Sales Corporation (DISC) program 313
dumping 228
Dunning, John 295

East Asian debtors 175–7, **177**
The East Asian Miracle: Economic Growth and Public Policy 357, 364
East Asian NIEs: Asian financial crisis and 357–9, 404; export-led growth strategies 354–5, **355**, 404; perspectives on success of 355–7, 405
Easterly, William 341–2, 370
economic and monetary union (EMU) 269–70
Economic and Social Council (ECOSOC) 22
economic liberalism 27
economic nationalism 58–9
economic(s): in IPE 3–4; openness, hegemony and 64–5; politics and 56–7, 79, 104–5
The Economics of Interdependence (Cooper) 85
economic union 256, 256
economism, defined 4
The Economist 32, 193
Eichengreen, Barry 154, 160
embedded liberal compromise 83, 142, 222
emergency measures in foreign debt crisis 186–7
emerging market economies: challenging DCs' dominance 26; in global trade relations 240–2; IMF membership and 143–5; membership in G20 27–9, 30, 31; members of KIEOs 40, **41–2**
Emmanuel, Arghiri 220
enabling clause 238, 267, 284
The End of Laissez-Faire (Keynes) 81–2
endogenous growth theory 96
energy issues: energy security 118; globalization 391–2
Engels, Friedrich 103–4
environmentalism 118–21, 120, 279–80
environmental issues: globalization 392–3; trade 244–6
epistemic community 115, 344
equity-asset ratio 199
Eurasian Economic Union 274
the euro 159–60, **268**
eurocurrency market 147–9
European Atomic Energy Community (Euratom) 268
European Central Bank (ECB) 156, 157, 159, 204

European Coal and Steel Community (ECSC) 262, 265, 268, 268
European Commission 204, 269, 271
European Community (EC) 154–6, 256, 268–9
European debt crisis 202–5
European Free Trade Association (EFTA) 256, 259, 268
European Management Forum 42
European monetary relations 154–7
European Monetary System (EMS) 151, 155–6
European Recovery Program *see* Marshall Plan
European Union (EU): agreements with LDCs 267–8; as customs union 256; European integration and **268**, 269–72; hegemonic prospects of 397; members of **154**, 154–5, 202, **203**, **260**; MNC regulation by 321–3; monetary union and 156; as supranational 268–9; theoretical perspectives on 272–5; TTIP negotiations 283
Eurosclerosis 269, 273
euro zone **154**, 154–7
exchange rates, PPP-based 32
excludability *120*, 120
Exon-Florio amendment 311–12
export-led growth strategies 354–7, **355**, 404
export substitution 315–16
external adjustment measures 136
external debt 137–8

fair trade movement 243–4
Faletto, Enzo 109
FDI flows 293–4, 385–6
FDI stock 293, 385
Federal Deposit Insurance Corporation (FDIC) 199–200
feminist theory 116–17
Ferguson, Niall 172
financial account, in balance of payments 132–5, **133**
financial contagion 195
financial crises: Asian (1990s) 194–8; austerity vs. government stimulus 205–7; definitions/ terminology 173; European debt 202–5; global (2008) 198–202; overview of 2–3, 172–3; *see also* foreign debt crisis (1980)
financing, for balance-of-payments deficit 136–9, **137**
fiscal policy 136
fixed exchange rates 21–2, 140, 142, 150–3
floating exchange rates 151–3, 162
Fordney-McCumber Tariff 20, 220
foreign aid 340; *see also* official development assistance (ODA)
foreign debt crisis (1980): European debt crisis vs. 202–4; foreign debt regime 178–85, **180**, **182**; IMF-World Bank functions 192–4; origins of 174–8, **177**; strategies for 185–90; transition economies and 190–2

foreign direct investment (FDI): from 1990 to present **301**, 301–4, **303**; Asian financial crisis and 194; determinants/effects of 304–7; EU/NAFTA regulation of 321–3; explanation of 134; home countries and 312–15; from mid-1940s to mid-1980s 298–301, **299–300**; MNCs and 293–5; OECD/WTO negotiations 323–5; in pre-World War II period 297–8; regime for 318–19
Foreign Investment Review Agency (FIRA) 310
forward vertical integration of MNCs 296
Fox, Vicente 276
Frank, André Gunder 109, 356
free trade 58–9, 81, 218–19
free trade area (FTA) 255, *256*, 276–7
Friedman, Milton 84, 159–60
Friedman, Rose 84
Fukuyama, Francis 66, 121
The Future of the Dollar (Helleiner & Kirshner) 157–63

game theory 86
GATT Article 24 265–6
GATT/WTO: development principle of 229; environmental issues and 244–6; FDI regulation and 323–5; RTAs and 263–8; transition economies and 234–6, 235; *see also* General Agreement on Tariffs and Trade (GATT); World Trade Organization (WTO)
Gazprom 68–9
gender: income inequality and 388; LDC women/SAPs and 362–3; unequal hierarchies and 116–17
General Agreement on Tariffs and Trade (GATT): Article 24 265–6; functions of 22; global economic role of 10, 17; global postwar trade regime and 221–2; more LDC participation (1980s to 1995) 238–9; trade regime principles of 222–9
General Agreement on Trade in Services (GATS) 230, 277, 323
General Arrangements to Borrow (GAB) 148
generalized system of preferences (GSP) 237–9, 241, 267, 270
The General Theory of Employment, Interest, and Money (Keynes) 82
geopolitical approach 139, 157–8, 163, 165
Germany 58–9, 132–5, **133**, 157–8
Gill, Stephen 65
Gilpin, Robert 51–2, 59, 60, 63
Gini coefficient 32, 37
Glass-Steagall Act (Banking Act of 1933) 199–200
Global Compact 321
Global Competitiveness Report 42, 396, 397–8
global economic management: functions of KIEOs 21–2;

KIEOs/United Nations in 22–3; postwar economic institutions 23, 26–31; post-World War II 17–18; pre-World War II 18–21
global financial crisis (2008) 43–4, 198–202
Global Information Technology Report 42
globalization: capitalist 105; civil society groups and 390–1; definitions of 6–7; democracy and 389; energy and 391–2; environment and 392–3; equality/poverty and 387–9; facts regarding 7–8; liberal views on 79–80; migration and 393–5; neomercantilism and 57; opposition to 94–5; overview of 384–5; regionalism and 258; the state and 386–7; triadization and 385–6
global trade relations: civil society and 242–4; environmental issues and 244–6; formation of WTO 229–32, *231*, **232**; GATT-based trade regime 221–2; influence of China/Brazil/India 240–2; overview of 215–16; stages of LDC participation 236–40; trade regime principles 222–9; trade theories 216–20, **217**; transition economies and 234–6, **235**; before World War II 220–1; WTO-based trade regime 232–4
gold exchange standard 141–2, 298
gold standard 20, 140–1
Gomulka, Wladyslaw 191
Gorbachev, Mikhail 183
Gourevitch, Peter 91
global governance, defined 89
governance, defined 89
government response to payments deficit 135–9, **137**
government stimulus, austerity vs. 205–7
Grameen Bank 365
Gramm-Leach-Bliley Act 200
Gramsci, Antonio 112–13
Gramscian analysis 62, 64, 279, 325, 340, 385
grant element of ODA 340
Great Depression 18, 60, 83, 141, 198–9
Great Moderation 2, 199
The Great Transformation (Polanyi) 83
Great Transformations (Blyth) 84
Greece 156–7, 203, 205, 206–7
greenfield investment 295
greens *120*, 120–1, 244–6, 392–3
Greenspan, Alan 196, 199
gross domestic product (GDP) 9–11, 67, 115, 138, 161, 215
gross national income (GNI) 9, 32–7, **33**, 337, 338, 342–4, **343**
gross national product (GNP), defined 9
Group of Five (G5) 26, 27, 29–30, 30, 143–4
Group of Seven (G7) 27, 30, 30–1, 153, 189
Group of Eight (G8) 29, 30, 179, 390, 395

Group of Seventy-seven (G77) 38, 185, 237
Group of Ten (G10) 148–51, 175
Group of Twenty (G20) **28**, 30, 31, 150
Group of Twenty-four (G24) 149

Haas, Ernst 272–3
Hamilton, Alexander 58, 351
Hancock, Kathleen 274
Hardin, Garrett 121, 393
hard power 65, 66
Havana Charter (Charter for an International Trade Organization) 221–2
Hayek, Friedrich 83
Heavily Indebted Poor Countries (HIPC) Initiative 189, 190
Heckscher, Eli 217
Heckscher-Ohlin theory 217–18
hegemonic stability theory 61–7
hegemony: American 9–10, 61, 64–7, 395–6; British 19–21, 61; definitions of 62; necessity/sufficiency of 64–5; replacing U.S. 397–9; strategies/motives of 62–4
Helleiner, Eric 17, 59
Helms–Burton Act 314
Hickenlooper Amendment 313
historical materialism: on Asian financial crisis 357–8; basic tenants of 103–5; critique of 121; early forms of 106–10; IPE and 6; NAFTA and 278–9; North-South relations and 340; rising regional integration and 263
historic bloc 113
Hobson, John 107
home countries 293, 312–15
Hong Kong 354–9, **355**
horizontal integration of MNCs 295–6
host countries: bilateral investment treaties 319–20; MNC relations with 293, 304–7; policies towards MNCs 307–12
Hufbauer, Gary C. 284–5
human development index (HDI) 32–4, **33**, **35**, 36; *see also* inequality-adjusted HDI (IHDI)
Hungary, foreign debt strategy 191–2
Huntington, Samuel 358
hydraulic fracturing (fracking) 69–70, 118–19
Hymer, Stephen 305
hyperglobalists 7

ideological superstructure 106
imminent default principle 184
imperialism 104, 107–8
Imperialism: The Highest Stage of Capitalism (Lenin) 107
import substitution industrialization (ISI) 109, 237, 350–2, 403–4
income inequality: economic development and 337–9, **338**; globalization and 387–9; HDI and 37, **38**

India 242, 397–8
individual, role of 55–6, 78, 103–4
individual rationality 88
Industrial Revolution 19, 58–9
inequality-adjusted HDI (IHDI) 37, **38**
infant industries 58, 68
infrastructure, described 10
institutional framework, pre-World War II 21
institutional liberalism 78, 119–20, 277
institutions, defined 85
instrumental approach, to U.S. dollar 157–8
instrumental Marxism 104–5
interdependence theory 85–6
internal adjustment measures 136, 139
International Bank for Reconstruction and Development (IBRD): criticisms/support of 349–50; foreign debt crisis and 192–4; functions of 22; global economic role of 10, 344–5; governance role 400; institutions comprising 347–8; international development and 344–50, 346; LDC development and 371–3; North-South relations and 22–3; providing SALs 359–63; shifting strategies of 363–9; transition economies in 181–4, **182**; United Nations and 22–3; United States influence 348–9; voting power within 345–6, **346**
International Center for Settlement of Investment Disputes (ICSID) 348
international development: China's strategy 369–70; export-led growth strategies 354–9, **355**; income inequality and 337–9, **338**; LDC strategies 350; official development assistance 340–4, **343**; orthodox liberalism and 359–63; perspectives on North-South relations 339–40; shifting World Bank strategies 363–9; socialist strategies 353–4; World Bank and 344–50, **346**; see also international political economy (IPE)
International Development Association (IDA) 347
international economic relations 56, 78–9, 104
International Energy Forum 391–2
International Finance Corporation (IFC) 347
international financial architecture 196–8, 357
internationalists 7, 82
International Monetary Fund (IMF): Asian financial crisis and 196–8; features/voting members of 142–5, **145**; foreign debt crisis and 185–7, 192–4; functions of 21–2; global economic role of 10, 17; governance role 399–400; North-South relations and 26; providing SALs 359–63;

relationship to EU 204–5; transition economies in 181–4, **182**; United Nations and 22–3
international monetary relations: balance of payments and 132–5, **133**; before Bretton Woods regime 140–1; Bretton Woods regime 142, 145–51; creation of IMF 142–5, **145**; current regime alternatives 153–4; European monetary relations 154–7; free-floating regime 151–3; functions/valuation of money 139–40; future of U.S. dollar 157–63; impact of 131–2; nature/purpose of 56; summary of 164–5
international organizations (IOs) 56, 88–9, 258, 294, 399–401; see also specific international organizations
international political economy (IPE): North-South relations and 339–40; overview of 3–4; security issues and 405–6; unexpected changes in 174–5; see also international development; IPE theoretical perspectives
international regimes 64–5, 88–9
international relations (IR) theorists 9, 115, 116
International Telephone and Telegraph Corporation (ITT) 320–1
interventionist liberalism: definition of 77–8; environmental issues and 119; Keynes influencing 83; NAFTA and 277; North-South relations and 93–4, 339; statism and 350
interwar period (1918–1944): economic instability and 20; global trade relations 220–1; lack of monetary stability 141; neomercantilism in 59–60
intrafirm trade 215, 293, 315–16
intraindustry trade 218–19
investment banks 95, 198–200; see also Asian Infrastructure Investment Bank (AIIB)
investor-state dispute settlement (ISDS) 320, 322–3
involuntary lending 186–7
IPE theoretical perspectives: adjustment, financing and 139; on Asian financial crisis 357–9; on corporate social responsibility 326–8; criticisms of 274–5; on East Asian success 355–7; on European Union (EU) 272–4; on globalization 385; on LDC development strategies 371–3; on NAFTA 277–80; overview of 4–6, 51–4; on regionalism 257–8, 283–5; on structural adjustment programs 360–1

Japan: FDIs and 313–15; hegemonic prospects of 397; policies towards MNCs 310–11; the yen's status 158–9
Johnson, President Lyndon B. 147
joint ventures 295

Kagan, Robert 65–6
Kanbur, Ravi 367
Kant, Immanuel 85
Katzenstein, Peter 90
Keohane, Robert 85–6, 89
Kerry, Senator John 315
key currency 67, 142, 146–9, 157–63
Keynes, John Maynard 17, 21, 78, 81–3, 206
keystone international economic organizations (KIEOs): changing North-South relations and 26–8; CPEs and 39–40, **41–2**; functions of 21–2; governance role 399–401; liberal principles of 78–9; neomercantilist view of 56; UN and 22–3
Kim, Jim Yong 370
Ki-moon, Ban 370
Kindleberger, Charles 305
Kohl, Helmut 156
Krasner, Stephen 56, 60, 89
Krauthammer, Charles 66
Kristol, William 65–6
Krugman, Paul 206, 359

labor, gender and 116–17
labor groups, MNCs and 315–16
labor theory of value 106
Lagarde, Christine 144
Latin American debtors 175–7, **177**
Latin American NIEs 354–5, **355**, 386
Latin American regionalism 280–1
Latin American structuralism 108
least developed countries (LLDCs) 11, 36, 239–40, 342
Least Developed Countries Report 39
Lehman Brothers 2–3, 200–1
lender of last resort 197
Lenin, Vladimir 104, 107–8
less-developed countries (LDCs): Article 24 and 266; debt crisis and 175–8, **177**; debt strategies for 185–9; development strategies of 350, 371–3; economic inequalities of 10–12; EU agreements with 267–8; foreign aid and 340–4, **343**; global trade participation 236–42; GNI and HDI rankings for 34, **35**, 36; import substitution industrialization and 350–2; initiatives for poorest 189; modernization theory and 93; RTAs among 266–7; socialist development strategies of 353–4; UNCTAD and 38–9; women and SAPs in 362–3
leverage 198–9
liberal feminists 116
liberal intergovernmentalism 273–4
liberalism: on Asian financial crisis 358–9; basic tenants of 77–80; cooperation and 86–8; critique of 95–7; development of 80–1; domestic-international interactions 90–2, 92; global governance and 89–90; institutions and 85–9; Keynes influencing 81–3; NAFTA and

liberalism (*Continued*)
277–8; North-South relations
and 92–4, 339; overview of 5; in
postwar period 83; present-day
94–5; regional integration and
262–3; return to orthodox 83–4;
view of IR 56
liquidity 145–8, 150–1, 173,
200
Lisbon Treaty **268**, 271–2
List, Friedrich 58–9, 67, 68, 351
loans 179, **180**, 340; *see also*
official development assistance
(ODA); structural adjustment
loans (SALs)
Locke, John 80
Lomé Conventions 267
London Clubs 184–5
Louvre Accord 153

Maastricht Treaty 156, 268, **268**,
269
managed floating 151
manipulative floating 151
Mao Zedong 181–2
market, relationship to state 3
market-based approach 157
market economy 77–8
market failure 4, 349
Marshall, George C. 39
Marshall Plan 22, 39, 63, 146, 261,
345, 400
Marx, Karl 103–4, 106–7
Marxism 51–2, 103–5
material facts 114–15
McNamara, Kathleen 155
McNamara, Robert 365
Mearsheimer, John 114, 261
mercantilistic period (1500–1750)
18–19, 57–8
merchandise trade 132–5, **133**
Mercosur (Common Market of the
Southern Cone) 280–1
mergers and acquisitions (M&As)
295, 311, 317
Merkel, Angela 160
Mexico: foreign debt crisis and
174–5; NAFTA and 275–80;
policies towards MNCs 311;
TPP and 283
Microcredit Summit 371
microfinance 367, 371
migration 270–2, 393–5
Millennium Development Goals
(MDGs) 341, 344, 370
Ministerial Conference, WTO
230, *231*
misalignment, under floating
regime 153
Mises, Ludwig von 84
Mitrany, David 262
moderate globalists 7
modernization theory 93, 350
monetary policy, for balance-of-
payments deficit 136
Mont Pelerin Society 83–4
moral hazard 197
Moravcsik, Andrew 273
mortgage-backed securities (MBS)
200
most-favored-nation (MFN)
principle 225
Moyo, Dambisa 341–2

Multilateral Agreement on
Investment (MAI) 28, 323–5
multilateral aid 343–4, 348
Multilateral Debt Relief Initiative
(MDRI) 189, 190
Multilateral Investment Guarantee
Agency (MIGA) 348
multilateralism 148–50, 257
multilateral trade negotiations
223, **224**
multinational corporations
(MNCs): bilateral investment
treaties 319; definitions/
terminology 294–5; development
of FDI 297–304, **299–301**;
employment and 1; EU/
NAFTA regulation of 321–3;
globalization and 7–8, 293–4;
home country relations with
312–18; horizontal/vertical
integration of 295–6; host
country relations with 304–7;
NGOs/civil society groups
325–6; North host country
policies toward 309–12; OECD/
WTO negotiations 323–5;
regulation and 318–19; South
policies toward 307–9; trade
liberalization and 215; UN and
320–1
multistakeholder model for WTO
243
Mundell, Robert 156, 159

Nader, Ralph 325
nation, state vs. 59
National Energy Program (NEP)
310–11
national security, free trade and
219
*The National System of Political
Economy* (List) 58
national treatment 225
negative list approach 277
negotiated currency 148
negotiated regimes 64
neocolonialism 104, 121
neoconservatives 66
neofunctionalism 272–4
neo-Gramscian analysis 112–14,
121
neoliberalism 84, 404–5
neomercantilism: on Asian financial
crisis 358–9; basic tenants of
55–7; critique of 70–1; Industrial
Revolution and 58–9; in
interwar period 59–60; as IPE
perspective 60–1; mercantilists
and 57–8; NAFTA and 278;
North-South relations and 67–8,
339; overview of 5; present-day
68–70; realism vs. 55; rising
regional integration and 261–2;
after World War II 60
New Development Bank (NDB)
370
New International Economic Order
(NIEO) 67–8, 238
newly industrializing economies
(NIEs) 11, 26, 179, **180**; *see also*
East Asian NIEs; Latin American
NIEs; transition economies
Nixon, President Richard M. 151

nondiscrimination principle of
GATT/WTO 225
nonexcludability 63, 120–1, 393
nongovernmental organizations
(NGOs) 243–4, 325–6, 390–1
nonrivalness 63, 120
nonstate actors 42–3
nontariff barriers (NTBs) 223–4,
229, 233, 280
North American Free Trade
Agreement (NAFTA): formation
of 275–6; free trade agreement
13, 255, 276–7; MNC
regulation by 321–3; theoretical
perspectives on 277–80
Northern Rock bank 202
North host countries 309–12
North-North relations: current U.S.
hegemony 395–6; international
institutions' role 399–401;
overview of 8–10, 12–13;
replacing U.S. hegemony 397–9
North-South relations: concepts
of development 402–3;
development strategies 403–5;
economic inequalities and
10–13; foreign debt crisis and
177–8; GNI and HDI rankings
and 32–6, **33**, **35**; increased
confrontation 238; inequality
of 401–2; IPE perspectives on
339–40; liberalism and 92–4;
neomercantilism and 67–8;
postwar economic institutions
and 23, 26–31
Nye, Joseph 65, 66, 85–6
Nyerere, Julius 96, 353–4

Obama, President Barack 370, 396
obsolescing bargain model (OBM)
306–7
official development assistance
(ODA) 179, **180**, 340–4, **343**
official development finance (ODF)
346
Ohlin, Bertil 217
Ohmae, Kenichi 7, 79
oil resources: environmental issues
and 118–19; globalization and
391–2; OBM and 307; price
increases 174
Oneal, John 85
Onuf, Nicholas 114
opportunity cost 216, 393
optimum currency area 156
Organization for Economic
Cooperation and Development
(OECD): Declaration and
Decisions on International
Investment and Multinational
Enterprises 319; Development
Assistance Committee 342–3,
343; members of 27–9, **28**;
negotiations regarding FDIs
323–5
Organization for European
Economic Cooperation (OEEC)
28, 261
Organization of Petroleum
Exporting Countries (OPEC) 11,
23, 26, 174
orthodox liberalism: definition of
77–8; environmental issues and

119; NAFTA and 277; North-South relations and 93, 339; return to 83–4, 404–5; revival of 359–63
outsourcing 315–16

Panitchpakdi, Supachai 26
paradox of thrift 206
Pareto-deficient outcome 87–8, 185
Pareto-optimal outcome 87–8
Paris Club 184–5
patriarchy 116–17
Paulson, Henry 201
pegged exchange rates 21–2, 140, 142, 150–3
per capita GNI 32–4, 33, 35, 36–7, 337
Perpetual Peace (Kant) 85
petrodollars 147, 174–5
Piketty, Thomas 37, 388
Plaza Accord 153
plutocracy 274
Poland's foreign debt strategy 190–1
Polanyi, Karl 83
Policy Framework for Investment 325
political union 256, 256
politicism, defined 4
politics 3–4, 56–7, 79, 104–5
Population Reference Bureau (PRB) 401
portfolio investment 194, 293
positive-sum game 5, 216, 340
postwar economic institutions: changing North-South relations 23, 26; G5, G7, G8 and G20 29–31; global financial crisis and 43–4; international development and 31–9, 33, 35; KIEOs and CPEs 39–40, 41–2; nonstate actors 42–3; OECD 28, 28–9
poverty and globalization 387–9; *see also* income inequality
Poverty Reduction Strategy Papers (PRSPs) 367
power 3–4, 11, 18–19
Power and Interdependence (Keohane) 85
Prasad, Eswar 162
Prebisch, Raúl 109, 220, 237, 350–2
preferential trade agreements (PTAs) 255, 258, 284
primary income, in current account 132–5, 133
Principles of Political Economy and Taxation (Ricardo) 216
prisoners' dilemma 86–8, 87, 121, 206, 394
private bank loans 179, 180
private goods 120, 120
program lending 192
proprietary trading 201
public goods 63, 120, 120, 146, 218
purchasing power parity (PPP) 32, 33, 161
Putin, President Vladimir 13, 68–70, 236
Putnam, Robert 91–2, 176

Quadrilateral Group 242
Quesnay, François 80

Ramo, Joshua Cooper 369
rational choice analysis 52–4, 86–8
Reagan, President Ronald 84, 141, 153, 307, 360
realism 5, 51, 55
Reciprocal Trade Agreements Act (RTAA) 21, 221
reciprocity principle of GATT/WTO 225–7, 227
Reciprocity Treaty 275
reformist CSOs 43, 390
refugees 270, 393–4
regime(s): definition of 88; for foreign investment 318–19; principles/norms 88–9; *see also specific regimes*
regime theory 88–90
Regional Comprehensive Economic Partnership (RCEP) 283
regionalism: European Union and 268, 268–75; first wave of 259; globalization and 258; Mercosur and 280–1; NAFTA and 275–80; regional integration and 261–3; RTA integration and 255–7, 256; second wave of 259–61; theoretical perspectives and 257–8; theoretical perspectives on 283–5; Trans-Pacific Partnership 281–3
regional trade agreements (RTAs); 13; GATT/WTO and 263–8; historical overview of 258–61, 260; levels of integration 255–7, 256
Rehn, Olli 204
Reinhart, Carmen 172
rejectionist CSOs 43, 390
relative gains 5, 56, 88, 219
remittances 132, 341
renewalists 64–7
the renminbi (RMB) 161–2
Report on the Subject of Manufactures (Hamilton) 58
research and development (R&D) 96, 295–6, 316–18
resource curse 34
revaluation, defined 140
Ricardo, David 81, 216
Rio Earth Summit 118
rivalness 120; overconsumption of resources and 120
The Road to Serfdom (Hayek) 83
Rogoff, Kenneth 160, 172
Roosevelt, President Franklin D. 199
Rostow, Walt 93, 350, 371
Rubin, Robert 196
Ruggie, John Gerard 83
rules of origin 264, 266, 277, 284
Russett, Bruce 85
Russia (Soviet Union): applying for WTO membership 236; energy neomercantilism of 68–9; G7 participation 30; relation to KIEOs 39–40; Ukraine and 272

Sachs, Jeffrey 341–2, 370
safeguard measures 228–9
Schengen Agreement 270, 272

Schott, Jeffrey J. 284–5
secondary income, in current account 132–5, 133
Securities and Exchange Commission (SEC) 199–200
security dilemma 56
security issues, IPE and 405–6
seigniorage 146
Servan-Schreiber, Jean-Jacques 310
services trade 132–5, 133
Singapore's export-led growth strategies 354–9, 355
Singer, Hans 350–1
Single European Act (SEA) 269
single undertaking 233, 238
Smith, Adam: criticism of 58–9; in defense of free trade 216; liberal IPE and 80–1; on mercantilism 18–19, 57; as orthodox liberal 78
Smoot-Hawley Tariff Act 21, 220–1
social facts 114–15
social greens *see* greens
socialist development strategies 353–4
societal groups 55–6, 78
soft power (structural power) 65–7, 349, 396, 399
solvency problems 173, 187, 203
South host countries 307–9
South Korea, export-led growth strategies 354–9, 355
sovereign wealth funds (SWFs) 304
Soviet Union *see* Russia (Soviet Union)
special and differential treatment (SDT) 236, 238, 247
special drawing rights (SDRs) 150, 163, 165, 398
specialized agencies 22–3
specific reciprocity 226–7
spillback 274
spillover 272–4
spontaneous regimes 64
The Stages of Economic Growth (Rostow) 93
stagflation 65
state 3, 55–6, 59, 78
Stiglitz, Joseph 366–7
Stolper–Samuelson theory 217–18
Strange, Susan 62
strategic trade theory 219–20
structural adjustment loans (SALs): conditions for 360; foreign debt crisis and 181, 184, 193–4; World Bank and 349
structural adjustment programs (SAPs) 360–3
structural Marxism 105
subprime mortgages 2, 66, 95, 200–2
Sub-Saharan Africa, SAPs and 361–2
supply chains 282
sustainable development concept 118–19, 359, 370, 402

Taiwan, export-led growth strategies 354–9, 355
Tanzania, socialism and 353–4
tariffs 220, 223, 224

terms of trade 109, 139, 190, 192, 220
Thatcher, Prime Minister Margaret 84, 307, 360
theoretical perspectives *see* IPE theoretical perspectives
The Theory of Moral Sentiments (Smith) 80
This Time Is Different (Reinhart & Rogoff) 172
tied aid 344
Tobin, James 197–8
Tobin tax 197–8
top currency 148
trade creation 264–5
trade diversion 264
trade liberalization principle 223–5, **224**
trade promotion authority (TPA) 282
Trade-Related Intellectual Property Rights (TRIPs) 230, 323, 324–5
Trade-Related Investment Measures (TRIMs) 230, 323–4
trade theories 216–20, **217**
Transatlantic Trade and Investment Partnership (TTIP) 283
transfer prices 296
transformist CSOs 43, 390
transition economies: foreign debt crisis and 190–2; global trade relations and 234–6; IMF/World Bank membership of 181–4, **182**; membership of **235**; *see also* East Asian NIEs; Latin American NIEs; newly industrializing economies (NIEs)
transnational advocacy networks (TANs) 43
transnational historic bloc 113
Trans-Pacific Partnership (TPP) 281–3
Treaty of Asunción (TOA) 280
Treaty of Rome 265, 267, **268**
Treaty of Westphalia 18
Treaty on European Union 156
triadization 385–6
trickle-down concept 364–5, 402
Triffin, Robert 147
Triffin dilemma 147
Troubled Assets Relief Program (TARP) 201
two-level game theory 91–2, *92*
2008 financial crisis *see* global financial crisis (2008)

UN Center on Transnational Corporations (UNCTC) 321
UN Conference on Environment and Development (Rio Earth Summit) 118, 120
UN Conference on Sustainable Development (Rio+20) 118, 120
UN Conference on Trade and Development (UNCTAD) 37–9, 40, 237
UN Development Program (UNDP) 350
unemployment, FDIs and 315
Unholy Trinity 152, 155
UN *Human Development Report* 32, **33**, 37, 372, 388–9
UNICEF *Adjustment with a Human Face* study 365
United Nations (UN): code of conduct for MNCs 319, 320–1; KIEOs and 22–3; Millennium Development Goals (MDGs) 341; system *24–5*
United States (U.S.): balance of payments data for 132–5, **133**; economic hegemony of 9–10, 61, 64–7, 395–6; global financial crisis and 198–200; global oil supplies and 69–70; NAFTA and 275–80; policies towards MNCs 311, 313–15; protectionism of 220–1; replacing as hegemon 397–9; subprime mortgage crisis 200–1; trade/current account deficits **137**, 137–9; TTIP negotiations 283; World Bank membership 348–9
Uruguay Round accord 229–30, 238–9, 246
U.S. dollar: approaches to 157–8; Bretton Woods regime and 146–8; crisis of confidence in 151; the euro vs. 159–60; future of 162–3; the renminbi vs. 161–2; the yen vs. 158–9

variable-sum game 56
Vernon, Raymond 306, 319
vertical integration of MNCs 296
volatility 141–2, 152–3, 387
Vollaard, Hans 274
voluntary export restraints 222, 228

Wallerstein, Immanuel 62, 111–12, 121

Washington Consensus 360, 373
wealth 3–4, 11, 18–19
The Wealth of Nations (Smith) 80
Werner, Pierre 155
Werner Plan 155
White, Harry Dexter 17, 39, 82, 345
win-sets 91–2
Wolfensohn, James 366–8
Wolfensohn period 366–8
Wolfowitz, Paul 368
women: feminism and 116–17; gender inequality and 388; structural adjustment and 362–3; World Bank and 366, 367
World Bank *see* International Bank for Reconstruction and Development (IBRD)
World Bank group 345
World Development Report 364, 365, 366–7
World Economic Forum (WEF) 42, 396
world-economy 111
world-empire 111
world-systems theory 111–12, 340
World Trade Organization (WTO): civil society groups and 242–4; directors-general of **232**; formation of 229–32; global economic role of 10, 22; global trade regime and 232–4; governance role 400–1; negotiations regarding FDIs 323–5; North-South relations and 26–8; safeguard measures 228–9; stabilizing effect of 215, 218–19; structure of *231*
World War I, British hegemony and 20
World War II: FDI growth before 297–8; FDI-home country relations and 313–14; global economic relations and 17–21; global trade relations and 220–2; institutional framework before 21; liberalism after 83; neomercantilism after 60

the yen 158–9
Young, Oran 119
Yunus, Professor Muhammad 365

zero-sum game 5, 56, 57
Zoellick, Robert 368–9